THE PORT OF IPSWICH, ITS SHIPPING AND TRADES

Title page: A view from the tower of St Mary-at-Stoke Church showing the yeast factory prior to its move to Felixstowe in the 1960s. The building, demolished in the 1980s in preparation for road widening, was originally Joseph Fison's flour mill, opened in 1852. At bottom right is the reinforced concrete Stoke Bridge that replaced the cast-iron bridge erected by Ransomes in 1818-19. (Colin Elsdon)

THE PORT OF IPSWICH, ITS SHIPPING AND TRADES

**RICHARD SMITH
& JILL FREESTONE**

MALTHOUSE PRESS, SUFFOLK 2011

Published by Malthouse Press, Suffolk,
17 Reade Road,
Holbrook,
Ipswich,
Suffolk, IP9 2QL

ISBN 978-0-9539680-4-6

© Richard Smith and Jill Freestone, 2011

British Library Cataloguing-in-Publication Data

A catalogue record for this book is available from the British Library.

All rights reserved. No part of this book may be reproduced, stored in a retrieval system, or transmitted in any form or by any means, electronic, mechanical, photocopying, recording or otherwise without the prior permission of the publishers.

Designed by Robert Malster
Typeset by John Walton
Printed in Great Britain by
Greenshoots, Ipswich

Contents

Preface

Chapter 1	The port and its trade	1
Chapter 2	Pilotage and other business	27
Chapter 3	Towage on the Orwell	47
Chapter 4	The coal trade	61
Chapter 5	Grain and animal feed	89
Chapter 6	Chemicals and fertilizers	143
Chapter 7	The timber trade	175
Chapter 8	Building materials	193
Chapter 9	General cargoes	219
Chapter 10	Public utilities	249
Chapter 11	Engineering	273
Chapter 12	Oil	287
Chapter 13	Passengers and yachting	314
Chapter 14	The port at war	330
Appendices		354
Index		369

Foreword

The Port of Ipswich has a long and fascinating history going back at least to Saxon times. Indeed, it is thought that the town was founded in the 7th century by the Wuffings, that East Anglian royal house whose most illustrious members were buried at Sutton Hoo, to serve as a port and trading centre for the kingdom.

The fortunes of the town have always been bound up with the Orwell and with the trade that was carried up and down that river. When in 1284 King Edward I seized the town, which had been self-governing since 1200, into his own hands on account of 'certain transgressions and offences to us donne by the Burgesses' it was the excellent service given him by the Ipswich seamen that persuaded him to restore the town's privileges.

In 1294 the town built a galley and its attendant barge for the King, and contrary to what is often written it is clear from the surviving records that these were by no means the first vessels to be built in the Ipswich shipyards. In a later period Ipswich became a prominent shipbuilding centre, building ships for the London merchants as well as for local owners.

Merchants who grew prosperous by exporting woollen cloth and importing wine, by bringing stockfish from Iceland and supplying victuals to the English armies fighting in the interminable wars with France built fine houses beside the river. The waterside was the business area of the town.

There was even a time when Ipswich aspired to become an English counterpart of Antwerp, that great centre of commerce and focus of world trade. The whole history of the town can be written against a maritime background.

The authors of this book have not delved so far back, confining their researches to the 19th and 20th centuries and showing how at a time of expansion and prosperity a multitude of important companies participated in the trade of the Orwell. Some like Ransomes and Fisons were known the world over; others like Mellonie & Goulder and Christopherson were of more local fame, but all depended on the river and its trade.

From their researches into the port records they have produced a most valuable account of a period when square-rigged sailing ships brought grain from Australia and from the west coast of America to feed the Ipswich mills and maltings, and when steamers brought the raw materials of the artificial fertiliser factories; when sailing barges provided a vital link with the London Docks and served the many wharves on both sides of the river; and when thousands gathered at Wherstead to witness the launching of vessels such as the East Indiaman *Orwell*.

It has been a privilege to be associated with the production of such a book as this.

Robert Malster

Acknowledgements

Many people have contributed to the production of this book over a very long period. We have been fortunate in being able to use personal accounts of the day-to-day life of the port, and for these we are extremely grateful to John Cresswell (Towage), Captain David Ingham (Pilotage 1950-2000), Captain Jerry G. Jones (The latter half of the twentieth century), Derek Lawrence (The ship's agent), Tom Polley (A barge trip to London) and Captain Roger Threadkell (Ship's business).

Before going on to mention others who have contributed to the work the authors offer their thanks to Richard's wife Joan for her painstaking work at the Suffolk Record Office extracting information on the numerous shipping arrivals and departures that form the basis of this book. Their thanks also go to Jill's husband Ken for the innumerable cups of tea and coffee he has provided during the lengthy discussions held throughout the book's preparation.

During the many years that the book has been in preparation we have spoken with numerous people who have provided us with a great deal of valuable information. We would particularly like to thank John Andreason (Cocksedges), Michael Ayden (life of George Glading), Bob Blastock (Wherstead Road Residents), Mr and Mrs Roy Colchester, Bill Ellis (motor minesweepers, Royal Netherlands Navy), Joy and Peter Holder (Eastern Counties Farmers), John Nunn, Russell Nunn (Fisons), Cyril Pendle (coal merchants), Michael W. Stow (Suffolk Chemical Company), Jean and Don Turvey (Ransomes & Rapier), Ann and Lionel Waldridge, and Len Woolfe. Members of the Suffolk Archaeological Service, including Keith Wade and Tom Loader, have also given us important information, as have several of the Suffolk Local History Council's history recorders.

We are most grateful to the Over Stoke History Group for a generous contribution towards the printing costs.

Many others have also assisted us over the years, including Mr James A.E. Burrows, whose superb photographs are among the illustrations. We thank them all, and apologise to those who are not named; it would take many pages to list everyone.

We have purposely avoided going into detail regarding the building and opening of the Wet Dock as this has been adequately covered by Bob Malster and Bob Jones in *A Victorian Vision* (Ipswich Port Authority, 1992). Further information concerning the local sailing barges and the big ocean-going sailing vessels that brought cargoes to Ipswich up to 1939 can be found in Richard's books *The Thames Barge in Suffolk* (2006) and *Blue Water Sail* (1997) respectively.

Finally, we owe much gratitude to Bob Malster for his generous help. He has made many valuable suggestions as to the content and layout of the book and has taken on the immense task of designing and publishing it. Thank you, Bob.

Richard Smith	Kesgrave
Jill Freestone	Stoke, Ipswich

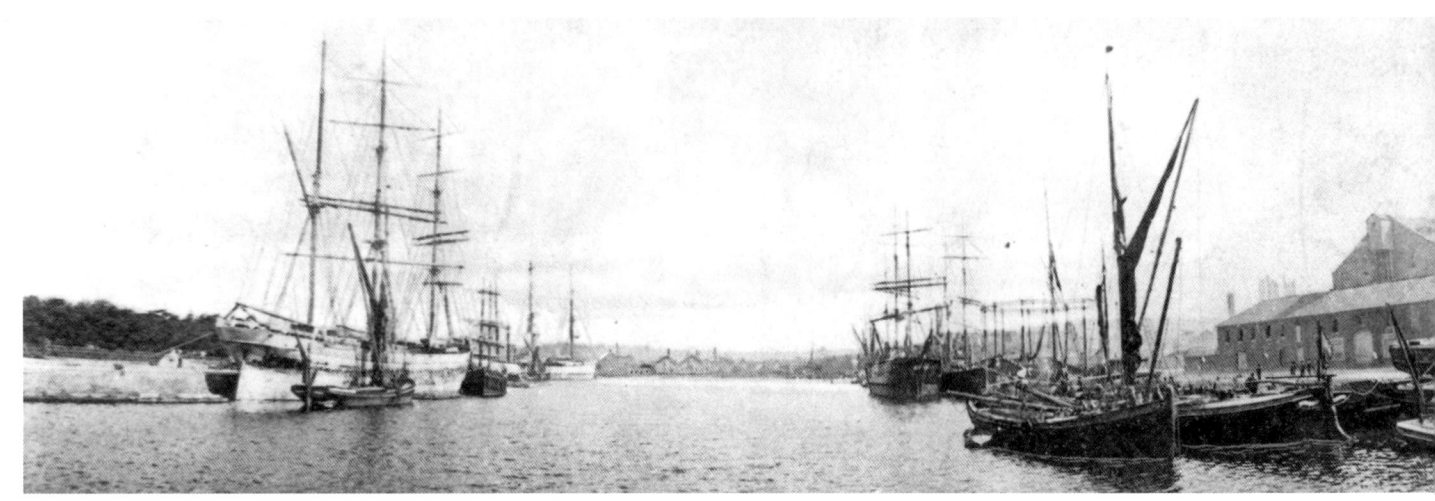

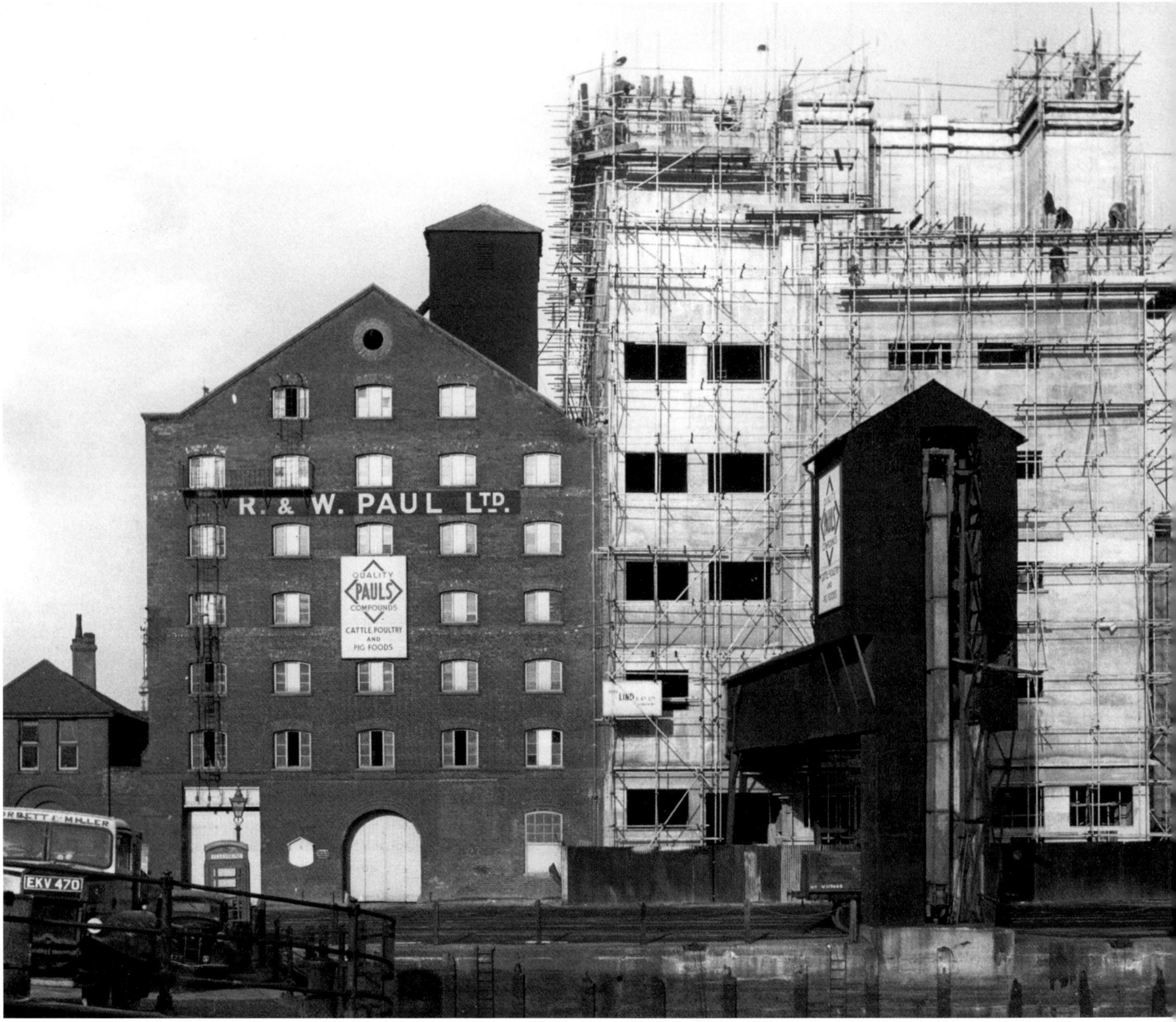
R. & W. PAUL LTD.
QUALITY
PAULS
COMPOUNDS
CATTLE, POULTRY
AND
PIG FOODS
EKV 470

Top left: A view of the Dock from the entrance lock at the beginning of the twentieth century, with sailing vessels and barges much in evidence.

Lower left: A new building under construction for R. & W. Paul on St Peter's Dock. At left is the former oil mill that was demolished after a spectacular blaze in recent years.

Below: F.T. Everard's motor coaster SPIRALITY unloading a cargo of grain at the head of the Dock at a time when mills, maltings and other commercial buildings lined the Dock. Built at Goole in 1939, the SPIRALITY *was typical of the vessels owned by the Greenhithe company, one of the larger British coaster owners.*

Right: One of the concrete dockside silos is demolished as the Dock is converted into the Waterfront.

The port and its trade   1

The estuary of the Orwell, otherwise known as Orwell Haven, has for centuries been a highway for trade. Roman, Saxon and Dane have sailed its reaches, indeed archaeologists carrying out excavations ahead of the redevelopment of Pauls' maltings and Cranfields' mills in 2006 found evidence of Roman occupation and the remains of a Saxon waterfront.

In the seventh century a small trading community was established ten miles inland close to the river crossing point now marked by Stoke Bridge. This community became the Anglo-Saxon settlement of Gippeswic that was to evolve into the town and port of Ipswich.

Although a thriving settlement at the time of the Norman Conquest, by the time Domesday Book was compiled in 1086 many of the town's burgesses were unable to pay the King's dues. Within the next hundred years however Ipswich was flourishing again. Wool and corn were exported to the Continent and wine, pottery and millstones were imported. Throughout its history the town has seen prosperity followed by stagnation, only for its fortunes to revive once more.

Recognised as one of the country's chief ports for foreign trade, the town was granted a Charter by King John in 1200. The Port of Orwell was described in the Charter as extending from Ipswich to le Polle or Polles Head just to seaward of the present Landguard Point. For centuries there was interminable wrangling between Ipswich and Harwich over the jurisdiction of Harwich Harbour until in 1863 the Harwich Harbour Act established the boundary of jurisdiction of the Harwich Harbour Conservancy Board and that of Ipswich as 'an imaginary line drawn across that river from Shotley Point to Fagborough Cliff'. Because of rapid expansion during the second half of the twentieth century by the Port of Felixstowe the boundary has since been set well above that position, it being changed in 1989 to a line between a marker on the Trimley Marshes and another on Shotley Marshes, permitting further incursion into the river by new quays at Felixstowe.

Ipswich was appointed a Staple Port in 1404 thus becoming one of the few ports in the country that could export wool. Ships were now travelling greater distances to and from the port and carrying a wider variety of goods. Products imported included iron, wine and pottery from the Rhineland, timber and furs from the Baltic, salt from Nantes, iron, oil, leather and wax from Spain and silk, spices and glass from the Mediterranean. Hides arrived from Ireland, fish from Scotland and coal from Newcastle. Some of this trade was handled at the Common Quay, which had probably been in existence since the thirteenth century, and small private quays were built by merchants for their own use on the north bank of the river, downstream of Stoke Bridge, close to their homes and warehouses.

The town continued to prosper during the fifteenth and sixteenth centuries. This was the time of the wealthy merchants and town benefactors, for example Henry Tooley who sent his ships on long voyages to Icelandic waters for fish.

Daniel Defoe, born in 1659, had childhood recollections of Ipswich when the town was a leading port in collier ownership. Several other ports in Suffolk and Essex owned ships engaged in the coal trade between London and Newcastle.

Opposite page: A deeply laden tiller-steered spritsail barge sails up the Dock perhaps bound for Cranfield Brothers' mill. In the background are two of the hulks used by R.& W. Paul for storage.

Visiting Ipswich in 1722 however, several years after the end of the Dutch wars, Defoe found that the collier trade had declined dramatically at the port. Large Dutch vessels, taken as war prizes, could be bought cheap and were in use by Yarmouth and London merchants and this had an effect on local shipbuilding. The cloth trade with the Continent was also in decline, resulting in a decrease in the amount of goods passing through the port.

A thriving coastal trade offset these losses however. Both the Navy and the rapidly expanding city of London had a need for the wheat, butter, vegetables, malt etc. that the fertile agricultural area surrounding the port was able to supply. These commodities could be transported to the capital by a quick and comparatively safe sea route from Ipswich.

During the latter half of the eighteenth century, some Ipswich shipowners and businessmen became involved in the Greenland whaling trade. In 1786 premises at the Nova Scotia Shipyard (now buried under the West Bank Container Terminal) were used for rendering down the blubber brought back by the vessels. The enterprise was ultimately unsuccessful and short-lived.

Shipbuilding was carried out on the riverbanks at Ipswich for many centuries. A galley was constructed for Edward I at the end of the thirteenth century, and during the seventeenth and eighteenth centuries several warships were built downriver at John's Ness just below Cliff Quay. By the early 1800s the major shipbuilding sites in the town were St Peter's shipyard near to Stoke Bridge, St Clement's yard close to the town quays, and the Halifax and Nova Scotia yards at the southern end of Wherstead Road. The zenith for shipbuilding was probably reached in 1816 when Jabez Bayley, of the Halifax shipyard near Bourne Bridge, laid down the keel of an East Indiaman, the *ORWELL*, of almost 1,400 registered tons. In 1840 the first iron steamer to be constructed at Ipswich, the *ORION*, was launched at Read & Page's Halifax yard. With a length overall

The East Indiaman ORWELL *almost ready for launching at Jabez Bayley's Halifax Yard in 1817. When she was broken up twenty-three years later the Suffolk oak of which she was built was found to be in surprisingly good condition.*

of 182 feet, the vessel was propelled by a pair of engines designed and built by Messrs. Lloyd & Easter of London.

The reclamation of marshes that had formerly been overflowed by the tides by the building of earthen river walls, probably between the twelfth and seventeenth centuries, altered the course of the estuary considerably in the lower reaches and caused such serious silting that in the eighteenth century vessels were forced to lighten their cargoes in Downham Reach between Woolverstone and Freston. So serious was the situation that the merchants, shipowners and businessmen of Ipswich called for an engineer's report on possible improvements to the upper reaches into the heart of the town. An Act of Parliament was obtained in 1805 under which River Commissioners were established who appointed a harbour master and purchased a primitive steam dredger.

The hoped-for improvements were forthcoming, and by the 1830s the Commissioners had set their sights on the construction of a wet dock, authorised by the Ipswich Dock Act of 1837. Under that Act the Ipswich Dock Commissioneers took on the role of the former River Commissioners and construction of the Dock began in 1838, the river being diverted into a new artificial tidal waterway, the New Cut, and each end of the broad right-angled bend in the river close to the Common Quay being dammed. The Dock was opened in January 1842. The old Customs House was demolished and replaced by the present building that opened in 1845. Railway access to the docks was progressively available from 1847. A larger, more convenient entrance lock was opened in 1881.

From the 1850s onwards, major changes were taking place in the shipping industry. For many centuries, British shipping had been protected by a series of enactments known as the Navigation Acts. These Acts succeeded in restricting the use of foreign vessels in the Nation's shipping trade and safeguarding the ability of the British shipping industry to supply the extra ships and seamen needed to strengthen the Navy during times of war. Not only did the Acts stipulate that exports must be carried in British ships but the carriage of imports also was restricted to either British ships or ships of the country actually producing the goods. In addition, participation by foreign vessels in certain English and Colonial trade was forbidden.

Other maritime nations passed similar Acts, and these were frequently reviewed as individual countries tried to monopolise the world shipping trade. Eventually the restrictions on the freedom of vessels to trade irrespective of their nationality were removed. This occurred in Britain during the early 1850s, although the right was retained to retaliate if restrictions were placed on British vessels in foreign waters. Until the Acts were abolished, the British coastal trade was restricted to British ships with a British Master. Afterwards, ships of any nationality could work in coastal trade.

Major changes were also being made to the ships themselves. The first screw steamship to bring cargo to the port was the newly built SS *HUNWICK* of London, arriving with 492 tons of coal for Prentice & Hewitt on 4th November 1853. She was the first steam collier to work out of Hartlepool. Hundreds of iron steam-driven ships were constructed during the 1860s and 1870s with the demise of the old wooden brigs, full-riggers and barques.

By the end of the nineteenth century the port was well prepared for the transformation of Ipswich from a purely agricultural community to a major industrial and engineering town. The improvements to the dock certainly lived up to expectations and the port's ability to cope with shipments ranging from coal and wheat to phosphate and petroleum was amply demonstrated.

The turret ship ss BELTOR of London, 2,025nrt, arrived on 1st October 1909 from Villa Constitution, some 240 miles up the River Plate near Rosario, with maize for Pauls. She sailed light for Shields on 10th October. The turret ship design enabled them to load 8% more without increasing the net tonnage, on which many port charges were calculated. Another benefit, and indeed a more important one, was that the design might also have contributed to improved stability, and thus the overall safety of the ship when carrying bulk rather than bagged grain. Such bulk cargoes encircling the Globe were unknown until grain began to be shipped to Europe from the Americas and Australia at the end of the nineteenth century. Many vessels were laid on their beam ends and lost when the cargo shifted in rough seas. (R.W. Smith Collection)

The opening in 1925 of Cliff Quay, just outside the Dock on the east bank of the Orwell, allowed much larger ships to be accommodated in the tidal deep-water berths there. Originally Cliff Quay was only 600ft (183m) long, but in the 1930s it was extended to 1,800ft (550m). This was especially important as the oil industry was developing and ocean-going tankers discharged within the borough boundary direct from oil fields in the Middle East and the Caribbean until changes within the industry altered the distribution patterns. The records show 2,319 vessels using the port in 1920 with a net registered tonnage of almost 200,000. By 1930, although the number of vessels that year had dropped by 21% to 1,832, their net registered tonnage had risen to 333,265, an increase of almost 67%. The importance of deep-sea shipping to Ipswich has never been thoroughly documented. Deep-sea shipping was particularly vital during both world wars when grain, timber and fertilisers still arrived despite Atlantic storms and the activity of enemy submarines, many of the ships being lost before peace returned. Colliers continued battling up and down the North Sea unremittingly. At times, the war came even to the Orwell itself and to its approaches.

The latter half of the twentieth century

by Captain Gerald C. Jones.

From 1943 onwards Gerry Jones was a midshipman and junior deck officer in Alfred Holt's Blue Funnel line. After the Second World War he progressed from Third Officer to Chief Officer with Blue Star Line on refrigerated vessels. In 1957 he became Superintendent Stevedore, loading and discharging vessels in Liverpool, with the West Coast Stevedoring Company. He became Assistant Harbour Master and Dock Superintendent with the Ipswich Dock Commission in 1968 and was Deputy Harbour Master and Dock Superintendent from 1969 to 1973. He continued as Deputy Harbour Master and Cargo Operations Manager with Ipswich Port Authority from 1974 to 1985, when he was appointed Harbour Master, a post he held until his retirement in 1990.

With the end of international conflicts in Europe the second half of the twentieth century saw many changes to worldwide shipping in all its facets. Ships became much larger, with a greater cargo carrying capacity, and with labour handling costs increasing all the time it was necessary for other parts of the transport industry to keep pace.

So far as the development of British seaports was concerned, the greatest changes lay in the methods used for the handling of cargoes, although the deepening of shipping channels and extension of the ground area required for the handling of the cargo were to play their part as the years progressed.

Associated with these alterations to the actual methods used for the handling of the cargoes was the general movement in this country to increase the use of road haulage, as opposed to the use of rail. The railways had been used for the inland carriage of bulk cargoes such as coal, chemicals, and fertilisers, to a far greater extent between 1900 and 1950. With modernisation, ports had to bear in mind the steady change from rail to road when planning the layout of new berths and the positioning and types of cranes, and also the access to and from the quayside within the dock estate. To some extent, the general road connections to the main highways, such as the new motorways, had to be taken into account to avoid unnecessary congestion to the daily traffic flow.

Health and safety at work also became far more important as time moved on. The general attitude to the well-being of the labour force had at long last begun to be considered when looking to the safety of the men at work and to the methods of working.

The use of derricks and steam winches for loading and discharging general cargo, which was in itself a hangover from the days of sail when the old square riggers used their spars with blocks and tackle attached, was slowly changing throughout the first half of the century. The greater use of cranes, both those fixed on shore and latterly those fitted aboard the vessels themselves, became the general practice throughout most ports.

For example, until about 1960 timber planks were handled aboard ships by gangs of eight holdsmen, with pairs of men in each corner of the hatch working together making up bundles into slings for discharging from the hold to the shore. Then the timber was relayed on bogies to an area of open land behind the quay, sorted to mark, and placed into various stacks prior to the planks again being manhandled for delivery to lorry or trailer, finally to be manhandled yet again on arrival at their new owners' depot. A far cry from the modern method of standard-sized, pre-strapped bundles, which are all lifted by high capacity cranes, and then moved around the quay with mechanical carriers, hardly requiring any manpower other than the driver. Consequently, the ships are turned round in hours rather than in days or weeks, with the added bonus of much less damage to the product.

These somewhat slow, labour intensive means of conveying general cargoes, using slings, grab hooks and trays, from the quay into the ship's hold and vice versa, were to change, firstly with the use of pallets and fork lift trucks on the quays, in the sheds, and aboard the ships themselves. Then in the late 1950s there was a dramatic change in the method of handling cargoes all around the world, with the introduction of the Standard Twenty-foot Container (TEU), and the up-dating of ex-wartime tank landing ships (LSTs), which developed into the modern roll on, roll off vessel, especially for the short sea trade routes and the vehicular ferry crossings.

At the same time as these new ideas for the handling of the cargoes were being invoked, the ships themselves were becoming still much larger, and of greater capacity. They were longer, of greater width, and most importantly as far as the ports of East Anglia were concerned they had deeper draughts. Many of the new freighters and particularly the bulk carriers dwarfed the pre-war passenger liners. The depth of water in the Harwich Approaches at the end of the century has been increased to twelve-and-a-half metres at Chart Datum to serve the needs of the Ports of Felixstowe and Harwich. This is far beyond the requirements of the Port of Ipswich which is governed by the depth of water in the River Orwell, this is 5.9 metres at LWOST, allowing for vessels of up to

The old method of handling timber: the NAVARINO of Glasgow delivering a cargo of timber from Portland, Oregon, via Grangemouth for William Brown and Gabriel, Wade and English in November, 1938.

THE PORT AND ITS TRADE

The sailing barge SPINAWAY C *and the motor barge* GLADYS *alongside Cranfield Brothers' mill at the head of the Dock in July 1966. (David Miller)*

140 metres LOA, and gives a depth in the channel of 9 metres at neaps and 9.8 metres at H.W. spring tides.

Recognition of all these facts meant that ports had to alter their facilities to suit, and the Port of Ipswich was no exception. In 1955 a major development came with a further extension of Cliff Quay by 1,450ft. down river, equipped with portal jib cranes running on dedicated railtracks with a 15 ton capacity, plus a fixed swinging derrick for handling heavy lifts up to 32 tons at 27.5 metres radius, and large modern Transit sheds for the storage of general cargo. All these berths were still fully connected to the main British Rail services, and for a while Freightliner ran a regular twice-daily train from Ipswich.

It was during the 1960's that in addition to the regular import/export of bulk chemicals, roadstone, timber, barley, grains, bulk petroleum, bitumen and general cargoes, the first regular use of an 8ft. cube 'Geest' container commenced, using a 15-ton slewing crane at Cliff Quay. These small containers were used for fresh produce inward and general goods on return to the Netherlands. This was the forerunner, in Ipswich, of the explosion to the standard 20ft, and 40ft, containers that are so widely used today.

Within the enclosed dock, timber was still the main source of business at End Quay, roadstone, chalk and general cargo being worked on a regular basis at South West Quay with a regular twice-weekly general cargo trade to Le Treport in France at Public Warehouse. The Gas Works had almost daily deliveries of coal by Coast Line vessels, and the northern end of the Dock was full of dumb barges used for grain storage by Messrs. Cranfields. Their mill and Messrs. R. & W. Pauls' mills were also frequently visited by numerous Thames sailing

Bob Roberts' barge CAMBRIA refitting on Pin Mill hard.

barges fitted with auxiliary engines (many since converted into pleasure craft) that traded cargoes to and from London. One visitor, the sailing barge *CAMBRIA* with Captain Bob Roberts, was the last of the East Coast Thames sailing barges still working commercially under sail only.

In 1966, to assist the various merchants using the port, a 40ft. long plate, 50 ton capacity weighbridge was built at Cliff Quay to cater particularly for the increase in bulk cargoes.

In 1968 cargo operations commenced at Orwell Quay in the enclosed dock, at a newly built quay and shed area on the site in Duke Street that the Dock Commission had purchased from Ransomes, Sims and Jefferies.

The regular GCB general cargo service to Hamburg, Germany was transferred from Cliff Quay to the newly installed Ro/Ro ramp at the north end of the quay, and the small Ro/Ro vessels *ARNEB* and *ARCTURUS* kept the No.8 Shed complex very busy until 1973 when the much larger West Bank Ro/Ro Terminal was brought into use. At the south end of Orwell Quay, general cargo trades (mostly to West Africa) started working into No.7 Shed, using mobile cranes, supported by a 32-ton fixed derrick similar to the one that had been installed at Cliff Quay.

The river berths at this time were very fully occupied with the tanker berths serving the fuel depots at the north end berths, timber being delivered to Greenwich Road, then the continued import of basic chemicals to Fisons with the compounded fertilisers being delivered by both ship overseas and by road to our own farmers throughout the UK. Stone was imported adjacent to the chemical berth and Geest containers occupied the next berth on a daily basis discharging then loading a full ship, sailing overnight to Rotterdam with an occasional extra service directly to Maasluis. There was the 32-ton fixed derrick that handled various trades heavy lifts as well as some of the early twenty-foot container shipments to the port. The area between the Heavy Derrick and the south end of Cliff Quay consisted of the main two general cargo berths which catered for trades ranging from Finland and the Baltic ports and Poland, to Yugoslavia, Italy and many ports in the Mediterranean as well as ports in West Africa

Following the Ipswich Dock Act of 1971 development commenced on the west bank of the River Orwell opposite Cliff Quay. Here, on the site of the

THE PORT AND ITS TRADE

former Stoke Bathing Place, and the mud flats reaching beyond Nova Scotia and Halifax, a new deep water quay and roll-on/roll-off terminal were constructed. This development became known as the West Bank. The first stage in 1973 saw the commencement of a Ro/Ro daily vehicle ferry to Europoort, and the transfer from Cliff Quay of the General Cargo Brokers general cargo/groupage service to Rotterdam.

In 1971 a second 40ft. plate, 50-ton weighbridge was built, this time at the back of the Public Warehouse, to serve the stone and other bulk cargoes being handled in the enclosed dock at South West Quay and Tovell's Wharf. The West Bank was also provided with a 50-ton weighbridge to cater for the regular Ro/Ro traffic.

On 24th July 1972 The Orwell Navigation Service was opened at the lock entrance. This provided assistance to all the users of the Port of Ipswich by giving a twenty-four hour radio and telephone service, and it acted as a central communicating point for the boatmen assisting with berthing. In more recent times these boatmen now use vans, however they are still referred to as 'the boatmen'. There was also liaison with the Trinity House Pilots who had an office in the same building.

In December 1973 The Ipswich Port Authority Order came into effect, thus marking the end of the Ipswich Dock Commission, which had been the guiding light for the Port of Ipswich since its formation in 1837, following on from the 1805 Act of Parliament that vested the conservancy of the River Orwell in a public commission. The 'River Commissioners' as they were called consisted at

The mv ARGO, *built in 1976 at Rendsburg on the Kiel Canal as a passenger and Ro/Ro ferry, was one of the earlier vessels to operate a Ro/Ro service from Ipswich.*

that time of seventy-two members who took over responsibility from the Town Authorities for the Port of Ipswich and the River Orwell down to Fagborough Cliff at Harwich Harbour. The Port Authority however was required to consist of fewer people having some experience or knowledge of the industry and better suited to the modern need of the shipping world, as distinct from the former Dock Commissioners who were mainly elected councillors.

The 1970's and 1980's saw many general Cargo lines calling at Ipswich, as well as the new Container and Ro/Ro berths being developed. These were in addition to the regular imports of timber, paper, and roadstone etc, at the south end, and the handling of bulk oils and spirits at the north end of Cliff Quay. There was however a reduction in the regular shipments of fertilisers from Fisons, but this was countered by increased exports of bulk grain, which reflected the changing conditions of farming in East Anglia.

At that time, the largest vessel that Ipswich could accept was 140.2 metres in length overall, due to the limited turning circle opposite the oil berths.

All ships, ports and trades rely very heavily on the support received from the army of pilots, ship's agents, cargo forwarders, customs, immigration, transport, and many other businesses associated with the movement of cargoes around the world. Ipswich is no exception; we were very fortunate and I can vouch, after nearly a quarter of a century working with the IDC/IPA, that we enjoyed very good working relationships with all our customers. That we had so many agents and cargo handlers to assist in the area was probably due to the fact that we had

A dramatic picture of spoil being pumped ashore for the construction of the West Bank Terminal in the 1970s. Framed in the 'fountain' is the Cliff Quay power station. (Bob Blastock)

neighbouring ports close by. The position of Ipswich, in a direct line between the Midlands and the industrial heart of Europe, must also be an important factor in bringing trade to our area. This emphasizes the need for a good road and rail network to the East Coast Ports.

In the first part of the twentieth century, dock labour was employed on a casual basis, which was not very satisfactory for the men concerned or for the firms employing them. However after the Second World War the Government of the day decided to nationalise the supply of labour, forming the National Dock Labour Board to employ all labour used to actually work aboard the ships. Various registered employers could then hire the number of men required to undertake the differing tasks on the shore side of the operation.

With this in mind the Ipswich Dock Commission formed a subsidiary Stevedoring Company to employ labour from the National Dock Labour Board to work aboard the ships, whilst they and other contracted employers directly employed the staff on the shore side of the operation. This system seemed to work very satisfactorily for a number of years. Ipswich was able to hold its own in competition with most of the larger ports.

The dock workers' union was a very strong organisation, and they used their power to great effect during this period. There were many heated arguments on the waterfront between the superintendent stevedores, and the union representatives, which had to be resolved before the job commenced. Usually the arguments would be about the rate for the job, but conditions, hours, and other factors could be involved.

The Port of Felixstowe, near neighbour to Ipswich, operated outside the 'scheme', and enjoyed very good labour relations compared to the nation as a whole. Although Felixstowe was expanding at an alarming rate, Ipswich too was extending its trade and becoming a very busy, medium-sized port with a good reputation in the shipping world.

In 1989 the National Dock Labour Board was dissolved and the employment of labour was placed in the hands of the Port Authority. On this occasion, shortly after the change over, Ipswich opted to hire most of its labour from an independent employer, as and when required, just keeping a nucleus of staff for continuity.

In 1997, another major change was to take place. The Port of Ipswich was to be 'unregistered', which was similar to its being de-nationalised, and sold into private ownership. In actual fact, the Port of Ipswich was an independent business in its own right; it was not owned by the Government, and the 'selling' of the port was hotly disputed.

However, after much Government and internal debate, the new owners turned out to be the Associated British Ports. The new owners injected some fresh thinking, and very soon made some alterations to the area by continuing the policy of 'swapping' with Ipswich Borough Council some of the land owned by the Port in the enclosed dock area for land further down river at the old electricity generator site. This policy enables them to have an area in which to develop further deep-water berths during the early years of the twenty-first century.

(End of article by Captain Jones)

Into the twenty-first century

By the beginning of the twenty-first century, many well-known manufacturing industries, including Cranfields, Pauls, Burtons and Ransome, Sims & Jefferies, had relocated away from the Dock or closed completely, while others moved into the technological age under new and sometimes foreign titles. Coal imports have been all but eliminated, not only for the retail market through long-established merchants but also for the gas and electricity undertakings due to closures. This has had a huge effect on the number and types of ships using the port.

Developers had begun moving into the Wet Dock area during the late 1990s with the construction of apartments on land near Fore Street, formerly occupied by Prentice Bros., Thomas Mortimer and Meux, and later leased by Hall & Co. Ltd. for storing aggregates. These flats were supposedly built in a style in sympathy with the former maltings.

At the time of writing (2007) the Wet Dock has largely been taken over by a subsidiary of the Port, Ipswich Haven Marina, with pontoon berthing and every facility for yachts. A completely new picture is emerging in this area, which is now referred to as 'The Waterfront'. The warehouses, silos and industrial premises are being demolished, to be replaced by high-rise apartments and

An aerial view of the Dock looking downriver, with the New Cut to the right. The three chimneys of Cliff Quay power station can be seen on the skyline.

leisure facilities. An ultra-modern, glass-covered building is springing up, set to become the centrepiece for the University Campus Suffolk (UCS). The merchant ships, working sailing barges and lighters that were once such a familiar sight in the Wet Dock will be seen there no more.

In spite of the loss of the Wet Dock, the port itself is still thriving under Associated British Ports. Manufactured fertilizers are now imported instead of the raw materials for the benefit of Fisons, now closed. A new timber terminal is in use on the extended West Bank and ABP has opened Sentinel Terminal for grain and animal feed handling at the southern end of Cliff Quay. In 2002 Southern Cement brought into use its £1.5 million terminal at Ipswich to handle imports of bulk cement and in 2004 ABP expanded its range of trade links after 4,500 tonnes of zinc ingots were discharged at Cliff Quay from Australia.

In June 2004 construction work begun on a new Ro/Ro berth at the port's West Bank Terminal. The £6.1 million capital project included the construction of a new 150m long quay wall, a hydraulically operated linkspan, and a tug berth. ABP undertook the project following an undertaking with Ferryways to extend the port's existing five-year agreement with the company by a further 20 years. Operating a Ro/Ro ferry service, Ferryways started at Ipswich in 2002 with the Ipswich-Ostend two-ship service and due to a surge in demand, the number of daily sailings doubled, resulting in the need for the second Ro/Ro berth. However in the summer of 2007 Ferryways NV collapsed, resulting in the loss of the sailings. Nevertheless, apart from this setback, the future for the continued growth of the Port of Ipswich looks bright.

Social activities and old timers of the river

Many of the dockside inhabitants either made their living from the dockside industries or were involved with the barges or coastal shipping. Until the Second World War the nearness of the river meant that the small amount of leisure time available to the local people was often spent on or near to the water. Public access to the port and the banks of the river was far less restricted than at the present time, and the area was considered an important and well-used amenity. One popular recreation spot was at Hog Highland, now occupied by Cliff Quay, where families picnicked on the shore and children paddled in the shallow water. Another popular place was on the Wherstead shore next to Bourne Bridge at Ostrich Creek, now the site of Fox's Marina.

The Promenade, long since gone, with its avenue of trees leading down from New Cut East to the lock gates and the so-called Umbrella shelter would all be decorated with bunting and coloured lights when the annual regatta was held. For many years spectators gathered to watch the various events taking place on the river and to witness the rivalry between the various rowing clubs. During such an event in 1905, the five occupants of a Petrel Rowing Club boat taking part in the coxed fours were lucky to escape with their lives when a paddle steamer sliced their craft in two while they were waiting for the start of the race. They had tried to row out of the way of the large vessel, which had suddenly appeared round the bend of the river near to Hog Highland, but did not have enough time to escape. Luckily, they could all swim and they were quickly rescued, to the delight and relief of the watching crowd.

Two other Ipswich-based clubs, the Naiad and the Orwell Works Rowing Clubs, had their wooden boathouses attached to the side of Stoke Bathing Place, near the timber ponds. Steps led down to the river from both buildings and the members were forced to stand with water up to their knees to launch their boats. This could not have been pleasant on a cold day when, with shoes full of freezing water, they had to complete their training session on the river and return to the boathouse to place the boat on the storage rack inside before being able to change into dry clothing. No hot water or showers were available in those days; a pail of cold water from the river or a swim at Stoke Bathing Place had to suffice. Sadly, the two boathouses caught fire shortly after the end of the Second World War, and the clubs never rose again as someone had forgotten to renew the fire insurance on the buildings.

The open-air swimming pool known as Stoke Bathing Place had already been in existence for some thirty years when it was advertised in 1874 as having 'every facility for visitors of sea bathing, as the baths are constantly supplied with pure seawater at every tide'. The fee at that time, including private dressing box, was 3d. and it catered for gentlemen only, although part of the north bank of the pool could be used free by the public. In later years Mr Harvey was the well-known individual in charge. During the 1920s and earlier an annual swimming race took place from West End Swimming Pool, passing under Princes Street Bridge and Stoke Bridge, to Stoke Bathing Place. Each swimmer had to be accompanied by a boat. At the end of the race swimmers changed at

A coxed four from one of the Ipswich rowing clubs in the New Cut. In the background are three of the paddle steamers working the Ipswich to Harwich service.

The Griffin Inn on the corner of Bath Street and New Cut West, with Charlie Smith, foreman at Christopherson's, second from left; standing next to him is Walter Podd, the local chimney sweep, then Mr Burgess and an unknown person standing next to ferryman Mr Bob Lumkin. On the right is Mr Herbert Rowland, the landlord of the Griffin, holding his dog Troski. Next to Mr Rowland is his young son Cecil, who later coxed a boat for the Naiad Rowing Club.

the Griffin public house, where they were supplied with tea and biscuits. Unfortunately, the bathing place did not survive the devastation of the 1953 floods and the site has now been swallowed up by the West Bank Container Terminal.

When the Ipswich Dock Commission announced in 1970 their intentions for the West Bank, there was little concern given to the local residents. Many people had come to live in riverside properties on the Wherstead Road in order to enjoy their interest in the river, have the facility to moor boats within easy reach of their back gardens and take pleasure in the splendid views available down the Orwell. These amenities had been enjoyed by the residents ever since their houses were built back in the 1920s. The Dock Commission plans were to infill right up to their garden fences to a height of about four feet, with security fencing on top, to install floodlighting and to stack containers at the bottom of their gardens. In an effort to get some degree of consideration from the IDC the residents challenged a Private Member's Bill in the House of Lords. Following the hearing, the residents withdrew their petition when a number of concessions were made in their favour by the Dock Commission, which no doubt had not expected a relatively small group of Ipswich people with very limited resources to challenge a Bill passing through the Lords. The Wherstead Road Residents' Association has been in existence ever since, and although sadly the people involved lost their riparian rights and river views they do have legally binding agreements with the port authorities.

Members of the public have often been allowed to go aboard various ships in the port. One Sunday afternoon in the summer of 1931, for example, visitors were allowed to look around the four-masted barque *MELBOURNE* after she had berthed at Cliff Quay with grain from Australia, the charge of sixpence per person going to a seamen's charity. At one event known as 'Port Sunday', held during the late 1970s, schoolchildren were encouraged to visit as many of the merchant ships in the port as they could manage.

Naval vessels, for example the submarine HMS *OPOSSUM*, launched in 1963, HMS *BRONINGTON*, a Coniston class minehunter refitted in 1977, and HMS *GRAFTON*, a Type-23 frigate, have all called at the port in recent years, *GRAFTON* enjoying a close affiliation with the borough for almost a decade. She sailed down the river for the last time on 23rd January 2006, facing decommissioning, having been sold to the Chilean navy. The Sail Training

Association's two vessels *MALCOLM MILLER* and *WINSTON CHURCHILL* and the Norwegian square-rigger *SORLANDET*, another training vessel, have all berthed in the Dock. Replica vessels have visited the Dock, allowing visitors to gain some idea of the conditions endured by the sailors aboard the original vessels. The three-masted barque *GODSPEED* came in 1985 before re-enacting the voyage across the Atlantic that led to the permanent English settlement at Jamestown, Virginia, in 1606/07. The man appointed to command the original *GODSPEED* was Bartholomew Gosnold, whose family lived at Otley, near Ipswich, and many of the seventeenth-century settlers came from Norfolk and Suffolk. A reconstruction of Sir Francis Drake's famous galleon, the *GOLDEN HINDE*, completed in 1973 by a group of people in San Francisco, visited Ipswich in 1985 and again nine years later. Two twenty-first century visitors have been the wooden sailing ship *GRAND TURK*, built in Turkey in 1977 and registered in London, and a replica of the fast schooner HMS *PICKLE* that brought the news of Nelson's victory and death to England in 1805. The latter vessel joined in the celebrations held at Ipswich in 2005 of the 200th anniversary of the battle of Trafalgar.

In 1992 council and port officials joined members of the Ipswich Maritime Trust, established in 1982, to celebrate the 150th anniversary of the Dock's opening. Visitors to Isaac Lord's warehouse enjoyed the borough council's 150th anniversary exhibition and a display of ropemaking. A Dunkirk Little Ships reunion took place, one of a few held in recent years at the Dock. 'Sail Ipswich', a weekend of events staged during the summer of 1997 to celebrate

The barge ARDWINA *under repair at Dock End Yard in 1980.*

maritime traditions, featured a gathering of tall ships, historic training vessels, traditional working craft and classic yachts gathered in the Dock for the public to inspect, together with exhibitions, musicians, and dragon boat racing. The last-named event, originating from China, took place on the eve of Hong Kong being handed back to that country. Visiting ships included the *POGORIA*, a 40m barquentine from Poland, *LA BELLE POULE* and the *ETOILE*, both square-riggers from France, and the sail-training square-rigger *KALIAKRA* from Bulgaria. A similar event was held in 1998. Since 2002 Associated British Ports have allowed annual exhibitions to be staged on the ground floor of the Custom House featuring various aspects of the maritime history of Ipswich. One or two barges, representing the tiny number still left in sail, are sometimes to be seen in the port. The spirit and fun of the first regattas are not entirely lost to the public in spite of the change from Wet Dock to modern Waterfront.

The welfare of the seamen was catered for during the second half of the nineteenth century by a floating church. A former 16-gun brig sloop, the *HELENA*, built at Pembroke Dock in 1843, was moored alongside the Quay at a spot now known as Helena Road and the vessel was in use as a seamen's church from 1869 to 1880. She had been granted by the Admiralty for that purpose following use as a coal hulk in 1861 and then a police hulk in 1863. It was said that she could seat between five and six hundred people. More recently, a former lightship moored in the dock was used by the Sea Cadets as their training headquarters.

Recollections still linger of some of the local characters whose lives were

The submarine HMS OBERON departing through the lock after a courtesy visit to Ipswich in 1985.

An advertisement of 1931 for C.H. Fox & Son Ltd, who had a boatyard at 499 Wherstead Road. A successor firm, Fox's Marina Ipswich Ltd, now occupies premises close to Bourne Bridge.

spent on the river, men such as 'Cocker', who would dive into the water from the top of the mainmast of a barge for one shilling. One man who might be described as a true waterman of the River Orwell, although unable to swim, was Mr Walter 'Budger' Flory, who lived for many years on a houseboat moored in the bight opposite Cobbold's Brewery. A cripple with one foot missing and the other turned inwards, he earned a living by helping to moor barges and other vessels to buoys as they waited for the lock gates to operate. He also cleaned and painted boats, repaired torn sails, spliced ropes and made fenders for boat owners in addition to fishing for flat fish and catching eels. His philosophy was that he was gifted with powerful arms to make up for losing the full use of his legs.

George Glading was the well-known skipper of the steam barge *TRENT RIVER* that traded between Ipswich and Bramford for a long time. Born in 1864, he lived close to the river all his seventy-three years. He was responsible for pulling several people, including children, from the river and was awarded the Royal Humane Society's bronze medal in 1902, its bronze clasp in 1905 and a Testimonial on Parchment in 1922. In later years he used the *TRENT RIVER* to tow barges to the vicinity of Bourne Bridge so that they could then set their sails for the journey downriver. He collected the five-shilling fee on the barge's return trip. At other times when the wind dropped he would tow barges into the Dock. Another individual, George Fulcher, performed the same service with his small motor-tug.

For many years a ferry boat was rowed between landing steps at the bottom of Bath Street, near to the Griffin Inn, and the Promenade. The ferry ran from early morning until dusk and the fare in later years was 1d. for adults and ½d. for children The ferrymen had a wooden hut at the top of the landing stage on the west side of the river. Workers at Ransomes & Rapier's and Cocksedge's were ferried across each day from the east bank, and similarly men from the Stoke area were taken across the river to their jobs at Ransomes, Sims & Jefferies. In the 1920s the ferrymen were Mr Bob Lumkin and Mr 'Caps' Smith, the latter man so called because he wore a style of headgear that today would be termed a baseball cap. After the Second World War one of the ferrymen was Mr W. Gostling. The ferry has not operated for many years now.

THE PORT AND ITS TRADE

Exempt lands

For several years the term 'exempt lands' referred to specific sites on the banks of the Orwell belonging to the larger landowners where no rates, dues or duties were payable on any goods loaded or discharged there. If such goods were, however, later moved from those locations to other places in the area they became liable for the dues.

This consideration was contained in the Act of Parliament for the improvement of the Port of Ipswich that received Royal Assent by George III in July 1805. A clause in this Act decreed that no cargoes loaded or unloaded on the lands of Philip Bowes Vere Broke between Ipswich and Levington Creek or on lands on either side of the river belonging to Charles Berners or Sir Robert Harland between Pin Mill and Freston Brooke should be liable to dues.

The same clause with variations was included in the 1837 Act that led to the setting up of the Dock Commission and also in another Act of 1852. The clause appears to have remained fundamentally unchanged in later Acts until its repeal by the Ipswich Dock Act of 1918. This exemption no doubt explains the absence of any records of barges discharging at places within the exempt lands including Pin Mill, the Cat House and Slumpy Lane Wharf before 1919. On the eastern side of the river the few arrivals mentioned on the shore or in Levington Creek were annotated 'Exempted lands' or 'Colonel Tomline's land'.

After 1919 the dock records note the arrivals of barges with coal, stone and shingle on both sides of the river, but trade to these places had ceased by 1929.

Harland's Dock photographed in the 1970s before it was filled in for the marina. (R.W. Smith)

Navigation — the approaches to Ipswich

The approaches to Harwich Harbour are naturally included in sailing directions in English published as long ago as 1588, the year of the defeat of the Armada. The reference to the Naze when coming from the Thames mentions only 'two trees stand upon a high hill; when they are both in one con North Northwest by the markes of Harwich untill you come before the Haven. . .' Trees and church spires were the only conspicuous objects along the relatively flat shoreline of the Thames Estuary, although there were a few primitive beacons and seamarks. Responsibility for erection and maintenance of these throughout England passed from the Lord High Admiral, Howard of Effingham, in 1594 to Trinity House by Act of Parliament. That august body, which began as a kind of benevolent association of ship masters, pilots and mariners and also happened to protect ships and cargoes, had received its Charter from Henry VIII in May 1514. Subsequent by-laws gave control and licensing of pilots in the Thames to the Corporation, and a decree of 1567 demanded that anyone taking down a steeple, tree or seamark was subject to a fine of £100 or even outlawry.

Two lighthouses, in effect leading lights, stood at Harwich from 1664 and with various rebuildings, resitings and modifications lasted until they were

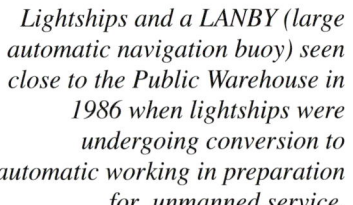

Lightships and a LANBY (large automatic navigation buoy) seen close to the Public Warehouse in 1986 when lightships were undergoing conversion to automatic working in preparation for unmanned service.

replaced by two screw-pile lights at Dovercourt, lit in 1863 and extinguished in August 1917. These Victorian lighthouses superseded the Harwich lights because of the relentless southerly extension of Landguard Point and were in turn displaced by new lighted and unlit buoys along the approach from the Cork Spit. Trinity House had taken over the Harwich lighthouses in 1837.

A lighthouse was put up in Landguard Fort in 1848 and moved to the beach in 1861. The latter burned down in April 1925 and was replaced by a lighted buoy at Cliff Foot. Many other leading lights and beacons have been established at Felixstowe and Landguard since the mid-nineteenth century.

A daymark on some early charts was replaced in 1720 by an 81ft octagonal brick tower on the Naze which stands to this day. A triangular mark, 50ft high, was built on the cliff at Bawdsey in the late eighteenth century, rebuilt in 1831 and again in 1837, and demolished because of erosion in February 1924.

The Cork light vessel, established in 1844, became well known to residents and visitors alike at Felixstowe and to passengers on paddle steamer trips from Ipswich. The Cork light vessel was withdrawn in 1975 and replaced by a LANBY (Large Automatic Navigational Buoy), 30 metres in diameter. Ten years later the LANBY was removed when a new approach channel was dredged, necessitating an entirely new system of buoyage.

The first buoy to be laid in the Harwich approaches was the Rough, placed in 1776 and lit in 1914, and several others were established leading into the harbour during the nineteenth century. The Beach End, laid in 1843, became the first in the area to be replaced by an iron one in 1866 and was lit in 1894. The Guard buoy was 'deemed advisable' in 1855. Shotley Spit buoy, later a beacon at the confluence of the Stour and Orwell, was laid in 1847 and lit eighty years later. It was moved in 1931 some 500 yards to the south-east and repositioned again as the Spit encroached upon the Harbour.

The first wooden buoys in the Orwell were laid in 1840, and replaced by iron ones from the 1860s. Before that many of the old hazards, shoals and hards had been marked by beacons or withies. The channel from Harwich Harbour to Ipswich Dock was dredged early in the twentieth century to 19ft (5.79m) at Low Water Ordinary Spring Tides (LWOST), a depth which has been maintained ever since. Dredging was done by a steam dredger served by hoppers in an operation which commenced in 1897 and ended on 23rd September 1931. On 10th November 1930 eleven lighted buoys were established, seven flashing white and four flashing red. The buoys conformed to normal practice: those on the starboard hand (sailing upstream) were black conical buoys while the port hand buoys were red can buoys. During the 1950s more extensive dredging was done to ensure the correct depth, some of the points were eased, the channel widened in places and another lighted buoy laid (No.12). The International Association of Lighthouse Authorities (I.A.L.A.) agreed to a standard buoyage system to come into force throughout European waters in 1977, starting in the English Channel on the Greenwich Meridian. In the new system the River Orwell had eighteen lighted buoys, of which ten were starboard hand buoys painted green and displaying a green flash instead of white and eight buoys on the port hand would remain painted and flashing red; unlit buoys also conform with the green and red colour code. By the 1980s all the buoys had been fitted with radar reflectors, and in the 1990s all lighted buoys were converted to use solar power instead of gas for illumination.

In 1972 the Ipswich Dock Commission established the Orwell Navigation Service (O.N.S.), a V.H.F. radio station on continuous 24-hour watch. Its call sign is Ipswich Port Radio and inward-bound ships report on entering the river and at specified buoys on the way up. Likewise outward-bound ships report prior to leaving the berth, on passing designated buoys and again on leaving the river, where they contact Harwich Harbour Radio. The service operates from a purpose-built tower by the lock gates and provides all necessary information to pilots and ships' masters, and other vessels including yachts keep a valuable listening watch. A dedicated telephone line connects the O.N.S. with the Ipswich pilots' lookout at Harwich. Pilots were a little wary of the idea at first, concerned that ships which had hitherto not been required to have a pilot but had still taken one might dispense with the service if enough information was passed over the radio to ensure a safe passage up the Orwell.

The Harbour Master at the time, Captain John Bain, was aware of the pitfalls the operators might fall into if they broadcast information which might have been construed as 'remote pilotage', including the offence of offering services while not holding a licence. There was also the risk of claims for damages caused if a ship came to grief after taking such advice. The pilots accepted Captain Bain's assurances and wholeheartedly supported the O.N.S. During this period many improvements were attributable to the Harbour Master after years of sometimes difficult relations between pilots and port authority. Indeed in 1973 the pilots moved from their lookout at Harwich to an office in the radio tower at the lock gates, paying a peppercorn rent. This provided as near an integrated service as possible while preserving the autonomous status of the self-employed pilots.

In the early 1980s closed-circuit television cameras were installed and radar scanners provided at Levington and the Orwell Bridge site, providing the O.N.S. operator with views of the river from Harwich. At the time of writing (2007) improvements have been made and very high definition, closed circuit television cameras are now in use.

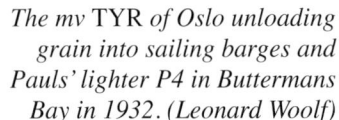

The mv TYR *of Oslo unloading grain into sailing barges and Pauls' lighter P4 in Buttermans Bay in 1932. (Leonard Woolf)*

THE PORT AND ITS TRADE

Buttermans Bay

Buttermans Bay is a broad deep reach on the south side of the River Orwell below Pin Mill which provides very sheltered moorings in almost all conditions. The Bay had for centuries been used as a safe anchorage, and the first screw moorings were laid in November 1878. There the big square-riggers and steamships moored fore-and-aft to the buoys until they had either discharged their complete cargo into barges and coasters or reduced their draught sufficiently to clear the lock-sill at Ipswich. If only lightening ship, they were towed up to Ipswich Dock after a week or ten days. Sometimes one of R. & W. Pauls' tugs was used, or perhaps a Dock Commission tug, the *90* or *STRONGHOLD*, or else one of the earlier steam mud hoppers, *FRESTON* and *DOWNHAM*, which were equipped with towing gear.

To work the cargo out of ships, gangs of dockers were taken downriver from the New Cut to Buttermans Bay each morning and returned in the evening aboard a 70ft steamer, the *PRIMROSE*. Steel-built at Great Yarmouth in 1903 for the Yare & Waveney Lighter Co. Ltd of Norwich, she was bought by Pauls in 1920 and is recorded as having towed one of Pauls' 350dwt steel lighters, the *P4*, empty from Woodbridge to Ipswich in June 1920. On the rare occasions that *PRIMROSE* was unavailable, the railway-owned Harwich Harbour passenger ferries were hired. One such instance was when *PRIMROSE* had been to Brightlingsea, possibly for repairs, and the LNER motor ferries *HAINAULT* and *BRIGHTLINGSEA* were used.

The length of channel through Buttermans Bay had been widened and dredged to 22ft by the new IDC dredger in 1897 and additional buoys were laid. Until the 1950s charts still marked twelve such buoys, four pairs inside and two pairs further apart; these were for bigger ships and were virtually in the middle of the dredged channel. Only three pairs remained by the 1970s and all were removed by about 1980.

Cliff Quay opened in 1925, providing much needed deepwater tidal berths. When the Cliff was fully occupied, ships continued to use the Bay until 25th August 1941 when the ss *IOANNIS FRANGOS* of Chios sailed for the Tyne, having brought wheat from Sorel for Pauls (653 tons), Cranfields (4,059 tons) and Marriages (221 tons). She had been launched as the *NOVINGTON* from Richardson, Duck's Yard at Stockton in 1912. The Bay moorings were no longer used because of the risk of mines laid by aircraft; the ss *SKAGERRAK* had been destroyed by a mine only two miles downriver on the day before the departure of the *IOANNIS FRANGOS*. If a ship lying at moorings in the Bay had been sunk it could have blocked the fairway to Ipswich. The *PAMIR* was almost certainly the last big square-rigger to moor in the Bay, in 1927, the 1930s arrivals all being towed to Cliff Quay.

Stores and coal had to be brought from Ipswich. When fresh water was required by ships in the Bay a water barge was towed down from Ipswich for ten shillings, with larger amounts, perhaps 50 tons, delivered by tug for a charge of £12 10s. These arrangements, including the charges, applied during the 1920s and '30s. In later years water came from Felixstowe aboard the little steam tug/water carrier *BHEESTIE*, built at South Shields in 1910 and owned by the

Felixstowe Dock & Railway Co. Many ships, however, would take water from the quayside at their next port of call.

Some minor problems were caused in 1926 by the Spanish steamship *HERCULES*, 2,758nrt, of Bilbao, launched at Middlesbrough in 1900. She had arrived at Harwich in October 1926 from Buenos Aires with 6,394 tons of maize for Pauls. A tug was ordered to take her from the harbour to Buttermans Bay on 16th October, but the ship had fouled her anchor and was unable to proceed until the 17th. She arrived in the Dock on the 27th to complete her discharge and eventually sailed on 6th November with a tug as far as Collimer Point. Nine days later her agents, Houlder Brothers, a shipping line who maintained an office on the Cornhill at Ipswich, were invoiced for £3 for the clearance of numbers 6 and 7 mooring buoys at Buttermans Bay that were fouled by the ship when one of her moorings parted on the night of 24th October. While at Ipswich the *HERCULES* took on 7,950 gallons of fresh water at a cost of £13 11s.

Ships' agents and users, including Lewcock & Pemberton, Houlder Brothers, R. & W. Paul Ltd., Felixstowe Dock & Railway Company, E. Marriage & Son Ltd and Free, Rodwell of Mistley, paid a subscription of one pound in January 1927 to a 'Guarantee Fund for the Pin Mill Public Telephone Office' which may have been a single contribution to establish an important service for ships' agents or masters, who could be rowed ashore to use a telephone in what was a remote area.

The following table shows grain ship arrivals in Buttermans Bay during 1935. The information is taken from the Ipswich Dock Commission's Pin Mill Harbourmaster's Register. Most of the ships shown brought Plate maize for R. & W. Paul amounting to about 104,624 tons. Pauls also received 9,184 tons of barley, Cranfield Brothers had 19,065 tons of wheat and E. Marriage & Sons of Felixstowe had 745 tons of the same, making a total of 133,618 tons discharged in the Bay.

Any sailing barges waiting for orders would find plenty of lighterage work when ships were being worked in the Bay. Most of the sailing barges loaded for Ipswich once or twice per ship and others served mills at Felixstowe, Colchester, Fingringhoe and Faversham, apart from London. Pauls steamships *OXBIRD*, *CROSSBILL* and *FIRECREST* sailed regularly to Yarmouth, Lynn, Wisbech and Boston. A few Dutch motor coasters were also engaged. During 1935 there were over 1,140 individual barge and coaster movements to and from the Bay as they arrived light and departed loaded from the ships. Of the vessels listed in the table, nine were still British owned. Of the 26 arrivals, the 18 marked with an asterisk were all British built, of which 14 had been launched at Sunderland, Shields, Stockton-on-Tees and Tyne yards, three from the Clyde and one from Hull. The rest were built at Rotterdam, Gothenberg, Kiel, Bordeaux and the *ALASKA* at Vancouver in 1918.

Taking as examples three arrivals, ss *PANTELIS*, ss *SCORESBY* and ss *TRAFALGAR*, in October 1936 with maize for R. & W. Paul, the following paragraphs show the arrangements made by the ships' agents, Lewcock and Pemberton, for these vessels and the costs.

PANTELIS required stores previously ordered through her owners and awaiting her arrival in the Public Warehouse. These amounted to 7 tons 13 cwt and were sent down aboard Packard's old steam barge *TRENT RIVER*, by then being run by her only master, George Glading. Towage from Harwich to the Bay cost £15 and swinging the ship head down ready for sailing cost £7 10s. Another £10 10s. (ten guineas) was required for the small motor boat *ORWELL II* to attend the ship from 5th to 16th October. She would take crew members to Ipswich on business or for a doctor, etc.

SCORESBY sailed on 29th October, but had ordered a tug for the 27th and 29th which cost £10 for standing by and £7 10s for swinging on departure. The launch *ORWELL II* had attended for eleven days, costing £9 12s 6d.

TRAFALGAR arrived on 17th October and required the assistance of a tug to swing at a cost of £7 10s. Evidently there was a strike at the time and the launch was on call for eight days for £4, plus 15 days discharging at £17 2s. 6d. Nine tons of stores in the Public Warehouse were sent down for £1 14s. 1d. On 2nd November the tug *STRONGHOLD* put the ship's crew aboard, charge £5, although whether it was a normal crew change is not known.

Grain ships unloading in Buttermans Bay, 1935. Details of the sailings were omitted from the records. *British-built vessel.

Arrival 1935	Ship	Reg	From	Cargo	Tonnage	Depart/Port
14 Jan	YNGAREN*	Gothenburg	Antwerp	P/C wheat	1,234	?
28 Jan	AGHIOS GEORGIOS*	Ithaca	Braila	maize	4,000	10 Feb to Cardiff
14 Feb	BULLAREN	Gothenburg	London	P/C wheat	1,783	19 Feb to Gothenburg
5 Mar	WAZIRISTAN*	Newcastle	London	P/C wheat	3,225	13 Mar to Swansea
17 May	TREGANTLE*	St Ives	River Plate	maize	5,500	30 May to Cardiff
16 Jun	EASTVILLE*	Newcastle	River Plate	maize	5,685	27 Jun to Tyne
21 Jun	MARIA de LARRINAGA*	Liverpool	River Plate	maize	7,671	8 Jul to Hull
1 Jul	TEMPLAR	Tonsberg	London	P/C wheat	1,490 + 745	3 July general to Bremen
12 Jul	EUTHALIA	Anapoy	Rosario	maize	6,324	25 Jul to Dover
25 Jul	KALLIOPI*	Chios	Rosario	maize	6,644	8 Aug to Rotterdam
2 Aug	VIRGINIA S*	Syra	Rosario	maize	3,535	12 Aug P/C to Ipswich
17 Aug	ELLIN	Andros	San Nicolas	maize	6,865	31 Aug to .Danzig
2 Sep	EL NEPTUNO*	Bilbao	San Nicolas	maize	6,008	23 Sep to Antwerp
26 Sep	CAPE CORSO*	Hydra	Theodosia	wheat & barley	4,072 + 2,491	11 Oct to Rotterdam
11 Oct	WESTMINSTER	London	Falmouth (for orders)	barley	4,123	21 Oct to Newcastle
5 Oct	ALASKA	Haugesund	River Plate	maize	7,088	21 Oct to Rotterdam
6 Oct	CHARLES L. D.	Dunkirk	Canada	wheat	4,271	12 Oct P/C to Hull
22 Oct	COULOURAS-XENOS*	Hydra	Southampton	P/C barley & wheat	580 + 2,990	27 Oct to Emden
27 Oct	ASPASIA*	Chios	River Plate	maize	6,600	11 Nov to Emden
27 Oct	GEORGE M. LIVANOS*	Chios	River Plate	maize	6,543	12 Nov to Emden
8 Nov	JOYOUS*	London	River Plate	maize	5,964	21 Nov to Rotterdam
22 Nov	AGHIOS GEORGIOS*	Ithaca	Odessa	barley	1,990	30 Nov to Newcastle P/C
26 Nov	TRAFALGAR*	Glasgow	River Plate	maize	6,512	?
21 Dec	ROXBY*	W Hartlepool	River Plate	maize	6,567	?
26 Dec	ANNA N. GOULANDRIS	Andros	Rosario	maize	6,176	13 Jan to Rotterdam
31 Dec	HAZELSIDE*	Newcastle	Rosario	maize	6,942	?
				TOTAL (tons)	133,618	

Harbour Masters at the Port of Ipswich

- 1837	Mr Robert Caston
1837 - 1864	Mr Samuel Smith
1864 - 1894	Captain Garwood
1894 - 1905	Captain Joseph Wing
1905 - 1924	Captain Stephen Phillips
1924 - 1948	Captain J.M. Coates
1948 - 1965	Captain J. Keldie
1965 - 1970	Captain Stephen H. Harvey
1970 - 1985	Captain John M. Bain
1985 - 1990	Captain Gerald C. Jones
1990 - 1997	Captain David H. Winter
1997 -	Captain John Swift

Port of Ipswich 1950 - 2006

1950   Mr Peter Bamford was Secretary and Solicitor and Captain J. Keldie was Harbour Master. They had both held these offices for a number of years.

1965   Captain S.H. Harvey succeeded Captain Keldie as Harbour Master.

1968   Captain G.C. Jones joined the Ipswich Dock Commission as Assistant Harbour Master and Dock Superintendent.

1969   Captain Harvey retired, Captain J.M. Bain became Harbour Master, and Captain G.C. Jones became Deputy Harbour Master and Dock Superintendent.

1975   Mr Bamford retired and Mr J. Evelyn became Chief Executive, during which time many major changes took place in the Port of Ipswich.

1985   Captain Bain retired. Captain G.C. Jones appointed as Harbour Master and Captain D. Winter as Chief Operations Manager.

1989   Mr J. Evelyn died and Mr M. Bealings, Chairman of the Ipswich Port Authority Board, became the new Chief Executive.

1990   Captain Jones retired. Captain D. Winter became Harbour Master.

1993   Mr Bealings was succeeded as chief executive by Mr Alan Howell

1997   On 25th March Ipswich Port Authority was sold to Associated British Ports, becoming Ipswich Port Limited with Mr J. Copping as Managing Director. The same year, Captain Winter retired and Captain John Swift became Harbour Master.

2000   Mr T. Docherty succeeded Mr J. Copping as Managing Director of Ipswich Port Ltd.

2001   Mr R. Smith succeeded Mr T. Docherty as Managing Director of Ipswich Port Ltd.

2006   Mr A. McFarland became Managing Director of Ipswich Port Ltd.

Pilotage & other business   2

The role of pilots on the Orwell was regularised in 1805 by the Act for 'improving and making more commodious the Port of Ipswich in the County of Suffolk', under which the men were to be licensed by the River Commissioners, and to act as a pilot without obtaining a licence would incur a fine of between £3 and £10. An 1808 Act empowered Trinity House to examine pilots, resulting in Harwich becoming an outport of London. A committee met the following year to examine services at Ipswich, and these were considered satisfactory.

In 1824, however, the commercial interests at Ipswich petitioned for a change of status. Consequently Ipswich became a Trinity House outport in the following year, rejecting the opportunity to merge with the Harwich pilots. Historically there had been long and bitter rivalry between the Corporations of Harwich and Ipswich, and this extended to the pilots; in 1899, when London and Harwich pilotage services were rationalised, the pilotage of Ipswich and Harwich remained separate.

```
Ipswich to Downham Reach and vice versa
Sloops and vessels with a single mast . . . . . . . . . . . . . . . . . . . . . . . . . . . 1s 3d. per foot draught
Vessels with two masts or more . . . . . . . . . . . . . . . . . . . . . . . . . . . . . . 1s 6d. per foot draught

Downham to Levington Creek and vice versa
Every British vessel . . . . . . . . . . . . . . . . . . . . . . . . . . . . . . . . . . . . . . 9d. per foot draught

Levington Creek to Harwich and vice versa
For every British ship . . . . . . . . . . . . . . . . . . . . . . . . . . . . . . . . . . . . . .6d. per foot draught

For every British ship coming from Harwich to Downham . . . . . . . . . . . 1s 3d. per foot draught

For every British vessel outward bound from Downham to Harwich . . . 1s 3d. per foot draught

And for every foreign vessel double the aforesaid rate to and from such part of the River Orwell as such foreign ship or vessel shall be piloted.
```

Pilotage rates for 1805.

Trinity House, after various reports and much discussion, produced new by-laws for Ipswich in 1838. These followed the 1837 Ipswich Dock Act in which a clause ruled 'That it shall and may be lawful for the Corporation of Trinity House of Deptford Strond, and they are hereby required to appoint proper and competent persons (not to exceed five or less than three persons) to act as Sub-Commissioners of Pilotage . . .and they are hereby authorised to examine into the qualifications of persons to act as Pilots for the said Port and adjoining coasts.' The spelling of the address, which goes back centuries, is still used for drafting new documents, etc. The Act provided for the Ipswich Sub-Commissioners to be responsible for managing the service through a Superintendent of Pilots instead of the Harbour Master. The Superintendent and pilots were subject to a stringent code of practice.

Pilotage was compulsory for vessels of 50 tons burthen or upwards between Downham Reach and the quays, and masters refusing a pilot would still be liable for full rates. Pilots were to conduct vessels to or from Harwich if required. Rates were based on the vessels' draught per foot and masters were to give true account of draught or incur a penalty of paying double pilotage plus a fine of not less than £2 or more than £10. Pilots were authorised to admeasure (determine) the draught. The Commissioners were empowered to alter rates of pilotage but no advance was to exceed double the rates mentioned.

Fifty years later and the charges had actually been reduced by about 3d off each rate, with vessels towed by a steam tug having to pay only two-thirds of the appropriate rate. Another hundred years on and the lowest pilotage rates in 1955 for sailing or steam vessels up to 100nrt was only 1s 6d per foot draught, comparing favourably with the rate of 2s 6d charged in 1805 to 50 tons burthen British vessels for Harwich to the River Orwell. In 1955, however, the rate for compulsory pilotage for vessels in the foreign trade was increased by sixty per cent.

Two pilot boats were moored in the River Orwell, one below Levington Creek and the other in Downham Reach. They were manned on a weekly basis and inward bound vessels had to take their pilots by turn but masters of outward bound ships could chose their pilots from those assembled at the Pilotage Office at tide time. One of the pilot boats listed in 1861 was named the *MULBERRY*, presumably after the Mulberry Middle shoal.

Ipswich pilots maintained a hulk anchored within the river near Shotley Spit, giving them accommodation. Pilots boarded and left ships by a rowing boat. This arrangement probably continued until the First World War.

The Ipswich pilot boats' history ended in 1925 after well over a century of accommodating pilots awaiting ships, the traditional Tide Waiters as they were once known. On 1st May 1925 the pilot boat *LENA*, owned by the Ipswich Dock Commission, was auctioned near the lock gates and realised £40 less £4 13s 10d

A four-masted steamship in the Dock close to the lock gates in the early years of the twentieth century. She is almost certainly the ss CARIB PRINCE of Newcastle, 1,305nrt, which docked on 23rd March 1904 from Limasol via London with a part cargo of locust beans for R. & W. Paul and is recorded as having a clipper bow & bowsprit. (R.W. Smith Collection)

PILOTAGE & OTHER BUSINESS

commission. Her specifications, revealing a higher standard of comfort aboard than the pilots would have enjoyed in her predecessors, were as follows:

> Length 68 feet, beam 14 feet 1 inch and depth 6 feet 7 inches. Hull and masts of fir, pine decking and oak scantling with 100 feet of cable and two-and-a-half-cwt anchor. Fore cabin with two bunks and water tank compartment. Second cabin with two bunks and two lockers. Saloon cabin 11 feet 6 inches by 11 feet, fitted with two nests of three drawers and two seats with cushions and fall-flap table. Aft cabin with four bunks, and aft peak with two bunks, lockers and cooking stove; to sleep twelve in all. Suitable for conversion into a house boat.

Rent payable to the Ipswich Dock Commission for *LENA* from April 1920 to March 1921 was £15 18s. This was calculated at 2s per man per week for three pilots, allowing for a 53-week period.

Inward-bound Ipswich pilots used the cutter at the long-established pilot station at the Cork light vessel until the 1920s when Trinity House built the 40ft motor boat *LANDGUARD* that became the means of boarding and landing pilots for Ipswich ships in the harbour.

The Ipswich men later had a small bungalow on the Green at Harwich where they could rest and wait for shipping. They had their own 18ft boat and a boatman quite separate from the Harwich pilots. A new pilot had to buy his share of boat and bungalow. There were four Ipswich pilots at the beginning of the Second World War and their licences were extended to the Sunk pilot station. Harwich men who were not transferred to the Clyde or elsewhere or called up for naval service were licensed to include Ipswich. After the war things reverted to normal and the two districts worked separately again. A new Trinity House launch, *VIGOUR*, was used from 1956 until 1966, when it was replaced by a new fast launch serving the Ipswich pilots in the harbour.

Barges clustered around the ss LUNEBERG as she lies at the mooring buoys in Buttermans Bay.

Pilotage 1950-2000

by Captain D. A. Ingham

Born in Surrey in 1933, David Ingham obtained an apprenticeship with the British Tanker Company in 1949. Deciding to specialise in Pilotage, he joined the short-sea trade to gain command quickly, which he did by the age of twenty-four. Captain Ingham was accepted as a Trinity House pilot for the Ipswich District in 1968, became a Sub-Commissioner in 1973 and for twenty-two years was an Examiner for the District. He held many varied appointments, including a secondment to Jeddah and operating the contractor's commercial vehicle ferry when the Orwell Bridge was under construction. He was one of the team to negotiate terms with the Harwich Haven Authority when that body took over the Ipswich Pilots in 1987, and he continued with them until his retirement in 1995.

After the Second World War the port expanded as Cliff Quay was extended in stages until it reached the power station coal jetty, which together with the coal yard and ash tip was used for general cargo work after the power station closed in 1983. In 1968 the first Ro-Ro service commenced from inside the Dock to Bremen and Hamburg. This was short lived as the West Bank development opposite Cliff Quay enabled much larger Ro-Ro ships to operate from a new link-span (ramp) in 1973. By the 1980s another berth was opened downstream of the West Bank, run by the Cast Line for daily container shipments to Antwerp or Zeebrugge.

The number of pilots increased from nine in 1967 to twelve in 1972, decreasing to eight at the time of amalgamation with the London (North Channel) Pilots in 1986. As the pilots were paid by results—no ships then no money—the number of pilots required was a complicated juggling act. The pilots needed a good income so generally avoided taking on additional men. The commercial interests of the port required an uninterrupted service at least cost. After the war Sir Robert Letch made a study of pilotage and the 'Letch Report' was born. Each port had a work index, which was the number of acts of pilotage that a pilot was required to do in a year taking in travelling and administration time. Ipswich pilots' work index was 273, hence 2730 ships per year needed ten pilots. They also had a recommended 'Letch' level of earnings. The fault with this system was that it fixed the charges for each ship on tonnage and draught, although the work statistics were always in arrears and not projected, coupled with the fact that industrial relations between the dockworkers and the ports nationally were not of the best. Protracted strikes caused a cessation of earnings for pilots, although they themselves never went on strike.

In 1972 Trinity House made an in-depth study of pilotage at Ipswich, resulting in the abandonment of the twenty-four-hour lookout required by by-law at Harwich. To keep twenty-four hours watch over 365 days required five pilots dedicated to that task alone. At the time the then Ipswich Harbour Master, Captain J.M. Bain, embarked upon an expansionist policy for the port that demanded complete co-operation of the pilots.

In consultation with Trinity House, the service was modernised. No lookout at Harwich—an office below the Orwell Navigation Service office at Ipswich

The masters of vessels like the collier CLIFF QUAY that used the port frequently could apply for a certificate allowing them to pilot their own ships.

was provided with a direct telephone line to the Harwich pilots, who had established an information centre in the old Low Lighthouse at Harwich. The pilots also employed a clerk to take pilotage bookings, liaise with ships' agents and keep statistics. Taxis were used to transport pilots from Ipswich to Felixstowe and vice versa. At this juncture, bearing in mind the modern development in ships including sophisticated rudders, bow-thrusters and radar, etc., the limitations placed on larger ships, at night or on the ebb tide, were removed, as was the daylight only rule for tankers. However the port rule that vessels longer than the width of the channel at Woolverstone required an escort tug from No.5 buoy, both inward and outward, was continued. The thinking behind this was simple. If a ship grounded and swung across the channel, grounding at both ends, the ship could break her back on a falling tide, thus blocking the port. In the 1960s and 1970s one of the Ipswich pilots, Captain J. Wright, was so convinced that this was a probability that he insured his earnings at Lloyds against the port being blocked at this narrowest part of the navigable river by this eventuality. It has not occurred YET.

In 1975 Argo Line, who supplied ships for the Rotterdam-Ipswich Ferry to and from the West Bank, announced that a second daily sailing would augment the existing once-a-day sailing. Two more pilots were taken on, but within a few days the proposed extra vessel was cancelled, and within the next three months the original ship ceased trading. The Rotterdam-Ipswich Ferry's revenue was collected in sterling and most of its expenses were in German DMs. A sudden change in exchange rates had scuppered the business.

Twelve pilots now had to share nine men's earnings. In 1976 two pilots, Captains Ingham and Clarke, successfully applied for positions in the Port of Jeddah. Obtaining release from the obligations of their licences for a year from the Ipswich Sub-Commissioners of Pilotage, they thereby solved their own and their colleagues' predicament.

A big effect on pilotage earnings was caused by EEC legislation that allowed hitherto precluded foreign shipmasters who were EEC nationals to sit for pilotage certificates, enabling them to pilot their own ships. Previously only British masters or mates could gain these certificates if they were frequent visitors to a port. In 1977 the Ro-Ro ferry to the West Bank re-started, using the *STENA NORMANDICA,* and was then taken over by P & O North Sea Ferries operating with one British and one foreign flagged ship. The operation was of no commercial value to the pilots as the masters of both vessels applied for and

A gang loading a barge at the timber stage outside Stoke Malting, pictured in the 1920s by the Titshall Brothers. (Courtesy Mr Doug Cotton)

obtained certificates. The ships were very efficiently run and the masters were required to undergo an oral examination by a licensed pilot and the Harbour Master lasting about forty-five minutes with another Sub-Commissioner present. When the Orwell bridge construction began, the Ipswich pilots secured a financial lifeline by winning the contract to operate a small ex-European vehicular river ferry, the *ST. ANTONIUS*, on behalf of the Stevin Construction Company, the bridge builders. The ferry allowed the transfer of plant and concrete from one bank to the other, avoiding unacceptable levels of construction traffic through the town. This was allowed by the Sub-Commissioners on the strict understanding that it did not impinge upon the pilots' normal work. It was estimated that the number of short 'hops' across the river added up to the distance to Australia and halfway back again by the time the bridge opened in December 1982.

In 1985 Felixstowe Dock & Railway Company announced that they proposed to extend into the mouth of the Orwell and in the area designated on the licences of the Ipswich pilots. The berths to seaward were all in the area of the licences of the London North Channel pilots who were based at Harwich. The London pilots claimed this new work should be theirs. Battle lines were drawn and both sides instructed expensive solicitors. In the end it was the strong but reasonable intercession by Trinity House and Captain Bain, the Ipswich Harbour Master, that forged a compromise resulting in Ipswich pilots being licensed to London and a number of London men likewise to Ipswich. All proceeds would go to the London pilots' common purse, of which Ipswich pilots would become equal shareholders. The system lasted until 1988 when the provisions of the 1987 Pilotage Act came into force.

The 1987 Act came about when the then Prime Minister, Mrs Margaret Thatcher, wishing to reduce the number of government employees, discovered that three civil servants were permanently engaged in sorting out pilotage matters under the old Acts. Port operators and shipowners wanted more direct control of the pilots, and relentless lobbying of the government and generous donations to party funds won the day. The new Act enabled selected ports to become Competent Harbour Authorities (C.H.A.s). Locally Ipswich, Felixstowe and Harwich Haven Authority became C.H.A.s but elected to refer all pilotage matters to Harwich.

Pilots could leave under severance terms with early pensions or could remain as employees of the ports. The North Channel and Ipswich pilots, only recently amalgamated, were split into two groups. Between thirty-five and forty pilots operated from the Sunk pilot station to and from the Haven Ports and the remainder supplied pilots from the Sunk to London. The old licences had to be relinquished and replaced by Authorisations with fewer powers. The pilots became paid employees with paid sickness, holidays and health insurance, all of which they used to have to find themselves when self-employed. They did, however, lose their autonomy, and previously when a pilot was unwell or overworked he could 'call-off', which meant losing his share of the common purse. Nevertheless, the system was beautifully self-regulating. A pilot in his sixties is not as fit as a man in his thirties, and if he felt below par he could 'call-off', leaving work to a younger and fitter person as well as the reward. Young pilots with the expenses of early married life welcomed the extra remuneration, while the older men appreciated a less demanding life. Under employed status, a pilot of thirty or sixty is expected to do the same amount of work, each being locked into a roster. Unfortunately, this led to more sickness than had occurred with self-employment. By the year 2000, another national forum was studying the effects of the 1987 Act. Disparities in qualifications and standards of training had become evident from port to port, highlighted by various maritime catastrophes such as the grounded tanker and resultant serious oil spillage in Milford Haven.

It should be remembered that the life of a pilot consisted of boarding and disembarking from every type and size of ships in all weathers and sea conditions throughout the year. At least half of these movements were not from the safety of a quayside but involved climbing up or down a rope ladder dangling from a vertical ship's side, either to or from a plunging launch in the North Sea. In the severest conditions, outside vessels may be requested to pick up a pilot in the entrance to Harwich Harbour, but this is at the master's discretion; he may prefer to anchor and wait for the weather to moderate.

The title of North Channel Pilots must not be confused at all with the English Channel. The term North Channel refers to the approach to the Thames from the north, which was from the Shipwash via the Sunk and leading outside the Gunfleet Sands (some three to four miles off the Essex coast) that were marked by the screw-pile Gunfleet lighthouse in 1850. During the early twentieth century the Barrow Deep, outside the Barrow Sands, came into use as trade increased and ships became larger. By the 1970s, with the advent of super-tankers and large bulk carriers, the Black Deep beyond the Sunk Sand came into regular use. It had been navigable during the two wars, marked by temporary buoys. The present unmanned Sunk light vessel is just visible from the cliffs at Felixstowe to the south-east and the old Gunfleet lighthouse may be seen to the south on a very clear day. It now marks the northern limit of the Port of London.

In March 1986 Ipswich and Harwich-based North Channel pilots merged and thirty-nine pilots became licensed for Ipswich. In October 1988 it was agreed that Harwich Haven Authority would run the Ipswich pilotage service. As a result of this, all pilots boarded ships at the Cork or Sunk stations from a fast cutter direct from Harwich and pilotage control from Ipswich ceased after almost two hundred years.

Ship handling at Ipswich

From the 1950s there were significant changes in ship design. Steamships became fewer as motor vessels became more reliable, and aids such as bow-thrusters made a pilot's job potentially easier. Patent rudder systems like the Kort nozzle, Jenckel rudder and active rudders appeared on all but the largest vessels. Voith-Schneider and Schottel propellers were fitted to smaller ships. Steering by a hand-held wandering lead or by a small bridge-front tiller was a great advantage. The advent of radar in all ships should have made life easier for pilots, but it could be argued that the reverse is the case. In the days before radar, ships remained in port or at anchor in dense fog. Nowadays it is the rule that ships sail in fog, although a pilot can recommend that in a particular ship the risk was unacceptable. However, commercial pressures and the all important 'berth occupancy' times have a major effect on decisions. The captain is under great pressure to keep the ship moving to satisfy the owners.

Techniques used by pilots have changed over the years. At the Ipswich gasworks quay, for instance, dock commission boatmen with a rowing boat ran the stern line ashore. Berthing starboard-side-to meant the stern cut heavily away from the berth, and a quick stern line was necessary to prevent the wind and the run-in from the lock gates from turning the ship round as way was taken off. Modern ships, now using the same berth with timber for Anglo-Norden Ltd, are usually fitted with bow-thrusters so the bow can be swung off (i.e. away from the quay), allowing the stern to come within heaving line distance. In the days of sail, before steam tugs were available, ships warped themselves into the dock from a buoy outside. Nowadays ships with as little as six inches to spare steam straight through. In August 2000 a Russian ship, too long to fit between the gates or to swing within the dock, entered the dock stern first at high water with tugs

The Ro-Ro ferry IPSWICH PIONEER II *has the aid of a tug as she swings when leaving her berth at the West Bank Terminal.*

at bow and stern. She brought packaged timber from Medvezhyegorsk, nearly 150 miles south of the White Sea at the northern tip of Lake Onega in Karelia.

At Cliff Quay power station, ships berthed stern to the flood tide, starboard-side-to. The port anchor, with about a shackle (90ft) of cable out, was dredged into the berth to prevent the bow colliding with the quay when going astern. The advent of bow-thrusters on the last of the modern motor colliers rendered this unnecessary, but it was still a good insurance in an emergency.

The large Ro-Ro ferries at the West Bank berthed port side to, and upon departure swung by the use of a short 'tether' from the starboard quarter to the south side of the berth. Keeping the tether just tight with the twin engines running ahead and astern, the bow swung through about ninety degrees until athwart the river, when the tether was let go, allowing the stern to swing clear. Clearance from tankers discharging at Cliff Quay was only of the order of a few feet.

Closed circuit television lookout cameras on either bow for berthing and specialised river-radars are now appearing on the short-sea vessels whose pedigree goes back to the highly manoeuvreable Rhine barges.

The ship's agent

With reminiscences contributed by Derek Lawrence

Born and educated in Ipswich, Derek Lawrence joined Lewcock & Pemberton, ship brokers, in 1962 at the age of twenty-two. At the time of writing in 2001 he was the manager of Cory Brothers Shipping Ltd, shipping agents, of Powell Duffryn House, Cliff Road, Ipswich, the name under which the original firm now trades. During his career, which has spanned almost forty years, Derek Lawrence has looked after more than 70,000 ships' voyages, and his recollections have contributed largely to this section.

When he joined Lewcock & Pemberton in 1962 the company was run by Mr Sydney Alexander, Mr W. Bellward and Mr Ivan Coleman, assisted by two accounts clerks, a secretary/telephonist and, later, an additional water clerk (shipping agent). The firm had been sold to William Cory & Sons Ltd a short time before, as had coal merchants and ships' agents Mellonie & Goulder. Both Lewcock & Pemberton, a private family firm of some eighty years standing, and Mellonie & Goulder carried out agency work in their own names for some time to come, L&P accounts being entered in the ledgers in black ink and M&G entries in red.

The company had moved from Prudential Buildings in the town centre to its Dock Head office in the late 1950s. Mr C. Pemberton, FICS, was still associated with the firm at that time. The whole company was sold in 1968 to Cory Brothers, a division of Powell Duffryn, at Cliff Quay, to where it transferred in 1976; it has remained there since. Both Mr Alexander and Mr Bellward retired after long careers that spanned the era of sailing ships to container vessels.

The stamp used by Lewcock & Pemberton as Spanish vice-consul at the Port of Ipswich.

Built as the wartime standard ship EMPIRE MALLORY by Connell & Co. in Glasgow in 1941, the ss BANGOR BAY, 2,805nrt, berthed at Ipswich on 2nd January 1952 with timber from Victoria B.C. for Browns, Gabriels and six other merchants, having come safely through the Atlantic gale that had resulted in the sinking of the ss FLYING ENTERPRISE in the Western Approaches. As the AMPLEFORTH she dragged ashore off Tel Aviv whilst bound from Cardiff for Haifa and Alexandria in 1947. Although she was refloated and arrived at Alexandria, she was declared a total constructive loss; in spite of this she was towed to Palermo and repaired. (R.W. Smith)

In the past, the ship's agent was appointed solely by the shipowner. Nowadays agents are usually chosen by charterers, cargo receivers or shippers, but the shipowner is still responsible for payments. Most reputable shipping agents are members of the Institute of Chartered Ship Brokers, which lays down scales of charges, looks after training for agency staff worldwide, and offers advice and legal assistance, together with protection and indemnity (P&I) clubs that also represent owners. Forwarding Agents are responsible for clearing cargoes to consignees.

Once an agent is appointed and told of the arrival time and cargo details of a vessel, then it is up to that agent to advise the owners of the expected cost of the ship's visit (known as a pro-forma disbursement account), inform the Port Authority (berthing master) and forewarn the cargo receivers or shippers of the position of the vessel. He also has to give provisional details to local pilots, and, in the case of tankers, notify any details of hazardous cargoes to Harwich Harbour and pilots, etc; this also applies to some dry cargoes and containers. A further task is to prepare Customs entries if the goods are from outside the EEC, and then pay Custom Duty if necessary.

With the advent of modern ship-to-shore communications, e.g. telex, fax, telephones and VHF, most vessels give regularly updated ETAs. The agent in turn keeps all interested parties duly advised. Once the ship is safely berthed, notice of arrival has to be given to receivers or shippers. This also has to be done if a ship has to wait for a berth. On arrival the vessel is boarded by the agent to assist the master to complete any necessary customs documents and discuss loading or discharging plans. Vessels have to be reported to HM Customs & Excise within three hours of arrival, and any documents required by port officials or stevedores have to be handed over. One important point is that no cargo may leave a ship until an original Bill of Lading, a Letter of Indemnity or the written authority of the owner is received. Otherwise, if things go wrong, an agent can end up with an extremely large debt.

As the owner's agent, the shipping agent acts for the owner and the master, who is, after all, the owner's agent aboard. During discharge or loading, the agent is in constant contact with the master, and arranges any requirements the vessel may have, for example, fresh water, stores, doctor, dentist, repairs, travel, cash, etc. In his career as a ship's agent Derek Lawrence arranged two funerals for crew members and a shipboard wedding.

Following discharge, documents to complete include timesheets, out-turn reports, etc., Customs clearance on completion if loading again, plus timesheets, manifest, Bills of Lading and arranging for a pilot, tug and ropemen when required. On departure sailing messages have to be sent and ETA given to the agent at the next port. On sailing, all documents have to be dispatched to the interested parties. Eventually, when all accounts are received, the final disbursement account is made up and sent to the owners. Strict rules are observed regarding credit. The company issues guidelines and if the owner of any vessel is not allowed credit, the agent has to receive payment from that particular owner by the time the vessel arrives. In these days of much larger ships than in former times, great care has to be taken to ensure that owners and masters are aware of length/air draft, draft restrictions and water available on the berth at low water. Otherwise, severe problems could arise.

The work just described is known in the trade as 'Tramp Agency', signifying working with vessels in the bulk cargo, timber, bags and tanker trade. Most container lines have their own 'In House' agency and some ships, for example small coasters, have no agent at all.

Consular work for the Swedish and Norwegian Consuls was also undertaken by Lewcock & Pemberton. The work consisted mainly of authorising ships' logs, signing crew on and off and dealing with passports. Mr Sydney Alexander was the appointed Vice Consul. The firm still has copies of pages from Norwegian signing-on books from about 1907, and a stamped invoice sheet from the same period signed by Mr Pemberton. Sadly, Cory Brothers no longer hold these vice-consulships. The company does still act as Lloyd's sub-agents and has to arrange cargo surveys, damage and draft surveys when required. Derek Lawrence was also an appointed Collector of Light Dues on behalf of Trinity House at Harwich.

Payments made to the Ipswich Dock Commission by Lewcock & Pemberton during the 1950s show some of the different services provided by the company

---

CALL THE AGENT

*If your vessel enters port, call the agent.,
If your berth appears too short, call the agent.
If your ship wrecks on a mole,
If she is drifting towards a shoal
Or your tug runs out of coal,
CALL THE AGENT.*

*If the doctor is too late, call the agent.,
If your gangs all have to wait, call the agent.
If 'Immigration' does not appear,
And delay is what you fear,
If this costs you too much beer,
CALL THE AGENT.*

*If the 'Customs' need more paper, call the agent,
And your patience starts to vapour, call the agent.
If they keep you from your letter,
From your wife or even better . . .
Those from principles do not matter,
CALL THE AGENT.*

*If the stevedores ruin your space, call the agent.
If you have your nerves to brace, call the agent,
If you have to stop for rain,
To wait for cargo all in vain
And all your gangs idle again,
CALL THE AGENT.*

*If you want to go ashore, call the agent,
To make some fun or maybe more, call the agent,
If the crew had been in fight,
Or more water to be supplied,
Urgencies all through the night,
CALL THE AGENT.*

*If you got fuel spilled on deck, call the agent,
If the gangway is a wreck, call the agent,
If the old man's on a blink,
Or crew falls in the drink,
If you have no time to think,
CALL THE AGENT.*

'Agent? What kind of agent— theatrical or literary?'

at that time. The bulk of the charges were for cranage, labour and tallying involved in the unloading of various cargoes. Coal, pig iron, wallboards, granite, pyrites, potash, sulphate of ammonia, basic slag and timber were among the cargoes discharged during 1952-53. When logs, sleepers and lumber, for instance, were unloaded from the ss *QUEEN*, Lewcock & Pemberton paid the cranage and labour charges involved in discharging the cargo from the hold to the vessel's rail. Gabriel, Wade & English Ltd then paid for the discharge of the sleepers from the ship's rail to trucks, and were also liable for the weighbridge and wharfage charges and the import rates. Similarly, William Brown & Co. Ltd paid the dock charges for unloading the logs and part of the lumber from the vessel's rail to lorries, trucks and the quay, the logs eventually going to the timber ponds in the river.

Lewcock & Pemberton made frequent payments, on behalf of the vessels' owners, for special locks, inwards or outwards; i.e. the use of the lock gates other than between the two hours before or after high tide. On numerous occasions, the firm settled charges levied by the Dock Commission for straw supplied to F.T. Everards' motor vessels. The amounts of straw, almost certainly used for packing cargoes, varied between one and four hundredweight. Other charges in 1952-53 involved lifting pistons from ss *SLESVIG* to a truck, and lifting an armature from mv *BEN HENSHAW* to a lorry standing by, and putting it back on board four days later. The firm arranged for a crane to hoist a lifeboat from a lorry to the quay and then aboard ss *THETIS*. On another occasion the spare anchor was lifted from ss *RIPPLEDYKE* to the quay, connected to the vessel and then lowered over the side.

Another charge settled by the firm involved lifting a generator into mv *APRICITY* from a lorry. Labour charges were paid to the Ipswich Dock Commission for receiving eleven superheater elements into the warehouse and later delivering them to ss *RITA*, and for taking three cases of brick samples from mv *WESTLAND* to the railway station. Other payments were for the cleaning and strawing of trucks after the discharge of basic slag. The firm settled a claim made by the Dock Commission for damage to the swing bridge by ss *LEICESTERBROOK*, involving payment for labour, materials and a survey fee. Another claim was for damage to a fender by ss *JOHN CHARRINGTON*. The firm paid for the services of the tug *RIVER ORWELL* to assist ss *PINEWOOD* at the power station jetty, and for towage assistance to ss *CITTA DI MOREALE* from Harwich to Cliff Quay and back. The money paid to IDC for all such services would be recouped by Lewcock & Pemberton from the owners involved.

'In conclusion,' writes Derek Lawrence, 'it has been shown that agency work is very demanding work, not least being available twenty-four hours a day for 365 days a year. Many an agent will recall spending Christmas Days, Bank Holidays and weekends on various quays and ships in the worst of weather, together with all the associated frustrations and loss of sleep, wondering what on earth he is doing there.

'Apart from the downside, however, there has been the enjoyment of socialising aboard many ships and dealing with thousands of people worldwide. The job has changed much over the last forty-odd years with the title of Ship's Agent evolving from what used to be called a Ship's Husband, Boarding Clerk or Water Clerk. As one last point of interest, Ships' Agents work in one of the few situations where an individual making a mistake, a wrongful declaration or an incorrect entry may be fined personally by HM Customs & Excise. Certainly a job with a difference.'

Ship's business

by Captain Roger Threadkell

Roger Threadkell was born in Ipswich in 1924 and attended Nacton Road and Northgate Grammar Schools. He inherited a love of ships and the sea from his father Stanley; both were long-time members of the Ipswich & District Historical Transport Society. Roger worked in R. & W. Pauls' office for a year after leaving school until he was eligible to join the British Tanker Company as an apprentice. B.T.C. was the shipping arm of the then Anglo-Iranian Oil Company, later British Petroleum. He soon gained his 2nd and 1st Mates' Certificates, four years of his service being during the Second World War, in the course of which he made several Atlantic crossings without harm. He progressed to Master and Extra-Master, coming ashore in the early 1960s as Marine Superintendant for the new BP Refinery at Rotterdam. He ended his career as Manager of BP's Ports Information Department in London and retired to live in Capel St. Mary in 1980. He became an Ipswich Sub-Commissioner for Trinity House and spent as much time as possible sailing his yacht around the Thames Estuary with his wife Beryl. He died in July 2001.

The business undertaken in the Baltic Mercantile and Shipping Exchange, or 'The Baltic' as it is more familiarly known world-wide, may seem remote in Ipswich, but in fact local commerce and shipping was very much bound to its historical and purposeful activities. Its origins, similar to Lloyd's of London, were in the early eighteenth century City of London coffee houses with names such as the 'Jerusalem' or the 'Virginia and Maryland'; Dickensian hostelries where the coffee was only surpassed by the excellence of neat punch or brandy. Shipping and trade in general grew swiftly in the first half of that century and the 'Virginia and Maryland', situated in Threadneedle Street, changed its name in 1744 to the 'Virginia and Baltic Coffee House', reflecting the growing influence of trade with the Baltic countries and the sugar plantations in Virginia. Before long a room was provided where clients could discuss business in these particular areas, and later a public sale room was added. The range of commodities dealt with included tallow, oil, hemp, seed, ships and slaves.

In 1810 the Baltic traders moved to the nearby 'Antwerp Tavern' which soon changed its name to the 'Baltic Coffee House', and the merchants and brokers established strict rules and a membership limit of 300 under a committee of management and a permanent secretary. The Corn Laws of 1815, designed to protect British agriculture by imposing duties on imported grain, were repealed in June 1846, opening the way within a few years for unlimited amounts of grain to be shipped to this country. The grain trade soon became one of the most important trades to be represented on the Baltic.

By 1856 one of the associated companies acquired the freehold of the famous South Sea House in Threadneedle Street. These premises served until 1903 when a new Exchange was built covering an acre of land in St. Mary Axe, off Leadenhall Street.

During the 1939-45 war this free style of trading ceased and all grain was imported by the Ministry of Food and allocated on a quota basis at a fixed price

The Comben Longstaff collier WINDSORBROOK *delivering a cargo to the gasworks in January 1960. Built in 1956, she and other ships belonging to the same company were frequent visitors to the gasworks quay, where they were unloaded by the two hydraulic cranes.*

to the millers or merchants. Grain can be a dangerous cargo if it is not properly stowed, and many ships have been lost through bad stowage. For this reason the British Board of Trade issued detailed regulations regarding the stowage of various kinds of grain, such as the size and construction of bins and feeders and the proportion of bagged cargo. Many countries such as the United States issued their own regulations and British ships loading in those countries had to comply with whichever rules were the most rigorous.

Some parcels of grain were sent to large ports by regular liner trade ships, but Ipswich-bound cargoes were fixed on the Baltic Exchange. R.& W. Paul had their London office conveniently located in nearby Seething Lane and every Tuesday morning one of the directors went by train to London to buy grain ex-ship, ex-wharf, or processed grain ex-mill.

The signing of various contracts and agreements is required in the shipping trade, each one involving precise terms. The process of getting cargoes for ships and vice-versa (in simplest terms) requires a *broker* representing an *owner* with a ship available, to agree with another *broker* representing a *shipper* to undertake a particular voyage. Once a deal is agreed with the traditional handshake the paperwork is completed at the respective offices.

A ship may be chartered for a single voyage or on a time charter basis for a number of voyages. Once the ship has been *fixed*, a document referred to as a *charter party* is drawn up and signed. This is a contract or agreement whereby a shipowner or master covenants for the use of the ship by the charterer for a specific voyage or time. Various forms of charter party are used for particular trades or voyages, but in all charter parties the master or owner warrants the ship to be tight, staunch, strong and fitted for the voyage, that is, she shall be seaworthy. The charter party specifies the commission payable to a shipbroker and penalties for non-performance. It also confirms the person or firm authorised to receive the cargo, or where agents are appointed as *consignees of the ship*. The following clauses cover a few of the principal points appearing in a charter party. The *freight clause* stipulates the amount of freight, and the time and manner in which payment is to be made. The *laydays* or *hours clause* specifies either the number of days or hours required for the cargo to be loaded or discharged, allowing for days on which perhaps cargo would not be worked, or else it fixes a date by which the cargo must be loaded. The *exceptions* or *negligence clause* excepts the ship from responsibility for acts of God, perils of the sea, fire, etc. Other clauses fix sums payable for *demurrage* (undue delay or

The Panamanian ss PETER, 909nrt, arrived at Ipswich on 6th January 1966 with timber for William Brown and sailed for Hull on 18th January. She had been built at Fredrikstad in 1916. (Richard Clarke)

detention), deviation or towing normally allowed in assisting other vessels.

When the cargo has been loaded, *Bills of Lading* are issued by the ship and signed by the master. These are the contracts of carriage between ship and shipper which set out in many clauses the conditions under which the ship agrees to carry the cargo and the shipper in turn agrees to ship the cargo. The original bill is a receipt for the cargo received on board and is a title to that cargo and a negotiable document. It is an officially stamped, negotiable document providing the only proper receipt for cargo proved to be on board. The ship's master will not sign the bill until all the mate's receipts are at hand to provide the physical check that all the cargo is on board. The bill is then delivered to the shipper who will forward it to the consignee. A bill of lading may change hands a number of times, especially with bulk cargoes like oil or grain. These may be bought and sold while the ship is on passage, but will eventually end up with the person authorised to collect the goods. Upon the holder tendering the signed bill of lading, the ship is bound to deliver the cargo. On arrival at the port of discharge the holder of the bill presents it to the master as evidence of his entitlement to the cargo.

Bulk grain cargoes were frequently bought on *C.I.F. terms*, that is, the importer paid for the cost of the cargo, the insurance and the freightage. He then has to bear the cost of discharging the cargo within the number of lay days, which, if exceeded, would be liable to demurrage charges.

To *tally* a cargo is to check and keep a record of all cargo loaded into or discharged from a ship and is an essential part of the cargo work to prevent claims upon the ship for short discharge. Tallying takes place on board the vessel as responsibility does not begin or end until the cargo crosses the ship's rail. The shipper and the consignee normally provide tally clerks.

The manifest is the comprehensive record of all cargo on board a ship. Against each bill of lading number is recorded the name of the shipper and consignee, the marks, numbers and description of goods plus weight and measurement of the consignment. The manifest is sometimes compiled by the ship's agent or by the ship's officers from their copies of the bill of lading. A manifest permits the checking of cargo during discharge and is of great assistance to the stevedores. Its greatest importance, however, is in satisfying Customs' requirements and at each port of discharge they will require a full copy. Manifests also provide the information used for completing the records of a nation's imports.

The Griffin Wharf Branch & Dock Tramway

By the time the Eastern Union Railway (EUR) arrived at Ipswich from London via Colchester in 1846, the Dock and the New Cut had been open for four years. The expansion of the railway, first to Bury St. Edmunds and later to Norwich, Cambridge, Ely and Peterborough, transformed the potential of the Dock and surrounding area, making the quays easily accessible to a large part of Suffolk and beyond. Before this time, the Ipswich and Stowmarket Navigation (a waterway with locks, opened in 1793 using the River Gipping) had provided the only means of transporting bulk cargo into Mid-Suffolk. As with all land transport until the railway age, the speed of the horse governed the movement of goods.

The Griffin Wharf branch

The first connection made by the railway with the tidal river opened in 1847 when a branch from Halifax Junction, just outside the original EUR station at Croft Street, bridged the Wherstead Road down to Griffin Wharf at the entrance to the New Cut. Initially the branch went only as far as Bright Street, but in 1898 it was extended the entire length of New Cut West almost to Dock Street. The extension served R. & W. Pauls' Stoke Maltings at the corner of Felaw Street and the Ipswich Malting Company's big maltings at the far end, where sidings

One of the tram engines used on the dock tramway running light over the swing bridge at the lock. In the background can be seen the waterless gasholder built in 1927 and Pauls' Eagle Mill, together with part of Ransomes' Orwell Works. (R.G. Pratt)

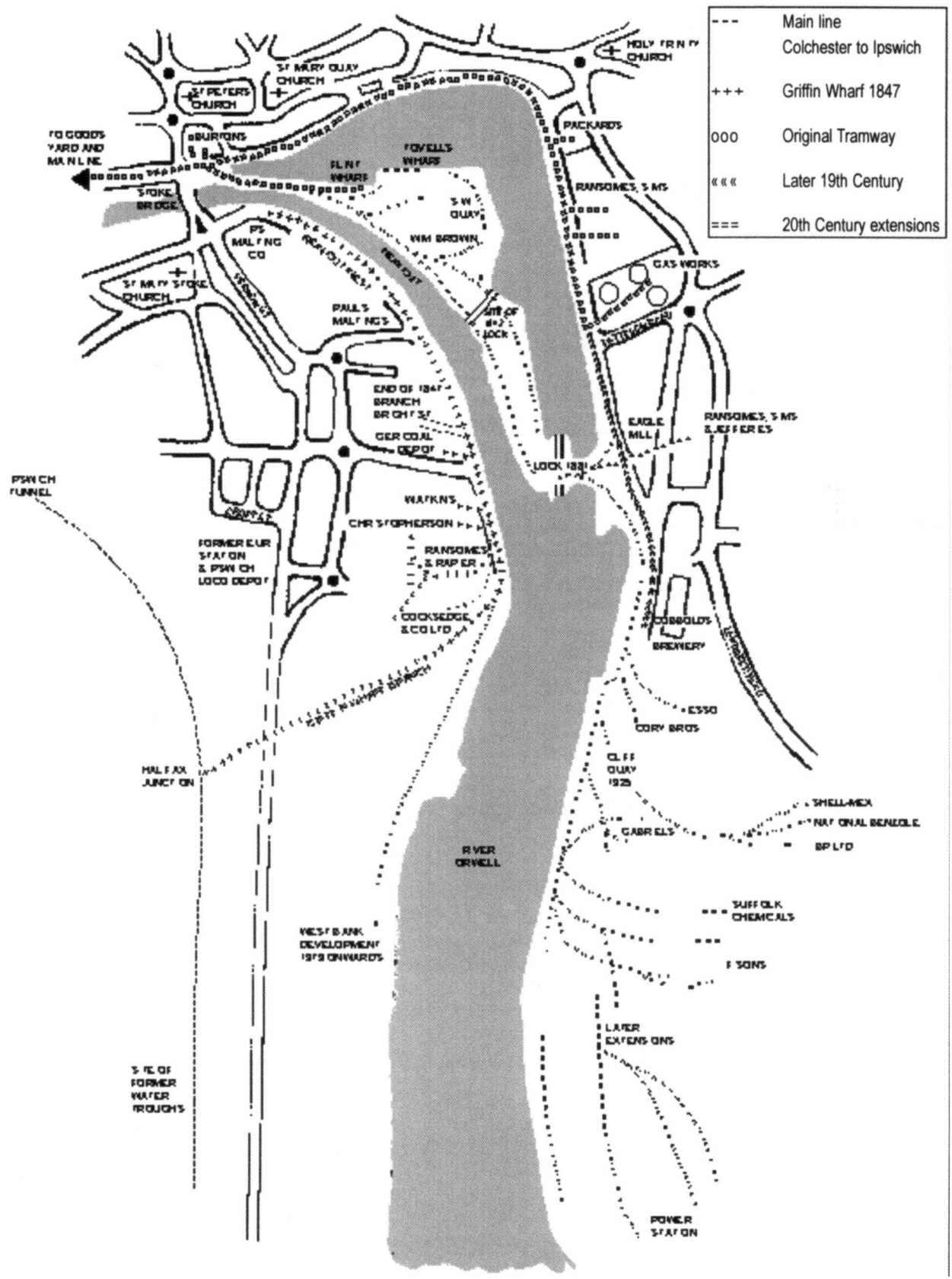

Sketch map of the Dock Tranway and Griffin Wharf Branch.

A Class 37 English Electric locomotive No. 37503, operated by English, Welsh & Scottish Railways, seen in July 1997 on the Griffin Wharf Branch. (Ken Freestone)

ran the length of their yard. Pauls did not have a private siding, and trucks were loaded or unloaded on a loop line on the roadway. Both had barley and coal inwards and malt out. The branch also served the GER coal yard in Bright Street with coal for the river steamers, Ransomes & Rapiers, Cocksedges, and Eldred Watkins's cement and lime works, all of which had their own sidings. Coal for the nearby Griffin Inn was delivered by a truck which was left on the railway line outside the front of the building, the coal then being unloaded and moved to a coalshed in the back garden.

Ransomes & Rapier had an extensive rail network to all parts of its works and operated a steam and later a diesel shunting locomotive, the latter well known as the *Biffer*. Steam engines always had access to Griffin Wharf. Horses were used for shunting trucks beyond the point to which locomotives were restricted, which was normally Bright Street, but the engines sometimes went as far as Felaw Street to Pauls' maltings. Otherwise horses served the whole of the extension to the Ipswich Malting Company's siding until tractors were available.

In 1973, when the West Bank Terminal was opened by the Ipswich Port Authority, a new siding was laid into the terminal to facilitate the handling of container traffic. One of the original main users was the Cast Company, which operated a feeder service to Zeebrugge for its North American box service from 1982 until 1992, when they withdrew from Ipswich.

During July 1997 traffic resumed on the Griffin Wharf branch with the delivery of heavy steel pipes from north-eastern England for export to the USA. The train, consisting of twenty container wagons adapted for pipe carrying, came to Ipswich regularly, travelling down the East Coast Main Line from Hartlepool. On arrival at Ipswich, the train was split into two parts, each of ten wagons, which were taken down the branch separately by the same engine. The pipes were removed by a straddle carrier while the engine stayed with the train, and were subsequently loaded on to 'lash' lighters berthed at the West Bank. These were then towed down the Orwell to Felixstowe for loading on to a Continent-bound barge-carrying ship and transhipment to an American-bound carrier.

The heavy diesel locomotive used for these trains contrasted with previous motive power seen on the branch. The track was, however, capable of carrying the very heavy machinery, including large steam railway breakdown cranes, manufactured and sent from Ransomes & Rapier's Waterside Works.

The Dock Tramway

On 27th October 1846 an agreement was reached between the Ipswich and Bury St. Edmunds Railway Company and Mr William May, a provision merchant, allowing the company to build a railway track from the main line, approximately half a mile from the northern entrance to the tunnel, to St. Peter's Wharf on the Orwell adjacent to Stoke Bridge. Mr May, who had premises on the site (later occupied for many years by Messrs. Burton, Son and Sanders) thus obtained a private siding along the quay, with a turntable and track into his building. Above all, the agreement allowed the railway access to Ipswich Dock.

By 1848, the Ipswich and Bury Railway had been absorbed into the Eastern Union Railway, John Chevallier Cobbold being chairman of both companies. The single-track approach to the Dock Tramway from the main line cut across what later became Ranelagh Road by means of a level crossing and then passed over the river. This route became extremely busy, linking as it did the Dock and the Lower Goods Yard alongside Commercial Road with the Upper or Top Yard and the main line.

The Dock Tramway initially served the northern and eastern sides of the dock beyond the Old Custom House and along past the corner of Coprolite Street as far as Patteson Road. There was also a siding to Flint Wharf that was owned by the railway on the opposite side of the Dock to where Pauls later established their maltings on Smart's Wharf. Private sidings eventually served two other premises on St. Peter's Dock (referred to in the agreement as St. Peter's Wharf), in addition to Packard's fertiliser works close to Coprolite Street, Ransomes, Sims and Jefferies Ltd, and the gasworks.

Piecemeal expansion of the Dock Tramway continued with a branch along New Cut East to the Public Warehouse next to the original entrance lock. The line on the eastern side was extended beyond Patteson Road to Pauls' maltings and Eagle Mill, and in 1901 to Cobbold's Cliff Brewery.

There were no additions on the Promenade side until the infilling of the old lock in 1902 enabled the tramway to be extended along New Cut East to the new lock, which had opened in 1881. The South West Quay and the swing bridge were not opened until 1904, when at last a circle of the Dock road and railway was completed. Thereafter new sidings were put in on the site of the old branch dock opposite Ransomes, Sims and Jefferies and on Tovells Wharf, opposite the Old Custom House, when the whole of that area was piled and developed in 1923-24.

The last major railway work was undertaken with the building of Cliff Quay outside the Dock, first used in May 1925. Sidings were laid to the Anglo-American Oil Co., Shell-Mex Ltd, B.P Ltd, National Benzole Ltd, Gabriel Wade and English, the Suffolk Chemical Company, and in the early 1930s to Fison, Packard and Prentice's new fertiliser factory. As Cliff Quay was extended, so the railway reached the post-war Ipswich power station, which closed in 1983. A freightliner terminal was established in 1984 with road connections.

New track for 100-ton bulk grain wagons bringing in barley and malt to Cliff Quay from Scotland and the north of England had been put in to serve the Ipswich Grain Terminal in 1983. This had a very short-lived career. Traffic to the oil companies' depots had ended by the late 1960s, and the timber and fertilizer work dwindled during the 1970s. Following closure of Fisons' acid-making plant, acid arrived at Cliff Quay in trainloads, this finishing when the entire works closed. All rail traffic on the original sections of the Dock Tramway ended in the early 1980s. Until that time Pauls were still sending malt away by rail as well as by sea from Albion Maltings. The Freightliners and grain trains stopped running to Cliff Quay, effectively marking the demise of the whole system, by 1992. The track has since been removed from St. Peter's Dock, thus preventing access to the whole system. The bridge carrying the branch over the river near Ranelagh Road was substantially rebuilt in 1995 at a time when the British Oxygen Company were discharging 100-ton tankers to road vehicles in the old Lower Yard. Ironically, this trade ceased not long after the costly rebuilding of the bridge.

Dock Tramway motive power

Horses were used throughout the Dock Tramway from its beginnings until replaced by steam tram engines in 1889 following agreement with Ipswich Corporation to permit engines to work on public roads.

The very short wheelbase of the tram engines was essential for working the tight curves of the dock tramway; if a conventional 0-6-0 tank engine had to be used, the side rods were removed from the leading axle, allowing more play by effectively converting it to a 2-4-0. The larger LNER 0-6-0 tank engine classes J66 and J67, built between 1886 and 1904, were used in the goods yards and along New Cut East to and from Cliff Quay.

Small Drewry and Hunslet diesel engines, complete for a time with cow-catchers and skirts, were in evidence from the early 1950s, and the first to work Cliff Quay was due to start on 5th May 1952. Thereafter steam disappeared from the dock area, and in the 1980s the more powerful British Rail 08 shunters handled the heavy grain and Freightliner trains.

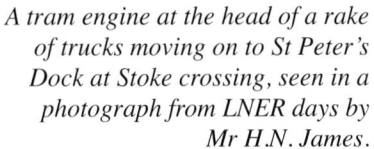

A tram engine at the head of a rake of trucks moving on to St Peter's Dock at Stoke crossing, seen in a photograph from LNER days by Mr H.N. James.

Towage on the Orwell   3

by John Cresswell

Since 1965, John Cresswell has had forty years' professional maritime experience, including eleven years as a commercial hard hat diver and eighteen as a tugmaster. He spent a number of years as a Coastguard volunteer prior to forming the Felixstowe Volunteer Coast Patrol Rescue Service. He is a member of the Suffolk Underwater Research Group and a R.Y.A. Advanced Instructor for Government Agencies, the Military and a training school. As a self-employed marine stunts co-ordinator, he supplies boats, staff and marine safety advice to the film, video and TV industries. His projects have included '999Rescue' and 'Crimewatch'.

The marine towage industry has always consisted of four types of operation; harbour, coastal, deep-sea towage and salvage. Tugs are stationed at most ports throughout the UK in readiness to be called at very short notice to assist a vessel to berth or unberth, and to give aid for any other manoeuvre. Tugs are employed particularly in the Orwell to help vessels negotiate the tight bends in the channel. The shore-side agent of the vessel will normally be aware of expected movements and will order a tug or tugs, together with a pilot and a mooring party. After that, it is up to the skills of the pilot and tug crews to ensure that the manoeuvring of the vessel is carried out efficiently and safely. Even in good weather conditions, a great deal of skill is required, especially in the tight confines of Ipswich Port.

Most manoeuvres, even down to passing a towrope to a vessel, require very precise close-quarter work to be done efficiently and without endangering either the tug or vessel. As with any marine work, the more difficult the conditions, the more important it is to do the job quickly and with the minimum of fuss.

Once the tug has a vessel in tow, the tugmaster and crew must be constantly alert to anticipate any sudden unexpected movements of the vessel and to be aware of the requirements of the pilot. A complete understanding between pilot and tugmaster is essential at all times. The skills that tug crews require cannot be learnt in a classroom, but only via hands-on experience. Most tugmasters have worked their way up through every aspect of the job; deckhand, relief mate, mate, relief master and finally tugmaster. Even then, the learning goes on.

While there has been a considerable change in tug design since the early paddle tugs, the towage methods remain very much the same, as are the weather conditions. Tug crews today have not evolved into robots or developed a sixth sense, they need to be just as skilled as they ever were, and more so with the array of electronic aids that modern technology has given us. To board a tug and steam out into the fairway or to display a tug's manoeuvrability is simple enough. To close-handle shipping, however, requires the same old planning, knowledge, skill and quickness of hand that was required in the days of steam. The designer, builder and owner may be dedicated people, but the tugman is even more dedicated. Out there, he has to make split-second decisions such as most people never have to do, based only on experience. A poor tug with a good crew is often safer than a good tug with a poor crew. Good seamanship depends on people; they are only assisted by their equipment.

Although it is generally accepted that around the coasts of England commercial marine towage began to flourish in or around the 1820s, we can go back even earlier regarding the River Orwell and Port of Ipswich. By 1281, Ipswich had an established community of merchants and shipowners. The port's first Collector of Customs had been appointed and tax returns for this period show that one in every eight of the townsfolk owned a boat of some description. Therefore we can assume that towage of some form must have been present to assist vessels on and off the Common or private quays. River towage was undoubtedly undertaken by the numerous smacks out of Ipswich, Pin Mill and Harwich. The average size of vessels using the port in 1805 was between 150 and 300 tons burthen, and a vessel of that size was considered large. In the early 1800s, it was commonplace for these heavily built and skilfully crewed smacks to assist with towage and salvage, and to tow out the volunteer lifeboats of the period. So important was this towage service seen to be that exemption certificates were issued to the smacks to protect their masters and crews from being 'pressed' into naval service.

The first hint of steam towage on the Orwell came in 1814 when a packet service was commenced between Ipswich and Harwich by the paddle steamer *ORWELL* under the command of Captain Rackman. However the *ORWELL* only ran between the two ports for a few weeks before being withdrawn, said to be due to the deficiency in the power of the steam engine. It was not until 1825 that steam again appeared on the Orwell in the form of the paddle excursion steamer *IPSWICH*, owned by the Ipswich Steam Navigation Company. During this period it was common practice for excursion steamers to unship their passenger

Captain John Cresswell in the wheelhouse of the tug MAXIMUS *as she heads upriver.*

regalia and revert to towage when required. A report at the time states that the steamer *IPSWICH* was by 1827 retained on the Orwell both as an excursion steamer and as a tug, and we know that she continued to serve as both until 1839. This is the first recorded mention of steam towage in the area. One year later, navigation on the Orwell was made safer with the laying of wooden cask buoys.

The first purpose-built tug to arrive in the Orwell was almost certainly the steam paddle tug *AMAZON*, built at South Shields in 1844 and registered at Hull. Her wooden clinker hull was 88ft 2in in length, her beam, athwart paddle boxes, was 18ft, and she was tiller steered and driven by a 37-hp engine, her maximum draft being 10ft. In 1855, the *Essex Standard* gave an account of a rescue by six smacks and a tug towing a lifeboat. The tug was named *AMAZON*, employed on harbour works at Harwich, the rescue involved the brig *STANTON*, and for their efforts the *AMAZON'S* crew was awarded £3.

The *AMAZON* is mentioned in various other accounts as being out of Ipswich. By the middle of the nineteenth century, steam towage was well established on the Orwell, as the Dock Commissioners issued a Notice to Mariners (16th July 1849) concerning the employment of steam tugs. The Commissioners did not have their own tug but relied on tug owners from elsewhere, and this was to remain so for many years to come.

The *AMAZON* was in the news again on 2nd July 1859 when the *Ipswich Journal* reported that the tug *AMAZON* had towed a distressed vessel into Harwich. Later during October she was holed on an underwater obstruction whilst towing in the Orwell. Four years passed before the *AMAZON* was again in the news. This time the *Essex Standard* for December 1864 reported that the

With the Orwell Bridge in the background, the MAXIMUS *brings the* HELIOPOLIS MOON *upriver in September 1987.*

Ipswich tug *AMAZON* had been awarded a salvage claim for assisting the Norwegian barque *FALCON*, found waterlogged on the East Barrow Sands.

By the 1860s ship towage had become a well-established industry, not confined to the North Coast where it was introduced in 1819. Numerous towage companies had been formed and competition was rife, especially in the North Sea, Thames Estuary and English Channel. Thus the era of 'seeking' was born. This was the tugman's term given to the practice of tugs being dispatched to these busy shipping areas to await the arrival of homebound sailing vessels.

The efficiency of the steamers was steadily improving, so that sailing vessels were finding it difficult to compete, and therefore became more and more reliant on steam towage to hasten their passage. This was known as 'taking steam', and seeking tugs would be on station near the Sunk ready to tout for work from any vessel wishing a speedy and safe passage through the Harwich approaches.

Meanwhile, *AMAZON* was still serving the Port of Ipswich, and an engraving of 1869 depicts her towing a brig and two barges into the New Cut. The port's shipping figures for 1879 show a decrease in the number of coastal sailing vessels, but an increase in the size of vessels arriving to include forty large sailing vessels and twenty steamers. During this time at Harwich, local barge owner John Watts had purchased the steam paddle tugs *LIVERPOOL* and *PROMISE*. The *LIVERPOOL* was built as an excursion steamer on the Tyne in 1870 and was licensed to carry ninety persons. Under the command of Captain John Carrington she was responsible for numerous successful salvage claims, yet John Watts's towage venture was short lived owing to bad management by his son, and it went bankrupt, forcing the sale of both tugs.

The next Harwich tug owner was John Vaux, a freemason and mayor of the town. He was also owner of the Navy Yard, where many a fine vessel had left the ways. His purpose-built tug *HARWICH* entered service in 1877 and was a wooden paddler of 123 tons, 100ft overall with two funnels and powered by a 50 hp engine. It is said that she was so heavily built of oak that she could only make ten knots at best. Under the command of Captain Si Keeble the *HARWICH* was used both as an excursion steamer and a tug. In 1881, the *HARWICH*, on this unfortunate occasion under the command of her owner, was criticised for failing to go to the aid of the large sailing vessel *INDIAN CHIEF*, hard aground on the Knock Sands. The *INDIAN CHIEF* became a total loss; seventeen of her crew drowned and eleven were rescued by the Ramsgate lifeboat. John Vaux died in 1884 and a year later his widow Julia sold the *HARWICH* to R. & W. Paul of Ipswich.

The year 1869 saw the introduction of the experimental screw propeller. The first practical screw steamers were tugs, although for many years after paddle tugs were thought far more efficient. One prominent London tug owner with vision was William Watkins, who realised that unless screw towage was taken up by some enterprising owner it would be slow to develop. With this in mind, he had the little iron tug *ERA* built at Blackwall in the same year with a screw propeller, so that he was able to look into her feasibility for towing. The *ERA* was a tug of only 30 gross tons, and her mean draft meant that she failed to grip the water as well as she might have done for towing duties. Even her propeller was an experimental variable-pitch type, driven by a Stewart & Nicholson patent continuous expansion engine that gave her a very fast speed of twelve knots against wind and tide. The *ERA* had a drop funnel for working under the Thames bridges, and being a river tug she rarely ventured further than the Nore. During 1878, the Watkins deep-sea tug *ANGLIA* was engaged to tow Cleopatra's Needle from Ferrol in Spain to Gravesend for the sum of £500. The

A steamer wrecked on the sands, with members of her crew taking refuge in the rigging. Ipswich tugs were sometimes involved in salvage and rescue work.

Needle, an ancient Egyptian obelisk carved from granite standing about 60ft high, and weighing 186 tons, was presented to the British in 1819. It was not until 1877, however, that plans were made for an iron pontoon to be built to enable the obelisk to be towed to England. During a gale in the Bay of Biscay six seamen lost their lives and the Needle was almost lost. The little *ERA* made good use of her drop funnel by completing the tow from Gravesend to the Needle's present position on the Thames Embankment. In 1887, the *ERA* finally left the Thames under the command of her new owner, Captain James Hooker, an Ipswich barge owner who had paid £1,000 for this revolutionary little tug destined to work the River Orwell.

The Port of Ipswich was now to see one of its oldest and most respected merchants enter marine towage. Maltsters and corn merchants R. & W. Paul were renowned for being owners of a fleet of fine sailing barges, and later for building them. Never a company to be left behind by progress, in 1886 they had a small steam coaster, the *SWIFT*, built for their Ipswich-London trade. It was not long before a second vessel, the *SPEEDWELL*, was put into service. Over the years the firm owned some seventeen steamers, and it is interesting to note that many were fitted with towing hooks and even towing arches. Although these were not true tugs, they had their fair share of towage and salvage work. The latter part of the nineteenth century saw sailing vessels increasing in size so that four-masted barques of 2,500nrt and over were commonplace, and very occasionally four or five of these barques were to be seen being lightened in Buttermans Bay. This, and their trait of being independent, may have prompted R. & W. Paul to acquire their first tug in 1889. This was the *LITTLE ENGLAND*, an iron-built screw tug launched in 1884 at Milford for her original owner W.H. Alexander, founder of the London Sun Tugs. Although the *LITTLE ENGLAND* was sound enough to have a Board of Trade passenger certificate, she seemed prone to disaster as she was reported as sinking on more than one occasion, although she was soon raised and back in service. Once, while racing her rival tug *ERA* to assist a steam collier, the *LITTLE ENGLAND* unfortunately collided with both tug and collier.

The next decade was to see R. & W. Paul invest heavily in towage and even have a tug built. However, by far their most successful tug was the 96grt *MERRIMAC*, purchased in 1890. The *MERRIMAC* was built of iron at North Shields in 1883 both as an excursion vessel and as a tug for service in the Bristol

Channel and on the West Coast. This large wooden paddler was 91ft overall with a beam of 18ft 2in. She was unique in that she was a registered trawler, number BL 1. The *MERRIMAC'S* arrival on the Orwell was noted by the contemporary press enthusiastically, saying, 'She is a paddle steamer of handsome appearance, so nice looking that she might be supposed to be one of the Great Eastern Railway steamers'. *MERRIMAC'S* master was to be Captain Ernest 'Delhi' Tovey, late of the *SPEEDWELL*, and already an experienced salvager. Captain Tovey was only thirty-one years old, in those days relatively young to hold such a prestigious command. However he had worked his way up through the 'hawse-pipes' and he knew every branch of the job. He also had that manifestation of a sixth sense possessed by every born sailor. A colourful character, he occasionally found himself on the wrong side of the law, albeit being described by other masters as a self-advertisement, very professional and having an instinct for salvage.

By October 1891, the *MERRIMAC* had received her first-blood when she went to the assistance of the ss *ACHILLES*, hard aground on the Shipwash. Much of a tug's work at this time was to assist the pulling lifeboats by towing them out and upwind of a casualty. During 1893, the *MERRIMAC* assisted at five such incidents, with Captain Tovey receiving praise from the RNLI.

MERRIMAC'S sturdy construction was proved when in 1895 she was in collision with the Esbjerg-Parkeston steamship, the ss *EXPRESS*. The tug was racing to assist a grounded vessel on the Shipwash when Captain Tovey misjudged his speed and distance and collided with the steamer, leaving her engine-room holed. R. & W. Paul's other tug, the *ROBERT OWEN*, was fortunately in the vicinity and soon ranged alongside the ship to take off her passengers. The *EXPRESS* was taken in tow for Harwich, where she was found to be severely damaged and was beached by the Guard. One week after the incident, *MERRIMAC* was again at the Shipwash to assist the grounded 1,350-ton barque *GUSTAV OMER* of Bremen. The list of salvage jobs undertaken by the *MERRIMAC* is far too numerous to mention here, and the same can be said of Captain Ernest 'Delhi' Tovey's exploits. He received a commendation from the RNLI and a Royal Humane Society testimonial for lifesaving. Once he appeared before Ipswich Magistrates charged with 'being in charge of a horse and cart whilst under the influence'. In his defence Captain Tovey said, 'I was not in charge your Worships, only driving'. Case dismissed.

R. & W. Paul's very successful towing venture had spanned a total of twenty-years in which time they had owned and operated seven tugs, including *LITTLE ENGLAND, GARNET, HARWICH, ROBERT OWEN, SPRAY, FOAM* and *MERRIMAC,* which was sold away to Liverpool owners in 1907. She was eventually filled with rubble before being built into the dock wall at Widnes in 1955.

Since the demise of R. & W. Paul's towage operation, the Port of Ipswich had been having to rely on outside towage mainly by London tugs and still having to utilise its three steam mud-hoppers, *DOWNHAM, FRESTON* or *STRATTON*, for towage. On 14th April 1914 the Commissioners held a meeting to discuss this issue, for they were now embarrassed by not being able to offer their own tug. A suggestion was made to several towage companies with the view that if they were willing to station a tug at Ipswich, any port dues would be waived in exchange for a few hours of free towage. Most of the tug companies that were approached said that it was not a viable proposition to have a tug committed to Ipswich for only a few jobs a month. However, a Great Yarmouth company was prepared to station its tug *GREAT EMPEROR* at the port, but the Commissioners declined the offer, saying that she was too large for quay work. The local firm of Dan Marine Motors had their tug *APOLLO* working up at Hull with her contract about to end and they could bring her to Ipswich if the Commissioners could provide a crew. An agreement was reached and the 67ft *APOLLO* served the port under various owners, including the newly established Ipswich Steam Tug Company, until 1921.

A towage saga of this period and worthy of mention is that of the *AMERKER BRUG 1*. During the First World War there was a dire shortage of timber in the UK, mainly because of the heavy losses of shipping caused by mines and attack by U-boat. The Admiralty still required a steady supply of timber for their own use, as did the country's tradesmen for essential war work. Captain Gardiner from the Ministry of Shipping came up with a Canadian idea used for transporting timber in bulk, which was to construct a massive timber raft and have it towed to its destination. This idea was approved, although many thought it to be lunacy and a waste of money. Captain Gardiner travelled to Hommenvik in Northern Norway where the raft was to be built.

The basic raft was first constructed on a slipway where its timber was sawn to give a bow and stern. It was then launched into deeper water where it was given a steel stern-frame and a two-ton rudder. A cabin was added, complete with stove, for the seven-man naval passage crew under the charge of Lieut. Onsley, RNVR. On completion the raft measured 360ft overall, had a beam of 42ft, a draft of 10ft 6in and a dry weight reckoned to be some 4,750 tons. To counter the unavoidable swelling of the timbers during the tow across, the wire hawsers that held the raft together were given heavy springs and turnbuckles so

The tug MAXIMUS *towing the* HELIOPOLIS MOON *past the power station in September 1987. On this occasion the* HELIOPOLIS MOON *loaded animal feed; it was the beginning of a regular service to Egypt.*

The timber raft AMERKER BRUG I *is towed into Ipswich Dock by the tug* RACIA. *(Leonard Woolf)*

that adjustments could be made underway. When the raft was ready for sea it was towed down to Trondheim and registered as a ship for insurance purposes, being given the name *AMERKER BRUG 1*. Captain Gardiner reported that the raft represented the cargo of five steamers.

The Ministry of Shipping's original idea was to tow the *AMERKER BRUG 1* across to the UK with four Royal Navy light cruisers in attendance. Fortunately, the Government's appointed authority on towage affairs was Mr John Watkins, of Watkins Towage London. He was quick to highlight the past disasters when towage was undertaken by warships, and convinced the Ministers that a purpose-built tug was their only hope of success. Even then, the weather had to be favourable and if not, then a dozen tugs could not prevent failure. On 22nd March 1919, the Watkins' tug *RACIA,* built in 1895, left Trondheim with the *AMERKER BRUG I* in tow. They soon encountered strong winds and heavy seas, so it was decided to anchor in Koppervik Fiord. This gave the *RACIA* time to steam into Bergen for extra bunkers. The tug and tow eventually left Norway on the morning of 31st March. However, only a few hours into the tow it was found that the raft's two-ton rudder was more of a hindrance than a help. The *AMERKER BRUG* had a severe bias to port even with the rudder put over hard-a-starboard. It was decided to remove the rudder while still in the lee of the land, and a pair of sheerlegs was rigged out of two baulks of the raft's timber. The rudder was soon hoisted free of its pintles and despatched to the bottom of the North Sea.

The tow across from Norway was uneventful, with only five lengths of timber lost. Captain Gardiner reported that the *AMERKER BRUG* rose beautifully in the heavy seas encountered, despite the raft's draft increasing by one foot through water absorption. On 27th April, the *RACIA* and her charge arrived off Harwich after a voyage of some twenty-eight days. A second tug had been requested to take the *AMERKER BRUG'S* stern for the tow into the Orwell, and with their usual gusto the Ministry had charted not one but three tugs, *DIRECTOR, GILBERT* and *VAUNTER*. The Ipswich pilot boarded the *RACIA* at the Guard buoy and the tugs and tow entered the Orwell, though not before the *AMERKER BRUG* had carried away the Shotley Spit buoy and collided with No. 1 Orwell buoy. The tow then commenced up through the lower reaches and the tortuous bends between Potter Point and Downham Reach. Suddenly, abeam of Hog Highland, the *AMERKER BRUG* took a sheer, forcing the *RACIA* to take the ground, but with the strong flood tide and the aid of the other tugs, the *RACIA* was soon pulled back into deep water. The procession continued towards the entrance to the dock, where the *AMERKER BRUG* was eased into the lock basin. Suddenly she came to an abrupt halt; it was discovered that one of her chains had parted and was now foul of the bottom of the lock pit. The port's own diver soon cleared the obstruction and the *AMERKER BRUG* was safely berthed at South West Quay, where the public were allowed on board for a silver collection in aid of the hospital.

Since the Ipswich Steam Tug Company had ceased trading in 1921, the port had again been forced to use outside towage, and it was not until 1924 that the issue of the port having its own tug was raised once more. The Commissioners now approached the Haven Ports suggesting that they could pool their resources and purchase a tug to serve them all. Harwich Harbour Board said that they would continue to use the London tugs, and the LNER at Parkeston Quay said that they normally warped vessels off their quays. The Felixstowe Dock & Railway Co said that their tug, the *BHEESTIE*, was sufficient for their needs, and for an annual subsidy of £500 she could be sent to Ipswich when required. The Commissioners, not knowing that Felixstowe even had a tug, were embarrassed and said that they were not in the business of putting money into another port's pocket.

Hearing of the Commissioners' dilemma, Maritime Salvors Ltd of London said that they presently had their tug, the 134-ton *REFLOATER*, engaged on wreck clearance off Harwich and for the annual sum of £2,370 she could be put at the port's disposal with her crew. Of course, the Commissioners found this offer unacceptable and the issue of a tug for Ipswich was again dropped for the time being, although they produced an estimate of running costs for future reference. With the opening of Cliff Quay, an increased record tonnage, and the arrival in 1926 of the largest vessel to berth at the port, the 8,350-ton tanker *SAN QUIRINO*, the Commissioners were left with little option but to purchase their own tug. Enquiries were made and a suitable vessel was found lying for sale in the London River. She was a Dutch-built tug of 99grt, registered in London during 1919. Her dimensions were 83ft overall, 18ft 6in beam, and with a draft of only 9ft 3in she was very suitable for the river. This handsome 135 hp tug was simply called the *90*, a name she would retain for several more years under the Commissioners' ownership. The *90* was put to work under the command of Captain Hawkes, and as well as handling the port's towage, she would assist with the dredging plant and tow the two dumb hoppers *SANDBANK* and *ROCKSAND* to and from the Spoil Ground off Harwich. It is said that Captain Hawkes was a deeply religious man, 'often the case with tugmasters', and that he had a voice like a chorister. He would sing hymns all through a towing job and especially with gusto when approaching the pier heads. The *90* was to serve the Port of Ipswich well until May 1933, when she was sold away to the Southampton towage firm of Hemsley Bell Ltd for £625 including all gear. She was renamed *MARION 2* before leaving the port under tow for Southampton.

The 6th November 1933 saw the arrival in the Orwell of the ship-handling tug *STRONGHOLD*, a very robust looking vessel that was to be the replacement for the ancient *90*. The larger and more powerful *STRONGHOLD*, built by the Goole Shipbuilding Company in 1931 for a Belfast tug operator, was a large tug of 95ft.6in with a beam of 22ft 5in and a draft of 10ft. 6in. The 150grt *STRONGHOLD* was powered by a 750 hp compound steam engine and was

classed by Lloyds as 100+A1 seagoing, which made her very capable of handling any vessel likely to enter the Orwell. She was soon registered at Ipswich and put under the command of Captain Jim 'Jummer' Orvis, with a crew of five. The wages were master £4 0s 0d, 1st engineer £3 17s 6d, mate £3 5s 0d, fireman £3 5s 0d and the two seamen £2 17s 0d per week.

The years leading up to the Second World War saw the STRONGHOLD assisting some of the famous large square-rigged sailing ships, all arriving at Ipswich after their three to four-month voyages from South Australia, including the last windjammer to visit the port, the ABRAHAM RYDBERG in 1939.

On 3rd September 1939 Britain declared war on Germany, and in December the requisitioning of vessels began, including ship-handling tugs from 80ft to 120ft in length and from 450 to 1,200 hp. At the beginning of hostilities there were some 350 suitable tugs in service at various ports around the UK. On Thursday, 30th May 1940, the Commissioners received a communication from the MOWT stating that their tug STRONGHOLD was to be requisitioned and stationed at Harwich for harbour duties. Although the Commissioners strongly opposed the requisition order, it proved futile and by June 1940 the STRONGHOLD was on station at Harwich in the company of another requisitioned tug, the Watkins-owned tug KENIA of 200grt. Her new master was Captain R. Strange, another Ipswich man. Captain Orvis was retained at Ipswich where he was to act as the Royal Navy's river pilot.

Although the STRONGHOLD was requisitioned for harbour duties, she was often sent to sea to assist with the numerous casualties on the busy East Coast convoy routes. On April 6th 1941 she was sent out to assist the rescue tug KENIA with the 7,479grt vessel GLEN FINLAS, which had been the victim of a vicious air attack off the Inner Gabbard. As if she had not suffered enough, whilst under tow from the KENIA and STRONGHOLD she was again attacked on her way into Harwich. It is said that her upper deck was so covered in blood that it was difficult to secure a foothold.

Not many weeks passed without the STRONGHOLD being despatched to sea, and time and time again Captain Strange took her as far north as Southwold and down south to the Tongue. She can be credited with numerous salvage jobs, and her crew were even paid special 'war risk money' for their hazardous work in 'E-Boat Alley'. STRONGHOLD'S most notable rescue mission was when she was sent out to assist with the burning spirit tanker SAN ZOTICO, for which her crew were awarded £600 salvage money. Even with the cessation of hostilities in 1945, the Commissioners were told by the MOWT that the STRONGHOLD would be retained at Harwich for some time and might even be sent to Portland naval base. The Commissioners strongly objected and said that Harwich had the Empire class tugs CEDAR and IMP, and it was vital for them to have their own tug at the port as a fire precaution, especially with the many large spirit tankers berthing at Cliff Quay. So it was that the STRONGHOLD and her crew arrived back at Ipswich on 20 December 1945, the crew thus spending Christmas at their home port. The STRONGHOLD continued to serve Ipswich well, but hard war service had taken its toll and a survey showed that she was in dire need of an extensive and costly refit. The decision was made to put her up for sale and look for a larger and more modern tug.

She was not on the market long before an offer of £25,250 was made from the Grangemouth & Forth Towing Co. This was quickly accepted and during May 1949 the STRONGHOLD left the Orwell for the last time under her new name DUNDAS.

During 1949 the Commissioners purchased a larger and indeed more modern

Opposite page: The Dutch-built tug 90 brings the Finnish barque ARCHIBALD RUSSELL *into Ipswich Dock on 21st May 1933. (James A.E. Burrows)*

tug from the Southampton-based salvage firm of Risdon Beazley Ltd. For the reasonable sum of £17,500, they acquired the 145grt seagoing tug *TOPMAST 9*, built in Germany in 1941 as the *LUMMI*. During the war the *LUMMI* had served with the German Navy as a submarine tender before being captured as a war prize. The 900hp diesel-powered *LUMMI* was soon registered at Ipswich as the *RIVER ORWELL*, and after a shake-down period was put under the command of Captain Orvis.

The *RIVER ORWELL* would serve the port well for the next twenty-three years. She was unique in having no ship's wheel but instead had an electric steering system. This had a handlebar affair which, when tilted to port or starboard, operated the steering telemotor. Although mainly efficient, this 'ahead of its time' system did give trouble. The tug's accommodation was very spacious, and her aft saloon or mess could probably have bunked more than a dozen naval ratings, or indeed submariners. Even into the 1970s oddments of German naval regalia could still be found on board, including old sea-charts bearing the eagle's head stamp; in fact, I do know that one of the *RIVER ORWELL'S* crew even wore a German naval officer's greatcoat at times. *RIVER ORWELL* was sold away to Ocean Services in 1972, only to become a total loss after grounding off North Africa.

The port continued to expand, with an extension to Cliff Quay and new warehouses, and Orwell Quay was built complete with Ro-Ro berth in the wet dock. There had been a substantial increase in tonnage from the 1950s to the early 1970s, a period that not only saw the £2 million West Bank Ferry Terminal developed with its daily Ro-Ro service between Ipswich and Rotterdam but also the establishment of the first Ipswich-based towage company for many years. Satim Towage was primarily involved in one of the port's oldest commodities, the ballast trade. Their small river tug *BRETT*, originally the steam tug *WALBERG 251*, was built in Holland in 1931, and in 1967 was purchased by the Horlock Dredging Company of Mistley. The 63ft *BRETT* was powered by a 400 hp MAK diesel, giving her a bollard pull of five tons through a fixed nozzle. Her duties would involve towing lighters of sea-dredged aggregate, usually three in tandem each day, from the dredger working in the Stour off Wrabness, to Hall's Redimix concrete plant at Mellonie's Wharf in the dock. This entailed the *BRETT* departing Ipswich at 04.00hr each morning with empty lighters for Wrabness and returning with loaded lighters of stone and sand, arriving at Ipswich to catch the tide after a round trip of some 28 nautical miles. This was usually an everyday occurrence, even in thick fog, as the *BRETT* had an efficient, albeit ancient, Marconi radar set. This trade took place between 1967 and 1978, during which time approximately 90,000 tons of aggregates were delivered per annum.

There is no better grounding for any tugmaster than towing dumb lighters with a mind of their own and no brakes through a busy harbour, then having to negotiate a lock entrance in a cross wind, sometimes twice or more a day. In addition to the ballast trade, Satim Towage had built up a reasonable ship handling business and had several firm contracts, albeit with the smaller vessels requiring towage. The larger vessels using the port, for example the Empros Lines vessels *ASTRANAFTOS*, *AGONISTOS*, *ANNA DRACOPOLAS* and the Ipswich-Rotterdam Ferry *IPSWICH PIONEER 2*, utilised the London tugs on charter to Gaselee Ltd of Felixstowe. The competition was fierce, and the London tugs believed that all towage between the Thames and Harwich was rightfully theirs! At this time Gaselee had the tugs *SUN XXII*, *EGERTON* and *SAURIA*, with the *SUN XXII* being stationed at the West Bank for the ferry contract. Even so, the *BRETT* was occasionally used as second tug for any two-tug jobs and Gulf Maritime Shipping, whose vessels on the West African run were prone to breakdowns, always used Satim. Then there were the colliers that brought almost a quarter of a million tons of coal for the Cliff Quay Power Station. Some of these were large enough to warrant two tugs, and even the smaller colliers required towage for swinging. The port had regular sailings to and from ports in the Netherlands, Germany, Italy, Belgium, Gibraltar, Cyprus, Greece, Poland, Yugoslavia and West Africa, and towage was on the increase.

Other contracts came Satim's way as their prices were very competitive and, above all else, they had built up a reputation for always turning out, even at very short notice, boasting that they could have a tug ready in fifteen minutes. It took at least an hour for a tug from Felixstowe to respond, and even with the *SUN XXII* berthed at the Ipswich her crew still had to come up from Felixstowe.

At this time an attempt was made to establish another Ipswich-based towage company with the arrival in the Orwell of the 1929-built 96grt diesel-electric powered lighterage tug *WORTHA* for general towage duties. A great deal of time was spent refitting the *WORTHA* for her new role under the command of her owner, Captain I. Ramsey. She assisted several vessels, but for various reasons was sold back to the Thames in 1974. By then Satim had been awarded the Ipswich-Rotterdam Ferry contract by General Cargo Brokers Ltd, and for some time the *BRETT*, under Captain Ken Pratt, managed both the ballast trade and the port's general towage. In order to handle the increasing towage another more

The STRONGHOLD *prepares to take the barque* ABRAHAM RYDBERG *to sea in July 1939 after she had unloaded Australian grain in the Dock. (James A.E. Burrows)*

powerful tug was acquired in 1976 to assist with ship towage and release the *BRETT* back to the ballast trade, where she would also be available as a second tug. The Dutch tug *ESWIL* of Rotterdam was built as a steam tug in 1930 but had been re-engined with a Deutz direct-reversing diesel engine rated at 650 hp and giving a seven-tonne bollard pull through a fixed nozzle. Although the *ESWIL* was a single-screw tug, she had power steering and twin rudders that gave her a very tight turning circle. This 88ft loa tug was soon given the name *ORWELL TOW* and registered at Ipswich, where she assisted some of the largest vessels ever to use the port over the next twelve years. During the late 1980s Satim charted the Felixstowe tug *GARY GRAY* to assist the *ORWELL TOW*, as the hard toil of the ballast trade had taken its toll on the *BRETT* and she had been laid up, to be sold away in 1989, only to founder off the Lizard while bound for Milford Haven.

The £2 million Cliff Quay grain terminal opened in 1983 and the port's record tonnage of over 3.5 million tons continued to increase with the arrival of numerous large vessels. The Port Authority had meanwhile made towage mandatory upriver from Pin Mill for vessels between 110 and 130m overall, and any vessels with a deadweight of 5,000 tons or more, even if under 110m, were forced to have one tug, while all vessels over 130m required two tugs. Large vessels such as the *VOLGA 40005* (460ft), *SUNSTAR* (478ft) and *LUX CHALLENGER* (476ft) loaded at the grain terminal, and all required two tugs. To handle these vessels and the large Ro/Ro ferries Satim Towage purchased the ship-handling tug *MAXIMUS* for £22,000. This 140grt tug was built at Cuxhaven in 1956 for Ridley Tugs of Newcastle-upon-Tyne. She arrived at Ipswich during March 1985, retaining the name *MAXIMUS*. The *ORWELL TOW* continued to work with the *MAXIMUS* for another two years before being laid up in the dock. To replace her, Satim purchased the small but robust harbour tug *TAYRA* in 1987. This 550hp tug was built in Holland in 1958 as the *ABEILLE 13* for the French salvage and towage company of Soc de Remorquaye et Sauvetage. Satim Towage was taken over by a road haulage firm in 1989 and in the September the *ORWELL TOW* was put up for sale as 'lying afloat—Ipswich and open to offers' and consequently she was sold for scrap and taken to Sheerness for breaking. Undoubtedly the 1980s were the boom years for towage at the Port of Ipswich, and it was not uncommon for *MAXIMUS* and *TAYRA* to handle up to eleven river tows, including numerous two-tug jobs, every week. Unfortunately this was not to last and the early 1990s were a difficult period for the port as the general economic recession meant that tonnages reduced.

Since then there has been a varying trend in cargoes, with general cargo substantially declining and the replacement of the large Ro/Ro ferries with the smaller vessels *GABRIELLE WEHR* and *THOMAS WEHR*, both of which do not require tugs unless for inclement weather or engine problems. At the time of writing (2000), the wet dock is in a commercial shipping decline and is now mainly given over to a very smart new marina. Satim Marine Services' tugs *MAXIMUS* and *TAYRA* remain as the port's main source of towage, although they are only crewed as and when required.

We cannot leave towage on the Orwell without mention of two of the largest tugs ever to visit the Port of Ipswich. The first occasion was in the 1970s when the Dutch Wijsmuller tug *UTRECHT* (716grt and 3,000hp) brought in the disabled *IPSWICH PIONEER 2* that had suffered a major engine problem. Then, in the early 1990s, the Greenpeace vessel *SOLO* berthed at Cliff Quay for public viewing. *SOLO* was built in 1977 as the 58.50m ocean-going tug *SMIT HOUSTON* of 16,000hp for Smit International Towage.

The coal trade 4

Coal was hardly utilised in Britain until the thirteenth century when it was burned in London by small businesses such as blacksmiths and used on a very small domestic scale by the rich. However by the middle of the sixteenth century the East Coast coal trade was expanding considerably, with London receiving some 15,000 tons of coal a year. One hundred years later this had increased to a quarter of a million tons. Pollution in London was a grave problem even then, the diarist John Evelyn referring in 1670 to 'a hellish and dismal cloud of sea coal—a filthy vapour corrupting the lungs'.

The expanding markets for British coal during the nineteenth century seemed limitless, with a burgeoning demand from the iron and steel industries, railway building and operating, gas making, and domestic fires. Coal was being burnt not only in this country but almost world-wide, with sailing ships and steamers loading return cargoes of coal outwards from Tyne, Tees and South Wales. A chain of bunkering stations for steamships eventually encircled the globe. The markets abroad lasted until soon after the 1914-18 war, by which time most foreign customers were served by their own country's coal mines or by hydro-electricity, while the development of the internal combustion engine heralded the end of steam power.

The story of the sailing colliers, the Geordie brigs, has been well told elsewhere. Great numbers of these vessels were engaged in the trade and they passed along the coast in their hundreds until steam took a hand in the mid-nineteenth century. Towards the end of the 1800s all the East Coast ports, including towns like Woodbridge and Manningtree, suffered from the silting of their estuaries; it was a problem which Ipswich had sought to overcome with the opening of the Dock in 1842. Nevertheless the fleet of flat-bottomed sailing barges provided the solution, the bigger barges carrying a tremendous amount of coal to the towns and villages along the east coast. They served the smaller coal merchants and users who would not need the carrying capacity of the big steamships but still required deliveries to obscure hards and wharves well into the twentieth century. Even so, the last collier brig survived until 1904 when the Whitby owned and registered *REMEMBRANCE* sank off Bawdsey without loss of life. She had been built at Middlesbrough in 1862 and was only 97ft in length, with a beam of 24ft, but in spite of her small size she sailed for over forty years in the most arduous of trades that crews and ships had endured for over 500 years.

The steamers which ousted the sailing collier were in turn replaced during the 1950s by diesel-engined ships. The last generation of coal-burning steam coasters, carrying 4,500 tons, were built for the Central Electricity Authority in the 1950s and ironically converted to oil firing during the 1960s because of the lower price of oil. At the time that the Cliff Quay Power Station closed in 1983, the gasworks had gone, the remaining power stations were oil fired or nuclear, and the domestic market had contracted so much that by the year 2000 only a couple of coal merchants remained within a ten-mile radius of Ipswich. The long era of King Coal was all but over.

Two units of capacity, the chaldron and the keel, were in common usage by the coal trade for many years. The Newcastle chaldron, varying from about

17cwt in the sixteenth century to 56cwt by 1818, was based on wagons used by the coal miners. The four-wheeled wagons, or 'chaldrons', were of wooden construction with outward tapering sides. Besides being used to carry the coal from the mine they were also used for loading colliers on the Tyne, being brought to the staithes by horses, first on timber wagonways and later on iron rails. Some East Coast ports used the Newcastle chaldron as their standard measure, but Ipswich coal meters favoured the London chaldron or King's Measure, which in later days was about half that of the Newcastle chaldron.

Before improvements were made to the Tyne, colliers loading on the river were also served by the local keels that brought coal downstream from the upriver mines. By the nineteenth century, most of the Tyne keels carried 21 tons, leading to the term 'keel' being used as a unit for the capacity of ships used in the coal trade. In the 1820s, for instance, the Ipswich Gas Light Company was reported to be unloading its coal ships at the rate of a keel, i.e. 21 tons, a day.

The coal imports, which for so many years played an important part in the trade of the Port of Ipswich, came mostly from the Tyne and the Northumberland and Durham coalfields. For many years Seaham Harbour was the provider of much of the coal. The first ship sailed with coal from this port, established by the third Marquess of Londonderry from his own resources, in 1831. After the development of the south Yorkshire and Nottinghamshire mines, coal was brought from that area, at first by rail and then by sea from Goole.

Tyneside coal is largely bituminous and volatile, ideally suited to household use, being easily lit with a good flame for heat. Another variety from the same area was coal of a dull appearance ideal for steam engines. The Durham coalfield produced coal for gas and coke making. Anthracite, a very hard coal, was brought round from South Wales. Because of its clean-burning properties it was used in the Ipswich maltings for at least the first fifty years of the twentieth century.

The ports supplying coal to Ipswich during the early nineteenth century before Seaham Harbour came into existence. Imports are given for the fourteen days from 23rd July until 5th August 1817. (Source: IDC)

Date (1817)	Vessel	PoR	Master	From	No. of chaldrons of coal
23 July 1817	ENDEAVOR	Ipswich	Thurlow	Sunderland	94
24 July	?	Sunderland	Scott, Peter	Sunderland	212
	HEMSLEY	Sunderland	Arrowsmith, Rt	Sunderland	266
	TYMGER	Ipswich	Mills	Sunderland	62
25 July	? GIVER	Ipswich	Newson, John	Newcastle	125
	MARIA	Ipswich	Orford?	Sunderland	66
	RIGLEY	Ipswich	Caston, R	Sunderland	117
	BURY	Sunderland	Nasham, Thos	Sunderland	184
26 July	OCEAN	Ipswich	Paine, John	Newcastle	63
30 July	MERNEVA	Harwich	Stewad, Rtchd	Newcastle	209
31 July	TORRIDGE	Sunderland	Dunn, Richd	Sunderland	128
1 Aug	DUNN?	Ipswich	Norman, J	Newcastle	117
	HERO	Sunderland	Blain, Thos	Sunderland	207
	HOPEWELL	Ipswich	Harris, Jno	Sunderland	54
2 Aug	?	Ipswich	Wiles, S	Blyth	17
	PENELOPE	Sunderland	Mints, Rt	Sunderland	120
4 Aug	BASTON	Sunderland	Ammer, Rt	Sunderland	109
	?	Sunderland	Gregson, Rt	Sunderland	236
	MANCHESTER	Ipswich	West, Wm	Sunderland	81
	VENUS	Ipswich	Lord	Sunderland	116
5 Aug	FRIENDS	Ipswich	Kettle, Thos	Newcastle	165
	VENUS	Sunderland	Smith, Rt	Sunderland	160
				TOTAL	2,908

Coal duties and remissions

Taxes or duties have been levied on coals for centuries by kings and governments. James I placed a tax on exported coals and duties were levied on coals landed at London to pay for rebuilding after the Great Fire. Coal taxes in general were abolished in 1831 after a recommendation by a Parliamentary Committee of 1829-1830 that it was *'a severe restriction on trade'*.

Ordinary dock dues were payable by owners of vessels on the net tonnage of each ship for maintaining the Navigation and facilities of the Dock. For years this was fixed by the Dock Commissioners, many of whom had vested interests as owners and merchants, at only a penny per ton for the smaller locally owned ships. This allowed little for future dredging and other improvement work. Duty on coal cargoes was assessed by the Coal Meters who attended and weighed the coal off every ship. The 1837 Ipswich Dock Act, which sanctioned the construction of the dock, also contained provision for the raising of additional money by duties or dues on coal. These were fixed at one shilling per ton 'prime' duties, i.e. paid on the quantity certified by the Master of the vessel, or twenty shillings per ton 'post' duties, i.e. any excess coal found after weighing by the Coal Meters.

The Act had given the Dock Commission the powers to appoint coal meters and weighers who had the right to seize vessels on neglect or refusal to pay duties. The original title of Coal Meter was an ancient one given to those checking the King's Duties and the holders were in fact excise men, unlike the Ipswich meters.

Additional funds were soon needed for additional work and in 1843 a Bill was put to Parliament seeking the right to collect, in addition to the duty set by the first Act:

'The duty or sum of sixpence (6d) for every ton weight of coals, coke or cinders and so on in proportion for any less quantity imported within the River Orwell or town of Ipswich, or otherwise brought or delivered within the limits of the first Act; which said additional duty shall and may be collected, recovered, applied and accounted for in the same manner as the duty granted by the first Act are thereby authorised and directed to be collected and recovered, applied and accounted for. . . . . '

There were queries why only the duty on coal should be increased, but it was easy to measure and calculate besides becoming an essential for industry. A percentage of the duties on coals became payable quarterly to Ipswich Borough Council, through the Borough Treasurer's office, less 5 per cent commission.

A further Act of 1852 however had introduced remissions (drawback) on coal *'conveyed by railway beyond the liberties of the town of Ipswich or which shall be transhipped beyond the River Orwell'* dependent upon distance from Ipswich. Remission was not to exceed twenty-three twenty-fourths of the duty. The operation of this engendered much aggravation amongst merchants and users. Drawback on coal duties referred to a formula calculated by the Ipswich Dock Commission whereby coal merchants could apply for a rebate on coal discharged by ship at Ipswich but subsequently sent beyond the borough boundaries by rail or water. The duty also applied from 1870 to coal brought in

---

**THE PATENT CONCRETE STONE COMPANY LIMITED
36, PARLIAMENT STREET,
WESTMINSTER SW1.**

Ipswich, June 20th 1864

My dear Sir,
I am duly in rect. of your favour of the 18th Inst but fear I shall be unable to attend the meeting of the Committee tomorrow as I expect to have to go to Town.

I am quite of the opinion that the Commissioners would do well to allow the amt. of drawback on Coke sent out of the port required by Booth & Taylor as I understand the probable quantity that will be taken by the Railway Coy. will be from 70 to 80 tons per week and this quantity will yield to the Com: a revenue of at least 1/- per ton after allowing a drawback of 1/5.

It should be borne in mind that the dues are first paid upon the Coals as imported and as nearly 13/4 tons coals are required to produce a ton of Coke and as the drawback is calculated upon the Coke and NOT upon the Coals producing it the Com. will get the full dues upon nearly half the quantity of Coals imported for this purpose whereas I strongly fear they will lose all unless this concession be made.

As regards the other application, you will recollect that at the last meeting of this Commission that I attended at the Chairman's house I expressed my opinion that unless the larger drawback were allowed on Coals going to Stowmarket & Finningham, land borne coals would take away a portion of our trade. I am still of this opinion and I know that arrangements are being made for bringing a considerable quantity of Coals by Rail from the North to Stowmarket which probably a prompt effort on the part of the Dock Comrs. may check.

I am my dear Sir
faithfully yours
Fredk. Ransome

P.B. Long Esq.

Letter from Frederick Ransome to the Ipswich Dock Commission concerning drawbacks. (I.D.C.)

Wherry Quay in the 1890s with the brigantine NAVIGATOR *on the inside by what became Isaac Lord's malting. Launched at Cardiff in 1865, she was owned by R.M. Church of Chichester. On the outside is the ketch* GOOD HOPE *and on the right are an unknown brig and a brigantinue.*

IPSWICH DOCK COMMISSION NOTICE

If any Master, Commander, Owner, Consignee, or other person having the Charge or Command of any ship or other vessel coming into the Port of Ipswich laden with Coals, Coke, or Cinders shall discharge, or cause to be discharged, any part of the Cargo of such vessel before he or they shall have produced the Invoice or delivered a true Particular to the Collector of Coal-Dues, and shall have paid the full Amount of the Dues payable on such a Cargo; such Master, Commander, Owner, Consignee, or other person, shall stand charged with and forfeit and pay, over and besides such Rates and Duties, the sum of Forty Shillings for every such offence, and which sum shall and may be recovered from such Master, Commander, Owner, Consignee or other person by the same means and in such manner as are directed for levying and recovering any of the Penalties imposed by the Ipswich Dock Act.

And if anyone evades or eludes payment of Duties or part thereof, they will be charged a sum of money equal to the Rates evaded or eluded. If anyone provides a false or incorrect Statement of the Invoice with intent to defraud the Commissioners of Duty, being lawfully convicted thereof, they shall be deemed guilty of a misdemeanour, and shall be punished accordingly.

[Signed] P. B. Long, Clerk to the I.D.C.

Notice referring to a bye law made by the Ipswich Dock Commission on 11th November 1842 following an incident earlier in the year when John Wesbroom, master of the schooner PROVIDENCE, *unloaded 20 to 25 tons of coal before payment of dues. (I.D.C.)*

Annual tonnages of coal taken away by railway from merchants' stocks imported by ship to Ipswich. (I.D.C.)

by train, which in itself caused a great deal of argument and protests from merchants who normally received rail-borne coals.

Complaints about the system included a rejection of drawback being allowed where coal was used as fuel on pleasure steamers, the Commission declaring it would only be allowed for cargo ships. Complaints were made by William Beaumont about anomalies in drawback payable for deliveries by rail to Burston, Eye, Finningham, Stowmarket and Needham Market, and requests made for the drawback payable to Finningham to be the same as for Elmswell. Coal to Norwich even, and Swainsthorpe, Tivetshall and Harleston was also likely to be lost to the railway. Others warned of the probable transfer of much sea-borne coal business from Ipswich to Lowestoft.

Booth Brothers raised the matter of coal brought in by the railway and duties paid but drawback not being allowed when that coal was then sent on beyond the boundaries by water. Their claim to the I.D.C. referred to 28 tons 12cwt. of coal arriving at Ipswich on 4th June 1871 in four of Booths' own railway trucks from Eckington in Nottinghamshire, and loaded into a barge for delivery at Shotley for Mr Hempson of Erwarton Hall. The amount in question, at 9d a ton, was £1 1s 6d drawback. The Commission held that the claim was not allowable under the Act.

With or without duty on rail-borne coals, the Port would soon lose a considerable amount of 'exported coal' traffic as the railway obviously began to attract the business. The link from Peterborough and the North to Ipswich opened when the section between Newmarket and Bury St Edmunds was completed in 1854, although the much sought after direct route via Spalding, Lincoln and Retford did not open until 1882. This particular line was promoted by the Great Northern and Great Eastern Railways with enormous potential for moving coal to East Anglia and East London.

The figures for 1875-6 reflect the downturn in coal "exports" from Ipswich.

Station	1863	1864	1865	1875	1876
Needham	2,137	1,819	1,655	491	555
Stowmarket	5,557	4,898	3,588	591	897
Finningham	2,382	2,004	1,259	143	48
Mellis	4,459	3,965	2,878	201	43
Diss	3,970	2,894	2,753	291	96

Interestingly the fertiliser works of Fison, Packard and H.Chapman must have been the reason for coals listed for *'Bramford by canal'* amounting to 461 tons in 1875 and 1,202 tons by 1876.

The term 'coal duties' did not mean a tax in the usual sense of the word but was, in reality, an additional part of the dock dues chargeable only on coal, coke and cinders. It was still levied at one shilling per ton by the Ipswich Dock Commission and its successor, the Ipswich Port Authority, until the 1990s, by which time regular imports of coal were a thing of the past and separate charges were dropped. Coal brought by sea for the Sproughton Road sugar beet factory in the year 2000 was the only coal imported for some time. Town Dues of $1\frac{1}{2}$d were paid quarterly to the Borough Treasurer's office.

Landborne coals referred to coals delivered within the Borough by the railway, and these were subject to the duty as described earlier. The Railway Company was expected to send a return to the Commission declaring all such deliveries to merchants and own account users whereupon the merchant or user would be sent an invoice for the appropriate amount due. This may not have always been the rule. It is possible that the Railway Company (post-1947 the Railway Executive) was charged for the amount delivered as carriers, in addition to the coal required for railway use before the advent of diesel traction. The last landborne duties claimed was from the Ipswich Co-operative Society for direct deliveries by lorry to their Derby Road yard prior to its closure early in the 1990s.

Drawbacks or remission of duties remained in practice, although it was rare,

Mellonie & Goulder's ss ELISE MELLONIE *(ex-*MILLWATER*), 365nrt, built 1921, seen under Mellonie's unusual crane c.1926. (R.W. Smith Collection)*

until 1968 when coke breeze was exported to Norway. Ironically, that particular case must have been one of the most testing of all occurrences of coals passing through the 'limits' to another place, given the original nineteenth century aggravation on the subject when coal was simply brought to the town by sea, transferred to rail and taken outside those limits. (Over the course of time, the 'limits' have been construed as being the boundaries of the Borough of Ipswich.) In this instance, coal was discharged for the gasworks and processed to make gas in the normal way. The coke breeze residue was then exported to Norway by sea out of the limits and drawback was rightly conceded by the Commission and a part of the duty returned, coke and cinders being specified in the relative Acts.

The coal merchants and their shipping

According to Pigot's Commercial Directory of 1830 there were some eighteen coal merchants in Ipswich with wharves or yards along the quayside or in adjacent streets, and a similar total is to be found in White's 1844 list. That was just two years before the railway arrived at Ipswich; by 1866 the number of merchants on the dockside had fallen to about thirteen, with others in business at the railway goods yard. Another eighty years on, in 1966, when domestic coal fires were giving way to oil-fired central heating, there were only three with dockside depots out of eight left trading in the town: Mellonie & Goulder, Ipswich Coal Company (A. Beaumont & Co. Ltd), and Isaac Lord. The others, including Thomas Moy, were served by rail, although M.M. Mitchell (with an office at 11 Northgate Street) and the Ipswich Co-operative Society received occasional cargoes by ship.

The brigantine WILLIAM PARKER, *built at Wells in Norfolk in 1840 and owned by William Beaumont, lying at the Common Quay in Ipswich, in a photograph taken by Ipswich photographer William Vick.*

THE COAL TRADE

Alfred Beaumont & Company

The Beaumont name has been evident in Suffolk since the Huguenots' incursion into East Anglia during the seventeenth century. At Ipswich, Beaumonts were involved with seafaring throughout the nineteenth century and probably earlier. One George Beaumont of Fore Hamlet was listed as a pilot in 1844 and William Beaumont of St. Clements Street (later Fore Street) was a coal merchant. By 1886 Alfred Beaumont resided at 'Park Side,' Bishops Hill, and was recorded as a coal merchant, ship owner and sailmaker at 130 Fore Street. He was also involved with brick and tile making. Frederick Beaumont ran a sailmaking and ships' chandlery business at the same address, which was close to Coprolite Street in the corner of the dock where the site remained as their coal yard until the 1940s.

The company was well known as a domestic coal merchant and coal was regularly delivered to Ipswich by rail and in Beaumont's own ships and barges. Alfred was listed in the 1884 Lloyd's Register as owner of five vessels: *GAZELLE*, a ketch barge built at Ipswich in 1877 by Curtis; an old wooden schooner *QUEEN*, also Ipswich built by Bayley; *REINDEER*, another of Curtis's ketch barges built in 1879; the *UNION*, an even older schooner from Bayley's Yard in 1819, and a brigantine, the *WILLIAM PARKER*, built at Wells in 1840.

In 1894 the number of coal ship arrivals for Beaumont was reduced to twenty-five, of which two came from Sunderland, the rest from Seaham. Although some coal may have been brought by rail, there were eight steamship arrivals and one or two other vessels of a higher deadweight tonnage than in 1883. Ten years on and only ten cargoes arrived in steamers, nine from Seaham, the other cargo from Sunderland.

The company owned several 10-ton coal wagons, and by 1922 there were no shipments by sea but just 207 tons were unloaded from thirty-two railway trucks in July and August, 124 tons being supplied to five ships for bunkers. By 1924, there were only two ships for Beaumont. The company moved across the dock that year, after the old branch dock had been filled in, creating Tovells Wharf. The name disappeared from the Dock Commission accounts by 1926, when the business was absorbed by the Ipswich Coal Company at their office address of

Coal ship arrivals for Alfred Beaumont in 1883.

NAME	RIG	POR	NRT	FROM Seaham	FROM Sunderland	FROM Newcastle	FROM Shields	REMARKS
UNION	Sr	Ipswich	99	4	1			b. Ipswich by Bayley 1819. Owner A Beaumont
QUEEN	Sr	Ipswich	99	6			1	b. Ipswich by Bayley 1838. Owner A Beaumont
WILLIAM PARKER	Bn	Ipswich	120	6	1			b. Wells 1840. Owner A Beaumont
GAZELLE	Kb	Ipswich	104	2				b. Ipswich by Curtis. Owner A Beaumont
REINDEER	Kb	Ipswich	113	1	2			b. Ipswich 1879 by Curtis. Owner A Beaumont
MARKET MAID	Sr	Harwich	93	1				b. Rye 1814
FAIR MAID		Goole	78		1			
JOHN LEE		Kings Lynn	66		1			
SEDGEMOOR	ss	Ipswich	112			7		b. Newcastle 1872. Owner E Packard of Ipswich
ANNA SARAH	Sr	Ipswich	139	1				b. Sunderland 1860. Owner Goddard & Co (Gas Co)
ADVENTURE	Bg	Montrose	165	1				b. Leith 1824 Owner R Lynn Montrose
ROBERT ADAMSON	Bn	Maldon	159		1			b. Sunderland 1865. Skipper/owner Bell of Maldon
LADY OF THE LAKE	Sr	Harwich	127		1			b. Milford 1840. Owner O Bendall
			Total	22	8	7	1	

24 Princes Street. The Ipswich Coal Company had originally traded as F.H. Forsdick, another well-known merchant. Both Beaumont and the Ipswich Coal Company were listed under the name of Manchester coal factors Thrutchley & Co. Ltd in 1926 at the same address. During 1926/27, all were taken over by Charrington, Gardner & Lockett Ltd. of 16 Mark Lane, London EC3. Between 1st April and 3rd November 1926, 5,640 tons of coal was discharged at Tovells Wharf for Forsdick/Thrutchley, and a further 3,034 tons was discharged to Charrington's account by eight ships from 23rd November 1926 to 30th March 1927.

Because of the good rail connections there was no serious trade by sea until the 1940s and 1950s, when Beaumont received part-cargoes with its associate the Ipswich Coal Company and another local firm, Mitchells. The Beaumont name was, however, still evident in advertisements placed by Charringtons in the Ipswich Dock Commission annual tide tables well into the 1950s. Like most of the other local merchants, they closed in the face of oil and gas.

Alfred George Bevan

Bevan's office was at 82 Fore Street, with a yard on the quay by the 1880s. He only had three coal cargoes in 1883. One was brought from Sunderland in the schooner *MARKET MAID*, built at Rye way back in 1814. The other two were brought by the Ipswich schooner *MARY*, belonging to F.A. Christie, which came twice from Seaham.

Eleven years later, during 1894, Bevan received fourteen cargoes, all from Seaham Harbour. The *HENRIETTA & LEONARD PRESTON*, a Sunderland-owned and registered brig, built in 1856 at Stockton, delivered four of them. Another schooner, *GODDESS* of London but Ipswich-built and owned, brought four more. *LUCY RICHMOND*, built by Robertson at Ipswich in 1875 and owned by the Richmond family of Burnham, arrived twice. The ketch barges *ALCYONE* of Harwich and *THISTLE* of Colchester each delivered a cargo, and R. & W. Paul's steamer *SEAGULL* came twice.

Although eleven shiploads came from Seaham in 1904, only one sailing vessel was included in these arrivals. The ss *DUDDON*, built at Preston in 1882, was first of the year and was followed by six visits of the ss *CAM*, registered and owned in Lynn by the East Coast Steamship Co. The ketch-barge *LORD ALCESTER*, built at Littlehampton in 1891, came next, then the ss *ENTERPRISE* of Hull, followed by the ss *SOLWAY QUEEN*. This vessel was Preston built of iron in 1883 for the Solway Steamship Co. of Whitehaven and had been sold to the North Eastern Shipping Company of Elgin and re-registered in Aberdeen in 1898. The last arrival for the year was the ss *T.W. STUART* of Newcastle, where she was built in 1896.

Within the next year or so after 1904 the company was taken over by Messrs. Sizer & Lord.

Booth Brothers

Booth Brothers of Eastwood near Nottingham were at Ipswich in 1870 as coal factors and merchants and most if not all of their coal came by rail. By the mid-1880s they may well have been in partnership as Booth & Mitchell with an office at 23 Princes Street and a large coal yard in the Great Eastern Railway goods yard off Chancery Road. A later company, M.M. Mitchell, possibly

THE COAL TRADE

related, had an office at 11 Northgate Street but by the 1950s were incorporated as R. Coller & Sons Ltd of Norwich and associated with Charrington, Gardner, Locket (London) Co.Ltd (merchants and factors), formed after amalgamation in 1922, who had branches at Newcastle, Nottingham and Hull. At Ipswich, Booth Brothers used the Northgate Street address but the coalyard was on Tovells Wharf. Charringtons had been established in 1731. Mitchells eventually joined with Beaumonts as part of Thrutchleys.

Booth & Mitchell had six cargoes arrive in 1888, four in the *HEDLEY* and two in the ketch barge *ALCYONE* of Harwich. All came from Seaham Harbour. Their imports were, however, somewhat sporadic.

Several ships berthed during the 1930s. There were for instance seventeen cargoes for Mitchell in 1933, sixteen in 1936 and ten in 1939. Forty-three cargoes arrived during the Second World War. Ships with part-cargoes came occasionally after the war, but this trade eventually ceased about 1960.

F. A. Christie

For a few years before the opening of the Dock, the Christie family received large quantities of coal from the North-east. In July 1839, for instance, they had five Ipswich-registered ships arrive with a total of nearly 670 tons. These were the *DISPATCH, LADY MIDDLETON, PROVIDENCE* and *ELIZA* (twice). During the 1840s and 1850s John Christie is recorded as both a coal merchant and a salt merchant in Salthouse Street.

William Christie, of Angel Lane, Ipswich, was master of the *PROVIDENCE* in 1839. In 1850 he had become master of the *HAPPY RETURN*, possibly the brig of that name built at St. Malo in 1838 and owned in Guernsey by 1884. He brought fourteen coal cargoes in this vessel for F.A. Christie between 27th August 1850 and 25th July 1851.

It was Frank Alexander Christie, of 6 Brook Street, Ipswich, who had set the pace by the 1880s. He was not only dealing in coal, salt and cake, but was also a shipowner and soon to become a timber merchant in Salthouse Street. In 1884, F.A. Christie's fleet consisted of the ketch-barge *FEARLESS*, built in 1876 by William Colchester at Ipswich; *JOHN AND MARGARET,* an Ipswich schooner

Christie's coal shipments of 1883, which are very similar to Beaumont's.

Name	Rig	POR	NRT	Seaham	Sunderland	Swansea	Llanelly	Remarks
JOHN & MARGARET	Sr	Ipswich	84	8	1			b. Leith 1827. Owner FA Christie.
FRANCIS		Ipswich	98	2				Not known
STAR OF THE SEA	Bn	Ipswich	99	6	1			b. New Brunswick 1856. Owner FA Christie.
FEARLESS	Kb	Ipswich	107	2	1			b. Ipswich by Wm Colchester 1876. Owner FA Christie.
VECTA	Bn	Harwich	132	1				b. France 1842. Owner JH Vaux Harwich.
TIGER		Goole	64		1			Not known
MARY	Sr	Ipswich	79	5				b. Ipswich 1825. Owner FA Christie.
MUTE	Sr	Ipswich	89			1		b. Portsmouth 1853. Owner W Bayley Ipswich.
ALDBORO	Sr	Ipswich	99	3				b. Yarmouth 1835. Skipper/owner S Hart Ipswich.
ALARM	Sr	Ipswich	99	1	1			b. Ipswich 1855. Owner EJ Robertson Ipswich.
SUMMER CLOUD	Sr	Aberystwyth	91			1		b. Burton Stather (R Trent) 1863. Owner T Lewis Aberystwyth.
TRIUMPH		Goole	86				1	Not known
ARIEL	Sr	Ipswich	84	1				b. Ipswich 1881 builder/owner EJ Robertson Ipswich.
Total number of arrivals for 1883				29	5	2	1	

built at Leith in 1827; the *MARU*, also a schooner, Ipswich-built and registered in 1825, and *STAR OF THE SEA* of Ipswich, a 114-ton brigantine built far away in New Brunswick in 1856.

In 1904 Christie's received only eight cargoes, five of which arrived in steamers. Six came from Seaham, one from Sunderland and one from Saundersfoot. In 1913, only two cargoes arrived, and as the coal interest was sold to Mellonie & Goulder in 1924, coal was probably delivered to the quayside by rail in the interim. Christie's warehouse still exists in the year 2007, although the premises were converted to modern offices during the 1990s.

Valentine D. Colchester

Valentine Desborough Colchester (1847-1921) was the son of William Colchester, whose varied company history has been described in the chapter on the fertiliser trade. Valentine Colchester advertised as a retail coal merchant besides needing coal for the patent manure factory on Griffin Wharf. He was Mayor of Ipswich in 1916 during the First World War.

The following table gives examples of Valentine Colchester's coal shipping for 1883, showing ten arrivals with coal, all from Seaham Harbour.

Name	Rig	POR	NRT	Trips	Remarks/Owner.
LADY OF THE LAKE	Sr	Harwich	127	1	b. Milford 1840/O. Bendall, Maldon.
EMPRESS OF INDIA	Kb	Ipswich	77	1	b. Ipswich 1876 by Curtis.
ROSE	Sr	Ipswich	97	1	b. Dundee 1828/W Flick, Ipswich.
N.E.V.A.	Bn	Lowestoft	146	1	b. Newport 1855.
QUEEN		Woodbridge	79	1	
MUTE	Sr	Ipswich	89	1	b. Portsmouth 1853/W.Bayley.
STARTLED FAWN	Kb	Harwich	117	3	b. Brightlingsea 1868/W.Griffith, Ips.
ALARM	Sr	Ipswich	99	1	b. Ipswich 1855/ E.J.Robertson, Ips.

Taking 1894 as another sample year, there were eleven arrivals, again all from Seaham.

Name	Rig	POR	NRT	Trips	Remarks/Owner
UNITY	Kb	Rye	126	2	b. Rye 1892. Known as *BIG UNITY*.
GODDESS	Sr	Ipswich	154	1	b. Ipswich 1842/C.Hart, Ipswich.
VANGUARD	Kb	Colchester	113	1	b. Sittingbourne 1885/J.Smith, Burnham.
LORD LANSDOWNE	Kb	London	109	1	b. Littlehampton 1890.
ELIZA H	Kb	Harwich	110	1	b. Harwich 1881 by Vaux/J.Holmes, Harwich.
MARTHA & ELLEN	Sr	Goole	82	1	b. Knottingley 1862./J.Crabtree, Goole.
ATHOLE	K	Shoreham	127	1	b. Littlehampton 1892.
ALCYONE	Kb	Harwich	107	1	b. Harwich 1884/Hempson, Shotley.
LUCY RICHMOND	Srb	Maldon	137	1	b. Ipswich 1875/Richmond, Burnham.
ADA GANE	Kb	Harwich	110	1	b. Harwich 1882 by Vaux for W.Gane.

In 1901, two notable barges brought coal for Colchester from Seaham Harbour. The first, *RECORD REIGN*, which arrived in January, had been built as a ketch barge with graceful clipper bow and counter stern by John Howard at Maldon in 1890. She was fitted with two engines when she became a Q-ship during the First World War. Afterwards the vessel traded as a motor ketch until her loss in February 1935 when she went ashore in fog near Beer in Devon. Wedged between rocks, she started to break up in the swell and so met her end. The other barge was *FRIENDSHIP*, a three-masted schooner barge built in 1890 to carry 490 tons. She delivered two coal cargoes to V.D. Colchester from

Seaham in March and August that year. *FRIENDSHIP* was run down off Spurn Head in February 1912.

By 1904, receipts of coal were down to four, all from Seaham. Beaumont's Ipswich ketch barge *REINDEER* came twice; the ketch barge *GLORIANA* of Harwich, built there by Vaux in 1871 for W. Middleton of Harwich, made one visit as did the Wisbech-owned and registered schooner *ZUMA*, built at Grimsby in 1856. Few, if any, further coal cargoes for V.D. Colchester are recorded.

Ipswich Industrial Co-operative Society

The Ipswich Industrial Co-operative Society was first registered on 3rd March 1869 and by the mid-1880s had its Central Stores in Carr Street and branches at Vernon Street, Bramford Road, Cauldwell Hall Road, Fore Hamlet and Holbrook. The Vernon Street store was the first branch to open in Ipswich, and a coal and coke depot was situated next to the premises. Coal on the 'divi' was obviously going to be important to its members and a regular supply by sea soon commenced. The table on this page gives an idea of the shift to different sources

Coal cargoes for the Ipswich Industrial Co-operative Society Ltd. 1883-1904.

Name	Rig	PoR	NRT	Seaham	Hartlepool	Middlesbro'	London	Goole	Remarks
1883									
UNIONIST		Hartlepool	69	1	1				
ALARM	Sr	Ipswich	98		1				b Ipswich 1855 owner EJ Robertson.
ZENOBIA		Yarmouth	57	2					
FRANCIS		Ipswich	97	1					
NILE	Bn	Wells	120		2				b Wells (Norfolk)1859 owner FB Southgate Wells.
FRANCIS		Ipswich	97	1					
1894									
LILY	Kb	Harwich	89	1					b Millwall 1873 owner G Underwood Southend.
ANNA SARAH	Sr	Ipswich	141	6					b Sunderland 1860 Goddard & Co Ipswich.
IVY P	Kb	Ipswich	79	3					b Ipswich 1893 b & owned by Robert Peck.
ONYX	ss	Ipswich	214			1			b Glasgow 1883 owner Edward Packard Ipswich.
REINDEER	Kb	Ipswich	113	1					b Ipswich 1879 by Curtis owner A Beaumont.
ANTELOPE	Kb	Harwich	116	1					b Brightlingsea by Aldous owner L Richmond Dovercourt.
MATILDA UPTON	Kb	Ipswich	90	1					b Ipswich 1887 by owners Orvis & Fuller.
THOMAS	Sr	Lowestoft	142	1					b Barnstaple 1837 owners T Stewart Lowestoft
1904									
SHAMROCK	sb	London	59				2		b 1899 Milton owner Wm Cory Ltd London.
SURF	sb	London	50				1		b 1900 E Greenwich owner Wm Cory Ltd.
NORSEMAN	sb	London	55				1		b Charlton 1902 owner Wm Cory Ltd.
JAMES GARFIELD	Kb	Ipswich	81					4	b Ipswich 1881 by Curtis owner J Hooker Ipswich.
BRACKENHOLM	Sr	Goole	99					1	b Skelton (Yorks) 1869 owner R Earnshaw Goole.
PEARL	Kb	Ipswich	88					3	b Ipswich 1889 by Orvis & Fuller owner W H Orvis..
EAGLE		Hull						2	
MADBY ANN	Sr	Goole	94					1	b 1865 Hylton (Durham) owner Wm Johnson Knottingley.
DAVENPORT	Kb	Ipswich	82					1	b Ipswich 1877 by W Colchester owner J Hooker.
		Total number of arrivals for 1883		5	4	0	0	0	
		Total number of arrivals for 1894		14	0	1	0	0	
		Total number of arrivals for 1904		0	0	0	4	12	

of coal over a twenty-year period. In particular it shows a change of contract from Durham to a Yorkshire colliery.

The four sailing barge cargoes ex-London, noted in the table during 1904, may have been of coke. Irregular shipments continued to come by sea and even in 1963 eight coasters arrived, seven of them British, one Dutch, and all from Blyth. In 1971, there were only four ships, mv *ARNEBORG* and mv *GUELBORG*, both of Delfzijl, from Antwerp, mv *TEESSIDER*, of Middlesbrough, ex-Germany, and the mv *ELOQUENCE* of Rochester from Amsterdam.

The Co-op had opened their large coal yard at Derby Road station, Ipswich, about 1911, and this stayed open until the Society sold what little retail coal business remained to British Fuels Ltd. in the early 1990s.

Ipswich Coal Company

The Ipswich Coal Company, managed by Mr. W.M. Birch, was well established at St. Peter's Dock by the 1880s with an office in the Exchange Chambers. The company moved the yard to Tovells Wharf about 1924 and was at that time advertising its association with Alfred Beaumont and J.R. Pendal. The office had moved down the road to number 24 Princes Street. Apparently Ipswich Coal Company never owned any ships.

The peak period for receiving coal by sea for many of these old-established Victorian companies appeared to be in the 1880s, and it is likely that they later obtained most of the coal by rail, perhaps because of the relatively small consignments required. The following table, like the others, is useful for noting at a glance the sources from where they bought coal.

Examples of arrivals for the Ipswich Coal Company in 1883 and 1894.

Name	Rig	POR	NRT	Departure Port				Remarks.
				Seaham	Shields	Harwich	Goole	
1883								
MUTE	Sr	Ipswich	89	2				b. Portsmouth 1853. Owner W Bayley of Ipswich.
IDELIA	Kb	Ipswich	123	1				b. Ipswich 1881 by W Bayley. Owner R&W Paul of Ipswich.
ARNO	Bn	Ipswich	107	8				b. S Shields 1818. Owner W Bayley of Ipswich.
MARY ATKINSON		Lowestoft	65	5				
DAYSTAR	Bn	Ipswich	148		1			b. Sunderland 1860. Owner E Goddard of Ipswich.
PROBLEM	Sr	Ipswich	128	3				b. Ipswich 1861 by builder/owner W Bayley of Ipswich.
VISITOR	Sr	Ipswich	127	1				b. Ipswich 1840. Owner E Goddard of Ipswich.
MASONIC	Kb	Ipswich	117	2				b. Brightlingsea 1876. Owner HD Smith of Ipswich.
DIRECTOR	sb	Rochester	29			1		
PROVIDENCE	sb	London	41			1		
ARTHUR	sb	Rochester	37			1		
1894								
ELIZA H	Kb	Harwich	110	2				b. Harwich 1881. Owner J Holmes of Harwich.
ROSE	Sr	Ipswich	97	1				b Dundee 1828. Owner W Flick of Ipswich.
ss SWIFT		Ipswich					1	b. Wallsend 1886. Owners R&W Paul of Ipswich.
DOROTHY	K	S Shields	99	1				
ANTELOPE	Kb	Harwich	116	4				b. Brightlingsea 1869. Owner Richmond of Harwich.
DAUNTLESS	K	Maldon	122	1				b. Sittingbourne 1873. Owner J Smith of Maldon.
ONWARD	Sr	Lowestoft	119	1				b. Bristol 1849. Owner J Stewart of Lowestoft.
		Total number of arrivals for 1883		22	1	3	0	
		Total number of arrivals for 1894		10	0	0	1	

THE COAL TRADE

ss JOHN CHARRINGTON, *885nrt, of London, at Ipswich with coal for Beaumont, Ipswich Coal Co., etc. on 6th October 1951. She was built at Sunderland in 1929 for Charrington, Gardner & Locket. (R.W. Smith)*

Eleven vessels arrived in 1904, seven of which were ketch-barges. *ALCYONE*, *FEARLESS*, *LAURA*, *HESPER* and *STARTLED FAWN* were Harwich registered and built at Harwich, Ipswich or Brightlingsea. *HESPER* and *STARTLED FAWN* were more familiar as colliers to Colchester gasworks. *COCK O' THE WALK* of Weymouth was built at Millwall in 1876 for Richard Cox who kept a small fleet of barges at Weymouth for use in the Portland stone trade. She was later skipper-owned by Captain H. Strange of Ipswich. *FRIENDSHIP* of Colchester was well known as a three-masted schooner barge 117ft in length, only drawing 3ft 6in when light but still dependant on leeboards. She could load 490 tons of coal and was built at Sittingbourne in 1890 for J. Smith of Burnham but was run down and sunk off the Spurn in 1912.

Another arrival in 1904 was the small steamer *KING JA JA* of Swansea. She was a screw schooner, Glasgow built in 1870 for the grandly titled Liverpool, Caernarvon & Menai Straits Steamship Company. The Padstow-built schooner *MARY SEYMOUR* of 1865, another schooner, *RICHARDS & EMILY*, built at Gainsborough in 1868, and the *JANTJE* of Hull (probably a billyboy) concluded the list for that year. Thereafter shipping dwindled to occasional cargoes and the company, with its associated A. Beaumont & Company, was absorbed by Thrutchley.

Isaac Lord

In 1900 Alfred Sizer and Isaac Lord took over the old-established firm of Cobbold & Company, which had been malting in the parish of St. Clement, on the site that became 80 Fore Street, since the eighteenth century. Malt and hops were sent by carriers' carts to small brewhouses attached to public houses in and around Ipswich, and bagged malt was sent regularly by sailing barge to the Red Lion Wharf at 261 Rotherhithe Street, Bermondsey. Malting continued until 1939-1940. Brewers' grains were collected from local breweries for drying and selling on as food for dairy cattle, a practice which continued into the 1950s from Cobbold's brewery by their own horse and tumbril, carrying on a while longer with lorries.

Bevan's coal yard, next door at number 82, was taken over by Sizer & Lord after 1904. Isaac Lord took over Alfred Sizer's share in October 1924 and some years on, probably in the 1940s, he acquired the coal interests of Wilfred

Christopherson, previously V.D. Colchester's on Griffin Wharf. Local coal factors Everett & Shepherd were bought out in 1966.

Retail coal deliveries were principally in the thickly populated town areas of the Rope Walk and Stoke. As the Priory Heath and Whitton estates were built during the 1920s and 30s trade increased, although only one daily delivery round was possible. One ton was the maximum for one horse going up Bishops Hill to Priory Heath, and any excess would have to be left at the bottom of the hill and retrieved after unloading a similar amount at the top. Sometimes a trace horse would be sent to assist.

In the 1930s the adjacent Ocean Queen Yard, site of a former corn mill and an inn round the corner in Salthouse Street was bought and stables and a garage erected there. The firm's first motor vehicle was a Morris 30cwt. truck purchased from local dealers Lock & Stagg Ltd. of Friars Road. The company was the first in the area to sell pre-packed coal, but with the swift reduction of the domestic coal market in the 1970s and 80s Isaac Lord ended their retail business in 1988, continuing as factors until Everett & Shepherd Ltd. was purchased by British Fuels Ltd. in 1994.

Mellonie & Goulder Limited

The prime mover in the founding of this ambitious company appears to have been Thomas Mellonie, of Norwich Road, Ipswich, a coal factor represented by agents in most market towns locally since the 1880s. He and his partner, Mr. Robert Goulder, of Little Ellingham Hall, near Attleborough in Norfolk, com-

The mv CENTURITY, 391nrt, built 1956 by Goole SB & Repairing Co. Ltd for F.T. Everard & Sons, discharging at Mellonie & Goulders' yard c.1960. She was sold in 1975 to Cypriot owners as TEMPESTA and was out of the register by 1987. (R. Josselyn)

bined in 1907 to provide a wholesale coal and shipping business, and the next year decided also to open a retail side by buying a small coal business at Stoke Bridge. A statement exists, signed by one Thomas Temple on 17th July 1908, referring to

Taking over in our mutual interests the coal and coke business hitherto carried on by myself, paying me the sum of £244 sterling including £125 for Goodwill of the said business, and you making a further payment to me on the 17th Day of July 1908 of £242 4s. 9d. for stock in trade as taken over by your Company on the 1st of July 1908, (such latter sum including part-payment to me of a sum agreed upon as being half the amount of Book Debts to be collected by your Company for myself as shown by my Books on the 30th June 1908.

The note went on whereby Mr. Temple

Agreed to bind myself absolutely not to engage in the coal trade as Principal or Agent, directly or indirectly or in any manner whatsoever in Ipswich or District, except it may be, or through, or in connection with your Company.

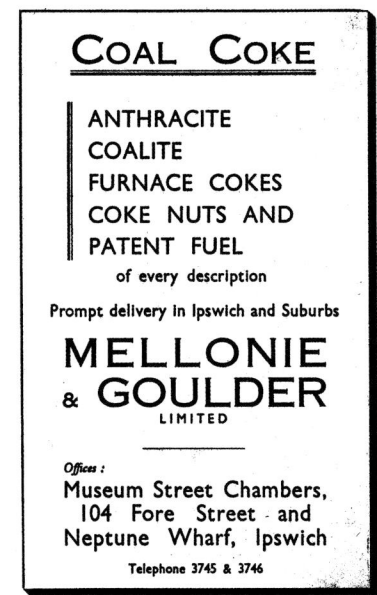

An advertisement for Mellonie & Goulder from an Ipswich directory of 1956.

The letter was signed by Mr. Temple and witnessed by Mr. Leslie Mellonie, of Holly Road, Ipswich. There is no Temple listed in Ipswich trade directories of the time, either as a coal merchant or under commercial or private residents. However, the first site used by M. & G. was on the west side of Bridge Street between Commercial Road and Fison's Eastern Union Mill, next to the railway crossing. The site had been occupied for years by coal merchant Joseph Bird, but before 1906 he had been joined by the Eastern Counties Coal Company, and their combined addresses were given as Bridge Street, with an office at 30 Westgate Street, Ipswich. Mr. Temple may have been connected with that company. At any rate, the 1909 directory shows Mellonie & Goulder occupying that site.

At first the company would have received most of its coal by rail, situated as it was close to the corner of the goods yard at Stoke Bridge. Among the very occasional arrivals was the small steamship *THAMES* of Hull, from Cardiff on 28th November 1908. The *MARY* of Marstal, on the Danish island of Aero, came from Hartlepool in November 1910.

Times were not easy for the new company, and in 1912 there was a coal strike, with a transport strike later in the year. Thomas Mellonie, in a letter to Mr. Goulder on 25th March 1912, expressed concern that it might take three months after the end of the dispute before they received further supplies of coal. He described the Government as weak-kneed but added that

Mr Asquith should be given credit of being firm on the real point, having refused to insert in his Bill a provision for the Minimum Wage as demanded but to leave it to each District to which the Owners [coal] have now agreed and if he stands his ground the men will give way at today's Conference.

Letters between the partners seem excessively formal by today's standards, particularly on Mr. Goulder's part. Whereas Mr. Mellonie would address him as 'Dear Mr. Goulder', the reply was invariably 'Dear Mellonie'!

On 15th November 1919 M. & G. agreed to lease coal ground and an office (12ft x 9ft) from the Great Eastern Railway at Westerfield. A year later, in 1920, the company purchased a yard on Neptune Wharf giving access to larger steam colliers and supplying ships' bunkers for vessels in the port.

Mellonie's first steamer, the ss MARJORIE MELLONIE, ready for launching at Chambers' yard at Oulton Broad in 1921.

The increased shipping associated with the move in 1920 to Neptune Quay coincided in 1921 with a national coal strike, and during June and July seven ships arrived from Ghent with the first foreign coal to be discharged at Ipswich. The first was the ss *ROBRIX*, one of J.R. Rix's ships from Hull, with 300 tons. She was discharged by volunteers with a police escort. (The company of J.R. Rix had been founded in the 1880s at Hull. There are still ships with the '*RIX*' suffix trading from the Baltic and elsewhere to Ipswich.) The ss *KNOWL GROVE* of Goole, built at South Shields in 1909, brought two cargoes, and the little ss *ROSIE*, only 64nrt, launched at Beverley in 1907, arrived on 5th June. The even smaller Glasgow-registered ss *SKARV*, Ardrossan built in 1911 and owned appropriately enough by Glasgow Steam Coasters Ltd., berthed on the 8th and 29th of June and 2nd July. On 24th June the ss *HEATHER LEA* of Cardiff arrived and the last two vessels were the ss *LUFFWORTH* of Newcastle and the *ELLINDA* of Hull, making ten cargoes all told.

Mellonie & Goulder took a risk in March 1920 by ordering a steamship for the coal trade from John Chambers of Lowestoft, at a cost of £52,210. The ship was to be 180ft long, 28ft 6in breadth and 13ft 5in depth, with a 575hp engine, the boiler for which would be 14ft diameter by 10ft long with a working pressure of 180lb. Delivery was due on or before the end of April 1921, and a trial trip of not more than four hours was to be run off the measured course near Lowestoft.

A subsidiary company, the Suffolk Shipping Company, had apparently been formed to operate the ship, but by late 1920 there appear to have been difficulties and agreement was reached with the London County Westminster & Parrs Bank, of 21 Lombard Street, EC3, for the company to overdraw to a maximum of £15,000. The firm's railway wagons, an incomplete steamship, its property and whole undertaking were to be regarded as floating security. A memorandum was issued on 12th January 1921, signed by Thomas Mellonie, a Mr. Sidney Allen and Mr. Cyril Constantine Ionides, the latter representing a London finance house. It proposed new Articles of Association be drawn up and Sir Wilfred Stokes, of Ransomes & Rapier, was appointed chairman. The board was to consist of Thomas Joseph Mellonie, Thomas Cyril Mellonie, Leslie Woodfield Mellonie, Sidney Allen, Andre Ionides, Cyril Ionides and Francis Bartrum Snell, and T.J. Mellonie should be appointed deputy chairman and managing director for seven years. It also required the Suffolk Shipping Company to be merged and the shares re-invested in M. & G. Valuations were to be made on the company's fleet of 190 ten-ton railway wagons.

Unfortunately the shipbuilders notified M. & G. that the ship would not be completed without assistance, due to the general trade depression. They agreed to reduce the purchase price by nearly £2,000, with £45,812 paid by 21st June 1921, and requested the sum of £4,438 in full discharge and for Mellonie & Goulder to advance John Chambers Ltd £5,000, interest payable at 7 per cent. They also asked for these payments totalling £9,438 to be paid at regular intervals for wages and materials. The ship was delivered in November 1921 and named *MARJORIE MELLONIE*. In spite of everything, the company acquired three more small coasters in 1921-22; the *ISABEL*, built at Bowling in 1898 for the curiously named Steamship 'Isabella' Co. Ltd. of Glasgow, the *ROSIE*, built 1907, which was re-registered at Ipswich, and the *MILLWATER*, new in 1921 and which was renamed *ELISE MELLONIE*. However, the ships were soon sold as the depression hit even more. The *ISABEL* was laid up in the Branch Dock close to the Public Warehouse in 1923, leaving light for London three weeks before filling-in began on April 23rd. She was the last vessel to use the Branch Dock before it was required to complete that corner of the Dock by the construction of End Quay and Tovells Wharf. The *MARJORIE MELLONIE* was last to be sold, in 1928.

Mellonie's ships were used more for general cargo than carrying coal for the company's business. One of the first voyages of the *MARJORIE MELLONIE* included bringing coal to R. & W. Paul from Swansea on 31st March 1922,

The ss MARJORIE MELLONIE fitting out at Chambers' No.3 yard with two other steam coasters building at the same time.

leaving light for Shields. She discharged again that year at Pauls on 1st September. *ELISE MELLONIE* meanwhile arrived at Ipswich on 25th June with basic slag for W. Christopherson, sailing two days later light for Bruges, where she picked up a cargo for Felixstowe, coming back in Ipswich on 1st July to load flour at Cranfields for Portsmouth. On 22nd January 1923 the *ELISE MELLONIE* arrived with coal for M. & G. from Boston, Lincolnshire, where coal was loaded from railway trucks from Yorkshire or Midlands pits. The ship sailed light for Ostend, loading for Felixstowe and docking at Ipswich again on 27th January, once more loading Cranfields' flour for Portsmouth and sailing on 30th January.

The coal side of the old-established Ipswich coal and timber business of F.A. Christie, whose premises were just along the quayside, was acquired in 1924, the timber side having been bought by William Brown & Son Ltd. Mellonie & Goulder also acted as shipbrokers, fixing ships and cargoes for such Ipswich firms as Fison, Packard & Prentice, the Suffolk Chemical Company and the original Ipswich power station.

Taking 1924 as a sample year, four years after the move to the dockside and four years before William Cory & Co. Ltd bought the company, no fewer than twenty-five coal cargoes arrived.

Coal deliveries to Mellonie & Goulder, 1924

Name	POR	NRT	Tyne	B'ness	Goole	Blyth	Remarks.
ss VALSCIAN	Liverpool		1				
ss ELISE MELLONIE	Ipswich	166	3	1	2	1	
ss MARJORIE MELLONIE	Ipswich	366	1				b. Lowestoft 1921.
ss OARSMAN	Ipswich	117			1		b. Northwich 1919. Owner R&W Paul Ipswich.
ss OXBIRD	Ipswich	112	1				b. Gt. Yarmouth 1916. Owner R&W Paul Ipswich.
ss SUNNYHILL	Newcastle		1				
ss BALFRON	Grangemouth	138				1	b. Scott & Sons Bowling 1920. Owner Shields SS Co.Ltd.
ss DALESIDE	Sunderland		1				
ss PENRHYN	Bangor	127				1	b. Scott & Sons Bowling 1895. Owner Rt Hon Baron Penrhyn.
ss JOLLY LAURA	London		1				
ss GUARDIAN	Newcastle					1	
ss HARTFORD	Liverpool	156				1	b. S Shields 1912. Owner Northwich Carrying Co.Ltd.
ss EDENSIDE	Sunderland	148	1				b. Newcastle 1921. Owner Rose Line Ltd.
ss BRAEDALE	Newcastle		1		1		
ss LEELITE	Methil	154		1			b. Rutherglen 1883.
ss LUDDICK	Aberdeen	214	1				b. Workington 1898
ss RAVENSCRAIG	Kirkaldy	132	1				b. Dundee 1899 for Kirkaldy Steamship Co. Ltd.
ss FODHLA	Glasgow	149	1				b. Scott & Sons Bowling 1893. Owner J Mitchell Glasgow.
		Total	14	2	4	5	

When the *MARJORIE MELLONIE* brought coal from Ghent during the so-called General Strike of 1926, a strike of transport workers in support of the coal miners lasting from 4th to 12th of May, the cargo was discharged with mounted and foot police present and the lock gates were operated by volunteers guarded by soldiers with fixed bayonets. Afterwards Mellonies received occasional cargoes from Rotterdam in the Dutch vessels *DRECHTSTROOM* and *AMSTELSTROOM,* both of about 2,000 tons dwt.

In 1928 the company was bought out by William Cory & Son Ltd. and the name was changed to Mellonie & Goulder (1928) Ltd. They continued trading under that title, but the office was moved to Cory's head office in Fenchurch Street, London. The name of William Cory & Son had been adopted in 1838 by

THE COAL TRADE

The MARJORIE MELLONIE *discharging at the Wouldham cement works at Grays in 1928. (Mr. S. Shipman)*

the much earlier Cory family firm of coal and collier owners, merchants and factors. It was not until 1896 that they were registered as a public company. William Cory & Son Ltd. also set up a chain of bunkering stations around the world and later became involved with oil bunkering and distribution. Ship bunkering was also provided at Ipswich and to ships moored in Buttermans Bay, coal being towed downriver in old wooden Thames lighters that had generally seen better days, and were also used as floating warehouses.

Although the company was using early lorries for deliveries, it still had several horses and in 1922 and 1929 drew up new tenancy agreements with Ipswich Borough Council for 36 rods of land, including stables and forage stores, in New Cardinal Street, Redan Street and Princes Street.

In September 1929 the London tug *BRITANNIA* towed the Cory lighters *VESPASIAN* and *FABIUS* on the 5th from London to Ipswich, and the *POMPEY* and *SEXTUS* on the 7th, for taking coal down from M. & G.'s yard to Buttermans Bay for ships' bunkers. Packards' barges had been used for this, but most of them had been disposed of, although the steam barge *TRENT RIVER* and the dumb barge *YARE* were taking coal to the Bay in March and June 1929. The two were in use again for M. & G. in 1931 and 1932, when two more Cory lighters, *CORIOLANUS* and *TARQUIN*, were brought from the Thames by the same tug. The lighters were used as floating warehouses, usually being kept laden in the Dock between trips.

On 29th April 1930 the relatively early motor coaster *INNISULVA*, built at Glasgow in 1914, brought 236 tons of Kent coal from the old Roman port of Richborough, not far from Betteshanger Colliery. This was the first of eight cargoes she brought until mid-August, out of a total of fourteen arrivals for M. & G. from Kent in that year. Twenty such shipments came in 1931, some arriving in the new steel sailing barges belonging to F.T. Everard of Greenhithe. Capable of loading 280-300 tons, they included the *ALF EVERARD* that came once and the *FRED EVERARD* that came four times. Everard's ketch barge *MARTINET*, built at Rye in 1912, brought one cargo and the rest came in small steamers and motor barges. Seven of Hay's Glasgow fleet of traditional steam coasters brought eighteen more cargoes from the north-eastern coast ports, *THE DUKE, THE DUCHESS, THE VICEROY, THE EMPEROR, THE COUNTESS, THE MONARCH* and *THE BARON*, all being very familiar ships in every port

One of Mellonie & Goulder's first coal carts outside the company's office close to the junction of Commercial Road and the approach to Stoke Bridge.

The ss CORMINSTER, *935nrt, built in 1928 at Sunderland for Wm. Cory & Sons Ltd., seen arriving ex-Blyth for Mellonie & Goulder. The last engines-amidships collier and the first ship to load coal at Dover from the new Kent coal mines, she was broken up in the early 1960s. (R.W. Smith)*

in the country and the near continent. Altogether no fewer than sixty-two coal cargoes arrived for M. & G. in 1931, and totals remained in the fifties and sixties each year until 1939.

Another example of the effects of the Cory buyout was the switch to the Scottish coalfields of Fife and Lothian, north and south of the Firth of Forth respectively, much of it brought to Ipswich in William Cory's own colliers from several ports close to the mines. Most of the ports had long histories of trade and shipbuilding prior to exporting coal for two centuries. Since the reduction in coal mining, the oil industry operating in the North Sea has provided business for some.

Many of Cory's ships discharged a whole or part-cargo of coal at Cliff Quay, where it was piled high at the south-western end, ready for bunkering ships, a worldwide activity for Cory's since bunkering stations were set up around the globe from the mid-nineteenth century. On 1st July 1929, for instance, the three-island type collier *CORMINSTER*, built by S.P. Austin in 1928 at Sunderland, berthed at Cliff Quay from Burntisland in Fife. She entered the Dock on 3rd July and was noted as William Cory's first arrival. Three days later *CORBRIDGE* arrived from Granton, west of Edinburgh in West Lothian, and in September *CORNESS* came in from Grangemouth, some eleven miles above the Forth Bridge. Likewise in October and November, *CORBEACH*, *CORMINSTER* and *CORPATH* all arrived from Granton.

1930 saw *CORMINSTER* load at Methil with part-cargoes for Mellonie & Goulder and Cranfield Brothers. As colliers grew bigger this became normal, ships discharging parcels for Mellonie, Mason's cement factory at Claydon, Cranfields or the Corporation power station in Constantine Road. In 1933, the ss *MOORFOOT*, built at Grangemouth in 1913, began to call regularly, usually with coal from her home port of Leith for the Corporation electricity supply or Mellonie & Goulder, the latter acting as agents and brokers for the ship, fixing her many Ipswich cargoes during the 1930s. *MOORFOOT*'s name referred to the Moorfoot Hills between Edinburgh and Carlisle. She belonged to George Gibson & Co. Ltd. of Leith, who owned nine colliers, all with place-names in the Lowlands. In 1935 *MOORFOOT* brought eleven coal cargoes, one from Blyth, two from Methil and eight from Leith, these being for various customers.

In their capacity of coal factors, M. & G. gained several local contracts to supply wholesale coal to such companies as BX Plastics Ltd. at Brantham and

THE COAL TRADE

Footman Pretty's clothing factory, and to local hospitals. They also stocked tons of Cheshire salt for water softeners and bakeries, and ground salt was sold to county councils for road gritting in later years. Cattle lick rock salt, obtained from places such as Spain, Chile, France and Poland, was stocked for farmers to enhance the diet of dairy cattle. During the 1939-45 war tons of logs and Scottish peat were sold for fuel.

In August 1948 the company's 150-ton lighter *CORIOLANUS* sank at the wharf laden with 58 tons of coke and 8 tons of lignite, a carbonised coal with a fibrous woody structure. The coke was recovered with no loss but the lignite became waterlogged and was written off. Valued at £35 6s.8d., it was taken away by the buyer of the barge, which was sold for £5. A year later, the lighter *SEXTUS* also sank in the dock with the loss of part of the coke cargo that spilled out.

Mellonie & Goulder averaged forty cargoes per year from 1939 to 1944, and in 1946 they received fifty-six. For the next three years they averaged seventy-seven, the numbers gradually diminishing during the late 1960s and 1970s. The table for 1963 shows the dominance by F.T. Everard's ships since the Second World War and the change to the Northumbrian port of Blyth as principal loading port. The mv *ALACRITY*, shown in the table, was wrecked off Cornwall

Everards' mv ACTUALITY overlapping the stern of sb CABBY in order to discharge her forward hold at Mellonie's wharf about 1960. The CABBY is at the BOCM warehouse with oilcake. The ACTUALITY sank on 27th October 1963 after a collision with the Dutch mv BETTY ANNE S in fog off Hastings.

in December that year. In addition to the coal cargoes, there were also two shipments of salt during 1963, one from Sousse in Tunisia.

During the late sixties competition, first from heating oil for factories and homes in the late sixties, then the introduction of natural gas in 1971 followed by the rush to convert from coal products to gas in the domestic market, signalled the end of much of the coal trade. Only six ships arrived in 1971. These were the Dutch coaster mv *PIROLA* and the Hamburg-registered mv *BIRTE O* coming from Emden with coal, the Rochester-owned mv *LADY SHEENA* and mv *LADY SYBILLA*, the *ORTOLAN* of the General Steam Navigation Company (a rare visitor to Ipswich) and Everard's *SCARCITY*, the last four vessels all arriving from Goole.

Having literally been a branch of William Cory for many years, Mellonie & Goulders' name finally disappeared about 1980 with the closure of their old yard.

Coal shipments for Mellonie & Goulder, 1963.

Details Of Vessel					Arrival Date	From
Name	NRT	POR	Owner	Built		
mv *ABILITY*	461	London	F.T.Everard	Goole 1943	27 Feb 2 Oct 24 Nov	Blyth Blyth Blyth
mv *ACTIVITY*	179	London	F.T.Everard	Greenock 1931	2 Oct	Blyth
mv *ACTUALITY*	499	London	F.T.Everard	Goole 1945	8 Aug 19 Oct	Blyth Blyth
mv *ALACRITY*	354	London	F.T.Everard	Goole 1940	23 Feb	Blyth
mv *ANTIQUITY*	147	London	F.T.Everard	Gt Yarmouth 1933	30 Mar	Blyth
mv *ATOMICITY*	304	London	F.T.Everard	Grangemouth 1947	14 Jan	Blyth
mv *CELEBRITY*	154	London	F.T.Everard	Italy 1947	17 Feb 3 Nov 27 Jan	Blyth Blyth Blyth
mv *CENTURITY*	389	London	F.T.Everard	Goole 1956	9 Feb 19 Jul	Blyth Blyth
mv *CONTINUITY*	329	London	F.T.Everard	Wallsend 1955	22 Jan 17 Mar 28 Mar	Blyth Blyth Blyth
mv *DIAL*	142	Appingham			26 Sep	Blyth
mv *EMINENCE*	291	Rochester	L.R.T.Co.	Aberdeen 1945	13 Feb	Goole
mv *FERNDENE*	313	Sunderland	T.G. Irving	Portsmouth 1949	8 Mar	Blyth
mv *GLENSIDE*	163	Sunderland	T. Rose	Holland 1938	15 Sep	Blyth
mv *INSISTENCE*	140	London	L.R.T.Co.	Delfzijl 1939	18 Apr 9 May 28 Sep	Blyth Blyth Blyth
mv *MARIAN M*	349	London	Metcalf London	Holland 1955	8 May 17 Aug	Tyne Tyne
mv *MICHAEL M*	343	London	Metcalf London	Holland 1955	22 Dec	Tyne
mv *MOIRA M*	346	London	Metcalf London	Goole 1937	26 Dec	Blyth
mv *MONICA M*	274	London	Metcalf London	Goole 1936	21 Feb	Methil
mv *ORDINENCE*	146	Rochester	L.R.T.Co.	Northwich 1941	13 Feb 1 Mar 18 May 22 Sep 4 Oct	Blyth Blyth Blyth Blyth Blyth
mv *PAUL M*	236	London	Metcalf London	Waterhuizen 1938	1 Nov	Blyth
mv *SAGACITY*	498	London	F.T.Everard	Grangemouth 1946	14 Oct	Tyne
mv *SCARCITY*	502	London	F.T.Everard	Goole 1948	13 Jan 28 Feb	Blyth Blyth
mv *SIGNALITY*	244	London	F.T.Everard	Greenock 1937	27 Jan	Goole
mv *SINCERITY*	333	London	F.T.Everard	Greenoch 1936	9 Mar 12 May 2 Jun	Blyth Blyth Blyth
mv *ST ABBS HEAD*	300	Leith	Henry & MacGregor	Waterhuizen 1956	19 Dec	Blyth
mv *THE MARQUIS*	151	Glasgow	F.T.Everard	Faversham 1934	25 May	Goole

THE COAL TRADE

Thomas Moy

Thomas Moy, a prominent citizen of Colchester who became mayor of that town, built up a large coal business in the eastern counties with depots in many a town and village railway goodsyard. Moy had his Ipswich yards on St. Peter's Dock and in the goodsyard along Commercial Road (now renamed Grafton Way after HMS *GRAFTON*). His other yard close to Derby Road station remained open for at least twenty years from about 1910.

With such a network of coal depots, Moy's name did not feature regularly in the Ipswich shipping arrivals, though in 1883 eight cargoes consigned to him were discharged at Ipswich by some familiar vessels. The Ipswich schooner *ALARM* came in May from Seaham, followed in June by the Harwich schooner *VECTA* from Sunderland, the *FRANCIS* of Ipswich also from Sunderland, the *DAYSTAR* of Ipswich from Seaham, and a stranger in the form of the Aberdeen registered *SPEED*, also from Seaham. The *VECTA* arrived once more in September from Saundersfoot; in November the Ipswich brigantine *PRINCESS ROYAL* berthed from Seaham, and in December the eighth cargo came in the schooner *MARKET MAID*, also from Seaham. She had been launched at Rye in 1814 only two years after Napoleon's retreat from Moscow.

The schooners *VECTA* and *PRINCESS ROYAL* brought five cargoes and one cargo respectively in 1888, five ex-Seaham and one ex-Sunderland. Another six arrived in 1894, including the Sunderland brig *HENRIETTA & LEONARD PRESTON* from Sunderland; the schooner *THOMAS* of Lowestoft (once from Seaham and once from Sunderland); the Lowestoft-registered *ELLEN H* from Seaham; the Ipswich *ROSE* ex-Seaham and the *MARTHA & ELLEN* of Goole,

Employees of Thomas Moy with the steam tractor the company operated at Ipswich..

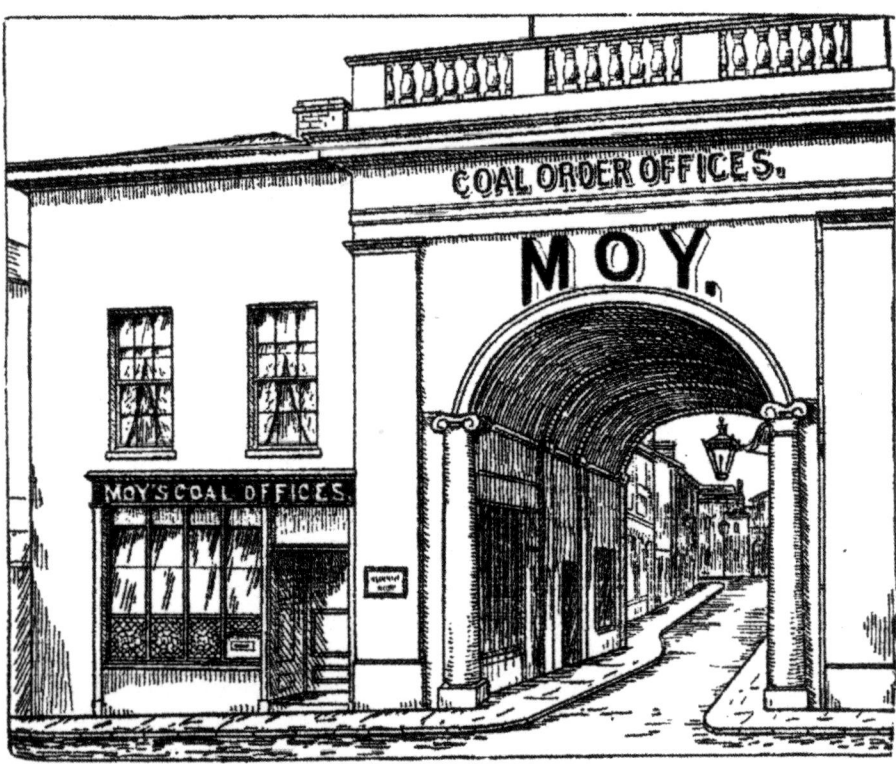

Thomas Moy's coal order office at the junction of Arcade Street and Elm Street, Ipswich, from the Suffolk County Handbook, 1904.

also from Seaham. Entries are very sparse from then onwards, and we may conclude that all Moy's coal then came by train.

J. R. Pendal & Sons

John Robert Pendal, born in Ipswich in 1866, married Julia Alice Hawes, daughter of William Hawes, a coal trader of Vaughan House, Wherstead Road, Ipswich, and subsequently became the owner of his father-in-law's business, marking the start of the Pendal Company.

Pendal's coal depot was established in the Great Eastern Railway goodsyard, off Princes Street railway bridge, and relied on railway haulage direct from the collieries. The company had a number of own-account coal trucks leased from Coote & Warren (coal factors) of Peterborough and painted in Pendal's livery. These were requisitioned during the 1939-45 war and not returned.

Coal was unloaded by hand into bays or weighed directly into one-hundredweight sacks ready for delivery. Orders were prepared in districts; attention had to be given to whether a particular area was hilly, and if two horses would be required for a certain delivery. Many customers paid in weekly instalments of 1/- or 1/6d. Problems occurred when the breadwinner was ill or unemployed, but the company was always sympathetic in those circumstances and few bad debts were incurred. The company usually had no more than two horses in its stables, situated in Prospect Street, off London Road, next to the greyhound track, an area redeveloped in the 1970s as a retail park.

Following the 1914-18 war Cyril Pendal, one of J.R. Pendal's four sons, became a partner and eventually sole owner in the 1930s. Cyril Pendal retired in 1950 and the business was sold to the Ipswich Coal Company Ltd. (A. Beaumont & Co. Ltd.), who carried on the Pendal name for several years but operated from Tovells Wharf in the dock, with offices at Imperial Chambers, 24 Princes Street.

THE COAL TRADE

The coal was by then usually brought in by sea, which was ironic as the Pendal family had long objected in the strongest terms to the duty imposed by the Ipswich Dock Commission on rail-borne coals coming into Ipswich, but to no avail.

W. Pipe

W. Pipe, of 83 Derby Road, Ipswich, was another domestic coal merchant who rented land at Cliff Quay in the 1930s. During the twelve months April 1935 to March 1936, the ss *SWYNFLEET* of the Ouse S.S. Co. Ltd of Goole brought 1,232 tons in four trips. Another 397 tons arrived in Stewart's *YEWMOUNT*, making a total of 1,629 tons. W. Pipe may well also have had coal delivered by rail via the Derby Road sidings, near to the Co-operative Society's coal yard.

The Shipping & Coal Company Ltd

The Shipping & Coal Company Ltd was a Dutch company that delivered coal from the north-east coast ports to Holland and other continental countries. Despite their title the ships were not British registered until the 1920s when their small fleet was given names with the suffix 'land'. A few were built in the 1950s, including the mv *QUEENSLAND*, built as *GREATHOPE* and renamed in 1964, which sometimes brought coal to Cliff Quay power station.

Unusually, the records for 1963 show four arrivals in January and February with coal from Blyth for the Shipping & Coal Co. Ltd. The cargoes all came in the Hamburg-owned mv *SEEFALKE*, built at Foxhol in Holland in 1939. This appears to be an isolated series of imports without any customer named. It may have had something to do with 1963 being one of the coldest winters on record, with the ground frozen to six feet down and severe problems experienced when trying to load ships at the coal ports.

The Isaac Lord warehouses at the rear of 80 Fore Street remain as the oldest surviving commercial premises in Ipswich.

Thrutchley

Thrutchley were old-established coal factors of Manchester who obtained contracts from local and national companies. They often received at Ipswich anything from twenty to over forty shipments a year, from the 1930s to the 1960s mainly to Tovells Wharf. In Ipswich, they absorbed local merchants such as Forsdick, Beaumont, the Ipswich Coal Company and J.R. Pendal & Sons, retaining some of the names for the retail business and maintaining a head office at 24 Princes Street. In the 1970s, however, Thrutchleys were bought out by Cawoods Ltd., an expanding firm of coal factors from Yorkshire based at Harrogate.

Cawoods was a name that probably surfaced at Ipswich during the 1960s. In 1971, there were no fewer than twenty-five arrivals for the company, nineteen of them coming from continental ports, including Emden and Nordenham in Germany and Rotterdam, where coal was imported from all over the world including Australia. Surprisingly only eight of these cargoes were brought in foreign ships, the British loading ports being Blyth, Middlesbrough and Goole.

Cawoods were taken over in 1977 by the modern British Fuels Ltd, who also bought out local factors Everett & Shepherd in 1994. This firm was originally established *c.*1910 by William H. Booth (perhaps no connection with Booth Brothers), and following his death in 1929 was called after his two managers; the company was acquired by Isaac Lord in 1966.

Own Account Coal Users and Factors

Sundry Ipswich factories were using considerable amounts of coal while others, needing less, had only railway truckloads. Starting with 1894, for instance, George Masons Paper Company had two barge loads from London; Tollemache Brothers had one cargo arrive from Seaham in the Goole-registered *FAIR MAID*; Cowell & Co. received one by the ketch barge *WILLIAM* of Ipswich from Seaham, and Cocksedge Ltd had one part-cargo in the ss *RINGMOOR* from Newcastle. Ransomes, Sims & Jefferies Ltd received six cargoes in steamships, three of which were Packard's ss *RINGMOOR*, ss *ONYX*, and ss *WINIFRED*, the last-named newly built in 1894 at South Shields. All came from Middlesbrough, Sunderland or Newcastle. Meanwhile Edward Packard had four cargoes brought in the same three ships; *ONYX* coming twice from the Tyne and the other two loading at Sunderland.

Ransomes' expansion by 1913 is evident by the arrival that year of the *WINIFRED* no fewer than twenty times, plus Packard's latest steamer, the *SHOTTON*, all from Hull.

The Cobbold family had brewed beer in Harwich since 1723, moving to the Cliff Brewery in Ipswich in 1746 to take advantage of the pure water from Holywells. The company opened a coal yard in Fore Street and had their own maltings, the largest of which was situated between the dock and Cliff Road; this was subsequently bought by R. & W. Paul, who later extended their Eagle Mill across the site.

Cobbolds needed coal for the brewery long before the Dock opened. In 1839 for instance, they received eight cargoes of coal, totalling 861 tons, during the month of July alone. Eleven vessels arrived in 1883 including Cobbold's own *ORWELL*, a three-masted schooner built at Ipswich in 1811, four years before the Battle of Waterloo; she arrived seven times from Seaham Harbour. The schooner *ALDBORO'*, Yarmouth built in 1835 and skipper-owned by S. Hart of Ipswich, and the brigantine *PRINCESS ROYAL* of Ipswich, built at Woodbridge in 1843, both came from Seaham. The *PETREL* of Ipswich arrived from Hartlepool and the schooner *MARGARET* of St. Ives, completed at Plymouth in 1838, came from Swansea.

In 1894, the Ipswich schooner *ALDBORO'* brought nine cargoes of Londonderry coal from Seaham for Cobbolds. The big ketch barge *VANGUARD* of Colchester, built at Sittingbourne in 1885, and the brigantine *DRIVING MIST*, new in 1854 from Sunderland, both came from Seaham while the Yarmouth-registered brigantine *HELEN MARSHALL*, built in 1863, brought Welsh coal from Swansea. She was owned by the old-established coal merchants Bessey & Palmer of Yarmouth. There are few regular cargoes for Cobbolds recorded after that decade.

HMS *GANGES*, the Royal Navy training establishment at Shotley, also received coal at Ipswich. They rented two or three rods of Tovells Wharf for a week at a time to enable the coal to be discharged to the quay, allowing time for the coal to be cleared by lorries. The rate was ninepence per rod per week and HMS *GANGES* was charged 1s. 6d. for two rods a week or 2s. 3d. for three rods. Between April 1935 and March 1936 five ships discharged 2,493 tons. They were the ss *BORDER FIRTH* of London, built in 1919 and owned by Border Shipping Co. Ltd; ss *EBBRIX*, built by Cochrane of Selby in 1917 for Rix of Hull; ss *RAYFORD* of Methil, built in 1894 by the Ailsa Shipbuilding Company of Troon; ss *SHERWOOD*, built 1924 at Stockton and owned by W. France, Fenwick Ltd of London; and the ss *YEWCROFT*, completed at Bowling in 1929 for J. Stewart of Glasgow.

Isaac Lord's coalyard when it was still operating in the 1980s.

Grain & animal feed 5

Throughout history grain has been the basic commodity for the production of flour, malt and feeding stuffs for beef and dairy animals. Cereals, together with various other crops, have also played an important part in enabling man to use animals for haulage. Many local firms in the dock area were involved in flour milling, malting and the production of animal feed, some companies having interests in more than one of the trades.

Flour milling

The often windy conditions of the East Coast and the upward slope of the ground from the Orwell estuary made Ipswich an ideal site for windmills grinding into flour the grain that came from the surrounding agricultural area. When William Cobbett visited the town in 1830 he counted no fewer than seventeen windmills in and around the town. Some of the early mills were water mills, the centuries-old mill standing close to Stoke Bridge harnessing the tides for power.

The earliest steam mill was probably Albion Mill at Blackfriars, London, powered by a Boulton & Watt engine in 1784. In Ipswich Joseph Fison had replaced the centuries-old tidemill at Stoke Bridge by the steam-driven Eastern Union Flour Mill by 1852. Less grain was being grown on East Anglian farms in favour of livestock farming, which required a smaller labour force, and that force was already being depleted as the drift to the towns gained momentum. The demand for imported grain of all kinds swiftly increased as steel roller mills were erected in close proximity to many of the great British ports at the end of the nineteenth century. The installation of auxiliary steam engines in watermills and windmills had only delayed the end of traditional local milling, although oil engines and electricity helped some small mills to survive, particularly those producing special and stone-ground flour. Cranfields' flour mill at Ipswich, where production started in 1884, was not by any means a pioneer in the industry.

Cranfields

John George Cranfield, the founder of Cranfield Brothers Limited, was one of four sons of William Cranfield of Park Farm, Buckden, Huntingdonshire, who had considerable farming interests in the area. John Cranfield, who was born in 1860, became interested in flour milling and travelled to America and other places developing his interest, especially in the new steel roller mills. Coming to Ipswich, he chose a site at the head of Ipswich Dock previously occupied by a variety of corn, cake and coal merchants, and there erected a flour mill using labour from his home village. John Cranfield was joined by his brother Thomas in the well-known partnership of Cranfield Brothers, situated at the Dock Roller Mills, Ipswich.

Cranfields' mill went into service on 31st March 1884 using machinery installed by E.R. & F. Turner of Ipswich. The first recorded shipment of wheat

Opposite page: Laden with wheat from London, the SPINAWAY C lies alongside Cranfield's mill at the head of Ipswich Dock in July 1966. (David Miller)

by sea, about ninety tons of wheat from London, arrived on 15th February 1884 in V.D. Colchester's sailing barge *LONGFIELD*. She came again on 9th March, to be followed by the Ipswich barges *CHAMPION*, later to be owned by R.& W. Paul, and *ALBERT*, built in 1840 and already owned by Pauls. The first shipment of wheat direct from abroad appears to have been one of about 190 tons from the East Prussian port of Konigsberg (later Kaliningrad) aboard the schooner *SOVEREIGN* of Fraserburgh, built at Peterhead in 1880. She was only 84ft in length, much the same as most of Cranfields' later sailing barges, but with a 21ft beam and 10ft depth. In 1886 there were thirty-five cargoes of wheat by barge from London, twenty-one of which were brought in eight craft belonging to R. & W. Paul. Cranfields did not apparently own any barges until about 1912, neither did they build up substantial shipments direct from overseas to Ipswich until the early 1900s.

In 1893 the ss *FANNIE* of Rostock delivered wheat on 28th February from Theodosia, on the Black Sea coast at the south-east corner of the Crimea, and on 9th April the full-rigged ship *ERROL* (ex-*CARISBROOKE CASTLE*, built in 1868 at Glasgow) arrived from Portland, Oregon. She came again from San Diego, California, in 1898. In 1894 the barque *BRIAR HOLME* of Maryport docked on 8th June from Adelaide and the full-rigged ship *PIAKO* of Elsfleth also arrived from the Spencer Gulf of Australia on 18th July. On 19th September the ss *CONCORD* of Whitby brought wheat from Mariopol, a port on the Sea of Azov in the south of the Ukraine. Two steamships, the schooner-rigged *JOHN ADAMSON*, built by Short Brothers at Sunderland in 1872, and the *EASTGATE*, laden with 2,550 tons of wheat, arrived in 1895 from the Ukraine ports of Odessa and Nikolaieff (now Nikolayev) respectively.

The company suffered a setback in February 1897 when the weight of wheat stored in the firm's silo caused the front of the building facing the quayside to burst open. A report described the silo as packed full of wheat and being some eighty feet tall with two feet thick walls but having no floors or piers to equalise the weight. Girders ran from side to side but not from back to front. It was probably these facts that led to the spectacular and frightening incident.

One or two ships came from the Ukraine between 1900 and 1903. The ss *LADY IVEAGH* of Dublin, bringing wheat from Theodosia, was one. In 1904 the *ANNA RAMIEN* of Elsfleth berthed from Adelaide, and the French barque *JANE GUILLON* docked, after customary lightening in Buttermans Bay, with wheat for Cranfields and barley for Pauls. She was wrecked, again bound for Ipswich, in 1906. Two steamers, the *ENFIELD* and *CASTLEFIELD*, arrived in November and December from Taganrog at the northern end of the Sea of Azov. The former was the first trunk-decked ship to visit Ipswich, one of a new design of cargo vessel similar to the turret ship current at the time. For the next five years two or three cargoes arrived annually for Cranfields, mainly from Black Sea ports, plus one or two from La Plata and Rosario in Argentina and a few part-cargoes in ships bringing barley for R. & W. Paul.

Initially, Cranfields' mill had produced eight sacks (one ton) of flour per hour. By 1906 the business was so successful that the original buildings and milling machinery were no longer adequate, so further land was bought between the dock and College Street. New equipment was installed capable of producing eighteen sacks per hour, with the possibility of doubling the output with additional machinery.

The death of John Cranfield in 1908 at forty-eight resulted in the firm becoming a private limited company with Samuel Armstrong as managing director, a position he held for fifty-one years until his death in 1959, when he

GRAIN & ANIMAL FEED

was succeeded by his son Douglas. Samuel Armstrong was for many years a member and chairman of the Ipswich Dock Commission.

From 1910 until 1914 there were six or seven wheat cargoes yearly for the company, a few being part-cargoes from Portland, Oregon, and many of them in sailing ships. In 1910 Packard's steam barge *STOUR* delivered a cargo of wheat from Great Oakley in the Walton Backwaters, contrasting with the arrival of ships owned by a widely-known nineteenth-century Cornish shipping line, Hain of St. Ives. In 1913 Hain owned more than thirty ships tramping worldwide, and its reputation was such that the P&O Steam Navigation Company acquired Hain's total shareholding in 1917.

All of Hain's ships were given names prefixed *TRE-*, and one, the ss *TREVARRACK*, the first of three of that name and built in 1895 by Readheads of South Shields, arrived on 19th August 1912 from Taganrog and again on 10th March 1914 ex-Novorissisk. The ss *TREVELYAN*, built in 1894 by Readheads, discharged wheat from Karachi in the Bay. She was torpedoed in December 1917 and beached down Channel, later to be salved by new Italian owners and broken up in 1924.

Four ships with wheat for Cranfields in 1914 were to be sunk in quick succession by German submarines three years later. The *EASTFIELD* of London, which had berthed on 8th January 1914 from Kherson, a Ukrainian port some miles up the River Dnieper, was torpedoed on 27th November 1917. The ss *REPTON*, built at Wallsend in 1894 and owned by the interestingly named Austin Friars Steam Shipping Company of London, berthed from Novorossisk

The tug FOAM *occupies the foreground of this photograph of two barques unloading grain in Ipswich Dock early in the 20th century.*

on 7th May 1914, and she was sunk off Matapan on 7th May 1917. The steamer *HARTBURN* of Newcastle, Blyth built in 1901, arrived from the Crimean port of Eupatoria on 8th May 1914, and went down on 15th October 1917. The ss *NESS* that arrived with Canadian wheat from Montreal on 12th July 1914 and came again on 14th December 1915 ex-New York, was torpedoed on 25th October 1917. All four were sunk within seven months, a pattern which reveals the losses incurred by the Merchant Navy as a whole.

By 1915 shipments were coming largely from United States and South American ports, including Portland (Oregon), Baltimore, Philadelphia, New York and Newport News in the USA and Rosario in Argentina. Cargoes were transferred to barges or coasters to supply several East Anglian millers from one ship; for example, in February 1917 ss *WYVISBROOK*, from Buenos Ayres and Rosario, had wheat for Cranfield, A.A. Gibbons and J. Fison of Ipswich, J. J. Colman of Norwich and E. Marriage of Felixstowe. In May the Norwegian steamship *HANSEAT* from Newport News supplied Cranfields, Thomas Mortimer, Marriages and Lee Barber of Great Yarmouth. Later in the year the ss *SICILY* of Liverpool arrived from New York with barley for Pauls & Mortimers, wheat for Cranfield, timber for Crossley and oil for the Royal Navy.

A programme of building standard ships was inaugurated by the Government to replace the final approximate total loss of two and a half thousand British merchant ships. Contracts were put out in Britain, USA, Canada, China and Japan, and some ships were launched in 1917. They included the ss *WAR SYREN* from the Uraga Dock Company of Japan. Registered at London, and of 3,368nrt, she arrived at Ipswich on 18th October 1919 from Port Augusta in South Australia with wheat for Cranfields, Pauls, Gibbons and Ipswich Malting Co. She was to become a victim of the Second World War when she was attacked by aircraft and sunk to the west of Ireland in February 1941, bound Philadelphia to the Clyde, as was the *WAR HALTON* on 2nd October 1940. This ship had been built by the Polson Ironworks in Toronto, Canada, in 1919 and in December of that year had arrived at Ipswich from Montreal. Her cargo was dispatched to Cranfields, Gibbons, Fison, Mortimers, Marriages, J.J. Colman and Lee Barber. During 1920 two ships berthed with consignments for nine importers, and the ss *BRYNTAWE* of Swansea had 5,500 tons of wheat from Bahia Blanca split between no fewer than eleven milling companies.

Cranfields' wheat trade continued through the 1920s with a yearly average of eight deep-sea arrivals. On 5th October 1920 one of the first few Japanese-registered vessels to come to Ipswich, the ss *TAKAI MARU*, moored in the Bay with some 5,000 tons of wheat for Cranfields and four other companies. The ships still came principally from North and South America during that decade, with one or two from the Black Sea, Karachi and Australia, but the range of loading ports had increased somewhat to include Bahia Blanca, La Plata, Necochea, San Nicolas, San Lorenzo, Santa Fe and Villa Constitucion, all in Argentina, and Galveston in the USA. The general increase in the size of ships meant that the practice of serving more than one importer carried on through the twenties. Part-cargoes were still being discharged for Marriages, Colmans, and Fisons, plus frequent barley or maize for Pauls. By 1930 several more vessels had returned to the Black Sea and Sea of Azov, to Leningrad and also to Braila in Romania. However, the 1930s will be best remembered in shipping annals for the so-called grain races, with wheat from the Spencer Gulf ports of South Australia carried to Europe by the last fleet of square-rigged merchant ships, including eight discharging at Ipswich for Cranfields.

In 1924, Cranfields had acquired the surviving flour milling business of

The four-masted barque ALTAIR *arrived at Ipswich from San Francisco with barley for the Ipswich Malting Company in March 1908. She was built of iron in 1890.*

Joseph Fison at Eastern Union Mills and Fison's mill was sold, according to the published records of Fison, Packard & Prentice. By the 1930s changes within the milling industry were taking place. William Green & Sons of Brantham had sold out to Cranfields, as had A.A. Gibbons. The latter business had been started by Alfred Alexander Gibbons, a corn merchant, in the 1880s, the company's West End Flour Mills being situated in Benezet Street in Ipswich. In 1936 Cranfields acquired a mill at Strood in Kent.

Two of the largest ships to have entered the River Orwell arrived from Australia in 1933. One was the Swedish-built motor ship *TUDOR*, more than 8,000 dwt and registered at Tonsberg in 1930. She moored in the Bay on 16th March from Sydney via Aden, Port Said, Dunkirk, Antwerp and Hamburg and sailed with a part-cargo aboard for Hull on 22nd March. The other was the ss *AUSTRALIA* of London, owned by the British India Steam Navigation Company. She had been built at Flensburg in 1912 with a deadweight tonnage of some 9,000 tons, and arrived in the Bay on 8th April, again by way of several ports of call, leaving on the 13th with part-cargo for London. In contrast a small Norwegian steamer built in 1917, the ss *ERLING LINDOE*, 751nrt, entered the dock on 9th September 1936 from Montreal and Fort William, a small port on Lake Superior at the far end of the Great Lakes that was accessible only to small ships until the opening of the St. Lawrence Seaway in 1959.

Interestingly, in 1932 the ss *CLINTONIA* and the ss *CYDONIA*, of North Shields, had arrived from Montreal. Both were owned by the Stag Line, founded in 1895 at North Shields, whose ships were all named after flowers ending in '*IA*'. The company's vessels were to become very familiar at Ipswich by the early 1960s after the Seaway had opened.

The outbreak of the 1939-45 war meant that once again wheat was shipped from the Americas, chiefly from the St. Lawrence River ports including Quebec, Sorel, Three Rivers and of course Montreal, plus St. John, New Brunswick, on the Bay of Fundy. The ships joined the Atlantic convoys at Halifax for the hazardous passage home among the U-boats and the North Atlantic weather.

Date	Ship	Reg.	Nrt	From	Built	+Part cargo / Customer / War damage, etc.
1939						
24 Mar	KATVALDIS	Riga	1976	Rosario	1907 Sunderland	
18 Apr	ZVIR	Susak(Yugo)	3518	Vancouver	1926 Glasgow.	+Wood for W. Brown.
17 Jun	DULWICH	London	2417	Rosario	1931 Stockton	+Marriage Damaged German prize Jun '40.
19 Jun	ABRAHAM RYDBERG	Gothenburg	1984	Port Adelaide	1892 Glasgow	To Stockholm 16th July.
13 Jul	STANLEY FORCE	Whitehaven	242	Caen	1930 Workington	
29 Jul	WOLSUM	Amsterdam	2195	Rosario		
11 Sep	SZENT GELLERT	Budapest	2915	Rosario		
28 Dec	BLAIR SPEY	Glasgow	2521	New York	Ardrossan 1929	+Marriage +Rankin +LPAGC.
1940						
16 Jan	KILDALE	Whitby	2310	R Plate	1924 Sunderland	+LPAGC. Bombed & sunk 3.11.40.
3 Feb	CAPE CORSO	Glasgow	2338	Santa Fe	1905 Glasgow	+LPAGC. Bombed & sunk 2.5.42.
10 Mar	DARCOILER	Glasgow	2544	Portland Maine	1928 Glasgow	+Paul, Marriage. Torpedoed 28.9.40.
11 Mar	DAYROSE	Cardiff	2605	Santa Fe	1928 Sunderland	+Paul, Marriage, Read. Torpedoed 14.1.42.
26 Apr	LANGLEEBROOK	Newcastle	2546	Phil	1929 Newcastle	+Paul, Marriage, Read.
29 May	PARTHENON	Chios	2030	San Lorenzo	1908 W Hartlepool	+Paul, Marriage.
30 May	EMMAPLEIN	Rotterdam	3155	Bahia Blanco	1926 Rotterdam	+Paul.
5 Jun	CZARDA	Budapest	2352	Sorel		+4 others.
23 Jul	DALEMOOR	London	3660	Sorel	1922 NC	Mined 15.1.45.
24 Jul	EMBASSAGE	Newcastle	2912	Montreal	1935 Sunderland	+Paul. Torpedoed 27.8.41.
20 Aug	DAYROSE	Cardiff	2605	Rosario	1928 Sunderland	+Paul +Marriage.
22 Aug	GRAIGLAS	Cardiff	2548	Vancouver	1940 Sunderland	+LPAGC +timber W. Brown.
17 Oct	SALVUS	Cardiff	2948	R Plate	1928 Newcastle	+Paul. Bombed 4.4.41.
17 Dec	BONNINGTON COURT	London	3012	Portland-Vancvr.	1929 Glasgow	Bombed and sunk off Sunk Iv, 19.1.41.
1941						
2 Feb	LOKE	Oslo	1431	Halifax	1915 Stockton	+Marriage.
12 Feb	BRABANT	Oslo	1287	R Plate	1926 Oslo	+Paul.
29 Mar	PHOTINIA	N. Shields	2457	Halifax	1938 Sunderland	+L. Page. Broken up 1974.
11 Apr	BONDE	Oslo	898	Halifax	Porsgrund	+L. Page.
4 May	TENNESSEE	London	1372	Portland(Maine)	1921 C'hagen	+LPAGC.
18 May	LOKE	Oslo	1431	Halifax		+Paul.
5 Jun	RIO BLANCO	London	2510	Boston	1922 Blyth	+Oak for W. Brown. Torpedoed 1.4.42.
26 Jun	NORTH DEVON	Newcastle	2239	St John NB	1924 S. Shields	+Paul. Damaged by bomb 5.7.41.
4 Jul	KEILA	Glasgow	2302	Quebec	1905 Sunderland	+Paul +LPAGC.
24 Jul	EUTHALIA	Andros	3023	Sorel	1918 Rotterdam	+Paul +LPAGC. Last sailing ex-B. Bay.
13 Aug	IOANNIS FRANGOS	Chios	2099	Sorel	1912 Stockton	+Paul.
16 Sep	SKJOLD	London	797	St John NB	1904 Sunderland	+Paul. Built for DFDS.
16 Sep	TENNESSEE	London	1371	Sorel	1921 C'Hagen	+Lorries (Govt.). Bombed 22.9.42.
4 Oct	EMPIRE SCOUT	London	1309	Montreal		+Wood for Ministry of Supply.
17 Oct	LOKE	Oslo	1431	Montreal		+Paul +wood for Ministry of Supply.
16 Dec	GLAISDALE	Whitby	2262	New York	1929 Sunderland	+Marriage.
1942						
21 Mar	KATINGO HADJIPATERA	Chios		Halifax	1913 Sunderland	+Ministry of Food. (6th name).
23 Apr	TIMOK	Susak	1971	Baltimore		+Paul.
1 May	IOANNIS FRANGOS	Chios	2099		1912 Stockton	+Wood for W. Brown.
16 May	RADHURST	London	2125	Boston		+Gibbons. Torpedoed 21.2.43.
19 Sep	EUTHALIA	Andros	3023	Montreal	1918 Rotterdam	+Ministry of Food
1943						
1 Mar	EMPIRE TYNE	Newcastle	2299	St John NB		+Gibbons +LPAGC.
29 Apr	CSIKOS	Panama	2468	St John NB		+Lorries & aircraft.
24 Jun	NICOLAS	Cephalonia	2910	+Gibbons	1910 Glasgow	
18 Aug	BEAUREGARD	Philadelphia	3700	Boston		+Milk, wood, phosphate, steel, lorries.
3 Oct	AGIOS GEORGIOS	Chios	2721	Montreal	1911 W Hartlepool	+Gibbons.
28 Nov	THEOMITOR	Chios	2750	Halifax	1910 Sunderland	+Gibbons +tank parts. Built as MOZART.
1944						
10 Feb	NADIN	London	2335	Halifax	1910 W Hartlepool	+Gibbons.
7 May	AGIOS GEORGIOS	Chios	2721	St John NB	1911 W Hartlepool	+Gibbons.
15 Jun	ARGOLIKOS	Andros	2962	Portland (Maine)	1921 Newcastle	+ Gibbons +Ministry of Food.
9 Aug	HENRIK IBSEN	Stavanger	2903	Sorel	1906 Middlesbro'	+Gibbons +LPAGC.
4 Oct	NICOLAS	Cephalonia	2910	Montreal		+Gibbons +Marriage +LPAGC +Govt stores.
27 Oct	HEINGAR	Bergen	1790	Quebec		+Marriage +LPAGC.
1945						
13 Feb	WILLOW PARK	Montreal	1656	Quebec		+Gibbons +LPAGC.
12 Apr	WILLOW PARK	Montreal	1656			?part-cargo via L'pool. +Gibbons LPAGC.
27 Apr	KATHARIOTISA	Ithica	1106			?part-cargo via L'pool. +Gibbons LPAGC.
17 Jun	SHELDERGATE	London	2691	Quebec		+Gibbons+LPAGC.
2 Jul	ALCOR	Rotterdam	2121	Montreal		+Gibbons +Marriage.
12 Sep	CEPHALONIA		2910	St John NB		+Gibbons + Marriage+LPAGC.
28 Oct	EGTON	Whitby	2535	Quebec	1938 Sunderland	+Gibbons + Marriage.
8 Dec	CAPE SABLE	London	2708	Montreal	1936 Glasgow	+Gibbons + Marriage.

Not only were the cargoes distributed between East Anglian millers but, with control over grain imports in the hands of the London Port Area Grain Committee (LPAGC), barges sailed from the Orwell to Kentish and Essex ports with their allocations.

The accompanying table is not a complete record of Cranfields' shipping for that period owing to many of the original books being damaged and some ships' names indecipherable. The records for 1942 are particularly sparse, but probably about 90 per cent of the total are listed, giving a clear indication of the pattern from 1939 to 1945. British ships were predominant before 1942, but merchant ships were being sunk at such an alarming rate by U-boats and aircraft that Greek vessels were much in evidence for the rest of the war. The number of British ships lost is starkly apparent from the table. At least twenty-two, having discharged wheat in previous years at Ipswich for Cranfields, were sunk, and many more were damaged. The *BONNINGTON COURT* was lost off the Sunk lightship and the *NORTH DEVON* was damaged off Sheringham after sailing from the Orwell light for the Tyne. Using the same Cranfield/Ipswich criterion, about thirteen vessels were lost in the First World War by submarine gunfire or torpedoes. Some ships are shown in the table arriving from Halifax, but as already mentioned this was the convoy assembly port and they would have loaded at the usual US and Canadian grain ports. Approximately fifteen ships discharged at the moorings in Buttermans Bay during 1940.

Most of Cranfields' imported wheat still came from Canada during the late 1940s. In 1948 two familiar steamships, *EGTON* of Whitby and *PENDEEN* of Falmouth, arrived from the St. Lawrence, from where in 1949 came the steamers *LA PAMPA* and *LA ESTANCIA*. The *LA PAMPA* had loaded at Three Rivers (otherwise known as Trois Rivieres) between Quebec and Montreal. *LA ESTANCIA* loaded at Montreal. Both ships were owned by the well-known British company Buries Markes Ltd of London and sported black funnels with prominent blue letters *BM* on red and white bands. The connection with the Stag Line resumed in 1949 with the *BEGONIA* berthing at Cliff Quay, also from Montreal. She had been completed in 1929 by Doxfords at Sunderland but sailed under a variety of owners and names until her acquisition by Stag Line in

Opposite page: The principal deep-sea arrivals with wheat for Cranfields, 1939-45.
*Sailed from Ipswich for the Tyne, 16th January 1941, and went down close to the Sunk light vessel.
LPAGC - London Port Area Grain Committee.

The ss BEGONIA *in the Orwell with wheat from Montreal for Cranfield Brothers on 9th August 1953. Registered at North Shields and built at Sunderland in 1929, she was owned by the Stag Line of North Shields, founded in the 1840s. Many of the Stag Line ships, all named after flowers ending in -ia, came to Ipswich with Canadian wheat until their new vessels became too big for the river. (R.W. Smith)*

1943. She was converted from coal to oil burning in 1949. Sold to Italian owners in 1956 and broken up at La Spezia in 1964, she had made at least five voyages from Canada to Ipswich as *BEGONIA*. Another of the fleet was *GARDENIA*, Tyneside built in 1930 as *BRIARWOOD* for Constantine of Middlesbrough and not purchased by Stag Line until 1945. She was also converted from coal to oil burning. She came to Ipswich at least nine times from Canada before being sold to Panamanian owners in 1964, and was scrapped in 1968 at Port Said after an engine room fire during repairs there. In the 1950s some of the old grain port names reappeared when the ss *IOANNIS FRANGOS* of Chios, which had been to Ipswich twice during the war with wheat, berthed at Cliff Quay from Odessa with wheat for Cranfields and Marriages and maize for Pauls, and in 1954 the Finnish vessel *MODESTA* of Abo came from Novorissisk.

In 1955 imports from a variety of sources began in January with *EGTON* from Mobile, the Liberian *NEVADA* from Argentina and ss *ATLANTIC CITY* of Bideford, owned by Sir William Reardon Smith, from Fremantle via London. The Greek *CORTHION* arrived from Sorel in May and on 24th October *BEGONIA* berthed from Port Churchill, Manitoba, in Hudson Bay where ice-free navigation for overseas ships lasts only from 20th July to 31st October. The white stag on a red and black funnel was very familiar on the Orwell by that time, and in the following year *GARDENIA* made two voyages from Churchill and *BEGONIA* came from Sorel. In 1953 the company had taken delivery of the first generation of smart dry-cargo bulk carriers with bridge amidships and engines aft, the *CAMELLIA*, and she was followed in 1955 by *CYDONIA*, both of about 8,000 tons dwt.

The opening of the St. Lawrence Seaway in 1959 allowed large sea-going ships to sail another 2,000 miles from the Atlantic to the western limits of the Great Lakes, giving access to Port Arthur and Fort William on Lake Superior, which are now amalgamated under the name of Thunder Bay. Detroit in Michigan, USA, at the western end of Lake Erie, was also accessible. Stag Line

A fleet of Thornycroft lorries operated by Cranfield Brothers in the 1930s. (Dunnett family collection)

GRAIN & ANIMAL FEED

was quick to take advantage of the Seaway, *GARDENIA* and *CAMELLIA* both making the passage only eight days after it opened. In 1960 *GARDENIA* arrived at Ipswich on 29th May and again on 27th July from Fort William. The table illustrates the final decade of deep-sea shipping to Cranfield Brothers.

Deep-sea shipping to Cranfield Brothers, 1961 to 1971.

*Foundered off the Norfolk coast on voyage from Goole to Shoreham in April 1973.

DATE	SHIP	REG.	NRT	FROM	BUILT	DETAILS
1961						
14 Feb	mv IRISH PINE	Dublin	2507	Halifax	1948 Readhead, Shields	
15 Jun	ss RIDGEFIELD	Monrovia	4431	Detroit	1944 Chester, Pa.	
24 Jul	LA BAHIA	London	2991	Montreal		To Port Churchill 1 Aug
3 Sep	LA BAHIA	London	2991	Port Churchill		
27 Sep	ss GARDENIA	N Shields	2463	Fort William	1930 Newcastle	ex-BRIARWOOD
26 Nov	ss ARISTIDES	Panama	2692	Fort William	1937 Ardrossan	ex-BARON ELPHINSTONE.
1962						
12 Feb	mv CURACOA	Montevideo	2124	Montevideo.		
24 Feb	mv SONNAVIND	Porsgrunn	2993	Haiti/St Domingo	1935 Vegesack	
22 Mar	mv ARCHIMEDES	Monrovia	4311	Vancouver via Hull		
16 May	TALON	Bergen	4209	Montreal		
27 Jun	TOBON	Bergen	4209	?via Hull P/C	1943 Clyde	
13 Sep	ss ELM HILL	London	4343	Great Lakes	1943 Montreal	ex-FORT LA PRAIRIE.
24 Oct	BRITISH MONARCH	London	3151	Port Churchill.		
29 Nov	ss GARDENIA	S Shields	2463	Fort William.		
1963						
6 Mar	ss CYDONIA	N Shields	3219	Halifax	1955 S Shields.	
26 Apr	mv CAMELLIA	N Shields	3168	Sorel	1953 S Shields.	
28 Jun	ss CYDONIA	N Shields	3219	Archangel	1955 S Shields.	
20 Jul	mv GOSFORTH	Newcastle	2806	Great Lakes	1962 Aberdeen.	
11 Sep	mv CAMELLIA	N Shields	3168	Port Churchill		To Great Lakes 19 Sep.
18 Oct	mv CAMELLIA	N Shields	3168	Great Lakes		To Nova Scotia 25 Oct.
4 Nov	USKOLE	Split	4460	?via Plymouth P/C		To St Lawrence River 9 Nov.
7 Dec	mv CAMELLIA	N Shields	3168	Nova Scotia.		
1964						
29 Jan	mv IRISH OAK	Dublin	2538	St John NB	1949 S Shields.	
4 May	mv CAMELLIA	N Shields	3168	Sorel		Sailed for Sorel 10 May.
4 Jun	mv CAMELLIA	N Shields	3168	Sorel		To Lt Narrows, Newfoundland.
19 Oct	ss SIDERIS	Monrovia	4654	Port Churchill	1943 California SBCorp	To Halifax 2 May.
1965						
4 Feb	mv CARRASCO	Montevideo	2646	Rosario	1946 USA.	
5 Feb	mv CAMELLIA	N Shields	3168	Halifax		
24 Jun	mv JW PAULIN	Abo (Fin)	2212	PortArthur	1936 C'Hagen.	
21 Aug	ss AGIOI ANARGYROI	Pireaus	3205	Port Churchill	1937 Hamburg	To Pt Churchill 28 Aug.
22 Oct	ss AGIOI ANARGYROI	Pireaus	3205	Port Churchill.		
12 Dec	ss CYDONIA	N Shields	3219	Quebec		To Casablanca 22 Dec.
1966						
13 Mar	ss GAROUPALIA	Pireaus	3204	St John NB.		
17 Apr	mv AMBERLEY	London	918	Rotterdam	1953 Grangemouth.	
17 May	mv CORBEACH	London	1072	Rotterdam	1957 Goole	*See footnote.
4 Jun	mv PENCHATEAU	Dunkirk	3341	St Lawrence Riv.	1960 France.	
19 Jul	ss TIRGU MURES	Constanza	2090	Constanza(Rom).		
1 Dec	mv CAMELLIA	S Shields	3168	Sorel.		
1967						
16 Mar	TRIPOLI	Bremen	3163	?via London.		
25 Mar	mv PENCHATEAU	Dunkirk	3341	Port Churchill.		
1 May	mv ORADA	Constanza	2086	Constanza.		
17 May	mv PENCHATEAU	Dunkirk	3341	Port Churchill.		
26 Jun	TRIPOLI	Bremen		Constanza.		
6 Jul	mv PENCHATEAU	Dunkirk	3341	Port Churchill.		
9 Sep	mv PENCHATEAU	Dunkirk	3341	Port Churchill.		
20 Nov	mv SUCEAVA	Constanza	2086	Constanza	1961 Galatz (Rom)	
1968						
30 Jan	ROTZBURG	Hamburg	2143	Constanza		
3 May	ss POLLUX	Flensburg	1637	?via Southampton	1944 Flensburg.	
16 Jun	VASYAALEKSEEV(?)	Leningrad	2215	Leningrad		
1969						
29 Jul	HARLYN	Oslo	695	Gdansk.		
1971						
21 Dec	PROF. RIBALTOVSKY	Leningrad	1553	Russia	1971 Stettin.	

Cranfield Bros. had worked continuously until the late 1950s using the 1906 machinery while the supply of flour was undergoing a transformation from the old jute sacks, delivered to back-street and village bakeries, to bulk deliveries. Railways in the second half of the nineteenth century and the development of motor transport in the twentieth allowed easier distribution of flour, cattle-feed and malt from the new mills, not only to the remotest parts but also to thousands of street corner bakeries and bake-offices in rapidly expanding towns and cities miles from the sea. The Second World War had delayed modernisation, but gradually Cranfields' interests spread to baking through their own automated plant bakeries. This was largely achieved by 1969 with the establishment of centralised bakeries, trading under the Betabake trade name, at Ipswich, Norwich, Chelmsford, Romford, Gillingham, Hayes and Luton.

Early in 1970 there began the removal and replacement of the old wheat-cleaning and milling machinery, with alterations to the building to install the new Henry Simon milling and processing plant. The new plant was at work within three months, producing nine tons an hour. The modernisation of the company included the acquisition of the former office building of Burton, Son & Sanders in College Street as head office, replacing the much altered original mill cottages in College Street. Major changes were still to come when in May 1972 the mill and bakeries were acquired by Associated British Foods Limited, the mill becoming a part of Allied Mills and Betabake of Allied Bakeries. The revolution in farming practices had seen home-grown wheat and barley make such enormous progress that thousands of tons have been exported from Ipswich since the early 1980s. These changes coincided with drought conditions in Spain, Eastern Europe and Russia, creating a huge demand for English wheat. Modernisation continued, new flour products appeared, and the centenary of Cranfield Brothers was marked in 1984.

Continuing drastic changes in the flour milling industry saw the name of Cranfields dropped in 1994, and plans for closure of the Ipswich mill were announced. The last of the workers finally left the premises five years later in

The Greek steamer THETIS, *2,462nrt, arrived at Ipswich on 30th May 1952 with wheat from Montreal for Cranfields (5,538 tons), Gibbons (221 tons), and the Ministry of Food (305 tons). Built in 1930 by W. Gray & Co. at Sunderland, she was owned by the Nereus Steam Navigation Co. She sailed on 9th June light for Southampton. (R.W. Smith)*

GRAIN & ANIMAL FEED

December 1999. Many other flour milling companies that had developed similarly were to merge under such famous names as Rank Hovis McDougall (RHM), and well-known names disappeared, including Marriage at Colchester and Felixstowe. Marriage's Felixstowe mill, which had opened in 1907, continued trading as part of the Rank Hovis McDougall group, but nearly a century of flour milling there ended in 2005.

Sailing Barges owned by Cranfield Bros.

Cranfield Brothers apparently did not own any sailing barges before 1912, but by 1915 they possessed the nine listed here. Later acquisitions are also shown.

DANNEBROG, *ORINOCO*, and *GLADYS* were the first of Cranfields' fleet to be fitted with auxiliary engines after the Second World War. The 80hp Ruston Hornsby engines, installed at Richards' shipyard at Lowestoft, had four cylinders and a compressed air start. Later, these engines were removed in favour of the three-cylinder, 66hp Kelvin engines that had already been installed in the next three barges to be fitted, namely *KIMBERLEY*, *ETHEL* and *BERIC*.

The barges *COLONIA*, *FLOWER OF ESSEX* and *PETREL* were all sold away by 1950. *EXCELSIOR* had been seriously damaged by incendiary bombs lying at Three Cranes Wharf early in the Second World War and was hulked outside the Dock. The smallest in the fleet, she was usually given to new skippers on promotion from mate. After her loss *PETREL* replaced her in that job. *PETREL* and *FLOWER OF ESSEX* became yacht-barges briefly *c*. 1950. *PETREL* was eventually burnt at Hoo *c*. 1965 and *FLOWER OF ESSEX* was hulked at Whitewall Creek, Rochester. The *COLONIA* foundered in 1956 near Whitstable, where she was owned by Daniel Brothers. Cranfield Bros. still owned four pure sailing barges and six with auxiliary engines in 1956, but more of the fleet were sold during the 1960s.

*Auxiliary engine installed 1940s-50s.

NAME	NRT	REG.	BUILT	ACQUIRED	PREVIOUS OWNERS / YEAR SOLD BY CRANFIELD
BERIC*	63	Harwich	1896, Harwich	1912	ex-Groom & J.W. Holmes, Harwich.
COLONIA	62	Harwich	1897, Sandwich		Ex-Groom, sold 1949. Sunk 1956.
EXCELSIOR	35	Maldon	1879, Sittingbourne		ex-G. Mason, Waldringfield.
GLADYS*	68	Harwich	1901, Harwich	1912	Whitmore, Harwich, and Howard, Shoeburyness.
MAY	57	Ipswich	1891, Harwich		ex-J. Hooker, Ipswich. Sold to Tate & Lyle subsidiary 1964.
ORINOCO*	70	London	1895, East Greenwich		ex-G. Mason, Waldringfield, sold 1966.
PETREL	52	Ipswich	1892, Ipswich		ex-G. Mason, Waldringfield, sold 1950 as yacht-barge.
SPINAWAY C	57	Ipswich	1899, Ipswich	1912	ex-A. Creasey, sold 1964 as yacht-barge.
VENTURE	58	Ipswich	1900, Ipswich	1912	Ex-Shrubsall, sold 1963 as yacht-barge.
Later Aquisitions					
DANNEBROG*	71	Harwich	1901, Harwich		ex-J. Groom, Harwich. Sold to R. & W. Paul 1967.
ETHEL*	68	Harwich	1894, Harwich		ex-J.W. Holmes, Dovercourt. Sold to Tate & Lyle 1970s for USA.
FELIX	68	Ipswich	1893, Harwich		ex-R.J. Smith, Trimley. Sold 1954 to R. Lapthorn of Hoo as mb.
FLOWER OF ESSEX	59	Ipswich	1890		ex-J. Howard, Shoeburyness.
KIMBERLEY*	65	Ipswich	1900, Harwich		ex-J.O. Fison. Sold 1970 as yacht-barge.

In 1960 *VENTURE* was the only one of Cranfields' three unpowered barges working to London for wheat, which she did thirteen times in that year, while *MAY* and *SPINAWAY C* were in use as floating grain stores and to lighten ships at Cliff Quay. *VENTURE* sailed to London two or three more times in 1961, with at least one passage back to Mistley. Probably her last round trip was to London on 26th May, returning light on 10th June. Thereafter she was used occasionally for lighterage from Cliff Quay.

BERIC and *GLADYS* still remained in 1972 to join Weston Shipping's fleet of motor ships as part of Mardorf Peach & Co. Ltd, grain brokers for Associated British Foods, the group which had acquired Cranfields in that year. *BERIC* was sold and re-rigged for promotional work in 1978 and *GLADYS* was re-rigged to full sailing condition for the company's corporate promotional work and has sailed into the 21st century owned by Associated British Foods' successor, Allied Mills Ltd.

Three motor barges lying at the head of Ipswich Dock, DANNEBROG on the outside and ORINOCO on the inside berth.

GRAIN & ANIMAL FEED

Life aboard

This section is based on material narrated by Captain Tom Polley. Tom grew up in the Stoke area of Ipswich, close to the river and the docks. Both his grandfather and his father were skippers of sailing barges. William (Coddy) Polley, Tom's father, was born at Harkstead in 1887 and was only eleven when he started work for Walter Wrinch, an Erwarton farmer, joining sb FARMER'S BOY as cook with his own father (Tom's grandfather), who was later drowned upriver at Nine Elms Wharf. The wharf was owned at the time by Wrinch, and was used to accommodate stack barges. In 1944, Tom Polley left school to sail with his father William, who by that time was skipper of Cranfields' sb BERIC, having previously been master of sb ORINOCO for twenty-five years (In the barging trade, the terms skipper, master and captain are interchangeable). William retired in 1956 and was succeeded by Tom, who carried on as master of the auxiliary-engined KIMBERLEY for two years. Then, with a young family to raise, Tom decided to give up barging and worked at Pauls' Stoke Maltings for seven years, followed by another seven years at the gasworks until its closure. He then returned to barging by joining his brothers Len and Bill aboard mb DANNEBROG, which by this time was owned by R. & W. Paul. Tom subsequently worked at Albion Maltings after the barge was sold, but in 1981 he became skipper of Pauls' ENA, which had been re-rigged in 1974 and was used for corporate entertainment. Tom retired in 1995.

During the early 1950s the working lives of the masters and mates of Cranfields' barges underwent a change when the best of the surviving Ipswich barges were fitted with auxiliary engines and the smaller craft were sold away.

The wages of Cranfields' skippers were originally based on a 50-50 share system that was dependent on the tonnage carried. The mates received a weekly wage, as did the skippers when they were refitting on the shipyard. Once an engine was installed, a 60-40 split in favour of the company was paid. Two-thirds of the forty per cent share went to the skipper, with one third going to the mate instead of his previous weekly wage. Additionally, all the diesel fuel costs were borne by the crew's share, though the firm paid for lubricants. These conditions were largely unsatisfactory, and after two or three years a weekly rate was agreed for skippers and mates. A skipper during the late 1950s might earn £10 to £12 per week, with his mate taking about four guineas. This was still roughly proportionally the same as the former share system. Cranfields never employed third hands, whereas R. & W. Pauls' barges had always been three-handed and weekly paid. There were no paid holidays, but conditions, especially in sail, were better than those of crews working for companies carrying different cargoes for a variety of customers. In these circumstances, the crews often spent long periods waiting for a cargo, especially during the depression years.

Cranfields' men supplied their own food. They took vegetables, meat and bread on board at the start of the trip and filled the sixty-gallon tank below deck with freshwater. The meat was hung in the mizzen rigging, and usually the mate did the cooking. Although seawater was used for washing up and for cooking the vegetables, freshwater posed a big problem. If the barge was to be windbound at Shotley for a week or more, the crew could restock with bread at the village shop. A run back to Pin Mill was involved, however, to obtain freshwater. A ten-gallon water barrel was stored on deck, and this was rowed ashore there and topped up. In the London Docks the crew was allowed only two free buckets of freshwater a day, this usually having to be fetched from quite a distance.

Once a year, Cranfields' craft went on Orvis's St Clement's Yard for a refit lasting five or six weeks, when an additional hand was employed to help with getting the gear down and up again, dressing sails and tarring round, etc. Other

Captain Tom Polley at the helm of the ENA.

work was done by the shipwrights. A barge would be positioned on four timber blocks, up to eighteen inches square, to enable work to be done on the bottom. The blocks, with ropes attached, were floated alongside a punt out to the barge, where the ropes were passed to the barge crew waiting on each side of the vessel. They then placed the blocks under the barge. One block went close to the stern, the second was placed at the middle of the main hold, the third was positioned near the mast and the fourth went close to the bows, the blocks being made fast aboard. Each block had wooden shoes bolted on at each end, the outer ones longer than the innermost to keep the barge level as she rose and fell on the shelving beach with the tide. Barge and blocks were hove in tight to the shore as the tide rose, enabling work to carry on for as long as the ebb and flow allowed.

The following account of a typical regular voyage, made between 1946 and 1950, illustrates well the period just before the fitting of auxiliary engines and when little had changed for almost one hundred years.

A barge loaded with 130 tons (2,080 ten-stone bags) of flour at Cranfields' mill on a Monday, for example, would leave the dock at high water on Tuesday morning, the crew having sheeted and battened down the cargo, which included a stack two-bags-high above the coamings. The skipper would have a Bill of Lading from the office and a green form from the Ipswich Dock Commission to hand to the lockmaster confirming the payment of Dock Dues. If the prevailing southwesterly wind was blowing, they brought up and anchored at Stone Heaps just inside the Orwell at Shotley. There the barge would be made ready for sea, the bowsprit lowered, dinner cooked and the crew turned in to be ready for the last two hours of the next morning's ebb that would carry the barge out to the Naze, where they would pick up the young flood enabling them to turn (tack) up the Wallet past Walton and Clacton against the south-westerly breeze. By the time the flood tide was done, the usual anchorage was at Shore Ends just inside the Crouch, or Burnham River as the bargemen called it. This was reached by keeping inside the Buxey Sand and sailing through the shallow Raysand Channel instead of crossing the Spitway between the Gunfleet and Buxey sands.

During fog, while tacking across between the shore and the sands, soundings were taken just before the time that the barge was expected to go about. The mate stood aft using the traditional lead line, which was hollow ended to pick up samples from the bottom, be it sand or mud. If sandy, the lead would hit the bottom with a thump. If mud, then the lead would dig in, requiring a sharp tug to release it. The barge would go about when the depth reached only two fathoms of water. William Polley, Tom Polley's father, was one of the last generation of barge skippers who, having spent years sailing the Thames Estuary along this course, knew instinctively where they were, without sight of the shore or the sands.

From Shore Ends, it was but a short sail on the Thursday morning down to the Whitaker, turning with the flood southwest up Swin and passing the Maplin Sands into Sea Reach and the London River. That night would be spent at anchor in the Yantlet, or maybe as far as the Lower Hope if the wind held. If the cargo were for Strood (just below Rochester Bridge up the Medway) then the anchorage inside Sheerness would suffice.

Still assuming a south-westerly breeze, the first of the flood on Friday morning saw the barge turning up the Lower Hope and into Gravesend Reach, making longer boards toward the Essex shore as the various reaches turned more to westward and even north-westerly in Northfleet Hope, Long Reach, Erith and Bugsby's. The next anchorage was in Gallions Reach, just below the entrance to the Royal Albert Dock. Here the skipper was sculled ashore to telephone for a tug, which was usually provided by London owners Tough & Henderson and contacted through Mr Riley, their agent.

Waiting for the tug meant an enormous amount of hard labour clearing a 'trench' through the stack of bags to almost deck level, allowing mast, sprit, sails and mizzen sprit to be lowered ready for the passage through the ten London road and railway bridges. The best six-inch bass rope aboard was handy for passing to the tug, with the end of the rope on the barge made fast to the windlass bitt-heads with perhaps a turn round the barrel. Once under way, the tug would pick up and let go lighters at various wharves upriver. If bound for Winchester Wharf, on the south bank at Southwark close to Cannon Street railway bridge, the barge would be set down against a lighter on the adjacent lighter roads. A line was sculled ashore and the barge hove-in to the wharf. However if Chester's Wharf, on the north bank at Pimlico, above Vauxhall bridge, was the intended destination, then upon reaching this wharf the rope was let go and the wheel put hard over, giving the barge a sheer toward the tideline. When the bow grounded on the beach, the anchor was touched down just off the wharf, until there was sufficient water to scull the boat across with a line to make fast ashore and the barge was hove alongside. Discharge would probably not start until the Monday morning, by which time the gear would have to be raised clear of the hatches to allow the cargo to be worked out by crane. A friendly crane-driver could sometimes ease the burden by putting a strop round mast and gear and gently lifting, the mate taking up the slack of the forestay on the windlass. Unloading could take from one to one and a half days. The gear then had to be lowered again and the barge anchored off ready for the tug.

Once the barge was being discharged, the master would telephone Cranfields' London office to inquire if there were any orders to load wheat back to Ipswich, perhaps from a ship in the docks. If there was nothing for Cranfields, then another call was made to agents Marcus Horlock, of the Mistley family, who also had a London office, for any other work. This might mean a cargo of maize, barley or cottonseed cake for Brooks of Mistley. Sometimes there could even be a cargo of English wheat ready to load at Mistley for Cranfields, which meant the barge was laden for all three passages.

If there were orders to load wheat back to Ipswich from the London docks, possibly the Royal Victoria, the barge was towed back to Gallions, where the gear was again hove up before entering the locks. An application was filled in stating name of barge and master, and the name of the ship from which it was intended to load. The form was handed over at the lock gates for the Port of London Authority to enter dock dues, etc., for forwarding to Horlock, as Cranfields' agent, for payment. The docks were full of Thames lighters, many of them adrift. The bargemen had to force a passage through them by muscle power using the dolly winch and line mounted on the windlass bitts, the line having to be made fast to a lighter or a bollard on the dockside each time a few yards were gained. If there was a fair wind, either up or down the dock, the topsail was set, although this was strictly against the Port of London Authority's regulations. There might be a wait to load from the giant floating hoppers alongside the ship. The hoppers were equipped with scales that measured the exact weight of grain sucked out of the ship and then shot into the hold of the barge. When loading was finished, the shipworker was found on board the ship to sign for the cargo and obtain a green customs form that was handed to the Lockmaster on departure. There was no Bill of Lading, the barge and cargo sailing under 'General Transire' rules. If there was a group of barges loaded and waiting to leave, a Port of London Authority tug was ordered to tow them all to

A laden spritsail barge sailing up the dock after having locked in at the end of a voyage from the London Docks.

the lock. Leaving as soon as the Lockmaster permitted toward high water, sail would be set as quickly as possible. With a fair wind, the ebb would ensure a quick passage down to the Yantlet anchorage, a distance of about thirty-three miles. It was by now the following Friday night.

Given that the southwesterly breeze held for another day, sail would be made shortly before high water on the Saturday, the ebb carrying the barge down to the Spitway. Here it might be necessary to wait an hour if it was low water before there was sufficient depth to cross. Then, with a fair wind, progress could be made over the flood down the Wallet. The barge could be in Harwich that evening to anchor at Stone Heaps for the night, ready for sailing up the Orwell in time for high water at Ipswich on the Sunday morning. The next day, the skipper reported to Cranfields that the barge was ready for discharge, which normally took between one and one and a half days. If the silos were full and discharge was delayed for more than five days, Cranfields then became liable for demurrage, which resulted in the skipper receiving a daily payment. If another company's barges were detained, then compensation was paid to that company for the loss of use of their vessels.

Malting & the animal feed trade

Several maltings existed close to the dock area, enabling local barley, and later imported grain, to be unloaded from barges and other vessels and to be stored close to the malting premises. The malting process begins by the removal of stones and other debris by a screening machine; the barley is then graded, small grains being taken away for animal feed. It is afterwards steeped in water, sometimes for several days, and the liquid is then drained away and the barley spread out on the malting floor for germination to take place. The grain begins to germinate and natural enzymes start to break down the starch within the grain. As it grows the grain has to be turned by hand using special turning shovels and plough rakes. The maltster has to use his skill to judge the right time to transfer the green malt to the kiln, when germination is brought to an end by heating. Different types of malt are produced by varying the basic process.

The malting firm of R. & W. Paul also produced animal feeds on a large scale and outlived all the other maunfacturers of animal feeds in Ipswich. It is difficult now to appreciate the sheer numbers of horses that were being used between 1870 and 1920 in London and in every town and city in the country as well as those employed in the countryside and on the farms. To give some idea of the many thousands of working horses, it might be noted that a large slaughterhouse in Wandsworth was disposing of about 25,000 horses each year: even the bones were sold either for button making or for use in the production of artificial manure, hence the bargeloads of bones arriving at Ipswich for the local fertiliser industry.

The thirteen horses employed on a 350-acre holding in Suffolk would each require a daily ration of 10lb. maize, 5lb. oats, 5lb. bran and 14lb. hay; the latter figure represents an annual 2.3 tons of hay. To supply this demand huge quantities of feedstuffs were imported from abroad, these being handled by a large number of local corn and feed merchants. A few of these were taken over by large firms, but many had disappeared by the 1920s as the numbers of working horses declined.

R. & W. Paul Ltd

The original business was started in Ipswich in the early 1840s by George Paul (1775-1852), a malt and grain merchant from Bury St. Edmunds. The firm was developed alongside Smarts and Albion Wharves by George's son Robert, who died in 1864 at the age of fifty-eight. The two sons of Robert senior, Robert and William, gave their names to the business, which in 1893 became a private limited company known as R. & W. Paul Limited, a title which endured for seventy years and which was recognised nationally and internationally for quality malt and cattle-feed products.

Pauls had bought land at the south-eastern corner of the dock near the new lock gates from Cobbolds Trustees for their maltings and a new feed mill, to be called Eagle Mill. The mill, built 1899-1900, took its name from the Eagle Iron Works previously on that site. In 1894 the company also had a warehouse, known as the Home Warehouse, built in Key Street by Fred Bennett. The premises were lit by electricity, which was also installed at Smarts wharf and Eagle Mill by the turn of the century. The Home Warehouse, so called because it was used to store grain produced on East Anglian farms, became a glass-fronted shipping company headquarters in the 1990s.

In 1899 the company purchased for £8,250 from the Board of Guardians the old Ipswich Union Workhouse at Felaw Street in Stoke, plus some old cottages along New Cut West. This provided a site on which were built large new maltings, augmenting the existing one adjacent to Smarts Wharf. Expansion of the business during the 1890s led the firm to hire several malthouses, including some small ones attached to public houses in the town. Among them were Cobbold's premises on the Mount, in Foundation Street, at the Compasses, Cowell's Ram and the Angel and also Thomas Mortimer's in Turret Lane. Further afield Pauls hired maltings owned by Clowes Walker in Needham Market, as well as others owned by Brooks of Mistley and Crisp & Sons of Beccles. They also used what were referred to as the Horn Maltings in Crown Street, Ipswich.

Deep-sea imports of maize, barley, wheat and oats in ships entering the dock and lying in Harwich Harbour or Buttermans Bay in the River Orwell were increasing during the 1860s. By the 1880s the sources of the various grains were already well established, although a few are no longer listed and difficult to identify after a hundred years. The shipping records for Ipswich naturally ignore the ships that anchored in Harwich Harbour with cargoes for Ipswich. For several years many vessels did this to avoid the more expensive dock dues at Ipswich, as the *East Anglian Daily Times* for 31st May 1884 pointed out:

> The Calvilla from Salonica, with 8,000 quarters of maize for Messrs. R. & W. Paul of Ipswich, arrived at Harwich on Thursday afternoon, and will discharge the whole of the cargo at that port. This is the fifth steamer which has discharged at Harwich during the present year for Messrs. Paul, the dock dues on these vessels, had they come to Ipswich, would have amounted to about £300.

The *CALVILLA* was an iron screw steamship 242 ft long, of 913nrt, built at Sunderland in 1879, owned by T.E. Hicks & Co. and registered at Scarborough, where in 1884 there were three shipping companies registered in the names of the Hicks family.

During the 1880s and 1890s, when steamships and new square-riggers were developing rapidly in power and size, Pauls' maize was already arriving regularly from ports as far away as Baltimore, Philadelphia and New York in the USA and Buenos Aires in Argentina. Maize and barley came from several Black Sea ports, oats from the Baltic and locust beans from Portugal and Cyprus.

Pauls' first steamer to work a regular passage service to London was their first *SWIFT*, built in 1886. In her first full year's work in 1887 she made no fewer than ninety-five round trips from Ipswich, a remarkable improvement on the sailing barges used in the hoy trade.

There were many shiploads of oats at that time to supplement the British crop. In 1883 for example two steamers, the ss *BERLIN* of Stettin and the ss *MAURITANIA* out of Liverpool, docked with oats and peas, the *BERLIN* from Riga, the other from Libau (now Liepaja). During the next six years oats also came from Vaasa in Finland and Smyrna in Turkey. However in May 1892 the

Swedish barque *DORIS*, registered at Helsingborg, brought oats from Bluff on the south coast of South Island, New Zealand. Later on most of the oats came from Cyprus.

On 22nd March 1889 the ss *ARNO* came with barley from an unfamiliar-sounding Dede Agatche in Turkey. Throughout the 1890s thousands of tons of maize arrived for Pauls from both Ibrail (later Galatz) on the Danube and Sulina, about 100 miles downstream at its mouth, and also from Poti in Turkey on the far eastern shore of the Black Sea. These cargoes were additional to those coming from the American ports.

Among ten deep-sea arrivals to berth in the dock for Pauls in 1893 were the Belfast barque *BLUEBELL*, arriving in March with barley from San Francisco, and two steamers with maize from Poti. The ss *BILLOW*, Hartlepool-built and registered in 1881, was also among these arrivals, coming with barley from Salonica, the Greek port on the north coast of the Aegean, known today as Thessaloniki. The Sunderland-built ss *BENEFICIENT* came from Sulina, the Swansea-owned barque *SINDBAD* arrived with maize from Buenos Aires and the iron barque *ISOLA*, Glasgow registered and built there in 1876, reached Ipswich from Valparaiso with barley. The full-rigged ship *RODERICK DHU* of Liverpool came from San Francisco with barley on 21st December of that year.

An almost legendary vessel that arrived from Faro in Portugal with locust beans on 29th June 1893 was the schooner *LADY OF AVENEL*, built at Falmouth in 1874. At 99ft in length, she was copper fastened and sheathed for ocean trading. She was re-rigged as a brigantine a few years after her launch and then had an auxiliary motor installed at the end of the First World War. She voyaged to Spitzbergen and to the Arctic before being moored at Falmouth as a schoolship, owned by Captain Dowman, who sold her when he acquired the *CUTTY SARK*. Subsequently she became derelict at Leith but was refitted as a yacht at Looe in 1933. She cruised the British coast for a few years and attended the naval review at Spithead in 1937. Under a new owner in 1939 she was unfortunately abandoned in Poole Harbour.

In October 1899 the ss *INDIAN PRINCE* of Newcastle, complete with clipper bow and bowsprit, delivered barley from Mersina on the Mediterranean coast of Turkey. As demand increased so more ships arrived from United States ports, including those on the West Coast where the trade was in the hands of the square-riggers that made the voyage out and home around Cape Horn. This particular work developed as scores of new French sailing ships entered the fray after 1900. Ships owned by Hain of St. Ives brought grain for Pauls, the ss *TRELYON*, built in 1882 at South Shields by J. Readhead, coming with maize from Sulina in September 1890 and from Poti in 1894. The *TREVILLEY*, launched in 1881 at South Shields, arrived in July the same year with barley from Kiliya, which was situated in the Ukraine on the delta of the Danube. *TREVILLEY* was lost without trace in 1901 bound from Spain to Glasgow with iron ore.

In addition to barges, lighters and steam coasters R. & W. Paul required road vehicles to serve their scattered premises. Until 1894 horse-power was the only means of local haulage apart from the railway, but in that year a traction engine and six wagons were bought from the well-known firm of Charles Burrell of Thetford for £1,148 18s. 6d. On 1st July 1898 five vans, six rulleys (flat four-wheeled carts), two trolleys, a tumbril and van covers were purchased for £283 10s from James Singleton, an Ipswich coachbuilder.

In November 1902 a steam lorry was bought from the makers, Manns Patent Steam Cart & Wagon Co. Ltd of Leeds, for £500 and the following year a similar lorry was purchased for £510. However it was not until 1948 that the company gave up using horses. Pauls went on to operate a large fleet of lorries, which by the 1950s consisted mainly of Leyland vehicles, some four-wheel trailers and some Scammell articulated 'Scarabs' with tank trailers to work bulk loads in the confines of their dockside premises at Ipswich.

Other intriguing entries show that the company had invested in the Eastern Counties Coal Boring & Development Company, which not surprisingly was in liquidation by 1899. A shame it was not in oil, although drillings in north Norfolk sixty years later proved equally abortive. Another unfortunate interest was in the Mid Suffolk Light Railway in 1901, when one hundred pounds worth of shares were bought. These were written off in 1906, although the railway did eventually open between Haughley and Laxfield in September 1908.

The principal arrivals for Pauls in 1908, including the ss QUEEN MARY.

Date	Vessel	nrt	Port of Registry	From	Cargo
19th Jan	ss ANTHONY RADCLIFFE	1,815	Cardiff	Constanza (Romania)	Maize
8th May	ss MILLWALL	1,546	Cardiff	Sulina	Maize
9th June	ss STRAITS OF MENAI	1,849	Glasgow	Rosario	Maize
20th June	ALICE	2,192	St Nazaire	San Francisco	Barley
18th June	ss AGNES		London	San Lorenzo	Maize
17th July	ss QUEEN MARY	2,262	Glasgow	San Nicolas / Buenos Aires	Maize
2nd Sep.	ss WENVOE	1,918	Cardiff	Rosario	Maize
6th Sep.	ELISA	1,408	Castellamara	San Francisco	Barley
9th Oct.	ss GUISEPPE ACCAME	2,212	Genoa	Rosario	Maize
27th Oct.	ss CHARTERHOUSE	1,928	London	Rosario	Maize
22nd Nov.	ss HORSA	1,901	W. Hartlepool	Rodosto (Turkey)	Barley
16th Dec.	ss PEERLESS	2,011	Newcastle	Buenos Aires	Maiz

On 17th July 1908 the ss *QUEEN MARY* of Glasgow arrived in Buttermans Bay from San Nicolas and Buenos Aires. The table shows the vessels involved in distributing her cargo of maize for R. & W. Paul Ltd. She entered the Dock on 22nd July to finish discharging and sailed light to Barry on 30th July.

Early in 1912 three ships, all under 1,000nrt, arrived from Algeria with barley. They were ss *DUVA* of Grangemouth, built 1909 at Campbeltown for J.T. Salveson of Grangemouth, coming from Philippeville; ss *SIVA*, built in 1902 at Grangemouth for the same owners, arriving from Mostoganen; and the

Vessels involved in distributing the QUEEN MARY'S cargo of maize for R. & W. Paul Ltd in July 1908.

Vessel	Port of discharge	Vessel	Port of discharge
sb AZIMA	Whitstable	sb ORWELL	Colchester
sb DORIS	London	sb ORWELL	London
sb EMILY	London	sb PRIDE OF THE ORWELL	Rochester
sb ENA	Newport, Isle of Wight	ss SEAGULL	London
sb FELIX	London	sb STOUR	London
sb GLOBE	Whitstable	ss SWALLOW	Poole
sb IDA	London	ss SWIFT	Southampton
sb MABEL	London	ss TERN	Southampton
sb MARJORIE	London	ss TERN	London
sb MARJORIE	Southampton		

GRAIN & ANIMAL FEED

ss *TAURUS*, built in 1895 and registered at Flensburg, and also coming from Philippeville.

By 1914 Pauls were receiving fourteen shipments of maize and barley a year from Sulina and South America, together with another five part-cargoes of wheat or timber from the Americas. In 1917 numbers were down to five, plus three part-cargoes, reflecting the effect of German submarine activity in the Atlantic and Western Approaches. The barge fleet also continued bringing imported barley and maize from London during the war. Between August and October 1917 about thirty-two cargoes of wheat were brought from London to Pauls in Government-built motor-barges that had been hastily constructed as landing craft for the disastrous 1915 Dardanelles campaign. Some were surplus and designated as H.M. Motorlighters, or X-lighters, for use in the coasting trade under the White Ensign. The list of arrivals at Ipswich includes the following numbers all prefixed 'X': *38*, *64*, *69*, *74*, *86*, *149*, *157* and *198*. After the war most were sold to barge owners, several surviving into the 1950s and beyond; one was hauling stone to the port in the 1990s.

The year 1919 produced a remarkable variety of ships entering the Orwell for R. & W. Paul. Four wartime wooden ships, the *DUNGENESS*, *SALMON*, *KIMTA* and *MANADA*, all built and registered in the USA, brought barley from San Francisco. At least three British standard ships arrived, including the ss *WAR SYREN*, built at the Uraga Dock Co. in Japan, from Port Augusta in

The Spanish three-masted schooner AMISADE SEGUNDO *unloading a cargo of grain in the Dock.*

South Australia with wheat for Pauls, Cranfields, Gibbons and the Ipswich Malting Company. The ss *WAR LEOPARD*, completed in July 1918 at Workman Clark's Belfast yard, docked on 27th November 1919 with rice, bran and oilcake for Pauls from Rangoon and Calcutta. Under her sixth name she was sunk in 1943 by American aircraft, having become Japanese owned in 1939. The auxiliary schooner *PAULINE* of New York arrived in October 1919 from 'Frisco with barley and wood, as did the four-masted schooner *ROLPH* in November 1919. Another American, the full-rigger *JAMES ROLPH* of San Francisco, formerly the British *CELTIC MONARCH*, moored in the Bay on 31st August 1919 with barley for Pauls and timber.

Probably of greatest interest that year, however, was the arrival of the Belgian schoolship *L'AVENIR* from San Francisco with barley for Pauls. The vessel attracted attention because of the composition of her crew and the misfortune that had occurred on the voyage back from 'Frisco, as described in an article in *Sea Breezes* in 1966. With the reduction in the Royal Navy at the end of the First World War sixty midshipmen opted for training in sail and were sent to join *L'AVENIR* at San Francisco, travelling first class to New York by Cunard and then by Pullman train across the USA to the West Coast, where they joined the ship on 1st May 1919. However, when they were asked to sign Belgian articles only thirty-eight agreed to do so, the remainder being sent home aboard HMS *CUMBERLAND* to the accompaniment of headlines in US newspapers declaring 'BRITISH NAVAL OFFICERS MUTINY'.

After nearly a month loading barley and fitting out, the *L'AVENIR* sailed for Falmouth for orders. The ship spent ten days beating round Cape Horn under topsails and fore-topmast staysail, and then the master became ill so the Belgian mate put into Bahia in Brazil, where the master was operated on successfully for appendicitis. They had already been 101 days at sea.

The pumps were manned night and day on the transatlantic voyage, and it was October before they neared the English Channel, where another two weeks of adverse weather delayed their arrival at Falmouth. There *L'AVENIR* received orders for Ipswich. The tug *VICTOR* of Falmouth brought her to the Orwell, to moor in Buttermans Bay on 23rd October. The boys were paid off the next day at £4 per month (1st May-24th October). They left the ship after months of hardship and squalor and put up that night at the Great White Horse Hotel in Ipswich. They must have been the only crew from such a vessel to spend their first night ashore in such opulent surroundings.

After the First World War Pauls still received almost all of their imported grain from North and South America. Then in 1923 the ss *EILBEK* of Hamburg arrived from Ibrail in Romania with maize. In 1924 ships came from Port Elizabeth and East London in South Africa with maize, two arrived with barley from Karachi and one came from Theodosia in the Crimea. In 1925 there was a cargo of maize from Beira in Mozambique, but the majority of shipments for the next decade and more were still from River Plate ports in Argentina such as Rosario, San Nicolas, Villa Constitucion, Necochea, Santa Fe and San Pedro. Relatively few came from the Black Sea.

During the 1920s the production of complete animal feeds for cattle, pigs and poultry was instigated. Maize meal and maize flakes were mixed in the feed mill with other ingredients, including oats, barley and wheat, to form the required diets. Locust beans were added to help in the appearance of the product and to provide a partial replacement for some cereal content. They were sweet and therefore commonly nibbled by mill staff, sales representatives, farmhands and farmers alike.

GRAIN & ANIMAL FEED

From its earliest days the firm dealt in grain imports and malting, but in 1902 they had linked up with Gillman Spencer Ltd of London, producers of maltsters' sundries. The year 1907 saw the introduction of Kositos cooked flaked maize for cattle feed, and in 1914 a former flour mill at Kings Lynn was converted into a feed mill. During 1918 the Hull Malt Company was acquired, as well as warehousing and distribution centres at Colchester, Great Yarmouth and Wisbech. As the demand for manufactured feedstuff and compounds for 'on-farm' production increased rapidly other mills were built at Manchester in 1929, Avonmouth in 1933 and Faversham in Kent.

Date	Ship	Nrt	Reg.	From	Built
20 Feb 1931	ss DALWORTH			Nikolayev	
28 Mar	ss NICOS VALMADIS			Nikolayev	
21 Apr	ss KOBE			Theodosia	
3 Jun	ss SHEAF SPEAR		Newcastle	San Lorenzo	Sunderland 1919
20 Jun	ss OOTMARSUM	2,205	Amsterdam	River Plate	Ysel 1920
17 Aug	ss HARBERTON	2,728	London	Rosario	Sunderland 1930
9 Sep	ss HOPECRAG	2,457	Newcastle	San Nicolas	Sunderland 1929
28 Sep	ss DELFLAND			Rosario	
7 Oct	ss PANTIAS			Nikolayev	
13 Oct	ss CSARDA	2,535	Budapest	Santa Fe	Sunderland 1917
29 Oct	ss PANORMITIS			Kherson	
24 Nov	ss KAYESON	2,873	Newcastle	San Nicolas	Newcastle 1929
30 Dec	ss BARON LOUDON	1,914	Ardrossan	Santa Fe	Port Glasgow 1925

Ships discharged in Buttermans Bay for R. & W. Paul in 1931.

A sample list is shown of vessels engaged in lightening the *SCORESBY* for R. & W. Paul in Buttermans Bay in 1936.

Vessel lightened In Butterman's Bay	Date	Vessel engaged in lightening	Master	Port Of Discharge
ss SCORESBY Reg. Whitby, 2,310 nrt Built Sunderland in 1923. Arrived 16th October 1936 ex-Rosario with maize. Sailed light 29th October 1936 to Cardiff.	16 Oct	sb AIDIE	Potter	Ipswich
	19 Oct	sb GRAVELINES I	Finbow	Ipswich
		ss CROSSBILL	King	Gt Yarmouth
		sb REMINDER	Stone	Mistley
	20 Oct	Lighter P4		
		sb TOLLESBURY	Webb	Ipswich
		sb EDME	Cresswell	Mistley
	21 Oct	sb ALICE MAY	Smith	Colchester
		sb HERON	Butcher	Faversham
		ss FIRECREST	Lucas	Boston
		ss CROSSBILL	King	Gt Yarmouth
		sb AIDIE	Potter	Ipswich
	22 Oct	sb RELIANCE	Greenleaf	Ipswich
	23 Oct	Lighter P4		
		ss OXBIRD	Goodman	Gt Yarmouth
		sb MILLIE	Martin	Mistley
		ss CROSSBILL	King	Gt Yarmouth
		sb MAYSIE	Bryant	Ipswich
		sb MYSTERY (Faversham)	Last	Ipswich
		sb FREDERICK WILLIAM	Smy	Ipswich
	24 Oct	sb FREDERICK WILLIAM	Smy	Ipswich
		sb MISTLEY	Page	Fingringhoe
	27 Oct	ss OXBIRD	Goodman	Gt Yarmouth

Once the Second World War started in 1939 most of the grain ships had part-cargoes shared between the London Port Area Grain Committee (LPAGC), Cranfields and Marriages, but a few whole shipments of maize were designated for Pauls. On 11th March 1940 the *DAYROSE*, 2,605nrt of Cardiff, arrived in the Bay from Santa Fe and on May 31st the Dutch ss *ZAAN*, of only 726nrt, entered the dock from Rosario. During the year coasters brought maize and meal transshipped from the Clyde, Mersey, Humber and Tyne. They included Kennaugh's *STANLEY FORCE* of Whitehaven; *BORNRIFF*, a Groningen-registered Dutchman; the Norwegian *ROYKSUND*, of Haugesund, and the General Steam Navigation Company's *CORMORANT*. The Belgian motor ship *BRABANT*, of Antwerp, brought maize from the Plate and commenced lightening in the Bay on 12th February 1941, finishing in the dock from 15th February to 4th March.

Subsequently there is little mention of direct maize or barley imports. There was naturally a priority for wheat shipments from the US and Canada, although it is possible that some imported maize could have come in by way of the West Coast ports and been brought to Ipswich by rail. Ships from South America would have been in convoy from Rio to Trinidad after Brazil entered the war and provided convoy escorts in the form of two ancient cruisers. The ships then went on to New York or Halifax to join north Atlantic convoys.

Barge traffic had lessened considerably between London and Ipswich during 1942-43, but by the middle of 1943 trade from the London docks had picked up again. Barges from several owners are recorded as loading from new American Liberty ships. The *CLARA* and *THISTLE* loaded wheat in May 1943 for Ipswich from ss *HANNIBAL*, built 1943 by the New England Shipbuilding Corporation in Portland, Maine. In April 1944 *SERB*, *ENA*, *VERONA*, *VARUNA* and *THETIS*

The sailing barge ENA *has her topsail set as she approaches her berth alongside one of Pauls' maltings in the Dock.*

loaded wheat from ss *WASHINGTON IRVING*, launched in June 1942 by the Oregon Shipbuilding Corporation at Portland, Oregon. By the end of the year large quantities of Plate and American maize was being transshipped in London while Scotch oats had come from Dundee and Arbroath. From 1945 Pauls appear not to have imported large amounts of grain directly to Ipswich, though in 1952 there were a couple of ships from Odessa with maize, the Turkish ss *SABAH* and the Greek *JOANNIS FRANGOS* with a part-cargo of wheat for Cranfields and Marriages. On 7th May 1958 the mv *KALISZ* of Stettin, arrived with maize from Rijeka in Yugoslavia. She went on to Rotterdam with general cargo to complete what was likely to have been her maiden voyage, having been completed that year at Stettin for the Polish Government. The Norwegian motor ship *HUMING* of Skiena, brought barley from Montreal on 23rd July. Deep sea arrivals for R. & W. Paul became very sparse as the Dutch mv *HASEWINT* of Groningen, laden with barley from Bayonne in France, docked on 25th September.

Of course Pauls' maltings still required barley and Eagle Mill still needed maize, etc., but most imported grains now came via London, and on to Ipswich by barge. In 1952 there had been no fewer than 230 cargoes brought mainly from London by barge.

During the 1960s sorghum was imported from the USA. A genus of plants that included millet, this was included in the animal feed mix. To make a complete feed, protein had to be added in the form of soya beans, groundnut and cottonseed extracts from which the oil had been removed, and locally-grown field beans were used to a limited degree. By that time the industry had become more competitive and sophisticated, as computers were introduced to produce diets for the least cost. The diets had to conform to detailed specifications. Tallow, or fat, has a high energy content and was therefore useful for formulating the high-energy diets, particularly those required by the poultry industry for broiler production. The company had come a long way from the original Kositos!

R. & W. Paul Ltd continued running their expanding malt and feed businesses on traditional lines and as late as 1958 the directors of the company were all direct descendants of the founder, George Paul. The many complex changes that were made to the company in the next thirty years were heralded in 1963 with the advent of Pauls & Whites, later Pauls plc, overseeing the operations of Pauls Agriculture Ltd and Pauls Malt Ltd. In 1985 Harrison & Crossfield, an international commercial and finance company, purchased the entire equity of Pauls plc. Numerous other companies had joined the group by 1987, including Associated British Maltsters (ABM), which was Pauls' main competitor with five maltings in England and Scotland. ABM was founded in 1928 by the amalgamation of Messrs. Gilstrap Earp of Newark, West Yorkshire maltsters Edward Sutcliffe of Mirfield, Samuel Thompson of Smethwick, W.J. Robson of Leeds and a subsidiary company, John Crisp of Beccles.

During the ten years from 1985 many of the acquisitions were sold. Among those remaining in 1995 were Robert Hutchison & Co. Ltd, a Scottish malting and flour milling firm established at Kirkaldy in 1825, Green Brothers flour mill at Maldon and Edward Baker of Great Cornard, former flour millers and more recently manufacturers of Omega pet foods, since closed down.

Pauls Malt Ltd continued the malting business and in 1983 opened the Ipswich Grain Terminal on Cliff Quay in partnership with the grain-trading firm of International Corn Company. BOCM Silcock, made up of the former British Oil & Cake Mills (established 1899) and R.Silcock & Sons, were a part of Unilever until October 1992 when they were bought from the Unilever Group to trade as BOCM Pauls Ltd, carrying on the animal feed business. On January 1st 1995 Pauls plc ceased trading and no members of the Paul family remained with an active role within the group for the first time in over 150 years.

During 1996, however, Harrison & Crossfield announced restructuring plans involving disposal of its food businesses. After an earlier unsuccessful attempt, by which time H & C had changed their title to Elementis, a management buyout was led by Mr Bill Mayne, managing director of BOCM Pauls, and Mr George Paul, for a time chairman of Harrison & Crossfield. With the help of private and outside finance the buyout was announced on December 1st 1998, together with assurances as to the firm's East Anglian based future. Unfortunately the end was in sight, and by September 2004 Pauls had produced its last load of malt. The maltings and silos were demolished during 2006 at exactly the same time as Cranfield's premises were treated likewise.

Vessels owned by R. & W. Paul Ltd

R. & W. Paul were significant owners of steamships and sailing barges for 130 years. At various periods since 1843 they owned seventeen steam coasters, forty-five barges, seven tugs large and small, and about thirty assorted lighters. Based at Harwich awaiting salvage jobs were some of the larger tugs, of which the *MERRIMAC* was best known, towing the Harwich lifeboat to sea on rescue missions or engaging in summer pleasure trips round the Cork Lightship.

Many of the lighters were old sailing vessels, mainly used as floating warehouses in Ipswich Dock although some of them could be towed round the coast by a tug or one of the company steamers. Four steel lighters were acquired by the company early in the twentieth century and these were named, rather simply, *P1*, *P2*, *P3* and *P4*. The largest of these was the sea-going *P1*, which was fitted with a cabin for the crew of four. She was built at Wivenhoe on the River Colne in 1915 and was often towed across the North Sea, loading at such ports as Antwerp. She was still used in the dock well into the 1950s.

The following table gives some examples of sea-going trips made by the lighter *P1* during the years 1915 to 1926. These trips were in addition to its normal lightering work from Buttermans Bay to the dock.

YEAR	DATE	ARRIVE / DEPART	CARGO	TUG
1915	7 May	Arrive Ipswich, ex-London	maize	*ATHLETE* built 1893, Blackwall
	9 May	To London	light	?
1916	9 Sept	Arrive Ipswich, ex-London	maize	ss *OXBIRD*, Ipswich
1923	12 June	Arrive Ipswich, ex-Keadby	coal (Gas Co.)	*R.W. WHEELDON* of Hull
	20 June	To Hull	light	*R.W. WHEELDON*
1926	July	To London	light	*REVENGER*
	July	To Kings Lynn, ex-Keadby	maize	ss *CONNISCRAG*
	11 August	To Antwerp, ex-Lynn	light	ss *OARSMAN*
	19 August	To Kings Lynn, ex-Antwerp	maize	*WARRIOR*

GRAIN & ANIMAL FEED

In 1936 the *P1* sailed with ss *OXBIRD* to Kings Lynn from Buttermans Bay, in addition to making thirty-eight trips to the Dock from the Bay, while the smaller *P4* loaded about thirty cargoes ex-Bay to Ipswich.

The sailing barge *BIJOU* was originally launched by R. & W. Paul as their first *ENA* in 1906, but later that year she and the *HILDA*, built in 1905, were chartered by Pauls to French owners and renamed *GRAVELINES II* and *GRAVELINES I* respectively. By 1912 both had returned to Pauls but by this time the company had acquired two further vessels named *ENA* and *HILDA*. The *GRAVELINES I* retained her name but *GRAVELINES II* was renamed *BIJOU*, always pronounced By-Joe. She was set on fire by incendiary bombs in an air raid on Mistley and sank near the quay in 1940. The second *ENA*, 73nrt, built at Harwich in 1906 and bought new by Pauls, was to be the company's last vessel. She traded under sail alone until 1948, when an auxiliary engine was fitted, and worked as a motor barge until 1974 when she was restored to sailing condition

Barges owned by R. & W. Paul, 1843-1974.
*Auxiliary engine installed 1940s.
†T.F. Wood of Gravesend owned several powder barges for the storage of explosives from ships in the lower reaches of the Thames until 1957, when PLA regulations were relaxed.

Barges owned by R. & W. Paul	NRT	Built	Dates owned by Pauls	Details
AIDIE	114	Brightlingsea 1925	1925-40	Abandoned at Dunkirk.
ALBATROSS	48	Ipswich 1869	1896-1918	
ALBERT	38	Newbury, Berks 1840	?-1889	
ALICE MAY	70	Harwich 1898	1927-1949	Converted to yacht-barge, houseboat.
ANDROMEDA	40	Ipswich 1867	1877-1907	Lost on Gunfleet Sands.
ANGLIA	54	Ipswich 1896	1940-1961	Converted to yacht-barge.
ANN	39	Greenham, Berks 1843	1843-1910	To store-barge for Kings at Pin Mill.
AUDREY	58	Ipswich 1903	1903-1941	bu 1941 after collision.
BARBARA JEAN	114	Brightlingsea 1925	1925-1940	Abandoned at Dunkirk.
BIJOU	79	Ipswich 1906	1912-1940	Ex-*ENA* (Paul's first), ex-*GRAVELINES II*, burnt 1940 in air raid.
CHAMPION	41	Ipswich 1861	1887-1894	
COLNE	56	Ipswich 1890	1890-1930	To ballast trade, houseboat 1946-1960.
DANNEBROG*	71	Harwich 1901	1967-1974	Ex-W. Groom, Archie Wife & Cranfield Bros.
DEBEN	74	Ipswich 1874	1911-1915	Used as lighter.
DORIS	62	Ipswich 1904	1904-1940	Sunk returning on tow from Dunkirk evacuation.
EMILY	57	Ipswich 1882	1882-1949	To Brown, Heybridge, as lighter. bu Woolverstone 1978.
ENA (Paul's first)	79	Ipswich 1906	1906	See *BIJOU*.
ENA* (Paul's second)	73	Harwich 1906	1906-1998	Converted to company yacht 1974.
GIPPING	33	Ipswich 1842	1868-1870	Lost off Orfordness 1870.
GIPPING	59	Ipswich 1889	1889-1938	To T.F. Wood† yacht-barge 1950s-60s, houseboat Pin Mill, b/u.
GRAVELINES I*	77	Ipswich 1905	1912-1965	Ex-*HILDA* (Paul's first). Engine fitted 1949, sunk Thames 1965, b/u.
HILDA (Paul's first)	77	Ipswich 1905	1905-06	See *GRAVELINES I*.
HILDA (Paul's second)	57	Ipswich 1895	1910-1927	Sunk Thames 1927, houseboat Walton, buried 1960.
IDA	130	Ipswich 1881	1881-1890	Ketch-barge sold to Whitstable owner for coal trade.
IDA	40	Ipswich 1895	1895-1948	To Brown & Son, Heybridge, as timber lighter, broken up 1980s.
INTREPID	57	Ipswich 1879	1903-1903	Sold same year to F. Strange.
JOCK*	86	Ipswich 1908	1908-1973	Last barge built by Pauls, became yacht-barge.
JOHN & THOMAS	42	Boroughbridge 1854	1868-	Converted to lighter 1871.
JULIA WOOD	45	Maidstone 1840	1843-1890	Lighter 1887-1890.
LADY DAPHNE	85	Rochester 1923	1937-1974	Original auxiliary engine fitted 1930.
LADY JEAN	86	Rochester 1923	1937-1973	Renamed *SIR ALAN HERBERT* for E.C.S. Trust.
LORD BEACONSFIELD	58	Sittingbourne 1878	1907-1917	
LORD PALMERSTON	48	Lambeth 1857	1903-1903	Re-sold same year.
MABEL	49	Ipswich 1875	1875-1919	
MARJORIE	56	Ipswich 1902	1902-1960	First barge built by Pauls sold 1960 as yacht-barge.
MISTLEY	64	Harwich 1889	1912-1940	Sold to Brown & Son, Heybridge, as a lighter, hulked.
ORWELL	51	Ipswich 1889	1889-1937	Sold to T F Wood†, sunk Thames 1950, houseboat, b/u. 1965.
PEGASUS	77	Strood 1891	1912-1919	Lost on wreck of HMS *ARETHUSA* off Bawdsey.
PRINCESS ROYAL	38	Newbury, Berks 1841	1863-1892	
SERB	75	East Greenwich 1916	1928-1949	Converted to yacht-barge, sunk English Channel 1951.
SOUTHERN BELLE	80	Ipswich 1885	1909-1930	Collision- damaged hull to Ipswich Sea Scouts.
STOUR	55	Ipswich 1891	1891-1932	Sold to H.A. Cunis, sunk on Buxey sand 1935.
THALATTA*	67	Harwich 1906	1933-1966	To East Coast Sail Trust for educational work.
TOLLESBURY*	70	Sandwich 1901	1912-1965	Sold as yacht-barge, houseboat at Pin Mill, rebuilt 1990s.
WAVENEY	54	Ipswich 1892	1892-1933	Sold as yacht-barge then houseboat. Derelict Emsworth 1964.
WILLIAM	38	Newbury, Berks 1841	1863-1889	Out of register 1894.
WOLSEY	65		1908-1949	Ex-*ROBERT POWELL*, wrecked Newhaven 1907, rebuilt as *WOLSEY*.

The mv DURRINGTON passing under the Orwell Bridge outward bound for Sardinia with a cargo of barley. She was built at Heusden for Stephenson Clarke Ltd. of London in 1981. Of nearly 12,000 tons deadweight and one of the largest vessels to have berthed at Ipswich, the mv DURRINGTON loaded over 10,000 tons of grain from the Grain Terminal for Mediterranean ports in August 1983. In 1986 a total of a million tonnes of grain for export was reached at the Grain Terminal, which is capable of loading ships at the rate of 700 tons per hour. (R..W. Smith)

and fitted out for corporate entertainment. *ENA* served at Dunkirk in 1940 and attended some of the five-yearly commemorative returns to Dunkirk. Sadly 1997 was her final active season working for Pauls, and she was put up for sale in 1998 lying at Smarts Wharf, Ipswich, her home port for ninety-two years.

By 1952 Pauls maintained only two pure sailing barges, *ANGLIA* and *MARJORIE*, and seven others were either auxiliary-engined or fully powered motor barges. They still owned the steam coaster *FIRECREST*, 259nrt, built at Aberdeen in 1929, but she was sold in 1953. During her career with Pauls she traded principally on the east and south coasts between Inverness and Cornwall, but especially went from London to Middlesbrough with scrap, bringing fertilizers back. There was always odd work to Boston and Goole, and once with coal from Seaham Harbour to Cowes. She had a long spell in the late 1940s sailing with general cargo from Tilbury to Ostend or Antwerp, and then from London to Rouen and Ghent with gypsum or pitch. She picked up various cargoes to Hull every few months for boiler cleaning but other repairs were done at Mills & Knights dry dock on the Thames where all Pauls' steamers were sent for work to be done. In six years from 1942-48 she visited Ipswich only five times. *FIRECREST* was scrapped in Holland in 1959.

Ipswich Malting Company Ltd

The Ipswich Malting Company was established about 1896 by Eugene Frederick Wells and Percy Crossman, who bought several small dwellings along New Cut West and Great Whip Street for demolition and in their place built a large maltings in two long parallel ranges divided by a yard. The entrance and office were on New Cut West. Two railway sidings that ran the length of the yard connected with the Great Eastern Railway's Griffin Wharf branch close to the end of Dock Street. The firm became a registered company in 1909.

GRAIN & ANIMAL FEED

Anthracite fuel was delivered at first by sea and then by rail to the maltings until they converted to oil firing after the Second World War. Steam locomotives were not permitted to work beyond Griffin Wharf and railway-owned horses, for many years in the charge of Mr Kemp, hauled the trucks to the maltings and collected wagons loaded with ten tons of malt, one at a time, for despatch. This was normally done by 4 p.m. in order to catch the five o'clock trip from the Griffin to Ipswich Goods Yard. In later years a tractor was used, and in the 1960s diesel shunting locomotives would sometimes work up to Felaw Street where Pauls' Stoke Maltings also used the railway.

The company owned at least three sailing barges for a few years; the *MARY ANN*, 46nrt, built at Ipswich in 1859, *LADY ELLEN* of Woodbridge, 45nrt, Ipswich-built in 1877, and *HECTOR*, a small barge of only 22nrt, built at Harwich in 1884. Barges were used to take malt to the London docks for export and were loaded at the timber staging near to Pauls' Stoke Maltings. Additional barges were also chartered from Pauls, although any barge available brought grain in. This was generally discharged at Flint Wharf at the head of the dock and delivered by horses and carts owned by John Woods, a well-known haulage contractor whose yard was formerly the Ipswich Tramway Company's depot and stables in Quadling Street. Lorries were later hired from a Mr Copping of Britannia Road, whose vehicles were eventually taken over by the company, which began operating its own fleet of four or five lorries serving their big maltings at Newark and delivering malt to breweries around the country.

Direct foreign imports seem to have begun for the Ipswich Malting Company in January 1899 with the arrival of the small sailing ship *HILDUR*, 135nrt, of

The Greek bulk carrier IRENE'S EMERALD *of Piraeus loading grain at the Grain Terminal in September 1991. Of 15,000 dw tons, she was built in 1977. (R.W. Smith)*

Marstal, from Kjertemunde in Denmark with barley. The sailing barge *EDITH AND HILDA* brought wheat from London in September. That was a small beginning; in 1900 fifty-two cargoes of barley and wheat came in thirty-two different barges from London, Harwich and Woodbridge and two schooners brought anthracite from Swansea.

It was also in 1900 that the company began importing grain from America. On 12th April the German full-rigged ship *ARTHUR FITGER*, ex-*BRITISH MERCHANT*, built by Harland & Wolff at Belfast in 1880, arrived from San Francisco. Her master, Captain Denker, arranged an outward chalk cargo for ballast which was brought to Ipswich from the great Thameside chalk pits in some of the new fleet of steel sailing barges owned by E.J. & W. Goldsmith of Grays, Essex. These were *ASPHODEL*, *SPARTAN*, *GRECIAN*, *SCOT*, all of 180 dwt, and their wooden barge *THETIS*. On June 6th 1900 another Bremen-registered full-rigger, the *MARIE HACKFIELD*, moored in the Bay with barley from San Francisco. She departed 11th July for the tow to Bremen in the charge of the big Dutch tug *TITAN* that had arrived that day from the Niew Diep. In November the first four-masted barque to enter the dock, the *EMANUELE ACCAME*, 2,092nrt, of Genoa, arrived from San Francisco with barley after lightening in the Bay.

During 1901 the Ipswich Malting Company received four sailing ships via Cape Horn from the West Coast. The French barque *MOLIERE*, built and registered at Nantes in 1899, came from 'Frisco. A part-cargo with Prentice & Paul was brought by the German full-rigged ship *LIKA* on June 16th ex-Portland, Oregon. The Italian full-rigger *DORA* of Castellamare also came from

Barges lightering grain cargoes from steamships moored in the Dock in the 1930s. In the right foreground is Pauls' lighter P.4.

Portland, and the fourth arrival was the *HARBINGER*, a full-rigged ship built at Greenock in 1876 for the Australian passenger work. She had been a cadet ship in the Melbourne trade since 1890 but was sold to Finnish owners in 1898 and arrived at Ipswich with barley from 'Frisco in the September of 1901. The number and types of ships with whole or part-cargoes for the company over the next twenty-five years is surprising, and some of these arrivals are shown in the accompanying table for the years 1907 and 1915.

Sailing barges continued to work to and from the Malting Company with barley from London and of course lightening ships from Buttermans Bay to Ipswich and elsewhere.

Once the deep-sea arrivals had tailed off, much of the barley arrived by rail, although thirteen barges from London discharged in 1926 and seventeen in 1930; seven barges left for London with malt in 1930 and another five in 1932. Throughout the rest of the 1930s, 1940s and 1950s there were only occasional barges sailing with malt for London until the short-lived era of ABM exports opened in 1968.

In 1957 the company was purchased by H.A. & D. Taylor of Sawbridgeworth, just prior to Associated British Maltsters (ABM), a consortium of previously independent maltsters, buying into the Taylor business. ABM eventually acquired the whole share capital in 1970.

In 1968 ABM Export Company Ltd sought agreement with the then East Suffolk and Norfolk Rivers Board to erect a jetty in the New Cut and to harden the bed of the Cut. A conveyor was established to load bulk malt direct to ships at the rate of twenty-five tons per hour. The German coaster *CLAUS JURGENS*,

Vessels bringing part cargoes for the Ipswich Malting Company in 1907 and 1915.

DATE	SHIP	NRT	RIG	POR	FROM	CARGO	+ PART CARGO FOR:
1907							
3 Feb	ss SHEIKH	2,828		Liverpool	San Francisco	barley	
18 Feb	MARGUERITE MOLINOS	1,774	Bk	Le Havre	San Francisco	barley & wheat	
24 Feb	ELISA	1,408	S	Castellemara		barley & wheat	Pauls
21 Mar	LATIMER	1,649	S	London	San Francisco	barley & wheat	
28 Mar	OCEAN	1,239	Bk	Mariehamn Nor.	San Francisco	barley & wheat	
10 Apr	MARECHAL DE TURENNE	1,939	Bk	Nantes		barley & wheat	
14 Apr	POLTALLOCK	2,139	Bk	London	San Francisco	barley	
14 Apr	GENERAL DE BOISDEFFRE	1,960	Bk	Nantes	San Francisco	barley & wheat	
26 May	MAGDALENE	2,686	Bk	Bremen	San Francisco	barley & wheat	Pauls
11 Jun	CLAN MACFARLANE	1,445	S	Gothenburg	San Francisco	barley	Pauls
14 Jun	SCOTTISH GLENS	1,999	S	Liverpool	San Francisco	barley & wheat	
10 Jul	GENERAL DE NEGRIER	1,946	Bk	Nantes	San Francisco	barley	
13 Jul	HOWARD D TROOP	2,080	Bk	Glasgow	San Francisco	barley & wheat	Pauls
8 Aug	COUNTY OF INVERNESS	1,612	Bk	Glasgow	San Francisco	barley & cascara bark	Pauls
3 Oct	VENDEE	1,776	Bk	Nantes	San Francisco	barley & wood	Crossley
10 Dec	ss ERNESTO ILARDI	1,764	-	Messina	Sfax & Bona	barley	Pauls
1915							
20 Feb	ss CRAIGINA	2,404		Glasgow	San Francisco	barley hops wood	Strauss Crossley
16 Apr	DUQUESNE	1,926	S	Nantes	San Francisco	barley	
12 May	BERENGERE	2,280	S	Dunkerque	San Francisco	barley	
29 Jun	CORTEZ	2,154	S	Tvedestrand Nor.	Portland, Ore	barley & wheat	Cranfield
26 Jul	SONGVAND	2,026	S	Christiansand Nor.	Portland, Ore	barley & wheat	
25 Sep	ss TREVERBYN	2,642		St Ives	Karachi	barley	
28 Sep	MACMAHON	1,952	Bk	Nantes	San Francisco	barley	
8 Oct	TOURAINE	1,778	Bk	Nantes	Portland, Ore	barley & wheat	T. Mortimer
11 Oct	ss VETURIA	3,528		Glasgow	San Francisco	barley	Strauss

the first of that name, was the regular ship to load, and after closure she and her successor of the same name still continued to take malt away from Pauls' Albion Malting in the dock to Becks' brewery at Bremen every two or three weeks, a connection lasting some twenty years.

Malt production actually ceased in 1972 after a serious fire at the maltings and was transferred to new ABM maltings at Bury St. Edmunds. The malt was sent to New Cut West by road and by a new fleet of bulk railway wagons for despatch abroad, using the conveyor to load ships. This provided work for a few more years, but the entire operation was closed in 1979 and all the buildings demolished shortly afterwards.

Other Importers

Apart from R. & W. Paul and Cranfield Brothers, there were other merchants who had already been in business for several years by the 1880s and who are now largely forgotten. They had their own wharves or premises close to the dock and relied on direct imports to Ipswich or transshipments by sailing barge from the London docks.

Among them was Etheridge Curtis, whose small wharf was at the corner of the dock near Coprolite Street and the Pilot Inn. The firm traded in corn, seed, coal, guano, oilcake and salt, and was an agent for Lawes chemical manures. Curtis imported oats straight from the Baltic ports, and barges and schooners arrived from London laden with lentils, maize, barley and peas. On 19th November 1883, for example, the Norwegian ss *NIORD* of Bergen, brought in oats from the Baltic. She was originally the *ROSE MIDDLETON*, built of iron at West Hartlepool in 1874. The wooden barque *STAR* of Liverpool, berthed on 28th November in the same year with guano, although this was probably a part-cargo as it is shown arriving from London. She had been built as the *ESTRELLA* at Bridport in Dorset in 1866.

Edward Fry was another corn and seed merchant on the dockside at the same time, as was Walter Southgate with premises on the quay for corn, coal and seed. Both of these companies imported oats from the Baltic.

Cowell & Co. had been in business at least since the early 1840s, when Abraham Kersey Cowell had premises in Fore Street and lived in Church Street, now Grimwade Street. By the 1870s the company was described as a corn and coal merchant. In July 1883 it suffered a setback to its business with the fall of its granary at the Quay but still continued trading.

Cowell's deep-sea shipments from 1883 to 1896 were all of maize from Baltimore, Philadelphia, Buenos Aires, and the Black Sea, including Braila in Romania. The three cargoes from Buenos Aires were all brought by Italian barques, *FELICE* of Livorno, now Leghorn, *ARTIERE GIOVANNI*, registered at Fiume, now Rijeka in Croatia, and the *ZOOGLI*, of La Spezia. Those from the USA and the Black Sea were carried in British ships, the ss *STAINCLIFFE* of Hartlepool, ss *FREE LANCE* of Middlesbrough, ss *SOLON* of Whitby and the last one in 1896, Stag Line's first *GARDENIA*, built in 1879.

In 1894 Cowells received a total of seventy-one barges; forty-two laden with

GRAIN & ANIMAL FEED

maize, fourteen with lentils and the rest with peas, barley, beans, wheat, linseed, oats and coal. In 1897 there were thirty-two bargeloads of maize, their principal import, from London, twenty-one in 1907 and thirty-nine in 1915. Cowells were sending agricultural goods, including bran, barley, maize and lentils, to Orford and Butley by sea before and during the First World War.

In 1919 the company received two shipments of maize from Rosario and La Plata. The ss *LEVNET*, 2,065nrt, arrived in 1920 from Rosario with 492 tons of

Vessel	Port of Departure	Cargo
sr *JOHN MARTIN*	Swansea	Coal.
sb *IREX*	Yarmouth	Barley
sb *HOCKLEY*	London	Wheat.
sb *ELIZABETH & SOPHIA*	Harwich	Oats
sb *STROOD*	London	Wheat.
ss *EMILY RICKET* reg. Danzig	Pillau	Wheat/Linseed
sb *SPINAWAY C*	London	Wheat.
sb *AMMONITE*	London	Wheat/Peas
sb *CONSUL*	Mistley	Oilcake.
sb *FAIRY*	—	Oats
sb *LADY ELLEN*	London	Barley.
sb *JOHN CLARK*	—	Maize/Wheat
sb *JANE*	London	Oats/Flour
sb *THE SISTERS*	Mistley	Barley
sb *ELIZABETH & SOPHIA*	Harwich	Oats
Sr *SEA VIEW* of Dublin	Llanelly	Coal
sb *MARY ANN*	Mistley	Barley
sb *ELIZABETH & SOPHIA*	Mistley	Barley
sb *CONSUL*	London	Wheat
MATHIAS PICKET of Marstal	Konigsberg	Oilcake
sb *ELIZABETH & SOPHIA*	Mistley	Barley
sb *MAY FLOWER*	London	Oats
sb *DOROTHY*	London	Wheat
sb *THE SISTERS*	London	Wheat
JORGAN LAPON of Thuro	Konigsberg	Oilcake
Sr *JANE KNOX*	Kirkaldy	Pollards
sb *HOCKLEY*	London	Wheat
sb *WILLIAM & LUCY*	Bradwell	Wheat/Barley
sb *THE SISTERS*	London	Barley
sb *NAUTILUS*	London	Barley.
CAROLINE of Svendborg	Libau	Oats/Peas
sb *MAY*	London	Barley
sb *ETHEL MAUD*	London	Wheat
sb *THE SISTERS*	London	Maize
sb *BEAUMONT BELLE*	London	Barley
sb *WILLIAM & LUCY*	London	Barley
sb *THE SISTERS*	London	Barley
sb *FRANK LUCEY*	London	Wheat
sb *SPINAWAY C*	London	Barley
sb *ARTHUR JAMES*	London	Barley
sb *THE EXCHANGE*	London	Oats
sb *EUREKA*	London	Oats
sb *EMMA MIZZEN*	London	Maize
sb *WILLIAM & LUCY*	London	Maize
sb *THE SISTERS*	London	Maize.

Arrivals for the Flint Wharf Company, 1897.

maize and berthed in Buttermans Bay. The company also received 1,272 tons of maize, 117 tons of maize-chop, 129 tons of maize meal and 178 tons of barley in fifteen barges in 1920, but there is no record of Cowells' activities after 1921.

The Flint Wharf Corn Company took its name from the wharf and warehouse that were near to the head of the dock, with access from New Cut East. The wharf and warehouse, together with a railway siding, belonged to the Great Eastern Railway until sold to the Ipswich Dock Commission in 1918. The company probably started trading in the 1890s and was soon handling a tremendous variety of grain and seed. During the first eight months of 1897 there were four shipments from the Baltic; a steamship, the *EMILY RICKET*, of Danzig, came with wheat and linseed from Pillau in Prussia, the *MATHIAS PICKET*, of Marstal, brought oilcake from Konigsberg (now Kalingrad) in East Prussia, the *JORGAN LAPON*, of Thuro, arrived from Konigsberg with oilcake, and the *CAROLINE*, of Svendborg, came from Libau (Liepaja) with oats and peas. During the same period there were thirty-eight sailing barge arrivals including two small craft, the 25nrt *FAIRY* and the 12nrt *ELIZABETH AND SOPHIA*, from Harwich. They brought maize (5 cargoes), wheat (12 cargoes), barley (15 cargoes) and oats (6 cargoes). Two cargoes of Welsh coal from Swansea and Llanelly came aboard the schooners *JOHN MARTIN* and *SEA VIEW*, the latter of Dublin but owned and built in 1861 at Arklow. A few deep-sea ships arrived with maize. In December 1895, for instance, the ss *LADY*

Barge arrivals for the Ipswich Corn Company, 1907.

Barge	Port of Registry	Port Of Departure	Cargo	Barge	Port of Registry	Port Of Departure	Cargo
I. BROUNCKER	Rochester	London	Maize	ORION	Faversham	London	Maize
SEXTUS	Harwich	London	Maize	AMMONITE	Ipswich	London	Maize
HARCOURT	Harwich	London	Maize	CYGNET	Harwich	Harwich	Oats
MARY ANN	Harwich	London	Maize	NILE	London	Mistley	Beans
TIT BITS	Ipswich	London	Gram	JANE	Rochester	London	Maize
GOOD INTENT	London	London	Gram	SEXTUS	Harwich	London	Maize
PRIDE OF THE STOUR	Harwich	London	Maize	VICTORIA	Ipswich	London	Gram
MARDY	Rochester	London	Dari Seed	MARDY	Rochester	London	Lentils
STROOD	Rochester	London	Maize	MADCAP	London	London	Wheat
GLEANER (30 tons)	London	Harwich	Peas	FRATERNITY	London	London	Maize
OCTAVIUS	Ipswich	London	Maize	NAUTILUS	Ipswich	London	Gram
TIT BITS	Ipswich	London	Meal	HECTOR	Harwich	London	Maize
DOVER CASTLE	Maldon	London	Wheat	ETHEL	Harwich	London	Gram
STROOD	Rochester	London	Maize	EUREKA	Harwich	London	Gram
SUNBEAM	Maldon	London	Maize	CYGNET	Harwich	Harwich	Oats
DAISY	London	London	Gram	MALVINA	Rochester	London	Maize
READY	Maldon	London	Oats	CORONATION	Ipswich	London	Maize
DEFENDER	Maldon	London	Maize	TIT BITS	Ipswich	London	Maize
CHARLES HUTSON	Rochester	London	Maize	VICTORIA	Ipswich	London	Maize
GLEANER (30 tons)	London	London	Middlings	MAFEKING	London	London	Maize
KIMBERLEY	Ipswich	London	Gram	UNIQUE	Colchester	London	Maize
DAISY	London	London	Gram	ETHEL	Harwich	London	Gram
LADY ELLEN	Woodbridge	London	Middlings	T M P	Rochester	London	Maize
STROOD	Rochester	London	Maize	MALVINA	London	London	Gram
FOSSIL	Ipswich	London	Maize	TERTIUS	London	London	Maize
FLORENCE	Harwich	London	Maize	IVERNA	Harwich	London	Gram
EASTWOOD	Harwich	London	Gram	steam barge EAGLET	Ipswich	Orford	Peas
ARTHUR AND ELIZA	Rochester	London	Maize	PRIDE OF THE ORWELL	Ipswich	London	Maize
CORONATION	Ipswich	London	Rice Meal	VALDORA	London	London	Maize
I. BROUNCKER	Rochester	London	Middlings	SUNBEAM	Maldon	London	Gram
CYGNET	Harwich	Harwich	Oats	VENTURE	London	London	Gram
MARY ANN	Harwich	London	Meal	SALTCOTE BELLE	Maldon	London	Maize
TIT BITS	Ipswich	London	Maize	TIT BITS	Ipswich	London	Maize
DAISY MAUD	Rochester	London	Oats	RATHBALE	Rochester	London	Meal
ARTHUR AND ELIZA	Rochester	London	Maize	DEBEN	Ipswich	London	Gram
GLEANER (30 tons)	London	London	Middlings	EASTWOOD	Harwich	London	Maize
EMMA SEAGER	Faversham	London	Maize	PHOENIX	Faversham	London	Maize
TIT BITS	Ipswich	London	Maize	CHARLES HUTSON	Rochester	London	Maize

IVEAGH of Dublin arrived with a part-cargo from Sulina in Romania, and during 1897 the ss *BUCKMINSTER* of London arrived from Baltimore and the ss *EVELYN* of West Hartlepool came from New York.

In September 1897 the firm changed its name to the Ipswich Corn Company, and another thirty-three barges delivered similar commodities for the new company before the end of the year. Three vessels came in 1898: Stag Line's *ROBINIA* arrived with maize from New York, the steamer *GLANSTWYTH* of Aberystwyth came from Gaza with barley, and the full-rigger *BORROWDALE*, 1,850dwt, of Liverpool, docked from San Francisco with barley. The *BORROWDALE* was an iron full-rigged ship built at Liverpool in 1868 and the pioneer ship of the Dale Line, operated by J.D. Potter of Liverpool, which made its name running a service to San Francisco. *BORROWDALE* often made the passages outward in about 107 days and homeward in 105. The Dale Line was dispersed in 1889 on the death of J.D. Potter, when *BORROWDALE* was sold with others of the Dale Line to Nicholson & McGill of Liverpool. Later she was sold again, to owners in Mariehamn in the Aland Islands, the home of Gustaf Erikson, who was in the process of acquiring ships for the last great fleet of square-riggers in the world. *BORROWDALE* was torpedoed as she left the Bristol Channel in May 1917, her crew getting ashore in the ship's boat at Milford Haven.

The Ipswich Corn Company had more than seventy barge arrivals in 1907 but only two steam coasters, with one Norwegian sailer discharging oats from the Baltic. The company also sent small parcels of grain to Orford by the weekly service provided by the steam barge *EAGLET*.

In February 1908 three barges arrived at Ipswich with phosphate of lime for Joseph Fison's fertilizer works. The *TOLLESBURY* and *GLADYS* (destined to enter the fleets of Pauls and Cranfields respectively) came from Dunkirk, and the *BRITANNIA* arrived from Ghent. They were joined by sb *JUSTICE* coming light from Orford, and all four loaded beans from the Ipswich Corn Company. *TOLLESBURY* left for Bruges, *GLADYS* for Brussels, *BRITANNIA* for Antwerp and *JUSTICE* for Newport. In May 1908 the small barge *FAIRY*, 25nrt, was engaged in her regular hoy trade to the Butley River and loaded lentils from the Corn Company for Butley among the rest of her mixed cargo. There seem to be no records of the company's imports/exports after that year.

Members of the Thurman family, Charles Edward, Isaac and David, were corn merchants and millers with premises at 20 Key Street in the 1860s. Twenty years later they had a mill at 2 Vernon Street, Stoke, and other premises at 33 and 79-81 Norwich Road. They also opened the Westbourne Steam Mills near the railway bridge at the corner of Cromer Road.

Thurmans received a few sailing barges per year. For example, in 1897 eight arrived from London with rice meal, maize meal, wheat, flour and offal. Only three were recorded in 1907, two with oilcake from Hull and one, the *EMMA MIZZEN*, with wheat from London. She was caught out at the mouth of the Ore in October 1916 and her remains, rarely visible, are buried beneath the stones at Shingle Street.

Vernon Street Mill was still in use in the late 1940s. Grain was crushed on the premises, different grades of flour were produced and the chaff used in rabbit food. The building then became a wholesale grocery warehouse and was afterwards used by an electrical goods supplier until demolition in the 1960s, when flats were built on the site. Westbourne Mills did not remain a mill for long and became an organ factory before being occupied by a succession of wholesale merchants.

Joseph and Edward Fison.

In addition to his direct involvement in the manufacture of artificial fertilizers and insecticides, Joseph Fison had erected a large steam-driven mill, Eastern Union Mills, next to Stoke Bridge. Earlier he had acquired the old tide mill, a timber-framed weatherboarded building standing on the town side of the bridge, and this structure was moved across the road to become part of his Eastern Union Mills complex. The tide mill was moved again in 1877, using hydraulic rams, to a position nearby when Joseph extended his premises. The tide mill survived until the early 1930s when the Eastern Union Mills became a yeast factory for British Fermentation Products Ltd.

Edward Fison meanwhile had interested himself in products made from malt and by 1868 had set up as a maltster, eventually occupying what had been Rainbird's malthouses situated between the river and Dock Street on the opposite bank to the tide mill. In the Napoleonic Wars these premises had been converted to a barracks. Edward Fison's registered office was in Dock Street. He was one of several smaller maltsters who catered for brewers and other food manufacturers' sundries but did not supply malt in vast quantities for brewing beer.

By 1920 two subsidiary companies were based in Dock Street, the Fiona Company (Edward Fison Ltd) making a wide range of liquid and dried malt extracts and malt flours, and the Pelmo Company (Edward Fison Ltd), food manufacturers. Fiona Malt Products prided itself that its malt was made exclusively 'from the famous golden barley of East Anglia, matured and

Joseph Fison's Eastern Union Mills just above Stoke Bridge seen in a photograph taken by William Vick in the 1880s.

GRAIN & ANIMAL FEED

mellowed in our Norfolk and Suffolk maltings and brought to Ipswich to be processed in our flour mills and malt extract factory'. In the 1930s and '40s the Pelmo Company was described as a bread, rusk and then sausage-rusk manufacturer. The Fiona Company disappeared in the late 1940s.

In 1954 only Edward Fison Ltd remained, and by 1958 Harold Sadd's Seeds Ltd had taken over his property, continuing there for another decade. Since then the premises have been an auctioneer's sale yard and builders' merchants, being converted to apartments and offices in the late 1980s.

The business of Edward Fison was acquired by Muntons of Bedford in 1935 but continued to trade independently under its own name. Munton & Fison Ltd, now Muntons plc, have continued as maltsters at Stowmarket.

In the early days Edward Fison had a small but steady incoming trade in barley by sailing barges that berthed in the New Cut alongside the lower end of the maltings. In 1907 there were ten cargoes of barley, all from London, amounting to almost 1,000 tons in all. The barges included *RELIANCE*, built in 1900, and *SARA*, built in 1902, both belonging to Horlock of Mistley. *EDITH MARY*, built in 1880 and owned by J.O. Whitmore of Ipswich, came twice, as did *ORION* of 1892 (later *GOLD BELT*), owned by William Green, the Brantham miller. Others were *JESSE* of Maldon, built 1865, and *WATER LILY* of 1902, both belonging to Clement Parker, the Bradwell-on-Sea farmer, *IMPERIAL*, built 1902 at East Greenwich for V.D. Colchester of Ipswich, and the old timer *SEXTUS*, registered and built at Ipswich by another of the Colchester family in 1849.

In 1914 ten barges arrived with barley. In 1927 only five came; the *D'ARCY*, built in 1894 at Maldon for farmer Richard Seabrook, of Tolleshunt D'Arcy in Essex but owned in the 1920s by Albert & Nelson Horlock, Horlocks' *PORTLIGHT*, and their *REDOUBTABLE*, which paid three visits. Twenty barges arrived in 1936 and ten in 1939, mainly belonging to Sully of London, all with barley, with a few more arriving during the 1940s.

Thomas Prentice & Co.

In 1799 Manning Prentice, the first of three to have that name, moved to Stowmarket from north-east Suffolk and founded a dynasty with complicated interests in fertilizers, malting, corn, coal, slate, timber, and the local gasworks, not to mention explosives. Thomas Prentice & Co., which was involved with malting and the corn, coal cake and artificial manure trade, was ensconced in Ipswich at a riverside wharf some years before construction of the dock. In 1839 it was importing a considerable amount of coal; in the first three days of July it received 126 tons from the *PROBITY* of Ipswich, 97 tons from the *MARGARETT* of Newcastle, 203 tons from the *DAVID* of Ipswich, and 132 tons from the *NANCY* of Mistley. Strangely enough, on 11th July 1853 it was the Stowmarket firm of Prentice & Hewitt that received 492 tons of coal out of the *HUNWICK* of London, the first steamship to discharge at Ipswich. Some or all of that coal would have reached Stowmarket in Gipping barges.

A selection of some deep-sea arrivals for the company between 1885 and 1899 is shown in the accompanying table.

Sailing vessels in the Dock about 1880, before the building of Pauls' Home Warehouse.

DATE	SHIP	RIG	NRT	PORT of REG	FROM	CARGO	YEAR/PLACE BUILT
10 Jan 1885	PO		558	Genoa	Cyprus	barley	
17 Jul 1885	SEATOLLER	barque	588	Liverpool	Port Pirie, Australia	wheat	1866 Liverpool
13 Aug 1887	MOUNTAIN LAUREL	barque	660	Liverpool	Perth, Australia	wheat	1865 Harrington
5 Nov 1888	GLAD TIDINGS	schooner	95	Aberystwyth	Hamburg	salt	1866 Aberystwyth
3 Oct 1891	ss LISBETH		438	Hamburg	Libau	salt	
24 Nov 1893	ss SHARON		857	Whitby	Taganrog	barley	1881 Whitby
9 Dec 1895	ss LADY IVEAGH		1,471	Dublin	Sulina	part-cargo maize	1892 Stockton/Tees
13 Jan 1899	FAMILIEN HAAB		81	Kjertemunde,	Kjertemunde, Denmark	barley	

Vessels other than sailing barges bringing grain and other produce for Thomas Prentice in 1894.

Thomas Prentice received a considerable number of cargoes annually from sailing barges. In 1894 there were more than a hundred arrivals, although some of these came with part-cargoes of wheat and maize, or beans and barley, etc., making the number of separate cargoes different from the total number of barges. That year the majority of arrivals came with wheat and maize, a smaller number brought peas and barley and there were a few cargoes of linseed, oats, oilcake, lentils, beans and coal. At that period, each barge probably averaged

DATE	SHIP	RIG	NRT	PORT of REG	FROM	CARGO	YEAR & PLACE BUILT
1894							
-- Jan	ss NORD		354	Bergen	Libau	oats	
1 Mar	ss CRAIGLANDS		859	Hartlepool	Kustendje	barley	
19 May	CITY OF AGRA	barque	987	Porsgrund	Melbourne	bran, oats, peas, wheat	1860 W Hartlepool
17 Jun	ss GEORGE DITTMAN		303	Hamburg	Libau	oats	
21 Jun	HERO	keel	69	Goole	Hull	peas	Goole 1876
22 Jun	REAPER	schooner	109	Truro	Amsterdam	moss litter	
30 Jun	JEHOVAH JIREH	ketch	60	Goole	Hull	peas	Grimsby 1886
30 Jun	ss LIZZIE CORY		768	Hartlepool	Galatz	barley & maize	
26 Jul	ss SAMLAND		350	Konigsberg	Libau	oats	
31 Oct	ESTRUP		128	Thuro	Kallundborg	barley	
3 Nov	AGENT LAGONI		109	Faaborg	Kallundborg	barley	
6 Nov	ss FRIGGA		109	Gothenburg	Ranea	barley	
9 Nov	ss DANA		308	Bergen	Bandholm	barley	
13 Nov	ss YRSA		218	Gothenburg	Nakskov Dk	barley	
21 Nov	ss YRSA		218	Gothenburg	Nakskov	barley	
23 Nov	ROSKILDE		80	Roskilde	Parajto	barley	
10 Dec	DINORWIC	schooner	98	Caernarvon	Saundersfoot	anthracite	Port Dinorwic 1862
13 Dec	JOHANNES		148	Rudkjoping	Rudkjoping	barley	

about 90 tons per trip. In 1914 only twenty barges arrived, showing how the trade had diminished.

In 1930 Thomas Prentice dispatched three shiploads of malt direct to Dublin. One was delivered in March by Horlock's coaster *MISTLEY*, followed by their *PHAEACIAN* in April and again in July. Both vessels were Harwich-registered steamships of about 200nrt, built at F.W. Horlock's yard in Mistley, *PHAECIAN* in 1920 and *MISTLEY* in 1922. Within a short while, however, Thomas Prentice's name was to disappear from Ipswich

Meux's Brewery Co. Ltd

Meux was a well-known London brewer established at the Horse Shoe Brewery, Nine Elms Lane, London SW8. In 1924 the company occupied the maltings on Neptune Quay that until 1922 had been used by Thomas Mortimer.

The seaborne trade was simple enough; barley in and malt out, mainly in F.W. Horlock's barges. In the twelve months beginning April 1925, 1,598 tons of barley arrived in ten barges and four small steam or motor ships, while fifteen bargeloads of malt, totalling 1,319 tons, departed, nine of them in Horlock's barge *MARJORIE*, Harwich-built and registered in 1899. Tonnages quoted, of course, relate only to the seaborne trade, and some barley or malt may have been moved by rail. Later on some 350 tons of coal a year was also delivered in 50 to 100 ton parcels by Horlock's steamer *PHAEACIAN*. Horlock's barge *MARJORIE* was chartered by Meux for a few years until 1934, when the brewery acquired the sb *PIMLICO*, built at Borstal in 1914. From April 1935 to March 1936 *PIMLICO* loaded nineteen of the twenty cargoes of malt, totalling 1,610 tons, for London. The vessel was used by Meux until the mid-1940s.

During the Second World War *PIMLICO* brought empty malt sacks to Ipswich with a couple of tons of the company's beer, wheat for Cranfields or barley for Pauls, and she took away the usual malt. Beer production was considered an important part of the war effort and carried on more or less normally. From April 1939 to March 1940 *PIMLICO* loaded malt fourteen times and Pauls' *GRAVELINES I* loaded once. The year 1944-45 saw *PIMLICO* bringing beer and loading malt nine times, and in January 1945 *PIMLICO* made her last voyage to Ipswich for Meux. A variety of barges took away twelve malt cargoes in 1945; the last to load were *JOCK* and *NORTHDOWN* in March and April 1946.

When the Danish brewers Carlsberg began to sell lager in Britain in the 1950s five small ships arrived at Ipswich from Copenhagen between May and August 1957 for Carlsberg and returned with empty cases, barrels and bottles. The trade continued in a small way into the 1960s.

Eastern Counties Farmers Co-Operative Association Ltd

The 'Farmers Co-op', as it was often called, was founded by a group of farmers in 1904. The organisation offered advantageous terms to members and customers for seed, corn, malting barley, animal feedstuffs, farm machinery, and, in later years, oil fuels and services including grass and grain drying. The registered office was at 86 Princes Street Ipswich, with a seed cleaning plant and warehouse in Hadleigh Road and a feed mill in Commercial Road. Branches were established throughout the Eastern Counties as the Association prospered for the next eighty years.

A new provender mill was opened on 20th September 1956 between Fore Street and the junction of Coprolite Street and the dockside. A bulk delivery service was available from the new mill as business continued to expand. The ECFCA meanwhile had changed its title to Eastern Counties Farmers Ltd (it later became a public limited company) and went on to achieve an annual turnover of £100 million and employed about 1,000 people. However, a decision was taken to end the manufacture of livestock feed after losses were recorded in the mid-1980s. The mill closed in 1990 and was demolished in 1994, the same year that Eastern Counties Farmers was put into receivership, a decision that shocked the farming community.

Although raw materials were brought in by ship and barge, especially to the new mill, there was not the seaborne trade through the Dock for Eastern Counties Farmers compared with the other cattle feed and seed suppliers. There were very few direct deep-sea shipments but there were some from the near Continent, and grain and seed from further afield was transshipped at London and brought by barge or coaster. A substantial amount of stock arrived or was

The cross in the topsail marks the sailing barge MARJORIE *as one of R. & W. Pauls' fleet.*
(A.J. Hubert)

dispatched in railway trucks and horse carts into and from the Public and other warehouses. In 1907, for instance, Wrinch's small barge *CYGNET* brought oats from a Stourside farm, the *NILE* of Rochester brought two cargoes of grain from London and the *IVERNA* brought one cargo. The Harwich-registered *MARJORIE* delivered oilcake from London and the Yorkshire billyboy *JOHN AND LILLIE* of Hull came with oilcake from that port, as did *BRILLIANT*, another billyboy registered at Goole and built at Leeds in 1841. She was still working at the age of eighty, a tribute to her builders. Taking 1914 as another sample year, there were sixteen barges recorded for Eastern Counties Farmers with similar cargoes and the ss *LEWIS* of London arrived from Rouen on February 16th with phosphate.

Storage and seed dressing machines were looked after by Ipswich Dock Commission employees, and rent and labour all charged to Eastern Counties Farmers. Other work included the weighing of seed, manures and grain for delivery, repair of sacks and the 'shooting' of grain from farmers' or Great Eastern Railway bags into Eastern Counties Farmers bags and vice-versa, plus the mixing of cattle and horse corn-feeds and the 'picking over' of seed potatoes. If we study entries for April 1920, apart from the above jobs, delivery and shipment charges arise for loading trucks and carts to and from the warehouse with some 200 tons of miscellaneous agricultural goods including:

basic slag, black oats, bone meal, castor meal, Clarendo Meal, clover, cottonseed meal, crushed oats, dried grains, dun peas, gluten meal, grass seeds, Kaffir corn, kainite salt, lupin beans, maize flour, maize germ, middlings, molassine meal, nitrate of soda, palm kernel meal, pig-meal, pollards, Poonac meal, rice meal, Sanfoin seed, seed linseed, seed tares, Singapore Poonac cake, sulphate of ammonia, Timothy seed, trefoil cosh and wheat.

Barley is listed under some farmers' names and came from railway stations at Salhouse, Lakenheath, Trowse and Leiston. Potatoes came with long forgotten names including Great Scot, King George, Ally, Up-to-Date, King Edward and Arran Chief. White seed oats arrived from Norfolk stations at Martham, Paston & Knapton, Melton Constable, Trimingham, North Walsham and Kimberley Park.

For the year 1920 there were close to 2,800 ledger entries, spread over seventy pages of the Dock accounts, for Eastern Counties Farmers, the most prolific of all the port's customers. This was chiefly due to the warehousing and handling of co-operative's commodities. In 1921 however the 'Farmers Co-op' built a new, five-storey seed cleaning establishment and warehouse, situated off Hadleigh Road at the junction with London Road, at a cost of £50,000. Ending within the premises was a railway siding that was one of a group of sidings serving nearby factories. For the rest of the 1920s Eastern Counties Farmers' activities were gradually transferred to the new warehouse, leaving only the fertilizers to be handled at the Dock.

Eventually there was only the occasional coaster, such as the small wooden motorship *HEATHERPET*, 93nrt, built in 1921 for Vickers Petter Ltd of Ipswich, which arrived in 1922 with superphosphate from Antwerp, and the little steam coaster *ST AIDAN*, 138nrt, Clyde built and owned, bringing 5,687 sacks of Scottish seed potatoes weighing over 284 tons in February 1934.

The opening of the new dockside mill in 1956, however, required regular shipments of meal, maize, oats, seeds, oilcake and soya. There were forty-two cargoes in 1957, most of them in the holds of fully powered ex-sailing barges, of which mb *WYVENHOE* brought ten cargoes and her sister ship *ATRATO* six. *WYVENHOE* had been built at Wivenhoe in 1898 and her sister in 1896. Other ex-sailers were *SCONE, MARIE MAY, ORINOCO, RESOURCEFUL* and *ADIEU*, plus five steel 200dwt motor barges built to replace the dwindling sailing barge fleet in the 1950s, including *NAUGHTON, SILVER, PEPITA, NICOLA DAWN* and *JOSH FRANCIS*. Marriages' steel barge *THE MILLER*, built at Liederdorp, Holland, in 1913, brought a couple of cargoes, one of groundnuts and one of malt. Six Dutch motor coasters, *ADARA, HILDA, HINK, OLIVE, DINKEL* and *ORANJE* brought the rest. Two years later, 196 vessels discharged at Eastern Counties Farmers in 1959. By 1970 overall numbers had dropped to 118, the ex-sailing barges having been largely sold out of trade, although *TRILBY* and *CELTIC* arrived from time to time during the 1970s. Ironically it was Eastern Counties Farmers who received the last cargo carried by a British merchant sailing ship when the sailing barge *CAMBRIA*, master Capt. A.W. (Bob) Roberts, berthed with ground-nut extract from a ship in Tilbury Docks. She locked out on 21st October 1970 and moored off Gravesend on the 23rd; the end of commercial sail.

Eastern Counties Farmers had formed their own shipping agency known as the A.B. Shipping Agency in 1961. The first vessel to be chartered was the mv *LUCTOR*, with 250 tons cargo capacity and a crew of five. By forming their own agency and chartering it was hoped to pass on to farmers in the region the saving on costs.

In 1991, just three years before being placed in receivership, Eastern Counties Farmers and another agricultural merchant unloaded 10,244 tonnes of bulk granular urea shipped from Nigeria in the mv *HAFNIA*. Commercially prepared urea, with its high nitrogen content, is used for fertilizers. At the time this was the largest cargo of urea ever dealt with at the Port of Ipswich, the discharge and distribution being undertaken by Eastern Counties Farmers' subsidiary A.B. (Handling) Ltd, operating out of No. 8 Shed.

The edible oil and seed trade

Cottonseed, together with linseed, once formed a considerable proportion of the total imports at many of the major ports of Britain. Cottonseed principally came from Egypt whilst linseed was obtained from flax grown either in India, where loading was at Bombay or Calcutta, or in the River Plate area of South America, the seasons being different between the two regions. Some linseed was also obtained from Russia via the Black Sea ports. Oil milling became big business in the second half of the nineteenth century at ports like Ipswich, where deep-sea ships could discharge, and Colchester, to where seed was brought from the London docks by barge, as was the case at Ipswich in later years. The oil was sent away by barge in wooden casks of 14cwt or 18cwt directly to the oil millers' customers in London, leaving the residue to be compressed into cattle-cake and supplied to feed merchants. Both types of seed were used for the production of cattle-cake, although linseed was the most popular. The oil was used in the production of paint, varnish and high-class linoleum. The varnish was especially popular with the paintshops of London Transport for the finish on trams and buses. Cottonseed oil was a major ingredient of margarine produced by Van den Bergh & Jurgens.

GRAIN & ANIMAL FEED

Owen Parry of Colchester owned a fleet of barges to serve his oil mills at Colchester Hythe and brought a dozen or so cargoes of oilcake a year to Ipswich. He had an oilcake store along St. Peter's Dock just to the east of Foundry Lane from c.1880, and when Cranfields required the site for their new mill in 1883 Parry leased a warehouse on New Cut East until 1920. The barge *UNITY*, 35nrt of Maldon, was regularly used and in 1894 brought nine of the ten oilcake cargoes for Parry.

Cubitt & Chatterton were oilcake merchants or factors, as well as handling other feedstuff, with an office in the residential Dalton Road, Ipswich, and an address at London Road, Kings Lynn. They were in business at Ipswich from approximately 1890 to 1906. Cubitt and Sons (any direct connection unconfirmed but possible) emerged shortly afterwards and rented warehouse space at Flint Wharf, New Cut East, later opening an office in Prudential Buildings, Princes Street. They vacated Flint Wharf about 1922 but maintained the office until at least 1975, trading in oilcake.

Much of Cubitt & Chattertons' business emanated from the Baltic and Germany. In 1894, a typical year, there were fourteen arrivals spread throughout the year, all with oilcake. Two only were from London, Pauls' ss S*EAGULL* and sb *LIVONIA* of Harwich; the little billyboy sloop *EDWARD*, 35nrt of Boston, came from Hull. One ship arrived from Konigsberg, one from St. Petersburg, two from Riga and no fewer than seven from Harburg, just below Hamburg on the Elbe, between them bringing close to 3,000 tons of oilcake. Only three were steamships, and three of the vessels from Harburg were Caernarvon-registered and were probably Portmadoc schooners that, having taken Welsh slates to the Continent, had managed to get return cargoes to England.

Vessels continued to arrive until about 1920. The small steamship *KELBOURNE*, 79nrt and owned, registered and built in 1910 at Leith, came from that port in June 1912 with pollards (fine bran sifted from flour). Occasional ships came from overseas, such as ss *WHINFIELD* of Newcastle, which brought a part-cargo with Cowells of maize from Rosario in 1919, as did the ss *LOISE HORN* of London that came from La Plata in the same year.

The German coaster KLAUS JURGENS *loading malt in the New Cut.*

George Mason Ltd

Oil milling was already a small industry in Ipswich before George Mason started his business, for Samuel Webber was crushing oil seed at Handford Mill in the 1840s. George Mason built an oil mill in St. Peter's parish in the 1860s and bought Handford Mill from Webber in 1873, but closed it down a few years later. When his oil mill at St. Peter's Dock burned down in December 1883 it was reported that the smell from the fire pervaded the town for many days afterwards. After the blaze Mason had a new redbrick mill erected with the gable ends facing north/south rather than the east/west facing ends of the original building. Many years later this structure met a similar fate to the one it replaced, the premises being engulfed in flames late on 13th April 2000, leaving only the shell and some of the cast-iron pillars remaining. The view from Stoke Bridge of St. Peter's Dock and the barges waiting to discharge or load was familiar for over fifty years and the subject of many picture postcards.

George Mason was very much the Victorian businessman. Born in 1812, the son of George Mason (1782-1865), builder and surveyor and one of the early dock commissioners, he was educated by his uncle, the Rev. Thomas Mason. His older brother William became an architect and was responsible for the design of the Union Workhouse in Great Whip Street, Ipswich, later emigrating to New Zealand where he designed Government House in Auckland. George started out as a young man with a timber and slate company in Greyfriars Road before establishing his oil milling business, and he later developed an important cement factory on the bank of the River Deben at Waldringfield that was later transferred to Claydon. He had some of his close relations in partnership with him, including his son George Calver Mason and Herbert Mason on the oil milling side and Frank Mason in the timber business.

The name of Mason was also associated with paper milling, and occasional shipments were received of china clay for use as a filler to give added weight and body to the finished paper. The clay came from Cornwall, where the industry began towards the end of the nineteenth century in the St. Austell area, previously a source of copper for which the harbour at Par had been built in the 1820s. Many of the claypits were owned by paper-making companies, but china clay had other uses including medicinal kaolin. During the period that vessels were loading for Ipswich, the clay was brought down to Par from the pits in heavy wagons drawn by two or four horses with a certain amount of hazardous racing for turn to unload. The port was modernised and expanded by English China Clays Ltd in the 1960s and is still exporting clay and granite.

Among the vessels to load clay for Mason, in what was very much a west countrymen's trade, were the ketch *HELEN AND ERNEST*, built at Cowes in 1876, which arrived at Ipswich in August 1892 and the schooner *SILVER SPRAY*, built in the same year at Dartmouth and owned at Salcombe, which arrived in the November. On 3rd March 1893 the cutter-rigged *LITTLE FRED* of Fowey, launched at Charlestown, Cornwall, in 1870, arrived at Ipswich and the *W.R.T.* of Truro, built in Penryn Creek near Falmouth, berthed in May 1902. The ketch *IRENE*, built and registered at Falmouth in 1884, arrived from Dartmouth on 10th October 1895 with the pigment umber for the Mason Paper Company.

GRAIN & ANIMAL FEED

George Mason was elected Alderman and became Mayor of Ipswich in 1875. The family were great benefactors of St Peter's Church near the Dock. The carved wooden pulpit, still to be seen in the now redundant church, was a gift from George Mason, having been designed by George Gilbert Scott, junior, (1839-97), the architect involved in the church's restoration during the 1870s and 1880s. This same architect designed a large residence in Belstead Road known as Lonsdale House for George Calver Mason. This was badly damaged by a bomb in the Second World War and was replaced by flats in the 1950s.

George Mason lived for several years at Broadwater, Belstead Road, in Ipswich. When he died in 1893 his funeral was held at St. Peter's Church and he was buried in Belstead churchyard. The smaller east window in St. Peter's was dedicated to his memory; a plaque underneath states that he had worshipped in the church for upwards of fifty years.

His oilcake business became a branch of the British Oil & Cake Mills in 1912, later catering for the increase in the poultry population during the 1930s by developing the production of poultry foods in the form of meals or pellets.

Examples of seed shipments for George Mason in the years 1883-1888 and 1898-1902.

Date	Vessel	NRT	Built	Port of Registry	Port of Departure	Cargo
1883						
13 Jan	SPON ACTON	733		Bristol	Alexandria	cotton seed
3 Apr	ss TAGUS	805		Newcastle	Alexandria	cotton seed
1885						
14 Feb	CALLIOPE NICOPULO (SSr)	996	1880 Sunderland	Syra	Alexandria	cotton seed
6 Mar	HIGHGATE (SBn)	927	1882 Whitby	London	Alexandria	cotton seed
1886						
15 Jan	CERIGO (SSr)	1,000	Liverpool 1881	Liverpool	Alexandria	cotton seed
10 Nov	ss RICHARD KELSALE	1,117		Shields	Alexandria	cotton seed
1887						
6 Jan	ss VOLMER	965		Danish	Alexandria	cotton seed
15 Apr	CHESAPEAKE (SSr)	933	Dundee 1872	London	Alexandria	cotton seed
16 Jun	ss ESME	1,061	Stockton 1882	London	Alexandria	cotton seed
28 Jul	LORD ESLINGTON (SSr)	1,116	Newcastle 1876	Newcastle	Alexandria	cotton seed
4 Dec	ss PARAGUAY	873		Middlesbrough	Alexandria	cotton seed
1888						
3 May	ss NORMAN MONARCH	970	Middlesbrough 1875	Middlesbrough	Alexandria	cotton seed
1898						
4 Feb	ss SIGYN	1,298		Stockholm	Alexandria	cotton seed
2 May	ss SN MADVIC	1,103		Copenhagen	Alexandria	cotton seed
28 Aug	MENZALEH (SSr)	1,052	Stockton 1870	London	Alexandria	cotton seed
3 Nov	ss SERAPIS	1,271	Middlesbrough 1877	Newcastle	Alexandria	cotton seed
1899						
2 Jun	ss MALABAR	1,203	Middlesbrough 1877	Newcastle	Alexandria	cotton seed
1900						
19 Mar	ss DINGWALL	1,365		Cardiff	Alexandria	cotton seed
6 Dec	ss NIORD	1,399		Bergen	Alexandria	cotton seed
1901						
11 Feb	ss ORLANDO	1,071		Sundsvall	Alexandria	cotton seed
6 Apr	ss SIGURD	1,342		Copenhagen	Alexandria	cotton seed
17 Oct	ss CELERITY	109	Middlesbrough 1878	Yarmouth	Hull	cotton seed
23 Nov	ss RUBENS	1,291		London	Alexandria	cotton seed
1902						
21 Mar	ss RAGNAR	1,339		Copenhagen	Alexandria	cotton seed

Name of vessel	nrt	Date built	Place built	Owner	Port of registry	Arrivals with seed	To London with edible oil
ALAN	61	1900	Battersea	LRTC		8	
ALDERMAN	73	1905	London	J. Groom	Harwich	11	3
ALINE	49	1863	Ipswich	J. Groom	Harwich	8	2
ARROW	54	1897	Rochester	LRTC		5	1
BRITISH LION	43	1879	Rochester	H. Surridge	Poplar	5	2
COLONIA	62	1897	Sandwich	Cranfield			1
CORONATION	58	1903	Ipswich	LRTC		5	
CORSAIR	72	1899	Deptford	E. Goldsmith	Grays	1	
CROUCH BELLE	65	1901	Hullbridge	LRTC		2	
DAWN	45	1896	Rochester	A.J. Knight	Rochester		1
EAST ANGLIA	46	1908	Rochester	LRTC		3	
FEDERATION	44	1901	Rochester	A.J. Curling	Strood	4	1
FIVE BROTHERS	46	1901	Rochester	LRTC		1	
FOXHOUND	56	1895	Conyer	Ramsgate Shipping Co.		5	
GEISHA	70	1898	Deptford	E.J. Goldsmith	Grays	1	
GENERAL JACKSON	49	1896	Ipswich	E. Watkins	Ipswich	1	
GLEANER	49	1885	Sittingbourne	G. Pudney	Maldon	7	2
GODWIT	50	1882	Milton	LRTC		1	
GRETA	46	1892	Brightlingsea	E. Hibbs	Brightlingsea	8	5
HERBERT	49	1890	Conyer	LRTC		5	2
JOHN EVELYN	57	1885	Deptford	W. Bowman	Southend	3	2
KIMBERLEY	65	1900	Harwich	J.O. Fison	Stutton		1
KNOWLES	63	1910	Frindsbury	LRTC		4	
LOUISE	46	1890	Poplar	LRTC		3	3
MAYSIE	54	1898	Limehouse	LRTC		1	
NEW TRADER	54	1865	Ramsgate	J. Groom	Harwich	1	
NIAGARA	79	1898	Wivenhoe	Tilbury Dredging Co		7	1
ONWARD	46	1872	Frindsbury	Eastwood & Co			2
PROMPT	42	1876	Rochester	H. Waller	Greenhithe		1
PUDGE	68	1922	Rochester	LRTC		5	
QUARRY	54	1886	Frindsbury	A. Hooker	Ipswich	11	3
RAVEN	46	1904	Rochester	LRTC		5	4
SAXON	80	1898	Southampton	E.J. Goldsmith	Grays	1	
SCONE	65	1919	Rochester	LRTC		4	
SEA SPRAY	48	1893	Rochester	Ellis	Stanford-le Hope	1	
SENTA	69	1899	Southampton	E. Goldsmith	Grays	1	1
SHIELD	50	1894	Rochester	LRTC		5	
SIR RICHARD	53	1900	Gravesend	LRTC		4	1
SQUAWK	46	1914	Strood	LRTC		3	2
SUNRISE	45	1889	Rochester	LRTC		2	1
THAMES							5
THE THREE DAUGHTERS		1864	Rochester	LRTC		1	
VIVID	48	1882	Blackwall	LRTC		7	2
WARDEN COURT	46	1870	Sittingbourne	LRTC		1	
WESTALL	46	1913	Strood	LRTC		5	3
WHIMBREL	46	1882	Milton	LRTC		3	1
WILLIAM CLEVERLEY	46	1899	Borstal	LRTC		4	1
WINIFRED	66	1893	Sandwich	LRTC		6	1
Unidentified vessels						none	4
Total visits						169	59
No. of different vessels						42	32

Barges bringing seed and taking away edible oil for George Mason during 1925.

British Oil & Cake Mills Limited

BOCM, as the company was usually called, was established in the late 1890s and soon acquired some small oil milling firms in Kent and elsewhere, including Ipswich, where Mason's oil mill at St. Peter's Dock was taken over. In 1900 BOCM established the London & Rochester Barge Company Ltd by purchasing two, very old, barge and lighterage companies for carrying oilseed to their mills. The L. & R. Barge Company's name was changed in the 1920s to the London & Rochester Trading Company Ltd with a large fleet of barges flying their houseflag, or bob, with a crescent moon device; it was this that gave the company the name of Crescent Shipping Ltd in 1982.

BOCM continued to trade in animal feed, in 1998 joining with the feed business of Pauls to become BOCM Pauls Ltd with its office at the former premises of R. & W. Paul in Key Street, Ipswich.

On 9th March 1922 the two lighters *OBAN* and *BEDE*, both London registered, arrived in Ipswich from London with the tug *SIMLA* to load BOCM oil for the capital, sailing on 12th March with the tug *RUMANIA*. Two months later, on 8th May, the lighters *OBAN* and *LENA* arrived with the tug *BREEZY*, departing for London on 10th May. These two lighters came to Ipswich again on 23rd July the same year.

A year later, on 22nd May 1923, the two lighters *ETHEL* and *INDUSTRY* came to Ipswich (both ex-London) to load BOCM oil for London, with the tug *FAVOROLE*. Similarly, on 31st May, the lighters *NEO* and *DEE* took oil to London with the tug *BREEZY*.

During the twelve months 1925-26 linseed made up almost half (49%) of more than 16,000 tons of material brought by river to Mason's oil mill at St.

Year	Name of vessel	No. of sailings
1925	*CO-OPERATOR*	5
1938	*BROILER*	29
April 1940 – March 1941	*BROILER*	35
1946	*PROWESS*	9

Motor vessel departures for London for sample years.

Peter's Dock, closely followed by cotton seed (45%), a small amount of groundnuts (3%), oilcake (2%) and soya beans (1%).

In 1939 arrivals with seed totalled 124 barges, comprising 51 vessels with cottonseed and 73 with linseed, totalling over 16,000 tons. Another fifty-four barges came with oilcake. The mv *BROILER* loaded more than thirty cargoes of oil, each of 100-110 tons. A similar number of barges arrived with seed and cake in 1940. During that year, however, linseed and cottonseed imports came under the control of the National Association of United Kingdom Oil & Oilseed Brokers Ltd, leaving the British Oil & Cake Mills Ltd to handle the oilcake business. The year did, however, see imports of linseed and groundnuts. Some linseed arrived in sb *IMPERIAL* on 18th May, and aboard sb *ROSME* and sb *ALAN* on 24th May, the groundnuts coming to Ipswich with sb *KING* on 5th May.

By then, however, the war at sea was beginning to have an effect on shipping to London, from where the seed had been transshipped to barges for Ipswich. In

June 1941 Winston Churchill told the House of Commons that shipping entering London had been reduced to a quarter of normal and traffic to East Coast ports was 'enormously shrunken'. The years 1941-1943 were lean ones for the Port of London and some fifty-six sea pilots were transferred to the Clyde.

During that time, therefore, many deep-sea ships were discharged at West Coast ports, and their cargoes were brought by coasters to Ipswich. On 22nd September 1941, Coast Lines' ss *LANCASHIRE COAST*, built at Middlesbrough in 1920, arrived with linseed from Liverpool, as did the Polish steamer *LWOW* of Gdynia on 4th.October. Two more coasters, the mv *EMPIRE CLIFF* and the mv *ROSE MARIE*, berthed with linseed in November and December respectively from the Clyde Anchorages Emergency Port, which had been planned early in the war.

The mv *BROILER* sailed for the last time on 19th December 1941 carrying 102 tons of oil. The *PROWESS*, successor to the *BROILER*, first appeared on 12th January 1942 and carried 210 tons of oil. The *PROWESS* was completed for F.T. Everard & Son Ltd in 1926 at Greenock. After a long career as a tanker, she was sold for breaking up in 1961.

In 1942 thirty-one barges berthed at St. Peter's Dock between 28th February and 17th May with 4,000 tons of cottonseed, and seventeen barges came between 1st January and 17th May carrying 2,265 tons of linseed. Seven coasters brought linseed from 11th May to 21st December: these were the ss *BUSIRIS*, built in 1929 at Troon, and the ss *FLUOR*, also Troon-built in 1925 and both Glasgow registered; the ss *VESTANVIK*, Swedish registered but built at Newcastle in 1906, and the ss *BIRGITTA* and the ss *LIDA*, both Swedish registered (Sweden was a neutral country during the war) and built in 1921 and 1920 respectively; the other two vessels were the ss *COLOMBIA* of Bergen and the ss *SOLDAT*.

The *BUSIRIS* had a lucky escape in April 1941 when during an attack by an aircraft off the Cornish coast a bomb landed on deck without exploding, but jamming the steering gear. After the crew had managed to move the bomb and heave it over the side, she made Penzance for temporary repairs. In May 1941, whilst at Liverpool for an overhaul, she was scattered with incendiary bombs during an air raid. These were hastily kicked over the side but a nearby ship laden with explosives caught fire. The skeleton crew on *BUSIRIS* raised sufficient steam to make use of the capstan to warp her clear, but she was covered with debris when the other vessel exploded. Such was the coasters' wartime trade. *BUSIRIS* survived until 1958 as the *KYLEGLEN*.

From 1944 the southern North Sea and Channel were clearer of German naval vessels, especially E-boats, but were not free from air attacks, mines, or the shore batteries near Calais. Ships began to return to the London Docks and 119 sailing barges had discharged linseed at St. Peter's Oil Mill by the end of December 1943. Two of W.S. Kennaugh's West Coast Shipping Company's coasters out of

Barges bringing oilcake to Ipswich from April 1942 to March 1943.

Barge name	Cargo	No. of Visits	Year built	Place built	Owner	Port of Registry	NRT
CONVOY	Oilcake	1	1900	Rye	F. Crundall	Dover	73
EDITH MAY	Oilcake	1	1906	Harwich	W, Barrett	Harwich	64
MAYOR	Oilcake	1	1899	Sandwich	J. Groom	Harwich	70
NORTHDOWN	Oilcake	2	1924	Whitstable	C. Burley	London	
ORINOCCO	Oilcake	1	1895	E.Greenwich	G. Mason	Ipswich	70
PORTLIGHT	Oilcake	1	1925	Mistley	F.W. Horlock	Mistley	
PUDGE	Oilcake	1	1922	Rochester	LRTC	Rochester	68
RAVEN	Oilcake	1	1904	Rochester	LRTC	Rochester	46
REPERTOR	Oilcake	1	1924	Mistley	F.W. Horlock	Mistley	69
RESOLUTE	Oilcake	1	1903	Harwich	F.W. Horlock	Mistley	60

GRAIN & ANIMAL FEED   137

Built at Kirkintilloch on the Forth and Clyde Canal in 1912 as the INNISBEG, *the 99 gross ton* BROILER *called regularly at the BOCM oil mill at St Peter's Dock for cargoes of oil.*
(Titshall Brothers photo, courtesy D. Cotton)

Whitehaven, *DALEGARTH FORCE* and *SKELWITH FORCE*, arrived on 4th and 5th May from London with linseed for the Ministry of Food. *DALEGARTH FORCE* was sunk in the Dover Strait by shore batteries in June 1944. Ninety-five barges, all with linseed, arrived during the first six months of 1944. Numbers were down to just over a hundred in 1945, although curiously between July and October that year twelve motor coasters arrived with 4,772 tons of linseed that had to be transshipped to barges in the Dock to reach St. Peter's.

The trade ended in 1946. The National Association of United Kingdom Oil & Oilseed Brokers Ltd were still handling the import of seed, although the British Oil & Cake Mills Ltd received oilcake and sent away the oil produced at St. Peter's Mill. Thirty-two sailing or auxiliary barges arrived at St. Peter's

Mill with linseed in the first three months of 1946. The last arrivals were *GLENCOE* and *NORMANHURST* on 24th March. The mv *PROWESS* loaded ten 220-ton cargoes of oil for London, her last one being on 14th July. The final barges with oilcake to St. Peter's Dock were *MARIE MAY* on 28th.March, *SCONE* on 5th April, *CABBY* on 23rd May, *SCONE* again on 15th June, *PUDGE* on 25th July and finally *PUDGE* once more on 16th February 1947. Thereafter BOCM received about half a dozen motor barges a year with cake at their warehouse on Neptune Quay, situated between Isaac Lord's malting and Whitmore's sail loft. The warehouse was in use for storing oilcake until the late 1950s. John Good Ltd used it for a few years after 1969 for storing general cargo. The premises have now been converted into an hotel.

An unidentified barge sailing by Stoke Bathing Place bound for the New Cut and Mason's oil mill. She is lightly loaded with a low stack above her hatch coamings, as was usual when loaded with oilseed. (A.J. Hubert)

Christophersons

Valentine Desborough Colchester of Griffin Wharf was described in the 1886 Kelly's directory as a coal, cake and manure merchant, ship owner and agent for the Sun Fire Office, with an office in the Ipswich Corn Exchange. He was the son of William Colchester, manufacturer of chemical fertilisers, whose business is described elsewhere in the book. The family company traded at Griffin Wharf until April 1911; in May of that year Wilfred Christopherson, V.D. Colchester's chief clerk, took over the animal feed and fertilizer business. He bought two or three Thornycroft lorries in the early 1920s and the sailing barge *MEMORY* in 1929 from J.O. Fison of Stutton Hall and Thomas Haste. The *MEMORY*, which had been built in 1904 at Harwich, worked under the company's house flag of a gold griffin on a red background. Captain Jack Pittock, who was master of the *MEMORY* for many years, was well known and respected and frequently fixed his own cargoes to or from Ipswich, Felixstowe (Marriages) and Colchester.

Christopherson enjoyed a prolific barge trade; in 1914 there were no fewer than eighty-five arrivals, but by 1927 there were only seventeen cargoes of meal, ten of them in the *MEMORY*. In 1939 more than twenty cargoes of meal and oilcake arrived, about fourteen aboard *MEMORY* and the rest in craft owned or managed by Sully & Co. of London, including *OXYGEN*, *PHOENICIAN*, *CONVOY* and *DOROTHY*. Neat guano from Chile was brought from Barking in Essex, where it had been bagged by a company called Depas Ltd. Chilean nitrate and slabs of oilcake measuring about 36in. x 12in. x 1in. were also brought in by barge. The cake was broken up by a machine driven by a stationary gas engine with an 8ft flywheel fuelled by the town supply. Cargoes were fixed by Cubitt & Sons Ltd, the old-established oilcake factors mentioned earlier. Wilfred Christopherson's head office was at 6 Dial Lane and his residence was 20 Park Road.

In 1943 the firm was bought out by Associated London Flour Millers. At that time the managing director was R. Bremner and the company secretary for many years was W. Gostling. There were at various times around ten manual workers employed plus a foreman (at one time Ben Brett) and three drivers. In the office there were another nine or ten people including a shorthand typist and two other typists, three lads and four or five more people including G.H. Cook and V.J. Cornish, who spent most of their time going to the local cattle markets selling fertilizer and cake whilst buying in corn for the parent company.

MEMORY was sold in 1951 to F.W. Horlock of Mistley. She continued trading without an engine until 1956 when a trust was formed to preserve a working barge, and *MEMORY* was the chosen survivor still working under sail alone. Unfortunately this was a fairly short-lived venture, and she ended her days unrigged as a headquarters for an organisation called Fellowship Afloat and as a clubhouse, becoming derelict in the 1990s at Tollesbury.

Wilfred Christopherson & Company survived into the late 1960s. Their buildings were demolished during the 1980s.

Last of the Hoy Barges

According to the dictionary, hoys are small vessels carrying passengers and goods especially for short distances. Many Thames sailing barges were employed as hoys until the end of the First World War when ex-army lorries became available, the purchase of these by hauliers and carriers marking the first real commercial threat to the trading sailing barge. Until this time the early steamships and the railways had not seriously affected the barges' work; there was in fact some interchange of cargoes at wharves having a rail connection. The coming of reliable motor transport however quickly spelled the end of the hoy trade on the East Coast.

From the beginning of the nineteenth century sailing barges were superseding the round-bottomed sloops and cutters engaged in regular or weekly voyages to London from such ports as Margate, Maldon, Colchester and Ipswich. R. & W. Paul's early barges were operating a regular hoy trade from Ipswich to London until the company began buying steamships by ordering the *SWIFT* from a Wallsend yard in 1886. This vessel could load 200 tons and cut the London sailing time to eleven hours. In 1887 *SWIFT* completed 95 round trips.

Two of the last services in the hoy barge tradition from Ipswich survived into the First World War. They were to wharves on the River Ore, and to Beaumont Cut far up the Walton Backwaters. The River Ore was served by the *FAIRY*, 25nrt, and built at Limehouse in 1861. She was owned for several years by William Groom of 40 Church Street, Harwich. Beaumont Cut was served by the *HECTOR*, 22nrt. Built at Harwich in 1884 for Hector Stone of Kirby-le-Soken, in 1915 she was owned by the Ipswich Malting Company.

Sailings to and from Ipswich by HECTOR *and* FAIRY *in 1912.*

Vessel	Arrived at Ipswich 1912				Sailed from Ipswich 1912		
	Date	From	Cargo	Customer	Date	Supplier	Cargo
HECTOR	18 Mar. 1912	Woodbridge	light		20 March 1912	Mason G.	Oilcake
						Paul R. & W.	Maize
						Cranfield Bros.	Bran
HECTOR	27 April	Woodbridge	Light		30 April	Mason G.	Oilcake
						Packard E.	Nitrate of soda
						Paul R. & W.	Gram
HECTOR	10 May	Woodbridge	Light		14 May	Mason G.	Oilcake
						Cranfield Bros.	Bran
						Packard E.	Superphosphate
						Paul R.& W.	Maize
HECTOR	22 May	Harwich	Light		23 May	Mason G.	Oilcake
						Paul R. & W.	Maize germ
						Packard E.	Superphosphate
FAIRY	3 Mar. 1912	Harwich	light		5 Mar. 1912	Cubitt	Middlings
						Cowell & Co.	Middlings
FAIRY	28 Mar.	Cattawade	light		30 Mar.	Fison J.	Bran
						Cubitt	Bran
						Cowell & Co.	Maize
FAIRY	19.April	Felixstowe	shingle	Cranfield Bros.	25 April	Paul R.& W.	Barley
						Mortimer T.	Peas
						Cranfield Bros.	Bran
						E.C. Farmers Co-op	Salt
						Fison J.	Middlings
FAIRY	2 May	Butley	light		5 May	Cowell & Co.	Maize
						Cubitt	Oats
						Paul R.&W.	Millet
FAIRY	28 May	Harwich	light		30 May	Christie F.A.	Coal
						Cubitt	Lentils
						Cranfield Bros.	Bran

Motor Barge Traffic 1977

The numbers of ex-sailing barges, both auxiliary and fully powered, declined rapidly during the 1960s due mainly to old age and small hatchways no longer suited to faster loading methods. Their traditional work in the Thames estuary and East Coast grain trade was carried on by a new generation of steel motor-barges built between 1957 and 1970. Most were owned and many actually built by the London & Rochester Trading Co. Ltd, shortly to become Crescent Shipping Ltd., which was later absorbed by the Hays Wharf Group. Loading 200 to 300 tons via single hatchways, the steel barges were capable of reaching the mills at Stambridge, Maldon, Colchester, Fingringhoe, Ipswich and Yarmouth from London and Tilbury Grain Terminal.

In 1977, for example, 160 cargoes of grain were brought to Ipswich from Tilbury, consisting of eighty-four cargoes of wheat, seventy-two of maize and four of barley. The following table details the actual craft engaged that year, some making several voyages.

In addition to the shipments from Tilbury in the larger coasters included above, some 15,250 tons of wheat, 18,500 tons of maize and 1,000 tons of barley were brought from Tilbury in the 'new' steel barges during 1977. A further 2,200 tons of wheat and 400 tons of maize arrived in four of the last half-dozen or so ex-sailing barges still in trade, namely *TRILBY, HYDROGEN, CELTIC* and *GAZELLE*.

Vessel	NRT	Built	Type	Cargo
ANDESCOL	254	Hoogezand (NL) 1961		Wheat, Maize, Barley
CAPTION	269	Hessle 1963		Wheat, Maize, Barley
CECIL GILDERS	224	Wivenhoe 1957		Wheat
CELTIC	234	Papendrecht (NL) 1903	ex-sailing barge	Wheat, Maize
FUNCTION	254	Hoogezand (NL) 1963		Maize
GAZELLE	254	Krimpen (NL) 1904	ex-sb *RUNIC*, ex-mb *GOLDRUNE*	Wheat, Maize
GILLATION	254	Strood 1964		Wheat, Maize, Barley
HYDROGEN	198	Strood 1906	ex-sailing barge	Wheat
LAFFORD	224	Wivenhoe 1958		Wheat
LOACH	295	London 1968		Wheat, Maize
LOBE	295	London 1969		Wheat, Maize
LOCATOR	315	Paull 1970		Wheat, Maize
LODELLA	315	Paull (Humber) 1970		Wheat
MARGARITA WESTON	449	Viervelaten (NL) for Cranfields' parent company	coaster	Wheat
MARY WESTON	905	1973 Hoogezand (NL) for Cranfields' parent company	coaster	Wheat
NAUGHTON	224	Berwick 1951		Wheat
NOBLESSE	590	Foxhol 1961	coaster	Maize
ROFFEN				Wheat, Barley
ROGUL	254	Paull 1965		Wheat, Maize
ROHOY	264	Strood 1966		Wheat, Maize
ROINA	264	Paull (Humber) 1966		Wheat, Maize
SEVERN SIDE	406	Sharpness 1952	coaster	Wheat
TRILBY	234	Rochester 1896	ex-sailing barge rebuilt 1947	Wheat

Chemicals & fertilizers 6

From the 1840s onwards, Suffolk played an important role in the development of the fertilizer industry due to the existence of local coprolite and the efforts and vision of local men such as the Revd Professor J.S. Henslow, Edward Packard, and members of the Fison and Prentice families.

From early times, farmers had recognised the value of animal droppings as an organic fertilizer. Later, waste materials such as ashes, bones, blood, soot, fishmeal and rags were used in efforts to replenish the fertility of the soil. However it was not until Justus von Liebig revealed in 1840 a method for producing soluble phosphate using sulphuric acid that the possibilities of artificial manure were suggested. By that time several investigators had recognised that certain chemicals were essential for plant growth. Liebig contributed to the gradual realisation that these chemicals, namely phosphorus, potassium, carbon and nitrogen, were the main ingredients needed for plant life and destroyed the long-held belief that crops could only assimilate fertilizers made from material that had once been living. Farmers and chemists joined to find solutions to agricultural problems. In 1842 Mr (later Sir) John Bennet Lawes (1814-1900), a farmer and landowner, treated coprolites with sulphuric acid at Deptford and soon afterwards he and his associate, chemist Henry Gilbert, started field experiments at Rothamsted. Some of the coprolite supplied to the experimental station came from beds discovered near Felixstowe by Professor Henslow, an outstanding Suffolk botanist, who had realised the coprolite's potential as a fertilizer. In addition, in 1843 and independently of John Lawes, Edward Packard commenced dissolving bones in sulphuric acid locally at Snape.

Coprolites found in East Suffolk and in Cambridgeshire, were irregularly shaped nodules consisting of the fossilised dung and skeletal remains of animals, together with shells. They were an important mineral source of phosphate and this could be converted with sulphuric acid into superphosphate, a form that could be taken up by living plants. Later the quarrying of coprolite became an important local industry. The stone-like objects were dug from shallow pits and trenches and were also picked up from the fields by women and children.

Imported material generally referred to as phosphate of lime was later used and the North African coast provided a useful source of supply for British manufacturers. Gafza rock was brought from Tunisia, which has vast supplies although of a lower grade than that of the rock phosphate which was shipped from Morocco. Nauru Island, a German colony taken over at the end of the First World War and administered by Australia, New Zealand and the U.K., was very rich in phosphates of a higher concentration than Morocco, and shipments of this material later came via Avonmouth. Another high grade of rock phosphate was sent from Christmas Island. The sulphuric acid or vitriol, needed to treat the natural or mineral phosphate to obtain superphosphate, was manufactured locally by burning imported pyrites or sulphur ore. During the Second World War, 'triple' superphosphate was imported from America, the fertilizer being produced by treating rock phosphate with phosphoric acid instead of sulphuric acid. As early as 1875 however Edward Packard had manufactured this concentrated form of superphosphate in Suffolk.

Opposite page: The ss STASSA, 758nrt, built in 1951 in Amsterdam as the ENEE, arrived on 26th May 1966 from Sofi with pyrites for Fisons, departing 28th May light for Flushing. (Richard Clarke)

The value of basic slag, a by-product of steel manufacture, as a phosphatic fertilizer was realised during the late 1880s. In addition to basic slag's ability to counteract soil acidity and release soluble phosphate, it contains iron, manganese, magnesium and useful trace elements needed by plant life.

Potash, in the form of potassium chloride, potassium sulphate and kainite (a mineral consisting of potassium and magnesium sulphate) was used as a fertilizer from 1870 onwards. It was imported mainly from France and Germany, although during the 1970s potash from Florida was transhipped to Ipswich from Rotterdam.

The nitrogen required for healthy plant growth was first obtained from nitrate of soda, mainly sent from the west coast of South America, or from imported guano, the latter being the excrement of gulls, cormorants and penguins, together with other animal remains such as feathers and bones. One ton of guano was reckoned to equal 30 tons of farmyard manure. By the 1840s, the most highly nitrogenous, and therefore the most valuable, guano was being imported from the Chincha Islands, off the coast of Peru. In Peru itself the guano deposits belong to the government of the country and exports have been forbidden. Guano was also one of the principal exports of the Seychelles. By the late 1880s guano imports had slumped and the use of sulphate of ammonia gradually took over. Ammonium sulphate was available as a by-product from gas and iron works and had been recognised as being a valuable nitrogenous fertilizer since the 1850s.

Edward Packard's first fertiliser factory at Ipswich, built about 1849 on the corner of what became Coprolite Street. A railway siding was laid into the works yard from the dock tramway through the central archway along the line of the infilled slipway of the old St Clement's Shipyard. (David Miller)

The Local Fertilizer Industry

The history of fertilizer production at Ipswich started in 1849 when Edward Packard, a chemist and a wine and spirit merchant of Saxmundham in Suffolk, bought the site of a flour mill close to the dock, the area remembered today by the name of Coprolite Street. He had already made discoveries relating to the manufacture of superphosphate, and at Ipswich he not only treated local coprolite with acid but also supplied other manufacturers with the crushed material. In 1851 he moved to Bramford, a village adjacent to Ipswich, served by the railway and the Stowmarket Navigation. Soon he had built his own sulphuric acid plant there and the factory continued with the manufacture of superphosphate for home and abroad.

Edward Packard & Co. Ltd was to amalgamate in 1920 with James Fison & Sons whose fertilizer factory, which in its early days used the coprolite obtained locally, was built by James and Cornell Fison at Two Mile Bottom near Thetford.

Joseph Fison, a nephew of the James and Cornell Fison just mentioned, had already set up a flour milling business in 1847 at the Eastern Union Mills at Stoke Bridge in Ipswich, having earlier hired the nearby tidemill from the Corporation of Ipswich. His brother Edward took over the maltings on the opposite bank shortly afterwards and continued with the manufacture of malt products. Joseph meanwhile had carried out independent investigations into the findings of Professor Henslow regarding the potential of coprolite as a fertilizer and in 1850 experimented with the possibility of grinding local coprolite to produce superphosphate. Finding his process a success, he moved production a short distance away to Halifax Works, Wherstead Road, situated on the river bank near Bourne Bridge. He stayed there until 1858, using purchased sulphuric acid, and then moved to a site adjacent to Edward Packard's factory at Bramford.

The business of Joseph Fison & Co. at Bramford soon expanded into the production of compound fertilizers, due to Joseph's lifelong interest in the differing nutrient requirements of plants. At the time of his death in 1878, aged fifty-nine, his firm was still engaged in flour milling in addition to fertilizer manufacture, his sons James and Edward carrying on the business. Halifax Works, the site of Joseph Fison's corn and coprolite mills, continued in use and various insecticides and sheep dips, including 'Tarbol', were manufactured with much of the output being exported, although this part of Joseph Fison's business was later sold to Cooper McDougal in 1923. By the end of the nineteenth century, the Halifax site was occupied by the Chemical Union Company, set up to supply fertilizers manufactured by Joseph Fison & Co. 'for greenhouse and garden'. Its catalogue listed special fertilizers for cucumbers, melons, vines, strawberries, potatoes and bulbs besides a soluble guano and an 'extra quality dissolved bone compound'. By 1904, the company's two main shareholders were Joseph Fison's two sons, James of Stutton Hall and Edward of Stoke House, Belstead Road (both with 4,900 shares).

Another important pioneering firm that eventually became part of the Fison group was Prentice Brothers of Stowmarket, the family chemical business that included a sulphuric acid and superphosphate works opened in 1856, and an explosives works launched in the early 1860s. The firm's origins went back to the corn merchant and maltster Thomas Prentice. The fertilizer side of the business was developed by Manning Prentice, whose aunt Deborah Prentice was the mother of Joseph Fison just mentioned. Prentice Brothers were at Flint

Wharf, Ipswich in 1869 and used the Gipping Navigation for transhipment of grain, phosphate, artificial manure and explosives to or from the Stowmarket factory. Much of the output of Prentice Brothers was conveyed by barge to Ipswich where it was put aboard larger ships in the dock for transportation to its final destination. In the late 1880s the superphosphate made by Packards at Bramford was similarly taken to Ipswich, mixed on the quayside and transported by Thames barge to London for shipment to overseas destinations.

The story of artificial manure manufacture at Ipswich would not be complete without a mention of the Colchester family. Benjamin Colchester (1759-1826) was a former wine merchant who became a soap and candle manufacturer with premises near the dock at Ipswich. Probably because of the need for oil in this trade, Benjamin had become a partner with others in the short-lived whaling trade from Ipswich. At the start of the 1800s, his stock included 15,000 pounds of candles, 20,160 pounds of hard soap, 25,000 pounds of tallow, 554 gallons of oil and 36,840 pounds of barrilla, an impure form of sodium carbonate obtained from the ashes of plants and used in the manufacture of hard soap.

Benjamin Colchester's son William (1813-1898) was a typical Victorian entrepreneur. William had been educated at University College, London and it was intended that he should become an architect. He spent time in Italy studying classical and medieval architecture, later visiting Russia. On his return, he joined John Chevalier Cobbold in a timber importation business and became both a shipowner and shipbuilder with a yard at St Clements. During the 1840s he had interests in the cement industry and dredged and sent stone (septaria) from Harwich to Devon for the Great Western Railway.

William was elected a Fellow of the Geological Society of London in 1857 and he later presented his collection of minerals and fossils to the Ipswich Museum. He reputedly shared an interest in coprolite with Professor Sir Joseph Prestwich who had investigated the prehistoric animal bones found in the Stoke Bone Bed during the building of the railway tunnel at Ipswich in 1846. William Colchester's obituary stated he was Chairman of the Lawes Chemical Manure Co. at Barking in Essex, and he had acquired a chemical works at Rainham in addition to establishing his chemical manure works and bone crushing mills at Ipswich. A rating assessment for 1864 shows him as the occupier of Griffin Mills on Griffin Wharf, where he ground and 'rectified' guano to make what he called 'Ichthemic Guano', possibly because of the resemblance of the fertilizer particles to fish scales or perhaps fish meal played some part in a procedure reputed to be 'non-odoriferous'. The product was exported to many countries. William Colchester was later joined at Griffin Mills by his sons Valentine Desborough Colchester (1847-1921), a ship owner and a coal and corn merchant, and Charles Maynard Colchester (1856-1909) who had a liking for travel and established extensive business connections both at home and abroad. For several years every autumn, the company held a barley competition with a gold cup awarded for the best sample of English grown barley from the company's Gold Cup barley fertilizers. When the company was wound up in 1913 the goodwill and trademarks of this company were purchased by Prentice Brothers of Stowmarket. The premises on Griffin Wharf were then occupied by Wilfred Christopherson, a corn and cattle feed merchant (see grain chapter).

George Henry Colchester (1857-1944), William's youngest son, also had links with the fertilizer industry. In 1886 he joined Mr Thomas Ball who owned a brickworks at Burwell, near Cambridge, and had set up a fertilizer works close by in 1846 using the local coprolite. When George joined, the name of the firm became Colchester & Ball. The business was later acquired by Prentice Brothers.

CHEMICALS & FERTILIZERS

At the start of the artificial fertilizer industry in the mid-nineteenth century guano, coprolite and vitriol were brought to Ipswich by a variety of small schooners, ketches and sailing barges ranging from those built in the last years of the eighteenth century to craft fresh from the ways in the 1840s and 1850s. Among the barges were the *QUARTUS* and *SEXTUS*, built in 1846 and 1849 respectively. Though both were built for Colchester's own use, the *SEXTUS* was later registered and owned at Harwich variously by John Watts, J. Groom and William Groom; she remained on the register for some ninety years. The ketch *ROSE IN JUNE*, Ipswich-built in 1798, and the barge *ECHO* of Harwich, built in 1839, brought at least twenty-one separate cargoes of the above commodities between May 1851 and October 1852. During the same period some forty other vessels between them delivered six cargoes of vitriol, twenty cargoes of guano and sixty-one cargoes of coprolite, the cargoes varying in weight from thirty to ninety tons each.

This 'local' trade was the general rule for the next decade and beyond, but by the 1880s most of the raw materials of fertilizer production were shipped to Ipswich in steamships from foreign sources. The following few foreign arrivals in 1883 are given as examples. In February of that year the schooner-rigged steamship *LLOYDS* arrived with phosphate of lime from Lisbon for Packards; she was built by Palmers of Newcastle in 1869 for Harris & Dixon of Gracechurch Street, London, who were owners of a fleet of fifteen iron steamships. On 16th March the steamer *ALBERTINA* arrived with sulphur ore for Packards from Pomeron and the same day the schooner-rigged steamer *MILLICENT* arrived with sulphur ore from Seville in Spain for the Seville Sulphur Ore & Copper Company. Both ships were Sunderland-built in 1882 and belonged to Fisher, Renwick of Newcastle, who had a fleet of twenty ships there before moving in 1894 to Manchester, then made accessible by the new Manchester Ship Canal. Taken over by Coast Lines in 1939, and changing their ships for lorries, Fisher, Renwick continued with road haulage into the 1970s.

Three more steamers brought phosphate of lime to Packards from Lisbon and the Coosaw River (USA) that year. There was also a small steam coaster, the London-registered *COME ON*, which, although only as big as a sailing barge of the period, delivered vitriol from London to William Colchester. She was showing the way for all the subsequent steam and motor coaster fleets soon to oust coastal sailing vessels, except for the Thames barges, from the British coast. The larger ships referred to above loaded six or seven hundred tons of cargo.

In 1887 the *LODORE*, an iron schooner-rigged steamship built at Newcastle in 1878, brought sulphur ore from LaLaja for Prentice Brothers, and the ss *HAVERSTOE*, 1,372 nrt and registered at Grimsby, arrived with phosphate of lime for Packards from Port Royal in South Carolina. By contrast, in that same year of 1887, several barges brought loads of coprolite from the Rivers Deben and Ore. They included the *VICTORIA*, built at Ipswich in 1868 and owned by V.D. Colchester, which brought nine cargoes from each river for Joseph Fison. Edward Packard was part owner of *DEWDROP*, 23 tons and built at Ipswich in 1867, which loaded three cargoes away from the Deben for Packards. One cargo was brought by Packard's own *AMMONITE*, built at Ipswich in 1859. *HASTE AWAY*, part owned by the Haste family with Joseph Fison as managing owner, arrived with one cargo for Fison.

Apart from *AMMONITE*, Packards also owned the sailing barges *FOSSIL*, 37 nrt, built at Blackfriars in 1853, and *NAUTILUS*, built at Ipswich in 1870. The latter was broken up at Pin Mill *c*.1960. *DEWDROP* was sunk down Swin in collision with the steam schooner *DUNDEE*, which was built in 1883,

An advertisement for William Colchester's barley competition from the 1904 Suffolk County Handbook.

registered in Dundee and owned by the Dundee, Perth & London S.S. Company.

Packards owned some small steam coasters at this time and had set up the Ipswich Steam Shipping Company in the names of E. Packard, jun. and H.W. Packard. Their three ships, *SEDGEMOOR*, an iron schooner-rigged steamer of 113 nrt, built at Newcastle in 1872, *DARTMOOR*, an iron screw steamer of 154 nrt built at Cubitt Town in 1882, and *EXMOOR*, were not engaged solely in Packards' work but carried general cargo and coal for other merchants from north-east ports and the Continent, as seen in the table.

SHIP	LOADING PORT	CARGO	NUMBER OF SIMILAR TRIPS
DARTMOOR	Newcastle	Coal	3
	Stockton on Tees	Coal	1
SEDGEMOOR	Middlesbrough	Slag	1
	Newcastle	Coal	6
EXMOOR	Antwerp	Phosphate of lime	1
	Middlesbrough	Coal	3
	Hartlepool	Coal	5
	Grangemouth	Coal	1

An average year's work for Packard's own account in 1887.

Packards also maintained a large fleet of lighters or dumb barges, plus a few steam barges, for use on the Ipswich & Stowmarket Navigation as far as Bramford. The table below illustrates some of the traffic by these craft, light from Harwich to Ipswich, although the actual destination of cargoes taken to Harwich is not known. They were probably of fertilizer, but details are sparse in the Ipswich port books of the period. The *ORWELL* was recorded as being the first steam barge to Bramford on 18 June 1868.

Traffic between Packards' factories at Ipswich Dock and Bramford is not recorded in detail but was quite intensive and included their other steamer, the *MERSEY*.

Traffic from Harwich to Ipswich in 1887.

DATE	STEAM BARGE (MASTER'S NAME)	LIGHTERS TOWED BY STEAM BARGE (MASTER'S NAME)
12 Feb, 1887	ORWELL (Halls)	SHANNON (Halls), WAVENEY (Peck)
19 Feb	ORWELL (?)	STOUR (Cook), WAVENEY (Peck)
26 Mar	CLYDE (Osborne)	
4 Apr	TYNE (Glading)	
10 July	CLYDE (Osborne)	HUMBER (Read)
7 Aug	ORWELL (Halls)	HUMBER (Read), ISABELLA (Rose)
12 Aug	ORWELL (Halls)	WAVENEY (Peck), STOUR (Cook)
13 Aug	CLYDE (Osborne)	HUMBER (Read), AVON (Anmer)
20 Aug	CLYDE (Osborne)	HUMBER (Read), AVON (Anmer), SHANNON (Halls)
27 Aug	TYNE (Glading)	
	ORWELL (Halls)	WAVENEY (Peck), ISABELLA (Rose)
3 Sep	ORWELL (Halls)	AVON (Anmer)
9 Sep	ORWELL (Halls)	AVON (Anmer)
10 Sep	CLYDE (Osborne)	WAVENEY (Peck)
17 Sep	ORWELL (Halls)	
24 Sep	TYNE (Glading)	
1 Oct	CLYDE (Glading)	

CHEMICALS & FERTILIZERS

Despite the progress made by steamships during the previous decade, some sailing ships were still making long hauls from America to Ipswich in the 1880s for the fertilizer industry. In 1889 the 202-registered-ton barquentine *OCEAN RACER* of Inverness arrived from Aruba in the Dutch Antilles with phosphate of lime for Packards. She had been built at Kingston on the River Spey in 1875, as had *ROB THE RANTER* in 1874, which brought phosphate of lime to Fisons from Antwerp in October 1891. On 6th December 1891 the 500-ton barque

Shipping for Prentice Brothers, 1884-1920.
POL - phosphate of lime.

DATE	SHIP	RIG	NRT	REGISTERED	FROM	CARGO	BUILT
16 Feb 1884	ss THOMAS ADAM	Bg	510	London	Seville	sulphur ore	1870, iron, Aberdeen
15 Jun 1884	SSr TYNEDALE		325	Barrow	Seville	sulphur ore	1868, iron, Sunderland
10 May 1885	SSr BAINES HAWKINS		480	Newcastle	Lalaja	sulphur ore	1881, iron, Blyth
21 Oct 1887	SSr LODORE		407	Newcastle	Lalaja	sulphur ore	1878, iron, Newcastle
28 Jul 1888	SSr EBOR		450	Middlesbrough	Lalaja	Pyrites P/C Packard	1868, iron, Hartlepool
10 Dec 1888	SSr ULLSWATER		578	London	Lalaja	pyrites P/C Packard	1872, iron, Sunderland
10 Feb 1889	SSr ISLE OF CYPRUS		744	Newcastle	Lalaja	pyrites P/C Packard	1883, iron, Sunderland
18 Mar 1889	ss CAIRNGOWAN		826	Newcastle	Lalaja	pyrites P/C Packard	1883, iron, Sunderland
9 Dec 1892	BERNARD BARTON	Sr	97	Woodbridge	Antwerp	POL.	
24 Apr 1893	SSr G E WOODS		678	Cardiff	Huelva	pyrites P/C Packard	1873, iron, Sunderland
31 May 1893	SSr CALANUS		1,025	Newcastle	Huelva	pyrites P/C Packard	1882, iron, Newcastle
10 May 1897	IONA		95	Padstow	Ghent	POL.	
20 Jan 1907	ss ISLE OF HASTINGS		1,003	Newcastle	Sfax	POL P/C Packard	1885, steel, Howdon
25 Dec 1907	ss WHITE SWAN		1,384	Newcastle	Sfax	POL	1903, Blyth
2 Dec 1910	ss JENNY		1,149	Terneuzen	Sfax	POL	
25 Dec 1909	ss CHINGFORD		1,100	London	Sfax	POL	1889, steel, W. Hartlepool
9 Jun 1911	ss PHOEBUS		2,013	Genoa	Sfax	POL P/C Packard	
28 Oct 1911	ss GUISEPPE		1,133	Spezia	Sfax	POL	
10 Dec 1911	ss NORTH BRITON		1,361	Cardiff	Sfax	POL P/C Packard	
19 Dec 1911	ss BOTHNIA		1,007	Jonstorp	Huelva	pyrites	
9 Apr 1912	ss MARY HORLOCK		488	Hull	Huelva	pyrites	1911 Sunderland
9 Apr 1913	ss PORTOS		1,101	Helsingborg	Sfax	POL	
13 Nov 1913	ss ERNA BOLDT		1,046	Rostock	Sfax	POL	
20 Jan 1914	ss CANADA		913	Jonstorp	Huelva	pyrites	
16 Feb 1914	ss SVANHOLM		848	Copenhagen	Sfax	POL.	
27 Jul 1914	ss HAWORTH		2,857	Newcastle	Tampa	POL P/C Packard	
3 Nov 1914	ss DURHAM		1,686	Sunderland	Sfax	POL P/C Packard	
9 Nov 1914	ss DON HUGO		1,249	London	Huelva	pyrites P/C Rio Tinto	
6 Dec 1914	ss BRAMHAM		1,269	London	Sfax	POL	
16 Mar 1915	ss CHINGFORD		1,100	London	Tunis	POL	
29 Mar 1915	ss KURLAND		1,220	Antwerp	Bona	POL P/C Packard	
20 Apr 1915	ss EGHOLM		822	Copenhagen	Sfax	POL P/C Packard	
27 April 1915	ss HARALD		1,208	Copenhagen	Sfax	POL P/C Packard	
8 Jun 1915	ss LOWLANDS		1,165	Hartlepool	Huelva	pyrites	
4 Aug 1915	ss ERIK III		1,202	Copenhagen	Sfax	POL.	
9 Dec 1915	ss FENAY LODGE		2,075	London	Alexandria	POL P/C Fison	
10 Dec 1915	ss GERMAINE		1,612	Pireaus	Alexandria	POL P/C Fison	
14 Jan 1916	ss ELPIDOPHORUS		1,448	Syra	Alexandria	POL P/C Fison	
17 Jan 1916	ss ATHINA		1,123	Pireaus	Alexandria	POL P/C Fison	
27 Jan 1916	ss DEMOSTHENES		1,437	Syra	Alexandria	POL P/C Fison	
28 Feb 1916	ss KNUD		1,201	Copenhagen	Sfax	POL P/C Packard	
8 Jun 1916	ss DANMARK		1,186	Copenhagen	Sfax	POL	
5 Aug 1916	ss HANS BORGE		873	Copenhagen	Seville	pyrites P/C Fison	
11 Aug 1916	ss HJORTHOLM		848	Copenhagen	Sfax	POL	
6 Sep 1916	ss TELESFLORA		2,655	Bilbao	Boca Grande	POL P/C Packard	
24 Jan 1917	ss ARNO		396	London	Huelva	copper ore	
14 Jun 1917	ss GEMINE		1,366	Cardiff	Tunis	POL	
8 Sep 1920	ss MOMBASSA			Glasgow	Tampa	POL P/C Packard, Fison	

VASA of Cronstadt came in from Buenos Ayres with bone ash for Packards. A topsail schooner of local interest was the BERNARD BARTON of Woodbridge, her birthplace in 1840, which arrived from Antwerp in December 1892 with phosphate of lime for Prentice Bros. The schooner-rigged steamer HALLAMSHIRE, 1876, of Hartlepool, arrived from Florida in 1892 with phosphate of lime for Packards, as did the ss VASCONGADA from Tampa in 1893. In June 1895 the steamship KATE FAWCETT, launched at Hartlepool in 1876, delivered some 1,300 tons of phosphate of lime for Packards from Tampa, Florida.

Relatively few cargoes arrived by sailing barge for Prentice Brothers. There were only seven arrivals in 1899, for instance, all with phosphate; COCK O' THE WALK, a ketch barge registered at Weymouth, came from Dunkirk, as did the spritsail barge VIOLET SYBIL. The other ketch-barges or boomies to arrive

Sailing vessels loading fertilizer at Ipswich in 1895.
*Built in 1870 at Padstow for the Newfoundland trade.

DATE	NAME	POR	NRT	FROM	IMPORTER / CARGO	EXPORTER / CARGO
1895						
17 Jan	GOOD HOPE	Rye	65	Swansea	Christie / coal	Fison / fertilizer
22 Jan	MAYFLOWER	Inverness	126	Seaham	Beaumont / coal	Packard / fertilizer
1 Feb	SUNBEAM	Bristol	79	Harwich	Light	Packard / fertilizer
14 Feb	DOUGLAS	Falmouth	141	Hartlepool	Crannis / coal	Prentice / fertilizer
4 Mar	PLYMOUTH	Padstow	78	Saundersfoot	Paul / coal	Fison / fertilizer
7 Mar	ANNIE CROSFIELD	Barrow	90	Milford	Cobbold / coal	Packard / fertilizer
8 Mar	ANNIE DAVEY	Bideford	62	Margate	light	Packard / fertilizer
8 Mar	OSPREY	Dundee	144	Whitstable	light	Packard / fertilizer
11 Mar	REGINA	Jersey	54	Mistley	light	Packard / fertilizer
22 Mar	JANTINA	Hull	59	Mistley	light	Packard / fertilizer
3 Apr	MARTHA ELLEN	Goole	72	Yarmouth	light	Fison / fertilizer
3 Apr	ROSE	Ipswich	97	Mistley	light	Prentice / fertilizer
4 Apr	SWAANTJE	Groningen	81	Groningen	Cowell / oats	Packard / fertilizer
6 Apr	ANDOWER	Holmestrand	262	Drammen	Palfreman / wood	Packard / fertilizer
10 Apr	ALFORD	Bideford	65	Saundersfoot	Paul / coal	Packard / fertilizer
24 Apr	TWIGGS	Goole	69	Middlesburgh	Christie / salt	Prentice / fertilizer
30 Apr	JANE KNOX	Goole	78	Mistley	Light	Prentice / fertilizer
1 May	ANNIE DAVEY	Bideford	62	Milford	Cobbold / coal	Packard / fertilizer
4 May	ANNIE	Littlehampton	64	Dartmouth	Masons Paper Co. / umber	Packard / fertilizer
17 May	ALFORD	Bideford	65	Saundersfoot	Paul / coal	Packard / fertilizer
17 May	MARMADUKE	Hull	56	Seaham	Beaumont / coal	Prentice / fertilizer
23 May	LIZZIE LEE	Goole	120	Yarmouth	Light	Packard / fertilizer
24 May	METTE	Marstal	109	Konigsburg	Prentice / oilcake	Packard / fertilizer
4 Jun	MARIE	Tonningen	96	Harburg	Cubitt & Chatterton / oilcake	Packard / fertilizer
15 Jun	HENRIKA	Papenburg	125	Emden	Cowell / oats	Packard / fertilizer
15 Jun	SKANDINER	Lorberget	189	Soderham	Mason / firewood	Packard / fertilizer
30 Jun	MARY MILLER	Barrow	93	Swansea	Cobbold / coal	Packard / fertilizer
17 Jul	FLOWER OF THE FAL*	Falmouth	98	Dunkirk	Fison / phosphate	Fison / fertilizer
5 Aug	MARY ELEANOR	Carnarvon	89	Stettin	Burton / sugar	Packard / fertilizer
10 Aug	WHIM	Brixham	111	Terneuzen	Fison / phosphate	Fison / fertilizer
9 Sep	ERMENILDA	Bridgwater	60	Bridgwater	Grimwade Ridley / Bath bricks	Fison / fertilizer
17 Sep	SARAH DAVIES	Aberystwyth	90	Harwich	Light	Fison / fertilizer
3 Oct	IRENE	Falmouth	66	Dartmouth	Mason Paper Co. / umber	Fison / fertilizer
4 Nov	ANNIE	Grimsby	56	London	Cowell / lentils	Fison / fertilizer
20 Nov	VOLUNTEER	Carnarvon	93	Stettin	Prentice / barley	Fison / fertilizer
28 Nov	MARMADUKE	Hull	56	Southampton	R.S. & J. / wood	Fison / fertilizer
3 Dec	FREDHEIM	Laurvig	440	Leith	Moy / coal	Packard / fertilizer
3 Dec	FLEETWING	Carnarvon	213	Aruba	Packard / phosphate	Packard / fertilizer
12 Dec	MARTHA AND ELLEN	Goole	72	Mistley	Light	Packard / fertilizer
19 Dec	JULIE	London	99	Harburg	Cubitt & Chatterton / oilcake	Prentice / fertilizer

CHEMICALS & FERTILIZERS

DATE	NAME	POR	NRT	FROM	CARGO / IMPORTER	CARGO / EXPORTER
1895						
10 Jan	ss GLENMORE	Middlesbrough	240	London	Light	Fertilizer / Prentice
28 Feb	ss JACINTH[1]	Glasgow	199	Hartlepool	Light	Fertilizer / Packard
8 Mar	ss TOPAZ	Glasgow	198	Bruges	Light	Fertilizer / Packard
3 Apr	ss SPINEL[2]	Glasgow	196	Lowestoft	Light	Fertilizer / Packard
18 Apr	ss JACINTH	Glasgow	199	Newcastle	Light	Fertilizer / Packard
5 May	ss SPINEL	Glasgow	196	Rouen	Light	Fertilizer / Packard
28 May	ss VIRGO	Gothenburg	242	Libau	Oats / Paul	Fertilizer / Packard
2 Jul	ss EUROPA	Lubeck	415	Shoreham	Light	Fertilizer / Packard
10 Jul	ss RIGA	Stettin	386	Libau	Oats / Flint Wharf Corn Co.	Fertilizer / Packard

Steamships loading fertiliser at Ipswich in 1895.
1 Built Paisley, 1888.
2 Built Bowling, 1893.

included *BONA* of Ipswich from Terneuzen; she was a new barge built by Harvey at Littlehampton in the previous year and skippered by Captain Haste, who later spent some years as a Trinity House pilot on the Orwell. Another was the *LUCY RICHMOND*, built in 1875 at Ipswich, which came from Antwerp. The spritties *CENTAUR* and *DUNKERQUE* arrived from Ostend and Terneuzen respectively, and the *MYSTERY* came with phosphate from London.

Taking 1895 as a typical year it is interesting to observe not only the cargoes of fertilizer shipped away from the port of Ipswich but also which other craft, besides those owned by Packard, Fison and Prentice, were available. During that particular year there were thirty-nine Thames barge cargoes sent away, chiefly to London for export. Twenty of that number were in the company barges, Packards' *NAUTILUS*, *AMMONITE* and *FOSSIL* and Joseph Fison's *HASTE AWAY*, *FRESTON TOWER* and *MAY*. The last three mentioned tended to arrive at the port either light or with wheat for Fison's flour mill or maize for Cowells before loading artificial fertilizer. Packards' barges meanwhile generally came in with own-account bones from London or Queenborough near Sheerness, bone-meal, or nitrate of soda. Of the other barges, nine arrived light to load, and some had phosphate of lime from Dunkirk and Brussels for William Colchester and Packards, including R.&W. Pauls' *SOUTHERN BELLE*, while their *STOUR* and *GIPPING* were loaded with barley for Pauls inwards and Packards' fertilizer out.

Pauls' small steamships *SWALLOW*, *SEAGULL*, *SWIFT* and *SPEEDWELL*, when engaged in their regular London sailings, loaded sixteen outward cargoes between them of Packards' fertilizer. In March *SPEEDWELL* arrived from London on the 24th with general goods, loaded fertilizer, was back in Ipswich on the 27th with general, loaded fertilizer again and sailed on the 28th. *SEAGULL* arrived on 29th March likewise, loaded fertilizer and sailed on the 31st.

Several other sailing vessels loaded fertilizer during 1895, by which time they were schooner or ketch rigged, the old brigs and brigantines having largely disappeared. Again it is interesting to note the diversity of ports of registry, loading and discharge during that time, as shown in the accompanying table.

Another table, at top of page, shows the nine other steamship arrivals, which, with the exception of *GLENMORE*, loaded fertilizer at Packards in 1895. All came light and probably loaded fertilizer direct for the Continent.

September 1897 brought the barque *SITA*, 916 nrt, to Ipswich with guano from the Peruvian island of Lobos de Afueros. The iron barque *LA QUERIDA* arrived from the same port in June 1899 with guano; she was from William Doxford's yard at Sunderland in 1876. Also from Lobos with guano, in September 1900, there arrived a well-known full-rigged ship of the time, *TENASSERIM*; she had been built in 1866 by Harland and Wolff of Belfast for T. & J. Brocklebanks' passenger and cargo trade to India and the Far East, soon to be taken over by steamships. Brocklebanks were founded in the 1770s and

Cargoes brought by Thames barge for local fertiliser companies in 1899. (K) indicates a ketch barge.

IMPORTER	BARGE	CARGO	FROM	NO. OF VOYAGES IN 1899
Edward Packard	AMMONITE	Bonemeal	London	1
	AMMONITE	Nitrate of soda	London	1
	ANDROMEDA	Phosphate of lime	London	1
	BEAUMONT BELLE	Phosphate of lime	London	1
	DUNKERQUE	Phosphate of lime	Dunkirk	1
	ETHEL	Potash of Lime	London	1
	FOSSIL	Bonemeal	London	2
	FOSSIL	Bones	London	1
	FOSSIL	Bones	Queenborough	5
	FOSSIL	Loam	London	1
	FOSSIL	Nitrate of soda	London	1
	IDA	Bonemeal	London	1
	MYSTERY	Phosphate of lime	Dunkirk	1
	NAUTILUS	Bonemeal	London	4
	NAUTILUS	Nitrate of soda	London	3
	PEARL (K)	Phosphate of lime	Dunkirk	1
	PERCY	Potash of Lime	Dunkirk	1
	ROSE BUD (K)	Bonemeal	Dunkirk	1
	ROSE BUD (K)	Phosphate of lime	Dunkirk	1
	STAR (K)	Nitrate of soda	London	1
	VIOLET SYBIL	Phosphate of lime	Dunkirk	1
Joseph Fison	ALERT (K)	Phosphate of lime	Dunkirk	1
	BONA (K)	Phosphate of lime	Dunkirk	1
	BRITANNIC	Phosphate of lime	Ghent	1
	CENTAUR	Phosphate of lime	Dunkirk	1
	DUNKERQUE	Phosphate of lime	Dunkirk	1
	FRESTON TOWER	Fish guano	London	1
	FRESTON TOWER	Nitrate of soda	London	2
	FRESTON TOWER	Phosphate of lime	London	1
	GENESTA (K)	Phosphate of lime	Antwerp	1
	GLENROSA (K)	Phosphate of lime	Dunkirk	1
	HASTEAWAY	Nitrate of soda	London	1
	HILDA	Phosphate of lime	Dunkirk	1
	ISABEL	Sulphur	London	1
	JAMES GARFIELD (K)	Phosphate of lime	Dunkirk	1
	JUSTICE (K)	Phosphate of lime	Dunkirk	1
	MAHALAH	Phosphate of lime	Dunkirk	1
	MAY	Nitrate of soda	London	1
	SUSSEX BELLE (K)	Phosphate of lime	Antwerp	1
	UNITY (K) (Ipswich)	Phosphate of lime	Dunkirk	1
	UNITY (K) (Rye)	Phosphate of lime	Antwerp	1
	UNITY (K)	Phosphate of lime	Dunkirk	1
	WILLIE	Phosphate of lime	Dunkirk	1
Prentice Brothers	BONA (K)	Phosphate of lime	Terneuzen	1
	CENTAUR	Phosphate of lime	Ostend	1
	COCK O' THE WALK (K)	Phosphate of lime	Dunkirk	1
	DUNKERQUE	Phosphate of lime	Terneuzen	1
	LUCY RICHMOND (K)	Phosphate of lime	Antwerp	1
	MYSTERY	Phosphate of lime	London	1
	VIOLET SYBtL	Phosphate of lime	Dunkirk	1
William Colchester	BYCULLA (K)	Phosphate of lime	Dunkirk	1
	DUNKERQUE	Phosphate of lime	Dunkirk	1
	GLENROSA (K)	Phosphate of lime	Terneuzen	1
	GLENROSA (K)	Phosphate of lime	Dunkirk	2
	JEWISH	Phosphate of lime	Dunkirk	1
	MAZEPPA (K)	Phosphate of lime	Dunkirk	1

survived for two hundred years, latterly within the Cunard Group. The nature of the guano cargo to Ipswich reflects the willingness at the end of the nineteenth century to obtain any type of work for ex-clippers like the *TENASSERIM*, which was about to lose her identity; on 29th October 1900 she became the *RYVINGEN*, registered at Mandal.

CHEMICALS & FERTILIZERS

DATE	SHIP	REG.	NRT	FROM	IMPORTER	CARGO	DETAILS
1899							
20 Jan	RESULT	Yarmouth	44	Ostend	J.Fison	Phosphate of lime	Dandy built Southtown 1880.
4 Feb	MARIA	Fowey	137	Terneuzen	J Fison	Phosphate of lime	Brigantine built Hayle 1865.
22 Mar	SSr ACCRETIVE	Sunderland	706	Huelva	J Fison	Pyrites	Iron built Sunderland 1881 by S.P. Austin. Owner Coatsworth of S'ld.
3 Apr	JANIE	Truro	97	Ghent	J.Fison	Phosphate of lime	Schooner built Malpas, Cornwall, 1876.
4 Apr	ss SIFKA	Grangemouth	657	Bona	Packard	Phosphate of lime	Built Leith 1898.
14 Apr	NETHERTON	Caernarvon	187	Aruba	Packard	Phosphate of lime	Brigantine built Salcombe 1872.
21 Apr	SUSAN VITTERY	Brixham	140	Ghent	J.Fison	Phosphate of lime	Schooner built Dartmouth 1859. Active without engine until lost 1953.
21 Apr	MYFANWY	Falmouth	149	Terneuzen	J Fison	Phosphate of lime	
22 Apr	ZUMA	Wisbech	79	Middlesbrough	Packard	Salt	Schooner built Grimsby 1856. Owned at Wisbech.
4 May	SSr SUPERNAL	Sunderland	732	Huelva	Packard	Pyrites	Iron built Sunderland 1873.
21 May	MALAPERT	Hull	62	Dunkirk	Packard	Phosphate of lime	Ketch built Dartmouth 1881.
2 Jun	LEVANT	Brixham	147	Antwerp	Prentice	Phosphate of lime	Wood schooner built Brixham 1868.
27 Jun	LA QUERIDA	Christiania Oslo	679	Lobos	Packard	Guano	Iron barque built Sunderland by Doxford.
8 Jul	MALAPERT	Hull	62	Dunkirk	Fison	Phosphate of lime	Ketch built Dartmouth 1881.
9 Jul	RESOLUTE	Fowey	98	Dunkirk	Packard	Phosphate of lime	Schooner built Peterhead 1877.
9 Jul	CONSORT	Hull	55	Dunkirk	J.Fison	Phosphate of lime	Dandy built Newhaven, Sussex, 1879.
19 Jul	MYFANWY	Falmouth	149	Antwerp	J.Fison	Phosphate of lime	
24 Jul	SSr SUPERNAL	Sunderland	732	Huelva	Packard	Pyrites	
26 Jul	MAY CORY	Liverpool	136	Dunkirk	J Fison	Phosphate of lime	Barquentine built Bideford 1875.
7 Aug	MARTHA EDMONDS	Fowey	159	Harburg	Packard	Salt	Wooden brig built Milford 1873, sunk 1917 by U-boat gunfire 125 miles off Lizard.
11 Aug	SARAH	Fowey	118	Antwerp	J Fison	Phosphate of lime	Schooner built Kingsbridge, Devon, 1858.
27 Aug	GENERAL LEE	Dublin	146	Treport	J Fison	Phosphate of lime	Wooden schooner built New Brunswick 1865.
12 Aug	CONSORT	Hull	55	Dunkirk	J Fison	Phosphate of lime	
15 Sep	FAIRY KING	Padstow	89	Antwerp	Packard	Phosphate of lime	Schooner built by Rawle of Padstow 1878.
1 Oct	SSr ACCRETIVE	Sunderland	706	Huelva	J Fison	Pyrites	
1 Oct	SPARTAN	Dundee	64	Treport	Packard	Phosphate of lime	Ketch built Goole 1890, owned (1899) at Mutford Bridge, Lowestoft.
6 Oct	MARY ANN	Fowey	138	Antwerp	J Fison	Phosphate of lime	Schooner built Par 1874.
7 Oct	THISTLE	Greenock	100	Ghent	J Fison	Phosphate of lime	Schooner built Bowling 1863.
19 Oct	GERMANIA	Brake	148	Hamburg	J Fison	Salt	
2 Nov	ss ISLE OF IONA	Newcastle	714	Huelva	Packard	Pyrites	Built North Shields 1889.
12 Nov	MARIO VITTPORIO	Genoa	777	Sfax	Packard	Phosphate of lime	
29 Nov	REAPER	Truro	109	Antwerp	J Fison	Phosphate of lime	3-masted schooner built Pill, Cornwall, 1875.
1 Dec	ss CASSIA	Newport	676	Huelva	Packard	Pyrites	Iron steamer built Port Glasgow 1883.
7 Dec	ss ALASSIA or ALASSIO	Newport	728	Huelva	Packard	Pyrites	Iron steamer built Sunderland 1883.

In 1897 Joseph Fison received about 1,000 tons of phosphate of lime from Dunkirk, brought in the holds of sailing barges. It is worth noting the cargoes brought by Thames barges for the Ipswich fertilizer companies two years later from France and Belgium and the imported cargoes coming from London. The traffic is shown in the table using the 1899 records. This is apart from the cargoes brought by deepwater steamships and sailing vessels.

The table above shows the rest of the 1899 arrivals and illustrates the variety of types of ship still common at the time.

By the turn of the century fertilizer traffic had adopted a fairly regular pattern which did not change to a great extent for forty years until the Second World

Cargoes for local fertiliser companies imported in other than Thames barges, 1899.

Berthed beside Edward Packard's factory, the ss WOODLAND of Ipswich is discharging cargo, probably potash, into Packard's steam barge TRENT RIVER, which was built at St Clement's Shipyard in Ipswich in 1916. Owned by the Duffryn Shipping Company of Cardiff, the WOODLAND was built at Grangemouth in 1903.

War, when North Africa was occupied and much more phosphate came from across the Atlantic.

In 1902 the barquentine *EVA LYNCH*, 457nrt of St. John, New Brunswick, brought guano for Packards from the Seychelles and Mauritius in the Indian Ocean, and in December 1908 the ss *VIRGEN DE LOURDES*, 2,105 nrt of Bilbao, docked with phosphate of lime from Sfax, Tunisia. In the following February another Bilbao tramp steamer, the *PAGARSARRI*, 2,077 nrt, brought a corresponding cargo.

On 9th April 1912 a new steamship, the *MARY HORLOCK*, 488 tons, registered at Hull and belonging to F.W. Horlock of Mistley, arrived with pyrites from Huelva, Spain, for Prentice Bros. Horlock was better known for his sailing barges and coasters, which continued trading into the 1950s.

During the First World War regular shipments of phosphate of lime and pyrites arrived from Huelva, Sfax, Bona and occasionally Tampa and Alexandria. Many foreign ships were in evidence toward the end of the war including Danish, Norwegian and Greek vessels, a portent of future trends. In the early 1920s the larger ships with phosphates were being discharged into barges at the buoys in Buttermans Bay. On 6th January 1921, for example, the ss *TREWYN*, 3,228 nrt, moored in the Bay from Boca Grande off the coast of Florida with phosphate of lime for Fisons and Packards. She was launched by J. Readhead & Sons of South Shields as *WAR GANNET* in December 1919 for the Shipping Controller but completed a year later as *TREWYN* for the Hain Steamship Co. Ltd of St. Ives. Several owners and flags later she was broken up at Hong Kong in 1962.

On 19th April 1922 ss *SUNDANCE* of Philadelphia arrived in the Bay from Boca Grande with a full cargo of phosphate for the Fertilizer Manufacturers Association, leaving for Charleston on 28th April. On 24th August the same year ss *AFOUNDRIA*, also of Philadelphia, arrived from Tampa, Florida, with a similar cargo for Fison, Packard and Prentice. Both ships were built by the

CHEMICALS & FERTILIZERS

American International Shipbuilding Corporation of Hog Island, Pensylvania, in 1919. Both were of the wartime standard class, fitted for burning oil, and just over 3,000 nrt. In contrast the ss *ELISE MELLONIE*, a newly built coaster belonging to local coal merchants Mellonie & Goulder, brought basic slag from Middlesbrough for W. Christopherson, who had taken over V.D. Colchester's Griffin Wharf business. On 15th October 1924 the 5,359 nrt ss *POLYBIUS* of Seattle moored in the Bay from Tampa with phosphate of lime for Fison, Packard & Prentice. She had been launched at Seattle in 1919 by the US Shipping Board.

It will be noticed that shipments were being consigned to Fison, Packard & Prentice as the original pioneer firms moved toward amalgamation during this time. The merger was due to several pressures. By the 1890s fertilizers made by Continental firms were entering the country. The First World War halted these imports but afterwards British firms were still finding it difficult to export and they were affected by a shortage of sulphuric acid, which was being diverted to the explosives industry. In 1922, just when Prentice Brothers were recovering from the effects of the War, their works at Stowmarket were almost destroyed by fire. When the suggestion was made of a merger between themselves and Packard and James Fison (Thetford) Ltd, and Joseph Fison & Co. Ltd, then Prentice Bros. Ltd agreed. Thus, in August 1929, Fison, Packard & Prentice Ltd was formed. It was in 1942, during the war, following the take-over of most of the remaining fertilizer manufacturers in the country, that the company's name was changed to Fisons Ltd with the head office in Gippeswyk Avenue, Ipswich. By the 1950s the headquarters had moved to the former Felix Hotel at Felixstowe and the company later came back to Ipswich to a new purpose-built office in Princes Street.

The barge trade on the River Gipping, as it was generally referred to, was still very busy in 1920. The original steam barges of 1887, *ORWELL*, *CLYDE*, *TYNE* and *MERSEY*, had gone and the work was done by the steam barges *STOUR*, built Ipswich 1903, *TRENT RIVER*, built Ipswich 1916, and *GIPPING*, with the working dumb-barge fleet consisting of *THAMES*, *WAVENEY*, *YARE*, *DEBEN*, *SEVERN* and *HUMBER II*. The steam barge *GIPPING* made six round trips between Ipswich and Bramford in January and February alone, the *STOUR* nine trips and the new *TRENT RIVER* nine, most of them towing barges. Four bargeloads of burnt ore were brought from Bramford to Ipswich on the 12th and 13th January to Ipswich for transhipment to the schooner *HARVEY* of Waterford, bound for the Tyne. The *HARVEY* was built 1873 in Harvey, New Brunswick, and owned in 1915 by Mrs K. Molony of Dungarvan, Co. Waterford.

By the mid-1920s the river trade to and from Bramford was obviously dwindling. Early in 1927 the traditional role of the Gipping barges was still in

VESSEL	NUMBER OF CARGOES TO BRAMFORD		
	ex-KNEBWORTH	ex-ANTEO	ex-FREDERIKSBORG
Steam barge *TRENT RIVER*	6	2	6
Steam barge *STOUR*	6	1	7
Dumb barge *DEBEN II*	4	1	4
Dumb barge *SEVERN*	4	1	4
Dumb barge *YARE*	4	1	4
Dumb barge *WAVENEY*	5	1	3
Dumb barge *HUMBER II*	4	1	3
TOTAL	33	8	31

Cargoes shipped from Ipswich to Bramford by Gipping barges between 15th January and 15th February 1927. The 72 cargoes, each of approximately 30 tons, total some 2,160 tons.

evidence when they loaded from three steamships, *KNEBWORTH* and *ANTEO* which arrived with phosphate of lime from Sfax on 14th and 31st January respectively and the *FREDERIKSBORG* of Copenhagen that arrived from Tunis on 2nd February, as seen in the table on the previous page.

Also in 1927, on November 16th and 24th, the steam barge *TRENT RIVER* arrived at Ipswich towing Packard's old barge *AMMONITE* shorn of her sailing gear and laden with sugar beet. She was the last of their three sailing barges; *FOSSIL* and *NAUTILUS* had both been disposed of, the latter existing for many years as a houseboat at Woodbridge and Pin Mill until broken up in the 1980s.

On 29th October 1928, the *SEVERN* was towed from Bramford to Pin Mill, never to appear in the records again. She was probably broken up, as was *HUMBER II* in October the following year, leaving only the *YARE*, *DEBEN II* and *AMMONITE* as lighters.

DEBEN II appeared not to work any more trips after the autumn of 1930 and she was taken to Orford on 21st November 1932, presumably sold. *AMMONITE*'s final sailing, on 18th April 1933, was to Pin Mill for breaking up. The *YARE* was taken to Ostrich Creek on 10th July and eventually towed to Pin Mill after the war and converted to a houseboat which is still used to this day, owned by Mr Jack Haste of the old barge-owning family. Edward Packard's name is still carved on her stern.

TRENT RIVER was sold in 1933 by Fison, Packard & Prentice Ltd to her skipper, George Glading, who had been employed by them since 1880. He continued carrying cargoes of shingle from Felixstowe to Fison, Packard and Prentice and to the gasworks, nine trips to each in 1936. He towed Cory's (Mellonie & Goulder's) lighters to the Bay with coal and sailing barges in and out of the dock. Significantly, the arrival of the ss *AIKU*, 666nrt, on 29th May 1933 from Huelva with copper ore was the last cargo for the Bramford factory. The river trade to Bramford had ended and the barges had been disposed of, so

Barge traffic for the Chemical Union Company between April 1924 and November 1925.

DATE	NAME	NRT	POR	CARGO		AMOUNT	BARGE OWNED / MANAGED
				Incoming	Out to London		
7 April 1924	MEMORY	65	Ipswich	-	Sheep Dip	91 tons	J.O. Fison
5 May	SAMUEL BOWLEY	47	London	sulphur	-	100 tons	Wills & Packham, Sittingbourne
18 Jul	MEMORY	65	Ipswich	-	Sheep dip	105 tons	J.O. Fison
1 Aug	THOMAS	55	Rochester	sulphur	-	99 tons	E. J. & W. Goldsmith, Grays
14 Aug	MEMORY	65	Ipswich	-	Sheep dip	65 tons	J.O. Fison
29 Oct	KIMBERLEY	65	Ipswich	-	Sheep dip	100 tons	J.O. Fison
4 Dec	MEMORY	65	Ipswich	-	Sheep dip	90 tons	J.O. Fison
7 Jan. 1925	CONVOY	73	Dover	-	Sheep dip	102 tons	F. Crundall, Dover
6 Mar	CONVOY	73	Dover	-	Sheep dip	76 tons	F. Crundall, Dover
24 Mar	FREDRICK WILLIAM	46	Ipswich	sulphur	-	100 tons	Eldred Watkins, Ipswich
6 May	MAJOR	67	Harwich	-	Sheep dip	78 tons	J. Chaplin, Brightlingsea
				-	Fertilizer	10 tons	
9 Aug	DOROTHEA	52	Harwich	sulphur	-	100 tons	A. Middleton, Harwich
18 Aug	CONVOY	73	Dover	-	Sheep dip	100 tons	F. Crundall, Dover
				-	Paint colouring	84 lb.	
				-	Tinned plates	1.2 tons	
				-	Blue	1.1 tons	
6 Nov	CONVOY	73	Dover	-	Sheep dip	132 tons	F. Crundall, Dover
				-	Blue	560 lb.	

CHEMICALS & FERTILIZERS

the cargo of approximately 1,200 tons would have been sent by rail.

Barges were also bringing and taking out cargoes for the Chemical Union Company at this time. The table on page 156 shows barge traffic for this firm from April 1924 to November 1925.

In 1929, the premises of the Chemical Union at Halifax, Wherstead Road, became the chemical works of Morris Little & Son Ltd and arsenic was discharged from Horlock's *DOROTHY, PRIDE OF IPSWICH* and the *SQUAWK* in February 1930 for this firm.

Deep Sea Shipments in the 1930s

Fisons, Packard and Prentice Ltd decided in 1931 to erect a large factory at Cliff Quay. Construction work took place during 1932-33 and production started soon after. Electric cranes and railway sidings were at hand and the site was adjacent to a deep-water quay able to accommodate the large sea-going vessels bringing in raw materials and taking out the manufactured products intended for export to all parts of the world. A covenant on the land meant that a sulphuric acid plant could not be built in the site so a plant was erected on top of the cliff behind. The factory was initially designed to produce 50,000 tons of superphosphate a year but soon afterwards the works were expanded to increase the output by 50 per cent.

The years of depression gave a longer lease of life to many British ships built in the early years of the twentieth century, several being snapped up by foreign users of second-hand tonnage after twenty or thirty years under the Red Ensign. Many old ships ended their days laden with phosphate or pyrites, the corrosive nature of the cargo not appealing to owners of new vessels. Consequently many British-built ships forty or fifty years old were bringing the raw materials to Ipswich during the 1950s under Yugoslav, Greek and Spanish flags. In the mid-1930s the ss *SEBRENO,* which had come from the ways of J. Readhead & Sons at South Shields in 1901, arrived three times with phosphate of lime from Sfax. Similarly, the interestingly named ss *SRGJ,* again from the Readhead yard in 1905, made three voyages to Ipswich between 1935 and 1937 from Sfax. Both vessels were then owned by Dubrovska Parobrodska Plovidba of Dubrovnik, who had more than twenty ships at that time.

Three Spanish steamships, *ARNOTEGI-MENDI*, built at Bilbao in 1921, *GORBIA-MENDI*, also launched at Bilbao in 1922, and *AIZKARAI-MENDI*, which was new in 1929 from Ropner's Shipbuilding Company, Stockton-on-Tees, came during 1932-35. All belonged to Cia. Nav. Sota Y Aznar, run by Sir Ramon de la Sota of Bilbao, a company owning more than forty-five ships at that time. One vessel which made five voyages to Ipswich from Sfax and Tunis between 1924 and 1931 and another in 1939 from Huelva with pyrites was the wartime standard ship ss *MOTIA*, built in 1918 as *WAR DIRK* by the Caledon S.B. Company, Dundee. Subsequently she was renamed *SICANIA* (1919) and then *MOTIA* (1920) of Trapani, Sicily, and scrapped at Viareggio, Italy, in 1959.

In January 1934 the German schooner *FLOTTBEK* arrived from Hamburg with kainite salt for Fison, Packard & Prentice, and in May came the 239 nrt ship *DUSKER* of Bergen with whale guano from Tonsberg, a prominent Norwegian whaling port. The Italian turret-decked steamer *SAN MATTEO*, with about 5,000 tons of phosphate of lime from Sfax, arrived on 7th February 1935. She had been to Ipswich previously in 1912 as the *WHATELEY HALL*, from

Captain George Glading, master of the steam barge Trent River for many years, and owner from 1933.

Doxfords of Sunderland. William Doxford pioneered the turret-ship concept, thus giving more strength and a six and a half per cent increase in deadweight capacity over a conventional ship's deadweight tonnage, and a related reduction in the net tonnage, on which most dock and Suez Canal dues were payable.

Three of Hogarth's Baron Line ships of Ardrossan berthed from Sfax in 1936. Both the *BARON LOUDOUN* that came on 17th February and the *BARON NAIRN* that appeared on 9th September had come from the Clyde yard of Lithgows in 1925 and both were lost to U-boats in 1940 and 1941 respectively. The third vessel, coming on 22nd April, was the *BARON NAPIER*, built by Hendersons on Clydeside in 1930. Sold to Liberian owners in 1957, she was stranded on rocks while bound for Japan in 1961 and was afterwards towed to Hong Kong and broken up.

DATE	SHIP	PORT Of REG	NRT	FROM	CARGO	TONS	LANDED	BUILT
1937								
8 Jan	ss *SRGJ*	Dubrovnik	2,317	Sfax	Phosphate of lime	5,857	Cliff Quay	1905 Readhead, South Shields
13 Jan	mv *ADVANCE*	Oslo	307	Menstad	Nitrate of Lime	300	Dock	1930 Kiel
17 Jan	ss *NEWLANDS*	Hull	854	Huelva	Copper-ore	2,315	Cliff Quay	1921 Paisley
7 Feb	ss *MERISAAR*	Tallin	1,288	Sfax	Phosphate of lime	3,175	Cliff Quay	1900 Trieste, Estonian owned
16 Feb	mv *HALLINGDAL*	Oslo	1,930	Nauru	Phosphate of lime	2,000	Cliff Quay	1929 Copenhagen, Burmeister & Wain
1 Mar	mv *HOLLAND*	Gaselternijveen	94	Hamburg	Kainite Salt	248	Dock	1935 Delfzyjl
5 Mar	ss *KEMI*	Vaasa	1,461	Sfax	Phosphate of lime	3,185	Cliff Quay	1900 Rostock
9 Mar	mv *AMAZONE*	Lubeck	89	Bremen	Kainite Salt	190	Cliff Quay	1932 Hamburg, 3-mast schooner
12 Mar	ss *OSMUSSAAR*[1]	Tallin	1,339	Sfax	Phosphate of lime	3,201	Cliff Quay	1909 Stockton-on-Tees
18 Mar	ss *SCANIA*	Arild, Swe	1,171	Huelva	Pyrites	2,910	Cliff Quay	1901 Sunderland, owned at Arild, Sweden
30 Mar	ss *SKAANE*	Copenhagen	724	Huelva	Pyrites	1,865	Cliff Quay	1918 Aalborg, owners DFDS
5 Apr	ss *SVERKER*	Simrishamn, Swe	234	Menstadt	Nitrate of lime	240	Dock	1916 Thorskog
9 Apr	ss *SARMATIA*	Koivisto	1,361		Phosphate of lime	3,382	Cliff Quay	1901 W. Gray, Hartlepool
21 Apr	ss *LISA*[2]	Hamburg	199	Menstadt	Saltpetre	238	Dock	1904 Glasgow by Napier & Miller
23 Apr	mv *ALBATROS*	Groningen	86	Antwerp	Kainite Salt	198	Dock	1913 Groningen, aux-ketch
28 Apr	ss *EVERARDS*	Riga	2,325		Phosphate of lime	5,693	Cliff Quay	
20 May	ss *ULMAS*	Cardiff	1,666	Sfax	Phosphate of lime	4,580	Cliff Quay	1910 W. Gray, Hartlepool Latvian-owned
15 Jun	ss *GARLINGE*	London	1,224		Pyrites	3,021	Cliff Quay	1918 Finch, Chepstow
5 Jul	ss *LIBRA*	Bergen	864	Huelva	Pyrites	2,027	Cliff Quay	1882 J. Readhead, Stockton
17 Jul	ss *EVERARDS*	Riga	2,325	Sfax	Phosphate of lime	5,747	Cliff Quay	1910 W. Gray, Hartlepool, Latvian-owned
25 Jul	mv *BARON DALMENY*[3]	Ardrossan	2,188	Nauru	Phosphate of lime	2,727	Cliff Quay	1924 Port Glasgow
21 Aug	ss *HEMINGE*[4]	Newcastle	1,465	Huelva	Pyrites	3,763		1919 W Gray, Hartlepool
16 Sep	*OOSTERSCHELDE*	Groningen	191	Bremen	Potash	295	Dock	1918 Zwartsluis, steel aux. 3-mast schooner
18 Sep	*BARON COCHRANE*[5]	Ardrossan	2,031	Sfax	Phosphate of lime	5,419	Cliff Quay	1927 Irvine
24 Sep	mv *CONTINENT*	Delfzyjl	313	London	Potash	211	Dock	1931 Martenshoek
					Nitrate of soda	363		
8 Oct	mv *REGEJA*	Groningen	180	Bremen	Muriate of potash	171	Dock	
					Sulphate of potash	166		
1 Nov	mv *WIM*	Groningen	196	Hamburg	Muriate of potash	200	Dock	
					Sulphate of potash	201		
3 Nov	ss *CANFORD CHINE*[6]	Swansea	2,094	Sfax	Phosphate of lime	5,113	Cliff Quay	1917 Stockton
7 Nov	mv *REGA*	Groningen	165	Hamburg	Muriate of potash	350	Dock	
9 Nov	mv *GRUNDA*	Delfzijl	136	Bremen	Potash Salt	330	Dock	1934 Delfzyjl
11 Nov	ss *NAVIEDALE*	Aberdeen	148	Hamburg	Muriate of potash	350	Dock	1906 Ailsa S. B. Co., Ayr
16 Nov	ss *NEPTUN*	Flensburg	943	Huelva	Pyrites	2,472	Cliff Quay	1928 Flensburg
8 Dec	ss *BARON KELVIN*[7]	Ardrossan	1,870	Sfax	Phosphate of lime	5,010	Cliff Quay	1924 Connell & Co., Glasgow
20 Dec	ss *ARKELSIDE*[8]	Hartlepool	948	Huelva	Pyrites	2,400	Cliff Quay	1924 Osbourne, Sunderland

CHEMICALS & FERTILIZERS

The table on the opposite page showing the 1937 arrivals to Fison, Packard & Prentice reveals the presence of the ubiquitous Dutch motor coaster that was making its mark at this time, to the detriment of British ships in the coasting trade. Only a few auxiliary-engined sailing vessels occur in the table.

There were few imports of fertilizers other than for Fison, Packard & Prentice during 1937. These included six for ICI from Middlesbrough brought by the ss *CONAN* of Glasgow, built 1917, ss *SOUTHWICK* of Sunderland, built 1917 by Swan Hunter, Sunderland, ss *FELLSIDE* (her fifth name) of London, built 1904 at Blyth, ss *SOUTHPORT* of Glasgow, mv *ARTHURTOWN* of London, and ss *YEWGLEN* of Glasgow, built 1915 at Ardrossan. The last-named vessel belonged to the well-known shipping company of John Stewart of Glasgow, whose steam coasters, all prefixed *YEW*, were familiar on the British coast. Wilfred Christopherson also received a cargo of fertilizer from Rotterdam aboard the Dutchman *JANTJE EPPIANA*, built at Delfzyl in 1935.

The imports in 1938 followed a similar pattern, with about four ships from Huelva with pyrites or copper ore, six from Sfax with phosphate of lime, and another cargo of phosphate of lime from Nauru in the ss *DALFRAM* of Newcastle, built by Scotts of Greenock in 1930. There were only four British-owned ships out of eleven, but at least another four were old British-built vessels.

The War Years

During the 1930s the port of Casablanca in Morocco began to show in the records as a source of phosphate cargoes to Ipswich, including one in 1939; thereafter no ships came from that port until late in 1943 because of the presence of the Vichy regime in Morocco and Algeria. American landings at Casablanca, Oran and Algiers all took place on 8th November 1942, coinciding with the British breakthrough at El Alemain. The American military convoys had sailed direct from America in such security that the invasion was a surprise, and hostilities ceased throughout Morocco and Algeria by 11th November. The Mediterranean was finally clear for convoys during May 1943.

Ships continued to arrive at Ipswich from Sfax in Tunisia until May 1940, when *BARON ERSKINE* brought phosphate, esparto grass and rags for Fisons and seven other importers. Built on Clydeside in 1930, she was later sunk by a U-boat with the loss of forty men in an Atlantic convoy bound for Loch Ewe, having loaded at Tampa in Florida, which, along with Curacoa, became a prime source of phosphates. The *BARON KINNAIRD* arrived on 18th October 1940 with phosphate of lime from Tampa via Halifax, the Canadian port where ships mustered and were allocated to eastbound convoys. From then on Tampa and Curacoa became the principal sources of phosphate until further cargoes arrived from Casablanca in 1943. Pyrites meanwhile still came in throughout the war from Huelva in neutral Spain. The *BARON KINNAIRD* made a similar passage to Ipswich in September 1941, but she was torpedoed in the North Atlantic with the loss of all forty-one crew outward-bound from Loch Ewe in March 1943.

Occasional shipments of pyrites came from Huelva during 1941 and until just after the war for the West Norfolk Farmers' Manure & Chemical Co-operative. This business, established in 1871, had allied itself with Fisons, Packard & Prentice in the 1930s, eventually being absorbed by Fisons in 1965. The ss *CARA* of Glasgow, built at Burntisland in 1929, arrived on 23rd March 1941 with such a cargo, as did the ss *VANELLUS*, built at Swan Hunters' yard in 1921, on 24th July.

The Dutch schooner OOSTERSCHELDE, *built at Zwartsluis in 1918, being discharged by crane on 16th September 1937. She was still visiting Ipswich during the 1990s on passenger carrying charter work. (J.A.E. Burrows)*

Opposite page: *Fertiliser traffic to Fison, Packard & Prentice, 1937.*
*1 ex-*DUDDINGTON
2 Built 1904 for Nobel Explosives Ltd. as LADY TENNANT, *1924 renamed* ELGIN COAST, *1930* KILKENNY, *1936* LISA. *Broken up 1974.*
3 Broken up 1960.
*4 ex-*RUDCHESTER, *ex-* LEICESTER, *ex-*WAR CURRANT.
5 Sunk by U123, December 1942.
*6 ex-*BRYNTAWE *1936.*
7 Sunk by U-boat October 1941.
8 Lost by enemy action 22nd September 1939.

The ss *OGMORE CASTLE* of Cardiff also berthed from Huelva on 5th January 1942, but from September 1942 until 1946 fertilizer traffic was in the control of the Ministry of Supply. This trade was complicated when, as frequently happened, other commodities were loaded, as in the case of the ss *CHARLES TREADWELL*, a wartime standard ship built by the Pacific Bridge Co., of Alameda, California, in 1943 for the Ministry of War Transport. She came via Middlesbrough with a part-cargo of fertilizer and sardines on behalf of the Ministries of Supply and Food.

American phosphate shipments to Fisons virtually ceased after 1942, Casablanca and Huelva becoming the regular ports for loading phosphate of lime and pyrites respectively, with one or two phosphate of lime cargoes from Sfax and Bona. One or two ships with pyrites came from Sofi in Morocco. Imperial Chemical Industries (ICI) had several small shipments of fertilizer delivered to Cliff Quay from Middlesbrough; in 1946 no fewer than forty-six ships discharged there for ICI. In November the same year one of the Canadian-built *FORTS*, standard ships for the Ministry of War Transport, brought a part-cargo of phosphate of lime via London. She was the *FORT BEDFORD*, built at Vancouver in 1943. One of her sisters, *FORT COULONGE*, Montreal built in 1943, had arrived from Casablanca via Hull with a part-cargo in August 1945.

Shipping from the end of the Second World War onwards

This pattern carried on routinely after the war ended in 1945, with a few exceptions. One was the arrival of the mv *HOEGH SILVERSTAR* with a part-cargo of phosphate of lime from Nauru via Immingham, the newspapers stating that she had brought the first cargo from that Pacific island since the end of the war. A few coasters brought potash from Bremen and a number of sailing barges delivered potash from ships in the London docks during the 1940s and 50s. The year 1951 saw twenty-nine barges with potash and ninety other ships for Fisons,

One of the biggest ships to have berthed at Cliff Quay up to that time, the Norwegian mv HOEGH SILVERSTAR, *3,260nrt, had brought phosphate from Nauru, a small rocky island in the Pacific at Lat. 0°, Long. l66°E. It was one of the first such cargoes to have reached Europe since the end of the Second World War, during which the island was occupied by the Japanese. She arrived at Ipswich on 28th July 1953 and sailed light for Antwerp on 7th July. Built in 1938 for Norwegian owners Leif Hoegh by Burmeister & Wain at Copenhagen, she was one of their fleet of nineteen ships.*
(R.W. Smith)

CHEMICALS & FERTILIZERS

and in the same year ICI imported through Ipswich fifty-four cargoes of ammonia and thirty-four cargoes of fertilizer and phosphate.

As mentioned much earlier, several elderly vessels ended their days delivering phosphate, one in particular springing to mind. The ss *AGIOS VIASIOS*, Greek owned and registered at Piraeus, arrived five times in 1950 with phosphate of lime from Casablanca. She had been built as a First World War standard ship in 1918 at Vancouver. Her first of six names was *WAR POWER*; she had been subsequently owned by the Chandris family since 1933, her fifth name having been *KARL CHANDRIS*. She was scrapped at Hong Kong in 1959.

The sixties witnessed the start of a revolution in merchant ship design and construction that rapidly took hold in the 1970s as demand increased for ever larger tankers and bulk carriers. This of course influenced the trade to Ipswich, as increased length and draught precluded the new ships from the smaller ports. By 1966 the old steamers had largely gone and direct shipments from North Africa

The Lebanese mv AGIA SOPHIA, *2,194nrt, discharging phosphate from Casablanca on 9th February 1966. Registered in Beirut, she was a Canadian wartime standard ship launched at Pictou as* CAMP DEBERT. *She subsequently bore the names* CRESCENT PARK *(1945),* JULIA *(1951),* LONA *(1951), and* SENATOR HAGELSTEIN *(1962). (Richard Clarke)*

The Portuguese mv AMBRIZETE, 3,267nrt, arrived on 12th January 1950 from Casablanca with phosphate, and sailed light for her home port of Lisbon on 21st January. She was built at Sunderland in 1949. (R.W. Smith Collection)

and Spain would soon disappear. In that year the oldest ship from Casablanca was the mv *AGIA SOPHIA*, which arrived in both February and May; a Second World War standard ship launched at Pictou, N.S., as *CAMP DEBERT* in 1943, she too was blessed with six names, and in 1966 was under the Lebanese flag registered at Beirut. Thus did the phosphate and pyrite shipping trade change for ever. The bulk ore carriers berthed at Antwerp or Rotterdam, the cargo being distributed by modern motor coasters, many of them Dutch and German, to ports like Ipswich.

In the 1980s the phosphate berth at Casablanca consisted of a 692-metre (2,274ft) jetty allowing three or four ships, dependant on length, to load, and a new 120-metre (393ft) jetty at right angles to its end. Loading was directly from trains at rates of 600 and 1,000 tonnes per hour. The long jetty would have accommodated six or seven ships like the *AGIOS VIASIOS* or *AGIA SOPHIA* at around 300ft long, illustrating the comparative dimensions of the new ore carriers.

At the beginning of the 1980s Fisons Ipswich factory was employing some 450 people until production was abruptly cut back in January 1981. There followed a buy-out by the Norwegian company Norsk-Hydro in 1982 and complete closure of the factory came in 1985 leaving empty berths from which so many venerable ships and men sailed into inevitable oblivion. Fisons' profits had dipped by 1992 and the company, by then a major drug manufacturer, was restructured. In 1994 the company completed the disposal of the fertilizer factory at Bramford with a buyout by Levington Horticulture. The name of the Bramford site changed again in 1997 when it was acquired by the garden pest control and plant food giants Scotts of Maryville, Ohio. Then in 2003, Scotts announced that the Bramford plant too was to close, ending 150 years of fertilizer production in the Suffolk village.

It seemed that the link between the fertilizer industry and the Port of Ipswich had been broken for ever with the cessation of shipments of phosphates, pyrites and copper ore in the 1980s, but in 1999 a new £2.5 million fertilizer terminal was opened at Cliff Quay on the site of the former Cliff Quay Power Station. Fertilizers and other bulk products from various locations are blended and bagged at the IAWS Fertilisers (UK) plant. In October 2002, two records were broken at the Port of Ipswich with the arrival of the longest tanker ever to use

CHEMICALS & FERTILIZERS 163

Approaching Ipswich with phosphate from Casablanca for Fisons on 27th June 1953 is the Jugoslav ss PLITVICE of Dubrovnik, 2,367nrt. She sailed light for Hartlepool on 11th July. She had been built by J. Redhead & Sons at South Shields in 1905. (R.W. Smith)

the port, carrying its biggest liquid bulk consignment. Hydro Agri (UK) Ltd, a major ABP customer and UK supplier of nutrients to the farming industry, imported the 10,000-tonne liquid-bulk shipment on board mv *FURE STAR*, a 145 metre-long tanker. The cargo, which originated in Germany, was discharged at Vopak's liquid-bulk terminal at Cliff Quay, ready for distribution to Hydro Agri's customers in East Anglia and beyond.

Owned by the Jugoslav Line of Dubrovnik, the ss KOZARA, 2,896nrt, berthed at Cliff Quay on 23rd February 1953 with phosphate from Casablanca for Fisons, sailing on 9th March light for Hartlepool. She had been built in 1927 at Port Glasgow as the RADCOMBE, a name she held until 1946. (R..W. Smith)

Guncotton

The Stowmarket firm of Thomas Prentice produced sulphuric acid as part of the manufacture of artificial fertilizer, and in 1863 opened a factory producing guncotton, an explosive made by dipping long staple cotton in sulphuric and nitric acids. The guncotton business was taken over by Prentice Brothers in 1868 and two years later a new factory went into production under the title of the Patent Safety Gun Cotton Co. Ltd. Unfortunately in August 1871 there was a major explosion killing 24 people but the factory was quickly rebuilt to be known as the Stowmarket Gun Cotton Co. Ltd. By 1885 it had become The New Explosives Company Ltd and sent guncotton down the Gipping Navigation to Ipswich and Harwich. Mr Walter Packard was quoted in a 1950s *East Anglian Magazine* recalling seeing a sailing barge occasionally going up to Stowmarket to the explosive works. A very small sailing barge named *IOTA*, of only 12nrt and owned by William Groom of Harwich, reached Stowmarket in the 1890s to load gun cotton. The *IOTA* is recorded as having arrived at Ipswich on 15th August 1894 light for Stowmarket and returning 'direct' to Harwich with gun cotton on the 18th. She returned on the 21st and 29th of August to Stowmarket, returning on 28th August and 3rd September. Packard's *AVON*, from Harwich, passed through Ipswich on the 30th August and the 11th October with gunpowder returning on the 11th and 18th of October with gun cotton for Harwich. There is no record of a tug but as a dumb-barge she must have been towed. On 29th November and 24th December the sb *JAMES* of Rochester arrived in Ipswich Dock light to load guncotton from the New Explosives Company brought from Stowmarket in Packards' *AVON*.

In 1896 the ketch *SWIN* of Harwich, 58nrt and the last round bottomed sailing vessel to be built there in 1883, came in light from Southampton on 3rd March to load guncotton from the *AVON* in Buttermans Bay, sailing on the 7th. She survived to appear in 1915 registered at Aberdeen and owned in Stonehaven.

The New Explosives Company had good access to the railway at Ipswich and Stowmarket and used the river less and less for moving guncotton after the late nineteenth century.

An advertisement for the New Explosives Company of Stowmarket.

CHEMICALS & FERTILIZERS

Salt

Salt (sodium chloride) is widely used as a condiment and for preserving food such as meat and fish. It is an important raw material in many chemical industries, particularly in the manufacture of soda and of chlorine bleaching powder. Rock salt has long been used for cattle licks and as a preservative for imported hides.

For centuries, salt was obtained by the evaporation of seawater in saltpans situated along East Coast estuaries from southern Scotland to Essex. The residue was allowed to dry out as the tide receded, and subsequently gathered and boiled in lead or iron pans. Evidence has shown salt extraction took place on local coastal estuaries at Trimley, Snape, Iken and Blythburgh during the Roman occupation.

In medieval times, many of the animals were slaughtered in the autumn due to lack of feedstuff during the winter months. Vast quantities of salt were required for preserving the meat, which was salted or steeped in brine. Much of the salt at this time was imported from the west coast of France. The Salters' Company in London can trace its foundation back to 1394, the Company's saltmeters measuring out and distributing the imported salt landed at Queenhithe. Although salt is normally measured by the bushel, a 'wey' was sometimes specified, equivalent to 40 bushels.

During the eighteenth century, North and South Shields at the mouth of the Tyne became an important centre for salt production, using cheap local coal to evaporate the seawater in numerous saltpans. Salt-boiling also took place in Worcestershire at the brine springs at Droitwich that were mentioned in the Domesday Book, and in Cheshire. Although the extensive deposits of rock salt in Cheshire were known to the Romans, the deposits have only been mined from the seventeenth century. Later in Cheshire the mining was superseded by pumping water into boreholes in the salt deposits and returning the liquid to the surface as brine. The soap and soda industry developed there partly because of the availability of sodium chloride, leading to the birth of the giant Imperial Chemical Industries (ICI). Salt deposits also occur in Europe, for example at Weiliczka near Cracow, and Stassfurt in Germany. For centuries, salt has been exported from the seaport of Setubal in Portugal, and from Sicily.

In England, a small import duty on salt was imposed at the beginning of the fourteenth century, and a salt tax was introduced in 1694. This tax reached its highest level during the Napoleonic Wars but was reduced in stages and was finally abolished in 1825.

At Ipswich, the salt business was to be found close to the river. The Salt Office, standing not far from Wherry Lane, gives its name to Salthouse Street, which runs from Fore Street to the Common Quay. In 1814, onions, apples and Westphalia hams were advertised for sale by auction in 1814 at the Hull Wharf, Ipswich, 'near the Salt Office'.

In the early eighteenth century, salt cargoes were brought to Ipswich from the mouth of the Tyne, with rock salt coming from Nantwich in Cheshire. At Ipswich in 1830, two salt merchants are listed, Thomas Bradlaugh at the Quay and James Thorndike at the Common Quay. By 1846 William Harrington and John Christie were thus described in Salthouse Street, where Christie also ran a coal business. His warehouse still exists, the oldest to survive along the Dockside since conversion to offices in the 1990s. Frank Alexander Christie continued the family business and in 1886, he was advertising as a shipowner, cake merchant,

An advertisemen of 1821 advocating the use of salt for agricultural purposes. (Dr. J. Blatchly)

> THE PUBLIC ARE RESPECTFULLY INFORMED,
> THAT
> # SALT FOR MANURE
> MAY BE HAD OF
> ## C. & G. JOHNSON,
> At a WAREHOUSE situated on the Premises of Mr. B. B. CATT,
> St. Clement's, in Ipswich,
> At 2s. 6d. per Bushel of 56lbs.
> PAYMENT ON DELIVERY.
> Messrs. SMART & BUCHANAN, of Stowmarket, will receive any communication on the subject.
> Messrs. LONGMAN, HURST, REES, ORME, and BROWN, of London, have lately published AN ESSAY ON THE USES OF SALT FOR AGRICULTURAL PURPOSES, AND IN HORTICULTURE, by CUTHBERT WILLIAM JOHNSON: it may be had of Raw, Ipswich; Dingle, Bury; Loder, Woodbridge; Wilkin and Youngman, Norwich; Meggy, Yarmouth; and all other Booksellers.
> March 1, 1821.
> [KING, PRINTER, IPSWICH.]

coal and salt merchant at the same address. In addition in 1886, William Kerridge, of 7 Key Street, described himself as a baker and a salt merchant.

As the salt industry became more centralised, e.g. Saxa Salt of Middlewich in Cheshire (at the time of writing a part of the Rank Hovis McDougal Group), so salt merchants disappeared and food and other companies using salt in large quantities had whole cargoes for their own processing. British salt came from Runcorn in Cheshire, which in the latter part of the nineteenth century became a very busy port.

Shipping

As the artificial fertilizer industry quickly expanded during the second half of the nineteenth century, there was a demand by Fison, Packard and Prentice long before they merged for kainite salt (hydrous magnesium sulphate with potassium chloride) that came largely from the same areas in Europe that had sodium chloride deposits. Unfortunately, in the shipping registers it would appear that kainite salt is sometimes simply referred to as 'salt'. It is therefore impossible to distinguish between the two imports in some cases.

Amongst the arrivals of the 1880s was *INGRID*, 98nrt of New Quay, Cardigan, which came in November 1883 from Runcorn with salt for Christie. The following table shows the six arrivals for 1885.

Some parcels of Cheshire salt came by way of the Coast Lines' liner service from Liverpool during the early 1900s, while on 13th April 1909 the Ipswich ketch-barge *LEADING LIGHT* arrived ex-Middlesbrough with salt for F.A. Christie, returning north with old iron for Newcastle on the 29th. By the 1930s most of the English salt was being transported on the railway and virtually all the old merchants had gone with the exception of Mellonie & Goulder who stored salt for cattle.

*Ships arriving with salt in 1885. *Loaded at Great Yarmouth, possibly surplus salt at the end of the herring season.*

DATE	SHIP	NRT	POR	FROM	CUSTOMER	BUILT
15 Jan 1885	HEDLEY sb	69	Ipswich	Yarmouth*	F.A. Christie	
21 Feb	JOSEPHINE MAGARETHA K	39		Yarmouth*	F.A. Christie	Edam, Holland 1875
6 Mar	MARY MILLER Sr	122	Kirkaldy	Runcorn	F.A. Christie	Irvine 1871
20 Mar	MARY ASHBURNER Sr	95	Barrow	Runcorn	Cobbold & Co	Barrow 1877
10 Dec	INTREPID sb	56	Ipswich	Yarmouth*	E. Curtis	Ipswich 1881
27 Dec	JAMES & EMMA sb	-	London	Yarmouth*	Cobbold & Co	Northfleet 1846

CHEMICALS & FERTILIZERS

The mv CHEMICAL LAUSANNE arriving at Cliff Quay on 18th March 1983. She left for Flushing the following day. (R.W. Smith)

Unloading fertiliser from Antwerp from the mv WATERDALE on 12th May 1982. (R.W. Smith)

Ethyl alcohol

The distillation firm known as the Suffolk Chemical Company was established at Cliff Quay in 1927 and the following year was taken over by Reckitt & Sons of Hull. During December 1927 plates for tanks and pipes and other machinery were delivered to the site by rail and road and then on 20th and 21st January 1928 ninety-four tons of machinery parts were discharged from the coaster ss *JOLLY FRANK* of London, more machinery being brought in by rail the following month.

There were eventually four large storage tanks to hold the molasses which were expected to be imported from the West Indies, Cuba and Egypt and from beet sugar factories in England and Europe. In addition to the molasses arriving by ship hundreds of tons were delivered in lorries from the nearest beet sugar factories, and from the late 1930s some molasses arrived in railway tank-wagons.

The company's basic product was ethyl alcohol (ethanol), distilled from the molasses for use in artificial fibres, perfumery, polishes and lacquers. Some research was undertaken in the laboratory toward the development of 'Dettol' disinfectant. The dark brown liquid known as molasses is a by-product of sugar processing and is that part of the cane sugar or beet sugar that will not crystallize. Known to the trade as Blackstrap Molasses, it was warmed in water to which was added cultured yeast grown on the site. Fermentation of the molasses sugar content quickly started, and after some days of fermentation, followed by

The tanker ATHELFOAM *arrived from Everglades, Florida, with molasses on 25th January 1952 and sailed two days later for Alexandria.*

a process of distilling, ethyl alcohol was produced. Three varieties of denatured spirit (containing wood naphtha to make it undrinkable) were manufactured: industrial, pyridinised and mineralised, the latter being the familiar purple methylated spirit consisting of ethyl alcohol to which was added wood naphtha (also known as wood spirit or methanol), along with a dye.

For many years the high duty on spirits had interfered with the development of many industrial processes. The remedy of adding wood spirit was supplied by Mr J. Wood, chairman of the Board of the Inland Revenue, and the measure was in place by the 1870s. A mixture of this kind is rendered permanently unfit for human consumption; at the same time, the spirit is not impaired for the many industrial uses for which it is intended and can be sold duty free. H.M. Customs and Excise officers monitored every process, and subsequent storage, to ensure that no spirit was used for unapproved purposes, for which task they maintained their own office, known as Ipswich 7, in continuous occupation at the works. Each process of fermentation and distillation was numbered, recorded and known as a period, normally lasting about one week.

The ocean-going tankers that served the company were with few exceptions owned by Tankers Limited and the Athel Line. Both were subsidiaries of the United Molasses Company Ltd and between them they owned no fewer than thirty-four ships in 1936. The parent company, United Molasses, which acquired Tankers Ltd in 1941 and Anchor Line in 1949, was itself created on 1st January 1926 as a holding company by The Pure Cane Company Ltd and British Molasses Ltd, plus another nineteen subsidiaries worldwide. The company was taken over by Tate & Lyle in April 1965.

The Pure Cane Company purchased its first ship in 1922, a Canadian 'Laker' built at Duluth on the US side of Lake Superior, and the company sought to give it and the ensuing fleet an identity with the prefix 'Athel' and associated houseflag. 'Athel' was an Anglo-Saxon word for 'noble' and the name of the managing director's house was 'Athelstane'.

The first part-cargo for the Suffolk Chemical Company arrived on 25th April 1928 in the Norwegian steamship *MARNA* from Vlaardingen. The vessel sailed three days later for Zeebrugge, loaded with molasses. She came again on 1st May loaded from Zeebrugge, sailing on the 4th once more with molasses, both outward cargoes for The Pure Cane Co. Ltd. On 26th May the ss *CASTANA* of New York brought the first molasses from Puerto Padre in Cuba. She had been built in 1920 by the American International S.B. Corporation of Hog Island, Pennsylvania.

The first Athel Line ship, the ss *ATHELSTANE* with a deadweight tonnage of nearly 800 tons, berthed with molasses from Hull on 30th January 1929, sailing on 2nd February for Liverpool with molasses. She made another four visits up to 11th June and returned twice in July 1930 with 780 tons each trip. The ss *ATHELFOAM* delivered 2,902 tons of molasses from the West Indies on 9th September 1929, sailing light three days later for Amsterdam. The year 1931 saw the arrival of ss *ATHELTARN*, completed in September 1929 by Cammell Laird at Birkenhead, which became the most familiar Athel Line tanker at Ipswich on coastal and continental work. She was sold in 1952 to F.T. Everard & Sons Ltd, who renamed her *ACCLIVITY*, replacing their first ship of that name which had sunk five miles off the Northumbrian coast in January 1952.

The first *ACCLIVITY* had been a frequent molasses trader to Suffolk Chemicals. Other Everard vessels were also engaged in the trade to Ipswich, *AUDACITY* and *ASPERITY* each bringing a cargo from Hull in 1932 and the mv *PROWESS* delivering five 250-ton cargoes from Kings Lynn. Built in 1926,

The ss ATHELTARN on the Manchester Ship Canal.

the *PROWESS* was not broken up until 1962. *ATHELTARN* meanwhile delivered four cargoes from the Thames and one from Landskrona in southern Sweden, and then the following year delivered one from Stege in Denmark.

Two other Everard ships, *TARTARY* and *SAUNTER*, were also employed in the trade. The steamer *TARTARY* had been built at Yarmouth in 1923 for the London oil company of Burt, Boulton but was purchased by Everards in 1929; she was lost off Winterton in February 1938, her crew being rescued by the Gorleston volunteer lifeboat *ELIZABETH SIMPSON*. The *SAUNTER*, built on the Tyne in 1915 as X106, one of the First World War motor lighters, made two trips from Lynn in 1933; she was eventually broken up in 1970.

A stready trade developed during the 1930s, exemplified in 1936 when the *ATHELTARN* completed nine voyages with molasses from the East Coast and the continent and the *ACCLIVITY* brought twenty-one in all from the Kings Lynn and Cantley sugar factories, the latter situated on the River Yare between Great Yarmouth and Norwich.

The original *ATHELFOAM* was replaced by a motor vessel of that name built at Birkenhead in 1930 which brought Egyptian molasses from Alexandria on 4th March 1937. A new *ATHELSTANE* arrived on 12th October 1937 and the *ATHELBEACH*, launched by Cammell Laird at Birkenhead in 1931, brought two part-cargoes of molasses from Cuba in 1938. Among the other ships bringing molasses to Ipswich was the ss *GLOXINIA*, owned by the Stag Line of North Shields; she had been completed as a dry cargo vessel of the conventional three-island type at Shields in 1921 but converted straight away to a tanker.

During the Second World War sources of molasses to the Suffolk Chemical Company included the Thames until June 1940, and then, due to increasing problems, the emphasis moved to Norfolk and the sugar beet factories at Cantley and Kings Lynn. *ASPERITY* brought six cargoes from the Thames, *AUDACITY* and *APTITY* one each and *ACCLIVITY* seventeen, making twenty-five in all between October 1939 and June 1940.

The trade is partly seasonal, so when a particular beet season's crop has been processed the amount of molasses produced is finite and the ships move on once the molasses tanks have been emptied. From August 1941 until 15th December *ACCLIVITY* loaded six cargoes at Cantley, totalling 2,675 tons. This appears to be all there was in that year, bearing in mind the distillery was closed briefly at some stage early in the war by the Ministry of Supply, but the Ministry allowed production to resume after a distillery elsewhere had been bombed. In the meantime a naval base had been established at Cliff Quay and some of the Chemical Company buildings were occupied by naval personnel. When the plant was allowed to re-open office accommodation had to be rented in High Street.

In 1942 ten cargoes totalling 6,108 tons were discharged and another 12,728 tons were delivered by road and rail. The *ACCLIVITY* worked out of Kings Lynn from May 1944 to October 1945, loading twenty-one times for Ipswich, and six cargoes were carried by *APTITY*. A further seventeen cargoes were brought by the new MOWT coastal tankers including the *EMPIRE DWELLER* (7), *EMPIRE AUDREY* (3), *EMPIRE HARVEST* (5), *EMPIRE TEGUDA* and *EMPIRE ANGLESEY* (1 each). Launched at Greenock for the MOWT, the *EMPIRE DWELLER* was managed by Everards. She was acquired by the company in 1946 and renamed *ASPERITY*, taking the name of a steamer torpedoed by an E-boat off the Norfolk coast in November 1941. Some 25,880 tons of molasses also arrived by road and rail during 1944.

Before the Second World War the industrial spirit was normally sent to Reckitts at Hull in 54-gallon barrels loaded aboard the steamships *PHAECIAN*

The Suffolk Chemical Company works on Cliff Quay.

or *MISTLEY* belonging to F.W. Horlock of Mistley, which ran a regular service from Ipswich to north-east coast ports. After the war, the spirit was sent by a smartly liveried 3,000-gallon bulk road tanker on contract hire from the Crow Carrying Company (motto 'As the Crow Flies'). The vehicle continued on to the ICI plant at Middlesbrough to load methanol, a substitute for wood naphtha as a denaturant.

Kings Lynn still supplied most of the molasses in 1946-47, thirty-two cargoes arriving in 1946, twenty-five in 1947 and twenty in 1948. The mv *SCOTTISH HEATHER*, built in 1928 and belonging to subsidiary company Tankers Ltd, arrived on 16th April 1948 from Cuba via Dagenham, sailing on the 21st for Cuba. *ATHELTARN* brought five cargoes from Lynn during July and August 1949 and the *SCOTTISH MUSICIAN* arrived in April and October of that year, reappearing in January and August 1950 from Cuba and San Domingo, now Santo Domingo, the capital and principal port of the Dominican Republic. On 11th May the *SCOTTISH HEATHER* berthed from Cuba via Dagenham, and *ATHELTARN* arrived twice in June from the Danish ports of Stege and Nakskov.

The new mv *ATHELBEACH*, completed at Hawthorn, Leslies' Tyneside yard in August 1950, appeared at Cliff Quay from the Caribbean on 28th October and again on 24th December from Port Everglades via Avonmouth, sailing straight back to Florida on the 29th. She could load 10,350 tons. Port Everglades in Florida had previously been only a harbour of refuge during the hurricane season, but it was judged to be first choice as the nearest convenient port to Cuba for small vessels bringing molasses for the ocean tankers, which by 1950 were getting too large for the smaller Cuban ports. Storage was initially provided for 200,000 tons of molasses, and it soon became a thriving port.

The *SCOTTISH MUSICIAN* arrived from Port Everglades on 3rd February 1951 and sailed to Georgetown on the 6th. *ATHELBEACH* came in on 11th March ex-San Domingo via Hull and again on 18th June from Cuba, and the *ATHELCREST* berthed on 4th August from Cuba and again on 4th November. *ATHELTARN* brought five cargoes of oil in November for Shell-Mex & BP Ltd from the Isle of Grain. The remaining seven United Molasses ships were by that time under the management of Tankers Ltd.

Another new *ATHELFOAM* arrived on 25th January 1952 from Alexandria via Dagenham, and *ATHELBEACH* berthed on 16th June from Cuba via Dagenham, as did *ATHELCREST* on 13th November. In 1953, *ATHELFOAM* arrived three times and *ATHELBEACH* came twice. In February and May 1954 *ATHELCREST* berthed from Port Everglades, and in 1955 *ATHELBEACH* returned on 7th May and 2nd September. Yet another new vessel, the *ATHELMERE*, launched in October 1954, arrived from Cuba via Dagenham. *ATHELFOAM* berthed on 2nd February 1956, sailing light to Bremen on the 6th. Interestingly, she came again on 21st September 1957 with a part cargo of whale oil for storage at Cory Brothers. There had been around half a dozen coastal shipments in 1955 and '56, but there were only three (from Rouen) during February 1957 in the mv *AMITY*, which had been built as *EMPIRE TEDMUIR* in 1946 for the MOT.

These cargoes probably marked the end of the Suffolk Chemical Company Ltd. Various economic factors and the political situation in Cuba at the time contributed to the closure of the Cliff Quay distillery about 1957. The last rent for the land and wayleave for the pipeline was paid on 24th June 1958. The premises were then used by Cory Brothers for oil storage and the site was taken over by the Ipswich Grain Terminal in 1983.

Calcium carbide

During the first quarter of the twentieth century calcium carbide was much in demand for producing the acetylene gas used for bicycle and motor vehicle lights. The action of water dripping from a reservoir on to the carbide contained within the lamp produced a gas that burned with a brilliant light. Carbide was easily and cheaply obtainable from motor dealers and cycle shops in cardboard canisters until the 1940s, by which time electrical batteries or bicycle dynamos were widely available.

The Carbide Trading Company is the first name noted as importers of carbide at Ipswich in the early years. By the 1920s, it was superseded by the Acetylene Corporation of Great Britain Ltd of 49 Victoria Street, Westminster. The company did not apparently have a warehouse of their own at Ipswich but rented land and part of the Public Warehouse at the Dock for a rent of £80 per annum. The handling and dispatch of carbide in drums was by I.D.C. employees. Arrivals and departures were sparse, ranging from none to two or three ships or barges a year. The trade ended by 30 August 1927, when entries for use of the Public Warehouse ceased.

One of the first vessels to discharge was the Fowey-registered schooner *LITTLE MYSTERY*, of 95nrt. She was launched in 1887 at Kingsbridge in Devon, and was one of hundreds of West Country schooners of that time built to trade from Europe and the Mediterranean to America with crews of only four or five. *LITTLE MYSTERY*'s voyages were typical of most of her sisters. She took cargo, possibly slates, to the Mediterranean and then loaded salt at Trapani in Sicily for Newfoundland, returning home with fish. Her voyage to the Mediterranean in 1914 brought her to Ipswich on 20th February with carbide from Civita Vecchia on Italy's eastern coast. She sailed light for London seven days later. *LITTLE MYSTERY*'s career ended abruptly after thirty years when she was captured by a German submarine on 30 April 1917, twenty-five miles S.S.E. of Portland Bill, and sunk by explosives, fortunately without loss of life.

CHEMICALS & FERTILIZERS

The sb *SQUAWK* of Rochester delivered carbide from Queenborough on 11th July 1917 and the mv *CARGO SHIPPER,* 273nrt of London, arrived in February 1921 with eighty tons from Sundsvall, on the eastern coast of Sweden in the Gulf of Bothnia. The ss *SIVA* berthed in November 1922 with 100 tons. In 1923, the barges *GODWIT* and *EAST ANGLIA* arrived in June and October respectively from London. *GODWIT* delivered fifty-seven tons, and *EAST ANGLIA* had 100 tons contained in 2,000 drums, each of one hundredweight. On 27th February 1924, sb *GLEANER* brought seventy tons in 1,400 drums. *GLEANER*'s cargo accounts were rendered to the Acetylene Corporation for the hire of three horses and carts for one day, each at fifteen shillings a day, totalling £2 5s. There appears to have been only sb *SQUAWK* with fifty tons arriving in 1925, another fifty tons coming in February 1926 aboard the ss *ST TUDWAL*, registered and owned at Cardigan by the Bristol & Cardigan Trading Company Ltd. She was built in 1895 at Wallsend.

The accounts reveal that, for a charge of two shillings, the IDC regularly delivered single drums to inns and public houses, such as the Running Buck and the Rose, for the carriers to deliver to outlying villages. The most frequently mentioned carrier was Mr Ernest List of Debenham, who operated from the Running Buck. IDC employees also delivered, possibly by handcart, single drums to local cycle shops, including Doddington & Son at 63 Foxhall Road. A charge was made for the usual opening and subsequent repairs to drums after all Customs inspections.

Another company handling carbide was Allen & Liversidge Ltd, of Victoria Station House, Westminster SW1. It would seem that they only traded at Ipswich for a year or two in the mid-1920s. They rented a part of the Public Warehouse in 1925 when two barges delivered drums of carbide. The sb *MADCAP*, one of E.J. & W. Goldsmiths' craft that was launched at Teynham in 1897, arrived on 17th June with 104 tons of carbide. This necessitated the hire of horses and carts for transferring the drums from ship to warehouse at a cost of £3 10s. 5d. Repairs were made to some of the drums in July, prior to delivery locally. On 8 December, sb *EAST ANGLIA* arrived with 70 tons of carbide for which the total charges, including import rates, wharfage and redelivery, came to £49 7s. 9d. Spritsail rigged, the *EAST ANGLIA* was Rochester built and registered in 1908 for the London & Rochester Barge Co. Ltd, later to be known as the London & Rochester Trading Co. Ltd.

Part of a page from an IDC day book showing charges relating storage and delivery of carbide.

A 'lash' (lighter aboard ship) lighter loaded with plywood being pushed up the Orwell after floating out of a 'lash' ship berthed at Felixstowe. The vessel operated a regular service to and from New Orleans, from where the lighters were pushed up the Mississippi River to the heart of the USA. (R.W. Smith)

The German schooner AAR unloading timber in Ipswich Dock. (R.W. Smith)

The timber trade   7

Three main types of timber satisfy the demands of the timber industry. Softwoods are obtained from the coniferous forests that extend across the Arctic and sub-Arctic zone of the northern hemisphere, parts of East Africa, the south-eastern United States and Central America. Growing in the north and merging with the softwoods are the temperate hardwoods, also obtained from Chile and Australasia. The rain forests of South America, Africa and South East Asia provide most of the tropical hardwood imports.

Nowadays, timber shipments to the Port of Ipswich are recorded in cubic metres and tonnes. Before the change to the metric system, the timber measure commonly used in this country was the load. This was equal to 50 cu. ft of squared timber, 40 cu. ft of unhewn timber or 600 sq. ft of 1inch planking. The term goes back to medieval times when it represented the amount of wood that could be loaded on to a one-horse cart or wagon.

Various terms exist for different types of sawn timber. A board is usually a long piece of timber, one inch or one-and-a-quarter inches in thickness. Planks are thicker than boards and battens are less than six inches in width. Deals are cut from fir, pine or similar softwood. Laths are very thin strips of wood. Robert Fulcher, a local timber merchant of St Peter's parish in Ipswich, used these terms and measurements in his inventory produced for the Government's Defence of the Realm Act in 1803 when the threat of Napoleonic invasion was at its height. Fulcher listed amongst his stock, 800 battens, 1,400 deals, 400 half deals, 150 loads of timber and 300 bundles of laths.

The English timber trade developed slowly from the middle of the twelfth century as the feudal system gradually declined and wooden-framed domestic and secular buildings appeared. By the middle of the thirteenth century, the Hanseatic League was exchanging Baltic timber for English cloth and it was recorded as long ago as 1273 that John the Carpenter went to Hamburg to buy timber to be shipped to Yarmouth for use in the building of Norwich Cathedral.

The demand for hardwood, especially English oak and elm, was sustainable until the sixteenth century when the rapid expansion of the Navy and to a lesser extent of the merchant service caused English supplies to dwindle. By the time Harwich had become a naval dockyard the forests in Essex were already depleted and private woods in Suffolk were scoured for suitable trees. Bordeshawe Wood at Boss Hall, Ipswich, near to Sproughton Road and the River Gipping, was cut down by the early sixteenth century, and documents a hundred years later describe the twenty acres of nearby Stokehall Wood as long since stubbed up, probably to make the land available for agriculture.

The succession of early French, Spanish and Dutch wars did not allow time for new plantations to mature in time to provide timber for shipbuilding. The shipbuilding industry therefore began to depend heavily upon the forests of Scandinavia and the plains of Russia and northern Germany for its materials. From Norway and the Baltic ports came the fir and spruce needed for boards, spars and masts, and the Baltic oak required for ships' frames. One timber import used by the shipbuilding industry was known as Danzig oak; although English oak was always considered superior, especially 'twixt wind and water', many ships were constructed of Danzig oak below the waterline. From the mid-eighteenth century imported oaks reached this country not only from the great forests beyond the ports of Danzig, Riga and Memel but also from the ancient woods of the Austro-Hungarian Empire through the port of Venice.

Compared with the Baltic and Russian ports, which were accessible during only that part of the year when the Baltic was free of ice, Norway was better placed geographically for trading purposes, owing to the Gulf Stream keeping her ports relatively ice-free. The forests reached down to the waterside and the wood could be loaded directly on to ships either in the fjords or on coasts sheltered by islands from the open sea. It was then a short passage to the English East Coast. Until the close of the eighteenth century Norway was by far the greatest supplier of timber to Britain. Among the principal Norwegian timber ports were Dram, Krageroe, Langesund and Porsgrund. After the Napoleonic Wars Sweden became the main source.

A major drawback to the development of sawmills in Sweden was that timber was required for iron smelting in those parts of the country rich in iron ore, and sawmills could not legally exist in protected areas where the iron mines were worked. Much of the hand-sawn timber cut in remote parts had to be rafted down rivers, causing discolouring of the timber; English merchants refused discoloured timber because customers would accept only 'bright' timber, which had been sawn at the port and loaded directly on board ship. Water-driven sawmills were swiftly erected as regulations were relaxed, and by the 1860s

A steamer in the Dock discharging timber for F.A. Christie & Son. In the foreground the timber is being made up into rafts.

steam sawmills were being introduced, resulting in a huge expansion of trade. English merchants began buying whole forests, together with the sawmills, and this flourishing trade continued until the early twentieth century when Russian timber from previously unexploited forests became available. Smaller trees were still plentiful, for which the developing pulp industry created a ready market within Sweden.

Poland was originally covered by spruce, pine, oak and beech forests whose exploitation required regulation as early as the mid-fourteenth century to protect Crown and other woodlands. Traders floated vast numbers of trees down the rivers to Danzig, Riga and Memel, where the timber was received and shipment arranged by merchants of the Hanseatic League.

Russian forests had remained largely undeveloped at a time when Scandinavian woods were already under threat from over-production. Hanseatic merchants were active in the thirteenth century at Novgorod, an independent trading republic, 100 miles south-east of St. Petersburg, and timber, furs and hides were exchanged for western goods through the Baltic ports. English companies had become by far the greatest concessionaires in the White Sea region. Rafts of timber travelled 1,000 miles northwards down the northern River Dvina to Onega.

The outbreak of the Napoleonic Wars led to the supply of Baltic timber to this country being restricted for several years. Timber merchants were therefore encouraged by the Government to turn to the North American colonies for their supplies. The problem of obtaining sufficient timber is illustrated by the fact that building a ship of the line required the felling of between two and four thousand oak trees. When Jabez Bayley built the 1,335-ton East Indiaman *ORWELL* in 1817 at his Halifax yard, 2,000 loads of oak timber (reported to be chiefly of Suffolk growth), 100 tons of wrought iron and 30 tons of copper were used in her construction. At the time, the building of the ship was regarded as being of local public benefit because of the construction giving employment, directly or indirectly, to several hundreds of people who could otherwise have become a burden on their parishes.

In America the drive for timber had spread south and west from New England to West Virginia, South Carolina, Georgia and Florida by the early 1700s. Just over a hundred years later millions of acres of forest became available due to the construction of the railroads, including short lines connecting the forests with coast or the great rivers like the Mississippi and Ohio. Eventually the trade increased dramatically on the West Coast, especially in the wake of the 1849 California Gold Rush and the end of the Civil War. News of the vast forests reached the lumbermen on the East Coast and plant and workers were loaded on ships bound round Cape Horn to California and Oregon, and businesses were set up along the Columbia River and Puget Sound.

In Canada, the forests bordering the St. Lawrence River were being cut down in the seventeenth and eighteenth centuries to satisfy the demand of the Royal Dockyards. Shipbuilding in New Brunswick and Nova Scotia became a vast industry; many of the new ships were loaded with wood for their maiden voyage, both timber and ship being sold together in Britain. Gradually Quebec and Montreal were developed as financial centres and merchants imported machinery, tools, textiles and other goods and exported much of the timber from the region.

Following the Fraser River Gold Rush of 1858 several small sawmills were built to provide sawn timber for the miners, and the first large mill was erected at Port Alberni by a London firm in 1861. Another at Chemainous started work

Owned at Hamburg, the ss REHHORST, 739nrt, brought timber for William Brown. Built in 1930 at Stavanger, she was ex-LILLGUNVOR (1951), ex-VARDIK (1935). (R..W. Smith)

in 1862, and both survived into modern times, sending timber to Ipswich until the 1950s. As in the United States, the coming of the railroads hastened the development of the West Coast lumber industry. Direct shipments to Europe were given a tremendous boost by the opening of the Panama Canal in 1914. Earlier, wood from Oregon had arrived at Ipswich from San Francisco as part-cargo on the square-rigged grain ships sailing via the Horn.

In England, the Industrial Revolution and a massive population increase during the nineteenth century necessitated a tremendous rise in house building and so the importation of timber increased. For the Port of Ipswich, timber formed a considerable part of the trade with merchants establishing themselves within the dock area, serving the local builders and becoming familiar names for many years.

As early as 1814 the *Ipswich Journal* was announcing the auction of 300 spruce firs at Ralfe Staton's timber wharf situated next to Jabez Bayley's shipyard on the river bank at Halifax, near Wherstead Road. Lots consisting of ten trees were on offer without reserve. The firs, averaging seven to nine inches in diameter at the butts or thicker ends, ranged from twenty to twenty-two feet in length. Staton and his landlord, William Ashmore, were in trouble that same year when Ipswich Corporation tried to recover possession of part of the ooze, as far as the high water mark, adjoining the ground occupied by Staton and used for the storage of his timber. The Corporation maintained that the defendants were using more land than was originally conveyed to them. Timber floating in the timber ponds situated on the foreshore next to Stoke Bathing Place, with the Griffin Wharf railway running alongside, would later become a familiar sight when in use by William Brown's and other timber merchants for the storage and seasoning of their timber.

William Brown & Company (Ipswich) Ltd was founded in 1799, and fifteen years later a map drawn by John Bransby shows the firm occupying a timber wharf next to the shipyard at Halifax, close to Ralfe Staton's premises.

Born in 1778 in Norfolk, William Brown practised as an architect and surveyor in Ipswich in addition to running his timber business. Curiously, another timber merchant of that time, Benjamin Catt of St. Clement's, was also

THE TIMBER TRADE

an architect and surveyor, later being listed as a coal merchant. When a competition was held in Ipswich to design the new Public Provision Market at the top of Silent Street the two best plans put forward were those of William Brown and Benjamin Catt. The designs were so similar that the prize money for the first and second places was shared between the two men, as was the responsibility for the market's construction.

William Brown's company was well established by 1830, with a yard in St. Nicholas Street. They later had premises in Friars and Greyfriars Roads (extending to Commercial Road), and Key Street and at the Dock, served there by Tovells Wharf and Timber Quay. In 1929, a large site on Handford Road was purchased and a joinery plant erected there for the manufacture of windows, doors and staircases, etc. Kiln drying and creosoting under pressure were also undertaken, and hardwood flooring was a speciality.

During the 1930s, in addition to home-grown timbers, the company was advertising British Columbian pine and all Empire woods for sale, with direct importation to Ipswich Dock, The company imported sawn wood from the larger Baltic ports such as Gefle, Soderhamn, Sundsvall and all the major ports right up to the Haparanda coast. Other imports came from Finland, the chief ports being Kem, Rafso, Abo and several others down into the Gulf of Finland such as Trangsund and Kotka. Considerable quantities from Russian sawmills were shipped at Leningrad, and occasionally from other ports on the Estonian, Lithuanian and Latvian coasts. Large cargoes also came from the White Sea ports of Archangel, Mesane, Onega, Kovda and Karet. A few years before the 1939-1945 War an important sawmill development in Western Siberia was

The ss BARON BERWICK of Ardrossan, 2,380nrt, berthed on 22nd February 1961 with timber from Vancouver for William Brown. She is seen here on 16th March sailing light for Ardrossan.

begun by the Russian Government, and large cargoes of the very highest quality European red fir were imported from Igarka and other ports situated on the Yenesei and Obi rivers. Cargoes, some as large as 5,500 tons, were directly imported to Ipswich from Vancouver in British Columbia and other ports on the Western Pacific coast. William Brown also obtained some timber from the great ports in the Gulf of St. Lawrence. Hardwoods were imported via London from such places as New York, India, Japan, Malaya and Siam.

The company was trading widely by the 1930s from London to the industrial Midlands and had taken over the timber interests of such old-established firms as Palfreman Foster & Co., George Mason and F.A. Christie (Christies were coal, salt and timber merchants with premises in Salthouse Street which were converted to a restaurant and offices in the 1990s, having been empty following their disposal in 1980). In recent times, the company also expanded as general builders' merchants.

In 1969 William Brown was acquired by countrywide timber merchants Montague L. Meyer (M.L.M.) and, combined with most other timber companies in Eastern England, came under the Jewson name in 1983 following a merger between M.L.M. and International Timber. Jewson & Sons' previous interests were in Norfolk, where they had started at Norwich in 1836, later occupying a long riverside wharf for imported wood in Southtown Road, Great Yarmouth. At the end of 1999 it was announced that Jewsons' administration centre in Norfolk was to be closed and the administration moved to Coventry and Huddersfield, following Meyer International's purchase of the Graham builders' merchants chain. The old William Brown premises in Greyfriars Road had already been demolished two years earlier in 1997 to make way for a new Virgin Multiplex cinema, but the Jewson and Graham companies still exist in the town.

The firm of Thomas Gabriel & Sons of London, founded in 1770, was later amalgamated with other timber companies to be known as Gabriel, Wade & English Ltd. They opened a depot at Suffolk Road, Ipswich, in 1919 and were one of the first tenants to occupy premises on Cliff Quay. Here they used up-to-date methods of handling timber in their electric sawmills and in their storage yards that had direct access to the railway at Cliff Quay. When the German steamer *JOHANNES C. RUSS* arrived at Cliff Quay on 24th July 1925 with timber from Kotka, hers was the first commercial cargo to be discharged at the new tidal quay.

Just prior to the Second World War, 80% of Gabriel's timber imports was of redwood, most of it originating from Finland with a smaller quantity coming from Poland, Russia and Sweden. A further 12% consisted of Douglas fir from British Columbia with the remaining 8% made up of cedar, wooden sleepers and western hemlock, again from Canada, and poles and whitewood from Norway. By 1946 the largest vessel importing timber dealt with by the company was the mv *ALIOTH* of 4,929nrt.

The company was acquired by Montague L. Meyer in 1969 and eventually absorbed by Jewsons in 1981-82.

Wrinch's of Ipswich was established in the 1850s close to Ipswich town centre by Alfred Wrinch. Following a fire in 1928, the business moved to St. Lawrence Works in Nacton Road, and by the 1930s was advertising itself as a pioneer of, and leader in, the garden furniture industry. Its customers were urged to choose teak for their garden, it being 'distinctive and elegant and requiring no upkeep'. Hose reels and wheelbarrows were sold, in addition to ladders, tables, ironing boards, plate racks, bed rests, lockers and cupboards for the home. The company survived until near the end of the twentieth century.

The timber shipping trade

The 1880s were times of change. Steamships began to make inroads into the timber trade, hitherto the province of sailing ships, many of which were seeing out their last years in the Baltic trade. The Danish *INGER MARGRETHE* of Skive brought firewood from Risor, Norway, on 26th April 1884 for the Ipswich Board of Guardians' Union Workhouse, demolished in 1899 to make way for Paul's Felaw Street maltings. The Norwegian *IRIS* of Tonsberg brought a similar cargo from Sundsvall, Sweden, in July 1889.

By this time, the engineering firm of Ransomes, Sims & Jefferies was consuming enormous quantities of wood that was delivered to Orwell Works by rail and sea. The Norwegian barque *AXEL* of Drammen arrived on 3rd August 1883, for example, with timber from Quebec for the firm. For about 110 years, until 1955, the sawmill at Ransomes' Orwell Works prepared the imported timber, mostly for the manufacture of threshing machines.

Between May and October 1885, when the Baltic Sea was free of ice, thirty

Imports of timber for 1885.

COMPANY	SHIP	PORT OF REGISTRY	PORT OF DEPARTURE
Wm. Brown	raft		Harwich
	ALPHA	Drammen (Norway)	Drammen (Norway)
	MATHILDA	Holosund ?	Fredrikshaven ?
	SRALEN	Wasa	Stockholm (Sweden)
	AUGUST	Woldact ?	Herdikswell ?
	sb CHAMPION		London
	sb CURLY BOY	Rochester	London
	SIRIUS	Fiskebak ?	Myhamn (Murmansk)
E.R. & F. Turner	four rafts		Harwich
Ransomes & Rapier	two rafts		Harwich
	sb NOVATOR	Harwich	London
	sb ADA		Poole
	ARIADNE	Gothenburg (Sweden)	Gothenburg (Sweden)
	GUSTAF ADOLF	Gothenburg (Sweden)	Gothenburg (Sweden)
Ransomes, Sims & Jefferies	STAFFORDSHIRE	Grimsby	Hull
	ss MADGE	Kings Lynn	Hull
G. Mason	HERBERTUS	Papenberg	Gothenburg (Sweden)
	THULE	Carlsholme	Soderham (Sweden)
	PROGRESS	Harsund	Cronstadt (Russia)
	sb ALINE	Harwich	London
	sb AUGUSTA MARY	Ipswich	London
	RATU	Tonsberg (Norway)	Soderham (Sweden)
	HIPPOLYTE	Middlesbrough	Fredrikstadt (Norway)
	VING ?	Arendal	Mobile (Alabama USA)
A. Long	raft		Harwich
	MARTIN	Okershamn ?	Pitea (Sweden)
	CAROLINA	Helsingor (Denmark)	Skelleftea (Sweden)
	ELIZABETH	Hoganus	Umea (Swe)
	sb NOVATOR	Harwich	London
W. Hewitt	MAUS ?	Helsingborg	Halstadt
	ARIEL	Rostock (NE Germany)	?
	NOVA SCOTIA	Fredrikstadt (Norway)	Soderham (Sweden)
	MOBIL	Stralsund (Germany)	Sundsval (Sweden)
O. Gibbons	GUSTAV	Uddevalla (Sweden)	Stockholm (Sweden)
	MARGETH	Fredrikstadt (Norway)	Fredrikstadt (Norway)
	BEINAT ?	Gefle (Sweden)	Gefle (Sweden)
Dawson	JOHN WRAY	Yarmouth	Hull

cargoes of sawn wood and baulks arrived at Ipswich directly from Baltic ports or via London or Harwich. The ships averaged 200 net registered tons, were barque, brig or brigantine rigged, and all but one were Scandinavian owned, often at small ports that are no longer listed. Some, including the one British ship *HIPPOLYTE*, registered at Middlesbrough, were built in the 1860s and '70s on Prince Edward Island, one of Canada's Maritime Provinces. However, the first arrival of 1885, on 24th April, had loaded timber for George Mason at Mobile, Alabama, a port approached from the sea by a channel thirty-two miles long and at the end of the Mobile and Ohio Railroad.

At that time ships with cargoes of grain and probably timber often discharged in Harwich Harbour to avoid the dock dues at Ipswich. The grain was lightered up to Ipswich in sailing barges, and many rafts of timber are recorded arriving at Ipswich from Harwich as the accompanying table for 1885 shows. An interesting arrival listed was the ss *MADGE* of Kings Lynn, a wooden screw steamer of length 87ft, beam 17.4ft, built at Blyth in 1884 for W.R. Smith, of Kings Lynn. The ss *FORTUNA*, built in 1880 and owned at Flensburg, Germany, is noted as the first 'proper' steamship, i.e. a steamer without auxiliary sails, to discharge timber at Ipswich; she arrived on 23rd September 1886 from Abo in Finland, then a part of Russia.

The trade continued steadily over the next three decades, steam having ousted most of the larger sailing ships by 1914. On 1st January that year the three-masted iron barque *AXEL* arrived from St. Petersburg with wood for Christies. She had been built at Glasgow in 1876 for J. Boumphrey & Co. of Liverpool,

The Swedish mv VARMLAND *passing through the lock on 9th August 1981 on her way to Sweden with a cargo of forest thinnings exported from Suffolk woodlands. They will probably return in due course in the form of paper.*
(R.W. Smith)

who owned her for some ten years before selling her to Nicholson & McGill, also of Liverpool, who renamed her *LOCHINVAR*. She was later sold by them to Swedish owners before becoming Aland-owned and registered at Mariehamn, when she received the name *AXEL* under which she arrived in Ipswich. She was one of the oldest vessels to survive the First World War.

Ships still brought some timber from Baltic ports, including Sundsvall (Sweden), Rafso (Russia/Finland), and Hommelvik (Norway), during the war, especially following the Battle of Jutland on 31st May 1916, after which fewer German ships were at large. Some of the grain ships, both steam and sail,

Timber imports for 1903.

COMPANY	SHIP	PORT OF REGISTRY	PORT OF DEPARTURE
Wm. Brown	*FORTUNA*	Arrensburg	Atta
	TRIO	Arendal	Hedikarall
	FINLAND	Arendal	Pensacola (USA)
	CHRISTIANIA	Quebec (Canada)	
	ss *RHEINLAND*	Brake	Archangel (Russia)
	ODIN	Fredrikstad (Norway)	Borga (Russia)
	raft 88 logs		Harwich
	+13 sailing barges		London
G. Mason	*NORNEN*	Fredrikstad (Norway)	Fredrikstad (Norway)
	ss *WILLIE*	Motala (Sweden)	Motala x 2 (Sweden)
	ELLIE	Korpo?	Abo (Finland)
	FO ANDERSEN	Copenhagen (Denmark)	Kemi (Finland)
	NAUTILUS	Uddavalla (Sweden)	Kotka (Finland)
	+ 1 sailing barge		London
F. Christie	*NYBORG*	Tonsberg (Norway)	Fredrikhold ?
	NYBORG	Tonsberg (Norway)	Wiborg (Russia)
	SKOVLAND	Sandefjord	Tom--?
	THORNHILL	Sunderland	Mobile (Alabama, USA)
	EVILENA	Aland (Finland)	Skelleftea (Sweden)
	ILAS	Mariehamn (Finland)	Rafso (Finland)
	HENRIK	Slite (Sweden)	Hernosand (Sweden)
	AUGUST	Denso ?	Umea (Sweden)
	+ 1 sailing barge		London
W. Hewitt	*EHRGLIS*	Riga	Norkopping
	GUSTAV	Fiskesgill ?	Gothenburg
Palfreman	*WILHEMINE*	Fredrikstad	Fredrikstad
	ss *PETERBOURG*	Archangel	Archangel
	ss *JARL*	Stavanger	Helsingfors
	THEKLA	Marstal	Rafso
	+ 3 sailing barges		London
Ransomes, Sims & Jefferies	*DANA*	Marstal	St John NB
	FLID	Sandefjord	Cronstadt
	WITUS	Aland	Cronstadt
	SVANEN	Aalborg	Cronstadt
	ss *RENOWN*		Hull
	GILLS		Hull
	FERN		Hull
	raft 138 logs		Harwich
	+ 21 sailing barges		London
Ransomes & Rapier	raft 24 logs		Harwich
	+ 3 sailing barges		London
A. Coe	raft 27 logs		Harwich
R. Girling	raft 61 logs	Harwich	
E. Gibb	3 sailing barges		London
Wrinch & Co.	1 sailing barge		London
R. & W. Paul	3 sailing barges		London

The timber raft AMERKER BRUG 1 which was built at Trondheim in the form of a ship and towed from Norway to Ipswich. In this photograph the raft is being pushed against the South West Quay in Ipswich Dock after her arrival. (Mr R. Bridges)

brought part-cargoes of wood from the USA ports of Portland, Seattle and San Francisco. On 29th May 1914 Furness Withy's new West Hartlepool built and registered steamship *CASTLE EDEN* arrived with logs for William Brown from Pascagoula, Mississippi, in the Gulf of Mexico. In September 1918 the ss *WAR GLEN* arrived with 5,000 tons of wheat and timber from Montreal, in full camouflage.

On 26th April 1919 a giant timber raft, the *AMERKER BRUG*, arrived from Trondjheim, Norway, after a nineteen-day passage under tow (see Towage chapter). Gabriel Wade & English were the importers. The 'cargo' of deal, intended for window frames and doors, etc., had become so waterlogged that it was sold for firewood. Other rafts had been more successful on shorter passages in the Baltic. In that same year, 6th September saw the arrival of the auxiliary-engined four-masted schooner *BRANDO* with timber and fish from Wasa in Finland. The ss *LAKE DYMER* arrived 8th March 1920 from Port Arthur, Texas, with 3,000 logs for Gabriel. Constantine's ss *HARLSEYWOOD*, built at Middlesbrough in 1907, docked at Ipswich on 27th April 1921 with a part-cargo of logs from Port Arthur; the ship had discharged the rest of its cargo at Rotterdam and Southampton. By that time only two major importers remained in Ipswich, Gabriel, Wade & English and William Brown.

For the rest of the 1920s and the 1930s until the Second World War timber imports to Ipswich came from the Baltic and White Sea, with regular shipments from Archangel and Igarka, from where William Brown imported five cargoes during the 1930s and an odd one in 1958. Igarka is situated at latitude 67 degrees 30 minutes north, longitude 86 degrees 40 minutes east on the Yenisei River, 689km south of the estuary of the Yenisei Gulf and the Kara Sea. Navigation at Igarka is possible only from July to October, whereas Archangel is viable from April to November and Murmansk enjoys year-round navigation. There were a few arrivals in the 1930s from the Americas, including the ports of New Orleans, Pensacola and Vancouver.

Events moved quickly following the start of the Second World War on 3rd September 1939, with Norway being overrun by the Germans in April 1940.

THE TIMBER TRADE

FIRM / DATE	VESSEL	PORT OF REGISTRY	FROM	CARGO
WILLIAM BROWN				
2 Jan 1923	sb ARDWINA	London	London	76 loads
14 Jan	sb ESTEREL	London	London	82 loads
23 Feb	sb FLOWER OF ESSEX	Ipswich	London	115 loads
5 Mar	Lighter BOMBAY	London	London	72 loads
8 Mar	ss LUSJNEALF	Hamburg	Memel (Russia)	944 loads
16 Apr	sb KLONDYKE	Ramsgate	Grimsby	129 loads
24 Apr	sb VARUNA	London	London	68 loads
6 May	sb MIMOSA	London	London	105 loads
19 May	JACOBA	Delfzjil	Christiania (Norway)	4,065 poles
23 May	ARGUS	Flensburg	Soderhamn (Sweden)	1,188 loads
18 June	HAMMERBURG	Hamburg	Pillau	739 loads
2 Aug	GRIEIJE	Delfzjil	Gothenburg (Sweden)	533 loads + 20 fathoms laths
2 Sept	ss ANNIE	Christianstadt	Viborg (Russia)	1,620 loads
3 Sept	ss ABINGTON	Newcastle	London	196 loads
14 Sept	ss BENLOS	Hull	Rafso (Finland)	1,650 loads
18 Sept	ss KRASNY PROFINTERN	St Petersburg	St Petersburg	1,669 loads
18 Sept	ss HARBOR	Christiania	Abo (Finland)	1,402 loads
1 Oct	ss JAKKMOKK	Kramfors	Gefle (Sweden)	1,933 loads + 4 fathoms laths
1 Oct	sb R.S.JACKSON	Rochester	London	65 loads
17 Oct	sb WAVENEY	Ipswich	London	12 fathoms laths
6 Dec	sb PEARL	Ipswich	London	119 loads
16 Dec	sb ESTEREL	London	London	66 loads
22 Dec	sb ASPHODEL	London	London	16 fathoms laths
24 Dec	sb BRITANNIC	London	London	123 loads
GABRIEL WADE & ENGLISH				
21 Jan 1923	sb NORMAN	London	London	109 loads
22 Jan	sb CALLUNA	London	London	99 loads
24 Jan	sb EUREKA	Colchester	London	81 loads
10 April	sb LANCASTER	London	London	77 loads
7 June	ss MANFRED	Werkeback	(Sweden)	881 loads + 1,129 poles
19 June	ss FRIDIUS	Gothenburg	Vestervig (Sweden)	806 loads
29 June	ss IMACOS	Tvedestrand	Viborg (Russia)	803 loads
3 July	ss FULTON	Bergen	Soroka	1,884 loads
17 July	ss MARIANNE	Trelleborg	Washlots	1,939 loads
19 July	ss BITINIA	Rome	Galatz (Romania)	1,036 loads
20 July	ss ANVALL	Oskarsham	Batskarsnas	1,315 loads
7 Aug	sb OUR BOYS	Rochester	London	73 loads
22 Aug	ss OPHIR	Bergen	Rafso (Finland)	1,665 loads + 16 fathoms laths
22 Sept	ss ASCANIA	Raa	Gefle (Sweden)	1,218 loads
1 Dec	sb TFC	Rochester	London	76 loads
18 Dec	ss FRIDA	Simrishamn (Sweden)	Sundsvall (Sweden)	571 loads
WRINCH & CO				
4 Aug 1923	sb GENERAL JACKSON	Ipswich	London	35 loads
8 Aug	sb SERB	London	London	71 loads
7 Oct	sb PUDGE	Rochester	London	84 loads
7 Oct	sb SPERANZA	London	London	93 loads
E.J. PEMBERTON (Agent)				
1923	WANJA	Helsingborg (Sweden)	Gothenburg	694 loads

Timber imports for 1923. Gabriel Wade & English's rent for 79 loads of logs lying in the timber pond from 30th September to 29th December 1923 was a penny per load per week.

Whereas in the First World War the Baltic had remained open to trade, in the second the occupation by Germany of both Norway and Denmark effectively blocked the Baltic trade routes, but lumber, together with potash and chrome ore, was still being shipped out of the White Sea port of Archangel as return cargo for merchant ships sailing in the Russian convoys on a route that took ships to within 750 miles of the North Pole. A few ships arrived from the White Sea at Ipswich during the war, and more than twenty came from the west and east coasts of the USA and Canada. Many are listed as arriving from Halifax, but this was the starting point for the eastbound Atlantic convoys with which the timber ships would have sailed and not their original port of sailing. It is interesting to note that on 12th October 1945, just four months after the war ended, the London-registered ship *JOHN W. AREY* arrived with timber from Brahestad, otherwise known as Raahe, 64 degrees north in the Baltic Sea. The *JOHN W. AREY* was a Liberty ship of welded construction built in 1943 at Superior, Wisconsin, in the United States, and operated by the Ministry of Transport on a bareboat charter from the United States Maritime Commission.

Immediately war was declared the Government implemented its plan to introduce timber control by the Ministry of Supply. It was not until November 1953 that all quotas and licensing for softwood, which constituted most of the Ipswich trade, were dropped. Much of the tropical teak and mahogany being imported went through Liverpool and London. The post-war arrivals soon showed a resumption of the Baltic trade from ports such as Lubeck, Kotka, Kemi and Leningrad, plus the important White Sea outlets of Archangel and Onega. Considerable amounts of timber continued to be supplied to Ipswich by Canada and the United States.

Some of the cargoes of the 1940s and 1950s were divided into extraordinary numbers of parcels for merchants across eastern England. On 31st March 1946

The ss ELIZABETE of Riga, 1,265nrt, arrived at Ipswich on 14th June 1939 from Archangel with timber for Browns and sailed light for Ostend on 29th June. Built in 1917 by the American S.B. Co. of Cleveland, Ohio, as the KIOWA, she was also known during her career as the KERZEME and the VALKA.
(James A.E. Burrows)

THE TIMBER TRADE

the ss *NOEMI* of London, a Sunderland tramp steamer built in 1914, arrived from Halifax. She had wood for J. Porter, John Sadd of Maldon, Jewson of Norwich, Brown & Son of Chelmsford, Ridgeon of Cambridge, Nottingham Mills Co. and also William Brown and Gabriel, Wade & English, all the timber to be distributed by rail and road. Similarly, in February 1948 the Panamanian steamer *TREBOL* of 1902 arrived from Yarmouth, Nova Scotia, and discharged timber for William Brown and Gabriel, Wade & English of Ipswich, Groom & Daniels

The Swedish three-masted auxiliary schooner KALMARSUND V, *built and registered at Kalmar, Sweden, in 1943, discharging her own cargo for William Brown on 16th January 1952. (R.W. Smith)*

of Colchester, John Sadd of Maldon, and Brown & Son of Chelmsford. Another arrival, on 16th December 1949 from Vancouver, was Sir William Reardon Smith's Bideford-registered *TACOMA CITY*, Sunderland built in 1938. One of the very last sailing ships to be launched, the *KALMARSUND V* of Kalmar, Sweden, a steel three-masted auxiliary schooner built at Kalmar in 1943, visited Ipswich twice, once in 1950 when she arrived from Kalmar with wood for William Brown, and again in 1952.

The record for the greatest number of consignments probably goes to the ss *REMBRANDT* which arrived in July 1951 with wood for nineteen merchants. She was built by Lithgows at Port Glasgow in 1941 for the Bolton Steam Shipping Company of London, a family firm established in 1884 with ships named after artists beginning with the letter 'R'. When war broke out in 1939, the company owned only three ships, with two more, including *REMBRANDT*, on order. Two of the original ships were lost by enemy action, but the fleet was built up again and by 1952 there were five new ships on order from yards in North-east England, such was the confidence in the British tramp shipping industry at that time. *REMBRANDT's* timber cargo was split among the following merchants:

> William Brown (Ipswich), Gabriel, Wade & English (Ipswich), C. Watson (Bury), J. Graham, Palgrave Brown (Gt. Yarmouth), A. Saul (Norwich), Groom & Daniels (Colchester), William Hughes (Bishops Stortford), W. Hewitt (Bury St Edmunds), Taylor & Butler (Manningtree), A.R. Taylor (Wroxham), William Ivens (?) & Sons, Saffron Walden Building Co. Ltd., Travis & Arnold (London), J. Hickman, C. Tebbutt Ltd., Sharp Bros. & Knight Ltd., Abraham Pyatt, Rippers Ltd (Castle Hedingham).

The year 1951 was a busy year for timber imports. The *SPRUCELAND* of Leith, a liberty ship built in 1942 at Sturgeon Bay, Wisconsin, and owned by the Currie Line, arrived from Archangel for William Brown and Gabriel, Wade & English. In August the *EMPIRE FROME* berthed from Canada and in September the *LOCH MADDY* arrived from Coos Bay, Oregon, some 180 miles south of the Columbia River, with timber for William Brown. On 10th November the Yugoslav ss *LOSINJ* of Rijeka, with a part-cargo via Southampton, attracted attention in the press as being crewed largely by 'displaced persons', a familiar term after the end of the war referring to the thousands of Europeans ousted from their homelands with nowhere to go. *LOSINJ* had been built in 1928 by J. Thompson at Sunderland as *HELMSGATH*.

On 2nd January 1952 the ss *BANGOR BAY*, of Irish Bay Lines, Belfast, arrived. Built in 1941 by Connells of Glasgow as *EMPIRE MALLORY* for the M.O.W.T., she was sold in 1946 and renamed *AMPLEFORTH*, and was later stranded near Tel Aviv, to be declared a total loss. In 1947, however, she was bought and repaired by Irish Bay Lines. After all these experiences she arrived in the Orwell with timber from Victoria, British Columbia, having survived the severe gale in the south-west approaches in which the ss *FLYING ENTERPRISE* was lost, ten days after the dramatic rescue of her 51 passengers and crew. *BANGOR BAY* was sold to Indian owners in 1954 and broken up at Bombay in 1961.

The ss *GRAIGLWYD* of Cardiff, launched by Wm. Pickersgill at Sunderland in 1943 as *CHERTSEY*, berthed at Cliff Quay on 15th February 1952 from Coos Bay. Williams Shipping Company of Cardiff was her third owner and in 1959 she received her fourth name, *NORDWIND*, when sold to the People's Republic of China. During 1953 and '54 ships from two prominent British lines arrived.

One, *CAPE SABLE* from Vancouver, belonged to the Lyle Shipping Company of Glasgow, and the other, Lamport & Holts' *DELIUS*, arrived from San Francisco via London with a part-cargo for William Brown, as she did again in August 1954 when she left for Hull with a part-cargo remaining on board.

Hogarth's Baron Line of Ardrossan had been in the shipping business since the 1860s, having started as ship-chandlers and sailmakers in Ardrossan, Ayrshire. Their ships had visited Ipswich with various cargoes over the years, and in 1960 and '61 the *BARON ARDROSSAN* and *BARON BERWICK* respectively arrived with timber. The latter, having arrived from Vancouver on 22nd February, sailed for Hartlepool with part-cargo R.O.B on 16th March, which reveals the length of time (over three weeks) it took to discharge timber by slinging a relatively few planks ashore at a time.

The 1960s and early '70s were the last years of traditional timber handling and also the last years of the older coal-burning steamships. These ships were easily recognised by their derricks mounted fairly high up the masts to allow stowage of considerable deck cargoes, which caused these vessels to take on profound lists to port or starboard, especially in the Baltic trade, causing grave concern to the uninitiated, but still the ships sailed on to their destination. The last two archetypal steamships in the trade to Ipswich were the *REHHORST* and the *PETER*. The *REHHORST* was built in 1930 at Stavanger, Norway, passed to German ownership in 1951 and was registered and owned by Johannes Ick at Hamburg. She made several voyages from the Baltic in her last years, arriving at Ipswich on 31st January 1961 ex-Kemi, Finland, and on 26th January 1962 ex-Kotka, Finland, and making three more visits in 1963 from the same ports. In 1964 she arrived four times; on 9th June, 13th July, 9th August (from Walkom, Gulf of Finland) and finally on 30th October from Kotka, returning light to Hamburg. *REHHORST* was the last coal-burner in the German merchant fleet. When she was withdrawn her master moved to the *PETER*, another coal burner in the Baltic trade which had been built at Fredriksstad, Norway, in 1916, and had had various changes of ownership and four previous names before being renamed *PETER* in 1960 and registered in Panama. This elderly ship came to Ipswich on 20th April 1965 and made three more voyages to the Orwell in January, May and July of 1966. The passing of these old ships and their sisters from their traditional routes made the Baltic and North Seas seem far lonelier waters.

Meanwhile the North American trade continued with bigger ships of more than 10,000 tons deadweight. In 1965 the Liberian mv *MARY* of Monrovia, built

Wartime timber imports, 1944-45. Imports for the earlier war years will be found in tables in the appendices.

DATE	SHIP	REG.	NRT	FROM	COMPANY	CARGO
1944						
21 Feb	ss *SVERTE*	Panama	2,614	Halifax (Canada)	MOS	Timber
5 May	ss *AMSLIE PARK*	Montreal	1,653	Halifax (Canada)	MOS	Timber
2 Jul	ss *ARMATHIA*	Pireaus	2,932	via Campbeltown (UK)	MOS	Timber
2 Sept	ss *DIVARA*	Susak (Yugo)	2,206	Halifax (Canada)	MOS	Timber
12 Nov	ss *EMPIRE GREY*	Shields	4,058	Camden (Philadelphia)	MOS	Timber
1945						
29 Jan	ss *BARBARA FREITCHIE*	Baltimore	4,380	Archangel (Russia)	MOS	Timber
10 May	ss *RUNSWICK*	Whitby	2,380	Camden (Philadelphia)	MOS	Timber
20 Jul	ss *BARON YARBOROUGH*	Ardrossan	2,034	Pugwash (Halifax)	MOS	Timber
12 Oct	ss *JOHN W AREY*	London	1,023	Brahestad (Norway)	MOS	Timber
7 Nov	ss *WILLIAM BREWSTER*	London	1,010	Halifax (Canada)	MOS	Timber

FIRM / DATE	VESSEL	NRT	POR	FROM	CARGO
WILLIAM BROWN					
5 Jan 1955	ss DAGNY	851	Mariehamn	Kotka	Deals 2,627 loads
25 Jan	mb VIKING	49	Rochester	London	Boards 84 loads
2 Feb	ss HENRICK PETERS	483	Hamburg	Gefle	Deals 1,268 loads
7 Feb	mb LEN. PIPER	90	London	London	Boards 138 loads
5 Mar	mb MARIE MAY	72	Rochester	London	Boards 134 loads
8 Mar	mb VIGILANT	66	Harwich	London	Boards 129 loads
21 Mar	mb ALARIC	63	London	London	Deals 84 loads
30 Mar	mv FRYKEN	464	Kristinehamn	Via Gt. Yarmouth	Part-cargo wallboards 261 tons
16 Apr	mv FALSTER	616	Kristinehamn	Via Kings Lynn	Part-cargo wallboards 204 tons
29 April	mv FERN	1370	Grimstad	Vancouver	Deals 3,572 loads
12 May	mv PEGNY	448	Mariehamn	Rauma	Plywood 37 loads Deals 1,060 loads
17 May	mv SANTA MARGHARITA	327	Groningen	Gefle	Deals 990 loads
23 May	mb CABBY	73	Rochester	London	Deals 132 loads
23 May	mb VARUNA	53	London	London	Deals 113 loads
2 June	mv MARTIEN	346	Amsterdam	Pernoviken	Deals 901
12 June	ss EASTDALE	891	London	Archangel	Deals 2,243 loads
25 June	mb WYVENHOE	83	Rochester	London	Deals 115
11 July	mv TUEN	336	Rotterdam	Norrsundet	Deals 837 loads
12 July	mb GEORGE & ELIZA	56	Rochester	London	Boards 84 loads
19 July	mb WYVENHOE	83	Rochester	London	Boards 88 loads
21 July	mv ST MARGARET	3,074	Newport	Vancouver via London	Deals 1,980 loads part- cargo
4 Aug	mb VARUNA	53	London	London	Deals 124 loads
16 Aug	mb ALARIC	63	London	London	Deals 80 loads
16 Aug	mb EDITH MAY	54	Harwich	London	Deals 72 loads
10 Sept	ss HENRICH PETERS	483	Hamburg	Kotka	Deals 1,377 loads
10 Sept	ss ADELFOTIS	1337		Igarka	Deals 3,175 loads
18 Sept	mb PUDGE	68	Rochester	London	Deals 96 loads
21 Sept	mv CALAND	317	Groningen	Kotka	Deals 848 loads
6 Oct	mb WYVENHOE	83	Rochester	London	Deals 99
11 Oct	mb MARIE MAY	72	Rochester	Felixstowe	Deals 25
18 Oct	mv APPIAN	1021	Bergen	Archangel	Deals 2,484 loads
3 Nov	mb WYVENHOE	83	Rochester	London	Deals 76 loads
2 Dec	mb WYVENHOE	83	Rochester	London	Deals 71 loads
7 Dec	mb MARIE MAY	72	Rochester	London	Deals 125 loads
8 Dec	mv PLANCIUS	321	Delfjyl	Helsinki	Deals 708 loads
9 Dec	mb CABBY	73	Rochester	London	Deals 112 loads
10 Dec	mb WYVENHOE	83	Rochester	London	Deals 69 loads
10 Dec	mv HERMAN BUISMAN	194	Zwaartsluis	Helsinki	Deals 545
GABRIEL, WADE & ENGLISH					
29 Jan	sb OXYGEN	72	Rochester	London	Softwood 84 loads
20 June	mv STEFAN	303		Karlshamn	Softwood 1,064 loads
23 June	ss HAUSESTADT HAMBURG	417	Hamburg	Mesame (Russia)	Softwood 1,178 loads
29 Aug	mv WIM	267	Groningen	Mantyluoto	Softwood 765 loads
1 Sept	mv TESSY	298	Lidkoping	Burea	Softwood 814 loads
3 Sept	ss LUNGO	831	Harnosand	Hamina	Softwood 2,477 loads
5 Sept	mv ZEUS II	287	Bremen	Lovisa	Softwood 652 loads

in 1949 by W. Gray & Co. at Hartlepool, berthed from Vancouver on 17th February with timber for William Brown. The third day of March saw the Liberian ss *SAN LORENZO*, ex-*JOHN LA FARGE*, arrive from America via Dublin with a part-cargo. A standard Liberty ship, she was built for the US War Shipping Administration in 1943 by the renowned Bethlehem Fairfield Shipyard at Baltimore. Another Liberty ship from the same yard, the

THE TIMBER TRADE

ss *MELTEMI*, arrived on 24th May from Vancouver via Hull, still with sufficient part-cargo on board to supply Gabriel, Wade & English and A. Taylor of Wroxham, Norfolk. By 1965 the vessel was Greek owned and registered by the Universal Tramp Shipping Company in Piraeus. On 2nd July the ss *PYRGOS* of Piraeus came in from Vancouver to discharge timber for four merchants, including William Brown and Taylors of Wroxham, before sailing on the 12th with part-cargo for Rainham, on the Thames. Also a Liberty ship, constructed in 1944 by the New England Shipbuilding Corporation of Portland, Maine, as the *GALEN L. STONE*, she would be known successively as *YANKEE STAR*, *DEMOSTAR* and *OCEANSTAR* before taking the name *PYRGOS*. On 8th October ss *MARIBLANCA* of Monrovia arrived from Port Churchill in Hudson Bay, a place usually associated with grain shipments. She was yet another Liberty ship, built by the Houston Shipbuilding Corporation in 1944, and having engines made by the intriguingly titled Iron Fireman Manufacturing Company of Portland, Oregon. The ss *GRACIA*, Norwegian built at Fredrikstad in 1950 and owned and registered in Vasa, Finland, arrived from Brazil on 4th December 1965 with timber for William Brown, Gabriel, Wade & English, J.T. Stanton of Kings Lynn, Palgrave Brown of Great Yarmouth, J. Davis of Hayes, Middlesex, and Travis & Arnold of London.

In addition to importing wood from Scandinavia, this country exported timber to that region for a time. The year 1920 saw the emergent Forestry Commission purchase 2,500 acres of heathland in East Suffolk, to be known later as Tangham Forest, followed by other acquisitions in the county. In 1922 the first of 51,000 acres of Breckland was also acquired for afforestation. Millions of Scots and Corsican pine trees, plus other species, were planted with varying success because of the quality of the land. Thinning took place according to a programme starting at eighteen years and thereafter every four years. 'Economic maturity' was prescribed as being reached sixty years after planting, bringing the first mature crop due for felling in 1980. Apart from selling to sawmills and the paper-making industry, as late as 1970 one-sixth of the crop

Built as EMPIRE TRAIL, *a D-class standard ship launched in August 1943 by the Shipbuilding Corporation Ltd., Wear Branch, the Glasgow-registered ss* LOCH MADDY, *2,805nrt, arrived at Ipswich from Coos Bay on 23rd September 1951 with timber for Christie and William Brown. She sailed light for Southampton on 13th October. Renamed* TRAIL *in 1947 for Maclay & McIntyre Ltd., she was renamed by the company* LOCH MADDY *in 1951. Sold to Panamanian Oriental Corporation, Hong Kong, in 1960, she was laid up damaged two years later and broke her moorings in a typhoon, sustaining further damage which resulted in her being broken up in Japan in 1963. (R.W. Smith)*

was still being cut for use as pit props in the coal mines. However, timber props were already being replaced by steel, and during the mid-1980s the mining industry itself became almost defunct.

In 1981, consequent upon the events described above, a new export trade developed in timber from Norfolk and Suffolk through Ipswich to Scandinavia. A company aptly named Forest Thinnings Ltd. obtained a contract with the Forestry Commission to handle the business. The Ipswich Port Authority made space available on parts of the site of William Brown's timber sheds and the former coal yard bordering Tovells Wharf and End Quay for 3,000 tons of trees to be brought in by lorry direct from the forests to await shipment every three weeks. Special labour agreements were introduced enabling 24-hour loading by the ships' own cranes. If the cargo was likely to increase the vessel's draught too much to clear the lock sill, the deck cargo would be topped up at Cliff Quay. Most of the logs exported went for pulping and returned to this country in the form of paper products. The Great Gale of October 1987 brought about the premature felling of the forests and the trade ended in the early 1990s, once the clearance of suitable trees had been completed.

For four decades, from the late 1950s onwards, the timber trade at the port had been in decline, heralding a time of considerable change both in the industry and in the methods used for the handling and transportation of wood. Looking back to 1947, for example, the two firms of William Brown and Gabriel Wade & English received fifty-six shiploads of timber between them that year, many of them aboard sailing and motor barges from the Surrey Commercial Docks, London. In 1959 the number was down to forty-four, and by 1970 a total of only thirty-six such shipments was recorded. However, between 1989 and 1990 a sudden increase occurred with timber imports jumping from 46,000 to 143,000 cubic metres. The revival continued throughout the decade, supported by new companies such as the Anglo-Norden Group, Northern Wood Terminals and later West Bank Timber Ltd. Pre-slung packaged timber now arrives at the port, mainly originating from Canada and the Baltic. New timber storage facilities for weather-sensitive wood have opened at the West Bank Terminal, followed by a timber treatment centre using the latest technology to enable wood to be protected against fungal decay and insect attack within hours rather than days of its arrival.

The Jugoslav Line steamship LOSINJ arrived on 10th November 1951 with timber from Russia for the Ministry of Materials and Palgrave, Brown Ltd, having already delivered a part cargo at Southampton. Her crew consisted largely of 'displaced persons', people who had been made homeless and stateless by the effects of the Second World War and subsequent events in Eastern Europe. (R.W. Smith)

Building materials 8

Although kiln-fired bricks were produced in this country during Roman times, brickmaking died out until the thirteenth century when fired bricks again made an appearance in East Anglia. From the sixteenth century onwards, small brickyards grew up all over Suffolk to supply local needs, the area possessing little stone for building purposes. Wolsey's Gateway, the only remaining fragment of Cardinal Wolsey's ambitious scheme for a college in Ipswich, provides an example of the red brick construction of the late Tudor period.

The raw material for brickmaking is brickearth, a mixture of clay and sand, dug from shallow pits and allowed to weather. It was then sprinkled with water and mixed to the required consistency, either by treading or by a pugmill worked by a horse or, in later days, driven by steam. The brickmaker threw the resulting 'pug' into a wooden mould fixed to his bench, producing one brick at a time. The 'green' bricks were air-dried before being fired in clamps which burnt for a week or in special kilns.

The presence of iron oxides in the clay affects the colours of most bricks. Suffolk 'reds' were the result of firing brickearth from the London clay areas of East Suffolk, including Ipswich, while Woolpit and other yards had deposits of clay containing chalk that produced distinctive 'white' bricks.

Many local brickmakers also turned out tiles, including E. & E. C. Gibbons of Wolsey Street, Ipswich, who were owners of brickworks near Romford and at Sudbury, Aldham (near Hadleigh), and Shotley on the Stour side, where a small creek became known as Gibbons' Creek. They also had the White Elm works in St Clement's Parish and the Valley Brickworks off Foxhall Road, which had a railway siding from the Felixstowe line close to Derby Road station. Edward Gibbon's head office was at 2 Corn Exchange Buildings, Ipswich, and they also possessed a London office at 143 Cannon Street E.C.

William Gardiner ran a brick and tile works on Hog Highland close to Greenwich Farm, until both were swallowed up by the development of Cliff Quay in the 1920s. Thomas Thorndike was operating a brickfield on the opposite bank of the river in Stoke, Ipswich, during the 1830s. This was later run by the Bennett Brothers, but was gone by the 1900s.

The brickworks at Woolpit were particularly well known. A number of makers carried on brickyards there from the sixteenth until the twentieth century. At the beginning of the twentieth century a railway was laid to connect the largest of the works with the Ipswich-Bury St Edmunds main line at Elmswell, this standard gauge line replaced an earlier narrow-gauge tramway that was possibly used for the occasional flurries of Woolpit bricks sent away from Ipswich by barge.

Other yards to have a railway connection were F. Rosher's brickworks at the Grove, off Henley Road, and the Dales works, the latter taken over in 1901 by Bolton & Laughlin, who made bricks there for over fifty years before closure in the late 1950s. Rosher was a major brickmaker by the 1880s, with wharves at New Cut East in Ipswich, at Chelsea, Blackfriars and Limehouse on the Thames and at Crown Quay, Sittingbourne, in Kent.

Brick Traffic

*The brick trade, 1885, with twenty-nine individual barges taking out from Ipswich fifty-four cargoes averaging about 22,000 bricks per barge. The Rochester barge CURLY BOY averaged 25,000 bricks per trip. *Owner 1904-1911.*

There was a considerable trade with bricks loaded within the port and river during the 1880s. Although their destinations are not recorded, it may be assumed that the larger barges went to London.

BARGE NAME	POR	NRT	BRICK EXPORTER	TRIPS	BUILT	OWNER
ALBATROSS	Ipswich	48	Cowell	1	1869 Ipswich	R. & W. Paul
			Gibbons	2		
ALICE & ELLA	Ipswich	45	Beaumont	1	1882 Wandsworth	George Roberts
AVEYRON		39	Beaumont	2	1881 Ipswich	
CHAMPION	Ipswich	42	Beaumont	1	1861 Ipswich	
CURLY BOY	Rochester	40	Beaumont	1	1871 Rochester	H. Wall, Stanford le Hope
			Borrett	1		
			Rosher	11		
DOROTHEA	Harwich	52	Beaumont	1	1880 Ipswich	W. Middleton, Harwich
EMILY			Gibbons	1		
FOSSIL	Ipswich	37	Beaumont	2	1853 Blackfriars	E. Packard
GOOD INTENT	London	44	Gibbons	1	1790 Chelsea	W. Middleton, Harwich *
HOPE			Beaumont	1		
JOHN & CLARA		19	E Fison	3		
MABEL	Ipswich	49	Gibbons	1	1875 Ipswich	R. & W. Paul
MARGARET	Harwich	49	Beaumont	1	1855 Brightlingsea	L. Richmond
MARIANNA	London	57	Gibbons	1		H. Shrubsall
MURIEL	Harwich	23	Beaumont	1	1880 Harwich	J. Groom, Harwich
NAUTILUS	Ipswich	50	Beaumont	1	1870 Ipswich	E. Packard
NINITA			Gibbons	1		
PEACE	Colchester	38	Rosher	1	1855 Brightlingsea	H. Howe, Colchester
POMONA	Rochester	42	Rosher	1	1878 Sittingbourne	
PROVIDENCE			Beaumont	1		
			Gibbons	1		
RACHEL & JULIA	London	41	Gibbons	1	1873 Milton	
RICHARD			E Fison	1		
RICHMOND	Harwich	49	Gibbons	1		Mrs M. Richmond
SPINAWAY	Rochester	46	Rosher	7	1875 Rochester	W. Gilbert
SWIFTSURE	Rochester	39	Gibbons	1	1879 Milton	
TERTIUS			Rosher	1	1844 Ipswich	
THOMAS & ANNIE	Ipswich	41	Gibbons	1		
UNION			Gibbons	1		
VICTORIA	London	43	Beaumont	1	1864 Faversham	W. Wrinch

BUILDING MATERIALS

During the autumn of 1886, thirteen barges left Ipswich carrying Woolpit bricks. These bricks were almost certainly delivered to Ipswich Dock in railway trucks and then transferred to the barges that were more economical for making journeys to London at that period. An average cargo carried by these barges was about 35,000 bricks, giving a rough total of 455,000 bricks transported.

Another thirty-one barges sailed from the port with bricks from other sources during the six months July-December 1886. At Ipswich, F. Rosher loaded nine brick cargoes, Beaumont loaded seven and E. Gibbons loaded six, while Edward Fison loaded nine cargoes at Hares Creek. At that time the Fison brickworks were in the name of Mrs. Catherine Fison of Stowmarket, who worked the small brickworks at Hares Creek in addition to the main works at Finborough Road, Stowmarket. Beaumont's works were in Cemetery Road, they having apparently disposed of their Eastern Counties Brickworks along Henley Road to F. Rosher & Co. Ltd.

The brickworks on Hog Highland in the early 20th century. (Robert Malster collection)

Bricks continued as a steady trade throughout the 1890s. By 1898, barges were arriving in increasing numbers from Holbrook Creek, bringing bricks made by the Holbrook Creek Brick Works Company. On 19th February sb *THE EXCHANGE*, only 36nrt, Rochester built and registered in 1866, delivered bricks for W. Barker. In July and August sb *FORMOSA* made three trips, and the *THOMAS WOOD* of Colchester and *PRIMA DONNA* (owned by John Watts of Harwich) each came once for Rosher. Later in the year, there were two more cargoes for Rosher in John Groom's small barges *PROVIDENCE*, 41nrt of London, built at Shadwell 1855, and the 25-ton *FAIRY*. Ipswich builder and merchant W. Pipe received three small bargeloads of bricks from Gibbons' Shotley works. One came in October 1898 in the ancient Maldon-registered *HAND OF PROVIDENCE*, also owned by Groom, and completed way back in 1826 at Lambeth. The other two loads came in the *WHY NOT* and *IOTA* during November and December. R. & W. Paul Ltd owned the *ANN*, 39nrt, built at Greenham, Berkshire, in 1843, which collected bricks from Holbrook for Pauls' own account on 4th November.

On 14th January 1899, the *IOTA*, one of a handful of very small barges owned by John Groom, of only 12 nrt and a likely carrying capacity of about 25 tons, delivered more bricks for Pipe from Shotley, returning to Harwich with oakum

Barges departing in the autumn of 1886 loaded with bricks from Woolpit.

DATE OF DEPARTURE	BARGE NAME	POR	NRT	ARRIVAL	DEPARTURE
22 Oct 1886	SPINAWAY	Rochester		Arrived with rice meal for Thurmans ex-London.	Loaded 30,000 Woolpit bricks.
29 Oct	ALBATROSS	Ipswich		Arrived light ex-London.	Loaded 35,000 Woolpit bricks.
29 Oct	WHY NOT	Ipswich	39	Arrived with peas from C.B. Cordy, Harwich Harbour.	Loaded Woolpit bricks.
1 Nov	LADY OF THE WAVE	Woodbridge	55	Arrived with maize ex-London for Cowells.	Loaded 36,000 Woolpit bricks.
3 Nov	UNITY	London		Arrived with cinders for E.R. & F. Turner ex-Colchester.	Loaded 35,000 Woolpit bricks.
4 Nov	ROBERT & THOMAS	Ipswich		Arrived light ex-Harwich.	Loaded 26,000 Woolpit bricks.
9 Nov	AVEYRON	Ipswich		Arrived ex-Thames with loam for R.S. & J. Ltd	Loaded 25,000 Woolpit bricks.
12 Nov	JOSEPH	Rochester		Arrived ex-London with maize for Cowells.	Loaded 25,000 Woolpit bricks.
19 Nov	SPINAWAY			Arrived ex-London with maize for Cowells.	Loaded Woolpit bricks.
6 Dec	PEACE	Colchester		Arrived ex-London with linseed for G. Mason.	Loaded 35,000 Woolpit bricks.
15 Dec	ROBERT & THOMAS	Ipswich		Arrived light	Loaded 35,000 Woolpit bricks.
17 Dec	SPINAWAY	Rochester		Arrived light	Loaded 35,000 Woolpit bricks.
18 Dec	JOSEPH	Rochester		Arrived light	Loaded 33,000 Woolpit bricks.

The little spritsail barge FAIRY, built at Limehouse in 1861 and owned at Harwich by Groom, which was engaged in the local brick trade.

picked by prisoners at Ipswich Gaol, no doubt for caulking new barges at one of the Harwich barge yards.

In 1900 George Kenney, an Ipswich builder working at the site of a former barge yard in Burrell Street (now Burrell Road), received fourteen brick cargoes from Holbrook between 24th April and 27th July, all delivered by two barges. Eight arrived in one of Groom's very small craft, the *ELIZABETH AND SOPHIA*, 13nrt, and six came in *THE SISTERS*, 33nrt of Maldon, which was built at Blackwall in 1863 and foundered in the Thames Estuary in 1913.

During those last years of the nineteenth century a revolution in brickmaking took place when brickmaking became mechanised and bricks began to be manufactured from the Lower Oxford clay found in the Fletton area near Peterborough. This shale clay had a moisture content that enabled bricks to be fired immediately after pressing, without any previous drying. The clay also contained about 10 per cent carbonaceous material that could be utilised during firing, leading to a reduction in the fuel requirements of the kilns. By the end of the century bricks were being manufactured in large quantities using large economical kilns and highly mechanised methods.

The small brickworks, which had provided bricks for the expansion of towns like Ipswich and of course London during the 1870s, 1880s and 1890s, could not compete and many closed down during the 1920s and 1930s. Some of the large works of Kent and south Essex survived into the 1960s, but long-established concerns continued to close as the great brickfields of the Marston Valley Brick Company, Eastwoods and the London Brick Company around Peterborough and in Bedfordshire quickly expanded. A few small yards such as Reade's at Aldeburgh survived by making bricks for special or building restoration needs and continued production into the 1990s.

The East Anglian barge trade in bricks was very small compared with that from the Kentish brickmakers such as Eastwoods, who had branches in various towns, including a depot in Cumberland Street in Ipswich. However, Eastwoods' barges, which numbered about a hundred until replaced by lorries during the 1930s, delivered clinker from Kent to the Aldeburgh Brickworks pier on the River Alde and loaded Suffolk red bricks away for special orders.

Certainly, the need for barge traffic from East Anglia had ended by the 1920s. The Great Northern Railway, to be absorbed into the London & North Eastern Railway Company at the grouping of 1923, concluded trials by 1922 with 50-ton capacity bogie goods wagons for transporting bricks from Peterborough to east and north London. Each truck was fitted with vacuum brakes and carried 20,000 bricks, a half of the number loaded aboard one of the larger barges in the trade. Over fifty wagons were in use by 1930, and it required only two of them to transport the equivalent of a bargeload of bricks, sufficient to build a pair of semi-detached houses, in hours rather than the two or three days taken by a barge. Eventually railway traffic and the labour-intensive transportation of bricks were superseded by heavy goods vehicles with the capability of one man unloading its palletized load of bricks with an on-board crane and delivering directly from the works to the building site.

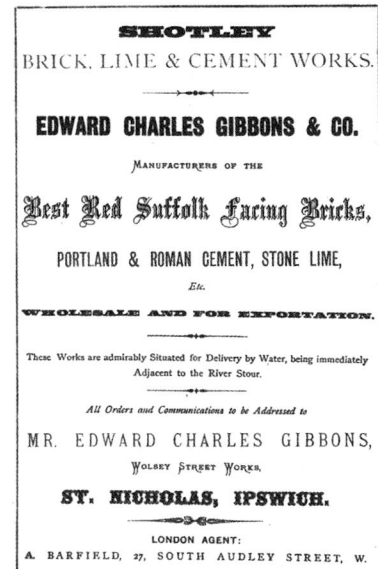

An advertisement for the Shotley Brick, Lime & Cement Works from White's directory of 1874.

Tile cargoes

There was never a prolific trade in roof tiles to Ipswich, and a perambulation of the town reveals a significant preference for slate roofs, at least in housing built prior to the 1920s, although numerous Victorian and Edwardian houses have since had their slates replaced by tiles.

A few Yorkshire billyboys, the indigenous ketch-rigged sailing barges of the rivers and coast of the north east, brought tiles from Barton-upon-Humber, close to the south end of the present Humber Bridge. In 1887 the *SANDRINGHAM* of Hull, built at Leeds in 1886, brought tiles for Ashton, Green Ltd, a London-based firm whose agent George Baker had a depot at Flint Wharf. The Boston-registered *HOLBEACH* and the *SAVILL* and the *SARAH,* both of Goole, all came from Barton for E. Catchpole, builders' merchants with premises in Princes Street until the 1960s. An ancient ketch barge, the Maldon-registered *ELIZABETH*, 63nrt and built at Maidstone in 1840, discharged tiles from the Humber for Rosher in 1885. In 1914 a ketch built at Hammilwarder in Germany in 1904, the *MARY ELIEZER,* owned by J. Gleadhill of Barton-upon-Humber and registered at Hull, also arrived with tiles for Catchpole.

During the 1920s occasional spritsail barges brought tiles from Antwerp and Dunkirk as well as Barton-upon-Humber. In 1924, sb *GWYNHELEN* of London came from Barton with 74,000 tiles (141 tons) for Wm. Brown & Co., builders' merchants. Two months later, sb *BRITANNIC*, 119nrt of London, arrived from Dunkirk with 146,093 tiles (251 tons) for Langley & Co. of 161 Borough High Street, London SE1. Twenty rods of land was required for stacking this last shipment of tiles, and it took two horses and three carts six and a half days to shift the cargo. Later the trade moved to other coasting vessels, including mb *HEATHERPET*, which brought tiles from Barton in 1927. She was owned by the diesel engineering firm of Vickers Petters of Ipswich. The ss *JOLLY MARIE* also arrived that same year with tiles from Rouen for Langley's. These tile shipments may have been intended for some of the 5,000 houses erected in Ipswich during the 1920s, thirty-eight per cent of which were built by Ipswich Corporation.

The steel billyboy KATHERINA, *uncharacteristically built at Stadskanaal in Holland in 1910, seen in a sketch by L. Jeffery.*

The slate trade

The Welsh slate industry, which flourished in the mountains surrounding the Vale of Ffestiniog in North West Wales, began in earnest early in the 1800s, although the trade had been carried on intermittently during the previous hundred years. Slate was obtained from quarries using primitive tools. It was brought down some 700 feet to river level on the backs of donkeys until tracks at the lower levels permitted the slate to be transferred to horse-drawn carts, each carrying a ton, for the six-mile trek to a wharf on the River Dwyryd. The slate was shipped from there to coasting vessels lying in the estuary by two-man boats, loading six tons apiece.

The slate trade might never have expanded as it did without the money and determination of a wealthy young man who came to the area in the 1790s and was fascinated by the combined estuaries of the Dwyryd and Glaslyn rivers. He succeeded, with the labour of hundreds of workers, in reclaiming 2,000 acres on the Glaslyn side and building a new market town named Tremadog, all within ten years. His name was William Alexander Madocks.

Encouraged by his achievement, Madocks applied for and received Crown Assent to build a mile-long stone causeway across the estuary, linking Carnarvonshire with Merioneth. This was only the beginning, however: Madocks obtained Parliamentary powers to construct a harbour, despite considerable opposition from some quarry owners and from the boatmen who carried the slate out to the waiting ships. Construction of a railway from Ffestiniog to the harbour began in 1821 and was completed in 1824. The boatmen were now able to stack the slates on the quay to await ships to load, houses were built and the harbour town of Portmadoc was born. Despite severe protests, the railway was opened in 1836 and covered over thirteen miles of extremely arduous territory, including Madock's great embankment known as the Cob. The slate wagons ran by gravity down to sea level and were hauled back up by ponies until 1863, when steam engines were employed. Today the steam engines haul passengers on the famous Ffestiniog Railway.

Shipbuilding and ownership was the next move. The name of Portmadoc was to be seen on square-rigged ships the world over during the 1860s and 1870s, the vessels loading slates whenever possible from their home port. The phosphate trade from the West Indies to any port in Europe proved very important for the homeward passage. Succeeding those ships were the smaller but fast vessels built for the fish trade from Labrador and Newfoundland. These vessels achieved wide recognition and a place in history as the famous Portmadoc schooners.

Although the last schooner did not leave the ways at Portmadoc until 1913, shipping there was already declining, due principally to increasing competition from steamships. The end came swiftly about 1917.

Smaller ketches and schooners, many of them built or registered at other Welsh ports, worked the hard coasting trade round Britain and the near continent. They were the slate carriers to Ipswich as the town expanded and new housing was built on the outskirts for such organisations as the Freehold Land Society, especially during the last two decades of the nineteenth century when slates were preferred to tiles for roofing in the town.

In addition to Ashton & Green and Wm. Brown, both already seen as importing roof tiles as well as slates, two timber merchants advertised in the 1880s that they also dealt in slates. One was the timber and cement merchant

George Mason, mentioned elsewhere in these pages, who occupied premises at Grey Friars Road and the other was Oliver T. Gibbons of Gipping Works, Wolsey Street, who promoted himself as a builder, contractor, slate, lime, cement and timber merchant.

By the 1920s tiles were proving to be more popular than slates as a roofing material in the town, but by then the railways and the roads had taken over the transportation of these bulky items.

Blockstone

The white limestone from Dorset, better known as Portland stone, achieved a reputation for use as building stone after it found favour with two great English architects, Inigo Jones (*c*.1573-*c*.1652) and Sir Christopher Wren (1632-1723).

Caen stone and Scottish granite have been transported to East Anglia by ship for centuries. One example illustrating the continuity of the trade in building

This table shows an important phase in the slate trade to Ipswich.

DATE	SHIP	RIG	POR	NRT	FROM	IMPORTER	BUILT	OWNER
1883								
18 Jun	SARAH ROWE	Sr	Milford	63	Portmadoc	Ashton & Green	1872 Cosheston	O. Jones
9 Oct	JOHN WILLIAMS	Sr	Aberystwyth	76	Portmadoc	Ashton & Green	1848 Portmadoc	W. Jones
14 Nov	MISS WILLIAMS	Sr	Caernarvon	79	Bangor	Ashton & Green	1880 Port Dinorwic	W. Jones
1884								
11 Mar	JOSEPH NICHOLSON	Sr	Newcastle	99	Portmadoc	Ashton & Green	1868 Nevin	D. Davies
6 Jun	EASTWARD	Sr	Aberystwyth	67	Portmadoc		1871 Rothsay	D. Davies
8 Jun	VICTORY		Carnarvon		Portmadoc	Wm. Brown		
17 Aug	MARIA CATHERINE	Sr	Beaumaris	89	Bangor	Ashton & Green	1841 Nevin	J. Ellis
16 Oct	MESSENGER	Sr	Aberystwyth	82	Portmadoc	Ashton & Green	1841 Aberystwyth	G. Davies
28 Nov	LADY LOUISA PENNANT	Sr	Beaumaris	73	Bangor	George Mason	1847 Bangor	J. Ellis
1887								
-	SECRET	Sr	Beaumaris	60	Portmadoc	Ashton & Green	1857 Rye	R. Williams
-	BLUE JACKET	Sr	Aberystwyth	100	Caernarvon	Ashton & Green	1860 Aberystwyth	J. Rees
-	JOHN WILLIAMS	Sr	Aberystwyth	76	Caernarvon	Ashton & Green	1848 Portmadoc	W. Jones
-	MAID OF MEIRION	Sr	Aberystwyth	60	Portmadoc	George Mason	1859 Aberystwyth	G. Lewis
-	MARY JANE		Caernarvon		Portmadoc	Ashton & Green		
-	JOHN AND MARGARET	Sr	Caernarvon	44	Portmadoc	W Brown	1857 Barnstaple	J. Jones
-	JOHN EWING	Sr	Caernarvon	105	Caernarvon	Rosher	1867 Whitehaven	E. Evans
1904								
31 Jan	SARAH MCDONALD	Sr	Chester	84	Portmadoc		1867 Perth	G. Millington
13 Apr	TINTARA	Spl	London	65	Dunkirk		1893 Bow	E. Whitmore, B'Sea
13 May	RHEIDOL VALE	Sr	Aberystwyth	76	Portmadoc		1859 Aberystwyth	D. Thomas
15 Jun	ST LAURENT		St Servian	48	St Malo			
30 Jun	CAMBRIAN	Sr	Aberystwyth	69	Portmadoc		1873 Aberdovey	T. Williams
14 Jul	JEAN BAPTISTE	60	Boulogne	60	St Malo			
17 Jul	UNITY	Kb	Ipswich	69	Dunkirk	E Mathews	1885 Ipswich	W. Rands, Ipswich
1 Aug	SILVER EAGLE	Sr	Jersey	59	St Malo	E Mathews	1875 Guernsey	J. Abbott
31 Oct	CALINEUSE		St Malo	61	St Malo	Broadbent		
22 Nov	LUCINDA	Sr	Jersey	59	St Malo	E Mathews	1869 Jersey	W. Steer, Plymouth

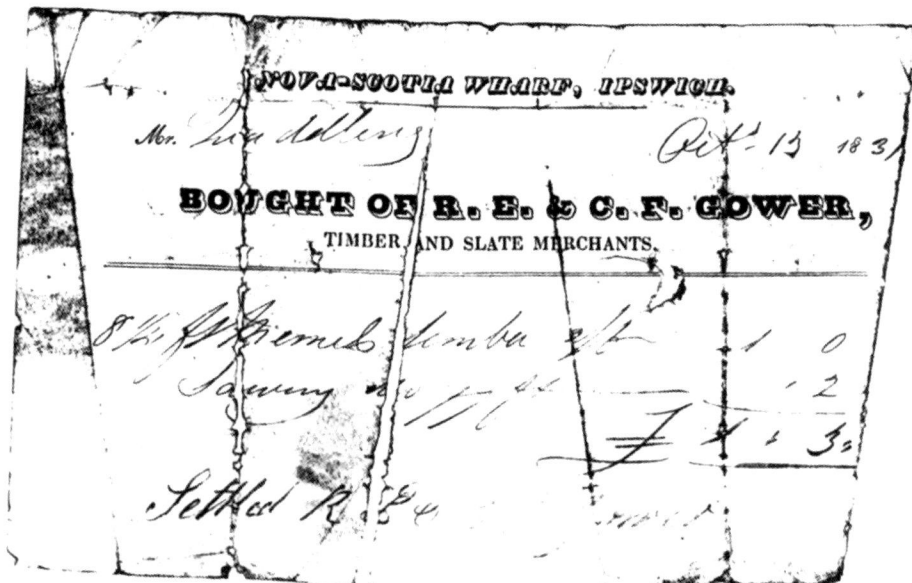

A receipt dated 1831 from timber and slate merchants R.E. and C.F. Gower of Nova Scotia Wharf, Ipswich. (Dr J. Blatchly)

stone is to be found in William Cubitt's weekly progress report of 8th June 1818 on the rebuilding of Stoke Bridge after flood waters had swept away two stone arches, drowning one of three men standing on the bridge. Cubitt, chief engineer at J. & R. Ransome, was responsible for the replacement cast-iron structure, the principal parts of which were made at an ironworks in Dudley, Staffordshire, and shipped to Ipswich from Gainsborough. He had requested the stone mason George Tovell 'to go to Scotland and get the stonework ready for laying down by the workmen in that country who are so much better qualified than any we can find hereabouts, and I expect by this rneans, much time will be gained as it is probable a freight of stones may arrive by the time the foundations are prepared for their reception'.

Stone shipments

From the middle of the nineteenth century stone was generally carried in sailing barges, as opposed to West Country schooners and ketches, because the barges were flat-bottomed with wide hatches. The first barges used were recorded in the 1850s and included Colchester's old *QUINTUS* that foundered off the Kent coast in 1866. The problem with using barges was that unlike bulk cargoes or those consisting of sacks or small packages that could be better distributed under the decks, stone came in large blocks that strained the hull, especially in rough weather.

Two stone cargoes came by sea from Portland for Alfred Harpham, ironmonger, stone and slate merchant of Ipswich, in 1884. The first arrived on 10th April and was carried by the ketch barge *SEPTIMUS* of Ipswich; the second came on 29th June in another ketch barge, the *MAY HAWTHORN* of Rochester.

Stone was a return cargo readily available to an East Coast skipper who had taken coal, cement or grain to Southampton or points west. It was not however a popular cargo or destination, the master having to decide whether to sail the additional forty miles from Southampton to Portland, usually against the prevailing winds. If, for instance, he had loaded cement on the London River, he would already have covered 190 miles from Gravesend to Southampton and considerably more when turning down Channel in adverse winds. Therefore with voyages to the south and west usually taking considerably more time than longer distances to the north-east coast, the master frequently decided to run back light, despite a possible loss of earnings for the barge, which would be negated anyway if the vessel were windbound for days at Portland. It was different if a barge was bound farther west to Exeter or Penzance, when a return cargo from Portland could be very useful.

Tons of block stone came by sea from the Isle of Portland to Ipswich for the first thirty odd years of the twentieth century. It was used for the restoration of old buildings, especially churches, for monumental masonry, and to embellish new buildings. Two principal companies were involved. Ernest Saunders & Company of 95 Cemetery Road (later at Sproughton Road) were in business from the early 1900s until the 1990s and Collins & Curtis Ltd began early in the 1920s at Handford Road. They remained there until 1986 when, having been bought out by Sadlers, the Ipswich building company, four years earlier, they moved to a small trading estate on Landseer Road, continuing there as Collins & Curtis Masonry Ltd beyond the year 2000. Both companies used natural stone quarried at Portland.

On 22nd November 1924, the sailing barge *RONALD WEST*, built at Teynham in 1903 for Samuel West Ltd, arrived from Portland with the first consignment of stone on which Ernest Saunders & Company were to carve the names of those soldiers who died at Ypres during the First World War. The panels of stone were intended for the walls of the famous Menin Gate Memorial at Ypres. More stone was discharged from Portland, appropriately enough by the sb *LORD HAIG* of Rochester, on 7th February 1925, and by a further visit on 4th May when 134 tons were craned off on to lorries. Unusually the steam coaster *EDENSIDE* of Sunderland, a regular collier at the Gasworks, arrived from Portland on 14th March with 155 tons of stone. Goldsmiths' *CETUS* arrived on 19th June with 150 tons. The *MAY*, which had been built and registered at Rochester in 1903 and was owned by Richard Cox of Weymouth for the stone work, came to Ipswich on 27th of August with 136 tons and again on 8th December carrying 133 tons. *LORD HAIG* was from the same Rochester yard run by Short Brothers as R. & W. Pauls' *LADY JEAN* and *LADY DAPHNE*, but she was all too soon run down and lost in the Humber. The *MAY* was also run down and the account of her tragic loss, written by Captain Bob Childs, is recorded here with his permission:

> The last cargo the *MAY* loaded was stone chippings at Alderney in May 1933. [Stone chippings for roadmaking were loaded by ships and barges at Alderney for many ports and the Portland-owned barges often filled in by bringing this roadstone to Portland.] Shortly before dawn on the following morning, when the barge was half way across the Channel en route to Portland, fog set in and the vessel was becalmed. With only another twenty-five miles to sail, no doubt the crew were looking forward to arriving the same day. Meanwhile, on her way down Channel outward bound for Australia steamed the Federal Line's ship *CAMBRIDGE*, a liner of some 10,800 gross tons. The ship's officers were of the best with all navigation rules adhered to strictly by the book. In such weather, the ship's siren would have been sounding a long blast every two minutes. Only those who have been on a small vessel without the benefit of radar will know the awful sense of anxiety upon hearing the mournful notes as the unseen ship approaches, not knowing from which side of the barge the danger is coming. At 4.11am, the *CAMBRIDGE* struck the *MAY,* which doubtless sank within a minute. Some smart work by the crew of the steamer followed in the almost hopeless task of finding any survivors, for her boats were swiftly launched. Just

as they were about to give up after a two-hour search a faint cry was heard and the boy cook was picked up. He was the only survivor. Once on board and after medical attention, he informed his rescuers of the name of his barge and her crew before he again fainted. Soon after the fog cleared, the *CAMBRIDGE* altered course for Tor Bay where the boy, Henry Hales of Reading, was landed and treated at Torbay Hospital for serious abdominal injuries. Lost with the barge were her master, George Chapman of Alderney, and mate, A. Hoxbe.

The loss of the Portland *MAY*, as she was generally known, brought to an end fifty-seven years of Portland ownership of some very fine coastal sailing barges.

There was not a regular trade to Ipswich from Portland by any means, just occasional cargoes in some years. Saunders, for example, received a few more loads by sea, including two in 1930. One was of 117 tons that came on l6th July in sb *MAGGIE*, Sandwich-built in 1898, and sb *VERAVIA*, completed in 1898 at Sittingbourne as the *ALARM*, arrived on 13th October with 135 tons. The sb *VALONIA* came on 4th July 1933 with 136 tons and again in 1935 with 125 tons; she had been fitted with an auxiliary engine in 1932. A small motor barge, the *GOLDACE*, built by Pollock of Faversham for Goldsmith of Grays in 1931, arrived with 120 tons on 30th September 1935, and another 88 tons was brought by the mv *REGUM*, possibly a Dutch coaster, in February, the following year. On 29th January 1938 the sb *VALONIA* arrived again and in November, the *CELTIC* berthed with stone for the new library at Colchester. She was one of the big steel sailing barges built at Papendrecht, Holland, in 1903 for Goldsmiths, to load about 250 tons. A newspaper cutting with the headline 'Ipswich-bound Barge's Buffeting—Cargo of Stone for Colchester's New Library' records her unfortunate voyage:

> 'The London sailing barge *CELTIC*, bound from Portland to Ipswich Docks with a cargo of Portland stone for Saunders Stone-masons (Ipswich) Ltd, suffered a terrible buffeting in Wednesday's gale. The vessel, which had left Portland a fortnight ago, had been held up by fog and contrary winds, and off the Foreland had her sails torn to shreds and her top mast was carried away. With decks awash, she was towed into Ramsgate by the Deal motor-boat *ROSE MARIE*.'

The last Portland stone cargo was probably that which came in the mb *SUCCESS* (ex-*CYMRIC*), also built at Papendrecht in 1903 and a sister ship to *CELTIC*. She berthed in July 1939 with 152 tons. *CYMRIC* had already been converted to a fully powered barge by that time, while in 1978 *CELTIC* was possibly the last ex-sailing barge to bring any freight to Ipswich. *VALONIA*, just mentioned, had been built in 1911 at East Greenwich and was lost during the Dunkirk evacuation in 1940. She had loaded pitch from Aylesford in Kent for Dunkirk and was due to load wheat, but the evacuation was about to begin and she was held back for taking off survivors. She was struck and holed by a Belgian tanker as she waited to leave and had to be abandoned.

The sailing barge *RONALD WEST*, spoken of earlier, was unfortunately run down and sunk by one of R. & W. Pauls' steamships, the *CROSSBILL*, when at anchor at Stone Heaps in the Orwell at 4.30 a.m. on 5th November 1935. The master, his wife and the mate managed to get on deck and board the *CROSSBILL*. The barge was raised, taken up to Pin Mill Hard and found unfit for further trading, and her registry was closed on l8th July 1936. It is thought she was broken up at Pin Mill.

Collins & Curtis generally had fewer seaborne stone cargoes. One barge cargo of 160 tons arrived for the company in December 1922 aboard the sb *EMMA* of Weymouth, which was launched at Strood in 1898 for Richard Cox. *EMMA* was wrecked in October 1931 near Scarborough when the barge was blown ashore, bound light Kings Lynn to Sunderland to load coal for Alderney. Her crew fortunately landed safely. Cranfields' *DANNEBROG* brought 132 tons in April 1930, and sb *BERYL,* Faversham-built in 1903, delivered 133 tons in October 1930. Among the company's contracts during the 1920s were the entrance to Ipswich Central Library and the Cenotaph in Christchurch Park. More recently, rebuilding work in the classical style was undertaken in London's King William Street, and a group of new houses was erected in Regents Park.

Cement

The two main types of cement used for building purposes are Roman cement and Portland cement, the first a quick-setting natural cement much in use before the invention of the cheaper and stronger artificial Portland cement. The manufacturing process for cement consists of the formation of silicates and aluminates of calcium by the intense heating of lime, derived from chalk or limestone, and clay.

From the beginning of the nineteenth century the need for hydraulic or water-resistant cement had begun to rise due to the building of canals, harbours and bridges. Later, with the coming of the railway, the demand increased even further. Roman cement is the traditional name given to a type of cement able to set rapidly under water, produced from stone containing a suitable mixture of lime, alumina and silica. James Parker took out a patent for manufacturing this 'natural' cement in 1796, using as his raw material septaria or nodules of argillaceous (containing a large amount of clay) limestone. The nodules consist of about 20 per cent silica and 15 per cent alumina. From the eighteenth century to the end of the nineteenth cement was produced by crushing, burning and grinding the rock to a powder.

In addition to the large quantities of stone found along the northern shore of the Thames estuary, septaria is present in parts of Suffolk. The nodules are found particularly along parts of the sea cliffs and in Harwich Harbour, the Orwell and Stour. Erwarton church was built with blocks of the stone and in recent years was restored using the same local material. As early as the sixteenth century, because of the awareness of likely changes to the Harwich approaches, strong protests were made against removal of the stone by Cardinal Wolsey for his new college in Ipswich when he expressed the wish for the building to be constructed of 'Harwich cliff stone'. Told that removal of the stone could endanger the safety of the town, he eventually ordered stone from the quarries at Caen.

From 1800 onwards septaria or cement-stone, earlier dug out of the cliff face, was dredged from the sea or riverbed by as many as 200 sailing smacks. These vessels, from Harwich, Pin Mill and Ipswich, dragged heavy dredges over the seabed. Great cromes or claws hooked to masthead tackle were used overside for the heavier lumps, which were broken into smaller pieces on deck. As many as thirty foreign vessels were recorded in April 1846 loading stone for the continent. A smack in the stone trade usually had three or four men aboard for what was extremely arduous and dangerous work, perhaps getting two tons of stone over the side in a day. The amount was assessed back in harbour by a

National Telephone—194.   Telegraphic Address—Eldred Watkins, Ipswich.

GREAT EASTERN LIME WORKS
(ESTABLISHED 1870.)

GRIFFIN WHARF & ROBINSON STREET, STOKE, IPSWICH.

ELDRED WATKINS,

Manufacturer of Grey Stone and Chalk Lime.

MEDWAY PORTLAND CEMENT OF THE FINEST QUALITY.

Whiting, Plaster, Hair, Lath, Parian & Keene's Cement Merchant.

Brick Rubbish, Whole Chalk Flints, Pit Flints, Wash Mill Flints, Granite, Rag Stone, Chalk, etc., for Road Making.

A 1904 advertisement for Eldred Watkins, who was a barge owner as well as a lime and cement manufacturer in Stoke, Ipswich, 1904.

'stone guesser' whose experience enabled him to judge accurately the weight of the cargo to everyone's satisfaction, and it was then unloaded at a wharf or on one of the heaps.

Over the years, thousands of tons went from Cobbolds Point at Felixstowe and Beacon Hill at Harwich, effectively widening the entrance and slowing the scouring of silt by the tides. Nobody was more concerned at what was happening than Captain John Washington, RN, of HMS *SHEARWATER*, who was engaged in surveying Harwich Harbour. He submitted a report to the Secretary of the Admiralty in January 1843 condemning the serious removal of stone, based on information from charts and plans of Harwich between 1709, 1756 and 1804. In the thirty years since about 1812, when the trade in cement stone begun, he stated he had been '. . . credibly informed that upwards of a million tons of this stone have been carried away from the shores in question'. Indeed Captain Washington asserted that the Board of Ordnance took 200,000 tons for the Government, reflecting that the Board had been running their own cement mill at Harwich since 1818. He criticised the removal of thousands of tons of stone from Felixstowe cliff (Cobbolds Point) that had served as a natural breakwater for the harbour causing two Mortella towers (as he called them) to collapse into the sea. This area was still being reinforced by importing stone to the beach in the year 2000.

His wide-ranging comprehensive report, with references to the fishing industry and the increasing trade to the harbour, included the following sentence. 'Under these points of view then, but chiefly as the Packet Station for all northern and central Europe, the preservation of this port appears to be of national importance.' Captain Washington later became Rear Admiral and Hydrographer to the Navy, and he is remembered today by the Washington Buoy in the Harbour approaches.

At one time there were five cement mills working in Harwich. By 1859, however, only John Pattrick remained in business with his factory at Dovercourt, alongside Bathside Bay. It was conspicuous by the 320ft chimney built in the 1870s to alleviate health risks from fumes and not removed until 1939, it being considered a prominent landmark for enemy aircraft. Pattrick changed to making Portland cement, but his premises closed by the end of the century and were put up for sale in 1906.

At Ipswich George Tovell was listed as a 'Roman cement maker', appearing in 1830 at St Matthews Street and in 1844 at Lock Road (New Cut East). He became a Dock Commissioner and his name is recalled today by Tovells Wharf, constructed as a part of the 'new works' in 1923-24, close to the site of his former cement factory.

William Colchester, referred to in the account of the fertiliser industry at Ipswich, also had an interest in the cement stone business. His barges, built at the Dock End Yard, sometimes loaded stone from heaps left by the smacks on the shore around Harwich Harbour. One such place in the mouth of the Orwell at Shotley is still known as Stone Heaps, and barges and smacks loaded from these heaps for Ipswich and other East Coast ports and further afield to other cement factories. In the 1870s E.C. Gibbons, of Shotley brickworks and Wolsey Street works in Ipswich, and George Mason, of St Peter's Wharf and later Greyfriars Road, were making Roman cement. By the 1880s both Oliver T. Gibbons, of Wolsey Street, and Mason were listed as cement merchants in the town.

Roman cement was gradually ousted by Portland cement, the term 'Portland' being first patented in 1824 by one Joseph Aspdin of Leeds, although this is contested in Kent where actual manufacture began in 1845 at Swanscombe. The name is thought to have originated by likening the strength of the new cement to the famous Portland stone quarried in Dorset. The modern cement industry began its expansion during the 1850s. The Portland cement works were particularly concentrated along the banks of the Rivers Thames and Medway, close to easily available sources of chalk and clay and with water transport and railway nearby.

William Brown, the timber and builders' merchant, received some cargoes of cement from John Pattrick during the 1890s. In 1892, for example, two of Pattrick's barges each brought five cargoes from Harwich to Browns at Ipswich. They were the *ONWARD* of Rochester, built at Sittingbourne in 1867, and the little *ALICE*, 22nrt, Ipswich-built in 1879. *ALICE*, one of several barges with that name, usually loaded local mud for Pattrick's works, similar to Mason's *KINGFISHER* at Waldringfield. In April 1898 the Maldon-registered *RENOWN* discharged cement from Leigh-on-Sea (where there had been a cement stone

Stone cargoes from Harwich delivered by smacks at Ipswich during the year 1857.

SMACK	MASTER	NRT	Jan	Feb	Mar	Apr	May	Jun	Jul	Aug	Sep	Oct	Nov	Dec	Totals
JUNIPER	Shilling	6	4	4	9	8	8	8	5	7	8	8	5	5	79
VIXEN	Biggs	8	3	3	6	7	0	8	3	5	4	5	4	2	50
WONDER	How	8	3		1		1								5
BEE	Webb	8	3	2	4	1									10
POLLY	Norman	8				4				3	6	2	3	1	19
ELLEN & MARY	Shilling	6			2	2	9			1	2	9	5	3	33
ALFRED	Robinson	8				2	8	8	4	6	8	8	6	3	53
LAURELL	Cook	8				1									1
DOLPHIN	Garrod	9					1								1
MARIA	Haste	7								4	2	5			11
MARGARET	Durrant	7								8	3				11
DORCAS	Norman	7								8	6	8	6	1	29
Total cargoes carried by smacks during 1857															302

works) for Eldred Watkins, a lime-burner and cement merchant at Griffin Wharf. In 1908 he received eleven bargeloads of cement from the Thames, ten of them in his own sailing barge *NOVATOR*, built at Ipswich in 1872, the other load in his *ETHEL ADA*, also Ipswich built, in 1897. One or two of Watkins' barges each month continued to bring in cement until the late 1920s. By the 1930s Masons Works (APCM) at Claydon supplied most of the needs in the area by road or rail. In 1939 William Brown supplemented his requirements for cement from the Thames by barge.

During the Second World War, however, the new airfields under construction for the RAF and the American Air Force needed thousands of tons of cement. For example, between 30th April 1942 and 31st March 1943 seven barges made a total of forty-one voyages and brought 10,736 tons to Ipswich from the Tunnel Cement Works, West Thurrock, as the following table reveals. This was out of a total of 249 barges with cement for those twelve months.

NAME	TONS (DWT)	CARGOES	OWNERS	BUILT
WILL EVERARD [1]	285	11	F. T. Everard, Greenhithe	Gt Yarmouth, 1926
CAMBRIA	170	9	F. T. Everard, Greenhithe	Greenhithe 1906
GREENHITHE	180	8	F. T. Everard, Greenhithe	Gt Yarmouth 1923
SARA	120	7	F. T. Everard, Greenhithe	Conyer 1902
LADY MARY	120	4	F. T. Everard, Greenhithe	Greenhithe 1900
LADY MAUD	125	1	F. T. Everard, Greenhithe	Greenhithe 1903
BANKSIDE [2]	140	1	Francis & Gilders, Colchester	Milton 1900

Voyages made by a sample of seven barges from West Thurrock to Ipswich with cement, 1942-43. 1 An account of the WILL EVERARD's *passage back to the Thames from Ipswich on 9th March appears in Captain J. Uglow's book Sailorman (Conway, 1975). 2 Mined Maplin Spit on 19th December 1942, with the loss of her crew of two.*

Airfield contracts had more or less ended by the summer of 1944 but cement has always been a regular commodity at Ipswich. In 2002, Southern Cement opened a £2.4m terminal at the port to handle imports of bulk cement and since then annual import volumes have grown to 150,000 tonnes. In November 2004, the 2,875-tonne mv *CEMSKY* made Ipswich its first port of call on its maiden voyage for Southern Cement Ltd, delivering 4,000 tonnes of cement to the Cliff Quay Terminal. The *CEMSKY*, converted by its Hamburg-based owners from an ordinary coaster to a specialized cement carrier at a cost of £1.5m, is the largest of six vessels serving the company's weekly dry-bulk import trade through Ipswich.

Mason's Waldringfield Cement Works

George Mason probably decided to manufacture cement in order to secure a local source of Portland cement to complement his timber business as a supplier to the building trade, and 'Mason's Portland Cement' became a familiar Suffolk trademark for over a century. The Deben estuary was navigable and busy in the nineteenth century, the railway only having reached Woodbridge in 1859. Waldringfield, with the channel close to the shore, was a practical choice therefore for George Mason, who purchased an old lime works there in 1875.

The materials needed, in addition to the river mud and chalk, were breeze for mixing with the slurry and coke to fire the kilns. The mud was dug from the river by floating a barge down to a spot just below Waldringfield, off White Hall Farm. As the tide left the vessel, the crew of two went overside and shovelled about twenty-five tons aboard before the water returned. Barges brought chalk from the Thames, and coke and coke-breeze from Deptford or other gasworks.

The mud was of a smooth consistency; it cut cleanly but had to have the salt removed by washing in piped fresh water from springs near the church. The chalk was also washed and mixed with the mud by adding eight to ten spits, or shovel depths, of mud to half a ton of chalk. The correct proportions were essential; in fact, insufficient care in the rule of thumb methods used earlier had delayed the successful use of Portland cement perhaps for twenty years.

The resulting slurry was allowed to stand and drain for two or three weeks in outside reservoirs, after which samples were taken by the foreman and tested by heating in ovens. When ready the mixture was laid up to ten inches thick on the oven floors for drying, and when dry it was placed in the bottle kilns, of which there were twelve. It was laid nine inches thick on alternating layers of faggots and coke some twenty feet high, with breeze spread on top to slow the burning process. The kilns were then bricked up and fired for about five days. After cooling for another two or three days the so-called 'clinker' was taken for grinding in a German-designed and installed ball-mill, the grinding being done by a ton and a half of iron balls that pounded the clinker to small pieces. It was then transferred for further grinding to another mill, from where it was removed as cement and taken for storage in quayside sheds before bagging. The cement was taken by barge either directly to London or by way of Ipswich, where oil in

Between 9th January and 21st April 1944 thirty-two barges arrived at Ipswich from the Tunnel Cement Works bringing more than 4,000 tons of cement.
*Part cargoes of cement and beer.
BSC = British Sugar Corporation.
MOF = Ministry of Food.

DATE	NAME	PORT OF REGISTRY	NRT	RETURN CARGO	EXPORTER	DESTINATION	DEPARTURE DATE
9 Jan 1944	ALICE MAY	Harwich	70				
10 Jan	GEORGE SMEED	Rochester	59	sugar	BSC	London	23 Jan
14 Jan	WILL EVERARD	London	150	sugar	BSC	London	27 Jan
19 Jan	TOLLESBURY	Ipswich	70				
19 Jan	DECIMA	London	67				
21 Jan	XYLONITE	Harwich	68				
23 Jan	REMERCIE	Harwich	67				
30 Jan	BRITON	London	80				
5 Feb	WILL EVERARD	London	150				
14 Feb	ALICE MAY	Harwich	70				
14 Feb	VERONICA	London	54				
14 Feb	WILL EVERARD	London	150				
17 Feb	TOLLESBURY	Ipswich	70				
17 Feb	PIMLICO	Rochester	53	malt	Meux Ltd	London	
19 Feb	SARA	London	50				
1 Mar	TROJAN	London	79	potatoes	MOF	London	9 March
1 Mar	ASTRILD	London	69	potatoes	MOF	London	9 March
2 Mar	GEISHA	London	70	potatoes	MOF	Rochester	9 March
6 Mar	CAMBRIA	London	79	sugar	BSC	London	15 March
- Mar	GLADYS	Harwich	68				
- Mar	LADY MAUD	London	59				
- Mar	VERONICA	London	54				
- Mar	PIMLICO*	Rochester	53	malt	Meux Ltd	London	
- Mar	LADY JEAN	Rochester	86				
- Mar	CARINA	London	64				
- Mar	THALATTA	Harwich	67				
- Mar	ANGLIA	London	54				
27 Mar	VERONICA	London	54				
28 Mar	LADY JEAN	Rochester	86				
29 Mar	LADY MAUD	London	59				
30 Mar	SARA	London	50				
21 Apr	WILL EVERARD	London	150	sugar	BSC	London	27 March

The kilns of the Waldringfield cement works can be seen in this photograph of about 1900 taken from the jetty in the Deben. (Robert Malster collection)

casks from Mason's oil mill was loaded for the capital. The vessels returned to Waldringfield laden with chalk, coke or breeze.

The works manager was Frank Mason, registered as the managing owner of seven or eight sailing barges. One was a small barge named *KINGFISHER*, used in the mud work. The others included *AUGUSTA*, 47nrt, built at Ipswich in 1874, *GRACE*, 50nrt, also completed at Ipswich in 1874, *ELSIE BERTHA*, 47nrt, Ipswich built in 1878 and *JUMBO*, 50nrt, built at Brentford in 1882. The barges were sold off after closure of the works and Cranfield Brothers bought the best three in the fleet; *EXCELSIOR, PETREL,* and *ORINOCO*.

In 1898 sixty-three cement cargoes from Waldringfield came to Ipswich for Masons, fifty-one of them in the firm's own barges. The other barges were *JANE* of Rochester, owned by J. Groom of Harwich, *OCEAN QUEEN*, owned by Peters of Southend, *THREE SISTERS*, owned by G. Miller of Dovercourt, and *FREDERICK WILLIAM* of Ipswich. Seven cargoes were brought by *LADY OF THE WAVE,* built at Brightlingsea in 1856 and part owned by her skipper, George Brooks of Ipswich.

In 1908 Waldringfield-Ipswich cement freights were down to thirty, carried by the *ORINOCO* (7), *JUMBO* (5), *EXCELSIOR* (5), *PETREL* (2), *GRACE* (7), *ELDRED WATKINS* (1), *GENERAL JACKSON* (2) and *OCEAN QUEEN* (1), Mason's own craft taking oil from his St Peters Oil Mills to London.

The Waldringfield works with its old-fashioned intermittent kilns closed down about 1910 and the business was transferred to a new works with modern rotary kilns beside Claydon station on the Liverpool Street to Norwich line, and with chalk and clay supplies close by. There is a story, probably apocryphal, that a member of the Mason family had spent the day hunting in the Great Blakenham area and had afterwards washed down his horse's legs. In doing so he noticed chalk and clay, the two ingredients of cement manufacture, adhering to the horse's legs. That discovery is said to have led to the decision to build the new works.

In 1948 the Claydon works were bought by Associated Portland Cement Manufacturers Ltd (APCM), formed in 1900 to amalgamate scores of small companies situated along the Thames and Medway, most of them owning a few sailing barges. By 1930 the 'Combine', as it was referred to, had accumulated a fleet of about 300 barges, but from that time onwards the barges were replaced by lorries that had by then become much more reliable. The APCM trademark, the Blue Circle (which latterly became the name of the group), was carried in the tops'l of the firm's barges.

The Claydon works was regularly considerably modernised from time to time, but it closed down in 1999. The final landmark of what was still known as Mason's Works disappeared in November 2000 when the factory chimney was demolished; it was the last vestige of the now-forgotten Victorian entrepreneur George Mason's little empire.

Road materials

From the mid-sixteenth century the upkeep of the king's highway was the responsibility of the parish. Each parishioner owning ploughland in tillage or keeping a plough was liable for the supply of a cart for four days a year and in addition each able-bodied householder or tenant was required to give a certain number of days' labour towards the repair of the roads annually. It was later possible to commute this obligation by making a payment or by providing a substitute person. The justices appointed a local official, the Highway Surveyor, who dealt with the payments and expenses involved. After 1835, statutory labour was abolished and a local highway rate was levied. Paupers were often put to work to collect or break the stones needed for highway repairs.

Turnpike roads became established in the eighteenth century, with local trusts able to charge a toll in exchange for the right to build and maintain a road, a tollhouse usually being built close to the highway for the use of the toll collector or pikeman. Cattle would typically be charged a farthing a head and a carriage horse 6d, while local cart traffic and persons going to church were excused the toll. One prominent turnpike road and bridge builder at that time was John Metcalf (1717-1810), who had lost his sight when six years old due to smallpox, hence his nickname 'Blind Jack of Knaresborough'. It was the setting up of his stagecoach business between York and Knaresborough in 1754 that led to his career as a pioneer roadmaker. Altogether he constructed nearly 200 miles of turnpike roads, the first of them between Harrogate and Boroughbridge.

In 1862 an Act was passed enabling the justices to unite parishes compulsorily into highway districts, and a Local Government Act followed in 1888

Cargoes of pitch ex-W.B. King unloaded at Ipswich, 1918. An approximate average of 130 tons per barge gives a total of 1,430 tons of pitch.
*Ketch-rigged or boomie barge.

Departure Date from Ipswich	Barge	POR	From	To	Built	Owner
13 Mar 1918	INTREPID	Ipswich	London	Calais	Ipswich 1881	J. Benstead, 4 Bolton Lane, Ipswich
13 Mar	ALDERMAN	Harwich	Calais	Calais	London 1895	J. Groom, Harwich
27 Mar	EDITH MAY	Harwich	Harwich	Calais	Harwich 1906	W. Barrett, Leytonstone
9 May	OLIVE BRANCH	Harwich	Calais	Dieppe	Harwich 1877	J. Hooker, Spring Road, Ipswich
9 May	INTREPID	Ipswich	Calais	Dieppe	Ipswich 1881	J. Benstead, 4 Bolton Lane, Ipswich
10 Jun	WOLSEY	Ipswich	London	Treport	Rebuilt Ipswich 1908	R. & W. Paul, Ipswich
10 Jun	DORIS	Ipswich	London	Fecamp	Ipswich 1904	R. & W. Paul, Ipswich
28 Aug	OLIVE BRANCH	London	Treport		Harwich 1877	J. Hooker, Spring Road, Ipswich
18 Nov	EMMA	Maldon	Maldon	Treport	Maldon 1897	S. Staines, Maldon
5 Dec	BRITANNIA*	Harwich	St Valery	Calais	Harwich 1893	J. Sparrow, Shotley
31 Dec	ALARIC	London	Treport	Treport	Sandwich 1901	W. Cory & Son

transferring the responsibility for main roads to the newly established county councils, local councils taking care of roads other than main ones by 1894. The 1888 Act also enabled county councils to assume responsibility for the majority of turnpike roads and the trusts involved were wound up.

The word Tarmacadam, a familiar enough title when describing road surfaces today, serves to remind us of one of the pioneers of modern road building, the Scottish engineer and surveyor John Loudon McAdam. He believed that a well-built and properly drained road could be constructed on subsoil surfaced with layers of compacted small broken stones. Another Scot, the civil engineer Thomas Telford, maintained that roads should have properly excavated foundations. Both gentlemen rebuilt roads across Britain and by 1836, the year McAdam died, 3,000 stage and 700 mail coaches were running timetabled services nationally.

The development of the steamroller in the mid-nineteenth century, most notably by Thomas Aveling of Rochester, facilitated the making of better surfaces, and by the early twentieth century road surfaces were being coated with pitch, found naturally in such places as the Pitch Lake in Trinidad, or tar produced in gasworks. The trade name Tarmac evolved after the discovery that tar mixed with 'macadam' made a smooth road surface. It was not until the 1920s, however, that modern road-building techniques using aggregate and concrete or else aggregate and granite chippings, together with bitumous products such as asphalt and tar, came to the fore.

Road material shipments

By the early 1880s Walter Burton King had established a Tar Distillery on an extensive piece of land situated between the last row of houses and the modern entrance to the West Bank, on the eastern-side of Wherstead Road near to Bourne Bridge. The location was a former ship-yard from where, in 1840, Messrs. Read and Page had launched the *ORION*, the first iron steamer to be constructed at Ipswich. Mr King himself lived on the site in a large detached, double-fronted house called The Elms, now converted into apartments. There were also two weatherboarded houses for staff known locally as Tar Cottages. These met an untimely end during the Second World War when the men on fire-watching duties there, having taken delivery of a new pump, decided to test its efficiency by setting alight some barrels of tar inside the empty cottages. Unfortunately the cottages' weatherboarding was also coated with several layers of tar and the resulting inferno was no match for the men's pump. The full-time firemen who had to be called remarked in no uncertain terms that it was bad enough dousing fires started by Germans without the natives setting the place alight.

Walter King's Company distilled tar from coal thereby producing a variety of by-products that included creosote, paraffin, soap and of course coke and coal gas. Surplus gas was later sold to the Ipswich Gas Light Company and the works eventually came into their ownership in the 1940s and remained a store for the Eastern Gas Board after nationalization in 1949 until it was disposed of in the 1980s.

The Company had their own wharf just above Ostrich Creek, accessible by sailing barges across the mudflats at high water. During 1889 for instance the sb *SWIFTSURE* loaded tar eight times, usually about 250 barrels a trip; sb *WHY NOT* of Faversham loaded 140 barrels; sb *ALICE* of Rochester (one of many of that name and registration) loaded pitch, as did the *ROSEBUD*, a small ketch barge built 1875 and owned for several years at Ipswich by W.H. Orvis. Prior to the start of the First World War in 1914, cargoes of pitch were being exported to France. In 1915, John Groom's kb *DANNEBROG* (built, registered and owned at Harwich and later to become one of Cranfields' fleet) arrived light from London to load pitch for Caen, sailing on 3rd August. She also arrived the following year on 25th March with maize for Pauls and sailed on 19th May with pitch for Treport. In 1917 two local boomies loaded pitch for Calais in May. They were the *BRITANNIA*, Shotley's own collier belonging to John Sparrow of the 'Bristol Arms' who was also the coal merchant, and the Ipswich *UNITY*, managing owner Walter Rands of 72 Spring Road. E. J. & W. Goldsmiths' steel barge *ASTRILD* sailed for Dieppe in August and the Maldon-registered sb *EMMA* sailed for Calais in the September.

Pitch was a filthy cargo. It was usually loaded in loose chunks that had to be trimmed while loading and then broken out for discharge after settling during the passage. It was available from many gas works and several barges were loaded at Beckton in East London. In addition to the unpleasant nature of the cargoes, by 1917 submarines and mines seriously added to the hazards of navigating to the French ports particularly during winter. As the war reached its end, pitch was much in demand for repairing the battle-scarred roads and the trade continued for a year or two after the war.

During 1918 the firm of Gatty, Saunt & Co., of 36-38 Victoria Street, London, rented 12 rods of land on the Promenade at New Cut East for storing pitch that had been delivered from elsewhere in railway trucks and which was intended to be loaded into barges. The following table records twenty-two barges sailing to France for the company with an approximate average tonnage each of 130 tons giving a total of 2,860 tons.

There was still plenty of trade to the Continent with pitch in 1919 with a total of forty cargoes sent away, of which twelve were from King's works and twenty-four from Gatty, Saunt & Co. The other four, to the account of an unidentified company named Earlback, went into Pauls' barges *PEGASUS, DORIS, ENA* and *BIJOU*. Of the remaining cargoes, thirty-three were loaded into barges, two went into small Dutch motor barges and one was loaded into the Irish-owned auxiliary ketch *TRALY* that had arrived from Ramsgate light to load for Treport. *TRALY* was one of two motor-ketches built of steel at Millwall in 1912. They were pioneering a new type of vessel, already tried by the Dutch, in which one of the new breed of oil engine could drive the ship in all conditions with sails acting as auxiliary power. The similar vessel rejoiced in the name of *THE MOTOKETCH*. The destinations for the first three months of 1919 were the same, that is Dieppe, Treport and Calais, but from the middle of April the remaining twenty vessels sailed to Antwerp.

Gatty, Saunt in 1920 sent a little over 600 tons of pitch away in the ss *LINCOLNSHIRE* and sailing barges *VICUNIA, SUNBEAM, MARGUERITE* and *HER MAJESTY* and then appear to have closed their account with the Dock Commission. In the same year Walter King dispatched a similar amount in *GLEN ROSA, EDITH MARY, ALARIC, UNITY* and *BRITANNIA*, and by 1922 it was down to 443 tons between *MATILDA UPTON, HAROLD* and the auxiliary barge *SEPOY*. The *SEPOY* was launched at Rye in 1901 for Frederick Crundall of Dover and is remembered for the remarkable rescue, by the Cromer lifeboat, of her master and mate off Cromer on 13th December 1933 when she had been blown on to the lee shore and was being pounded by heavy seas and breaking up. The rescue is famous in the annals of the RNLI and made headlines in the national newspapers.

BUILDING MATERIALS

Only 260 tons of pitch were loaded into the *INFLEXIBLE* and *MYSTERY* in 1923, with 150 tons going into Captain Mynheer's *PEARL* in February 1924. The *BRITANNIA* loaded 135 tons in 1925 and *SHAMROCK* 145 tons in January 1926. It appears that trade in pitch ended after the mv *MARTHA* loaded 145 tons in the following December. Occasional cargoes of shingle had been delivered to King's works, probably for filter beds.

Shipments of granite and stone to be used for the Dock Commission quaysides, the new sewage disposal works and the tramways, arrived during the 1880s from Guernsey, Penzance, Aberdeen and Portland. The table on page 214 reflects the vessels in order of arrival with stone in 1889.

Sure signs of changing times were revealed in 1909 when fifteen out of twenty stone cargoes were delivered in steamships and a firm with the title 'Road Maintenance Supply Company' was in business. A. & F. Manuelle of London, the company contracted to the Borough Council for the development of the electric tramway, received five cargoes of granite from Guernsey and one from Cherbourg. One arrival was the ss *THRIFT*, a collier of Aberdeen, built of steel there in 1903 and owned by the Northern Co-operative Company Ltd, also of Aberdeen. Another ship bringing stone from Guernsey was the ss *TURQUOISE*, built and registered at Glasgow in 1893 and constructed of iron and steel. The cargo from Cherbourg came in the *HELEN MARSHALL*, a wooden brigantine built at Garlieston, Galloway, in 1863. She was owned by W.H. Bessey, the coal merchants of Great Yarmouth, where she was registered.

Cargoes of pitch per Gatty, Saunt & Co, 1918.
*Ketch-rigged or boomie barge.

Departure date from Ipswich	Barge	POR	From	To	Built	Owner
23 Aug 1918	SCOTIA	London	London	Treport	Greenhithe 1903	F.T. Everard
29 Aug	INFLEXIBLE	Ipswich	Treport	Treport	Ipswich 1889	J. Hooker, 70 New Cut West
3 Sep	PEARL*	Ipswich	Treport	Treport	Ipswich 1889	G. Mynheer, 97 Back Hamlet
9 Sep	MYSTERY*	Faversham	Treport	Treport	Milton 1875	W. Pipe, Park Road, Ipswich
11 Sep	EDITH MAY	Harwich	Harwich	Treport	Harwich 1906	W. Barrett, Leytonstone
11 Oct	MATILDA UPTON*	Ipswich	Brightlingsea	Calais	Ipswich 1887	W. Dove, Brightlinsea
17 Oct	HAROLD*	London	Boulogne	Calais	Milton 1900	Garnham, 33 Belle Vue Rd, Ipswich
25 Oct	MATILDA UPTON*	Ipswich	Calais	Calais	Ipswich 1887	W. Dove, Brightlinsea
7 Nov	SUSSEX BELLE*	London	St Valery	Dieppe	Rye 1892	Garnham, 33 Belle Vue Rd, Ipswich
11 Nov	LORD NELSON*	London	Dieppe	Dieppe	Littlehampton 1889	A Parker, Bradwell
15 Nov	ALICE MAY*	Ipswich	St Valery	Calais	Harwich 1899	R.J. Smith, Trimley
15 Nov	HAROLD*	London	Calais	Dieppe	Milton 1900	Garnham, 33 Belle Vue Rd, Ipswich
22 Nov	LANCASTER	London	London	Dieppe	Brightlingsea 1898	Stone Bros, Brightlingsea
22 Nov	MELISSA	London	London	Dieppe	Southampton 1899	E.J & W. Goldsmith, Grays
25 Nov	UNA	Harwich	St Valery	Dieppe	Harwich 1882	W. Whitmore, Harwich
17 Dec	OLIVE BRANCH	Harwich	Calais	Dieppe	Harwich 1877	J. Hooker, Spring Road Ipswich
17 Dec	MATILDA UPTON*	Ipswich	Calais	Calais	Ipswich 1887	W. Dove, Brightlinsea
24 Dec	HAROLD*	London	Dieppe	Dieppe	Milton 1900	Garnham, 33 Belle Vue Rd, Ipswich
30 Dec	LORD NELSON*	London	Dieppe	Dieppe	Littlehampton 1889	A. Parker, Bradwell
31st Dec	ALICE MAY*	Ipswich	Calais	Dieppe	Harwich 1899	R.J. Smith, Trimley
31st Dec	WOLSEY	Ipswich	Calais	Treport	Rebuilt Ipswich 1908	R. & W. Paul, Ipswich
31st Dec	INFLEXIBLE	Ipswich	Dunkirk	Treport	Ipswich 1889	J. Hooker, 70 New Cut West

The Road Maintenance Supply Co. received four ships with granite ex-Cherbourg. One was the *WILLIAM DYER*, a wooden brig laid down at Sunderland in 1865 for Mrs. M. Dyer of Weymouth. This vessel was registered in Guernsey in 1909. Others were the ss *ZEPHYR*, London registered but built at Dundee in 1905 for the Sunderland Lighterage Company, and the ss *ALGEIBA* of Shoreham, owned by Sidney Penney of Brighton, which had been built as the *CLARENCE* at Bowling on the Clyde in 1902. Of particular interest in 1909 was the arrival from Cherbourg of R. & W. Pauls' steamer *SWALLOW* (62nrt), Paisley built. Also in 1909, Pauls' *SWIFT*, the second of that name and Paisley built in 1904, delivered granite from Guernsey to Ipswich for the Granite Stone Company, as did the schooner *MARIAN* of Padstow, laid down at Barnstaple in 1877. Mowlem, a very familiar company of civil engineers surviving into the twenty-first century, had one cargo of granite from Guernsey, purpose unknown, arrive in the ss *JAMES TENNANT*, built and registered at Newcastle in 1893. The Brighton-owned *ALGEIBA* and the ss *BISHOP ROCK*, built in 1895 for Alfred Rowland of Liverpool (some of whose coasters were named after prominent seamarks), both returned to the port with Guernsey granite for Fry Brothers. The St Keverne Stone Company of Cornwall sent stone from Falmouth in one of James Nurse's well-known Bridgwater ketches, the *CLAREEN*, completed at Plymouth in 1884. Some of these ketches, including *CLAREEN*, were familiar at Ipswich, having brought anthracite to the maltings.

On 13th March 1914 the big Faversham-registered schooner *RESOLUTE* berthed from Cherbourg with stone for A. & F. Manuelle. She was a former barquentine out of Peterhead, built at Aberdeen in 1868, and one of several elderly sailing colliers bought up by the Whitstable Shipping Company and still earning a living in the coal and rough trades until the increasing perils of war stopped them in 1916. During 1915 the ss *VIANNA* arrived from Cherbourg on 28th.June and again on 14th July with stone for E. Brookes (?). Not much is known about her, except that she was an interned German vessel. Little if any more stone was imported for the rest of the war years.

Three major roadstone companies were starting up at Ipswich and renting land from the Dock Commission in 1925. The best known was probably the East Anglian Roadstone & Transport Company Ltd of Queen Anne's Chambers, Tothill Street, Westminster SW1, usually referred to as 'EARAT', who rented a large chunk of the South West Quay. In their first full year the company received over 4,000 tons of broken granite, and 2,772 tons of tarmacadam was weighed outwards at the IDC weighbridge. At about the same time the Tilbury Contracting & Dredging Company arrived, but all the ships' cargoes were

Vessels arriving at Ipswich with cargoes of stone, 1889.

NAME	NRT	RIG	POR	FROM	CARGO	IMPORTER	REMARKS
MUTE	89	Sr	Ipswich	Guernsey	granite	IDC	Built 1853 Portsmouth, owner W. Bayley, Ipswich.
BLANCHE	68	Kb	Ipswich	Guernsey	granite	J. May	Built 1884 Ipswich, owner Garnham, Chelmodiston.
ELIZABETH	88	Bk	Ipswich	Goole	stone	Sewage Works	Built 1840 Yarmouth, owner J. Morton, Ipswich.
SEPTIMUS	75	Kb	Ipswich	Portland	stone	A. Harpham	Built 1860 Ipswich, owner Hayward, Pin Mill. Sunk Humber 1893.
SYLPH	95	Kb	Harwich	Goole	stone	Sewage Works	Built 1878 Harwich, owner Gooch, Harwich. Run down River Scheldt.
MUTE	89	Sr	Ipswich	Guernsey	granite	IDC	-
LYMINGTON	163	Sr	Harwich	Guernsey	granite	I. Noy	Built 1880 Harwich, owner Vaux, Harwich. Wrecked Holm Sands, October 1889, ex-Sunderland with coal.
PEARL	88	Kb	Ipswich	Guernsey	granite	I. Noy	Built 1889 Ipswich.

discharged to railway trucks, probably for transport to premises or customers elsewhere. Interestingly, Tilbury's London office address was the same as EARAT's. Both companies received broken granite from Inverkeithing on the Firth of Forth, sometimes part-cargoes for each. The ships were frequently those belonging to Henry & MacGregor of Leith, and all suffixed '*HEAD*'. For example, on 28th July 1926 the ss *ST. ABBS HEAD* berthed from Inverkeithing with granite for both companies. Alexander F. Henry & MacGregor Ltd began owning their own ships in 1907 after running a ships' agency, adopting their '*HEAD*' suffix in 1910. In 1936 they operated twelve steam coasters, of which the ss *BARRA HEAD* (built 1930), ss *DUNNET HEAD* (built 1921) and ss *ST. ABBS HEAD* (built 1914) were frequent traders to the EARAT berth. New motor ships were built during the 1950s, 1960s and 1970s. The company was absorbed by the London & Edinburgh Shipping Co. Ltd in 1941 and by the 1970s had associations with Christian Salvesen, also of Leith, when some of their new bulk carriers brought the last coal cargoes to Cliff Quay power station.

The steamers *RATTRAY HEAD, DUNNET HEAD, BARRA HEAD, NOSS HEAD, MARWICK HEAD* and *ST. ABBS HEAD* combined with three other vessels to make forty-four voyages to Ipswich during 1933. The total tonnage of broken granite or chippings for the year ending in March 1936 amounted to 31,880 tons, in addition to a few thousand tons of large rubble and the occasional ten to thirty tons of kerb stones. Apart from Inverkeithing, several cargoes came from Jersey.

Penlee Quarries Ltd, of 67 Queen Street, Bristol, had 10,134 tons of broken granite discharged to railway trucks during the twelve-month period April 1925-March 1926. They continued to handle roadstone by rail in some years, probably to their contractors or customers, in the same way that the Tendring Rural District Council at Great Bentley in Essex received two shiploads of broken granite, one in the ss *OUTWOOD* on 27th October 1927 and the other in ss *YEWBANK* on February 15th 1928, making a total of 716 tons. Both cargoes were discharged to railway trucks at Tovells Wharf and Cliff Quay, presumably for transport to Great Bentley station close to the council yard or to another site for their road mending.

George Hodsman & Sons Ltd, of 7 Martin Road, Middlesbrough, rented land at Tovells Wharf for making tarmacadam in the mid-twenties. In 1925 they are recorded as completing a tenancy agreement with the IDC 'in respect of a tarred slag works', taking delivery by rail of an iron tarmac drier, a boiler and other machinery plus the laying of a siding to the premises. In the twelve months April 1927 to March 1928, forty cargoes totalling 18,700 tons of slag stone were delivered by sixteen ships, most of it coming from Middlesbrough. At some stage during the 1930s a link developed with Woodmancy & Co. Ltd, Felixstowe coal factors, roadstone merchants and shipbrokers, to whom accounts were sent in the 1940s. Woodmancy & Co., which bore the name of a Yorkshireman who became manager of the Felixstowe Dock & Railway Co. in 1891, operated the tarmacadam plant at Tovells Wharf mentioned above.

In December, February and March 1927 Edward J. Edwards, of Plumstead Road, Norwich, began importing granite through Ipswich. Four cargoes totalling 1,800 tons arrived during those months, one in the ss *ROSALIE*, built at Goole in 1906, two in the steamship *JOLLY HUGH* and one in ss *JOLLY BRUCE*. These last two vessels, belonging to Walford Lines of London, are not to be confused with F.W. Horlock's later Mistley coasters prefixed *JOLLY*. Already established as a road-mending contractor at Norwich, E.J. Edwards owned a Norfolk wherry named *UNKNOWN* but renamed by Edwards with

Tovell's Wharf, seen here about 1930, was constructed in 1923-4 following the filling in of the old branch dock using ballast dredged from the Dock. The name commemorated George Tovell, a member of the original Ipswich Dock Commission, who owned a small cement works on part of the land around which the development took place.

amazing flair to become *MACADAM*. She plied the broads and rivers unloading road materials at local staithes for road repairs. By the mid-1930s the business at Ipswich was flourishing, as over 11,000 tons of broken granite was imported. Stone came from Newlyn and from Crookhaven in the far south-west of Ireland near Mizen Head.

Crow Catchpole & Co. Ltd of Aldwych House, London WC2, with depots across the south of England, began operations at Ipswich in the early thirties, renting land at Cliff Quay in front of Fisons' factory. Twenty-eight cargoes of slagstone and granite were discharged there in 1932 from Middlesbrough or Dundee.

In the mid-1920s the Limmer & Trinidad Lake Asphalt Company opened a yard in Seven-Acre Field, Portman Walk, beyond the Constantine Road power station. West End Road was later opened and Limmer & Trinidad had their yard close to the new river bridge at Handford Lock. In 1927 they received 700 tons of sand from six barges, and 1,415 tons of asphalt in barrels and 115 tons of oil in drums out of eleven barges. All of this was delivered by lorries from the dock. They continued throughout the 1930s to receive cargoes of asphalt and granite dust in barrels by sailing barge. The company, with its head office at 34 Victoria Street, London SW1, later went on to receive cargoes of stone taken by lorry to West End Road. In 1955 they had one cargo from Dundee, three from nearby Newburgh and one each from Jersey and Newlyn. In 1958 fourteen cargoes were discharged and there were eight in 1970.

During the 1939-1945 War stone imports dropped from eighty-seven in 1939

BUILDING MATERIALS
217

Another view of Tovell's Wharf with its travelling cranes, with the oil mill and Meux's maltings in the background on the other side of the Dock. The ss ALICE MARIE, built in 1920 to replace an earlier vessel of that name that had been torpedoed in January 1918, is being unloaded into railway wagons. Owned by the Rodney Steamship Company of Newcastle, she struck a mine in the Barrow Deep in 1940.

to eleven in 1940, with none in 1941 and 1942, before recovering a little from 1943. The companies meanwhile were receiving some supplies by railway. EARAT, which had moved its head office to The Thatched House, Wargrave, in Berkshire, had the ss *SARNIA* with 885 tons of roadstone arrive in March 1940, ss *JERSEY QUEEN* discharge 1,175 tons in April, and two more vessels arrive in May, the ss *IPSWICH TRADER* with 490 tons and ss *TREMAIN* with 900 tons. The ss *THORA HAFTER*, with 747 tons, appears to have been the last arrival in July. Another 6,580 tons arrived by rail by March 1941. E. J. Edwards received

Ships arriving with stone for G. Hodsman, April 1927 to March 1928.

SHIP	NRT	POR	NO. OF CARGOES	BUILT	OWNERS
ss *SKINNINGROVE*	217	Middlesbrough	14	1895, Thompson, Sunderland	Skinningrove Ironworks
ss *BRYNAWEL*	163	Glasgow	7	1893, McArthur, Paisley	G. Canning
ss *CROFTER*	?		3		
ss *CROHAM*	154	Aberdeen	3	1912, Fullerton, Paisley	J.S. Cole
ss *RIVER LUNE*	118	Barrow	2	1898, Paisley	R. Little, Lancaster
ss *BEESTON*	192	Liverpool	1	1921, Cochrane, Selby	Overton SS Co.
ss *NOSS HEAD*	171	Leith	1	1921, Hall, Aberdeen	Henry & MacGregor
ss *AIRDRIE*	?		1		
ss *NORHAM*	?		1		
ss *CLYDE FIRTH*	?		1		
ss *SHELLIE*	130	Dundalk	1	1905, Dublin	S. Lockington, Dundalk
ss *STREAM FISHER*	191	Barrow	1	1919, Appledore	J. Fisher, Barrow
ss *BANGOR*	134	Beaumaris	1	1894, Bowling	O. Jones, Bangor
ss *ASHDENE*	125	Sunderland	1	1893, S. Shields	Ferrum SS Co., Newcastle
ss *NORTHGATE*	155	Stockton	1	1925, Hawthorn Leslie, Newcastle	
ss *DEMPSTER*	?		1		
Total number of cargoes			40		

one stone cargo aboard the ss JIM in July 1940 and another 5,737 tons by rail for the next nine months. Hodsman had 5,122 tons during same period by rail.

Once peace had been restored in 1945 the trade resumed, but with fewer tarmac contractors. Crow, Catchpole remained but were taken over by Tarmac Roadstone Ltd, tarmacadam manufacturers of Cliff Quay, and eventually only the successors to EARAT survived. The office had moved to 60 Bracondale, Norwich, and the company was soon to become Tilbury (EARAT) Ltd although still situated at the S.W. Quay.

In 1964 thirty-three cargoes of roadstone were brought to Ipswich in eighteen ships. There were fifteen cargoes for EARAT and eighteen for Tarmac Roadstone Ltd. Nine of these cargoes arrived from Inverkeithing, nineteen from the Tees, one from the Continent and, surprisingly, four from Porthoustock, a village on the Lizard peninsular in Cornwall, close to the Manacles rocks, from where the occasional cargo had come since the 1930s.

Tilbury (EARAT) Ltd continued to unload ships throughout the 1980s at the S.W. Quay, although by then these were mainly Dutch motor vessels from Teesport. However, stone began to be delivered by road in the 1990s and traffic by sea ended. The business remained and by the year 2000 had been absorbed by Tarmac Quarry Products Ltd at the S.W. Quay.

A processing plant for marine dredged aggregates opened on the north end of the West Bank Terminal in 1992. Aggregate producers Wilding and Smith Ltd were following guidelines encouraging more use of resources from the sea rather than the opening of new land-based quarries. In addition to sand and gravel processing, the plant is also used for the importation of crushed rock by sea.

Ships arriving at Ipswich with stone for EARAT during 1949.

SHIP	NRT	POR	FROM	NO. OF CARGOES	BUILT	OWNERS
ss YEWCROFT	410	Glasgow	Newlyn	1	1929, Scott, Bowling	J. Stewart
ss RIVER FISHER	451	Barrow	Inverkeithing	1	1941, Vickers Armstrong, Barrow	J. Fisher
ss ASTERIA	319	Glasgow	Inverkeithing	1	1926, J. Lewis, Aberdeen	W. Robinson
ss LANCASTERBROOK	490	London	Newlyn	1	1948, J. Lewis, Aberdeen	Comben Longstaff
ss BARRA HEAD	326	Leith	Inverkeithing	10	1930, Goole SB Co.	Henry & MacGregor, Leith
ss THE PRESIDENT	481	Glasgow	Newlyn	1	1936, Ailsa SB Co., Troon	J. Hay, Glasgow
mv POLLY M	183	London	Newlyn	1	1937, Van Diepen, Waterhuizen	Metcalf, London
ss LEICESTERBROOK	490	London	Newlyn	2	1948, J. Lewis, Aberdeen	Comben Longstaff
mv SUMMITY	287	London	Inverkeithing	1	1939, G. Brown, Greenock	F.T. Everard, London
ss HIGHLAND QUEEN	570	London	Newlyn	1	1945, Ardrossan Dockyard	Queenship Navigation
ss NORDIC QUEEN	582	London	Newlyn	2	1945, G. Brown, Greenock	Queenship Navigation
mv AUSTERITY	305	London	Inverkeithing	1	1947, Grangemouth Dockyard	F.T. Everard
ss WINDSOR QUEEN	561	London	Newlyn	1	1943, Burntisland SB Co.	Queenship Navigation
mv SCARCITY	300	London	Inverkeithing	1	1948, Goole SB Co.	F.T. Everard, London
mv SERENITY	286	London	Inverkeithing	1	1941, G. Brown, Greenock	F.T. Everard, London
ss ST ABBS HEAD	256	Leith	Inverkeithing	3	1914, J. Fullerton, Paisley	Henry & MacGregor
ss TUDOR QUEEN	582	London	Newlyn	1	1941, Burntisland SB Co.	Queenship Navigation
mv ACTUALITY	499	London	Inverkeithing	1	1945, Goole SB Co.	F.T. Everard
ss THE DUKE	387	Glasgow	Newlyn	1	1927, Ailsa SB Co., Troon	J. Hay, Glasgow
Total number of cargoes				32		

General cargoes 9

The seventeenth and eighteenth centuries saw civil unrest abroad, religious disturbances at home and the Dutch Wars, which were unpopular because a great deal of our trade was with Holland. Most of the trade left to Ipswich was sending provisions and other commodities to London, a trade that can be illustrated by examples from the shipping records of 1670:

DESIRE of Ipswich
    587 firkins of butter
    12 hundredweight of cheese
    2 barrels of walnuts
    6 broad cloths
    raisins and other goods

JAMES of Ipswich
    750 firkins of butter
    21 hundredweight of cheese
    1 barrel of brawn
    1 basket of pewter and other goods

MARYGOLD of Ipswich
    1,200 cheeses
    55 firkins of butter

SPEEDWELL of Ipswich
    25 firkins of butter
    10 hundredweight of cheese
    10 bags of carrot seed
    2 hogsheads of apples
    3 barrels of beeswax
    2 broad cloths
    1 firkin of brawn
    1 bag of cotton yarn
    5 quarters of peas

MAYFLOWER of Ipswich
    30 pairs of oars
    2 dozen pieces for hard spikes
    4 firkins of butter
    2 loads of planks

(*Firkin*; a measure equal to 56 pounds of butter, and one-quarter of a barrel or nine gallons for brewing.)

    Cargoes to London changed little during the next 150 years. In August 1817, for example, the *FRIENDS OF ELIZA*, 101 tons and built in 1792 at Ipswich where she was registered, carried an assortment of goods to the capital. Her master and owner at the time was Edward Caston and she had on board wheat, flour, malt, beans, sugar, butter, cheese, a cask of mustard, a pianoforte, 45 bags of rags, three dozen ploughshares, paint and leather.
    In the third quarter of the nineteenth century the schooner *MAY FLOWER*, 60nrt and built at E.J. Robertson's yard in Ipswich, was sailing regularly to Rotterdam for her owner John May, who was a wholesale grocer with a warehouse on St Peter's Dock. One John May, junior, was listed in 1836 as a wholesale butter and cheese factor at the Common Quay, with a William May of St Stephen's Lane in the same business. In 1844, William May was established at St Peter's Wharf and Yarmouth, and John May was living in St Peter's Street and working on the Common Quay. Fifty years after John May, junior, was listed with his premises at the Common Quay, John May & Company is described as provision merchants of Commercial Road.
    In 1883 the *MAY FLOWER* under Captain Hawkins arrived at least half a dozen times from Rotterdam with cheese, brushes and baskets, and on two

occasions also brought sugar for Burton & Son. On 18th March 1884 another schooner, *AMY*, 98nrt and Ipswich built and registered in 1827, brought from Rotterdam a part cargo of sugar for Burtons, the rest being iron rails for the Ipswich tramway. The little 33nrt *HANDY* of Jersey and the *LYDIA*, also of Jersey, arrived from Cherbourg with butter for H.W. Raffe, a wholesale grocer of St Peter's Street and Rose Lane. Raffe received several similar cargoes, including butter from Cork in the schooner *AMELIA AND JANE* of Guernsey in 1905. She was of 51nrt and owned by George Louis Kent of Jersey, where she was laid down in 1874. These are examples of regular cargoes of the period, with Rouen also a regular port of loading.

For over thirty years, from the early 1880s onwards, two small locally-owned coasters, *EAGLET I* and *EAGLET II*, served the farmers and residents of the Orford area by maintaining trips backwards and forwards from Ipswich throughout the seasons of the year. The regular sailings of the two *EAGLETS* may not seem remarkable but achieving more than forty round trips a year in these small relatively low-powered craft with not too much freeboard needed perseverance and hard work. There was little time to lose sheltering from the weather despite the fact that the sea passage of only ten miles from Harwich to Orford had to be made in the winter months of east and south-easterly gales when that coastline was very exposed to the seas.

EAGLET I (20 gross tons, 14 reg. tons, official no. 86618) was built of wood in 1883 by Curtis at Ipswich. She was 50.3 feet in length, 13.5 feet in breadth and had a hold of 3.9 feet in depth. The vessel was a screw steamer fitted with a two-cylinder steam engine made by E.R. & F. Turner of Ipswich. She had various owners, the first being Richard Blake, corn merchant, with a 48/64 share and William John Haste, master, with the remaining 16/64 share. In 1898 she went to Arthur Heywood and in 1906 to Kenneth Clark, both men living at Sudbourne Hall. In 1910 she was sold to Dan Marine of Ipswich, the builders of *EAGLET II*. In 1911 the vessel was re-registered at Hull and renamed *HYCOL*. William Pearson Ltd, of 15 Elm Street, London, was her last known owner.

The larger *EAGLET II* (44 gross tons, 20 reg. tons, official no. 122978) was built of steel in 1910 by Dan Marine of Ipswich where she was registered. She was 62.8 feet in length, 13.2 feet in breadth and the depth of the hold was 5.8 feet. The 30 hp screw motor vessel was fitted with a Dan Marine 2-cylinder paraffin engine. Her first owner was Kenneth Clark of Sudbourne Hall, the former owner of *EAGLET I*. The *EAGLET II* was disposed of in 1918 when the coastal trade dwindled with ex-army lorries becoming available and Orford losing some of its remoteness. It is thought the vessel went to Southampton followed by moves to Herne Bay (?), Southampton, Rouen and Greenwich owners until in 1922 she was mortgaged to Barclays Bank after which her registration soon closed.

The master of the *EAGLET I*, Captain Haste, frequently delivered goods and groceries to order from Ipswich to Orford. Sailing barges carried general cargo when required and in 1910 when the new *EAGLET II* was due, sb *FRESTON TOWER*, owned by the Haste family, made six such voyages from May until October.

EAGLET II made her first sailing from Ipswich to Orford on 21st November 1910. In March 1912 she brought a cargo of coal from Orford to Burtons at Ipswich and the following year she loaded coal for Ransomes Sims & Jefferies. There are no coal mines in Orford and Ransomes had about twenty part-cargoes of coal delivered by steamship from the north-east coast to their works in 1913 so why this coal was available at Orford is curious at a time when sailing barges were still bringing it to Orford from the north.

GENERAL CARGOES

As the following tables show, when making the round trip between Ipswich and Orford, return cargoes were frequently available, sometimes hay for the merchants and horse users of Ipswich. For example, Frederick Fish of Tavern Street, well known furnishers in the town, had such a cargo in 1886, as did George Fisk, a grocer of Queen Street. The Fiske family of Thornbush Hall, Bramford, also owned Havergate Island in the River Ore from where in 1887 *EAGLET I* loaded hay for Fiskes. In 1913 *EAGLET II* brought two loads of hay back to Ipswich for Canham & Sons, proprietors of livery stables in St Matthews Street.

Hay cargoes were sometimes brought from Orford by *EAGLET II* for Alfred Cooper, an Ipswich hay and straw company. When the sailing barge *ALINE* of Harwich brought hay from the Deben in November 1885 for Cooper, his address at that time was St Margaret's Green. Cooper's later Crown Street yard was burnt out in a very spectacular fire in the 1950s.

Messrs. C. Warren & Son of Lower Orwell Street, Ipswich, was another hay and straw company surviving into the twentieth century. This company received

Voyages made by the EAGLET I *between Orford and Ipswich from 9th January to 22nd March 1888.*

Vessel	Arrived Ipswich from Orford 1888			Departed Ipswich for Ordord 1888		
	Date	Supplier	Cargo	Date	Supplier	Cargo
EAGLET I	9 Jan.	A.T. Pratt of Chillesford	Wheat	17 Jan.	R.& W. Paul	Maize & oats
					Cranfield Bros.	Bran
					James Bird	Oilcake
					Cubitt & Chatterton	Oilcake
					N.& O. Parry	Oilcake
					G. Wilson	Offal
EAGLET I	2 Feb.	Minter of Boyton	Wheat	Feb.4	Cubitt & Chatterton	Oilcake
					G.Wilson	Pea meal
					J.Fison	Bone manure
					A.Heywood	Rod iron
					W.Wilson	Bran
EAGLET I	13 Feb.	Brinkley & A. Heywood, Sudbourne	Wheat	15 Feb.	R.& W.Paul	Oats
					Bird	Oilcake
					Cranfield Bros.	Offal
					Wilson G.	Barley Meal
					Mason G.	Oilcake
EAGLET I	20 Feb.	T. Brinkley	Wheat	23 Feb.	Unknown	Peas & oats
					Wilson G.	Barley meal
					Wilson W.	Oats
					Fison J.	Oilcake
					Mason G.	Oilcake
EAGLET I	3 Mar.		Light	5 Mar.	Cubitt & Chatterton	Oilcake
					Mason G.	Oilcake
					Bird Jos.	Oilcake
					Paul R. & W.	Oilcake
					Brown Wm.	Cement
					Mason G.	Oil
					Wilson G.	Offal
EAGLET I	12 Mar.	A.T.Pratt of Chillesford	Wheat	13 Mar.	Paul R.& W.	Oats & maize
					Cranfield Bros.	Bran
					Prentice	Moss litter
EAGLET I	20 Mar.		Light	22 Mar.	Fison J.	Manure
					Colchester W.	Nitrate of soda
					Wilson W.	Offal
					Mason G.	Oilcake
					Wilson G.	Offal

Vessel	Arrived Ipswich 1914				Departed Ipswich 1914			
	Date	From	Cargo	Customer	Date	Destination	Cargo	Merchant
EAGLET II	26 April	Orford	Hay	A.Cooper	28 April	Orford	Oilcake	Mason G.
							Molascine	Packard E.
							Coal	Cory & Son
							Lime	Brown Wm.
							Bran	Cranfield Bros.
							Oilcake	Christopherson
EAGLET II	2 May	Orford	Hay	A.Cooper	6 May	Orford	Bran	Cranfield Bros.
							Oilcake	Cubitt & Sons
							Wood	Brown Wm.
							Coal	Ipswich Coal Co.
							Coke	Ipswich Gaslight Co.
							Oilcake	Christopherson
EAGLET II	13 May	Orford	Light		19 May	Orford	Coke	Ipswich Gaslight Co.
							Maize	Cowell & Co.
							Maize	Paul R. & W.
							Middlings	Cubitt & Sons
							Bran	Cranfield Bros.
							Cement	Brown Wm.
EAGLET II	23 May	Orford	Light		24 May	Burnham-on-Crouch	Oilcake	Christopherson
EAGLET II	29 May	London	Manue	Christopherson	3 June	Orford	Barley	Cubitt & Co.
							Wood	Brown Wm.
							Bran	Cranfield Bros.
							Oilcake	Christopherson
EAGLET II	5 June	Orford	Hay	A.Cooper	9 June	London light		
EAGLET II	12 June	London	Manue	Christopherson	16 June	Orford	Oilcake	Christopherson
							Cement	Brown Wm.
							Bran	Cranfield Bros.
							Rice meal	Cubitt & Sons
EAGLET II	18 June	Orford	Hay	A.Cooper	22 June	Queenborough		Light
			Wheat	Cranfield Bros.				
EAGLET II	24 June	Queenborough	Manure	Christopherson	27 June	Orford	Bone & meat meal	Christopherson
							Maize	Cubitt & Sons
							Maize	Damant W. F.
							Oilcake	Mason G.
							Bran	Cranfield Bros.
							Maize	Cowell & Co.
							Lime	Brown Wm.
EAGLET II	1 July	Orford	Light		6 July	Orford	Wood	Brown Wm.
							Bran	Cranfield Bros.
							Wood	Crossley A.B.
							Wood	Bennett & Snare
EAGLET II	8 July	Orford	Light		14 July	Beccles	Barley*	Ipswich Malting Co.
EAGLET II	18 July	Cantley	Protos	Christopherson	22 July	Beccles	Barley*	Ipswich Malting Co.
EAGLET II	24 July	Beccles	Light		27 July	Burnham-on-Crouch	Oilcake	Christopherson
EAGLET II	30 July	Burnham	Light		4 August	Orford	Oilcake	Mason G.
							Oilcake	Christopherson
							Barley	Cowell & Co.
							Bran	Cranfield Bros.
							Lime	Brown Wm.
							Coal	Cory Wm. & Sons
							Goods	Haste J.

Trips made by the EAGLET II *from the end of April to the beginning of August 1914. Note the variety of cargoes carried to Orford and the hay brought back for Alfred Cooper, forage contractor.*
*ex sv CHAMPIGNY

very little trade through the Dock however apart from perhaps a couple of barge loads of hay arriving from Harkstead and Levington. Charles Warren rented land around the port from the Ipswich Dock Commission during the First World War and into the 1920s. This was initially for the storage of hay or straw brought to the town for the company's contract with the army to supply forage that was sent either to France or to Ipswich Barracks. The company also paid for the regular parking of a steam lorry and trailer for the financial year April 1920 to March 1921. There were over fifty entries for parking but the total for the year only came to £2 15s 6d. In 1922 two railway trucks were each loaded with two-and-a-half tons of chaff. During 1923-1924 eighty-seven tons of chaff, two tons of hay and four-and-a-quarter tons of oats were sent away on the railway. By 1925 though, only two tons of hay were loaded into truck No.19826 at a charge of $2\frac{1}{2}$d per ton, giving a total account of 5d for that twelve-month period. Because of the swift drop in demand by the Army and other customers changing to motor transport, the firm closed in 1927. Their yard quickly sold to become the Eastern Counties Bus Company's workshops.

North Sea work by ketch barges

At a time when the trading activities of the ketch barge were probably at their height and typical of the period in 1898, it is worth recording in detail the North Sea crossings and long coastal voyages made by these vessels to load cargoes for Ipswich companies.

The *FRIENDSHIP*, the first vessel mentioned in the table below, was a big schooner-barge owned by John Smith of Burnham-on-Crouch for the coal trade and registered at Colchester. She was built at Sittingbourne in 1890, flat bottomed and with leeboards, but could load nearly 500 tons. Rigged with square sails on the foremast she drew less than four feet of water when light. Although not a regular trader to Ipswich, she was to arrive three times in 1901 with two coal cargoes for William Colchester's works from Seaham and one of anthracite from Swansea for Pauls. She was run down off the Humber by a steamer in 1912.

Arrivals and departures of ketch barges in 1898.

Arrival	Barge	Reg	Nrt	From	Importer	Cargo	Depart	Exporter	Cargo
9 Jan	FRIENDSHIP	Colchester	199	Seaham	Beaumont	coal	1 Feb	J Fison	burnt ore
16 Feb	BYCULLA	Ipswich	79	Calais	Colchester	phosphate	5 Jan		light
12 Feb	ROCH CASTLE	London	90	Harwich		light	28 Feb	Lewcock	old iron
23 Feb	BRITANNIC	London		Brussels	Packard	phosphate	9 Mar	Packard	fertilizer
28 Feb	MAZEPPA	Harwich	79	Dunkirk	Colchester	phosphate	14 Mar		light
15 Apr	JUSTICE	Harwich	73	Bruges	Packard	phosphate	23 Apr		light
15 Apr	HILDA	Ipswich	57	Dunkirk	Colchester	phosphate	27 Apr		light
21 Apr	ROSE BUD	Harwich	59	Grimsby	Berners	coal	5 May		light
25 Apr	BRITANNIC	London		Brussels	Prentice	phosphate	2 May		light
8 May	FELIX	Ipswich	67	Poole		light	13 May	Prentice	fertilizer
17 May	MATILDA UPTON	Ipswich		Terneuzen	Prentice	phosphate	6 June	Slater	trees
22 May	LORD CHURCHILL	London	72	Cologne	Burton	sugar	26 May		light
23 May	BRITANNIC	London		Ghent	Prentice	phosphate	28 May		light
24 May	ELIZA H	Harwich	98	Ghent	Fison	phosphate	10 Jun	Whitaker	trees
6 Jun	STOUR	Harwich		Rotterdam	Curtis	moss litter	10 Jun		light
6 Jun	DUNQUERQUE			Dunkirk	Fison	fertilizer	20 Jun		light
13 Jun	BYCULLA	Ipswich	79	Cologne	Burton	sugar	23 Jun		light
18 Sep	LOTHAIR	Harwich	179	Antwerp	Fison	phosphate	30 Sep		light
26 Sep	RECORD REIGN	Maldon		Grimsby	R & R	timber	30 Sep		light

GENERAL CARGOES

Later general cargo services

The company known as Coast Lines Ltd was formed in 1913 by the merger of three Liverpool shipping companies, all of which could trace their origins back to the early nineteenth century. It was known as Powell, Bacon & Haugh Lines Ltd but the name was changed to Coast Lines Ltd in 1917. It became a public company in 1919, by which time it had already been acquired by several major shipping companies including Royal Mail Line, Union Castle, Elder Dempster and others.

Twenty-one ships had been brought together in 1913 and it was decided that all present and future vessels be suffixed *'COAST'*. The company's trade

Opposite page: The barquentine TWEED of Faversham in Ipswich Dock with one of Packard's steam barges alongside. The TWEED was built at Newburgh in Fife in 1863.

Visits of Powell, Bacon & Haugh Lines vessels to Ipswich during 1908, showing the varied cargoes brought to the port.

Vessel	Arrived at Ipswich 1908				Departed Ipswich 1908	
	Date	From	Importer	Cargo	Date	Destination
DEVON COAST	11 Mar.	Liverpool via Shoreham	Wrinch & Co.	Boards	13 Mar.	London (sailed light)
			Ribbans	Tinplate		
			Keeble W.	Tinplate		
			Curtis E.	Oilcake		
			Packard E.	Cat food		
			London & Ipswich SS Co.	Soap		
			Masons Paper Co.	Soda ash		
			Grimwade Ridley	Bicarb of soda		
			Ipswich Gas Light Co.	Soda ash		
			Burtons.	Bicarb of soda		
			Colchester V.D.	Feeding cake		
			Mortimer T.	Oilcake		
DEVON COAST	15 May	Liverpool via Lowestoft	Grimwade Ridley	Bicarb.of soda	16 May	Liverpool via Rochester
			Pain & Bayles	Bicrb. of soda		
			Masons Paper Co.	Soda ash		
			Curtis E.	Oilcake		
			Colchester V.D.	Oil Cake		
			Ribbans	Tinplate		
			Mason G.	Nuts		
			Brewer W.	Nuts		
			London & Ipswich S.S. Co.	Soap		
DEVON COAST	29 Jul.	Liverpool via Poole	Ribbans	Tinplate	30 Jul.	Liverpool via London
			Burtons	Bicarb.of soda		
			Grimwade Ridley	Bicarb of Soda		
			Gooding	Feeding cake		
			Lewcock	Feeding Cake		
			Curtis E.	Oilcake		
			Mortimer T.	Meal		
			London & Ipswich S.S. Co.	Soap		
CORNISH COAST	8 Sept.	Liverpool via Dover	Simmonds Hunt Montgomery	Oilcake	11 Sept.	Rochester
			Curtis E.	Oilcake		
			Mortimer T.	Oilcake		
			Pain & Bayles	Soda		
			Mason G.	Soda		
			Grimwade Ridley	Soda		
			London & Ipswich S.S. Co.	Soap		
DEVON COAST	29 Sept.		Details not available			
DORSET COAST	22 Oct.		Details not available			
DORSET COAST	4 Nov.	via Dover	Details not available		5 Nov.	Liverpool via Gravesend
CORNISH COAST	4 Dec.	via Lowestoft	Details not available		5 Dec.	Liverpool

extended from the Irish Sea to the south and east coasts including London, and it owned warehouses and offices at many of the ports it served. The company's title Coast Lines was not just coincidence; coastal cargo-liner services operated on specific routes just as passenger liners sailed scheduled services across the Atlantic. Passenger accommodation was available on many ships, especially to Dublin and Belfast and also to London, many people taking the opportunity to visit other coastal ports en route in cruising fashion. Road transport and a remarkable variety of other companies with interests in shipbuilding and bunkering services were acquired over the years

Coast Lines reached its zenith in the mid-1950s with just over 140 ships, after which it faced competition from the new ro-ro and container operators. Coastal shipping, dependent upon traditional general cargo, was in decline, and some of the constituent companies were sold off and the company was itself acquired by P & O in February 1971.

The shipping table for 1908 on page 225 shows the type of trade in which Coast Lines specialised at Ipswich. The 1930 table reveals dwindling tonnage and type of cargoes, probably giving a clue as to why their ships appear to have cut out calls to Ipswich soon afterwards. In fact, as if to prove the point, the port accounts for 1933 show that Calthrop Bros. Ltd of Liverpool were charged for unloading five consignments of approximately 10 tons each of oilcake and meals from railway trucks to the Public Warehouse. Over twelve months $56\frac{1}{2}$ tons were received and later loaded into lorries for dispatch to customers. Road and rail transport was beginning to take over.

During the early 1920s two short-lived general cargo services were running between London, Colchester and Ipswich. One was operated by the Eastern Steam Packet Co. Ltd of 14 Key Street, Ipswich, the other by the Eastern Counties Water Transport Co. Ltd of 66a North Hill, Colchester. Goods were sent in the odd barge or else in two small motor ships, the latter incongruously prefixed WESTERN, one being the WESTERN MAID of Southampton, and the other the WESTERN BELLE of Guernsey. As an example of the occasional flurries of provisions brought by sea to Ipswich, the table on the opposite page shows arrivals for 1921. The cargoes were discharged to a rented warehouse on Three Cranes Wharf.

The mv WESTERN MAID arrived only twice in April 1922 for the Eastern Steam Packet Company, bringing six tons of oranges and two tons of onions on the first trip and eleven and a half tons of oranges and one ton of condensed milk on the second, making a total of only twenty and a half tons.

Oranges had been imported direct at least once before as a part cargo with Mason's linseed from Theodosia in the Crimea when the ss MARY of Whitby berthed on 28th December 1891.

For about eighteen months during the 1930s the Free Trade Wharf Company Ltd, with an office at Sutherland House, Broad Street, London and a warehouse at Ratcliffe Highway, Stepney, provided a general coastal cargo-liner service

*This table shows the reduced number of cargoes brought to Ipswich by Coast Line vessels in 1930. *Special lock.*

Vessel	Arrived at Ipswich 1930				Departed Ipswich 1930		
	Date	From	Discharged	Importer	Date	To	Loaded at Ipswich
DEVON COAST	20 Feb.*	Liverpool via Portsrnouth	164 tons oilcake meal	Bibby and Calthrop	21 Feb*	London via Dover	2 tons pig meal
SUFFOLK COAST	1May	Liverpool via Dover	117 tons oilcake & meals	Bibby & Calthrop	2 May	London	Details not known
HAMPSHIRE COAST	9 Aug.*	Liverpool via Shoreham	136 tons general	Bibby Calthrop & BOCM	11 Aug.	London	4 tons oilcake and meal
DEVON COAST	21 Dec.	Liverpool via Portsmouth	142 tons oilcake etc.		22 Dec.	London via Dover	12 tons oilcake

operating round trips from London to Kings Lynn and Boston. The regular ships on the service, calling at Ipswich about once a week, were the *SANDHILL*, 242nrt of Newcastle, the smaller ss *BELFORD* (ex-*JOLLY LAURA*, ex-*MICLEHAM*), 147nrt of Sunderland, and the new Groningen-built mv *ETAL*, 93nrt of London. Other vessels, including Horlocks' ss *PHAEACIAN*, called occasionally.

The first cargoes to Ipswich were brought on 5th February 1933 by the *SANDHILL*, arriving with 86 tons of sugar and coming again on 23rd February with five tons of sugar and six tons of glass. On 1st March she returned with $27^1/_2$ tons of sugar and was back again a week later with 26 tons of the same commodity. The mv *ETAL* arrived on 11th March with 35 tons of sugar and 23 tons syrup and the *SANDHILL* brought 60 tons of sugar on the 15th. By the end of April, loads had rapidly diversified to include 1cwt of wood pulp containers, $1^1/_2$cwt of paper serviettes, a quarter of paper cups, three tons of custard powder, five tons of cordials, one ton of soda ash, seven tons of school requisites and four tons of preserves. The largest consignments were of sugar, syrup and soap, with the emphasis on groceries and other retail commodities. By the end of 1933 no less than 30 tons of Christmas crackers had arrived.

Some 500 tons of goods were being dispatched monthly by rail to Kelvedon, Saffron Walden, Thaxted, Haverhill, Newport, Halesworth, Beccles, Luckin Smith of Chelmsford, Cullen's Stores at Walton-on-the-Naze, many Co-operative Wholesale Society branches and the Bradfield Poor Law Institution. Lorries served the village stores nearer Ipswich, including Hopgoods of Stowmarket, Kearly & Tonge Ltd (International Stores), and Messrs Squirrel & Cleveland, the well-known Ipswich grocery wholesalers with premises in Museum Street. This last-mentioned firm also distributed to shops direct from the Public Warehouse. The Free Trade Wharf service was destined to be short lived; by the summer of 1934 cargo consisted only of soap, sugar and syrup. The mv *ETAL* berthed on 4th September with the last shipment by sea of four tons of syrup and 159 tons of sugar. Some more came by railway, but the account closed on 9th February 1935 when the last goods were loaded to lorries and trucks.

Developments from the 1960s onwards

Regular general cargo services began during 1960 by General Cargo Brokers Ltd (GCB), who were running a service every three or four days to Rotterdam, and Lockett Wilson started a weekly service to Le Treport. Within two years, the Rotterdam-registered *IPSWICH PIONEER* and *IPSWICH PROGRESS* were providing extra capacity on the GCB route. Both ships were built at Bremen in

Cargoes of provisions unloaded at Ipswich during 1921.

DATE	SHIP	POR	NRT	CARGO
13th Apr. 1921	sb *ROSE*	Maldon	42	51 tons Quaker Oats
11th May	mv *WESTERN BELLE*	Guernsey	50	53 tons condensed milk
13th Jun	sb *GEORGE*	Maldon	40	51 tons sugar, 51 tons condensed milk
27th Jun	mv *WESTERN BELLE*	Guernsey	50	79 tons condensed milk
31st Jul	mv *WESTERN BELLE*	Guernsey	50	118 tons condensed milk
26th Aug	mv *WESTERN BELLE*	Guernsey	50	31 tons condensed milk
10th Sep	mv *WESTERN BELLE*	Guernsey	50	75 tons condensed milk
10th Sep	mv *WESTERN BELLE*	Guernsey	50	31 tons flour
2nd Oct	mv *WESTERN BELLE*	Guernsey	50	10 tons sugar
20th Oct	mv *WESTERN MAID*	Southampton	44	38 tons sugar
10th Nov	mv *WESTERN MAID*	Southampton	44	25 tons Quaker Oats

1955, and each loaded just over 500 tons. Lockett Wilson began sailings to Rouen and Paris with mv *CREMONA* in 1967. Geest vessels *GEESTDIEP*, *GEESTSLUIS* and *GEESTDAM*, all of 400 tons DWT and Dutch-built in the early 1960s, made a hundred, sixty-nine and five calls respectively in 1966 as their business got underway.

In 1969, on 15th April, the first Ro-Ro service to and from Ipswich commenced when mv *ARNEB*, 247nrt, arrived at the new berth near Coprolite Street from Hamburg, sailing on the 18th for Bremen. *ARNEB* completed forty-six voyages during the remainder of 1969. On 21st April, ss *JAROSLAW DABROWSKI*, 3,040nrt of Gdynia, launched at Blyth in 1950 and owned by Polish Ocean Lines, arrived for the first time at Cliff Quay with general cargo for a new Polish service by GCB lasting for over ten years.

In 1970 three cargoes of rod iron and one of pig iron arrived from Sydney, Nova Scotia, on behalf of shippers Shaw Lovell in the steamers *EMIL REITH* of Hamburg, *LEINSTER BAY* of Copenhagen, *PENCHATEAU* of Dunkirk and the *AGIA MARINA* of Famagusta. In the same year Glover Bros. introduced a short-lived service, which included containers, calling at Ipswich to and from Boston USA and the Continent. The ships were all German-registered and appear to have been named only briefly as *BOSTON EXPRESS*, *BOSTON SAND*, *BERNARD WESCH II* and *HARTFORD EXPRESS*. On 4th November 1970 mv *ARCTURUS* joined *ARNEB* on the Ro-Ro service from Orwell Quay. *ARCTURUS* remained working from Ipswich and Harwich for many years, having conventional hatches instead of an all-steel deck.

The momentum at which the general cargo services increased is illustrated in 1971 when GCB had 362 shipments, Geest 355 and Lockett Wilson 119 to the near Continent. Gulf Maritime entered the fray about 1971 with regular services from within the Dock at Orwell Quay to Turkey, Greece (Piraeus), Cyprus, North Africa (Tripoli-Benghazi) and West Africa (Lagos-Apapa-Tema). Most of their ships were prefixed '*GULF*' and in November 1973 they introduced the recently renamed *GULF IPSWICH*, which at 306ft was 29ft longer than the lock. She had been built in Germany in 1957, and her first Ipswich-based voyage was to Bisan in Guinea and Tema (Ghana). The *GULF ANGLIA* became their seventh ship in June 1975.

A regular liner trade developed to Yugoslavia in 1972 with a Jugolinja ship departing every ten days to Rijeka, Pula and Split, frequently with machinery, especially dump trucks, and returning with beechwood, tinned fruit and pulped fruit in barrels. Another company, Lovell's Shipping & Transport Group, began a twice-weekly service from Ipswich to Flushing in May 1975 with the 100 TEU capacity ship *NORDBALT*, which in turn was replaced the following March by the *BARBARA BRITT*. Sailings increased to thrice weekly with one call at Hull. Empros Line commenced fortnightly services in February 1976 to Piraeus, where the owning Dracopoulos family was based, to Salonika, Chalkis, Volos, Istanbul and Tripoli. Also in 1975, the Polish Ocean Line's (POL) service to Gdynia was augmented by links with the United Baltic Corporation to a weekly liner trade by the *BALTIC CONSORT* and *BALTIC ARROW* and POL's mv *JASLO*, 3,350DWT, launched in 1967 at Aalborg.

Cliff Quay power station had closed in 1983, and the associated coal yard was acquired by the IPA in 1986. It was soon used for the import of Norwegian stone in ships with self-discharge equipment, sea-dredged aggregates and the export of grain ex-lorries via mobile conveyors. The actual power station building (subsequently demolished) and ash tip was purchased by ABP in 1998, giving another forty-four acres. A rail/road container terminal was established on Cliff

Quay in 1985 for Freightliner Ltd, its main user being Geest North Sea Line. An earlier but short-lived service was revived in 1984 when Hafskip UK Ltd offered a weekly sailing to Iceland (Reykjavik) in three days with all kinds of goods. In 1987 other connections were made to Cartagena (Spain) and Tripoli (Libya) by Flamar Line of Zeebrugge, and weekly sailings operated to Bilbao (Portugal) by Compagnie Maritime Belge (CMB). In the same year Geest had augmented their fleet with the introduction of mv *CANOPUS* (204 TEUs) serving Emmerich (on the Dutch-German border) weekly, in addition to its normal Rotterdam traffic.

A setback had occurred back in August 1976 when the Ipswich-Rotterdam ferry *IPSWICH PIONEER II* ceased operation despite normally full loadings. At the beginning of 1977 negotiations were taking place with North Sea Ferries Ltd, part of the P&O Group, to replace the lost ro-ro connection, which in fact opened in March 1977 with the chartered vessel *STENA NORMANDICA*. She provided six sailings a week but was soon replaced by North Sea Ferries' own *NORSKY*. She in turn was superseded in 1983 by the larger *NORSEA*, ex-*IBEX*, built by Mitsui Eng. & SB Co. Ltd at Tamano in 1979, and her later running-mate *NORCAPE*, introduced in 1986. Unfortunately the service was withdrawn in 1995, leaving the port without a North Sea ferry. It was not until the year 2000 that a new service was inaugurated from the West Bank, but this was to Ostend, only 87 nautical miles away, compared with the Hook at 113 nautical miles.

The Canadian Cast Container Group, which began in 1969 with its own shipping line connecting Antwerp with Montreal, signed a fifteen-year agreement with the IPA early in 1981 for a new dedicated container terminal to be constructed along the West Bank below the Ro-Ro berth. This opened in 1982 for a twice-weekly service to Zeebrugge by the *CAST RACCOON* and a Saturday sailing by the *CAST PORCUPINE* to Sweden, Denmark and Germany, giving an annual throughput of over 70,000 TEUs. This traffic ceased in 1993 when Cast announced their intention to divert their transatlantic vessels to Felixstowe and dispense with the feeder service. Contrary to popular opinion, Ipswich has generally not been affected by expansion of the Port of Felixstowe. The two ports provide for quite different trading routes, customers and of course size of ships; there is not normally direct competition for business.

Not all of the smaller shipping lines operating out of Ipswich during this period are mentioned. Some remained for only a short time, and to account for every one would be repetitive as the bulk of the trade had shifted to general cargo hidden in boxes. The origin and final destination of their contents is not revealed in arrival and clearance records.

Burton, Son & Sanders

The firm of Burton, Son & Sanders Ltd was originally established in 1824 by Charles Burton who purchased a retail grocery business in Tavern Street. Successive members of the family ran the concern, and during the 1880s it began trading on a national basis. It was at that time that Mr Bunnell Burton and Mr William Burton, both sons of Henry May Burton, joined the firm. William was considered one of the country's finest amateur helmsmen and in 1913 he was asked to sail a new racing yacht, Sir Thomas Lipton's *SHAMROCK IV,* in the America's Cup Race the following year. 'Mr Burton will have his work cut out in tackling these Americans, for they are absolutely determined that their cup shall never leave their shores,' reported the *Evening News*. Unfortunately

A steam coaster lying at the head of the Dock discharging a cargo of sugar for Burton, Son & Sanders about 1912.

the outbreak of war in August 1914 intervened: the New York Yacht Club sent a cable to the Royal Ulster Yacht Club on 6th August asking as to the arrangements for the America's Cup and received the reply: 'After consultation with Sir Thomas Lipton they would be glad if a postponement of one month could be granted in regard to the 1914 racing dates; in the event of war still being in progress this postponement to be extended so as to enable the races to be sailed in 1915. . .'. As things turned out SHAMROCK IV was laid up in New York until 1919, and Sir William, as he became, did not get his turn at the helm.

In 1897 Sanders & Son of Colchester amalgamated with the Burton firm, and by 1908 Burton, Son & Sanders Ltd incorporated William Jolly, John May & Co. and Wainwright & Sons. In due course the slogan displayed on their own substantial lorry fleet was simply 'Burton, Son & Sanders Ltd, Bakers' Sundries'. As the company rapidly became one of the foremost of its kind in the country its head office remained in Ipswich, with branches and factories in London, Hull, Newcastle, Glasgow, Belfast, Manchester, Birmingham, Bristol, Portsmouth, Norwich and Colchester. Their premises at St Peter's Dock had access to the railway via a wagon turntable on the quayside. A great many of their raw materials arrived by rail and their products were dispatched nightly by the same means until road transport took over most of their traffic.

They were dealers in tea, groceries and provisions, and they pioneered the production of pulverised castor and icing sugar. They were also the first processors of almonds in Britain; almond processing was a seasonal job ending in December, after which there would be no more work for many. Some of the almonds were used to make marzipan, and the company supplied preserved peel and fondants for the bakery and confectionery trades. Sugar was the main ingredient to come by sea due to the quantities involved, and most of it was probably for their jam factory in nearby Greyfriars Road. Burtons printed their own labels for their produce at their College Street premises.

Soap was another of Burtons' products, their own production being augmented in the 1890s by barge loads from London, fixed by Pickfords. The soap was for the wholesale grocery trade, and during the early 1900s it was part of the regular cargoes brought to Ipswich by Coast Lines' ships in the liner trade from Liverpool.

Burtons' shipping requirements appear to have been dealt with for many years by Pickfords, who were shipping agents as well as carmen and furniture removers, with an office at 40 Princes Street, Ipswich from the 1880s. Records from 1896-97 show the sb *SCARBORO'* of Rochester arriving almost weekly, especially during 1897 when she made forty-four round trips from Harwich with sugar, eggs, or 'goods' for Burtons, plus parcels of maize or barley for Pauls and wheat for Cranfields. It is not clear if some of the cargo was taken on board from vessels in the harbour or whether some of it, particularly the sugar, was imported by the regular railway-owned continental cargo ships from Rotterdam. *SCARBORO'* (41nrt) was built in 1877 at Rochester; in the 1890s William Chandler, of 104 Myrtle Road, was the managing owner. In addition to the *SCARBORO'* many other barges brought sugar from London on Pickford's account for Burtons. The most frequent arrival was the *LIVONIA* (43nrt) of Rochester, Ipswich built in 1873. She made about twenty round trips from London, and a few from Harwich. Additionally another twenty-six cargoes, return freights from London, were discharged from several of Pauls' barges. The ketch barge *CORINTHIAN* of London, built at Yarmouth in 1892, had loaded at Cologne.

In 1898 at least six vessels from the continent arrived with sugar, including the ss *JENNY*, 474nrt of Danzig, which came from her home port in January. In September *OCTAVIUS*, 79nrt of Dublin, a schooner built in 1878 at Bridgwater and owned and registered there until 1883 when her registration changed to Dublin, came from Stettin, whence the schooner *WALTER ULRIC*, 91nrt, had arrived on 30th July. The *WALTER ULRIC* was another Portmadoc schooner, completed in 1875 and registered at Carnarvon; she would almost certainly have taken Welsh slate to Germany and there fixed a return cargo of sugar for Burtons. *WALTER ULRIC* sailed light, probably to Portmadoc, a week later. The ketch barges *ROCHESTER CASTLE*, 90nrt and built Sittingbourne in 1889, *LORD CHURCHILL*, completed at Littlehampton in 1885, and *BYCULLA* of Ipswich (where she was launched in 1887) all brought sugar from Cologne, some 215 miles up the Rhine from the Hook of Holland.

Taking 1907 as a typical year of the early twentieth century, Burtons received thirty-three cargoes of sugar, nineteen of them brought by barges from Harwich, presumably having been transshipped in the harbour there. Among these were three cargoes in the little Harwich-built *HECTOR* of 1884, only 22nrt and owned by the Ipswich Malting Company, plus one in the same company's *MARY ANN*, Ipswich-built in 1859. F.W. Horlock's Harwich-registered barge *EXCELSIOR* delivered four, William Colchester's old *TERTIUS* of 1844 delivered another two, with Groom's ancient *EASTWOOD*, built at Southwark in 1822, also arriving with two. Fourteen other sugar cargoes came from the continent including three by R. & W. Pauls' steamers *SWALLOW*, *SWIFT* and *TERN*. Two foreign steamships, the ss *KULLIN* of Kristinehamn on Lake Vener in Sweden, and ss *ODIN* of Haugesund, just north of Stavanger on Norway's west coast, arrived from Stettin. The ss *GLENO* of Newcastle, built at Larne in 1902, came twice, once each from Treport and Dunkirk. Another British coaster, the ss *ACTIVE*, completed at Dundee in 1898, came from Dunkirk. A Dutch sailing vessel, the *VERTROUWEN* of Amsterdam, arrived from Rotterdam, and Pauls' barge *AUDREY* came twice from Dunkirk, as did the Rochester barge *ALAN*. The Maldon *EMMA*, 64nrt and built there in 1897, also arrived from Dunkirk. She was part owned by John Sadd, the Maldon timber merchant, and her managing owner was Simeon Stanes of Ipswich, who later became master of the ketch barge *RECORD REIGN*.

The sailing barge *EXCELSIOR*, 45nrt, built at Harwich in 1885 by Cann Brothers for Horlocks, carried from Harwich to Ipswich thirty-six cargoes of presumably European sugar for Burtons between 2nd January and 29th July 1914. At that time Herbert Cann was her managing owner. War was declared in August and that particular trade ceased abruptly.

In July 1923 a spectacular fire destroyed Burton's warehouses in College Street. Starting just before ten o'clock in the evening, the blaze was watched by crowds of people gathered on Stoke Bridge and New Cut West. In a statement made after the fire Sir William Burton explained that the main premises had been erected by Mr Fred Bennett some twenty-five years earlier and they had since been extended considerably. There were really three buildings running into one on the quayside with floors resting on iron pillars and girders. The walls had been so well built that in spite of the heat they were still standing at one o'clock the next morning, though the interior and roof were wrecked. Giving details of the layout of the buildings, Sir William explained that the cellars were used entirely for cold storage and the ground floor was devoted largely to bacon. The first floor was a delivery floor for the whole of the factory and the second, which also extended into the property recently purchased from E.R. & F. Turner, the engineers, was used for the confectionary trade. The upper three floors were devoted to the almond business, and it was thought that this was where the fire had started. There was an enormous quantity of sugar stored in the premises that were destroyed.

The firm's other buildings next to Cranfield's mill were damaged by water, but fortunately all the buildings and stock were fully insured. During rebuilding of the premises, the company hired Flint Wharf Warehouse at an annual rate of £575. Additional items hired were hoists and electric motors, chains and pulleys, two sack barrows, electric light fittings plus shades, a sack machine room, and an office desk and drawers.

During the 1920s Burton, Son & Sanders were importing sugar in barges via London. In 1922-23, for example, the company received 3,533 tons. There were

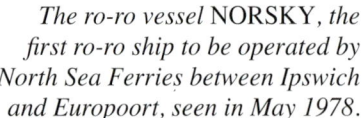

The ro-ro vessel NORSKY, *the first ro-ro ship to be operated by North Sea Ferries between Ipswich and Europoort, seen in May 1978.*

fifty-six barge arrivals during the twelve months April 1925-March 1926, with 4,590 tons of sugar. Of those twenty-one individual barges, fourteen were owned by various members of the Horlock family of Mistley, i.e. *DOROTHY, MARJORIE, MILLIE, KITTY, PRINCESS, EDME, D'ARCY, RELIANCE, RESOLUTE, REMERCIE, REDOUBTABLE, PORTLIGHT, VIGILANT* and *CHARLES HUTSON*. Almonds often came in by sea; 162 tons were discharged in parcels of about thirty-six tons in 1926-27. By April 1930, however, sugar tonnage was down to about 1,000 tons, without need of the warehouse, and it amounted to 1,312 tons in 1935. Indeed by 1939 there were only 800 tons of sugar discharged, and none during the war years of 1940-1945. After the Second World War a few tons of sweetened fats and other confectionery products arrived, but the earlier seaborne tonnage was no longer there, although in the early 1960s a few cargoes of orange peel for Burtons were discharged from Seville and Messina. Peel was transported in brine in hogsheads (casks of fifty-two and a half gallons).

In the 1950s and 60s various companies were acquired by Burtons, thereby adding a number of diverse interests to their traditional bakery and grocery business. The company merged with Matthews Holdings Ltd in 1970 and seven years later Matthews Holdings was in turn purchased by Thomas Borthwick & Sons Ltd By then the firm was specialising in edible cake decorations and was concentrating on exports, sending considerable quantities of their products through other ports such as London. Even during the 1980s, substantial amounts were sent to the Middle East, winning the company an export award.

Burtons' Ipswich jam factory finished in the 1980s and, following a decline in profits, the entire business closed in 1993 following its sale by Borthwicks.

The IPSWICH PIONEER II *was fitted with bow thrusters that enabled her to swing in the confined space between the ro-ro berth and Cliff Quay without the aid of a tug.*

Potatoes

During the 1950s and 1960s potatoes were regularly imported. There were several wholesale fruit and vegetable merchants in the town at the time, including J.J. Wilson Ltd of White Elm Street, Millington & Company, R. Jackson (Ipswich Ltd) and B.H. Ellis & Sons. These last three were based at a former 1950s Ransomes' service centre in Russell Road, having recently moved there from their original depots. All these firms were importing Dutch potatoes in the mid-1950s, thirty-two cargoes arriving in 1958 alone. During 1961, however, Jacksons received only six such shiploads, these coming from Belfast, Dundee and Montrose.

A new trade in fresh produce started at the end of 1999 with containerised shipments of potatoes being exported to the Canary Islands, via the port. Transported to Ipswich by road and rail from Scotland and East Anglia, a sizable portion of the cargo was received on pallets and loaded into containers at Ipswich. The season for the seed and feed potatoes runs from October to February and follows the onion handling season at the port. One of the vessels taking the potato shipments was the mv *ADELE J.*, with the London-based shipping company Agrolon (UK) Ltd handling the cargo.

Beet sugar

Beta Maritima is a beet with a sweet content known to the Romans, but it was not until the eighteenth century that chemists became aware of its sugar-yielding potential. In 1747 a chemist working in Berlin produced sucrose from this beet, and it was clear that sugar could be profitably extracted from the plant in a European climate. It attracted wide scientific attention and Frederick the Great helped finance future development, enabling the first beet sugar factory to be established in 1801 in Silesia. It was Napoleon who encouraged beet cultivation and processing because of the Royal Navy blockade cutting off French cane sugar supplies. By the end of the Napoleonic Wars in 1815 there were 213 French factories producing 4,000 tons annually. In Britain, however, opposition was strong to beet sugar trials. Hostile remarks were made in Parliament referring to the enormous investments made in cane sugar production from the plantations abroad and in established British refineries, and the belief was expressed that the British Navy was impregnable in case of war.

In Britain the first commercial attempt to produce sugar from beet began when Robert Marriage built a small factory at Ulting near Maldon. He came from a well-known Essex milling family and was a member of the Society of Friends, which was fiercely against slavery in the plantations. Money problems caused the factory to close within two years. Although one or two other similar short-lived projects were started, it was 1868 before another serious attempt was made with a substantial factory being erected by James Duncan, of Silvertown, at Lavenham in Suffolk. In 1874 this also closed. An attempt to get it going again ten years later was also unsuccessful when the crops failed.

In addition to relying on the sugar cane plantations throughout the British Empire for the nation's sugar, the industry's growth in Britain was further hindered by European governments creating a set of artificial conditions by ordering exorbitant prices to be charged in Europe while selling sugar to Britain at less than cost price. In 1903, however, a Brussels Convention abolished the subsidies paid to European countries that had enabled Britain to import cheap beet sugar.

The first of the modern beet sugar factories in this country was set up at Cantley in Norfolk in 1912, a year after the Board of Agriculture and Fisheries had given help and encouragement to the industry. For the first time in Britain direct state subsidies were being used to aid a brand new industry. This could not save the situation during the First World War, when European supplies vanished and the country was faced with blockades in the Western Approaches. Much of the fighting during the war had been in beet growing areas on the Continent and Britain was faced with exports drying up and the price of sugar increasing. This led in the 1920s to the building of many sugar beet factories as part of a Government-supported programme, and by 1928 there were eighteen factories at work, mainly in East Anglia. They were run by various companies including Tate & Lyle, who opened one at Bury St Edmunds. In 1936 all the factories were linked together with Government representatives to form the British Sugar Corporation; Tate & Lyle later withdrew from beet sugar refining.

It was in April 1925 that the first machinery was shipped from Rotterdam to Ipswich for a beet sugar processing factory being built by the Ipswich Beet Sugar Factory Ltd on the site of a dark pinewood known as Devil's Wood along the Sproughton Road half way between Bramford Road and Sproughton village. The first shipment of boilers arrived on 29th April in the ss *VECHTSTROOM* of Amsterdam, an engines-aft coastal steamer of 442nrt that had been launched as *ENERGIE II* at Haarlem in 1918. Her cargoes were brokered by the British Amsterdam Maritime Agency of 150-151, Fenchurch Street, London. There were apparently seven voyages by *VECHTSTROOM* from the end of April to 9th July, bringing 2,184 tons of machinery and 210 tons of boilers. Her last visit with machinery also included about 12 tons of furniture in two three-ton vans that were craned off and then back aboard when emptied, all topped up with 150 pints of wine that we may assume was used to seal the contract! The first 2,323 tons of coal arrived at the dock on 7th July 1926 aboard the ss *LOUIE ROSE*, 955nrt and built at Paisley in 1924, and was taken by rail to the factory, which was opened in time for the 1926 season under its Dutch manager, Mr Van der Heyden. The annual campaign, as it was usually called, lasted roughly from the end of September to the end of February, depending upon the weather. Thousands of tons of beet were delivered by rail from country stations to the factory's extensive sidings, and deliveries by rail continued until the 1960s. Beet loaded at farm wharves by hand from tumbrils was brought to the dock by barges and transferred to railway trucks for the short journey to Sproughton Road.

At the beginning of the first season Packard's steam barge *TRENT RIVER* left Ipswich on 20th October 1926 with fertilizer for Great Oakley dock in the Walton Backwaters and returned with sugar beet, picking up two of Packard's dumb barges, *WAVENEY II* and *DEBEN II*, with beet from Pin Mill, apparently towing them up the Gipping directly to the factory on the 24th. This may not have been repeated, as the cargo would probably have had to be shovelled across the towpath at the factory, but Packard's craft brought several more beet cargoes from the Deben and Stour to Ipswich Dock, where the beet were doubtless transferred to railway trucks.

At the start of the 1927 season the ketch barge *LORD HARTINGTON*, built at Ipswich in 1887, loaded sugar beet on the Deben for Ipswich twice, arriving on 30th October and again on 12th November. She was then owned by Captain Skinner of Woodbridge, who worked the last two or three barges owned there at the time. The *LORD HARTINGTON* was lost in the Schelde after a collision in 1928. Barges continued to bring beet direct from riverside farms certainly until 1937.

Molasses was delivered to dockside tanks near Flint Wharf by road tankers, and dock workers were also employed repairing damaged bags. Sugar was loaded either directly from lorries and railway trucks or for many years from Flint Wharf Warehouse, which was let to the beet factory and first used in February 1927. Number 3 Shed and some of the land at the Public Warehouse was rented to store dried pulp. In 1935-36 twenty-four vessels, including eight of Everards' sailing barge fleet, loaded 3,777 tons of sugar, an increase of 1,402 tons on 1927. No bulk molasses went by sea and the railway carried most of the dried pulp, although road transport was beginning to carry significant quantities. In 1941 seven ships carried 3,614 tons of pulp away.

There is no record of any ships leaving with sugar in 1939 or 1940 and only one in 1941 when Everards' mv *ACTIVITY* sailed on 10th February. In February, March and April 1942 fifteen ships sailed with some 7,800 tons. Traffic increased annually for the rest of the war and until 1950, when it appeared to peak; sixty-one cargoes, amounting to 21,954 tons, were loaded by twenty-nine ships, all owned by F.T. Everard & Sons Ltd. The total fell to forty-eight cargoes, 17,458 tons, in the 12 months from April 1952 to March 1953 and dropped to forty-five cargoes, 16,239 tons the following year.

Throughout the years of sugar sailings ex-Ipswich it was nearly all coastal traffic to ports including Plymouth, Exeter, Southampton, Chatham, London, Bridlington, Hull, Goole, Selby, Middlesbrough, Sunderland and Newcastle. The sugar tonnage fell to 2,260 tons by 1955-56, loaded into six ships direct

The container ship CANOPUS sailing from Ipswich for Emmerich on the Rhine in September 1987 on her regular sailing for Geest North Sea Lines.

from lorries, and during 1957 mv *FIXITY* loaded one cargo and mv *FUTURITY* loaded two for Goole; few if any other seaborne cargoes of sugar left Ipswich. The trade had diminished very quickly as sugar was moved by rail and road until the factory sidings were closed in the 1960s; after which everything went away in lorries.

After many optimistic years of modernisation followed by threats of rationalisation, some East Anglian factories have been enlarged considerably since the 1980s and smaller ones closed. It was nevertheless totally unexpected when it was announced in January 2001 that the Ipswich factory would close at the end of the campaign in March 2001.

Motor vehicles

Ipswich has long been recognized for the export of agricultural machinery, steam engines and walking draglines. Less well known is the fact that cars, caravans and lorries were shipped from Cliff Quay for a number of years, commencing in 1958. In that year the mv *ILA* of Trondheim, arrived on 2nd May to load cars for Milwaukee via Falmouth. For a brief period from the end of the 1950s to the mid '60s, several cargoes of vehicles were exported to various countries in Europe. In 1963 for example, no fewer than ninety car-laden ships left Ipswich, mainly for Scandinavia, as shown in the accompanying table.

Stockholm received thirty-seven such shipments, Abo twenty-eight, Oslo eight, Bremen and Amsterdam one each and the remaining fifteen went to

The Dutch ship ELANDSGRACHT *discharging onions direct from New Zealand at Cliff Quay in May 2002. Onions from the other side of the world provided an annual cargo for a few years.*

Trelleborg, Turku and Helsinki. It is probable that these were nearly all Vauxhall products.

Shipments continued into early 1964, fixed by Mann & Co. The first of these was on 7th January when the mv *RIGOLETTO* of Bremen loaded cars and caravans for Hamburg, and on the 16th the *PARSIFAL* returned to load lorries for Stockholm. The *GUNDULA* berthed again on the 26th for cars to Oslo and once more on 5th February when she loaded lorry chassis for Oslo, sailing the same day. The trade was short-lived, however, as by the mid-1960s ro-ro ships were operating from other ports. Eventually the export of vehicles virtually ceased and the massive importation of foreign cars from Japan, etc., was undertaken in huge specially-built carriers which, on the East Coast, were handled at Sheerness.

The US Army occasionally used Ipswich. For instance on 26th June 1971 the *JAMES E. ROBINSON*, 4,549nrt of New York, discharged general cargo and cars from the USA, sailing for Rotterdam two days later.

The Beardmore Inflexible

An unusual cargo arrived at Cliff Quay aboard the ss *ARDGANTOCK*, 415nrt of Greenock, on 5th September 1927. Built in Scotland by William Beardmore & Company and at the time the largest aircraft in the world, the all-metal Beardmore Inflexible was shipped in large pieces to the port of Ipswich for assembly and testing at RAF Martlesham Heath. Powered by three 650h.p. Rolls-Royce Condor engines, the Inflexible had a wing span of $157\frac{1}{2}$ ft and a length of nearly 76 ft, and stood 21 ft tall.

The IDC accounts show that discharging the aircraft parts on 6th September took fifteen hours at a cost of £1 per hour, the cranage of eleven tons at six shillings per ton came to £3 6s. and the wharfage cost 2s. 4d., making a final total of £18 8s. 4d. that was paid by Beardmore & Co. The ship sailed late on the 6th. The RAF at Martlesham bore the expenses of loading the aircraft parts from the

Car exports from Ipswich in 1963.

Ship	NRT	POR	Vessel Details	No of cargoes carried in 1963
mv *BORE VII*	275	Abo	Built 1963 Oskerhamn	3
mv *BORE VIII*	233	Abo	Built 1957 Foxhol	2
mv *BORE IX*	277	Abo	Built 1960 Druten	1
mv *BORE X*	275	Abo	Built 1963 Oskerhamn	2
mv *BOTILLA RUSS*	416	Hamburg	Built 1959 Rendsburg	1
mv *EDITH*	251	Helsingborg	Built 1959 Solsborg	1
mv *GUNDULA*	274	Hamburg	Built 1954 Lubeck	8
mv *HERMINE*	-	-	-	1
mv *MAARIT*	741	Helsingfors	Built 1945 Aalborg	1
mv *MARGIT*	443	Gothenburg	Built 1935 Landskroner	4
mv *MATHILDA*	227	Rotterdam	Built 1957 Schiedam	12
ss *NORDANO*	751	Harnosand	Built 1946 Helsingborg (*ex-MANGEN*)	1
mv *NOVA*	307	Norrkoping	Built 1963 Gefle	1
mv *PARMA*	563	Helsingfors	Built 1944 Gothenburg (*ex-AHUS ex-BOTHNIA*)	1
mv *PARSIFAL*	244	Bremen	Built 1959 Bremen (*ex-HELMUT PARCHMAN*)	21
mv *RUSS*	-	Hamburg	-	1
mv *SIEGFRIED*	379	Bremen	Built 1961 Cologne (*ex-KARL-HEINZ ex-PARCHMAN*)	20
mv *TRAVIATA*	779	Stockholm	Built 1955 Kiel	2
mv *VAASA*	-	-	-	5
mv *WORTHYDOWN*	1,814	London	-	1
mv *YRSA*	976	Mariehamn	Built 1949 Middlesbrough	1

The Norwegian mv ILA *loading cars for Scandinavia about 1951. Owned by Lykkes Rederi A/S and registered at Trondheim, the* ILA *had been built at Wesermunde in Germany as the* LUNA *in 1938. (A.J. Hubert)*

quay to lorries, involving three hours work during the day at 12s. 6d. an hour, three nights work totalling nineteen hours at 15s. per hour and use of the quay lights and clusters for three nights at 12s. a night, making a total of £17 18s. 6d. The job of transporting the large parts from the dock and through the streets of Ipswich on their way to Martlesham near Woodbridge was found to be very tricky, the corners of some buildings in the town avoiding damage only by inches.

The first flight of the Inflexible was made in March 1928, and in 1931, having successfully served its purpose, the plane was tested to destruction, dismantled and the sections left outside to check corrosion levels on the metal coatings.

During the 1930s the RAF at Felixstowe paid the IDC £1 each per year for two mooring buoys laid in Buttermans Bay. They were used by sea planes and flying boats brought up from Harwich Harbour to shelter in the lee of the woods at Pin Mill during stormy weather.

Scrap metal

Iron foundries such as those operated by Ransomes and E.R. & F. Turner at Ipswich used a mixture of old scrap iron and pig iron for the production of iron castings, including the chilled iron ploughshares that were so distinctive a product of the Ransomes works. The necessary pig iron provided many a cargo for Ipswich-bound ships; in 1846 no fewer than ninety cargoes of pig iron, some 14,000 tons, were unloaded in the Dock. Later in the nineteenth century the rapid development of the steel industry led to the growth of a ready market for scrap metal, especially in the steel towns of Northeast England, and 'Old iron,' as it was often called, was collected by rag and bone men or scrap merchants and sent away by sea or train for recycling. During the last years of the nineteenth century vessels frequently loaded scrap as a return cargo after discharging coal from the Northeast coast ports. Ketch barges were soon engaged in this traffic when working in the coal trade, and this continued into the second half of the twentieth century.

The following shipping examples are typical of the turn of the nineteenth century. The ketch barge *ROCHESTER CASTLE* loaded with old iron outward in February 1898. In 1901 the handsome ketch barge *RECORD REIGN* and the schooner barge *FRIENDSHIP* both loaded coal at Seaham Harbour, the *FRIENDSHIP* for V.D. Colchester of Ipswich, *RECORD REIGN* discharging at Colchester and arriving light from there; both vessels returned north with old iron. The ketch barge *CORINTHIAN* brought phosphate from Dunkirk on 4th March 1908, sailing with iron for Newcastle on the 18th. The *LEADING LIGHT* of Ipswich, one of Harvey's Littlehampton boomies, launched there in 1906, arrived light from Harwich on 15th June 1910 and again on 8th July to load old rails for Newcastle, and she did the same in August 1911. The boomies *EVELYN*, of Rye, and *ADA GANE*, of Harwich, both returned north with scrap to Newcastle in April 1914.

W. H. Southgate & Sons Ltd and H. Skinner

It was inevitable that out of the numbers of rag and bone men in every town, one or two would dominate as they moved into the old iron trade. In Ipswich, Walter Southgate, who was a marine store dealer at 34 Pottery Street in the 1880s, went into the scrap business and by 1923 had moved to nearby Long Street. During the 1920s and 1930s Southgate sent occasional cargoes of 150 to 200 tons of scrap away by sea, which included in 1935 the boiler of Fison's steam barge *WHALE*. H. Skinner of Bond Street, Ipswich, also sent a few shiploads away a year. In fact, between April and September 1937 five Dutch coasters (two motor vessels and three with auxiliary engines) loaded 1,033 tons altogether. In addition to cargoes bound for British ports there were several to the near continent. Skinners sent scrap to Antwerp by the Dutch auxiliary *ALBATROS* in April 1937, and Sackers (see below) loaded the mv *CORTENAER* for Duisburg on the Rhine in September 1938. Duisburg is now a major inland port comprising nineteen docks in the Ruhr area of Germany, some 120 miles from the Hook of Holland.

A rare visitor to Ipswich with a general cargo was the Ellerman liner CITY OF LICHFIELD, *seen here on 23rd September 1978.*

Loading a Danish ship with bagged potatoes for the Argentine at Orwell Quay in 1972.

S. Sacker Ltd

Sidney Sacker, who moved from Colchester in the early 1920s and opened a yard in Handford Road, soon became the largest local dealer in scrap metals and began shipping out scrap metal by sea in the mid-1920s. He sent away 1,037 tons in five Dutch and German motor vessels, the ZEEHONDE, VEGA, IRENE, BERTHA and SCHWAN, between April 1927 and March 1928. Some iron, rags and bones were sent by rail. By 1935, Sacker was renting land on the South West Quay and the tonnage had risen to 3,800 in ten ships, with another 1,200 tons going by rail.

The drive for scrap metal from the start of the 1939-45 war required an enormous amount of transport which early in the war was restricted to the railways, on which thousands of tons left Ipswich. During the twelve months from April 1942 to March 1943, however, there were eleven coastal shipments. The ships included the ss *SLATEFORD* of Montrose, built in 1903 at Workington, Horlock's ss *MISTLEY*, the ss *GROS PIERRE*, which sounds as if it was a Free French vessel, and the ss *SOUTHWICK* of Sunderland, where she was completed in 1917. Pauls' ss *OXBIRD* loaded two cargoes, as did the war-built *EMPIRE PUNCH*; the *EMPIRE REYNARD* loaded once. There was also Metcalf's 1937 Dutch-built mv *POLLY M*, which survived for some 30 years, and the little ss *FAIRY* of Kings Lynn, built at Paisley in 1902 and well known on the East Coast. They carried 3,708 tons down the coast, averaging 337 tons each.

Similar to other scrap metal merchants, Sackers also dealt with waste paper. During the Second World War the firm was using advertisements to persuade the public to clear out unwanted paper that was taking up valuable space and was needed urgently by the nation. Sackers offered prompt cash for large or small quantities and enquiries from corporations and public bodies were especially welcomed.

By the 1950s Sackers had moved to Riverside Road in Ipswich. The company still rented a considerable area of land around the South West Quay and occupied St Clement's Shipyard for a few years. In 1952 they sent eighteen shipments of scrap metal away, five to Immingham and thirteen to Grimsby. For the period April 1955 to March 1956, some 8,700 tons, consisting of borings, cast iron, steel and tins, made up thirty-nine cargoes in a variety of coasters including seven cargoes in Rix's ships, another seven in the ex-sailing barge *OLIVE MAY* and the remainder mainly in Dutchmen. Only 41 tons went away by rail and 550 tons in lorries.

A mere 1,200 tons were dispatched, between five ships, during 1959-1960. The use of land at the Dock ceased during the mid-1960s, although a few shipments did continue; for instance the London & Rochester Trading Company's mv *GILLATION* arrived light from Snape in October 1967 to load for Antwerp. In 1981 Sackers moved to a yard at Claydon on the site of the wartime aviation fuel depot and its railway sidings. They used the railway at first, but later turned entirely to road transport while remaining at Claydon into the twenty-first century.

A. King & Company, Ber Street, Norwich

King's name had appeared at Ipswich by the early 1950s, and they dispatched a cargo of scrap to Hull and four cargoes to Great Yarmouth in 1952. In 1959 the company was responsible for sending away the first bulk cargoes to the Far East from Ipswich. The scrap arrived in trainloads from Norwich, creating an interesting but short-lived trade lasting into the 1960s, as illustrated by the table.

Many of the ships engaged in this trade were between twenty-five and forty-five years old and destined for the scrap yard, making a one-way passage. Some were already sold and re-registered under a new name and foreign flag. The mv *ASHBURTON* of London, for example, had arrived on 16th March 1962 light from Newcastle and she sailed on 19th March with scrap for the Atlantic Steel Company as the mv *PACIFIC BREEZE*, bound for Japan. She had been launched in 1946 by Denny of Dumbarton. The 1960s apparently saw the end of King & Sons' brief interest in shipping scrap metal out of Ipswich.

Cargoes of scrap sent to the Far East by A. King & Sons.
1 A. King & Sons were charged £69 13s. 7d. for the cost of repairing damage done to newly laid concrete slab and construction joints at Cliff Quay by vehicles carrying scrap metal during the loading operations of ss WOLFSBURG.
2 There was a surplus noted in the accounts of 1,532 tons for the ss ALFHEM, subsequently loaded into four Dutch coasters sailing 27th July-4th August.
3 Yawata, now part of the Japanese industrial city of Kitakyushu, N. Kyushu Island, has a dock to handle materials for the Nippon Steel Corporation mills.

Arrival / departure date	Ship	NRT	POR	From	Tons Loaded	For	Built
1959							
16 Jan/5 Feb	mv VILJA	3106	Oslo	Oslo	8,131	Kobe	1942 Copenhagen
26 Feb/16 Mar	mv SOLVEIG RICKERSON	3536	Hamburg	Aarhus	8,325	Osaka	
5 May/25 May	ss WOLFSBURG[1]	3289	Hamburg	Rotterdam	8,237	Tokyo	
5 July/18 July	ss ALFHEM[2]	2781	Uddevalla	Copenhagen	6,019	Tokyo	
1962							
24 Jan/9 Feb	ss CHRISTOPHER OLDENDORF	2926	Lubeck	Rotterdam		Aviles Spain	
15 Feb/8 Mar	mv KALAMAI	2666	Merpsailyz	Hull		Jakarta (Java)	1932 Copenhagen
8 May/25 May	ss RIVADELUNA	3632	Bilbao	Sujon		Aviles	1919 Birkenhead C/Laird
1963							
14 Jan/14 Feb	ss ARDGEN	4164	Hong Kong	Tees		Alexandria	1943 Belfast H&W
14 Mar/3Apr	ss UNION FAIR	5166	Monrovia	Rotterdam		Osaka	1945 Sunderland
20 Nov/14 Feb	ss GRAND	4454	Kaohsiung	Antwerp		Yawata[3]	
1967							
18 Apr/6 May	ss DIOPSIDE	4353	Panama	Karlstad		Hartlepool	
14 May/!8 Jun	ss HYDRAIOS 111	3102	Piraeas	Avonmouth		China	1938 Rotterdam

Fish

The Orwell has been used as a fishery for as long as man has dwelt by its shores, and a thriving fish market existed within the town of Ipswich for centuries. During the sixteenth century Ipswich merchants were involved in fishing for Icelandic cod and efforts were made in the 1700s to participate in the Greenland whaling trade (see first chapter). Since then, however, very little fish trading has taken place in the town. There were still active oyster beds in the river in the early twentieth century, historically owned by Ipswich Corporation, the owners of the river bed. Ipswich men have long kept small vessels in the Orwell or the New Cut, catching fish for sale locally. At the beginning of the 1900s, for instance, fresh fish was sold from the broad pavement on the town side of Stoke Bridge, the scene featuring in several postcards of the time.

At the end of the nineteenth century most of the visiting boats from nearby ports were bringing in sprats and other fish in season. For example, in 1883 at least six smacks, the Harwich bawleys *WHO'D A THOUGHT IT*, *EMILY*, *ALARM*, *PAUL*, *MARY JOHANNA*, and *LITTLE LADY*, all arrived with sprats in October, November and December. Dried herrings were unloaded from the *WANDERER* of Southwold in January 1884. In the December of that year the *WHO'D A THOUGHT IT* delivered three loads of sprats, as did *ETHEL* of Harwich, *ERNEST* of Harwich and *PAUL & EMILY* of Ipswich, plus the *FANNY* with herrings. On 22nd November 1885 sprats were unloaded by the *ELLEN* of

The German mv SOLVEIG RICKERTSEN loading scrap metal from railway trucks about 1957. She was built in 1930 by Burmeister & Wain at Copenhagen as the MINERVA. (Aubrey Frost)

A fish stall at St. Peter's Dock in the early years of the twentieth century, shown on a contemporary postcard. (R. Blastock)

Ipswich, *KINGFISHER*, *PAUL*, and the *MARCH* of Colchester, with the *ADAM HILL* of Harwich arriving with herrings. The *BLACK EYED SUSAN*, 24nrt of Lynn, discharged sprats in February 1888.

Moving on to 1896, *FLORENCE* of Colchester arrived three times with sprats, *EMILY* and *START,* both of Colchester, came once each, and the *DIADEM* brought oysters. Unusually, the *DUCHESS* and *COURAGE SANS PEUR*, a beach yawl, both of Lowestoft, delivered fish. In 1899 *PETREL* of Colchester (Skipper Francis) brought seven cargoes of oysters, with *MARCH* and *FASHION*, both of Colchester, one cargo each. The Colchester smacks *MASONIC*, *PALESTINE*, and *CLAUDE* and the Harwich *KINGFISHER* brought sprats in 1902, while *JOHN & EMMA* and *PEARL* each delivered two cargoes of whelks and the *CLAUDE* one of oysters. In 1903 two Harwich smacks, *PEARL* and *JOHN & EMMA* brought whelks, the Colchester *CLAUDE* twice and *ELIZABETH ANN* (Skipper Cranfield) once with sprats while the Colchester *CLAUDE* came on eight occasions with oysters. It is possible that these quantities of oysters were for replenishment of the local stock. Although the Essex smacks were registered at Colchester, either Brightlingsea or West Mersea were their home ports.

With the modern methods of fishing and refrigeration, the swift transportation of the frozen catches by road and rail, and the imposition of fishing quotas, there seems little likelihood that the fishing trade will ever be revived at Ipswich.

Ice

Closely linked with the introduction of ice cream in the seventeenth century, icehouses were common features in the parks of many country houses. Designed to preserve blocks of ice cut from frozen ornamental lakes in winter for use during the summer, icehouses were generally situated close to the source of the ice. In Ipswich, for example, there was an icehouse in Christchurch Park near the Round Pond, and another almost certainly existed in the grounds of the former Stoke Park Mansion, off the Belstead Road, as the tithe map of 1840 shows an 'Icehouse Plantation' there. A further icehouse has been excavated in the grounds of another grand house in Belstead Road now occupied by St Joseph's College.

An icehouse usually consisted of a pit about 25ft deep, lined with bricks or stone, with a north-facing entrance. A drain was dug at the bottom to dispose of the melt-water, and the chamber was topped by a domed roof for ventilation. Layers of straw provided insulation and ice could be kept for two or three years in this way.

By the mid-nineteenth century, ice from America was being shipped to this country. The Wenham Lake Ice Company, for example, cut ice from the frozen Wenham Lake near Salem, Massachusetts, and exported the blocks to England in the holds of sailing ships. Unlike in America, the fashion for iced drinks and chilled beer did not become popular in England until many years later, the imported ice being mainly used by ice cream makers and fishmongers. The Norwegians, benefiting from their closer proximity to England, took over the American 'frozen water trade' to this country from the 1850s onwards.

From the early 1880s, if not before, three or four cargoes of ice a year were imported into Ipswich from Norway. The cargoes were usually loaded in the small ports of what is now called Oslofjord, near to Christiania (now Oslo). The ice, generally sawn into two feet square blocks, was usually obtained from frozen freshwater lakes in the mountains where the water was reputed to be the purest in Europe. Ice cutting was an important winter occupation in Norway, the blocks of ice being stored in icehouses until the spring, by which time the blocks could have lost about half their original weight. Long wooden chutes were built from the lakeside to the edge of the nearest fjord, and the ice blocks were slid down these to the waiting ships. In an attempt to insulate the cargo and stop it freezing into an unmanageable mass, the blocks were separated by thick layers of sawdust, which itself presented a problem in certain conditions due to the risk of spontaneous combustion.

Discharge usually took place at the Common Quay at Ipswich using a gin-wheel suspended in the rigging, over which a rope was run with a windlass on one end and a spiked scissor-grab on the other. The spikes were knocked into the ice to get a grip for lifting and swinging the blocks ashore, where they were placed on rulleys (flat wagons) and taken to the importer's icehouse. Cargoes were generally received from late May to September.

Block Ice Merchants and Shipping

Glancing at forty years of shipping records from 1885, we note that the ships bringing ice to Ipswich were usually Norwegian, around 100 to 200 nrt and registered at ports along the south coast of Norway. There were also some Danish ships, and nearly all were relatively small sailing vessels, often schooner-rigged and nearing the end of their trading days.

In Ipswich Meadows & Bennett, furnishing and general ironmongers of 24-26 Tavern Street, were advertising in 1883 as block ice merchants with ice stores in Princes Street near the railway station. The company also manufactured kitchen ranges, dealt in electro-plated goods and cutlery and imported marble chimney pieces. In 1885 William Mills, of the Ipswich Cream Yeast Stores at 52A Westgate Street, advertised as a dealer in Wenham Lake Block Ice (mentioned earlier), offering the commodity all the year round. He received bargeloads of ice from London, two particularly in April and June 1889 aboard *AVEYRON* and *WHY NOT* respectively. Whether this ice was imported from America, Norway or elsewhere is not clear. Mills later moved to the Ivy Leaf at 54 Westgate Street where he advertised as a yeast and ice merchant and beer retailer. In 1885, 130 tons of ice is the amount specifically recorded as discharged from the Danish Thuro-registered *SPESET FIDES* from Porsgrund for William

Mills. With the blocks weighing three or four hundredweight each, this corresponds to a total of between 600 and 900 blocks. The other ship to berth in 1885 was the *BRATSBERG,* recorded as being of 913 nrt and registered at and from Porsgrund. If the tonnage were correct then this would be the largest ice-laden vessel to arrive in the Orwell. She is recorded at Pin Mill moorings, that is Buttermans Bay, but it is unclear if she was actually lightened or unloaded there.

Clifford Stegall Orriss, a cement merchant of 28 Cobbold Street, followed Mills in the ice trade. Orriss received his first vessels in the late 1880s, one being the *LOUISE,* 178nrt, with 225 tons of ice. The vessel was registered at Sandefjord and loaded at Laurvig (Larvik), both places situated on the western side of Oslofjord (then Christiana Fjord).

Orriss was succeeded in 1904 by the Ipswich Ice Company, which also had the odd barge freight of ice from London, one arriving in 1907 from Gravesend. The proprietor of the Ipswich Ice Company, situated in Turret Lane, was Robert C. Barker. Three cargoes arrived for the Ipswich Ice Company from Christiana in 1904, one in June and two in August. They were brought by the *ANSGAR,* registered Christiana, which berthed on 5th June and again on 22nd August, and the *VIKJNGEN* of Selvik on the Dramsfjord off Oslofjord, which arrived on 3rd August. The next year, 1905, the *CAROLINE* of Halbaek in Denmark, berthed quite early on 24th March and returned in June, July, August and September.

The trade continued into 1914 when the Marstal-registered *AERIAL* arrived from Christiana on 27th March and sailed eight days later with a cargo for part of her return passage to the Baltic of scrap rails, probably ex-tramway, to Bo'ness on the Forth. She was followed by the *ANNIE* of Fredrikstadt, with three cargoes from Christiana; she loaded return cargoes of gas coke home, one to Moss and two for Fredrikstadt in June, August and September 1914. The Ipswich Ice Company could store up to 250 tons of ice at its premises in Turret Lane, and appeared to be the sole importer in the later days of the trade, which ended in 1926. The firm, which was described in directories as an ice manufacturer, continued in business until the mid-1960s manufacturing butchers' sundries.

Ice traffic to Ipswich between 1922 and 1926. All the cargoes were for the Ipswich Ice Company.

Year	Date	Ship	Nrt	POR	From	Ice tons	Annual Total
1922	14 May	SIERS KRANSEN	-	-	-	253	926
	24 June	HYDRA	130	Tonsberg	Porsgrund	188	
	13 July	SIERS KRANSEN	-	-	-	230	
	11 August	SIERS KRANSEN	-	-	-	255	
1923	18 April	LEIF	-	-	-	225	540
	18 June	NJELS	146	Marstal	Langesund	215	
	26 August	mv HENRY	-	Nykobing	-	100	
1924	20 May	ROSSING	193	Thuro	Langesund	-	-
	18 July	ROSSING	193	Thuro	Langesund	-	
	24 August	ROSSING	193	Thuro	Langesund	-	
1925	28 May	ELISABETH EFF	155	Thuro	Porsgrund	258	755
	6 July	ELISABETH EFF	155	-	Porsgrund	264	
	13 Aug	ELISABETH EFF	155	-	Porsgrund	233	
1926	7 June	GERD	-	-	-	229	676
	1 July	GERD	-	-	-	232	
	28 July	GERD	-	-	-	215	

The Italian founders of the firm of Peters Ice Cream, Maria and Napoleone Zagni, produced their ice cream with the help of ice collected from the Dock when they pioneered their product in Ipswich in 1897.

The trade ceased during the 1914-18 war, and resumed for a few more years in 1922. As shown in the table, 1926 appears to be the final year of the traffic. Artificial ice manufacture and refrigeration had taken over by then and the ice trade with Norway was no more.

Twine

The company of Craven & Speeding Brothers had a relatively small but interesting part in shipping to Ipswich from Sunderland where they manufactured rope. The business was established in 1860 by Hiram Craven, an engineering contractor. His father was John Craven from York who had achieved much in civil engineering and associated railway construction in northern England and Scotland during the 1840s and 50s. His company, John Craven & Sons, was engaged in the construction of South Dock at Sunderland *c.* 1852. It was at this time that Hiram Craven married Mary Jane Speeding, daughter of Thomas Speeding, and went into partnership with James and Edward Speeding (Hiram's brothers-in-law) with whom he founded a rope-making company trading as Craven & Speeding Brothers. Hiram's sons, John and Hiram junior, joined the company, the latter becoming the driving force soon after the manufacture of wire ropes began in addition to traditional fibre ropes. The wire ropes were in use as ships' rigging, and for hauling and lifting work in many collieries.

The line that achieved the greatest and longest lasting success was the making of baler twine for self-binders used in the cornfield. Sisal was used, the only reliable material for the automatic knotting apparatus used by the binders at harvest time. Production continued after the introduction of combine harvesters that were followed in the fields by mechanical balers. In addition to binder-twine, other cords and twines were made for different purposes, one of which was for manufacturing hardwearing carpets.

The works machinery, originally driven by steam engines, was converted to gas in 1898, and in 1902, the first of three diesel engines was installed. By 1932, electricity had become the main power source. The introduction of mechanically produced ropes heralded the end of many small rope-making concerns traditionally associated with using rope-walks. Several such rope-walks had existed in Ipswich and can be seen marked on nineteenth century maps of the town.

In 1924, the company became a founder member of British Ropes Ltd, although this did not show until June 1929 when all IDC accounts were to be forwarded to British Ropes Ltd of 32 Cavendish Square, London W1 and only duplicates were sent to Sunderland. The company no longer produces fibre ropes.

Trade at Ipswich during the 1920s and 1930s amounted to the annual arrival of a coaster from Sunderland carrying between 90 and 140 tons of binder twine in 56lb bags, always at the beginning of July ready for the coming harvest. (Four thousand bags equalled 100 tons.) The twine was then sorted into specific amounts as required, labelled and dispatched from the Public Warehouse usually by rail direct to the customers, most of which were in Suffolk, Cambridgeshire and Norfolk. In 1940, 52 tons was received ex-lorries at Flint Wharf Warehouse. Nothing further is recorded. Binder twine was displaced by plastic with the introduction of giant bales during the 1970s and 1980s.

Public utilities   10

The development of coal gas is usually credited to William Murdoch in the last decade of the eighteenth century. Small gasworks were set up in factories in Birmingham and Manchester and a few street-lighting experiments made during the following ten years. The Chartered Gas Light and Coke Company was founded in 1812 by some London businessmen to supply the public from a main gasworks and to provide coke as a smokeless fuel, for which there was already a commercial demand. The company lasted until nationalisation in 1949, and the word 'chartered' in the title reveals its legal status. Gas companies needed not only to create local monopolies but also to have the right to lay pipes and mains under the public highway, which required statutory powers granted by Acts of Parliament.

It was in 1817 that three eminent Ipswich businessmen, Robert and James Ransome, partners in the company of Ransome & Sons, and John Shewell, a draper in Tavern Street and great-uncle of Frederic Corder, proposed a gasmaking plant to supply the town for public, domestic and commercial purposes. The three subscribed £2,600 as capital and erected a plant in Ransomes' original foundry, the site still remembered by the name Old Foundry Road, in the town centre.

The first engineer was William Cubitt, who at the time was chief engineer at Ransomes' works. He was later to be acknowledged as one of the best engineers of his time, becoming President of the Institution of Civil Engineers and being knighted for his work in connection with the Great Exhibition. The son of a miller, he had invented a patent sail for windmills and a treadmill for use in prisons. The latter had a very wide wheel of relatively small diameter that could be trodden on the outside by several prisoners at once. When two stone arches of Stoke Bridge were swept away by floodwaters in 1818 Cubitt was responsible for the erection of the replacement cast-iron structure.

At the start gas pipes were laid in Carr Street, Tavern Street and the Cornhill and some houses were connected to the supply. As the public saw the benefits of gas over oil lamps opposition to the scheme was overcome and it was decided to form a company to build and operate a full-size gasworks; the three founders offered to relinquish all their rights on the formation of the Ipswich Gas Light Company. An Act of Parliament for lighting the Town and Borough of Ipswich with gas received the Royal Assent on 28th May 1821. It was an extremely comprehensive Act containing sixty-five clauses regarding the operation of the works and company management.

The demand for gas would soon mean larger premises were needed, and in 1822, with incredible foresight and initiative on the part of the founders, ground was bought by a small creek on the east bank of the River Orwell in the parish of St Clement. Not only did this allow for the better handling of coal coming in by sea directly to the works but twenty years later the site was within the area of the enclosed Ipswich Wet Dock. Expansion of the business followed as gas mains were extended through the town, with the demand doubling between 1842 and 1846. From July 1846 to June 1847 seventeen sailing vessels delivered 2,516 tons of coal to the gasworks, an average of 148 tons each.

Discharging the coal was normally done by 'coal-whippers'. A gang of men in the hold shovelled the coal into wicker baskets, and four men on deck climbed

Opposite page: A view across the gasworks showing the 1928 waterless gasholder, the first of its kind to be built in Britain. (Aubrey Frost)

upon wooden staging erected for the purpose; each man had a rope tail spliced into a single rope (sometimes referred to as 'Paddy's bell rope') which passed through a gin wheel in the rigging and down into the hold, where it was hooked on to a basket of coal. At the foreman's command the four would jump as one on to the deck, causing the basket to ascend swiftly from the depths in response to the descending weight of the four 'whippers'. The usual procedure was for the foreman to unhook the basket on the deck and tip the coal into vats for measuring, or down a chute positioned over the side of the vessel to the wharf, but the gas company's account of this operation differed in that it described the baskets or skips as being carried on men's backs up a ladder to the deck and to the storage area ashore. About twenty tons a day was unloaded in this manner.

The early shareholders included many of the county's finest people: Dykes Alexander, Arthur Biddell of Playford, William Brown, Thomas Clarkson of Playford (the 'Friend of Slaves'), members of the Cobbold family and Daniel Poole Goddard, who as company secretary is credited with the initial success of the new company. After Daniel Goddard's death in 1842 he was succeeded by his son Ebenezer Goddard, who had been apprenticed to Ransomes and had worked for the marine engineers Maudslay on the Thames. He served as company secretary and engineer for forty years.

In 1846 sixteen cargoes of coal, totalling some 2,230 tons, were delivered by eight schooners and collier brigs. The *HAPPY RETURN* arrived fourteen times between 9th July 1850 and 25th July 1851. Was this the ship that gave her name to the public house situated opposite the entrance to the gasworks until the 1970s? It may well have been; the 1884 register shows a wooden brig, the *HAPPY RETURN*, 185nrt and built at St Malo in 1838; the vessel was still active for Guernsey owners at that time.

Imagine the anticipation and possible apprehension of the good folk of Eye in north Suffolk when their gasworks opened in 1850. The nearest railway station was at Mellis, nearly three miles away, and a branch line to Eye was not opened until April 1867. We must assume that the 120 tons of coal discharged at Ipswich by the *JANE* of Whitby on 5th August 1850, plus the 100 tons from the *CRUIZER* of Blakeney on the 7th, all for the Eye Gas Company, were loaded to railway trucks for Mellis and there transferred to horses and carts for onward carriage to the gasworks.

Four vessels brought 360 tons of coal to Ipswich for the gasworks at Bury St Edmunds, and this coal would have been transferred to the railway. This may have been a trial run, because Bury had been linked to the sea and coastal shipping at Kings Lynn since 1715 by the rivers Lark and Great Ouse, especially for the transport of coal.

Charges to customers were at first based on contracts providing for gas to be used through particular types of burners for so many hours per night per half-year, the consumer undertaking to extinguish his lights at the appointed time. Those who cheated were threatened with having their supply cut off. Gas meters were developed only later in the course of the nineteenth century. Street lighting began in 1818, and by July 1863 the last street oil lamp was removed, except for one or two temporary oil lamps, the company receiving instructions on the laying of mains and placing of lights from the Corporation Paving and Lighting Committee. A chairman of that committee introduced the ruling that the distance between two street lamps was to be such that a person standing at night midway between the lamps should be able to read his pocket watch.

The use of gas expanded so rapidly that additional powers were obtained in 1864 enabling the company's capital to be increased to £100,000 for improve-

Leaving the gasworks is the ss VISCOUNT CASTLEREAGH, built of iron at Sunderland in 1878 for the Marquis of Londonderry, of Wynyard Park, Durham.

ments and a new gasholder. In 1876, an offer was received from Ipswich Corporation to purchase the undertaking, but the terms were not acceptable to the shareholders.

A new retort house was built in 1878 and another new gasholder erected in 1881. By 1882 the output had increased by 1,600 per cent and the price had dropped considerably. By that time a steam crane was in use for discharging coal from the vessels' holds, but the use of steamships demanded modernisation. On 10th March 1885 the Gas Light Company installed two Armstrong hydraulic cranes, lifting manually filled buckets. The ss *HARTON* was the first vessel to be discharged in this manner. Grabs later replaced the buckets, and the first ship to be worked at the rate of one ton of coal per minute was the ss *ONYX* with Tyne coal on 26th August 1901. The cranes were able to move a short distance on rails along the gasworks quay between the ships' holds. The coal was lifted into overhead hoppers, from where it was mechanically conveyed to the yard. So efficient were these cranes that they remained in service until the gasworks closed in 1971. The Eastern Gas Board offered the cranes for preservation, but regrettably no offer was forthcoming and they were broken up after eighty-six years' remarkable service.

The Corporation again attempted a buy-out in 1883, which the directors approved, and an Act authorising the takeover received the Royal Assent on 2nd August. However, a meeting of ratepayers in October opposed the scheme and it was not carried out.

Ebenezer Goddard died in 1882 and was succeeded by his son, Daniel Ford Goddard, who had served his time with E.R. & F. Turner and had later studied chemistry as applied to coal and gas in London and Newcastle. After only five years, however, he resigned his position with the company to pursue his interest in public work. He was to become a town councillor and was later elected an alderman and J.P., and was Mayor in 1892. Three years later he was returned as Member of Parliament for Ipswich, awarded a knighthood in 1907, and made a Privy Councillor in 1916.

The original gas mains in Ipswich were two inches in diameter, but a hundred years later the trunk main was two feet in diameter, with a total of eighty-eight miles of mains laid from the works. Many developments had taken place during this period. Ebenezer Goddard had invented and patented what was probably the world's first gas-heating stove (known as an 'Asbestos Gas Stove') by the 1870s and had designed gas cookers and gas-heated baths, many of which were made

The ss EDENSIDE (ex-CARDIFF CITY) at Ipswich gasworks. Built at Paisley in 1909, she was owned by the Wear S.S. Co. Ltd of Sunderland.

at the Ipswich gasworks and used widely in the town and elsewhere. In 1882, the popular and long-lived domestic gas fire was introduced.

Lighting underwent a revolution after Dr. von Welsbach invented the incandescent gas burner in 1885, and ten years later almost all the street lamps had been converted to this system. In 1890 the gas geyser for heating water, which had first appeared in 1868, was developed for instantaneous heating as the water flowed. Pre-payment meters were introduced in the 1890s, accepting either pennies or shillings. Exhibitions of gas appliances were held in the Public Hall for several years, resulting in further new business, and a new office and showroom were opened at the Corn Exchange building in 1884, superseded in 1892 by impressive new offices and showroom erected by prominent Ipswich builder Fred Bennett.

The company owned four sailing vessels in 1884 and these are listed in Lloyd's Register for that year in the name of Ebenezer Goddard of Oak Hill, Ipswich. (They are marked with an asterisk in the following table.) In that same year there were only two steamships, both belonging to Edward Packard, working regularly to the gasworks; the *SEDGEMOOR*, approximately 230dwt, and *DARTMOOR*, about 300dwt; each brought four cargoes from the Tyne.

Deliveries of coal to Ipswich gasworks in 1884.

Name	Rig	POR	NRT	From	Owners	No. Of Cargoes	Remarks
ss SEDGEM00R		Ipswich	113	Newcastle	E Packard, Ipswich	4	b 1872 Newcastle
MUTE	Sr	Ipswich	89	Shields	W Bayley, Ipswich	1	b 1853 Portsmouth
ECONOMY *	Snow	Ipswich	133	Shields	E Goddard, Ipswich	6	b 1831 Peterhead
VISITOR *	Sr	Ipswich	128	Shields	E Goddard, Ipswich	6	b 1840 Ipswich
DAYSTAR *	Bn	Ipswich	149	Shields	E Goddard, Ipswich	10	b 1860 Sunderland
ss DARTMOOR		Ipswich	154	Newcastle	E Packard, Ipswich	4	b 1882 London
IDA	Kb	Ipswich	136	Shields	R&W Paul, Ipswich	1	b 1881 Ipswich
ANNA SARAH *	Sr	Ipswich	141	Shields	E Goddard, Ipswich	7	b l860 Sunderland
SARAH LIZZ1E				Shields		1	
SNOWDROP	Sr	Ipswich	100	Shields	W Turner, Ipswich	1	b 1859 Ipswich
PRINCESS ROYAL	Bn	Ipswich	135	Shields	W Cole, Ipswich	1	b 1843 Woodbridge
LYMINGTON	Sr	Harwich	163	Sunderland	Vaux, Harwich	1	b 1880 Vaux Harwich. Wrecked 1889 Holme Sand. Three-masted schooner barge loading 350 tons.
					Total number of cargoes	43	

By 1888, four years later, the steamships *HARTON* (20 cargoes), *BIRLING* and *CLEOPATRA* (each with one cargo) spelled the end of the gasworks coal trade under sail. *HARTON,* built at Sunderland in 1872, had a deadweight tonnage of nearly 600 tons and was owned by the Harton Coal Company; H. Philipson of Newcastle managed the vessel. This comparison of 1884 and 1888 effectively demonstrates the dependability and regularity of the steamships, which delivered an additional 2,000 tons in 1888 with half the number of vessels.

By 1894 the gasworks business had further increased with over thirty cargoes arriving that year. Four of these cargoes arrived from Seaham Harbour in the *GARRON TOWER,* built at West Hartlepool in 1876 for the Marquess of Londonderry. From that time, and for several years to come, much of the coal for Ipswich gasworks came from Seaham in Lord Londonderry's own ships. Presumably a new contract for Londonderry coal had been drawn up. Nineteen cargoes were brought by the *HARTON,* the rest by the *KINGSLEY, BOLSTRUP*, and *RINGMOOR* of Ipswich, *ETHELBERT* of London and the 1883 Sunderland-built vessels *HARTSIDE* and *KINGSCOTE*. These all came from Tyneside. Many of the ships brought small parcels of coal for gasworks at Hadleigh, Halstead, Earls Colne and Stowmarket, the coal being forwarded by the railway.

In 1903 another Act was introduced authorising a capital increase to £350,000 and the company's limits were extended to include Bramford, Whitton, Westerfield, Rushmere, Nacton, Wherstead, Belstead and Sproughton. Progress had also been made in dealing with residuals from the gas-making process. One ton of coal produced about 10cwt of coke that could be screened in various sizes for sale. The tar that for years had been consigned to tar pits near the works became a valuable product not only for road making but also for providing pitch, creosote, carbolic acid and naphtha. Saccharine and certain dyes could also be made from tar. Toluol and benzol were obtained from coal distillation and sulphate of ammonia could be derived from the liquor produced.

In 1913, thirty-six vessels arrived. Many of the cargoes were split three ways between Ipswich, Hadleigh and Stowmarket. In fact, seventeen part-cargoes went to Hadleigh and the same number to Stowmarket. The *HOLMSIDE* brought fourteen shipments, all for Ipswich; she was of 1,000 tons dwt and built in 1893 for W. Swanston of Newcastle. The rest of the gasworks fleet in 1913 included the Marquess of Londonderry's *VANE TEMPEST, VISCOUNT CASTLEREAGH* and *LORD LONDONDERRY*, all from Seaham Harbour and all with parcels for Hadleigh and/or Stowmarket. This practice continued until the 1914-18 war, during which Ipswich gasworks received some coal by rail because of the shipping problems on the East Coast, although some coal was still getting through by sea; for example in 1918 the ss *EDEN* of Maryport brought coal for the Colne Valley Railway from Amble and the ss *BLUSH ROSE* of Liverpool and the Shoreham-owned ss *ALGETHI* discharged coal for the Great Eastern Railway.

A handful of iron screw steamships had been built in the 1840s with the London coal trade in mind, but they were in effect sailing vessels with low-powered steam engines. In 1852 Palmer Brothers at Newcastle launched the iron collier *JOHN BOWES*; she was schooner rigged, but the sails were no more than an auxiliary source of power. She loaded 650 tons of coal and has been widely accepted as the first successful steam collier. Palmers were aware of the potential of new London gas company contracts and between March 1853 and September 1854 launched no fewer than ten ships, each carrying about 750 tons, of which the *NORTHUMBERLAND* was one. This vessel was one of two ships, both classed as barges but each conveying 700 tons, which were towed up and down the North Sea by the tug *ATHLETE* in 1916-17 with Tyne coal for the gasworks

An employee of the Ipswich Gas Light Company in his working uniform.

at Ipswich. The *NORTHUMBERLAND* arrived in the port on five occasions during this twelve-month period. The other ship on tow was the *ANNIE*, built in 1869 as a sailing vessel, which came to Ipswich seven times during 1916-17.

Coke was bought by local merchants and large customers, some of whom shipped out coke in sailing barges. Trips were made to Bawdsey, presumably for the Manor boiler house, for where in 1907 the barges *JOHN* and *HANNAH* loaded in January and the *GENERAL JACKSON* loaded in November; this trade continued until at least 1929. The *JOHN* and the *HANNAH* also took a load to Slumpy Lane wharf on the Berners estate at Freston, and other loads were taken by barge to Rochester and Sittingbourne.

Gas oil, produced by the fledgling oil companies and generally referred to later as diesel oil, was capable of being distilled to produce gas, hence the name. This distillation was done in many gasworks and the gas produced was blended with the coal gas. Early deliveries of gas oil were made by the sailing barges *HYDROGEN* and *NITROGEN*. They, together with *OXYGEN*, had been built with tanks fitted in the holds. *HYDROGEN*, built at Rochester in 1906, arrived with gas oil twice in 1907, interestingly sailing light on both occasions for Grangemouth on the Firth of Forth. In the following year *HYDROGEN* arrived with oil seven times. *NITROGEN* was built of steel as an auxiliary sailing barge and fitted with an oil engine at South Shields in 1912 for Burt, Boulton & Haywood of London, a small but old-established oil company who had a depot at Prince Regent Wharf on the Isle of Dogs. It gave the name of Regent to a once familiar petrol company. Burt, Boulton was bought about 1930 by Trinidad Leaseholds who had already established a refinery in Trinidad and sought an outlet in Britain. Burt, Boulton used *NITROGEN* extensively, coming regularly to Ipswich gasworks, arriving ten times in 1916.

Through the 1920s and 1930s the gas oil was brought in by two steam coastal tankers owned by the Eagle Oil Transport Company that from 1919 was managed by Royal Dutch Shell. The ships were *SAN DARIO*, built by Short Bros. of Sunderland in 1918 as a fleet oiler, and *SHELL-MEX IV*, built 1921 at Queensferry for the Anglo-Mexican Oil Company. By 1939 Rowbotham's coastal tankers were delivering perhaps two cargoes of gas oil a year. They were very well known ships around the coast, with names all ending in '*MAN*'. mv *STEERSMAN*, Dutch built at Alblasserdam in 1936, and mv *RUDDERMAN* from the same yard, both arrived at Ipswich in 1939.

Another by-product of coal distillation for gas was benzine or benzol. This was found suitable for blending with petrol, and in 1919 the National Benzole Co. Ltd was formed to market National Benzole Mixture. The first depot in Ipswich opened next to the gasworks, on the corner of the Dock and Patteson Road, in 1923. In that year two cargoes of coal from Keadby on the Trent arrived for the gas company in R. & W. Pauls' 500-ton lighter *P1* towed by the tug *R.W. WHELDON* of Hull.

Competition from the new Corporation electricity generating station, opened in 1903, did not seriously affect the gas company, whose gas sales increased by seventy-five per cent between 1903 and 1920. In 1920 the Government brought in a Gas Regulation Act changing the way in which customers were charged for gas. It was realised that gas was used for heat-giving purposes and customers were thereafter charged on heat value, with prices calculated on so much per *therm* instead of per 1,000 cubic feet. By 1932 the famous and popular 'Ascot' water-heater was in use in many houses, resulting in more gas being consumed by the domestic user.

In 1926, the year of the General Strike and the lengthy coal miners' strike,

Date	SHIP	Reg	NRT	Built	Owners	Cargo tons	From
1920							
27 Mar	VISCOUNT CASTLEREAGH	Sunderland	397	Sunderland 1878	Marq. of Lond.*	732	Seaham Harbour
31 Mar	SUNNISIDE	Goole	447	Sunderland 1905	Wear S.S. Co Sunderland	774	Sunderland
15 Apr	VISCOUNT CASTLEREAGH	Sunderland	397	Sunderland 1878	Marq. of Lond.*	720	Seaham Harbour
25 Apr	NEWTOWNARDS	Sunderland	425	Sunderland 1912	Marq. of Lond.*	1011	Seaham Harbour
9 May	HOLMSIDE	Newcastle	531	Bill Quay (Tyne) 1893	Wm Swanston, Newcastle	1166	Tyne
9 May	NEWTOWNARDS	Sunderland	425	Sunderland 1912	Marq. of Lond.*	1025	Seaham Harbour
20 May	VISCOUNT CASTLEREAGH	Sunderland	397	Sunderland 1878	Marq. of Lond.*	754	Seaham Harbour
7 Jun	SUNNISIDE	Goole	447	Sunderland 1905	Wear S.S. Co, Sunderland	821	Tyne
10 Jun	VISCOUNT CASTLEREAGH	Sunderland	397	Sunderland 1878	Marq. of Lond.*	750	Seaham Harbour
25 Jun	VISCOUNT CASTLEREAGH	Sunderland	397	Sunderland 1878	Marq. of Lond.*	748	Seaham Harbour
27 Jun	HOLMSIDE	Newcastle	531	Bill Quay (Tyne) 1893	Wm Swanston, Newcastle	1142	Tyne
7 Jul	NEWTOWNARDS	Sunderland	425	Sunderland 1912	Marq. of Lond.*	1019	Seaham Harbour
17 Jul	VISCOUNT CASTLEREAGH	Sunderland	397	Sunderland 1878	Marq. of Lond.*	752	Seaham Harbour
5 Aug	THRIFT	Aberdeen	209	Aberdeen 1905	Northern Co-op Co, Aberdeen	546	Seaham Harbour
5 Aug	HOLMSIDE	Newcastle	531	Bill Quay (Tyne) 1893	Wm Swanston, Newcastle	1157	Tyne
15 Aug	VISCOUNT CASTLEREAGH	Sunderland	397	Sunderland 1878	Marq. of Lond.*	750	Seaham Harbour
2 Sep	VISCOUNT CASTLEREAGH	Sunderland	397	Sunderland 1878	Marq. of Lond.*	753	Seaham Harbour
15 Sep	HOLMSIDE	Newcastle	531	Bill Quay (Tyne) 1893	Wm Swanston, Newcastle	1151	Tyne
18 Sep	SUNNISIDE	Goole	447	Sunderland 1905	Wear S.S. Co, Sunderland	819	Tyne
29 Sep	VISCOUNT CASTLEREAGH	Sunderland	397	Sunderland 1878	Marq. of Lond.*	762	Seaham Harbour
9 Oct	VISCOUNT CASTLEREAGH	Sunderland	397	Sunderland 1878	Marq. of Lond.*	698	Seaham Harbour
11 Oct	HOLMSIDE	Newcastle	531	Bill Quay (Tyne) 1893	Wm Swanston, Newcastle	1170	Tyne
12 Nov	NEWTOWNARDS	Sunderland	425	Sunderland 1912	Marq. of Lond.*	1003	Seaham Harbour
23 Nov	NEWTOWNARDS	Sunderland	425	Sunderland 1912	Marq. of Lond.*	1005	Seaham Harbour
28 Nov	HOLMSIDE	Newcastle	531	Bill Quay (Tyne) 1893	Wm Swanston, Newcastle	1175	Tyne
9 Dec	VISCOUNT CASTLEREAGH (probably last trip)	Sunderland	397	Sunderland 1878	Marq. of Lond.*	738	Seaham Harbour
24 Dec	HOLMSIDE	Newcastle	531	Bill Quay (Tyne) 1893	Wm Swanston, Newcastle	1155	Tyne
25 Dec	NEWTOWNARDS	Sunderland	425	Sunderland 1912	Marq. of Lond.*	1013	Seaham Harbour
1921							
6 Jan	mv ADMIRAL KEYES	London	175		Goole	459	Goole
14 Jan	NEWTOWNARDS	Sunderland	425	Sunderland 1912	Marq. of Lond.*	1020	Seaham Harbour
19 Jan	ESKWOOD	Middlesbrough	370	Middlesbrough 1911	Meteor S.S.Co, Middlesbrough	927	Goole
26 Jan	HOLMSIDE	Newcastle	531	Bill Quay (Tyne) 1893	Wm Swanston, Newcastle	1185	Tyne
14 Feb	HOLMSIDE	Newcastle	531	Bill Quay (Tyne) 1893	Wm Swanston, Newcastle	1158	Tyne
18 Feb	NEWTOWNARDS	Sunderland	425	Sunderland 1912	Marq. of Lond.*	998	Seaham Harbour
5 Mar	VANE TEMPEST	Sunderland	440	W Hartlepool 1884	Marq. of Lond.*	810	Seaham Harbour
9 Mar	HOLMSIDE	Newcastle	531	Bill Quay (Tyne) 1893	Wm Swanston, Newcastle	1156	Tyne
14 Mar	DICKY	Liverpool	210	Maryport 1901	Goole & Hull Steam Towing Co.	661	Goole
18 Mar	HOLMSIDE	Newcastle	531	Bill Quay (Tyne) 1893	Wm Swanston, Newcastle	1176	Tyne
20 Mar	NEWTOWNARDS	Sunderland	425	Sunderland 1912	Marq. of Lond.*	1017	Seaham Harbour

Cargoes to Ipswich gasworks, April 1920 to March 1921.

*Marquis of Londonderry.

coal supplies to Ipswich were maintained one way or another. The small motor coaster *LINTON* arrived in June from Rotterdam with coal for Bury Gas Company, and in August the ss *PRIMA* of Flensburg came from Hamburg with a cargo for Cambridge gasworks. The highlight of 1926 must have been the arrival of the Dutch steam coaster *VLIESTROOM* from Amsterdam with sections of the new waterless gasholder that was erected in 1927 and which was a significant Ipswich landmark until its demolition in the 1980s. The benefit of this holder was that the gas, when it went into the mains, was not saturated with water vapour, unlike the gas stored in the rest of the gasholders at Ipswich that were inverted over a tank of water.

The next generation of colliers kept the works supplied during the 1930s, as the table for 1931 reveals. The steamships brought a total of fifty-six cargoes from various East Coast coal ports.

In 1933 the total coal discharged was up by only about 4,000 tons from 1916, revealing a levelling-off as electricity became the choice for lighting on the new council and private housing estates being built around the town. Gas, however, remained the favourite fuel for cooking.

The emphasis had changed by 1939 from Seaham Harbour to Goole as the principal source of gas coal from the South Yorkshire and Nottinghamshire coalfields. Although Constantine's and Hargreaves' ships were still frequent visitors, colliers belonging to A.W. Atkinson's Ouse Steamship Company of Goole became familiar with their '*FLEET*' suffixes; *FAXFLEET*, the first ship to be aquired by the company, built at Paisley in 1916 and immediately sent to Scapa Flow as a fleet collier, *YOKEFLEET* (ex-*BRENTHAM*), Clyde-built in 1910, and *SWYNFLEET*, built as the *BEIGE* at Sunderland in 1914. In 1924 Atkinson's subsidiary company, Ebor S.S. Co., bought the *AVONWOOD*, built in 1915, and renamed her *BROOMFLEET*. She left Goole for Ipswich gasworks on 13th December 1933 and sank with all hands in bad weather off Sheringham.

Coke availability was subject to seasonal or industrial demand, and most gasworks had to bring in coke from elsewhere from time to time. In 1939 eighteen cargoes were delivered to Ipswich gasworks using twelve steel barges built at Deptford or Southampton during 1898-99 for E.J. & W. Goldsmith of Grays, plus two of their wooden craft. About 1,800 tons came from London (almost certainly Beckton) from January to April and another 900 tons arrived from Southend in August and September.

To cover a shortfall in August 1941 the Norwegian steamship *SKAGERRAK*, sailing under the British flag, had loaded coke at Newcastle for Ipswich. Having

The steamships that brought coal to the Ipswich gasworks during 1931.

Name	POR	NRT	Owners	Built	Place Built	No. of Trips
ss *LEVENWOOD*	Middlesbrough	374	Jos Constantine S.S. Line Co	1924	Workington	11
ss *COPSEWOOD*	Middlesbrough	537	Jos Constantine S.S. Line Co	1925	Sunderland	6
ssS *HOMEWOOD*	Middlesbrough	426	Jos Constantine S.S. Line Co	1927	Workington	2
ss *LARCHWOOD*	Middlesbrough		Jos Constantine S.S. Line Co			9
ss *HARFRY*	Goole	438	Jas Hargreaves Ltd., Leeds	1924	Goole	8
ss *SANFRY*	Goole	481	Jas Hargreaves Ltd., Leeds	1930	Goole	12
ss *BORDER FIRTH*	London	250	Border Shipping Co	1919	Swan Hunter, Newcastle	2
ss *DICKY*	Liverpool	210	Goole & Hull Steam Shipping Co	1901	Maryport	2
ss *ARDGARROCH*	Greenock	497	P McCallum & Sons	1918	Ardrossan	2
ss *GRETA FORCE*	Whitehaven	456	W Kennaugh & Co	1928	Paisley	2
					Total trips	56

The ss FAXFLEET, 420nrt, was a regular trader to Ipswich gasworks. She made 49 round trips from Goole in 1950, and her sistership YOKEFLEET made 42 trips that year. Built in 1916 at Paisley and registered at Goole, she was owned by the Ouse S.S. Co.Ltd. (R.W. Smith)

safely entered the Orwell, she detonated two parachute mines dropped the previous night and was blown in two approaching Collimer Point with the loss of seventeen crew out of twenty-two and the Ipswich pilot.

SWYNFLEET was another war casualty. Acquired in 1919, she was a typical three-islander with engines amidships and able to load over 1,600 tons. She was lost on 25th January 1941 inbound for Ipswich gasworks. Approaching Harwich Harbour just outside the swept channel on the Landguard side she struck a mine and sank in shallow water. It proved impossible to salvage the wreck, and it remained there for the rest of the war. *FAXFLEET* and *YOKEFLEET* were to continue regular voyages to the gasworks until the early 1950s; in 1950 *YOKEFLEET* arrived forty-two times and *FAXFLEET* no fewer than forty-nine, supplying almost all the requirements for the year between them.

The next major Gas Act in 1949 nationalised the industry. Twelve area boards were set up guided by the Gas Council. By then the end of the steam coaster was in sight. Constantine's and Hargreaves' were two of the companies to build motor ships, and Comben Longstaff & Co. of London, whose vessels had names of counties ending with the suffix '*BROOK*', were another. They were soon to be the main shippers of coal to the gasworks. The *KENTBROOK* arrived at Ipswich gasworks on Tuesday 2nd February 1954 with coal from Goole, and after a lengthy stay sailed the following Wednesday evening. Twenty-four hours later she radioed for assistance, having gone ashore three miles north of Orfordness. Lifesaving rocket brigades from Aldeburgh and Orford went to the scene and brought a man ashore. Attempts to refloat her failed, and it was decided to wait until the next spring tides on the 17th, leaving a skeleton crew aboard. The Yarmouth tug *RICHARD LEE BARBER* stood by and bulldozers worked on the shingle, but to no avail. On 13th March an onshore gale buffeted the ship and the vessel was declared a total loss on 7th May. She was broken up on the beach.

In 1955 ss *LANCASTERBROOK* brought no fewer than sixty-two cargoes from Goole, plus two ex-Rotterdam, ss *LEICESTERBROOK* brought three, ss *LINCOLNBROOK* five and ss *LONDONBROOK* eight, out of eighty-five during that year. These four steamers were all built by John Lewis & Sons Ltd of Aberdeen in 1946-48. Three traditional steam coasters brought four more cargoes: these were the ss *THE COUNTESS,* built 1928, *THE DUKE,* built 1927, and *THE EARL* built 1936. Unusual in having the definite article as a part of their name, they were all launched by the Ailsa Shipbuilding Co. of Troon for J. Hay & Sons of Glasgow. Hays were a very well-known coastal shipping firm that was taken over by F.T. Everard & Sons Ltd in 1956. The three ships just mentioned were broken up in 1960-61.

The mid-1960s saw ships arriving at Ipswich that were owned by Stephenson Clarke Ltd, a company with roots going back to the eighteenth century. The firm had become London coal factors in the early nineteenth century before taking shares in ships and managing collier fleets, whilst building up a large fleet of their own, most of them named after Sussex villages and towns.

In 1963 Stephenson Clarke's *BROADHURST*, 1,525 dwt, built 1948, *BEEDING*, 1,597 dwt, built 1950, *HENFIELD*, 1,530 dwt, built 1950, and the company's first motor ship, *SEAFORD*, 1,510 dwt, built 1947, brought thirty-one cargoes between them. By that time, Comben Longstaff were also well to the fore with a new generation of ships, all built in Holland. They included *DORSETBROOK*, 1,360 dwt, built 1957, *DURHAMBROOK*, 1,734 dwt, built 1955, *WARWICKBROOK*, 1,405 dwt, built 1956, *WESTMINSTERBROOK*, 1,406 dwt, built 1961, *WINCHESTERBROOK*, 1,418 dwt, built 1960, and *WINDSORBROOK*, 1,360 dwt, built 1956. These vessels delivered thirty-six

The mv KOMET, 278nrt, registered and built at Hamburg in 1963, loading coke breeze at Ipswich gasworks for Hamburg or a Scandinavian port in the late 1960s.

cargoes in 1963. During that year, the two companies' ships delivered sixty-seven out of a total of sixty-nine cargoes, all from Goole. Comben Longstaff gradually turned to deep-sea ships and were bought by Everards in 1980. In addition, during 1963 sixteen loads of gas oil, approximately 3,000 tons, arrived from Thameside in the 1916-built mb *BICKLEY HALL,* owned by Bowker & King of London.

Coke breeze (small coke siftings) was in demand for making breeze blocks for the building industry, and in 1956 forty motor barges loaded this material for London. There was a ready export market to Norway during the 1950s-1960s, and in 1960 eight Scandinavian motor ships berthed light from London, Newcastle, Shoreham and Grimsby to load return cargoes of from 500 to 1,200 tons. Two ships sailed for Mo I Rana at the head of the Ranafjord, normally ice-free all year at lattitude 66°N, about 250 nautical miles north of Trondheim and very close to the Arctic Circle. Another left for Porsgrunn on the south-eastern coast, and other ports to which cargoes were consigned included Kristiansund and Svelgen on the west coast. Another thirty-six cargoes of breeze went to London in the equivalent of the sailing barges, steel motor barges able to load 200 tons. Ten had brought grain or cattle-cake to Eastern Counties Farmers Ltd or timber for William Brown, or had arrived light from Felixstowe. They included *SILVER, GOLD, PEPITA, JOSH FRANCIS, CECIL GILDERS, NAUGHTON, NICOLA DAWN,* and the former sailing barge *WYVENHOE,* built at Wivenhoe, Essex, in 1898, since restored to sail and still active in the year 2001.

Tar was another occasional commodity outward. In 1960 seven loads were taken to London in the 200 dwt motor tanker *BRADFIELD,* owned by Bowker & King Ltd of London and built in 1917 as one of the craft intended for war service.

Natural gas was discovered in Holland in 1959 and large reserves were found under the North Sea, resulting in the 1965 Continental Shelf Act that staked out North Sea gas areas. The 1965 Gas Act recognised that the local generation of gas was all but finished and confirmed the Gas Council as the key organisation with a Gas Corporation proposal in 1971. A national gas grid was established on the assumption that natural gas would be available to all parts of Britain by 1980.

In 1968 there were sixty-seven arrivals with coal, but the end of a long era was at hand. By 1970 only forty-four ships came, including *SEAFORD, WESTMINSTERBROOK,* and *WORCESTERBROOK,* also Everards' mv *SAGACITY,* built 1946, and mv *CENTRICITY,* built 1955, plus mv *GLADONIA,* built 1963 and belonging to Keadby owners J. Wharton Ltd.

In the event, gas production and distribution ceased at Ipswich in March 1971 after householders and other users had had their existing cookers and other appliances adapted in a major campaign. Gasholders, or as they used to be called, gasometers, were gradually taken down, leaving only the latest one, erected in the 1950s off Hadleigh Road, connected to the grid and still in use in 2000. The last one in the old gasworks (since in use as a timber importers yard) was dismantled in November 1999.

The closure of the gasworks in 1971 meant that only four shipments were required that year. They were by the mv *WINCHESTERBROOK* on February 4th and the mv *WORCESTERBROOK* that discharged on 17th January and 9th February and arrived with the final cargo of coal on 19th March 1971. Subsequent privatisation of the industry is no part of this story, that has sought to tell something of gas production in Ipswich and the hundreds of North Sea colliers and crews that kept the town's gas flowing throughout wars and winter storms for a hundred and fifty years from 1821 to 1971.

The Power Stations

The change to electricity for the public was perhaps not so dramatic as had been the introduction of gas light half a century before. Previously, candles or rushlight (obtained by dipping rushes into tallow) had provided lighting for most people, the wealthy having beeswax candles. Before the introduction of paraffin, the first oil lamps used smelly animal fat (usually tallow) or imported colza and rape oil, often in a lamp consisting of a pot with a rag or fibre wick. People tended not to go out at night except when there was a full moon and the 'parish lantern' guided the traveller. Even when compared with gas, the importance of electricity to those inhabitants and industries using it for lighting and power cannot be exaggerated. The flick of a switch made available bright lights and power for domestic appliances in the home. In industry, electricity gave power to individual machines on the factory floor and did away with the need for troublesome and sometimes dangerous line-shafts driven by a central steam engine. Many farms in East Anglia, however, did not receive electricity until the 1950s and '60s, and wind-powered Lucas 'Freelite' propeller generators on poles were for a time familiar in the landscape.

It was in 1831 that Michael Faraday put together the principles of the dynamo to generate direct current (DC), the alternator producing alternating current (AC), and the transformer for varying voltages. An electric motor was invented soon afterwards, but the development of necessary equipment to create an electricity generating industry took another fifty years or so to bring about. Engineers, municipalities and private companies unfortunately managed to

An aerial view of Constantine Road power station, with the refuse destructor shaft dominating the area. Most of the coal used was transhipped from colliers in the Dock and delivered by rail to the siding at bottom right. (CEGB)

The Constantine Road power station viewed from above the railway tunnel. The chimneys of the Railway Hotel can be seen at bottom right, and the lettering on Moy's and William Brown's premises can just be made out. (Kevin Higgins)

contrive enormous confusion amongst themselves over the relative merits of AC/DC, frequencies and would-be suppliers. All the companies were set against any form of a national supply. Two Electric Lighting Acts of 1882 and 1888 served only to make more restrictions, although by 1900 there were more than 300 mainly municipal power stations.

The electrical pioneer Charles H. Merz, born in 1874, recognised and advocated the advantages of a national electricity supply system through a trunk mains network, but in spite of further Electricity Supply Acts in 1919 and 1922 nothing much happened except the introduction of the word 'supply' in place of 'lighting'. These Acts reflected the fact that electricity had become a major source of power, especially for urban transport. The confused situation is best illustrated by the fact that an AC electric clock could not necessarily work in both London and the provinces because of differing frequencies. At last in 1926 another Electricity Supply Act set up a Central Electricity Board to push ahead with national standards and a grid of transmission lines connecting power stations, although the Board itself was unable to own stations. The National Grid, as it is called, developed quickly from the 1930s under the auspices of the C.E.B. Confusion, however, was not entirely ended until the nationalisation of the whole industry by the Electricity Act of 1948 which vested everything into the British Electricity Authority. The 1957 Act established the Central Electricity Generating Board that, as its name implies, took over the generation side and distributed power through twelve area boards. Since the 1980s the industry has been privatised and split into many different companies, all competing for customers with differently priced electricity tariffs, and in some cases also supplying gas.

Constantine Road power station

In February 1899 the Ipswich Corporation Parliamentary Committee was empowered to purchase the Ipswich Tramway Company, which had run horse trains in the town since 1880. As that system was extended during the decade, four ships brought in some 1,200 tons of granite blocks from Aberdeen to be used for road building. The vessels included the schooner-rigged steamer *RANGER* of Montrose, listed in the 1884 Lloyd's Register as built in 1846, an early steamship.

The Ipswich Tramway Company system was purchased by the Corporation for £17,000 and it was decided to build an electricity generating station on Seven Acre Field owned by the Corporation, close to the River Gipping from which fresh water was available for cooling purposes. The generating station, with a workshop, car shed and offices attached, was erected by Ipswich builder S.A. Kenney, work commencing in October 1902. The station itself consisted of a boiler house with four marine type boilers and an engine room containing four compound high-speed engines made by Reavells of Ipswich and four German-manufactured dynamos (the two larger pairs providing current for the trams and the other sets for electric lighting). There was also a battery room. A refuse destructor, or incinerator, was included and its square shaft, $178\frac{1}{2}$ft high, became a well-known landmark. Outside was a coal yard and railway sidings connected to the G.E.R. Lower Yard close to the bridge bringing the line across to the north side of the tidal Orwell.

For the construction of the power station and new electric tramway, a huge amount of shingle (most of it for the concrete track bed), granite setts and rails all came up the Orwell to the dock. Most of the shingle was landed close to the site above Stoke, Princes Street and the dock branch railway bridges. During the first three months of the construction time of the new tramway, at least 8,000 tons of shingle was delivered by the small sailing barges owned by William Groom of Harwich. They included the *MURIEL, FAIRY, PROVIDENCE, ARNOLD HIRST, EASTWOOD, SEXTUS* and *JANE*, plus one or two others. The barges brought approximately 130 cargoes between January and March 1903, nearly all discharging above bridges. Loading straight off the beach, getting the sailing gear down at Stoke Bridge and up again to clear the hatchways for unloading, down again to negotiate the three bridges and then up once more for the sail to Harwich or Felixstowe in the middle of winter must have proved a most arduous job for any bargeman. *MURIEL, FAIRY* and *PROVIDENCE* each did four round trips in January alone.

The consignee for the shingle was Messrs. Dick, Kerr & Company of London, well known as developers of tramway systems and one of the main contractors. They had also been associated with the setting up of the horse tramway. Other contractors included W. Griffiths, who laid the granite setts, importing these from Fredrikstad and Sarpsborg on the Glomma River near the entrance to Oslofjord. Two Norwegian steamers, *ERNA* and *BREMEN*, arrived in the dock on 12th January with up to 1,000 tons between them. Dick, Kerr & Company. and Levick & Company imported the rails from Middlesbrough and Antwerp between 27th January and 6th November 1903.

The ss *GERTRUDE* of Middlesbrough, a ketch-rigged steamer built in 1873 at Stockton, brought rails from Middlesbrough on 27th January and 1st March.

PUBLIC UTILITIES 263

On 27th August, the ss *TEESDALE* of Middlesbrough, where she was built in 1876, had also loaded there. Another Middlesbrough steamship, the *WILLIAM DAWSON,* built Sunderland in 1872, made five voyages from Middlesbrough. The ss *GLENO* of Newcastle, built of steel at Larne in 1902 but only 75nrt, brought yet another load of ironwork from Middlesbrough. Strangely, all the rails from Antwerp arrived in sailing barges.

Electricity supplies to the town of Ipswich for lighting and power became available at the same time as the tramway developed, and the change from gas street lighting went ahead steadily following the first conversion in 1909. Parts of the Dock, however, remained lighted by gas until 1960. By the end of March 1940 there were 3,132 public lamps in service and 28,149 households and commercial establishments consuming electricity in a population of 96,500. By the 1930s Ipswich power station was supplying electricity to Woodbridge, the

Date	Ship	Tonnage Discharged for Power Station	Additional Cargo Discharged (tons)		
			Mellonie & Goulder	Masons Cement	Sugar Beet Factory
10 Apr '33	ss *YEWDALE*	962			
25 Apr	ss *MELROSE*	754	1464		
23 May	ss *HOOKWOOD*	559	556	916	
29 May	ss *LULONGA*	378			
30 May	ss *YEWVALLEY*	998			
20 Jun	ss *YEWMOUNT*	397			
20 Jun	ss *DRYBURGH*	447	403.	672	
30 Jun	ss *MOIDART*	547	462		
10 Jul	ss *DRYBURGH*	672			
26 Jul	ss *LAURIESTON*	694	925		
10 Aug	ss *DONNA FLORA*	1161			
18 Aug	ss *YEWMOUNT*	418			
22 Aug	ss *FERNWOOD*	638	652	1174	
15 Sept	ss *WHITWOOD*	635	649.	678	
25 Sept	ss *YORKBROOK*	1534			
26 Sept	ss *MAYRIX*	936			
12 Oct	ss *YORKBROOK*	607	910		
21 Oct	ss *EASTWOOD*	540	494	1063	
13 Nov	ss *DILSTON*	510	389	1051	
18 Nov	ss *YEWTREE*	1001			
20 Nov	ss *HOLYWOOD*	1510			
28 Nov	ss *HOLYWOOD*	526	418	1101	
15 Dec	ss *YEWARCH*	970			
21 Dec	ss *HUNSTANWORTH*	485	873	1428	538
28 Dec	ss *DILSTON*	2006			
8 Jan '34	ss *THE SULTAN*	989			
16 Jan	ss *MOORFOOT*	482			
19 Jan	ss *PYLADES*	392	394		
26 Jan	ss *LESRIX*	544			
5 Feb	ss *KENRIX*	788			
14 Feb	ss *MOORFOOT*	494	1048	1070	
26 Feb	ss *SHEAFGARTH*	1408		582	
13 Mar	ss *WHITWORTH*	395	822	503	
15 Mar	ss *YEWMOUNT*	929			
25 Mar	ss *MOORFOOT*	552	1299	732	
TOTAL (tons)		26,858	1,1758	1,0970	538

Power station coal tonnage discharged 1st April 1933 to 31st March 1934.

The corrugated-iron end wall of the original Constantine Road power station that facilitated simple extensions if required. (CEGB)

Deben peninsula and several parishes around the town, in addition to providing current to the trolley-buses which superseded the trams in 1923-26. The withdrawal of the last trolleybus in 1963 ended sixty years of electrically-powered public transport.

The Constantine Road power station eventually ceased generating in 1965 and closed altogether in 1966, sixteen years after the official opening of the new power station at Cliff Quay.

For a few years the refuse destructor supplied steam to the generating station, but in 1915 a loan of £3,100 was raised for a coal handling plant. It cannot be established how much rail-borne coal unloaded in the private sidings was used as the station expanded. Trucks with coal required for immediate use were towed one at a time to the end of the siding, placed on to a tippler (a frame for gripping and rotating trucks) and turned over to shoot the coal into a hopper. The fuel was then conveyed to the top of the building, from where it was fed to the boiler room. If the coal was to be stored in the yard it was unloaded by a Stothert & Pitt crane travelling on an overhead gantry. Lorries disposed of the ash. The Destructor was used again briefly early in the 1939 war for the sterilisation of pig food that was collected in bins placed at street corners. The chimney of the Destructor was demolished in the 1950s.

Coal was not brought in any quantity until the 1930s. Usually ships' cargoes were split two or three ways between, for example, the Corporation, Mellonie & Goulder, Mason's Cement Factory at Claydon and the Sproughton sugar factory, coal for the last two being transferred from the dock by railway. The Corporation rented a part of Tovell's Wharf for storage until the coal was moved by lorry to Constantine Road.

In the early 1950s, after the opening of Cliff Quay power station, coal was discharged at the Cliff Quay coal jetty and moved by road to Constantine Road power station. 13,904 tons of coal were transported during 1955-56. The rented space at Tovells Wharf was no longer required and was leased by the I.D.C. to Thrutchleys (Beaumonts).

Cliff Quay Power Station

In 1937 the Ipswich Borough Electrical Engineer, Hampton E. Blackiston, initiated a proposal to build a new power station by the River Orwell, on a site that was at the time well beyond Cliff Quay. Borrowing powers under the 1897 Ipswich Electric Lighting Order and the Ipswich Electricity (Extension) Special Order of 1930 meant subsequent loans of £250,000 for the buildings and £1,000,000 for generating plant were acquired on 1st September 1939. Work began during that year, but on the outbreak of the 1939-45 war ceased for the duration of the war.

Nationalisation of the industry on 1st April 1948 saw work on the project taken over by the British Electricity Authority (B.E.A.); the deeds of the unfinished station were formally handed over to Lord Citrine, Chairman of the B.E.A., by Alderman S. C. Grimwade on behalf of Ipswich Borough Council. The B.E.A. was renamed the Central Electricity Authority (C.E.A.) in 1955, and in 1957 became the Central Electricity Generating Board (C.E.G.B.).

The ash from the power station furnaces was dumped in a huge adjoining area downstream of the coal jetty and transported to worked-out aggregate sites and road building projects, including the dualling of the A14 and the construction of the long embankment at Claydon.

The first cargo of coal (4,110 tons) to be discharged at the power station arrived from Sunderland on 21st October 1948 in the ss *BUSHWOOD*, built by S.P. Austin of Sunderland in 1942 and owned by William France, Fenwick & Co. Ltd of London. She returned on 26th and 29th November, and again on 6th January 1949, having delivered an initial total of 16,038 tons in preparation for

Date	Electricity	Beaumont	Beaumont	Charrington	Suffolk Chem.
12 Apr	550			550	
28 Apr	555	527	603		
18 May	582		561	552	
19 Jun		566	551	567*	
10 Jul		539	582	559*	
24 Jul		1091		558	
2 Oct	1155	528	591		
16 Oct	1169	539			
9 Nov	1709	498			
18 Nov	1708				
28 Nov	1178	506		563	
7 Dec	1108		522	571	
18 Dec	571	1091			
12 Jan	1158		521		
22 Jan	1708	526			
29 Jan	1123	527	573		
5 Feb	1113	551			
12 Feb	1687				
20 Feb	1078	558			540
26 Feb	1140		514	561	
12 Mar	1119			536	
22 Mar	1131	481	518		
Total tons	21,542	8,528	5,536	5,017	540

Cargoes for Electricity Supply and other customers brought in by ss JOHN CHARRINGTON between April 1950 and March 1951. Another 44,822 tons for the power station arrived during this time, made up of three part-cargoes brought by the ss MONKWOOD and one brought by the ss MOORWOOD.
*Coal discharged at Cliff Quay for Charringtons to be used in ships' bunkers.

Some of the colliers that brought coal to Cliff Quay power station in 1950.

Name of collier	Number of visits	Owners
CORGLEN	7	William Cory & Son Ltd.
CORMARSH	4	
CORMEAD	3	
CORMIST	25	
CORMOAT	6	
CORMOUNT	11	
CORSEA	2	
CHELWOOD	3	France, Fenwick Ltd.
HAWKWOOD	3	
PINEWOOD	1	
HUDSON RIVER	5	Hudson S. S. Co. Ltd.
HUDSON STRAIT	12	

Arriving from Sunderland with the first coal cargo to the power station on 21st October 1948 is the ss BUSHWOOD of London, 1,588nrt. She was built at Sunderland in 1942 for Wm. France, Fenwick & Co. Ltd. (Ken Hammond collection)

the start of commercial generating on 22nd March 1949. The next cargo of 3,875 tons, on 15th April that same year, was in the ss *GRANTA*, ex-*EMPIRE STRAIT*, built at West Hartlepool in 1940 and renamed *GRANTA* in 1945 by her managing owners, Witherington & Everett of Newcastle, replacing their first ship of that name and similar tonnage, built in 1927, which had been mined off the Norfolk coast on 12th January 1940.

The B.E.A. had yet to take delivery of new ships built to their order and it was not until 7th June 1950 that the ss *CLIFF QUAY* arrived, ready for the official opening on 9th June by Alderman Grimwade. Until then, and since the

arrival of the *GRANTA,* some eighty-two cargoes had arrived in twelve chartered vessels, as shown in the table. All the vessels belonged to old-established collier owners. During this period, approximately one half of the incoming ships had loaded at Sunderland, the rest coming from the Tyne, Blyth, Immingham or occasionally Hartlepool.

The ss *CLIFF QUAY* was the first of the new generation of B.E.A. colliers and entered service in June 1950. She and her sister ship *BARFORD,* which first arrived at Ipswich on 30th July, were able to load over 4,500 tons. The whole new fleet had revolutionary standards of accommodation, with single cabins for seamen and firemen and greatly improved officers' quarters. The new ships were all named after power stations and personalities within the electricity industry. Barford, for instance, was a modern power station near St Neots. During the rest of 1950, the *CLIFF QUAY* discharged here eighteen times, *BARFORD* twenty times, *PINEWOOD* three times and the *CORMULL, CORMOAT* and *CORMOUNT* each discharged once. Another new B.E.A. vessel, *LORD CITRINE* (completed in September), arrived on 13th November. She was named after the first Chairman of the B.E.A., Walter Citrine, who had been General Secretary of the T.U.C. for twenty years from 1926 during which time he was knighted. He became a peer in 1947 on his appointment to the new National Coal Board.

The ss CLIFF QUAY *brings a cargo of coal to the power station she was named after. Above is Captain Mosley, the master, pictured after her first arrival at Ipswich on 7th June 1950.*

During 1955, forty-eight vessels brought coal from Rotterdam, eleven from Ghent, thirty from Antwerp, twenty-seven from Stettin, and one from Gdansk. These foreign shipments were possibly due to an industrial dispute. For the twelve months April 1955 to March 1956, one hundred and sixty-five ships brought 707,200 tons of coal. The *CLIFF QUAY* and *BARFORD* brought one hundred and five cargoes, the *LORD CITRINE* arrived with one cargo and another fifty-nine chartered vessels carried the remaining shipments. Some of these vessels were previous arrivals, and some belonged to Stephenson Clarke's fleet, including *BORDE, MINSTER, BOWCOMBE, HEYSHOTT,* and *LAMBTONIAN.* This company was founded in 1850 but its ancestry may be traced back to 1730. Its ships were almost all named after Sussex towns and villages and some of the present fleet still trade to Ipswich in the year 2000.

In 1982, a fire occurred at the Cliff Quay power station. Although nobody was hurt, a helicopter had to assist in the rescue of a fitter trapped on the roof. The blaze spelt the end for the power station, since despite not suffering severe damage, the structure was considered uneconomical to repair. The final cargo for Cliff Quay power station arrived on 31st October 1983 in the mv *WARDEN POINT* (6440dwt), built at Solvesborg, Sweden, as *RED SEA* in 1978 and managed by Hudson S.S. Company.

However, the power station, using up all its coal stocks, did not cease generating until May 1985. The three chimneys of the power station were probably the best-known landmarks in the town area and many people expressed sadness at the news of their proposed demolition. Thousands of sightseers lined the Strand at Wherstead and other vantage points to see the chimneys toppled, in quick succession, on the morning of Sunday 27th November 1994. After a relatively short working life, Cliff Quay power station was no more.

Cliff Quay power station, fronted by the coal dump from which the pulverised fuel was fed by conveyers to the boiler rooms.

Sewage disposal

Despite an unfavourable report submitted to the Town Council in 1848 by a prominent civil engineer on the general sanitary conditions in the town, nothing positive was done to provide any means of disposing of sewage until the 1880s. The consulting engineer, Henry Austin, observed that Ipswich was virtually without any kind of sewerage system: slops and refuse were thrown from houses into the street, with the waste merely draining to cesspools or dead wells, and consequently the foundations of the town were saturated with foul and polluted water. During the mid-nineteenth century Ipswich had one of the highest death rates of any of the large towns in England, and there was little improvement by the 1870s, typhoid fever, and diarrhoea being common killer diseases. The river between Handford Mill and Stoke Bridge was in a dreadful state owing to the effluent and waste going into it from the slaughterhouses, tanneries and other industries situated near its banks.

When the Dock was built such drains as existed were intercepted and diverted to outlets at St Peters Dock and just below the present lock gates. At the time of Austin's report, Ipswich was concentrated around the town centre and the surrounding river and Dock areas. Many inhabitants of the small and badly-ventilated cottages, built in rows or courts near the river, obtained their water from shared wells sunk in the polluted ground. Although some areas of the town received water piped from local springs, a vastly improved fresh water supply was necessary for any kind of sewerage system to be effective.

Henry Austin's comment on one matter was, in retrospect, a sign of things to come. He thought Ipswich had an advantage over many large towns arising from the fact that 'the excrementitious matter is of sufficient value in the neighbourhood as manure to render it worth tolerably punctual removal'.

In 1857 the railway and civil engineer Peter Bruff, a resident of Ipswich, was asked by the Corporation to design a drainage system for the town. After prolonged discussion and amidst much diverse opinion, the first low level-sewer and disposal works were constructed in 1882 downstream of Hog Highland on the site of the present works situated close to the Orwell Bridge. Progress in the provision of sanitary arrangements for the town was undoubtedly due the passing of the Public Health Act of 1875, when extensive powers were given to the local authority. Because of the rapid expansion of what had become a swiftly growing industrial town, the initial works could not cope with the discharge of storm water and effluent to the river at high tides and, coupled with the primitive screening process, the system was soon in need of urgent improvement. It was not, however, until fifty years later, in 1932, that a new high-level sewer and outfall works were completed.

For many years the sludge left over from the sewage treatment works was available to parishes in the immediate vicinity of the river, including Nacton, for use as manure. Until the mid-1920s barges took thousands of tons of the treated sludge to riverside farms for the farmers to spread on their land by horse and cart.

Six such cargoes were loaded during the last three months of 1904. The *FANNY* of Rochester and the *WILLIAM* of London, built respectively at Brentford in 1878 and Shadwell in 1868, each loaded sludge. The *WATERLOO,* which had been completed in 1865 at Christchurch in Surrey, arrived on 21st

September from Mersea Island and sailed on 10th October with sludge, arriving light from Holbrook on 20th October. The vessel sailed on 25th October, returned light ex-Wrabness on 29th October, loaded and was away on 10th November and back nine days later with shingle from Felixstowe beach, leaving with sludge again on 29th November. Occasional freights continued and in 1906 the *MARY JANE* of Rochester, built at Milton in 1877, sailed three times with sludge to Orford.

The sb *PRIMUS*, built at Ipswich by William Colchester in 1841 and owned for many years by John Robson Pattrick, the Harwich cement manufacturer, loaded twelve times for Holbrook during 1907; the Rochester *GEORGIANA* loaded three cargoes for the same place and the *LONGFIELD* did a trip to Shotley. The next year saw *PRIMUS* very busy in the trade with cargoes to Slumpy Lane (Freston) and Pin Mill as well as at least ten trips to Holbrook. She sometimes loaded a return cargo of firewood, to the account of Frederick Suckling of the Rose public house in Harkstead, for Edwin Roberts of Rectory Road, Ipswich.

After 1913 sewage sludge was delivered regularly to Pauls' farm at Kirton and discharged at the wharf in the creek. One of the first barges to engage in this particular work was the *ARTHUR AND ELIZA*, built at Faversham in 1862 and part-owned by John Sparrow, the Shotley coal merchant. The old *LADY OF THE WAVE* of London, built at Brightlingsea in 1856, was skippered by her managing owner George J. Brooks of 23 Tomline Road, Ipswich, at this time. She made nine voyages from the Outfall to Kirton Creek between 9th July and 21st November 1914, at least six trips in 1915, twelve in 1917 and ten in 1918, and

Right: The mv SWEEP *arrived at Ipswich from London on 10th February 1916. She had been built at Leidersdorp in Holland in 1910. (R.W. Smith collection)*

Left: The second bulk sludge vessel belonging to the Mayor, Aldermen and Burgesses of the Borough of Ipswich, the mv SWEEP II, *86nrt, was built in 1928 by John Chambers at Lowestoft with an engine by Petters of Ipswich. She was sunk by a mine off Harwich in 1940 with the loss of her mate, George French. (R.W. Smith collection)*

carried on until at least 1920 when she delivered six cargoes. At about this time she stranded on the ebb tide with a cargo of sludge nearly opposite the Cat House at Woolverstone just to the north of the channel and never came off. Her remains are still there, visible at low water springs. Meanwhile an 1854 Brightlingsea-built craft, the *CHARLES AND ANN* of Ipswich, owned by Frederick Knights of Chelmondiston, did a couple of trips in 1919 as did the *THREE SISTERS*, Maldon-registered and built there in 1865, and by 1915 owned by George Miller of Dovercourt. She went on to make at least seven voyages in 1923, with possibly a one-way passage to Kirton in that year, because she was abandoned there at about that time with no further work in prospect, and her master and mate walked home to Ipswich. *THREE SISTERS* remains in the creek.

In 1916 the small motor vessel *SWEEP*, built at Leidersdorp, Holland, in 1910, had been purchased by Ipswich Borough Council to carry the sludge out to sea for dumping. She had a length of 99ft 6in, a beam of 18ft 1in and a depth of 6ft 4in. Fitted with a 38hp oil engine, she was of 88nrt. *SWEEP* arrived at Ipswich on 10th February 1916 and made ten trips to sea in that year. She worked until 1927 when she sailed for Hull on 24th August, and was later re-registered at Middlesbrough.

SWEEP II, her imaginatively named successor, was launched at Lowestoft by J. Chambers Ltd in 1928 and arrived at Ipswich on 2nd May that year, starting work on 4th June. This vessel was fitted with two 2-stroke single-acting oil engines by Petters (Ipswich) Ltd and measured approximately another foot all round. Despite the humble name carried by both vessels, their owners were listed at Lloyd's as 'The Mayor, Aldermen & Burgesses of the Borough of

Ipswich'. By 1938, she was making up to 189 round trips to the spoil ground a year and had completed thirty-six trips in January and February 1939 alone.

On lst June 1940, German aircraft dropped several mines in the Harwich approaches and *SWEEP II*, discharging her cargo on the 4th, exploded one and was sunk with the loss of her mate, G. French. He and his ship are remembered on the Merchant Navy Memorial at Tower Hill.

The next major construction of the sewage works began in the early 1970s, resulting in the abandonment of the former premises. A new jetty was constructed to enable the revival of shipments of sludge to the spoil grounds once more. When the new facilities were completed, one of the first sludge vessels to operate from Ipswich was the mv *FALSTONE,* built by L. Smit & Zoon of Kinderdijk in 1934 as a hopper barge for the Dutch waterways. In 1964 she was purchased by the well-known collier owners Stephenson Clarke Ltd of London for conversion into a sludge carrier, becoming one of their smallest seagoing vessels. During the 1980s Effluents Services Ltd took over the contract, tankers used including *ERRWOOD*, built in Holland in 1950 and working under her fifth name; *YARROW,* built 1967, and the *PERCY DAWSON*, renamed *HAWESWATER* by the company in the late 1980s after working from Ipswich under her original name. She had been built at Port Glasgow in 1968 for North West Water to convey Manchester sewage sludge down the Manchester Ship Canal for dumping in Liverpool Bay. The last ship in regular use was the *ALSTON*, formerly the *LEADSMAN*, of Rowbotham Tankships Ltd. The specified area (spoil ground) for pumping the cargo out was in the triangle formed by the NE Gunfleet buoy, the Sunk lightvessel and the wartime Roughs Tower.

The service from Ipswich ended in 1996, the year before the entire trade was banned by EEC regulations prohibiting the practice of dumping sewage at sea. In 1997, a £33 million scheme, 'Project Orwell', was begun by Anglian Water including the provision of a three-and-half mile tunnelled main sewer and major improvements at Cliff Quay treatment works. The new works were commissioned in the year 2000. The sewage is now converted to a biosolid and transferred by road tanker to other plants operated by Anglian Water, and made available as 'Nutribio'.

The HAWESWATER *undergoing repairs to her bows on the slip at Ipswich.*

Engineering 11

The heavy engineering side of Ipswich industry, which had grown up during the nineteenth century, expanded considerably during the last thirty years of the Victorian era. New companies like Ransomes & Rapier Ltd, Cocksedge & Co. Ltd and Reavell Ltd appeared, all specialising in their own particular field and building upon the worldwide reputation already established by Ransomes, Sims & Jefferies Ltd and E.R. & F. Turner Ltd. Other firms such as Bull Motors Ltd, the Manganese Bronze & Brass Co. Ltd and Crane Ltd followed in the twentieth century.

Some of these firms imported pig iron and loam through the port, but not all made use of the docks for the export of their goods since the majority of their products could be transported within the railway loading gauge or by road. The following pages give details of those companies that did utilise the port or contribute to the port's activities in one way or another.

Ransomes, Sims & Jefferies Ltd

Robert Ransome, a Norfolk Quaker born in 1753, had completed his apprenticeship and had already set up his own small iron foundry in Norwich before deciding to move to Ipswich in 1789. The detailed history of the company he founded is well recorded elsewhere, but it is relevant to mention the move in 1849 to purpose-built new premises, Orwell Works, along the dockside, from a site near the town centre where the name of Old Foundry Road still recalls his presence.

Ransome's business was built on the production of agricultural implements, aided by his invention of hardened cast-iron ploughshares, patented by him in 1803, and diversified into civil engineering when the end of the Napoleonic Wars brought an agricultural depression. When the antecedent of all lawnmowers was invented by Edwin Budding in 1830 the Ipswich firm obtained a licence to manufacture the new machines, which eventually became a Ransomes' speciality. Apart from the agricultural business, which expanded considerably later in the century, the company made all kinds of ironwork for the new railway industry and even became involved in work on astronomical instruments in conjunction with Charles May and Astronomer Royal Sir George Biddell Airy, who lived at Playford. This work included castings for the Northumberland refractor telescope, which is still at Cambridge University Observatory, and a new transit telescope for the Greenwich Observatory that still defines the prime meridian of the world. Charles May, who joined the firm as a partner in 1836, was a member of the Royal Astronomical Society and an associate member of the Institution of Civil Engineers. In 1846 the firm adopted the title of Ransomes & May and a few years later successfully exhibited at the 1851 Great Exhibition.

Both the railway work and the export of agricultural implements expanded in such a way that in 1869 a new company, Ransomes & Rapier Ltd, was formed specifically to make railway equipment and plant across the river at Waterside Works, allowing the original firm more space to devote to the production of ploughs and other farm implements. As new partners came into the business the original firm became Ransomes, Sims & Head in 1869, Ransomes, Head & Jefferies in 1881 and then Ransomes, Sims & Jefferies in 1884, becoming a public limited company in 1911. The Orwell Works was extended from time to time until it stretched for some distance along the east side of the Dock and also on the far side of Duke Street. The works began moving to a new site at Nacton in 1948, and the link with the Dock was finally broken in 1966, after which the famous Orwell Works was sold to the Ipswich Dock Commission.

For nearly one hundred and fifty years vast numbers of ploughs and cultivators, followed by portable steam engines, traction and stationary engines, and thrashing machines were made at the works. Later, Ransomes began producing electric trolleybuses and battery electric vehicles, electric and motor lawnmowers, and during two world wars munitions, including aeroplanes in the First World War. After the Second World War combine harvesters briefly joined the range of products that poured from Orwell Works and Nacton Works to be sent across the world.

During the 1970s and 1980s, however, the company was unable to compete with major international companies. The manufacture of combine harvesters ended in 1974, and the entire agricultural machinery business was disposed of in 1987 to Electrolux, famous for vacuum cleaners.

Ransomes' quay about 1880 with the timber destined for the production of thrashers and other agricultural implements. Some appears to be arriving by rail.

As a result of so much of the product range (otherwise known as the 'family silver') being sold off, only the grass-cutting (turf care) side remained. In 1998 that was inevitably acquired by a global multi-national company, Textron Inc., a name quite unknown to Ipswich residents. Happily the name of Ransomes was reinstated some time after the takeover when the American owners realised the prestige that went with the name.

Early shipping records show that during the 1880s and 1890s Ransomes, Sims & Jefferies received five or six cargoes a year of pig iron from Grangemouth or Cardiff, mainly in steamships. The year 1884 typically included the ss *FLORENCE* of Stockton, built and owned at Middlesbrough in 1881, the ss *FOX* of only 94nrt, launched at Middlesbrough in 1869 for the Boston & Hull S.S. Co. Ltd, and another two Middlesbrough-built vessels, the ss *BEDLORMIE*, built in 1878 for Glasgow owners, and the ss *MASCOTTE*, built in 1883 and owned by her builders, W. Harkess. The schooner *MINNIE*, launched at Padstow in 1866, arrived in 1889. There were also about five barges a year with loam.

Ransomes Sims & Jefferies engine no. 23266, built in 1910, which was used for exhibition purposes and later as the firm's yard engine. It is seen shunting rail wagons at the works in 1935. (R.G. Pratt)

Coal was an essential requirement and often shipped as part-cargo. For example, the 1894 arrivals were ss *VULCAN* and ss *TAY*, both of Dundee, the latter of only 73nrt, steel built at Dundee in 1885, the ss *HARTON*, an iron collier of 326nrt launched at Sunderland in 1872, and three Ipswich vessels owned by Edward Packard. These were the steamships *ONYX* of Ipswich, originally launched as the *STRATHNESS* in 1883, *RINGMOOR* and *WINIFRED*. In 1913, no fewer than twenty-one part-cargoes of coal arrived, twenty of them in ss *WINIFRED*, built South Shields in 1894, the other in their ss *SHOTTON*, built at Selby in 1909.

In each of the 1914-18 War years, Ransomes received a few hundred tons of pig iron and a dozen or so bargeloads of loam, the majority of them in the *AZARIAH*, then skippered by 'poor old Charlie Butler' of Ipswich who had a kindly reputation for hard luck and hard work. From April 1920 to March 1921 three vessels discharged 410 tons of iron, the *AZARIAH* brought 1,440 tons of loam and there were two bargeloads of shingle.

By 1922 the company was enjoying the start of a long association with the ss *PHAEACIAN*, launched in 1920 at Mistley by and for F.W. Horlock & Co. Ltd (Ocean Transport Co. Ltd), the barge and ship owners and builders of that parish. She was 144ft long and 25ft in the beam, with a net tonnage of 220. Her triple-expansion steam engine was by W.B. Allen & Co. Ltd, agricultural engineers of Bedford. For many years the *PHAEACIAN* ran a fortnightly liner trade from Ipswich to Hull and Middlesbrough with general cargo. She discharged 400 tons of pig iron in 1922. The small steamship *ROMA*, 68nrt, loaded the only outward cargoes that year consisting of 64 tons of machinery in February and a $4^{3}/_{4}$ ton steam engine and $28^{1}/_{2}$ tons of plough castings in March. The *ROMA* was built in 1903 and rebuilt ten years later by the Larne S.B. Co. Ltd for A. Capper of Belfast.

In 1927 there were no outward cargoes, but 2,800 tons of pig iron arrived ex-Middlesbrough and sb *AZARIAH* delivered eight freights of loam. Two other vessels brought 194 tons of ash trees and 775 poles. Much of the timber was used for thrashing machines. The only quayside movements from April 1935 to March 1936 entailed 26 parcels of pig iron, totalling 3,470 tons, unloaded from ss *PHAEACIAN* on her fortnightly round voyages. A diver and gear were occasionally hired from the Dock Commission to find any pig iron that had slipped overboard during discharge.

During 1939-1940 the *PHAEACIAN* unloaded nineteen part-cargoes of pig iron and sb *AZARIAH* brought two cargoes of loam on 5th May and 12th August.

This was possibly *AZARIAH*'s last visit to Ransomes, since she was lost near the Whittaker off the Essex coast during the winter of 1940-41. *PHAEACIAN* landed 3,960 tons of iron on the quay for R.S. & J. between April 1940 and March 1941, managing seventeen voyages despite the wartime conditions. During this time roughly 500 tons of loam were brought by Horlock's barges *EDME*, *D'ARCY*, *REMINDER* and *RESOLUTE*, the latter barge being mined and lost in January 1943. *PHAEACIAN* made nine trips in 1942-1943 and there were four barges with loam. By 1944, however, loam was the only commodity discharged. Similar amounts came until 1949 when seaborne trade to Ransomes apparently ceased. A charge was made at about that time for the cost of laying a new railway siding into the old foundry from the quay. In later years an occasional cargo of combine harvesters from R.S. & J. left the port. For instance, on 18th March 1964 mv *VALDIVIA* of London arrived light from her home port, leaving Cliff Quay on 20th March for Barcelona loaded with combines. These must have been brought from the Nacton Works to the docks by road.

Ransomes & Rapier Ltd

The firm of Ransomes & Rapier was founded in 1869 by James Allen Ransome (1806-1875) and Robert James Ransome (1830-1897), father and son, in partnership with Richard C. Rapier (1836-1897), who had been manager of the railway materials department at Ransomes well-established Orwell Works. The Waterside Works, as it became known, was set up in a cornfield between the river and Wherstead Road. It was intended that the company should take over the manufacture of railway equipment from the Orwell Works on the opposite side of the river, enabling the parent company to concentrate upon its agricultural engineering commitments. The new company produced rail points and crossings and continued with the design and manufacture of railway equipment and small

Twelve Ransomes portable steam engines, possibly for export via London docks, on a train being hauled under the Princes Street bridge by G.E.R. class T18 engine No.315, which was completed at the Stratford Works in 1886. This class was the Cinderella of the G.E.R., performing all the dirty work. (R.S. & J.)

locomotives. During the middle of the 1870s the firm was involved in the construction of China's first railway, which was closed down by the mandarins after having only a short life. The Chinese ambassadors who visited the works during the project were entertained by Robert Ransome at his residence at nearby Stoke Hall (now demolished) next to St Mary-at-Stoke-Church and close to the river. The company achieved a world-wide reputation for the production of turntables, traversers, buffer stops, loco hoists and breakdown cranes.

Ransomes & Rapier also engaged in other spheres of engineering. Their sluice gates were to be found in most countries of the world, they were pioneers in the development of concrete mixing plants and they were heavily involved in the manufacture of excavators, cranes of many kinds and giant walking draglines. Unusual engineering jobs were also undertaken in later years, the firm being responsible for the revolving stage at the London Coliseum, aircraft catapults for ships and the revolving restaurant on the Post Office Tower in London.

During the 1970s Ransomes & Rapier was linked with Newton Chambers and other firms. In the early 1980s a deal involving an American dragline firm proved to be a costly mistake. Opportunities to diversify were also missed during the world recession of the mid-1980s; chances were not taken for instance to enter the market for the construction of oil and gas rigs. Finally the firm was bought out by Stothert & Pitt of Bath, part of Robert Maxwell's organisation, and swiftly closed in 1987. A local newspaper mirrored the feelings of the townspeople when it headlined an article on the firm's closure, 'A Great Talent Gone to Waste —118 years of Care, Courage and History at an End'.

Throughout its life Ransomes & Rapier always had an excellent railway connection straight to the main line via the Griffin Wharf Branch and depended considerably on the railway for traffic in and out. The firm had its own steam, and later diesel, shunting engines on its private sidings. However, many ready-made assemblies were too large for the loading gauge and so went by sea. Coasters, sailing and motor barges left Ipswich loaded with large sections of

The motor barge REMINDER, *a former sailing barge built of steel at Mistley in 1929, loading water control equipment for transhipment in the London Docks, c.1960. (R..W. Smith collection)*

Part of a consignment of thrashing sets ordered from Ransomes, Sims & Jefferies Ltd.. by the Estonian Government in August 1920 loaded on to railway well wagons, probably for delivery to the London docks. (R.S. & J.)

The small Dutch coaster mv ORION loading Ransomes & Rapier products for the Continent. Built in 1926 at Groningen, she traded under three owners before being sold to Tanzania in 1968. Her cargo of sand ballast shifted on the delivery voyage and she sank, but the crew were rescued. (R.W. Smith collection)

The coaster CONDOR loading machinery at Waterside Works ex-Packing Department via the works railway track. (R.W. Smith collection)

machinery, especially sluice gates for export via the London Docks or direct to the near Continent. The steel used by the firm was largely imported from Grangemouth.

Early shipments of loam, pig iron and timber were made to Waterside Works. In 1884, for instance, six Ipswich-owned barges arrived with loam, namely *PRIMA DONNA* (twice), *NOVATOR* (twice), *AZARIAH* and *OCEAN QUEEN*. At least ten cargoes of pig iron came in six different ships from Grangemouth, Bo'ness and Middlesbrough. One vessel was a schooner with the foreign-sounding name of *LEON RAYMUNDO*; in fact she was built at Rye in 1856 and owned by H. Crundall, a well-known Dover barge owner. Other vessels were the ss *BASIC*, fresh from the ways in 1884 at North Shields for Crawford of Grangemouth, ss *VIGILANT*, an iron and wood screw ketch of only 62nrt, *PETREL* (with five cargoes), ss *FLORENCE* of Middlesbrough and the schooner *RED TAIL* of Runcorn. There were also three barges from London with old iron (scrap).

From April 1922 to March 1923 some 1,150 tons of machinery was sent away in fourteen bargeloads to London and 335 tons of loam and 420 of shingle were brought in, although in 1927 there was a slight reduction to twelve barges loading machinery. During 1929-30 eighteen loaded, including the auxiliary ketch-barge *SARAH COLEBROOKE*, built at Rye in 1913 for the Sussex Colebrooke family. She had an engine installed when commandeered and renamed *BOLHAM* as a Q-ship in the First World War which she survived; she was sold away to end her trading days on the Mersey in the 1930s. Another interesting vessel at Ransomes & Rapiers in 1929 was the auxiliary ketch *HALCYON* of Hull, a Yorkshire billyboy built of steel at Hessle in 1903. For the first time there was a noticeable presence of eight foreign motor vessels, mainly Dutch, loading machinery, and in the following year the die was cast when twenty-two barges and twenty-six Dutchmen loaded.

The barges loading in 1930-31 included the auxiliary ketch barge *RECORD REIGN*, destined to be wrecked on the Dorset coast in 1935; *BARBARA JEAN*, one of Pauls' big steel barges, to be lost at Dunkirk, and Horlock's brand-new *BLUE MERMAID*, which was destroyed by magnetic mine in July 1941 with the loss of both her crew.

There was an increase in seaborne traffic in 1935-36, when six cargoes of loam came in, five in Eldred Watkins' *GENERAL JACKSON* and one in his *ETHEL ADA*, which also discharged 240 tons of shingle. The small steam coaster *WISBECH*, 108nrt, built in 1916 at New Holland in Lincolnshire and engined by Dodman of Kings Lynn, loaded five cargoes of machinery grossing 442 tons. Thirty-two Dutch coasters arrived for machinery, of which thirty sailed for Antwerp, but only two motor barges, *RESOURCEFUL* and *CELTIC*, and sb *NORMAN*. The sailing barge *GENERAL JACKSON* brought 480 tons of loam. Thirteen Dutchmen loaded machinery in 1939 before October and the mb *RESOURCEFUL*, sb *MEMORY* and the 1915-built landing craft mv *SPITHEAD* also loaded in that year. There were few other movements from Griffin Wharf until after the Second World War, although the company rented land at S.W. Quay and Cliff Quay for storing cases of machinery.

Traffic was back to pre-war levels by 1950, when more than thirty machinery cargoes were handled by mb *REMINDER* (eight cargoes), mb *RESOURCEFUL* (two cargoes), auxiliary barge *REDOUBTABLE* (three cargoes), mb *ADIEU* (four cargoes), mv *SPITHEAD* (ten cargoes), and one or two other motor vessels. Some fifteen vessels were loaded during 1959-60 including *REMINDER*, *RESOURCEFUL*, *ADIEU* and *SPITHEAD*, but the days of seaborne traffic were

---

COASTAL TRADE RIVALRY

"DUTCHMEN" OUST BRITISH

MOTOR VESSELS V. STEAMSHIPS

FROM A SPECIAL CORRESPONDENT

Those picturesque, grey-and-white, bluff-bowed vessels that you see in the Thames and other British rivers and in the little ports all round the coast are an ornament to any stretch of water.

They attract attention anywhere with their great deck-house aft. Sometimes they sport a great sail, and often there are pots of geraniums at the port-holes, and perhaps a buxom Dutch woman bustling about in a big apron.

Pleasing to the eye they undoubtedly are, but by competing on unfair terms they are doing grave damage to a section of Britain's shipping.

Seven years ago they were almost unknown in British ports. Now they are everywhere. Every month sees more and more of them coming into our ports from the Continent. They are even snatching from British ships cargoes to be transported from one British port to another.

FAMILY ENTERPRISES

Many of the crews are family affairs, with the skipper, his wife, and his sons to work a vessel of 150 tons. Even when one of these vessels carries a paid crew the men rarely receive wages on the scale which applies in our own industry.

"These 'Dutchmen,' as they are called among sailormen, whether they be Dutch, Belgian or French, are always motor-driven, and they buy their fuel in their home ports," said an official of a London shipping firm to a representative of THE DAILY TELEGRAPH yesterday. "The British ships which lose trade to them are steamships, and buy their coal in England. Thus every time a 'Dutchman' gets a cargo in these waters our collieries lose an order.

"The British ships in competition with the 'Dutchmen' are vessels of 1,000 tons and upwards, and are fully manned. We have no complaint to make of regular foreign lines, for their ships compete with us on level terms and have full crews which pay 'fair' wages.

"But the 'Dutchmen' are in quite a different category. Being of shallow draft they can go alongside little wharfs away from the regular docks and unload cargo direct to the spot where it is wanted.

"The unloading is done by unskilled men for whatever pay they can get, whereas the work of unloading of our bigger vessels is done by skilled dock workers who know their job, and expect—and get—high wages for it."

BRITISH RETALIATION

A number of British shipping firms which have been harried by the operations of the "Dutchmen" are now beginning to fight back with the foreigners' own weapons. They are ordering small motor vessels of similar type, but with many modern improvements, and there is every reason to hope that by these means the coastal and cross-Channel trade which has been "sniped" by the "Dutchmen" will be recaptured.

One of the directors of a great London shipping firm which has large interests in the coastal cargo traffic said that his company is now considering a general policy aiming at the replacement of the present

Part of a report in the Daily Telegraph in February 1934.

A Rapier W2000 walking dragline working on an opencast coal site in Alabama, USA. (Don Turvey)

numbered; Griffin Wharf was soon to become almost isolated by the West Bank development in the early 1970s and by flood prevention works.

The trade just described shows clear evidence of the incursion into the British coastal trade of the ubiquitous small Dutch motor vessel since the 1920s. They were usually family run, and being of shallow draught could easily reach the small traditional barge ports as well as comparatively deep-water places like Ipswich. The subject remained a bone of contention for decades, because the Dutch were allowed to trade between one British port and another whereas continental regulations excluded British ships from taking part in the continental coasting trade. The Dutch ships made severe inroads into the traditional coasting work, forcing many bargeowners to lay up their craft or fit auxiliary engines and also seriously affecting the coastal steam and motorship fleets.

Cocksedge & Company Ltd

In 1879 James Cocksedge moved to Ipswich from Stowmarket, where he had been a partner in an engineering business known as Woods, Cocksedge and Warner, and bought a small engineering works in Grey Friars Road to found the general engineering firm of Cocksedge & Company Ltd The premises (later occupied by Burtons' jam factory) consisted of a small foundry, a pattern shop and engineering shop and provided employment for only a small number of men. When the premises became too small they were supplemented by a property on the opposite side of the road where the firm established a much larger foundry and engineering workshops. James Cocksedge died in 1887 and his eldest son, J.W. Cocksedge, carried on the business, later being joined by his brother, E.H. Cocksedge, who had been engaged for some years in large constructional engineering work in India. The firm saw that there was an opening for constructional steelwork in the Ipswich area, since most steelwork for buildings was being imported into the town.

The business, which until that time had been a general engineering one, ultimately developed into two distinct spheres of structural and mechanical engineering. With the increase in business the firm decided to move in 1903 to a five-acre site on the west bank of the river adjacent to Ransomes & Rapier's Waterside Works, and here at Eagle Works the company was to develop its structural steelwork production even further. The firm's offices remained in Grey Friars Road.

The company grew rapidly and achieved international recognition, bringing prestige to Ipswich. For many years the manufacture, erection and maintenance of steel-framed buildings brought orders from the sugar-beet industry for silos and other equipment. The steelwork used for the new buildings for both Pauls and W.S. Cowell at Ipswich was fabricated and erected by Cocksedge. The company also specialised in hangar-type buildings for holiday camps, sports grounds and racetracks, and in large farm buildings. The contract for much of the steelwork for the giant Goonhilly Downs satellite tracking station was won by the firm; another project was the building of monorails at Butlin's holiday camps.

The mechanical side meanwhile produced a variety of agricultural equipment such as fruit graders and slicing machines and parts for cranes, tractors and gasworks. The company also gained vast experience in ship repairs, both mechanically and structurally, and they frequently worked on ships at Ipswich Dock, making repairs to broken-down pumping equipment on tankers discharging at Cliff Quay. An immense amount of work was done during both world wars, especially the second when Cocksedge Ltd maintained and repaired the Ipswich minesweeping fleet round the clock for the duration. Altogether well over 2,000 ships, naval and merchant, were repaired by the firm during this time. Armour-plated ammunition boxes, gun mountings and turrets, searchlight housings, and Bailey bridge components were produced, as were hangers large enough to accommodate aircraft as large as the B-17 Flying Fortress.

Unfortunately for the firm pre-cast concrete was gaining in popularity by the 1980s and the demand for steelwork had started to decline sharply. In addition, the British Sugar Corporation decided at this time to employ its own draughtsmen and maintenance men, and more and more Cocksedge jobs were lost, leading to the closure of the company in 1985, just two years before the collapse of its neighbour, the great Ipswich engineering company of Ransomes & Rapier.

Cocksedge Ltd had its own private railway siding, by way of which most of the steel came to its premises via the Griffin Wharf Branch. Aside from occasional cargoes of loam, pig iron and steel, there were no regular shipments in or out of the port by the firm, but the importance of the company's involvement at the port during the Second World War cannot be over-emphasized.

Reavell Ltd

William Reavell, Charles Gaskell and William Scott agreed in 1898 to purchase two and a half acres of land fronting Ranelagh Road from the Great Eastern Railway for their new works in which they proposed to manufacture high-speed steam engines and compressors, though they did not proceed with steam engines after 1904. Reavell compressors were soon to be sent to many countries around the world to be used aboard motorships of all kinds to start the main engines. Their compressors were also used in submarines and torpedoes, by gas and sewage works along with all the local engineering works, and by civil engineering companies for air locks in tunnel construction. They were also utilised in the Ipswich trolleybuses for braking.

The company's seaborne trade appears to have been limited to the import from Kent of loam for the foundry by barges, usually loading at Erith. Until the mid-1930s a barge's crew needing to gain access to Reavell's works dropped the gear (masts, sails and rigging) on deck in the New Cut. The barge was taken through Stoke Bridge and along the river either by hauling from the towpath or by using sweeps, under Princes Street bridge and the railway bridge connecting the lower goods yard with the main line, and berthed at the rear of the factory. Once there the gear had to be raised to clear the hatches for discharging, after which the whole process, extremely hard work, would be repeated in reverse.

Two to four cargoes were taken up to Reavells every year until about 1935, when the loam began to be craned out within the dock into lorries for the short trip to Ranelagh Road. The motor barges *CABBY*, *PUDGE* and *ATRATO* all discharged in 1959-1960. This proved to be the last remaining trade in loam for the foundries of Ipswich.

In 1959 the factory was used for the setting of the film The Angry Silence, starring Richard Attenborough, with crowd scenes shot in Cowell Street, near to Cocksedge's engineering works.

In recent times the company has become known as CompAir Reavell and since 1985 has been owned by one of the country's largest and most diverse engineering groups, Siebe PLC. At the beginning of 2004 the firm announced

A Cocksedge advertisement from the 1904 Suffolk County Handbook.

E.R. & F. Turner's chilled roll shop with rolls in various stages of manufacture, photographed about 1930.

that it was ending its production of special castings and closing the foundry to concentrate solely on the manufacture of compressed air and gas systems. In 2005 the firm decided to move away from its historic factory site in Ranelagh Road to new premises on the Landmark Industrial Park off Whitehouse Road in Ipswich, freeing the area for the building of new homes, offices and shops.

E.R. & F. Turner & Co. Ltd

Initially known as Bond, Turner & Hurwood, the company was established in July 1837 by Mr. Walton Turner and two business partners. The premises were situated at St. Peter's Works, close to Wolsey's Gate in College Street, and it is interesting to note that the present-day Foundry Lane took its name from the original foundry. Walton Turner died in 1847 and his son, Edward Rush Turner, became a partner, to be joined later by his brother, Frederick Turner. With the other partners dropping out, the company adopted the name of E.R. & F. Turner and became a private limited company in 1897.

Early production consisted of agricultural machinery, stone mills and small steam engines. In 1849 their success warranted expansion to the new Greyfriars Works on the corner of Quadling Street and Wolsey Street. At the same time, the firm introduced its first portable steam engines, one of which was exhibited at the Great Exhibition of 1851, gaining Turners a world-wide reputation as engine builders and boiler makers.

The company pioneered the introduction of steel roller mills, which they started manufacturing in 1863, and in the 1880s they were installing complete milling systems with steam motive power, including Cranfield Brothers' new mill in 1884. The company later became specialists in making cereal flaking machinery, seed cleaning apparatus, flax processing plant and grain drying and storage facilities.

In 1919 Turners became a member of the ill-fated Agricultural and General Engineers Ltd (A.G.E.) that controlled a number of East Anglian engineering firms. In 1924 Bull Motors, an important member of the A.G.E. group making electricity generators and small electric motors, moved into St. Peter's Works from Stowmarket, where it had been founded in 1898 by Napier Prentice, a member of the well-known Prentice family who had considerable interests in corn, malt and chemicals. Bull Motors became an integral part of E.R. & F. Turner in 1932 when the company, unlike some of their contemporaries, survived the receivership of Agricultural and General Engineers Ltd. In their centenary year of 1937 Turners, including Bull Motors, moved from the dock area to new premises on a nine-acre site, formerly a brickworks, in Foxhall Road, Ipswich. The company, which had produced lathes for shell manufacturing and other armaments work during the First World War, turned to electric motors and portable generators in the second.

A company trading under the E.R. & F. Turner name moved to an industrial estate in Knightsdale Road, off the Norwich Road, in the 1980s. The Bull Motors business, however, remained on Foxhall Road until December 1999, when it abruptly ceased trading. Turners have continued into the twenty-first century, still specialising in cereal-flaking machinery for the production of all kinds of corn flakes, besides making mills for oil seed extraction and for the production of pet and animal feeds, for companies worldwide.

In the early manufacturing days much of the pig iron was brought in by sea. In August 1883, for example, the *LAUNCESTON* of Bideford arrived from Grangemouth, a port opened at the eastern end of the Forth and Clyde canal in 1777 and still very much in use. In 1884 Turners received at least three vessels with pig iron including the schooner *ZENOBIA*, built at Ipswich in 1870, and five bargeloads of loam from Kent. In May 1885 Packard's barge *AMMONITE* delivered millstones from London (possibly imported), and more arrived aboard sb *CHAMPION* in March 1888. In the 1890s Turners were offering milling equipment complete with steam engines, and in May 1893 the iron barquentine *ELIZA*, arrived with special lifting tackle to load a complete roller mill for Brazil. The *ELIZA* was Liverpool registered and owned, and was built as a barque in 1876 at Greenock.

In 1900 three barges, *PRIDE OF THE ORWELL*, Ipswich-built in 1863, Pauls' *WAVENEY* and the *AZARIAH*, a small ketch-barge built at Ipswich in 1878, all discharged pig iron from London, where it would have been transhipped from another vessel. Iron and loam imports appear fairly constant at that period, with three bargeloads of loam in 1910, two of them in William Colchester's old *TERTIUS* of 1844. Cranfields' *SPINAWAY C* and *COLONIA* brought one cargo each in 1916 and Eldred Watkins' *INTREPID* arrived with two in 1918. There were none, however, in 1921 and few if any after that. By that time loam and pig iron might well have come by rail.

Crane Ltd

Initially known as Crane-Bennett Ltd, the company was founded as a twin enterprise between the Crane Company of America, a group established in Chicago in 1855 which had an international reputation for the production of pipe fittings and associated products, and the English business headed by James E. Bennett established in 1906 to produce similar products. The American founder, Richard Teller Crane, who had family connections with Ipswich, Massachusetts, was resolved to conduct his business 'in the strictness of honesty and fairness, to avoid all deception and trickery; to deal fairly with customers and competitors; to be liberal and just towards employees and to put his whole mind upon the business'. It was in 1920 that company officials, looking for a suitable site for a factory in Ipswich, England, decided on forty acres of heathland off Nacton Road. Foundations for the first buildings were laid in 1921 and although machinery was quickly installed, the poor economic climate after the First World War leading to the Great Depression of the 1930s stopped any further progress and it was not until 1925-26 that production finally commenced at the site.

A railway siding from the Felixstowe branch line was laid in 1927 on which sufficient fuel and raw materials were delivered right into the premises to make it worthwhile for the company to buy its own steam locomotive. By that time the factory was in full production making malleable iron pipe fittings, etc. A precisely-controlled mechanised foundry was opened and the factory was extended in the same year. Another foundry constructed in 1929-1930 made castings for domestic heating boilers and radiators, which became a significant line for the factory, as did the manufacture of valves and flanges for the oil industry and others.

After the war more buildings were added, and a new machine shop was completed in 1947 in preparation for manufacturing steel valves and pipe fittings for the new oil refineries. A few more years and the company's name, which in the intervening period had changed to Crane Ltd, became Crane Fluid Systems and as such survived until 2008.

The company, with its excellent rail facilities, had no reason to use the Port of Ipswich to any great extent. There was a cargo of loam brought by Cranfields' barge *PETREL* on l9th March 1927 'per Child & Pullen' who were very old established Ipswich haulage contractors. A load of pig iron came from London aboard Goldsmiths' *CAMBRIA* in 1931. The next year more loam freights arrived; one in Pauls' *GRAVELINES I* in June, another in August aboard *KARDOMAH*, one in November and one in December, each by the *GERALD*, the last two barges being Rochester-owned. The small steamship *ABERCRAIG*, built and registered at Dundee in 1902, discharged pig iron from Cardiff in April 1932 'per Guest, Keen & Baldwin'. Loam imports apparently ended in January 1934 with a total of 1,653 tons having arrived in barges, including the three listed above plus *BRITISH OAK, RONALD WEST, LADY GWYNFRED, GWYNHELEN, MADRALI* and *GLENBURY*. In April and May 1935 120 tons of cast iron fittings were dispatched in five parcels by the ss *WISBECH*, which was loading other materials from Ransomes & Rapier at the time. There is little else to record about shipping traffic to or from Cranes.

The little coaster HEATHER PET, *probably used as a test bed for marine engines made by the Consolidated Diesel Company Ltd.*

The Consolidated Diesel Company Ltd

At the end of March 1912 the Diesel Oil Engine Company announced its plan to establish itself at Ipswich on land off the Hadleigh Road between the River Gipping and the Yarmouth railway line, affording easy access from both railway and river. A local newspaper reported that the works were to be modelled to a large extent on the workshops of Carel Freres of Ghent, who had been engaged in the development and manufacture of the Diesel engine for some ten years. Engines of the kind designed by Dr. Rudolf Diesel, both for working on land and for marine use, from 40 hp upwards and four-stroke and two-stroke, were to be produced. The factory was to be equipped with the latest form of labour-saving machinery for the accurate production of interchangeable parts. Referred to originally as the 'Ipswich Works', the extensive works had opened by 1913 to manufacture oil engines Indeed, Dr. Diesel was on his way to visit the works when he was reported missing from the Antwerp-Harwich steamer on 29th-30th September 1913. That same year, Ipswich Corporation invited plans for the layout of a 'Garden City' on their land close to the London Road to house the expected growth in population.

Known during 1913 as the Consolidated Diesel Company Ltd, the works received cargoes of foundry sand/loam, pig iron and old iron when production began that year. Loam and pig iron came from Grangemouth on 29th June, l7th July, 27th August and 29th October in ss *JESSIE* of Grangemouth, completed at Ayr in 1901, and also on 10th August in ss *ALASTAIR*, launched and registered at Aberdeen in 1902. The ss *BRAESIDE*, Sunderland built in 1909, however, brought loam apparently from Antwerp on 15th September of that year.

A strike, lasting only a short time, occurred at the Diesel Works in May 1913. The works were closed from 20th June 1914 until 15th February 1915, when the factory was re-opened by Vickers Ltd. It was during this time that the engineering firm of Manganese Bronze & Brass Co. Ltd developed ten acres of land adjoining the Diesel Works and in 1916 opened their Handford Works, where at first they were paid largely by the Government to produce specialised materials for munitions.

Submarines from Harwich were frequently in the dock, and it was said with some authority that Vickers maintained and repaired their engines. Shipments of raw materials may have been suspended during the 1914-18 War and materials brought by rail, but loam traffic was under way again during the 1920s, by which time Vickers were in partnership with Petters of Yeovil, who also manufactured oil engines. Loam was discharged by the old sb *AZARIAH* in January 1921 and by the new mv *HEATHER PET* on August 13th. *HEATHER PET* was back in the Orwell at Pin Mill from 5th-8th November 1921, bound from London to Fosdyke with oats and barley. It may be that she put in for some attention to her engine from the makers, but she went on to make numerous visits to Ipswich during her career with various cargoes.

HEATHER PET was a wooden vessel built by the well-respected Kentish barge builders Wills & Packham Ltd of Sittingbourne for Vickers Petters Ltd in 1921. She was of 94nrt, 94ft x 23ft x 8ft and fitted with a two-cylinder oil engine by Vickers Petters of Ipswich. She may have been ordered as a working test-bed for their engines as she entered the general cargo trade but was sold after only two years to C. Mann, of Kings Lynn. Bought by F.T. Everard & Sons in 1927, she was renamed *ASSURITY* in 1934 and a Newbury Diesel Company engine installed. She carried on in general trade, having another Newbury engine in

1942. This engine was removed in 1956, when her hull was used for training Everards' shipwrights at their Greenhithe yard until being broken up in 1959.

Another vessel built by Wills & Packham, the sailing barge *OLIVE MAY*, was fitted with a Vickers Petter engine when she was launched in 1920.

One of the most significant jobs Vickers Petters gained at Ipswich was the refurbishment of the four-masted schooner yacht *FLYING CLOUD*, owned by the Duke of Westminster during 1922 and 1923. The yacht, 177ft loa, had been built of wood and was launched in June 1918 as *ELIZABETH RUTH* from the slips of the Mississippi Shipbuilding Corporation at Biloxi, Mississippi, with two oil engines by Vickers Petters of Ipswich.

A new *FLYING CLOUD*, built of steel and 192ft loa, was completed at Leghorn (Livorno), NW Italy, in 1928 and was fitted with two oil engines inscribed 'Modified by Vickers Petters, Ipswich 1922'. Subsequently the first *FLYING CLOUD* disappeared from the register.

Vickers' name was deleted from the port records from January 1926, but Petters still rented land on the SW Quay until March 1926. The firm had probably closed by 1927/28; the factory buildings stood empty for years, and in a special historical supplement published by the East Anglian Daily Times in 1930 hope was expressed that the works site, with its excellent rail, road and water transport facilities, would be recognised by some enterprising firm and the wheels would once again be set in motion inside the modern, lofty and spacious workshops. This was not to be, however, and the land was eventually cleared for the building of the Hadleigh Road Industrial Estate in the 1960s. The two-storey red-brick office block, criticised at the end of 1913 as being 'too palatial', is all that remains. An Ipswich-built oil engine is preserved at the Prickwillow pumping station near Ely.

The Duke of Westminster's schooner yacht FLYING CLOUD, *which was equipped with both propulsion engines and auxiliaries by the Consolidated Diesel Company.*

Oil 12

The first oil cargoes to reach Ipswich came in sailing barges owned by R. & W. Paul, twenty such cargoes being unloaded in 1883 and 1884. It has been suggested that the oil age really began in 1850 when James Young, a Scottish chemist, patented shale oil upon discovering that it was commercially possible to obtain oil from shale, a clay rock found in the Scottish Lothians to the west of Edinburgh. By roasting the rock at 550 degrees centigrade and refining the resulting oil, a mixture of liquid hydrocarbons, known in the trade as kerosene, but more popularly called paraffin, was produced.

Young formed a company, Young's Paraffin Light & Mineral Oil Company, but his patent lapsed in 1864 and within six years ninety-seven other firms had been founded; thirty of them failed by 1870. The business reached its peak in 1913, after which it declined until only six shale oil companies remained. William Fraser, managing director of the Pumpherston Oil Company (established 1883), guided their amalgamation into Scottish Oils Ltd, which was acquired in 1919 by the Anglo-Persian Oil Co. Ltd (APOC), later the Anglo-Iranian Oil Co. Ltd (AIOC) and British Petroleum (BP), which helped modernise the shale oil industry. Fraser, who started work with his father's Pumpherston Oil Company in 1909, went on to become managing director of the APOC/AIOC from 1923 to 1956. The shale industry produced over two and a half million tons of paraffin in 1907, one and a half million tons in 1938, and little more than half a million tons by 1960. The business ended in 1962.

Kerosene or paraffin was much sought after during the second half of the nineteenth century to replace lamp oils derived from tallow, colza (India), rape (China), shark and whale oil. Back in 1838, over one million pounds worth of oils for illumination was imported, and by 1880, Britain was using 200,000 tons of tallow, half of which was imported.

British oil has been discovered in many different places. Wells were sunk in Nottinghamshire and Dorset, for instance, Dorset being the most prolific today. The Finance Act of 1928 levied the first tax of 4d. a gallon on imported oil while exempting indigenous oil, thus helping the shale oil industry and aiding research into means of obtaining oil from coal. Oil was distilled from coal, but scarcely on a commercial scale, despite efforts by the Anglo-Persian Oil Company and I.C.I., and the project ended by 1940. Coal oil came on stream in 1936 but was still commercially unsuccessful, and the plant at Billingham turned to the manufacture of creosote.

In other parts of the world oil deposits were close to the surface and known to ancient civilisations, particularly in parts of America, Greece, Rumania and Burma. In 1859 a significant reserve of oil was discovered only seventy feet down in Pennsylvania, and the modern industry was born. During the 1880s and 1890s large fields were producing 'petroleum' in Russia, Rumania and Burma. At that time oil was generally referred to as petroleum and used for lighting. The product later known as petrol, motor spirit or gasoline was not then available. Not until the arrival of the internal combustion engine and motor cars was there a requirement for an energy-producing fuel. Well into the twentieth century the description used when shipping kerosene (paraffin) was 'petroleum (burning)' or 'oil (burning)'.

In 1863 John D. Rockefeller, already a successful businessman at the age of twenty-three, entered the 'new' petroleum industry by building a refinery at Cleveland, Ohio. In 1870 his company became the Standard Oil Company, flourishing for forty years. In 1911, however, because of the influence the company was able to exert on the international oil stage, the U.S. Supreme Court decreed that the company be split into no fewer than thirty-four unrelated companies. Standard Oil, a name known so widely and not to be lost easily, was retained in the new arrangements by the new companies becoming Standard Oil (Ohio), Standard Oil (New Jersey), and so on. In 1888 Standard Oil had already formed an affiliated company in Britain, the Anglo-American Oil Company, or Esso as it became in 1934, derived from the phonetic version of the initials of the parent company, the Standard Oil Co. (New Jersey).

Anglo-American had set up a depot at Purfleet in 1888, next to the Anglo-Russian Oil Company depot on the Thames, from where some of the early oil cargoes arrived at Ipswich. The oil at that time was shipped in wooden barrels each containing 42 U.S. gallons or 34.972 imperial gallons. Later it was transported all over the world in five-gallon drums, two at a time in a wooden crate, from which it became known as case oil. This could be transported in merchant ships in the same way as general cargo, until leakage made the holds unsuitable for other commodities.

Russian oil came from Baku, west of the Caspian Sea, and was shipped down the Volga in the 1870s from Astrakhan to the Black Sea. During the 1880s oil was being exported from the Baltic port of Libau, where it had arrived by rail, finding a ready market in Britain as Russian Oil Products or simply as R.O.P. A thousand tons of Russian oil arrived from Libau at the Regent's Canal Dock in London and was pumped through a pipeline to a depot at nearby Bow. The first bulk oil had arrived in Britain. The ss GLUCKAUF is credited with being the world's first steam ocean-going oil tanker, built on the Tyne in 1886 for a German company. During the 1890s more tankers were under construction, advancing

Sailing barge traffic with oil to Ipswich, 1883-1884. While some relevant shipping records are missing and the list might be incomplete, as much information as possible is included to present a reasonable overall picture.

DATE	NAME	POR	FROM	LISTED CARGO	CONSIGNEE
30 Jan 1883	sb ANDROMEDA	Ipswich	London	Paraffin	Grimwade Ridley
6 Apr	sb MABEL	Ipswich	London	Petroleum	Grimwade Ridley
13 Jul	sb PRINCESS ROYAL	Ipswich	London	Paraffin 270 barrels	Grimwade Ridley
1 Sep	sb ANDROMEDA	Ipswich	London	Petrol	Grimwade Ridley
1 Sep	sb MABEL	Ipswich	London	Petrol	Grimwade Ridley
5 Oct	sb JULIA WOOD	Ipswich	London	Petrol	Grimwade Ridley
8 Oct	sb ALBERT	Ipswich	London	Petrol	Grimwade Ridley
17 Oct	sb EMILY	Ipswich	London	Petrol	Grimwade Ridley + Cornell
21 Dec	sb PRINCESS ROYAL	Ipswich	London	Petrol	Cornell & ER & F Turner
15 Feb 1884	sb CHAMPION	London	London	Petrol	Grimwade Ridley
14 Mar		Ipswich	London	Paraffin	Grimwade Ridley
19 May	sb CHAMPION	London	London	Petrol	Grimwade Ridley
10 Jul	sb JULIA WOOD	Ipswich	London	Petrol	Grimwade Ridley
14 Jul	sb ALBERT	Ipswich	London	Petrol	Grimwade Ridley
30 Jul	sb AZARIAH		London	Petrol	Grimwade Ridley
10 Sep	sb ANN		London	Petrol	Grimwade Ridley & Gostling & Co
15 Sep	sb JULIA WOOD	Ipswich	London	Petrol	Pauls (probably Pauls' A/C) Grimwade Ridley
30 Oct	sb ANDROMEDA	Ipswich	London	Petrol	Grimwade Ridley
10 Nov	sb JULIA WOOD	Ipswich	London	Petrol	Grimwade Ridley
25 Dec	sb PRINCESS ROYAL	Ipswich	London	Paraffin	Cornell

quickly in size and technology. The case oil trade continued well into the twentieth century, however, serving remote parts such as the Pacific islands.

All the sailing barges in the table, with the exception of sb *AZARIAH*, were owned by R. & W. Paul Ltd, the work providing useful return cargoes to Ipswich before the launching of Pauls' steamer *SWIFT* in 1886. The *SWIFT* managed ninety-five round trips between Ipswich and London in her first full year, and often brought paraffin in barrels with other general cargo.

By that time, however, the coastal paraffin trade was being augmented by deep-sea shipments to Ipswich from America, usually in old wooden barques of Scandinavian or Italian registry. In 1885 the sv *SECUNDA EMILIE* of Arendal, Norway, arrived on 17th August from New York with 'petroleum' for Grimwade Ridley, a firm established early in the nineteenth century in Ipswich as wholesale chemists. The following July a similar vessel, the *SIDON* of Arendal, came from Philadelphia with paraffin for the same firm, who in the twentieth century became better known as wholesale grocers and chemists. On 28th July 1887 the Italian *TOMASO* of Genoa brought paraffin from New York and on 24th August 1888 the Italian barque *SCUTOLA* of Castellammare discharged 2,714 barrels of petroleum from New York for Grimwade Ridley, sailing light on 7th September. The coasting trade still went on, however: an ancient schooner the *POLKA* of Maldon, built at Sunderland in 1845, arrived from the Thames on 28th July 1889 with petroleum. The refined product known as petrol, motor spirit or gasoline was not then available.

Direct imports to Grimwade Ridley continued for a few more years. In July 1892 the sv *HIERVERY* of Fagerstrand, twelve miles south of Oslo, arrived from Philadelphia, and on 8th November the same year the sv *GIOVANI*, registered at Venice, came from New York. The following year saw the sv *GYLLER* of Kragero, Norway, arrive from New York, and in 1894 the *ITALIA* of Castellammare di Stabia, on the SE shore of the Gulf of Naples, berthed at the end of a voyage from Philadelphia. Two ships arrived in 1895, both from New York, the *ANNA WICKHORST* of Blankenese on the Elbe, just downstream of Hamburg, and the *AMICITIA* of Kragero. Two British sailing ships docked in 1897 from New York, the *ZAYDA*, a schooner built at Bideford in 1869, and the *ARETAS*, a wooden barque, like most of the vessels in this trade, which was launched at Bideford in 1871 and registered in London.

Shell, BP and Esso refineries serving Ipswich.

Originally the oil companies considered it practical to refine the crude oil as close to the oilfields as possible, a policy which was reconsidered later after the effects of two world wars and problems in the Middle East. Consequently only limited refining capacity was available in the UK until the 1950s, and it is of interest to note the developments that affected oil companies with depots at Ipswich or in East Anglia served by the new refineries.

An Act of 1871 permitted the then Thames Conservancy to limit the import of petroleum to Thames Haven on the north bank of the river above Canvey Island, and stipulated that the oil be transported further upriver in covered barges. A petroleum wharf was constructed in 1875 and storage tanks added shortly afterwards to be run by the London & Thames Haven Wharves Ltd. Thames Haven had been linked to the London, Tilbury & Southend Railway in 1855 by a short branch line from Stanford le Hope. The Port of London Authority, created in 1908, extended the petroleum limit to above Purfleet, where Anglo-American had built its first depot in 1888, though until 1908 it had been forced to keep most of its stock at Thames Haven. Until Anglo-American's Fawley refinery near Southampton was modernised and re-opened in 1951, Purfleet and Thames Haven were the main sources of Esso products for Ipswich, although from 1951 coastal tankers used all three installations.

The Anglo-Persian Oil Co. opened small refineries at Llandarcy (named after William Knox Darcy, founder of Anglo-Persian) in South Wales in 1921 and at Grangemouth, Scotland, in 1924. Despite relatively small additions being made afterwards, it was not until the early 1950s that both were considerably enlarged and modernised. Although wartime petrol rationing did not end until 1950, it was obvious that additional refining capacity would be required, and the Isle of Grain refinery in Kent opened in 1953. Supplies were brought to Ipswich from both Grangemouth and Llandarcy as necessary.

Sources of BP products within the UK dried up considerably in the 1980s when the company refineries at Llandarcy and the Isle of Grain closed, leaving only Grangemouth on the Firth of Forth, from where tankers for Ipswich loaded. During the 1990s BP came to an agreement with the Mobil Oil Company for a limited amount of integration, but this was short lived, ending by the end of the decade. BP, however, purchased the Mobil Coryton refinery near Thames Haven, enabling the company to bring its own refining capacity back to the south of the country. This plant had been first opened in 1922 by Cory Brothers, who purchased the site of the former Kynoch Explosives Works, and Mobil rebuilt the refinery to modern standards in 1954.

Escorted to Ipswich by the London tug CONTEST, *the ss* ACHATINA *approaches Cliff Quay in March 1934 with motor spirit loaded in Curacoa, having left a part-cargo at Shellhaven. The IDC tug* STRONGHOLD *is astern. The* ACHATINA *was owned by Anglo-Saxon Tankers (Shell).*

In 1916 Shell began refining in a small way at Shellhaven, downstream from Thames Haven and just upriver from Coryton, which was also wholly redeveloped into a modern refinery during the 1950s. Shellhaven was an ancient fishing settlement and it was coincidence that it proved such an ideal site for the Shell Company. The refinery closed in 1999 and is now redeveloped as a large container terminal. Until then, like the BP Isle of Grain refinery on the other side of the estuary, it provided an easy source of products for Ipswich. A normal passage for ships took about six hours, which meant that round voyages were usually completed within twenty-four hours.

Anglo-American Oil Company Ltd

The company's first Ipswich depot was established in 1906-7 at Chancery Road, adjacent to the Great Eastern Railway goodsyard, and was supplied by rail from Purfleet. The company must have bought out the storage tank and substantial lamp-oil trade from Grimwade Ridley, the oil and colour merchants who had built a large storage tank on the site and from 1899 received paraffin from Purfleet. This was brought in a small steam tanker to Stoke Bridge, from where the cargo was pumped to Chancery Road through a pipeline laid under the ground by the river towpath, under Princes Street bridge and across the goodsyard to their storage. Shipments continued until a new depot at Cliff Quay was opened in 1925.

The new depot was conspicuous by big capital letters spelling the name PRATTS, with one letter on each of the storage tanks. Charles Pratt was a friend of J.D. Rockefeller and an early director of Standard Oil. In 1896 Charles Pratt's name became the trade name, 'Pratt's Perfection Spirit', for the company's petrol until 1935, when the acronym ESSO was used for all products except lubricating oils, which retained his name until the 1950s. On 28th March 1951 the company's name was changed from Anglo-American to Esso Petroleum Company Ltd. It finally closed its operations at Ipswich in 1987, the depot being taken over by Powell Duffryn Ltd, who had the adjoining fuel oils and chemical storage.

Esso Shipping

The first Anglo-American Oil Company ship to work to Ipswich was the ss *OSCEOLA*, of 380 dwt, built in 1897 at Port Glasgow for the company as a bulk tank ship. Her engines and accommodation were amidships, and she was fitted with towing gear aft. She brought the first paraffin cargoes from Purfleet to the Stoke Bridge pipeline for Grimwade Ridley and continued to do so until 1908, when her cargo is recorded for Anglo-American. In 1899 she discharged at Stoke Bridge in March, May, July and November, and she made six trips in 1900. She continued making three or four trips a year, and from about 1908 delivered occasional part-cargoes, the balance being taken to Anglo-American's depot on Lake Lothing, Lowestoft. From the beginning of the First World War in 1914 *OSCEOLA*'s visits tailed off. She still traded, however, because she is recorded as being attacked in the North Sea by aircraft in 1915, although she was undamaged. This was probably one of the first air attacks on shipping. She was eventually broken up in 1935 at Stockton after 38 years' service, having spent her last years working on the North-east coast. *OSCEOLA* was joined on the Ipswich run by the 1912 Belgian-built steam coaster *LUFFWELL*, originally a general cargo ship owned by Steam Traders Ltd of London. Anglo-American fitted her hold with tanks when the company bought her in 1916. She, too, was broken up in 1935. Her first voyage to Ipswich was probably on 7th July 1917 with a part-cargo to Lowestoft, and she carried on completing four or five trips a year until December 1924.

Cliff Quay was opened in 1925, and the Anglo-American Oil Company was one of the first tenants, the initial cargoes by sea arriving in September. On 8th September, the company motor vessel *OSAGE* arrived at Cliff Quay from the Thames with 1,108 tons and 19cwt of the quaintly termed 'petroleum (burning)' or paraffin. She made another four trips to the end of December with motor spirit and paraffin. Her sister ship mv *JUNIATA* berthed on 25th September with a part-cargo of 715 tons of motor spirit, the rest being for Sunderland. Both tankers were built in 1914 for the Royal Fleet Auxiliary, *OSAGE* being launched at Devonport Dockyard as *FEROL* and *JUNIATA* by Short Brothers of Sunderland as *SPRUCOL*. Both were the principal vessels delivering Anglo-American oil products to Ipswich throughout the 1930s, together with their steamer *ALLEGHENY*, launched at Connahs Quay on the River Dee in 1921. *JUNIATA* was sunk by the Royal Navy as a blockship at Scapa Flow in 1940. *OSAGE*, having traded regularly to Ipswich until May 1940, was sunk by aircraft a few miles north east of the Arklow light vessel in the Irish Sea in December 1940.

The post-war oil market

The demand from industry and the retail petrol market increased considerably in the 1950s. There were 78 cargoes delivered to Esso in 1954 for instance. During the early 1950s, regular coastal tankers at Cliff Quay were four 200ft loa company coasters bought from the Ministry of War Transport, all wartime standard steamships based on the *PASS OF BALMAHA*, 850dwt of 1933, owned by the Bulk Oil S.S. Company.

The mv *ESSO OTTAWA*, ex-*EMPIRE COAST*, 340dwt, was one of two smaller vessels from the MOWT. She was built at Northwich, Cheshire, in 1943.

Chartered tankers discharging in 1954 were F.T. Everard's mv *AMITY* (built 1945), ss *ADHERITY* (built 1942), mv *ATONALITY* (built 1950), mv *AUSTERITY* (built 1947), and ss *AUREITY* (built 1942). Others included the Bulk Oil Steamship Company's *PASS OF BALLATER* (built 1928), Metcalf's *ANTHONY M* (built 1944) and three vessels owned by C. Rowbotham & Sons of London, the *HELMSMAN* (built 1937), *BRIDGEMAN* (built 1939) and *RUDDERMAN* (built 1934). The majority of cargoes were loaded at Purfleet, with some from Fawley refinery in Southampton Water, and others from Saltend, Hull.

The oil industry was at its zenith during the 1960s. In 1970, 123 tankers unloaded at the Ipswich Esso Terminal prior to drastic pruning by all the oil

The coastal tankers acquired by Esso from the Ministry of War Transport.

Name	Built	Place built	Former name	Details
SS *ESSO DAKOTAH*	1942	Grangemouth Dockyard	EMPIRE GAWAIN	Broken up 1962 Belgium
SS *ESSO GENESEE*	1943	Grangemouth Dockyard	EMPIRE HARBOUR	Broken up 1961 Belgium
SS *ESSO JUNIATA*	1941	Grangemouth Dockyard	EMPIRE LASS	Broken up 1969 Belgium
SS *ESSO TIOGA*	1943	Grangemouth Dockyard	EMPIRE WRESTLER	Broken up 1963 Forth.

companies in the aftermath of the enormous price explosion of 1973, triggered by events in the Middle East. This ultimately led to the search for alternatives for industry and the domestic market, which North Sea gas helped to satisfy.

Esso coastal tankers unloaded at Ipswich in 1970 were the *ESSO HYTHE* (built 1959, of 1300dwt), ESSO IPSWICH (built 1960, of 1,576dwt), *ESSO CAERNARVON* (built 1962, of 1,570dwt), and the *ESSO PURFLEET*. The last vessel, built in 1967, was the largest at 4,430dwt and the most sophisticated to date, being able to carry twelve grades of oil products. Chartered motor vessels included Everard's *AGILITY* (built 1959), *ASSIDUITY* (built 1964), *ASPERITY* (built 1967), and *ACTIVITY* (built 1969). Metcalf's regulars were *JOHN M* (built 1963), *NICHOLAS M* (built 1965) and *FRANK M* (built 1964 and 1,600dwt). Most if not all these ships loaded at Fawley refinery, which opened in 1951 on the site of a small refinery constructed in 1921. Fawley was connected with Purfleet by pipeline in the 1970s, but much of the oil storage at Purfleet by then served London. The other main loading port was Milford Haven, where a new refinery was opened in 1960 for Esso's business on the West Coast.

The 1980s brought to an end the major oil companies' presence at Ipswich, Esso being the last to close in 1987. The final cargo to the Cliff Quay site under Esso management was aboard the *ESSO PENZANCE*. She and the *ESSO INVERNESS*, both completed at Appledore in 1971 and of 3,402dwt, had delivered most of the final years' products.

Ironically, the distribution of Esso petrol and other oils in the Ipswich area would henceforth be by road tanker from Purfleet.

The BRITISH PLUCK, *built at the Swan Hunter yard on the Tyne in 1928, on her trials. Renamed* SHELBRIT 1 *when chartered to Shell-Mex & BP Ltd in 1937, she was sunk off Inverness on 17th September 1940.*
(Shell-Mex & BP Archives)

Petroleum products at Shell-BP Ipswich

Before the First World War different products were obtained from crude oil by primitive distillation including gas, which if not used within the refinery was burned to waste, gasoline (petrol), kerosene (paraffin), lubricating oils and fuel oil. By 1913, the mixed residue of these processes was considered fit to replace coal for ships, railway locomotives and some industrial boilers. Paraffin (as lamp oil) was the main refined component, motor spirit being originally a by-product.

Improvements in motorcar engine design, however, called for something more than straight distillation, leading to more research within the industry which resulted in the 'cracking' process that greatly improved the quality of separated products of the motor spirit range by the application of heat and pressure. Apart from motor spirit improvements were made to paraffin, gas oil (diesel) and aviation fuel, the latter particularly valuable during the Second World War. The introduction during the 1950s of 'catalytic cracking' brought about more sophisticated refining processes, including even more extraction of solvents, etc., resulting in less wastage from the crude. The words 'petrol' and 'paraffin' are not used within the industry. The terms motor spirit and kerosene (now spelled kerosine) are used for these basic products in Britain, other names denoting particular grades or company brands of either product.

Kerosene was sold by all the major petroleum companies as burning oil to the retail trade or commercial consumer. The cheaper brand was also used as a cleaner in workshops. Shell-Mex & BP Ltd maintained an enormous winter trade throughout the late 1940s into the 1960s with their cheaper Royal Standard paraffin and premium grade Aladdin pink paraffin. The latter was the finest available and was known officially as White May. Dye was originally added as a 'marker' at the retailer's site (usually a small corner grocery or hardware shop) by the driver emptying the contents of a stipulated number of slender glass phials of pink dye into the churns. The dye was the guarantee to the consumer of the quality. White May was sold especially to farmers and other non-retailers without marker. Esso's best paraffin was White Rose, with its cheaper alternatives Tea Rose and Royal Daylight, and the company competed fiercely during the 1960s with Esso Blue. Some parts of the county were served by old-established travelling hardware and oil merchants who built up considerable retail businesses during the autumn and winter. Shell-BP used to supply Hopgood's of Stowmarket with about 3,000 gallons of paraffin a week in cold weather, distributed by Hopgood's familiar vans that were hung with buckets, pans, brushes, tools, candles and every type of hardware on their weekly rounds.

In early days paraffin was expensive and used only by the better-off, but by the end of the nineteenth century it was down to 6d. a gallon. Esso bought out the oil-stove manufacturers Valor, just as Shell-BP later purchased the Aladdin stove makers. Because paraffin was still of such importance to a large section of the population without other adequate forms of heat or light, governments decreed that a legal maximum retail price would apply. The price of best paraffin in the 1950s therefore increased only from about 1s. 6d. to two shillings per gallon. Some rural areas in Suffolk were not connected to the electric supply until the late 1950s or early sixties, after which the price was de-regulated, and it soared. Pink paraffin all but disappeared, but the original cheaper 'Royal Standard' brand was soon in demand for oil-fired central heating; it has continued to be used in country areas not supplied with mains gas. A versatile product indeed, used for jet aircraft and country cottage alike.

The SHELL SEAFARER, *seen here in the Orwell, and the* BP HUNTER *represented the final breed of coastal tankers employed by Shell-Mex and BP in the 1980s, prior to the major oil companies' withdrawal from Ipswich.*

Motor spirit as we have noted was swiftly improved and tetra-ethyl lead was added as an anti-knock agent. It was in the late 1950s and 1960s, however, that competition between the major companies brought about even higher specifications. Additives were introduced to the premium grades, at first by adding a quart-measure of chemical to a certain number of gallons at the loading point. Originally, these additives were Shell ICA and BP08. The companies steered away from an octane-rated sales pitch that the public tended to want, and although 'super-plus' brands were introduced at filling stations with octane ratings in the high nineties, these were phased out after a few years. Brands were eventually classed by the number of 'stars' given to grades of petrol, e.g. two-star or four-star, which is still in use. A 50-50 rating of three stars was sold for some years. This was obtained for example by mixing 250 gallons of two star with 250 gallons of four star motor spirit on the delivery vehicle and selling as 500 gallons of three star. Since those days, different company brands have concentrated on the 'star' system with no real differences in quality, so that one company may draw supplies from a competitor's stock. The competition has moved to pricing in pence and decimal parts of a penny per litre at the service stations. White spirit (turps substitute) came to Ipswich by road and was sold principally to dry-cleaners.

Diesel and gas oil for road vehicles (DERV) were the same product. Indeed until the mid to late 1950s there was no difference between them. Five hundred gallons of each could be delivered to different customers from the same 1,000-gallon vehicle compartment, although a tax similar to that on motor spirit was levied on DERV. Gas oil was soon to be coloured red at source to satisfy Customs & Excise, who could easily check if a road vehicle was running on tax-free red gas oil. The gas oil business grew enormously as industry turned from coke and coal-fired heating. Motor ships were swiftly taking over from steamers, and a considerable amount of bunkering was undertaken at Ipswich and also at Felixstowe Dock, Colchester, Mistley and Harwich.

Light (black) fuel oil, trade name Britoleum (not normally heated), was stored at Ipswich, where it was mainly sold for factory or horticultural heating. Heavier grades of fuel oil were stored in lagged heated tanks at Cory Brothers' tank farm on Cliff Quay after 1953 and were graded as 'KG' and 'B', the 'B' resembling tar. These oils were delivered all year round to many factories and laundries, etc., and seasonally to grass dryers and beet sugar factories across East Anglia, from Colchester to Peterborough, and Kings Lynn to North Walsham and Great Yarmouth. It was also delivered to large oil-burning steamships. Road tankers, designed for use solely for gas or black oils and allocated for black oil deliveries during the winter season, were washed out with specified amounts of gas oil until clean, before loading gas oil for actual deliveries. It was not until around 1957 that plastic lined tanks, fitted on new vehicles, permitted all products to be loaded according to seasonal demand.

Vaporising oil was a product in the range between motor spirit and kerosene, exempt from tax and sold in huge amounts to farmers to fuel their post-war tractors, which were normally run for long periods under steady conditions without need of sudden bursts of power. Officially known as Tractor Vaporising Oil (TVO), it was further refined in the early 1950s and given the brand name of Shellspark. By the 1980s, however, as tractors grew in size and power, it had been almost completely displaced by diesel fuel, except that small supplies are still required by enthusiasts with vintage tractors or stationary engines.

High octane aviation fuels were not available at Ipswich and deliveries to local aerodromes were brought from Shellhaven. Jet fuel, or Aviation Turbine Fuel (ATF), which is basically kerosene, was kept at Ipswich under very strict quality control from the late 1940s. It was supplied by road to RAF and USAF bases throughout Norfolk and Suffolk until the last surviving airfields were connected to the pipeline system in the 1990s. Transport of aviation fuel usually involved the use of independent contractors, for example Thomas Allen Ltd of Stanford-le Hope and Crow Carrying Company Ltd of Barking. The latter had served the oil companies since 1920 by transporting petrol in two-gallon cans under their trade mark 'As the Crow Flies'.

Packaged and bulk lubricating oils were supplied by road from a blending plant at Fulham. Until the mid-1950s bulk oil was sold in forty-gallon barrels, hand-pumped out on site, or five-gallon churns were filled in the oil store for emptying to customers' oil cabinet tanks. From that time, a bulk lorry was used

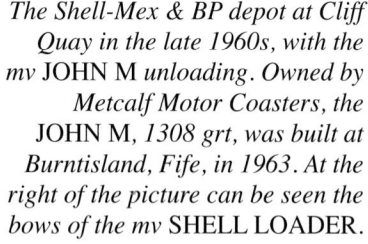

The Shell-Mex & BP depot at Cliff Quay in the late 1960s, with the mv JOHN M unloading. Owned by Metcalf Motor Coasters, the JOHN M, 1308 grt, was built at Burntisland, Fife, in 1963. At the right of the picture can be seen the bows of the mv SHELL LOADER.

at Ipswich, as garages developed lubrication bays, and packaged lubricant distribution was put out to contract.

A high-pressure tank for Liquefied Petroleum Gas (LPG), i.e. Propane, was installed in 1962 and the gas delivered to Ipswich from Shellhaven or Kent refineries in twenty-ton railway tank wagons. The old sidings had been disused for a few years and one was brought back into use for about ten years until it was decided to fill in the sidings area for lorry parking. LPG was then brought by road tanker until the 1980s, when it was no longer distributed from Ipswich. At first its main use was heating for the expanding poultry industry in Norfolk and Suffolk, then as a clean fuel for forklift trucks, ice-cream van refrigerators and greenhouses.

National Benzole Company

The National Benzole Company, of Wellington House, Buckingham Gate, London, SW1, which was founded in 1919, marketed a mixture of benzine (a byproduct of coal-gas manufacture) and petrol. Its first depot at Ipswich opened in 1923, close to the gasworks on the corner of Patteson Road and St Helena Road, i.e. the roadway on the south-eastern side of the dock between the gasworks and the lockgates. This was the first bulk storage depot for motor spirit in the town; the depots in Chancery Road only had bulk storage for paraffin. It was situated across the quay from the petroleum stage erected to receive all petroleum products arriving at the port (at that time in barrels), thus enabling ships to comply with new bye-laws issued by the Commissioners in 1872 under the 1871 Petroleum Act. A pipeline was laid under St Helena Road from the stage to the depot in 1923 at an annual rent of £20 for the wayleave.

The small company-owned tankers were all prefixed *BEN*. National Benzole supplied benzole to Fawley refinery and agreed to market the products of the refinery that opened in 1921 on Southampton Water. The refinery had been built for the American-based Atlantic, Gulf & West Indies Petroleum Corporation Ltd (AGWI), which was taken over by Anglo-American in 1926.

The first tanker berthed at Ipswich with 153 tons of Benzole spirit on 3rd November 1923 from Fawley. She was the ss *BEN ROBINSON*, a brand new vessel built in Utrecht with a Beardmore engine. On 19th January 1924 mv *BEN JOHNSON* arrived with 54 tons. This vessel, built in 1913 at Vlaardingen, Holland, for Burt, Bolton & Haywood of London, had previously delivered gas oil to the gasworks since 1914 under her original name of *IALENE*. The *BEN ROBINSON* came again on 5th February 1924, the ss *BEN HENSHAW*, Norwegian built in 1915, arrived on 29th July and *BEN ROBINSON* delivered 108 tons in March 1925. The National Benzole Company and its Mr Mercury trade-mark became popular with motorists, and the business expanded so that in the twelve months from April 1927 to March 1928 approximately 2,500 tons of motor spirit, loaded at Fawley or on the Thames, were discharged.

Trade increased during the early 1930s to the extent that a larger depot outside the dock was needed. By 1933 seven special locks were ordered to save waiting to allow tankers to enter and leave the Dock at a cost of £1 each passage. A small available area of Ipswich Dock Commission land at the corner of the new Landseer Road and Greenwich Road, adjacent to the Shell Mex & BP installation, was duly leased to National Benzole at a rent of £131 per annum.

Metcalf's coastal tanker FRANK M, seen off Levington with petroleum products for Cliff Quay in September 1985.

Work started in the summer of 1935; a pipeline was laid from Cliff Quay and a railway siding installed by continuing up Greenwich Road from the Shell Mex & BP sidings.

In the financial year from April 1937 to March 1938, National Benzole received twenty-six shipments of motor spirit, eleven delivered by the *BEN READ* and fifteen by the *BEN HENSHAW*, making a total of 8,200 tons. Loading ports were Hamble, Thames, Hull, Middlesbrough and Sunderland. Part-cargoes were sometimes shared with Great Yarmouth, where a National depot existed on the South Denes into the 1950s. Rail amounts were small. In the first quarter only 26 tons 14cwt arrived, and in the third quarter 40 tons 9cwt came, at a total charge (described as rental) to the company by the Ipswich Dock Commission of £3 7s. 3d.

BEN READ and *BEN HENSHAW* continued into the early days of the Petroleum Board, and things did not really get back to normal until 1948 when they were regularly joined by the *BEN SADLER* and *BEN HEBDEN*. National Benzole received thirty-nine cargoes in 1954 by the *BEN HENSHAW*, *BEN HEBDEN* and *BEN HITTINGER*.

Tankers discharging motor spirit at Ipswich in 1927-28.

BEN JOHNSON		BEN HENSHAW		BEN READ		BEN ROBINSON	
Date	Tons	Date	Tons	Date	Tons	Date	Tons
31 May 1927	123	6 April 1927	105	21 June 1927	117	27 Aug 1927	72
11 July	124	23 April	179	20 July	90	10 Sept	165
29 July	102	13 May	140				
11 August	121	11 June	87				
25 August	68	28 June	60				
26 Sept	81	25 Nov	134				
11 Oct	96						
29 Oct	103						
22 Dec	141						
21 Jan. 1928	104						
26 Feb	165						
22 March	105						
Total	1333		705		207		237

Ship	NRT/GRT	Built	Remarks
MV BEN JOHNSON	78NRT	1913 at Vlaardingen as IALINE.	
MV BEN OLLIVER	49NRT	1935 by Rowhedge Ironworks.	
SS BEN ROBINSON	105NRT	1923 at Utrecht with Beardmore engine.	
SS BEN READ	169NRT	1923 at Bristol with Beardmore engine.	
MV BEN SADLER	161NRT	1931 by Rowhedge Ironworks.	
MV BEN HENSHAW	168NRT	1933 by Rowhedge Ironworks.	1957 as STOWMEAD (Dredger).
MV BEN HEBDEN	184NRT	1947 by Rowhedge Ironworks.	1960s to Penfold of London.
MV BEN JOHNSON	100NRT	1938 by Rowhedge Ironworks.	1964 as VARKIZA to Greece.
MV BEN HITTINGER	522GRT	1951	To Shell-Mex & BP Fleet*
MV BEN HAROLD SMITH	325GRT	1952	To Shell-Mex & BP Fleet*
MV BEN BATES	565GRT	1956	To Shell-Mex & BP Fleet*

From 28th March 1955 to 25th March 1956, forty-four cargoes, or about 13,650 tons, of motor spirit were discharged at Cliff Quay for the company, thirty-nine of them by BEN HENSHAW, four by BEN HEBDEN and one by BEN HITTINGER. The rental due to the I.D.C. was £131, the same as in 1923, some thirty years earlier. One charge made by the Commissioners was for supplying a diver with crew and gear to retrieve a rope from BEN HENSHAW's propeller on 29th June 1955. The cost was £10.

The company became an integral part of Shell Mex & BP Ltd in 1957, although continuing to trade separately until the mid-1960s, when some of the remaining tankers transferred to the Shell-Mex & BP fleet.

National Benzole's tankers.

The tank barge BP ALERT coming alongside as the motor tanker SHELL CRAFTSMAN clears the Cliff Quay berth on 7th May 1982. The BP ALERT was able to bring products from Shellhaven to Ipswich and return within the crew's twelve-hour shift.

Shell

The evolution of the many companies trading worldwide under the Shell name is extremely complex. Actual beginnings are identified with the Samuel family, who lived in Victorian London. Marcus Samuel, father of eleven children, ran a successful business, M. Samuel & Co., trading in rice, grain and sugar, with several contacts in the Far East. When he died in 1870 his eldest son Joseph carried on, to be joined by his brothers Marcus and Samuel, who received in 1878 a share of their father's estate. Marcus in particular was the adventurous type who, through a shipbroker during the 1880s, ventured initially into the case oil trade, despite the threat of ruin or takeover from Standard Oil and their near worldwide monopoly.

Marcus Samuel's visionary idea included the transport of bulk oil, free from American involvement, from Russia to the Far East via the Suez Canal that had opened in 1867. The main drawback was that only case oil was permitted to pass through the canal. With enormous influence from business friends and a certain amount of secrecy, and backing from the Rothschilds, a contract was signed to load kerosene, brought overland from Baku on the Caspian Sea, at the Black Sea port of Batum. A bulk tank ship named *MUREX* was built to the highest specifications of that period at West Hartlepool and launched in May 1892. The vessel was classed 100A1 by Lloyds, which coincidentally conformed to new Suez Canal requirements which came into force from the July of that year allowing bulk tank ships to pass through. *MUREX* passed through the Canal in August 1892, by which time storage tanks had been constructed at Singapore, Bangkok, Hong Kong, Djakarta, Penang, Saigon, Shanghai and Kobe in Japan.

Ten new ships, each able to load from 5,000 to 5,400 tons, were in the service of M. Samuel & Co. within the next eighteen months, and with the infrastructure already in place by the end of 1895, sixty-five similar voyages had been completed. The design of the ships had incorporated an efficient steam-cleaning system for the cargo tanks, enabling return cargoes of rice, grain and tea to be safely loaded without contamination. By that time Marcus Samuel had decided that his company should no longer be dependant on outside sources of oil, and the company should invest in its own supplies. That too was accomplished early in 1897 by drilling in Borneo.

Seven more ships, including four general cargo vessels, and a new London office in Leadenhall Street were acquired in the same year. Discussions took place with the Royal Dutch Petroleum Company, which was also drilling in Borneo and Sumatra, about possible amalgamation. The Royal Dutch were seeking outlets and transport for their oil, but the talks came to nothing. However, the year 1897 was significant when the decision was taken by the Samuels to form a new company. A part of their father's original business was importing exotic seashells from the East for decorating souvenir gift-boxes or ornaments for the British market. From the *MUREX* onwards, their ships were all named after seashells, and so the name of Shell was first used in the founding of the new company, Shell Transport & Trading Co. Ltd, in October 1897. The world-famous trademark name, from which so many different national companies were spawned, had been born.

In 1902 an agreement was reached with Royal Dutch to form a new company, Asiatic Petroleum, in which Shell, Royal Dutch and Rothschilds were equal partners. Marcus Samuel became Lord Mayor of London in the same year. Following colossal commercial pressure from Standard Oil, which nearly finished Shell in 1905, negotiations with Royal Dutch resulted in the formation of two companies in 1907, the Bataafsche Petroleum Maatschappij to produce and refine oil and Anglo-Saxon Petroleum to own the ships and transport the oil. Royal Dutch and Shell Transport became holding companies, to be known later as the Royal Dutch/Shell Group. Shell oil exploration and drilling commenced in Rumania in 1907, in Russia in 1910, Oklahoma in 1912, Mexico, California and Trinidad in 1913 and Venezuela in 1914. The latter field, centered on Lake Maracaibo, forty miles from the Gulf of Venezuela and accessible through a channel only twelve feet deep at low water, proved a major find. Fortunately by 1917 a fleet of purpose-built shallow draft vessels was transporting the oil to Curacoa, in the Gulf, which, most importantly, had been a Dutch colony since 1634. The Mexican Eagle Oil Company, founded in 1908, established the Eagle Oil Transport Company in 1912, which joined with Anglo-Saxon after a long association in 1960.

Shell in Great Britain and Ipswich.

Having examined principal elements in the history of the Shell organisation and its international role, it is important to make the local or 'downstream'

Built as EMPIRE COPPICE *for the Ministry of War Transport in 1943, the ss* SHELL FITTER *is seen here discharging at Cliff Quay on 25th September 1961. From 1948 to 1952 she was owned by Kuwait Oil Company as* AMIR, *and afterwards her owners were Shell-Mex & BP Ltd. In 1964 she was sold to Greek owners as* ALIKI.

connection with Ipswich. The company agreed in 1912 that the small independent British Petroleum Company should distribute Shell products in Britain. In 1917 Shell Marketing Ltd was formed and within a year it also had its own rail-fed depot in Chancery Road, Ipswich, where BP and Anglo-American were already based adjacent to the railway goods yard. Shell Marketing amalgamated in 1921 with the Anglo-Mexican Petroleum Company to become Shell-Mex Ltd, the marketing company for the Shell and Eagle Oil Groups, and soon absorbed the business of several small companies including the Bowring Petroleum Company and the St Leonards Wharf Company. In 1926 Shell-Mex Ltd opened a depot at the new Cliff Quay, enabling supplies to be brought by ships. Railway sidings were installed and other depots in East Anglia were served by rail from Ipswich until the 1950s. When the new depot was built, it included stabling for horses, and the mangers remained until demolition in the early 1960s.

The Anglo-Persian Oil Company Ltd

To quote the first line of introduction to one of the company histories, 'The story of BP is multi-layered'! It began in 1901 when the Shah of Persia granted wealthy businessman William Knox D'Arcy a concession to explore, produce and sell oil and related commodities, and, conditional upon a company being formed within two years, to exploit any finds in order to pay the near-

The ESSO PENZANCE *about to berth with the final cargo for the Esso depot before closure in December 1986.*

impoverished Shah and his Empire an initial 'cash' payment of £20,000. D'Arcy never did go to Persia but sent geologists and an engineer, George Reynolds. Sufficient traces of oil were found to form an exploitation company but more funds were needed. Approaches were made to the Admiralty and other possible providers to no avail, and in June 1903 all operations in Persia ceased. D'Arcy was introduced to another oil company, Burmah Oil, which was having problems in Burma. Burmah had been founded in 1886 by a group of Scottish businessmen to find and produce oil in that country. In 1904 Burmah agreed with D'Arcy to form a new Concessions Syndicate to take over from the Exploitation Company. However, it was not until May 1908, following three years of awful conditions, that oil was discovered at 1,180 feet.

The Anglo-Persian Oil Company was founded in 1909 as work continued in the desert. A 138-mile pipeline was laid from the Masjid-i-Suleiman oilfield to Abadan by 1911, and a refinery was under construction. The first consignment of Persian oil was shipped from Abadan in May 1912. The whole project, set in motion back in 1901, was producing oil but the company was in financial trouble. It was time to revive interest by the Admiralty, then more than anxious to secure a British fuel supply for the Navy. At last in May 1914 the Government put in two million pounds of new capital and acquired a majority shareholding, ratified by a request by Winston Churchill, First Lord of the Admiralty, to the House of Commons to pass the Anglo-Persian Oil Company, Acquisition of Capital, Bill. The company's first ships, ordered late in 1914 from Armstrong Whitworth and Swan Hunters, consisted of one 5,000-ton and three 10,000-ton tankers. A new

One of a new breed of coastal tankers able to load 3,000 tons of petroleum products, the mv B.P.HUNTER was built at Appledore, Devon, in 1980 for BP Oil Ltd. She is seen on the Orwell in September 1982. Vessels of this class provided single cabins for all seamen for the first time. (R.W. Smith)

subsidiary was formed in 1915 to manage the growing fleet. Of equal importance to the international company was the need to distribute Anglo-Persian oils in Great Britain. To this end, a ready-made company was purchased. This company was itself a subsidiary of the German-owned Europaische Petroleum Union, which already held the agency for selling Shell products in Britain. Because of its German ownership, the subsidiary was classified as an enemy concern and taken over by the Public Trustee for Enemy Property, from whom Anglo-Persian purchased it. The name of that subsidiary was no less than The British Petroleum Company.

The Anglo-Persian Oil Company soldiered on through the depression years of the 1920s and early 1930s, when it joined Royal Dutch Shell in the formation of Shell-Mex & BP for distribution in Britain. Persia changed its name to Iran in 1935 and the company quickly adopted the title of Anglo-Iranian Oil Company. The Second World War resulted in the loss of forty-four company tankers and 657 crew members. After the war Iran became increasingly nationalistic, and by 1950 it seemed inevitable that despite hefty increases in taxes and royalties paid to Iran, the company would be nationalised. Several well-known mediators, including Ipswich MP Richard Stokes, who had vast international business experience, all tried to save the situation but failed. In 1951, families of staff were evacuated as the head office was taken over by Iranians in June, and the International Court endeavoured to regain control of the company without success. Remaining staff were evacuated on 4th October. It was apparent in the aftermath that nationalist feelings would not diminish, and eventually in 1954 the Shah assented to a new consortium, Iranian Oil Participants (IOP), running the industry. This included Anglo-Iranian (40%), Royal Dutch Shell (14%), five US major oil companies (8% each) and a French company (6%). AIOC retained a stake in the Iranian oil industry and was awarded compensation. The industry was back in business as the tanker *BRITISH ADVOCATE* loaded at Abadan for the IOP on 29th October 1954.

In December 1954 the name of the company was changed to British Petroleum. It broadened its horizons by exploration in the North Sea and Alaska, to become a truly international organisation. By the year 2000 it had acquired substantial interests in the American Mobil and Amoco companies. BP Oil Ltd was formed to carry on British Petroleum's distribution business in the UK after Shell-Mex & BP Ltd was divided in 1975.

British Petroleum at Ipswich.

The German-owned British Petroleum Company came into existence in 1906 by the amalgamation of the Consolidated Petroleum Co. and the General Petroleum Co. (Consolidated Petroleum had already absorbed, among other firms, the Anglo-Caucasian Petroleum Co.). The company held the agency for the distribution of Shell products in the UK until 1917 when Shell Marketing Ltd was formed. That same year, 1917, Anglo-Persian purchased British Petroleum, turning the BP trademark into an icon almost on a par with the popular Shell image, both surviving into the twenty-first century.

The original British Petroleum Company had rail-fed premises from 1909 to 1928 in Chancery Road, where Anglo-American had also commenced operations in Ipswich. The company's new depot, alongside Shell-Mex Ltd at Cliff Quay, was officially opened on 18th September 1928. The tank farm had a storage capacity of over three million gallons and was to be served by coastal and deep-sea tankers. Railway sidings and a loading gantry enabled ten tank wagons to be filled simultaneously, and a weighbridge and electric capstans to shunt wagons were provided.

1930s competition

By 1930 there was mounting competition from a number of smaller firms, including the Texas Oil Co. and Cleveland Petroleum Products, a Manchester firm founded in 1920 to sell white spirit. Cleveland began to market its own brand of motor spirit nationally in 1930 with alcohol as an additive. The company was absorbed by Anglo-American in 1938 and renamed Cleveland Petroleum Ltd. In the mid-1960s the depots and road tanker fleet were integrated with Esso, and the name of Cleveland was dispensed with in 1973. At Ipswich Cleveland operated from one of the old Chancery Road depots until the merger, when they moved into the Esso Cliff Quay depot.

Russia had long been a petroleum-producer from fields in the Caucasian Mountain area. By 1924 Russian Oil Products (ROP) was vigorously competing in Britain with sales values of £500,500 in 1924 rising to almost £4,000,000 within five years. ROP opened several depots but their market share decreased in the mid-1930s. The company had opened a rail-fed depot in Stanley Avenue, Ipswich, on the eastern side of Derby Road station and goods yard, which was listed in 1933-34, and the site continued under the management of the Ipswich Oil Company. ROP was bought out in 1948 by the Regent Petroleum Company who, like the rest of the oil companies, used authorised distributors for agricultural sales and deliveries from the 1950s. Regent appointed the Eastern Counties Farmers Co-operative Association to run a service in East Anglia, and they continued operations at Stanley Avenue until the 1970s.

British-Mexican Petroleum had a complex history in the USA, and it was registered in Britain in 1919 but its British interests were sold to the Anglo-American company (later Esso) in 1925. The particular interests included storage depots and a vehicle fleet working under the title of Redline Motor Spirit Company. The deal also included shares in the Atlantic, Gulf & West Indies Petroleum Company (AGWI) that in 1920 had begun the construction of the refinery at Fawley in Southampton Water, later to be developed by Esso in the 1950s. The Glico Petroleum Company was founded in 1888, the same year as Anglo-American, who bought Glico in 1927 and combined it into Redline-Glico Ltd. This company operated a rail-fed depot at Ipswich next to ROP in Stanley Avenue from about 1934 until the late 1940s. Redline-Glico was voluntarily wound up by Esso in 1962.

Two other petrol companies, Power Petroleum Company and Dominion, were acquired by Shell-Mex & BP Ltd in 1934, although they traded separately until the 1960s. Power was formed to sell and distribute products from the Medway Oil & Storage Company's depot in Kent (MOSCO as it was referred to), on the site where the BP Isle of Grain refinery was built in the early 1950s. The National Benzole company originated in 1919 selling petrol (National Benzole Mixture) mixed with benzine, a by-product of producing coal-gas. A depot opened next to Ipswich gasworks in 1923, moving to Landseer Road in 1935.

A postcard view of Gainsborough Lane as it was about 1900, looking north towards the farmhouse and buildings of Greenwich Farm. The area was recorded in Domesday Book as Grenewic.

Shell-Mex & B.P.Ltd

There was relief for BP and for Shell-Mex Ltd when, in the face of all the competition, their parent companies Royal Dutch-Shell and the Anglo-Persian Oil Company (BP) agreed to combine the marketing and distribution sides of both companies by merging the two British-based organisations. A new company, Shell-Mex & BP Ltd, was sixty per cent Shell and forty per cent BP. It became a market leader with its partner over the Border, Scottish Oils & Shell-Mex Ltd, for forty-three years in the UK with its HQ at Shell-Mex House in the Strand, London. It inherited over 350 depots across the country including Ipswich, Beccles, Bury St Edmunds, Thetford, Diss, Haverhill, Lowestoft and Saxmundham, all of which were still open in 1950. Ipswich, Lowestoft and Saxmundham had two depots apiece, the result of Shell-Mex Ltd and BP each having their own depots within those towns. By good fortune, the two at Ipswich faced each other across Greenwich Road, 400 yards up from Cliff Quay, and became one installation. Those at Saxmundham and Lowestoft, however, were in different parts of the towns.

Only ten years before the merger there would have been double the number of depots. The original network was based entirely on the railway system in the first two decades of the twentieth century, coupled with the area that could be covered in a day's work by horse and cart delivering paraffin in five-gallon open-top cans, and petrol in two-gallon cans. Prime examples in the 1920s were BP's depot in the goods yard at Wickham Market and Shell Marketing with another at Marlesford station, both companies also having their own depots in Saxmundham. Once sufficient motor lorries were available, the depots at Marlesford and Wickham Market closed.

Upon the Ipswich depots' move to Cliff Quay, many of the remaining country depots were more conveniently and cheaply supplied by rail from Ipswich with sea-borne products. As road tankers grew larger and more reliable by the 1950s, the amount distributed by rail soon diminished. At this time, the company owned the largest private lorry fleet in the UK with 2,400 road wagons, 7,000 rail tank wagons and eleven coastal tankers.

A similar view in September 1982 looking between Gabriel's timber yard and the Shell-Mex & BP installation. The farmhouse was situated where the timber stacks can be seen.

In 1953, Shell Mex & BP put the whole of its agricultural business out to authorised distributors. In East Anglia the trade was handled by William Cory & Son Ltd, a part of an old coal owning and distribution company founded in the early nineteenth century. The remaining country depots, vehicles and staff were taken over by Cory, unless they preferred to move to Ipswich or to one of the larger installations still run by Shell Mex & BP. All the non-agricultural business in East Anglia was then handled by the remaining company depots at Ipswich, Great Yarmouth and Kings Lynn. A new fleet of larger lorries was ordered, standardising on 2,000-gallon articulated vehicles rather than 800 to 1,200-gallon tankers for the retail and commercial trades. The boundaries from Ipswich were extended to include south Norfolk, all of Suffolk except for the Lowestoft area, and north Essex from Mersea Island to Finchingfield. Instead of working an eight or nine-hour day, eleven hours became normal. Other major companies like Esso and Regent adopted the same policy of using authorised distributors.

Shell-Mex & BP continued to serve most of the principal industries in Ipswich, including Ransomes & Rapier, Cranes, Reavells, R. & W. Paul, Ipswich Malting Company and Fisons. Ship-bunkering was undertaken, plus the huge task of supplying the US and RAF air bases in East Anglia with aviation fuel. For decades staff levels at the Ipswich installation remained between eighty and ninety strong, including forty to forty-five drivers, three or four garage staff, twenty installation hands and about ten clerks in the office. Geographically, Ipswich was always considered to be ideally situated as a centre for distribution, with good access by road, rail and sea from the refineries at Shellhaven and the Isle of Grain and those further afield. As the volume of business increased, so coincidentally did vehicle weight and road speed regulations, from the twenty-two tons gross maximum and still only twenty miles an hour for lorries over three tons (unladen weight) in 1950. In fact, the twenty-miles-an-hour limit was increased to thirty during the early 1950s and to forty with a twenty-four-ton maximum weight during the 1960s. The 1968 Act permitted thirty-two-ton articulated vehicles, which during the 1980s and 1990s increased to thirty-eight and forty-four-tons, plus higher maximum speeds. All this, combined with road improvements such as the dualling of the A12 London road, eventually meant that deliveries could be made within the hours regulations direct from Thamesside depots. New pipeline-fed depots were operating in Hertfordshire and near Wymondham in Norfolk, all of which rendered the Shell, BP and also Esso installations at Ipswich redundant.

In 1975 the parent companies decided to end the partnership effectively from 1st January 1976 and Shell UK Ltd was formed to serve the downstream business of the Shell Group. In Ipswich, however, the former Shell-Mex & BP terminal was allocated to BP to operate, and the Shell interest was confined to loading facilities, maintaining an order office, facilities for drivers and vehicle maintenance and parking.

BP Oil Ltd announced the total closure of their operations at Ipswich in 1983. The terminal, as it was now called, was taken over and operated by neighbours Powell Duffryn to become a general oil storage depot for many different firms. The staff of BP Oil Ltd moved to other terminals or were made redundant, as were Shell UK staff when that company left Ipswich in 1988.

The impact of the discovery of oil in the North Sea by British Petroleum in 1970, and its subsequent arrival on shore in November 1975, turned the downstream map of petroleum product flow in Britain upside down. Since the beginnings of the industry in the Middle East, the lines of distribution moved north and west from that part of the world, even across the UK. The major refineries were largely in the south, and traffic radiated northwards even from the depots across the country. As we have seen, most of the products came to Ipswich from the refineries at Fawley, Shellhaven and Kent, and were then distributed by road or rail northward and westward with as few miles as possible covered in the opposite direction. North Sea oil was brought ashore at Cruden Bay near Peterhead for refining at Grangemouth, thus reversing the flow as coastal tankers came south. This, coupled with the road and vehicle improvements, gave additional impetus for the depot and refinery closures mentioned earlier.

A Scammell 3150-gallon, 22-ton fuel oil tanker discharged by compressed air at Ipswich in 1961. Its regular driver was Percy Hawes, who rarely exceeded 22mph when lorries over three tons were restricted to 20mph. He learnt to drive a Ford Model T van when working for Cuttings, the Mendlesham grocers, and in 1942 was directed to drive Petroleum Board tankers delivering 100-octane aviation fuel to Suffolk airfields. In 1945 he found himself allocated to Shell-Mex & BP.

OIL 309

Cory Brothers/Powell Duffryn

In 1953 the last 'greenfield site' along Cliff Quay, between the Esso Depot and Gabriel Wade & English, which had been used casually for storing timber, was occupied by a new tank-farm run by Cory Brothers. In the late nineteenth century this company set up many ships' bunkering stations for Welsh steam coal, and diversified into oil storage. Similarly, Powell Duffryn had considerable coal interests in South Wales that included the management of several coal mines and the Powell Duffryn Steam Coal Company. They in turn took over Cory Brothers' storage on Cliff Quay by the 1970s. Initially heavy grades of fuel oil were stored on behalf of Shell Mex & BP, in addition to various edible oils, palm oil and for a period whale oil.

When the Suffolk Chemical Company closed in the late 1950s, Cory Brothers moved into their office and yard with a small tank farm to handle fuel oils for Esso. Gradually, the business expanded. Light oils were stored for small domestic heating firms, and chemicals were housed for a variety of purposes, including weed killer manufacturing in West Suffolk. In 1996 the Powell Duffryn sites at Purfleet, Barry and Ipswich were taken over by Van Ommeren Tank Terminals, a Dutch company involved in the oil industry since the 1890s.

Shell & BP Shipping

Work on the new depot at Cliff Quay for Shell-Mex Ltd continued for much of 1925 with the assistance of the Ipswich Dock Commission, which provided timber for shuttering, truck haulage, two tons of ballast, bags of iron nails, etc., and also the labour for cutting out manholes in the quayside and for cutting bolts for pipe hanging below the quay. This was all paid for out of the I.D.C. Trade Facilities Accounts. The rent for the land was set at £370 per annum.

*The first of the fleet to be repainted in the new company livery in 1954, this 22-ton AEC Mammoth Major with a 3,600-ton capacity was collected with pride from the forecourt of Shell-Mex House by driver Ted Gostling, a former commando who cleaned the vehicle when discharging its loads and achieved much admiration from customers and colleagues alike. When it was sold off in the 1960s the tank was replaced by an open buck and the vehicle was used by Pointers Haulage of Norwich to carry sugar beet from field to factory.
(Courtesy BP Archive.)*

The Shell-Mex shore steam station at Cliff Quay built in 1925 to supply steam to the cargo pumps of steam tankers which were required to draw their fires when discharging motor spirit.

The first ship to discharge at the new depot was the mv *SHELL-MEX I* from the Thames, probably Shellhaven Refinery that opened in 1916. She was Dutch built as *LARA* in 1915, owned by Anglo-Saxon Petroleum Co., and berthed at Cliff Quay on l6th January 1926 with 800 tons of motor spirit. The second arrival on 6th February was a big Dutch lighter, the *NEERLANDIA*, towed by the steam tug *VLAANDEREN*, both of Rotterdam, with 1,073 tons of spirit. The two sailed the next day light for the Thames. The third ship marked the beginning of a new, if brief, era at Ipswich when the first ocean-going tanker to come to Ipswich, the Eagle Oil Transport Company's ss *SAN QUIRINO*, berthed on 24th February with a part-cargo (2,478 tons) of 'petroleum (burning)', better known as paraffin. Built in 1923 by Armstrong Whitworth at Wallsend, she had delivered the rest of her cargo at Hull en route from Tampico, Mexico, and was attended in the river by the London tug *VANQUISHER*, built at South Shields in 1899. Tugs were usually ordered to attend a vessel by the ship's agents. At Ipswich, the agents were normally Lewcock & Pemberton, of Prudential Buildings. They had ordered a tug for 23rd February but *SAN QUIRINO* did not arrive until the 24th, involving a charge of £10. The *VANQUISHER* attended her from Harwich to Cliff Quay, and the next day outwards from Cliff Quay to Buttermans Bay, for £15 each day.

On 19th March 1926 mv *SHELL-MEX I* delivered 810 tons of spirit from Shellhaven, and similar amounts on 2nd and 20th April. On 30th April ss *SAN ROSENDO*, Wallsend built in 1922 and scrapped in 1935, arrived from Tampico via Shellhaven with 2,407 tons of paraffin, accompanied by the tug *VANQUISHER*. She sailed the next day for New Orleans. On l0th and 20th May the oil-burning ss *HICKOROL* brought 900 tons each trip. Owned by the Admiralty, she had been built at Dumbarton in 1918. She was followed on l0th June by *SHELL-MEX I*, which also arrived with three cargoes of 820 tons each of motor spirit during July and August. The smaller *SHELL-MEX II*, built at Dordrecht in 1915, delivered 438 tons on 16th August. The 24th August 1926 brought the ss *LUMINOUS* of Liverpool, from Tampico via the Thames, with 2,454 tons of paraffin for Ipswich. She was owned by the Lumina S.S. Co., managed by H.E. Moss & Co. and built by Russell & Co. of Port Glasgow in 1913 as the *VITRUVIA*.

The last day of August saw the first arrival of one of the Bulk Steamship Company's fleet of tankers, all prefixed '*PASS OF*'. The company, whose address was 130-135 Minories, London, was a subsidiary of James W. Cook & Co. Ltd, who built and repaired ships and lighters at Wivenhoe until the 1980s. The ss *PASS OF MELFORT*, a new ship launched in 1926 at Glasgow, arrived from Shellhaven with motor spirit on 31st August, the first of three trips that year. Another Eagle Oil ship, ss *SAN MACEDONIO*, arrived from Tampico with 2,989 tons of paraffin and *SHELL-MEX I* brought another three 820-ton cargoes of spirit. On 10th December, the oil burning ss *SUPERGA* berthed from Beaumont, Texas, up the Neches River some forty miles above the Sabine Pass. She brought 2,684 tons of paraffin, and was Italian built, owned and registered. *SHELL-MEX II* arrived from Shellhaven with 426 tons on 11th December and 418 tons sixteen days later. Such was the first year's trade to the Shell-Mex depot.

Cliff Quay shore steam station

The Shore Steam Station was designed and built in 1925 by Shell-Mex Ltd to supply steam to the shipboard cargo pumps of the ocean-going steam tankers at a time when port authorities considered it undesirable to maintain the ship's fires when discharging motor spirit. On berthing, the fires were drawn and steam taken from the boilers ashore, although this usually meant that the ship's galley could not provide hot food and mess rooms at the dock gate supplied meals to the crews. The company paid £3 per day for this service, and in addition, a charge was made for the cost of electricity and gas consumed over two days. Lewcock & Pemberton usually took care of these payments.

Two vertical Cochrane boilers were installed in the building, 100ft from the quayside. One 4in steam pipe led straight to the point on the quay where a flexible pipe connected to the ship's steam pipes. Six-inch and 8in pipes branched off 400ft to the northern end of the quay, where another tanker could berth. The pipes were laid in wooden troughs filled with insulation material. The boilers were attended throughout the discharge of the vessel, which usually lasted from 24 to 48 hours, the boilermen working 12-hour shifts feeding the fires.

Petroleum Spirit in Harbours Order

Immediately after the declaration of war an order came into force permitting local port authorities to waive regulations prohibiting ships using their own steam for pumping cargo to shore installations. Keeping the fires going meant that a ship had a better chance of moving quickly in the event of an air raid and possible fire in the area. The old regulations were not enforced after the war and the procedures described in the previous paragraph were not revived at Ipswich. In any case, the majority of tankers, especially coasters, were by that time motor ships. The boiler house was stripped of all its equipment and was used to store hoses and fittings for connecting the ship's discharge lines to the depot pipelines. The building was eventually demolished in 2002.

It is perhaps worth looking at a few of the deep-sea tankers that arrived in

Shell, Eagle Oil Group and chartered ocean tankers delivering to Shell-Mex Ltd at Ipswich 1927-36 (from 1932 Shell-Mex & BP Ltd). A few ships might not be included owing to gaps in the records, but the list does give a fairly accurate picture of the substantial ocean tanker traffic to Ipswich during the period.

the 1930s in more detail. The ss *MYTILUS* was built as a coal/oil burner by Swan, Hunter on the Tyne in 1916 and sailed with the Anglo-Saxon fleet, although registered and managed at Arendal in Norway. She berthed two or three times at Ipswich and survived the war. By the late 1940s she was restricted because of age and general condition to working in the sheltered waters of the Banka Straits off Sumatra and needed special dispensation to sail the 250 miles to and from Singapore for dry-docking. She was broken up after nearly thirty-five years' service in 1950.

The mv *SLIEDRECHT* was launched in 1924 at Rotterdam, where she was registered and owned by N.V. Maats. Motorschip 'Sliedrecht'. She arrived at Cliff Quay from Abadan at least four times, twice in 1938 and again in February

DATE	SHIP	NRT	FROM	BUILT	OWNERS	BROKEN-UP
5/4/27	ss *OPHELIE*	3488	Port Arthur US	1922 St Nazaire.	Reg Leflavre	
15/6/27	ss *CORDELIA*	4178	Beaumont US	1912 Wallsend	CT Bowring Liverpool.	
27/9/27	ss *SAN ROBERTO*	3611	Mexico	1922 Armstrong Whitworth Wallsend		1949
24/11/27	ss *SAN ROBERTO*	3611	Tampico	See 27/9/27.		
10/12/27	ss *LUCELLUM*	3233	New Orleans	1913 J Laing Sunderland	HE Moss Liverpool.	
6/3/28	ss *MUREX*	8887[1]	New Orleans	1912 HM Dockyard Portsmouth	Anglo-Saxon.	
21/3/28	ss *SAN ROBERTO*	3611	Tampico	See 27/9/27		
20/6/28	ss *SOLEN*	3385	Curacoa	1922 Swan Hunter Sunderland	Anglo-Saxon.	
21/6/28	ss *AMALTHUS*		San 'Fisco	1921 Union Constr. Oakland Cal.	Anglo-Saxon.	
28/8/28	ss *SAN LEOPOLDO*	3149	Tampico	1921 Globe SB Co Baltimore		
15/9/28	ss *SAN UGON*	3619	Los Angeles	1921 Standard SB Corporation New York		1935
19/11/28	ss *CORDELIA*	4178	Curacoa	See 15/6/27.		
29/1/29	ss *CYBELINE*	3760		1927 W Hamilton Port Glasgow	CT Bowring.	
7/2/29	mv *INTA*	3421	Tampico	Armstrong W/worth Wallsend	Reg Bergen.	
24/3/29	ss *SAN ROBERTO*	3611	San Pedro	See 27/9/27		
12/6/29	ss *SAN UBALDO*	3684	Mexico	Standard SB Corp New York.		Tyne 1955
18/7/29	ss *SAN TIRSO*	3951	Tampico	Swan Hunter Newcastle		Troon 1953
20/729	ss *SAN LEOPOLDO*	3149	Tampico	See 28/8/28		
i0/9/29	ss *SAN MACEDONIO*	3613	San Pedro	1922 Palmers Newcastle		Blyth 1935
13/12/29	ss *SAN QUIRINO*	3577	Tampico	1923 Armstrong W/worth Newcastle.		
13/1/30	mv *OILSHIPPER*	-	Tampico			
10/2/30	ss *SAN SALVADOR*	3547	Mexico	1924 Armstrong W/worth Newcastle		1949
25/4/30	ss *SAN MAEEDONIO*	3613	San Pedro	See 10/9/29.		
27/4/30	ss *SAN VALERIO*	4054	Mexico	1913 Palmers Newcastle		1953
16/7/30	ss *SAN LEONARDO*	3261	Los Angeles	1921 Globe SB Co Baltimore		Blyth 1935
15/8/30	ss *LUNULA*	3776		1927 Hamilton Port Glasgow	HE Moss Liverpool.	
12/9/30	ss *SAN VALERIO*	4054	Tampico	See 27/4/30.		
16/12/30	ss *SAN EDUARDO*	3959	Tampico	1912 Swan Hunter Newcastle		1934 Glasgow
30/1/31	ss *SAN LEONARDO*	3261	Los Angeles	See 16/7/30.		
19/3/31	ss *SAN MACEDONIO*	3613	Mexico	See 10/9/29.		
23/5/31	mv *IMA*	4026	Singapore	1930 Doxfords Sunderland	Norwegian-owned Reg Oslo.	
9/7/31	ss *SAN MACEDONIO*	3613	Mexico	See 10/9/29.		
28/8/31	ss *DAGHESTAN*	3532	Constanza [3]	1921 Short Bros Sund	Common Bros.	
14/10/31	ss *SAN EDUARDO*	3959	Aruba	See 16/12/30.		
4/11/31	mv *SCOTTISH MUSICIAN*	4019	Mexico	1922 Vickers Barrow	Tankers Ltd London.	
11/1/32	ss *VARAND*	3681	Constanza	1927 Armstrong W/worth	Baltic Trading Co Lon.	
514/32	ss *WILLY*	3465	N Orleans	1916 at Wilmington Delaware		
16/7/32	ss *DAGHESTAN*	3532	N Orleans	See 28/8/31.		
2/12/32	ss *RADIX* [2]	4082	Curacoa	1919 gen cargo		
20/1/33	ss *MUREX*	8887[1]	Curacoa	See 6/3/28.		
18/4/33	ss *GUNDINE*	3575	Curacoa	1921 Bethlehem S B Corp. Maryland	Norwegian.	
7/6/33	ss *MYTILUS*	3421	Curacoa	1916 Swan Hunter Sunderland	Norwegian/reg Arendal	
29/8/33	ss *PETRICOLA*		Curacoa			
30/9/33	ss *MYTILUS*	3421	Curacoa	See 6/6/33.		
7/11/33	ss *MUREX*		Curacoa	See 6/3/28		

and August 1939. Coincidentally she was managed by the Van Ommeren shipping group of Rotterdam.

Another visitor in the late twenties and thirties was the ss *LUNULA*, registered at Liverpool and completed at Port Glasgow in 1927 for the Aral S.S. Co. Ltd (H.E. Moss & Co). The same company's *LUMINETTA* and *LUMINOUS* also berthed from Abadan or Tampico via Shellhaven. *LUNULA* was central to a wartime disaster on 9th April 1941 when coming alongside at Shell Haven with 8,000 tons of petroleum spirit. Someone had reported a mine close to the berth, so she moved on the short distance to Thameshaven. *LUNULA* probably had a line ashore, as one of her tugs had left and the other, Watkins' *PERSIA*, was standing by her stern when a mine, apparently hidden between the piles of the jetty, exploded. The ship's back was broken in the explosion and flames estimated at 100 yards high surrounded the crippled ship. None of the crew of the tanker or of the tugs survived, and petrol spilled into the river, literally setting the Thames on fire. It was said the fire lasted for ninety-seven hours or more. Adjoining wharves and buildings were set alight and desperate efforts were made to close off pipelines and tanks ashore. The ship was later raised and taken away for breaking up.

The Eagle Oil Transport Company

Founded in 1912, the company operated ships conveying oil produced by the Mexican Eagle Oil Company to Europe and especially to Great Britain; the ships were named after saints in the Mexican calendar. In 1919 the company's founder Lord Cowdray entered into an agreement with Royal Dutch Shell, who took over the management of the company. In 1930 the name changed to Eagle Oil & Shipping Co. Ltd, and in 1952 it became the Eagle Tanker Company Ltd. The Royal Dutch Shell Group acquired the company outright in July 1959 and their tanker fleets integrated. At least fourteen Eagle Oil tankers brought refined petroleum products to Ipswich, principally from Mexico.

The Anglo-Saxon Petroleum Company

Following the reorganisation of Shell in 1908, Royal Dutch Shell and the Shell Transport & Trading Company became holding companies of the new Anglo-Saxon Petroleum Company, formed to transport and store products for the whole group, including the Dutch tanker fleet. The ships were commonly regarded as Shell owned, but not until 1953 did the group register a new company, Shell Tankers Limited, to manage Anglo-Saxon ships. Two years later Shell Petroleum Company bought out Anglo-Saxon's assets, though leaving Shell Tankers Ltd to manage the ships. Change came once again in 1964 when Shell Tankers was divided into Shell International Marine Ltd and Shell Tankers (UK) Ltd, remaining so into the 1990s.

Passengers & yachting 13

Before the introduction of the first primitive steamers on the Orwell, passenger traffic was largely confined to the small two-masted wherries which ran a service between Ipswich and Harwich, probably using oars in calms and aided by the ebb tide to Harwich and the flood for the return journey, day or night. Surprisingly a few primitive paddle steamers worked briefly on the Orwell quite early in the nineteenth century: in August 1815 the first paddle steamer *ORWELL* plied for just five weeks between Ipswich and Harwich. The intention had been to carry up to 200 passengers, plus goods and parcels daily, Mondays to Saturdays, during the summer months, but the service ended prematurely and was not resumed the following year.

Three prominent Ipswich businessmen, merchant F.F. Seekamp, banker Dykes Alexander and shipbuilder George Bayley, established the Ipswich Steam Navigation Company in 1824 and ordered two steamships in October 1824. The first vessel was the paddle steamer *IPSWICH*, launched on 12th September 1825 at George Bayley's St Peter's yard, which began a service to London on 14th April 1826. She was joined by paddle steamer *SUFFOLK* in September 1826, but for seven weeks only, during which period the *IPSWICH* did not run. *SUFFOLK* alone was used in 1827. Passengers were few, however, and both vessels were offered for sale by auction in London in April 1828.

Another paddle steamer *ORWELL*, launched in 1839 at Blackwall on the Thames, became familiar on her regular voyages to and from London, usually calling at Harwich and Walton-on-the-Naze. Her master for many years was Captain S. Rackham. She was owned by the Ipswich Steam Navigation Company whose office was adjacent to Stoke Bridge; passengers embarked at Flint Wharf Stairs, situated just downstream on the east bank of the New Cut. The *ORWELL* was purchased in 1853 by Alfred Cobbold, a director of the Eastern Union Railway (EUR), the first railway to serve Ipswich, when the Ipswich Steam Navigation Co. was in liquidation. The *ORWELL* and the Ipswich-built *ORION*, which sailed to London on alternate days from St Peters Dock, together with their few contemporaries, offered alternative travel to the stage and mail coaches to the capital, and they continued after the railway had linked Colchester with London in 1843. Even after the Eastern Union had opened their line from Ipswich to Colchester in 1846 some passengers still appreciated the voyage of some seven hours (only four hours at sea) in preference to the long and sometimes fraught journey by train all the way to London in those days. The vessels went up the Thames to Blackwall for passengers to join the London and Blackwall broad-gauge cable railway, which had opened in 1840 to the City. Fenchurch Street Station became its terminus a year later. In a way this marked the beginning of an association between the River Orwell and the railway companies that was to last until 1930.

Peter Bruff, engineer to the EUR, purchased the *PRINCE ALBERT* in 1853, she had been built at Walker-on-Tyne in 1842. Bruff had a year earlier bought some coastal paddle steamers from various owners, including the *ORION* of 1841 and the *PEARL*, new from a Blackwall yard in 1835. Other smaller vessels

Opposite page: Edwardian yachtmen on the Orwell.

better suited for the Ipswich-Harwich service were the *RIVER QUEEN* of 1839, *PRINCE*, Ipswich-built in 1852, *CARDINAL WOLSEY*, built 1845, and *ATALANTA*, built at Deptford in 1841. All were purchased by either Peter Bruff or Alfred Cobbold for Eastern Union services using Griffin Wharf, and most were sold on to the Eastern Counties Railway in 1854 when that company absorbed the Eastern Union.

In 1850 the *ORWELL* made about eighty-one London voyages, plus a few excursions. The trade became much more popular during the 1850s and the *ORWELL* is recorded with the same number of voyages in 1853. In addition that year there were the EUR Directors' new acquisitions; the *PEARL* that completed seventy voyages with a couple of excursions and *ORION* with twenty-six voyages. *PRINCE ALBERT* managed fifty-five voyages between 14th June and 8th October. On 1st September 1854 the *ORWELL* made a day excursion to Dunkirk that was repeated on the 13th, although bad weather on that occasion forced her to return light on the 15th, her passengers possibly having returned by way of Dover and the railway. These early steamers were laid up annually at Ipswich for periods varying from three to five and a half months.

Steamship business on the Thames meanwhile had flourished as companies mushroomed. 'Trade wars' on the river became common and racing caused many accidents as tens of thousands of passengers were carried to work and on weekend excursions. However, the coming of the railways into Kent (especially to Gravesend) and also to the Essex shore captured an enormous number of the regular travellers, and with new regulations being introduced, many steamship businesses began to go under and their boats were sold off. The Thames Steamboat Company operated between Hungerford Market wharf, close to Charing Cross, and Gravesend. Two of their ships, *SONS OF THE THAMES* and *FATHER THAMES*, were launched in 1844 but were withdrawn the following year. The latter vessel was taken over by the Diamond Steam Packet Company. Both were working to Ipswich in 1858, *SONS OF THE THAMES* making at least twenty voyages during May and June, and *FATHER THAMES* sailing on eight occasions in July. Captain Rackham is noted as master of both craft. The *LADY ELIZABETH*, a small steamer of which little is known, sailed on 5th September with an excursion to Aldeburgh and another on the 17th to Woodbridge. A Mr Dorling of Ipswich began operating pleasure steamers on the Orwell in May 1857, they were *ALMA I* and *ALMA II*. The service lasted until October 1867.

In 1862 two new vessels belonging to the Woolwich Steam Packet Company,

The paddle steamer ORWELL *of 1839 and other shipping below Ipswich, with the steamer* RIVER QUEEN *on the extreme right. Both vessels were acquired for the Eastern Union Railway's service.*

QUEEN OF THE THAMES, built at Woolwich 1861, and QUEEN OF THE ORWELL, launched at Govan in 1862 (both Ipswich registered for some reason), operated a daily service, Sundays excepted, to Ipswich, leaving London Bridge at 9.30 am and calling at Blackwall, North Woolwich, Tilbury, Clacton, Walton, Harwich and Felixstowe.

The two ships were still serving Ipswich in 1870, when the QUEEN OF THE THAMES made five voyages in May, eight trips in June, thirteen in July, twelve in August and six in September. QUEEN OF THE ORWELL arrived twice in late August and fourteen times in September. They were joined in July by the same company's OREAD, launched at Rotherhithe in 1854, which made ten voyages in July and twelve in August. The Woolwich Steam Packet Company's PETREL and DORIS each made one trip in August. The company was taken over in 1875 by the London Steamboat Company, which purchased the GLEN ROSA in 1883 from the associated Thames & Channel Steamship Company that had owned her since 1881. She had been built at Greenock in 1877 for Clyde owners and had come into Ipswich Dock in July 1881, chartered to carry the great and the good to celebrate the opening of the new entrance lock. Many of her passengers, including the President of the Board of Trade, the Rt. Hon. Joseph Chamberlain, had arrived by special train from London for a day of official ceremonies that also included the opening of the Ipswich Museum and the General Post Office.

By that time the once-vast passenger trade on the Thames had gone into decline, depleted by further extensions to the railways, including the electrified District Line, and fierce competition from the omnibus companies. QUEEN OF THE THAMES was still sailing between London and Ipswich in the summer of 1883, but most of the steamship companies had been finding it difficult to keep going. The London Steamboat Company closed in 1884.

The paddle steamer GLEN ROSA *enters the new lock on 27th July 1881 with the President of the Board of Trade and other notables on board celebrating the inauguration of the improved entrance to the Dock.*

The Great Eastern Railway paddle steamer NORFOLK, *built on the Thames in 1882, setting off for Harwich with the helmsman high up on the rudimentary bridge abaft the funnel. At the extreme left can be seen a three-masted schooner on the slip of the Cliff shipyard. (Robert Malster collection)*

The first Great Eastern Railway (GER) paddle steamer for excursion work from Ipswich, yet another *ORWELL*, was built in 1873 on the Thames. The same company's first *NORFOLK*, launched in 1882, also on the Thames, was used for regular summer work to and from Harwich and the GER Felixstowe Pier, adjacent to Felixstowe Dock entrance in Harwich Harbour. By July 1885 *NORFOLK* was also voyaging to Clacton. In 1888, *GLEN ROSA* returned to make twenty-four trips. In the interim, she had worked seasons from Ramsgate to Calais, Boulogne and Dunkirk, and on the East Coast to Clacton and Yarmouth after her first appearance at Ipswich. *QUEEN OF THE ORWELL* reappeared in September and in the same year the *ALEXANDRA*, built at Port Glasgow in 1865 for the Woolwich Steam Packet Company, arrived four times in the August. Another GER paddler, the *STOUR*, a sister to their *ORWELL* and built in 1878, began with a sea trip to Orfordness via Harwich Pier on 4th September that year and offered sea trips from Ipswich in the 1880s. An interloper appeared in July 1892 in the shape of the *MERRIMAC*, a 91ft-long iron paddle tug/excursion steamship built at North Shields in 1883 for Bristol owners but purchased by R. & W. Paul Ltd for salvage work out of Harwich. In her first season in 1892 she managed seventy-five trips to Clacton, Brightlingsea and Aldeburgh and short sea trips. She was also used to tow the Walton and Harwich lifeboats to wrecks and to stand by them. On 27th August 1906 *MERRIMAC* sailed to Liverpool to become a towed barge under new owners.

What was remarkable, considering the plight of the Thames steamboat owners, was that by the end of the century the summer trade to the East Coast was flourishing. The General Steam Navigation Company, founded in 1824, had already established their London to Great Yarmouth services and 1890 saw the formation of the parent companies of the well-known Belle Steamers. The *WOOLWICH BELLE*, launched on the Clyde in April 1891, opened their services from Ipswich in 1894 to Harwich, Felixstowe and Clacton, by arrangement with the GER for the use of the railway-owned piers. The vessel quickly became a popular ship on the Orwell, berthing at Ipswich for the first time on 27th April and making at least 173 trips from a long floating stage, extending from the lock entrance, between May and September before sailing for winter lay-up and refit. She was joined at Ipswich on 27th May by Belle

Steamer's coal hulk *WOLFS COVE*, formerly a 126ft wooden barque of 626nrt built at Quebec in 1831. (Wolfes Cove was a small settlement from which General Wolfe launched his assault on Quebec in 1759.) By the 1880s she was owned by H. Faucus, of Newcastle, in the coal trade. The hulk was usually towed away out of season and was topped up with coal by sailing barges. She was eventually broken up after seventy years' service in November 1901.

In 1895 the first of three paddle steamers ordered by the GER to operate from Ipswich was launched by Earle's of Hull. She was the *SUFFOLK*, double-ended with perpendicular twin funnels and masts. She was joined the next year by the *ESSEX*, built by Earle's on similar lines but slightly larger, and then in 1900 the last paddler to be constructed for the GER was launched from Gourlay Brothers' yard at Dundee. She was the second *NORFOLK*, the first having been sold in 1897. She had only one funnel and was ten feet longer than the *ESSEX* at 184 feet. These three were dedicated to the very popular Ipswich services to Harwich and Felixstowe, with evening sea trips competing with the *WOOLWICH BELLE*.

The *SUFFOLK* first appeared at Ipswich on 28th April 1896, sailing with passengers on 1st May, *WOOLWICH BELLE* arriving three weeks later. *SUFFOLK*'s next season in 1897 ran from 15th June until 9th September. She was joined on 29th May by the *WOOLWICH BELLE* and her 'support vessel' *WOLFS COVE*, plus the sailing barge *AUGUSTA MARY* with coal. The *WOOLWICH BELLE* frequently worked to Clacton, often connecting with a Belle steamer from London. The new *ESSEX* appeared on 31st May 1897. In 1900 the *NORFOLK* arrived on 12th June to complete the trio of railway steamers. *WOOLWICH BELLE* berthed on 1st June. Unusually, two more

The later Great Eastern Railway steamer ESSEX, *built of steel at Hull in 1896, at her moorings on Griffin Wharf*

The decorative cover of the 1927 Belle Steamers guide, which cost just one penny.

'*BELLES*' arrived at Ipswich on the 3rd and 4th of September, the *YARMOUTH BELLE* and the *SOUTHWOLD BELLE*, both from London, each calling here another four and five times respectively within the next ten days.

The four resident paddlers came year in, year out with few alterations until 1913, although the *WOOLWICH BELLE* offered some day trips to Margate in 1907. The *ESSEX* was sold in December 1913, and with war imminent services were curtailed at the end of July 1914 for the *NORFOLK*, *SUFFOLK* and *WOOLWICH BELLE*. The *SUFFOLK* and *NORFOLK* frequently came to Ipswich from Harwich with personnel and stores.

PASSENGERS & YACHTING

The WOOLWICH BELLE in the New Cut at Ipswich, seen in a postcard issued in the first decade of the twentieth century. (Robert Malster collection)

After the First World War, NORFOLK and SUFFOLK carried on. To illustrate the brief but intensive passenger services on the river, in 1923 when the London & North Eastern Railway absorbed the GER, the details are as follows: the NORFOLK (Captain Morton) began the season on 12th May and ended on 29th September, having completed 324 round trips; SUFFOLK (Captain Tyrell) started on 14th May, finishing on 15th September, with a total of 284 trips, sometimes doing as many as five round trips a day.

Unfortunately, the railway service ended in 1930. NORFOLK's season began on 27th May that year and ended on 28th September, SUFFOLK sailing with her first passengers on 29th May and making her final trip on 14th September. SUFFOLK departed for Rotterdam, probably under tow, for breaking up on 2nd May 1931. The NORFOLK sailed to Stockton-on-Tees on 20th December 1932 and was sold to Scottish owners, but there is no evidence of her being in service again.

The WOOLWICH BELLE was refitted in 1922 by Dennys of Dumbarton, who actually bought the ship. Afterwards she was sold on to Channel Excursions Ltd of Brighton and renamed QUEEN OF THE SOUTH. Her South Coast days were limited and in 1924 she was sold to the New Medway Steam Packet Company to continue on the East Coast for a while at Yarmouth. In 1932, the old WOOLWICH BELLE, later QUEEN OF THE SOUTH, was broken up at Thomas Ward's yard at Grays.

Seen taking in passengers at Harwich, the WOOLWICH BELLE acted as a feeder ship linking Ipswich with the Belle Steamers services between London and Yarmouth. (Robert Malster collection)

The Nineteen Thirties

The New Medway Steam Packet Company had been incorporated in 1919 to take over and operate vessels owned by the Medway Steam Packet Company, including the paddler CITY OF ROCHESTER (built 1904) and the twin screw CITY BELLE (built 1917); the company renamed the latter vessel ROCHESTER CITY BELLE. On 20th June 1931 they introduced at Ipswich the paddle steamer CITY OF ROCHESTER for sailings to Clacton and sea trips until 21st September; she had been built at Kinghorn in Scotland in 1904. The LNER incidentally sent their Felixstowe-Harwich motor ferry BRIGHTLINGSEA on at least one excursion to Pin Mill with a capacity crowd of 150 passengers.

In 1932 CITY OF ROCHESTER and ROCHESTER CITY BELLE arrived at Ipswich on 10th June and adopted various routines, which for example over two days in June may be shown thus:

Day 1. CITY OF ROCHESTER departs Ipswich-Clacton-Ipswich-Cork light vessel-Ipswich.
ROCHESTER CITY BELLE departs Ipswich-Harwich-Ipswich-Harwich-Ipswich
Day 2. CITY OF ROCHESTER departs Ipswich-Cork light vessel-Ipswich-Clacton-Ipswich.
ROCHESTER CITY BELLE departs Ipswich-Harwich-Ipswich-Harwich-Ipswich

There were also day trips to Clacton and Southend, and ROCHESTER CITY BELLE called at Felixstowe too. Both vessels returned to Rochester on 9th September.

The BRIGHTLINGSEA also brought passengers into the Orwell in season from Harwich and Felixstowe. The following year, 1933, only CITY OF ROCHESTER

Having passed to the London & North Eastern Railway at the grouping in 1923, the SUFFOLK *is seen setting off from the New Cut.*

spent the season at Ipswich from 17th June to 8th September, and included trips to Clacton and Southend, with evening trips to the Cork lightship. An ancient paddle steamer appeared on the river on 1st June 1934; built at Southampton in 1897 as the *DUCHESS OF KENT* for the Isle of Wight services of the London Brighton & South Coast Railway, she was purchased by the New Medway Steam Packet Company in 1934 and renamed *CLACTON QUEEN* for the season at Ipswich. She completed some 15 trips to Harwich, 71 to Clacton and a few round the Cork lightship before returning to the Medway on 10th September.

ROCHESTER CITY BELLE worked from 10th June to 12th September 1937. Thereafter the *CITY OF ROCHESTER* returned and did 69 trips to Clacton from 8th July to 21st September 1938. She came back to the Orwell on 1st July 1939 and completed about 25 Clacton trips before returning to the Medway on the outbreak of war. The *CITY OF ROCHESTER* was seriously damaged by aircraft bombing in the Medway in 1941 and scrapped. It was the end of an era.

Post-war services

In July 1947 the railway-owned mv *BRIGHTLINGSEA* returned to Ipswich to run occasional river trips from New Cut West, and she came back in June 1948 with the *HAINAULT*, one of the Harwich to Shotley railway-owned ferries. Meanwhile an open launch named *ORWELL QUEEN* began a series of two or three trips a day from the New Cut, some to Felixstowe Dock. In that same year another motor vessel, the *MERRY GOLDEN HIND*, registered at Dover, sailed from New Cut during July, August and September. Nothing else is known about her.

The mv *TORBAY PRINCE* appeared from Dartmouth on 10th April 1949. She was only two years old and owned by the Devon Star Shipping Company, for whom she normally worked with the Western Lady Ferry Service in the Torquay and Brixham area. The latter company operated five ships including *RIVER LADY*, which arrived at Ipswich on 27th May 1949 to begin a long association of that name with the River Orwell. She was a typical wooden naval motor launch of the Fairmile B class, completed by Thornycroft in 1941. She appears in Lloyd's Register of 1950 already registered at Ipswich. She was joined in 1950 by a similar vessel, the *RIVER LADY II*, both running river trips from the end of June. One of them continued operating cruises until at least 1961, but by then the attraction of river trips had waned considerably and the service probably ended in that year.

British Railways closed the Harwich-Felixstowe-Shotley ferry service in 1960 and *BRIGHTLINGSEA* was sold for further work in the harbour. She was offered for sale again in the late 1970s, going to Captain Alan Pridmore, a tugmaster, who used her for the Felixstowe service combined with river trips. In 1982 she made some public cruises on the Orwell from Ipswich, and in November and December 1990 a few Christmas shopping excursions to Ipswich from Harwich were arranged in connection with Ipswich Buses. There was very little demand, however, and the vessel was put up for sale; unfortunately she has not operated since. *BRIGHTLINGSEA* was built at Rowhedge in 1925 for the LNER.

For four seasons in the early 1990s the 40ft motor launch *PINMILL* operated two-hour trips from the Harbour Master's Steps on New Cut East, depending on the tide. She had been completed at the Dan Marine Yard close to Cobbold's brewery in 1910 as a typical open passenger launch of the period, fitted with a Dan two-cylinder paraffin engine. In 1912 the GER obtained the ferry rights for

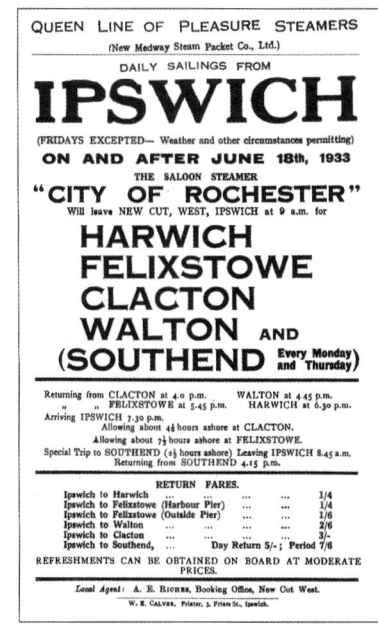

An advertisement for the Queen Line ship CITY OF ROCHESTER *for the 1933 season. A special excursion was run to Southend on Mondays and Thursdays, allowing $2^{1}/_{2}$ hours ashore in the Essex resort.*

The mv BALMORAL approaching the Orwell Bridge in September 1991.

The motor launch PIN MILL after being acquired by four members of the Ipswich Maritime Trust.

the Felixstowe-Harwich-Shotley services from the Marquess of Bristol, for which they acquired the *PINMILL*. She was retained as a ferry until joined by the new Rowhedge-built *BRIGHTLLNGSEA* in 1925, when she became a workboat/relief ferry. In this capacity she remained until 1988, when the railway passenger fleet was disposed of after privatisation and *PINMILL* was no longer of use. She was laid up at Parkeston Quay and bought by four members of the Ipswich Maritime Trust, who renovated her to carry twelve passengers on popular river trips from Ipswich. Due to an event beyond the control of her owners or the Port Authority she was laid up ashore in her ninetieth year. Ownership was transferred to the Ipswich Maritime Trust, who eventually sold her for a nominal sum to undergo restoration at Faversham, hopefully in time for her centenary. Probably the vessel will afterwards be used in the West Country rather than on the Orwell.

The *PINMILL* had been joined in 1915 on the ferry service by the GER motor boats *EPPING* and *HAINAULT*, both built in that year by Vospers at Portsmouth. They served until the mid-1950s and were also used for river trips from Harwich, sometimes bringing passengers up to New Cut West for disembarking. They were also hired to carry dockers from the Dock to Buttermans Bay to discharge ships moored there.

Many Ipswich people were delighted to see the return of a pleasure steamer in 1988 when the Paddle Steamer Preservation Society initially scheduled their screw motor ship *BALMORAL* to berth at Cliff Quay on the 2nd and 3rd of May for two cruises for schoolchildren and an evening cruise for the public. She is a passenger vessel launched from Thornycroft's yard at Southampton in 1949 for the Isle of Wight ferry service, having a small car deck. On 25th September 1989 the last sea-going paddle steamer in the world, the *WAVERLEY*, arrived for a public cruise to Clacton, an evening estuary trip, and a cruise to London on the following day. Clyde-built in 1947 for the LNER's services on the Clyde, she was taken over by the British Transport Commission on Nationalisation in 1948.

Since their first visits the two ships have annually worked their way round the British coastline earning money for the society and visiting Ipswich regularly in spring and autumn, providing river and sea trips, usually including passages to London that have proved extremely popular. Cliff Quay and the former power station coal berth have been used for the two vessels, with passengers taken direct to board the ships by Ipswich Buses from the town centre. However, these berths are no longer available and the *BALMORAL* uses Orwell Quay within the Dock. As the *WAVERLEY* is too beamy to pass through the lock, her Orwell trips now start and finish at Harwich.

Passengers can also enjoy trips on the local river during the 21st century aboard a newcomer to Ipswich, the *ORWELL LADY*. Regular cruises are operated between April and September to Harwich Harbour or Pin Mill, in addition to various seasonal and special theme nights.

On the Quayside

We have already noted that the early passenger vessels loaded at Flint Wharf Stairs in the New Cut and Griffin Wharf at the entrance to the Cut. The Great Eastern Railway, incorporated in 1862, rented landing stages on the east side close to the original lock for the use of their steamers, and a series of landing stages were later erected along the western side of the Cut from Felaw Street to Bath Street at the ends of which cab ranks were put in for the horse cabs to wait for returning passengers. The Corporation electric tramway opened its through route from Whitton to Bourne Bridge, with a branch down Bath Street to serve the steamers, in November 1903. The branch was used only when the GER paddle steamers were operating, and on fine summer days until 1914 as many

The paddle steamer WAVERLEY berthed at the power station quay during a visit to Ipswich in 1990.

as three tramcars would wait at the bottom of Bath Street for the last boats to return. Their passengers would be conveyed to various parts of the town including the railway station, from where passengers from as far as Bury St Edmunds could get home by train.

These stages became home to the railway steamers and the New Medway Steam Packet Company in the 1930s, one remaining until the 1960s used by the *RIVER LADY*. The structures have disintegrated since then and small craft like the *BRIGHTLINGSEA* have used the Harbour Master's Steps—in fact a ramp leading into the mud outside the old lock entrance and the former Harbour Master's Office, and accessible within about two hours either side of high water.

Space for a ticket office throughout the 1920s was charged by the IDC at four guineas per annum. Charges were naturally raised against labour for loading of coal and supplying water to the vessels. During the year April 1920-March 1921 the *NORFOLK* and *SUFFOLK* were supplied with 916½ tons of coal in total. The GER had a coal yard for the steamers, with a rail siding in Bright Street off New Cut West. The *NORFOLK* was supplied with 79,700 gallons of water and *SUFFOLK* received 103,200, at the rate of eight shillings per 1,000 gallons. The *HAINAULT* had 1,000 gallons in the same period.

From 1931 the New Medway Steam Packet Company of 365 High Street, Rochester, paid rent for the ticket office space at the same annual rate of four guineas. The company continued to pay these charges throughout the Second World War, possibly anticipating their return, but it never happened. Instead, the owners of the *RIVER LADY*, who in 1955-56 were the River Orwell Cruising & Ferry Service of Wembley, were charged £15 quarterly rent for Stage No.2, plus fourteen shillings a year fire insurance.

The Reserve Fleet laid up in the Stour was one of the attractions offered in this advertisement for the RIVER LADY in the early post-war years. The local agent for the owners, the Devon Star Shipping Company, was E.W. Howe of the Steamboat Tavern, New Cut West.

Last year's Popular and Comfortable Twin-Screw Cruising Vessel.

'RIVER LADY'

Licensed by Ministry of Transport to carry 230 passengers

IPSWICH—FELIXSTOWE Service

Sailing every **Wednesday** and **Sunday.**

Depart IPSWICH	a.m.	p.m	Depart FELIXSTOWE	a.m.	p.m.
(New Cut West)	10.30	5.30	(Sea Front)	11.30	6.30
Arrive FELIXSTOWE			(Dock)	11.45	6.45
(Dock)	11.35	6.35	Arrive IPSWICH		
(Sea Front)	11.45	6.45	(New Cut West)	12.50	7.50

Special Buses convey passengers without extra charge between Felixstowe Dock and Sea Front.

SINGLE 2/- CHILDREN 1/-   FARES   RETURN 3/6 CHILDREN 2/-   To Felixstowe Dock and back NON-LANDING Fare 3/-. Children 1/6

RIVER AND SHORT SEA CRUISES from IPSWICH.

SAILING: TUES., WED., SAT., and SUNDAYS. (NEW CUT WEST). Viewing the Delightful RIVER ORWELL, also PARKESTON QUAY, and the RESERVE FLEET off HARWICH.

Depart: 2.30 p.m.   Return: 5.15 p.m.   FARES: 4/- CHILDREN 2/-

For further details and special terms for parties (25 upwards), also ADVANCE BOOKINGS, apply:
IPSWICH: Booking Office, New Cut West ('Phone Ipswich 51838), or Stratfords, 27, St. Matthew's Street.
FELIXSTOWE: Clarke's Booking Office, Sea Front.
Local Agent: E. W Howe, Steamboat Tavern, New Cut West, Ipswich.

Devon Star Shipping Co., Ltd., London, Torquay and Ipswich

Yachting on the Orwell

Gentlemen's yachts were sailed for pleasure on the Orwell during the mid-nineteenth century, some being laid up in the Dock for autumn and winter. As sailing slowly came within reach of a wider populace a number of yacht or sailing clubs were formed, one of these being known as the Orwell Yacht Club.

Although an earlier Orwell Yacht Club had existed in the nineteenth century, the present club of that name was established in 1918 in Ostrich Creek and has since gone from strength to strength on the same site. Stoke Sailing Club was formed in 1935 on a site adjacent to the old Stoke Bathing Place and had to move to its present site at Slumpy Lane Wharf, Freston, in 1972 when the area it had occupied was needed for the West Bank development. Pin Mill Sailing Club was also formed in 1935 and for a time its headquarters was in the ex-sailing barge *FLORENCE* berthed on the foreshore at Pin Mill. The club later moved to a clubhouse upstream of the Butt and Oyster. The club has for many years arranged the annual Orwell barge match.

In the 1960s a modern yacht marina known as the Suffolk Yacht Harbour was dredged out of what had once been drained and embanked land at Stratton Hall, Levington. It was equipped with floating pontoons enabling yachtsmen to board their craft at any state of the tide and had all the modern facilities of a slipway, workshops, chandlery and washrooms, etc. The Haven Ports Yacht Club was set up, based at the Marina, with its headquarters aboard a former lightship.

The Royal Harwich Yacht Club had meanwhile pioneered the establishment of 'real' yachting, bringing together people from Harwich, Ipswich and the Deben who had organised local regattas and yacht races since the end of the

The mv RIVER LADY, *a former Royal Navy Fairmile B type motor launch built in 1941, at her moorings in the New Cut. In the background are the kilns of Pauls' maltings at the bottom of Felaw Street.*

One of Cranfield's lighters, converted into a floating clubhouse for the Stoke Sailing Club, is towed out of Ipswich Dock on the way to Freston in 1972.

eighteenth century. The club was formed in 1844 with its headquarters in Harwich, and remained there until moving to Woolverstone in 1946. The 1970s saw the development of Woolverstone Marina upstream of the shared Cat House Hard referred to in other chapters.

Ipswich Haven Marina now occupies much of the Wet Dock at Ipswich, with pontoon berthing and facilities for yachts.

The great days of the 'Big Class' yacht racing towards the end of the nineteenth century saw the Prince of Wales's *BRITANNIA*, the German Emperor's *METEOR*, Sir Thomas Lipton's 23-metre *SHAMROCK*, Mr Kennedy's *WHITE HEATHER* and the 19-metre *MARIQUITA* all competing in the Royal Harwich Regattas until 1914. Later, the introduction of the J Class America's Cup challengers like *SHAMROCK V*, *ENDEAVOUR*, *ASTRA*, *CANDIDA* and *VELSHEDA* brought about great public interest for the first time, due to newspaper coverage and striking photography. The J Class yachts visited Harwich for the last time in 1936. These yachts moored within the harbour but never came to Ipswich, although some of their illustrious predecessors, the elegant Victorian and Edwardian steam yachts, did visit the port.

Among these in the late 1880s was the 186ft *THISTLE*, registered at London, an iron screw three-masted schooner built and engined by Blackwood & Gordon of Glasgow in 1881, with sails by Lapthorn & Ratsey. Owned by the Duke of Hamilton, of Brodick Castle, Buteshire, and Easton Park, Suffolk, she arrived at Ipswich at least four times in June and July 1887, twice from Boulogne and twice from Amsterdam under Captain Kerr. She visited Ipswich several times in 1889 between 22nd June (from Cowes) and the end of August, sailing to and from Calais, Amsterdam, Trouville and Boulogne.

Three steam yachts berthed in 1901 including the 146ft steel screw schooner *SUNFLOWER*. Registered at Southampton, she was launched and engined there in 1898 by Day & Summers, with sails by Beaton. Her owner was Sir E. Walter Greene, Bart., of Nether Hall, Bury St Edmunds, and she arrived from Southampton under Captain Powell. The next to arrive was *EUPHROSYNE* of Cowes (Captain Parnell), a 131ft wooden screw schooner completed by Camper

& Nicholson at Gosport in 1889, with engine by Thompson & Co. of Dundee and sails by Lapthorn & Ratsey. The third to come was *FINGAL* (ex-*LANCASHIRE WITCH*) of Glasgow, an iron screw schooner built in 1872 by Laird Brothers of Birkenhead, who were also responsible for her engine. Her master was Captain Turner and she was owned at the time by Bunnell H. Burton, of Broad Oak, Ipswich (see Burtons, General Cargoes chapter).

MORNA (ex-*FINGAL*, ex-*LANCASHIRE WITCH*) berthed in 1903, bearing her third name since she was laid down in 1872 and her second since arriving in Ipswich in 1901 as *FINGAL*. The *SUNFLOWER* also called in 1903, as did sy *ILIONA* (ex-*CASSANDRA*), another steel screw schooner, l04ft in length, built by the Culzean Shipbuilding & Engineering Co. Ltd of Culzean, Ayrshire, and engined by Kincaid of Greenock, with sails from Fergusons.

In 1908 the *AGATHA* (Captain Knox) steamed in. She was owned by Sir E. Walter Greene, Bart., the former owner in 1901 of sy *SUNFLOWER*, which had since been sold and renamed *GARLAND*. The *AGATHA* (164ft) of Southampton was schooner rigged but had twin screws and been launched, engined and equipped with electric light by Day & Summers at Southampton in 1905.

Ipswich was never on the popular list of ports at which wealthy yachtsmen would wish to call, and so visits were few and far between. These vessels normally frequented the Solent or Clyde, not to mention the coast of France, but at least three of these yachts, all very much a part of the period, were owned by men with Suffolk addresses and associations. Many steam yachts were laid up at Brightlingsea, Wivenhoe or Rowhedge, where the *SUNFLOWER* had her winter berth.

A yarn that became popular within the fraternity told of one of the steam yachts whose owner had connections with a Suffolk estate and enjoyed a little yachting on the 'other side' and a little steam barge that had a habit of snuggling up to the counter stern of the yacht, allowing various barrel-shaped items to be lowered to her deck before she set off with her usual general cargo for a nearby estuary port. An estuary port, moreover, that was hardly a night's horse and trap ride from the big house! Probably nothing in it!

A painting showing a large steam yacht lying off the dock entrance. The accommodation ladder is rigged to enable the owner to go ashore and guests to come on board.

Sub.	Year, no. of visits to Ipswich					Builder / Date	Remarks
	1914	1915	1916	1917	1918		
C 3				1		Vickers 1906	Blown up Zeebrugge Mole 23 April 1918.
C 21				1		Vickers 1908	
D 1		1				Vickers 1908	Sunk as a target 1918
D 3			1			Vickers 1910	Sunk 15 March 1918 in English Channel by French airship in mistake for enemy sub.
D 4		1				Vickers 1911	First to carry a gun on deck.
D 6		2	1			Vickers 1911	Sunk off N. Ireland by U-boat 28 June 1918.
D 7		1				Chatham DY 1911	
D 8		2				Chatham DY 1911	
E 2		1				Chatham DY 1912	
E 4		1	1		2	Vickers 1912	
E 5		1				Vickers 1912	Lost North Sea 7 March 1916. Cause unknown.
E 7		2				Chatham DY 1913	Sunk by enemy, Dardenelles 4 September 1915.
E 8		1				Chatham DY 1913	First sub. out of Harwich, 6.30 am on 5 August 1914 with E6 and Harwich Force. Scuttled at Helsingfors to avoid capture 4 April 1918.
E 10	2					Vickers 1913	Hit German mine while patrolling with E 5 and lost off Heligoland 18 January 1915. All 31 men aboard vessel, commanded by Lt Cdr William St J. Fraser from Harwich, perished. Wreckage not found until 2002 and now designated a war grave.
E 12		1				Chatham DY 1914	
E 13		1				Chatham DY 1914	Damaged by German destroyers' gunfire while stranded Saltholm 18 August 1915. Interned at Copenhagen 3 Sept. 1915. Sold to Danish shipbreakers in March 1919.
E 22			2			Vickers 1915	Fitted briefly with ramps for launching 2 seaplanes but too vulnerable when launching. Sunk by U-boat North Sea 25 April 1916.
E 23			2			Vickers 1915	
E 26			1			Beardmore 1915	Lost North Sea 6 July 1916.
E 29		1	1	2		Armstrong 1915	
E 31			1		1	Scots 1915	
E 33				1		Thornycroft 1916	
E 35			2			J. Brown 1916	
E 37			3			Fairfield 1915	Lost North Sea 1 December 1916. Cause unknown.
E 38			1			Fairfield 1916	
E 41			1	1		Cammell Laird 1915	
E 42			1		2	Cammell Laird 1915	
E 45				1	1	Cammell Laird 1916	
E 47			1	1		Fairfield 1916	Lost North Sea 20 August 1917. Cause unknown.
E 51				2		Scotts 1916	Minelayer.
E 55			1			Denny 1916	
E 56			1	1		Denny 1916	
F 1			1			Chatham DY 1913	
F 3			2			Thornycroft 1916	
G 8			1			Vickers 1916	Lost North Sea 14 January 1918. Cause unknown.
H 5		1				Canadian Vickers 1915	Sunk in Irish Sea by collision 6 March 1918.
H 7			1	1		Canadian Vickers 1915	
H 9			1			Canadian Vickers 1915	
H 10			1	1		Canadian Vickers 1915	Lost North Sea 19 January 1918. Cause unknown.
H 25					1	Vickers 1918	
H 26					1	Vickers 1917	
S 1		1				Scot 1914	Ceded to Italian Navy 1915.
V 1				1	1	Vickers 1914	
V 2			1	1		Vickers 1915	
V 3			1			Vickers 1915	
totals	2	18	26	18	10		

The Port at war   14

There was little business for the military at the Port of Ipswich prior to the so-called Great War. Just a few shipments of 'government stores' had come from Woolwich for the Artillery Barracks at Ipswich, and ominously 'war materials' had arrived in 1896, some two years before the beginning of the Boer War. However, the Dock played an important role during the First World War by providing a secure base for the repair of submarine engines by Vickers staff from the newly established factory in the town (see chapter 11).

War was declared at midnight on 4th August 1914. The Harwich Force had been established in the harbour on 30th July, when the First and Third Destroyer Flotillas, consisting of thirty-nine ships, arrived from Portsmouth, the Grand Fleet going north to Scapa Flow. Harwich Force under Commodore Tyrwhitt (1870-1951, later Admiral of the Fleet Sir Reginald Tyrwhitt) had orders to patrol the North Sea between 50 degrees and 52 degrees north. The Eighth Submarine Flotilla, with ten boats, which was independent of the Harwich Force, arrived at Harwich on 31st July under Commander Roger Keyes (1872-1945, later Admiral of the Fleet and first Baron Keyes of Zeebrugge). The separate flotillas were augmented during the war, a flotilla of seven light cruisers joining Harwich Force in 1915, and there were also patrol and minesweeping flotillas. Additional submarines joined as fast as they came off the ways. Ships of Harwich Force engaged the enemy more than any other part of the Royal Navy, Harwich being the nearest harbour to Germany.

The submarines and destroyers had their respective depot ships, HMS *MAIDSTONE*, HMS *WOOLWICH* and HMS *DIDO*, in the harbour, and these were used for minor repairs not requiring dockyard attention. For any problems affecting the new Vickers engines, however, it was convenient to tow the submarines up to Ipswich to seek the care of trained fitters. The time spent by the submarines at Ipswich ranged from one to sixty-six days, with a stay of thirteen days being the most frequent. HM submarine *C3* was an exception, however, arriving at Ipswich on 4th July 1917 and remaining for eighty-seven days. This long visit was possibly connected with the involvement of the vessel in the raid on Zeebrugge in April 1918. At least forty-five submarines paid more than seventy visits to Ipswich, with classes D and E submarines being the most numerous. Fourteen of these visiting vessels were lost during the period of hostilities. A memorial stands in Shotley churchyard to all the officers and men of the 8th and 9th submarine flotillas who gave their lives during the war.

The E-class vessels, built from 1912 onwards, suffered particularly badly, due to their very intensive commitments throughout the war. D-class vessels were launched from 1907 onwards and fitted with the first successful diesel engines. Earlier B and C classes were designed by the Admiralty and Vickers Ltd and largely built by Vickers at Barrow-in-Furness between 1903 and 1909, though a few were built at Chatham Dockyard. They had petrol engines made by the Wolseley Company, requiring storage for 4,500 gallons of petrol aboard. Submarines of the H-class, *H1–H10*, were assembled by the Canadian Vickers Company of Montreal, and they crossed the Atlantic under their own power.

At least eight of the submarines that participated in the raid on the airship

Opposite page: Submarines visiting Ipswich for repair and maintenance, 1914-18.

sheds at Cuxhaven, in North West Germany, on Christmas Day 1914, visited Ipswich at some stage of the war. The eleven vessels taking part were *E6*, *E7*, *E10*, *E11*, *E12*, *E13*, *E15*, *D6*, *D7*, *D8* and *S1*. Nine seaplanes were to be craned over the side of seaplane tenders converted from railway cross-channel ferries to carry out the raid. The task for the submarines was to patrol the whole area and to act as markers for the returning seaplanes and to assist on the surface if necessary.

The *C1* and the *C3*, both built in 1906, were picked to destroy the viaduct linking the Mole at Zeebrugge with the shore during the famous action on St George's Day, 23rd April 1918. The intention was to prevent German warships entering or leaving the Bruges Canal by sinking blockships inside the Mole, thus rendering the whole port useless. Submarine *C3*, which had spent almost three months at Ipswich during 1917, as mentioned previously, was loaded with five tons of Amatol explosive, and effectively destroyed the viaduct with one enormous explosion. Members of her skeleton crew, along with the crews of the blockships, were taken off by motor boats immediately beforehand. The amazing twenty-minute action resulted in over thirty torpedo boats and twelve U-boats being put out of commission for the rest of the war as a result of the destruction of the entrance to the canal that had given access to the repair facilities at Bruges.

There was other war-related traffic to the port. Within the first year of hostilities two ships were brought in as war prizes, having been captured by the Royal Navy with their cargoes of grain intact. First was the full-rigged ship *OSSA*, originally launched at Dumbarton in 1902 as *S.T. MARGHARITA* and purchased by German owners before 1914, registered at Hamburg and renamed. On 17th October 1914 she was brought into the Dock wearing the Red Ensign above her German colours, having been captured by a British warship down Channel. Her cargo of barley and wheat, which had been loaded at Portland, Oregon, was discharged for the Ipswich Malting Company. After a war-prize court had been held in January 1915 the ship was bought by London owners and renamed *KILPURNEY*. Ironically she was later torpedoed and sunk by the German Navy.

Another prize was the ss *SIGYN*, 1,169nrt of Stockholm, a neutral Swedish vessel built in 1897 at Campbeltown. The ship was recorded as carrying grain from Baltimore that was designated by the Admiralty Marshal as a prize cargo, so we must assume it was destined for a German port. She arrived on 18th May 1915 and sailed on 6th June, light for Sunderland.

A few steam trawlers including the Grimsby-registered *ADRIAN*, the Scottish *FORWARD* of Banff and the drifter *CLUNY HILL* of Inverness arrived in June 1915 for three to four weeks. These had all been hired as patrol vessels or minesweepers and they may have come for repairs at St. Clement's Shipyard. Another war prize captured earlier was the small sailing vessel *FRIDA*, 48nrt and re-registered at London, which arrived from Hull on 20th October 1915 with oilcake for Christopherson. She sailed on the 30th with Cranfields' flour for Portsmouth.

Various motor-boats called during 1916. The Dock area narrowly escaped damage at that time when a Zeppelin dropped a bomb on buildings in nearby Key Street. A casualty of the raid was Stoke Bathing Place, just outside the Dock. The site of this open-air pool, which was filled and emptied by the tide, is now occupied by the West Bank Container Terminal.

In the following year, on 22th June 1917, HM Tug *NETTLE* loaded torpedoes for Harwich, and the minesweeping drifter HMS *CITRON* berthed on 30th June 1917, ex-Harwich, and returned the same day. One intriguing entry for 23rd July 1917 shows HMS *DORANDO*, a Grimsby trawler, arriving with fish from Harwich and departing same day with 'fish OHMS'. Might she have also loaded torpedoes? On 31st July 1917 an interesting little steamer, the ss *GEM*, 46nrt, arrived from and left for Harwich having loaded timber OHMS. Built of iron at South Shields in 1881 and owned by Joseph Beckwith, a bargeowner of Hythe Hill, Colchester, the *GEM* worked in Beckwith's regular hoy trade between London and Colchester with general goods for local shops and businesses. The Royal Fleet Auxiliary *ELMOL* arrived in the Bay from Harwich to load oil directly overside from the ss *SICILY*, a Liverpool-registered ship in from New York on 5th November 1917. The *SICILY* had barley and wheat for Mortimer and Paul, timber for Crossley and oil (possibly lubricating oil) for the Royal Navy.

Early in 1918 a number of Dutch fishing vessels were brought in by Customs and interned. On 15th January the *GETRUDE*, *ADRIANA* and *VOORWARTS II* of Scheveningen were brought to Ipswich, and on 5th February the *WILLUM CORNELIS* of the same port came in. Seventeen days later the steamer *GOEREE* of Rotterdam was also interned, and on 21st May the steam trawlers *OTONO*, *ELISEBETH*, *HOLLAND V* and *DERIKA XII* all arrived courtesy of HM Customs. All were detained until February and March 1919, when they returned respectively to Scheveningen, Rotterdam and Ymuiden, two of the last batch not sailing until June and August. Holland was neutral during the First World War and unoccupied, and the reason for internment of these vessels is uncertain. It is possible they transgressed their neutrality; they were often in a position to observe movements of the Harwich Force.

The full-rigged ship OSSA *lying in the Dock after being brought in as a prize of war following her capture by a British warship down Channel.*

The memorial at the Shotley cemetery to officers and men of the 8th and 9th Submarine Flotillas who died in the 1914-18 war.

During hostilities, Commodore Tyrwhitt organised a kind of convoy protection plan for the few British vessels that still traded with Holland on a weekly basis. The idea of the ocean convoy system was not introduced until quite late in the First World War, although in the Second World War the convoy principle was instituted at once despite the fact that there was an initial lack of escort ships to offer the desired protection.

Several of the French bounty ships that visited Ipswich, before or during the First World War, were sunk by the Germans during the hostilities. These vessels

The wartime fate of some of the French bounty ships that visited Ipswich.

Ship and Date of Visit to Ipswich	Details of Sinking
ANNE de BRETAGNE 1913	Captured in South Atlantic by German raider *Kronprinz Wilhelm*. Stores taken before ship sunk by gunfire and ramming, November 1914.
BAYONNE	Captured by *U84* on passage New York to Ipswich with barley and maize, February 1917. Ship blown up after being abandoned by crew who came ashore next day at Lyme Regis.
BERANGERE 1904, 1915	Sunk by *U6* in May 1917, 100 miles south of the Fastnet.
CAMBRONNE 1903	Stopped in South Atlantic by the German armed raider *Seeadler* commanded by Count von Luckner who transferred 263 prisoners to her and cut down her topgallant masts. She was ordered to make a slow passage to Rio de Janeiro to land her 'passengers'. She sailed from Rio for Nantes in April 1917, only to be sunk by *U72* in July. Crew landed by boat two days later at Sein Island, south of Ushant.
ERNEST REYER 1910, 1911	Sunk by *U69* off the Western Approaches, April 1916.
JEAN 1909, 1914	Intercepted by German raider *Prinz Eitel Friedrich* and towed to Easter Island, December 1914. After her coal cargo had been plundered, the barque was towed to sea and used for target practice until she sank. Crew picked up later from Easter Island by a British steamer.
JULES GOMMES 1911, 1915 (twice)	German U-boat threat was at its height during the vessel's last visit to Ipswich, so she stayed a few weeks in the dock after discharging her cargo of barley. Sailed in February 1916 but was stopped by the *U62* 105 miles WSW of the Bishop Rock. She was blown up but her crew were saved.
LA ROCHEFOUCAULD 1916	Captured by the German armed raider *Seeadler* in February 1917, just north of the equator in the Atlantic, and sunk by gunfire after her crew had been taken prisoner.
LA ROCHE JAQUELEIN	Loaded with wheat at San Francisco for Ipswich, vessel was sunk fifteen miles south of the Lizard in November 1916.
MARECHAL de VILLARS 1910	Sunk about fifty/sixty miles north-west of Ushant by the German submarine *U18* while on passage from Seattle to Ipswich with wheat and barley in September 1916.
PIERRE LOTI 1910	Bound to Harwich with barley from San Francisco, she was captured and sunk by the raider *Prinz Eitel Friedrich*.
VILLE du HAVRE 1916	Vessel had discharged barley from San Francisco at Ipswich in January 1916 and had sailed in March light for Buenos Aires but was intercepted and sunk off Ushant by the *U32*. Her crew, except one, were saved by two steamships.

THE PORT AT WAR

were sailing ships constructed by the French between 1897 and 1902. Historically the French Government had given far more support to its maritime profession than any other country with strong seagoing traditions, especially Britain. The conditions governing manning observed by the French merchant service eventually put their ships at a commercial disadvantage, and in 1881 the first subsidies or 'bounties' were introduced by the French Government. The bounty payments led to a dramatic upsurge in French shipbuilding between 1897 and 1902, and in that period more than two hundred new sailing ships slid down the ways at Nantes, le Havre, St. Nazaire, Rouen and Bordeaux.

These so-called bounty ships brought cargoes to Ipswich from the east and west coasts of America, some coming to Ipswich more than once. Between 1900 and 1922 some eighty-six individual ships arrived, with one or two appearing four or five times. They sailed around Cape Horn laden with wheat for Cranfields or barley for R. & W. Paul or the Ipswich Malting Company. They proved very vulnerable to attack by German submarines or surface raiders in the Atlantic and the Western Approaches, and of those eighty-six vessels at least twenty-four were sunk by enemy action. Another twenty or more bounty ships that had visited Ipswich during the same period were lost due to bad weather or other misfortunes.

The First World War ended with the Armistice of 11th November 1918 and the German submarines were ordered to rendezvous off Lowestoft at 4.30am on 20th November to be escorted to Harwich in a five-mile-long convoy. Eventually 170 boats surrendered, their crews being sent home in a German transport as soon as their vessels were safely berthed. The captured U-boats were visited at Harwich by members of Ipswich Corporation on 5th December 1918, and on 16th January 1919 the German submarine UB148 was on public view in Ipswich Dock. Harwich Force gradually dispersed after four-and-a-half years of action in close co-operation with Commander Keyes' submarine flotilla, whose boats had become so familiar at Ipswich for repairs and maintenance.

Eight C-class submarines alongside HMS GANGES II *in Harwich Harbour. These boats all date from 1909-10. Of the craft seen here at least three were lost: C31 off the Belgian coast and C33 in the North Sea in 1915 and C34 sunk by U52 off the north of Ireland in 1917.*

Left: Survivors from a German vessel climb aboard a warship of the Harwich Force. It might just be that they are survivors of the minelayer KONIGEN LOUISE, sunk off the Suffolk coast on 5th August 1914. In that instance many of the prisoners aboard HMS AMPHION died with members of the crew when the cruiser struck one of the mines laid the night before by the KONIGEN LOUISE.

Below: H-class submarines lying alongside their depot ship HMS ALECTO at Shotley c.1919. The four boats seen here were all built in 1918-19. Nine of this class survived to serve in the Second World War.

The Second World War

Little more than twenty-one years after the end of the Great War, itself described as the 'war to end all wars,' hostilities again broke out between Great Britain and Germany on 3rd September 1939. This time the River Orwell and Ipswich would become more closely involved in the action. Thousands of mines were laid by German vessels and aircraft, not only at sea but also in harbours and estuaries. Merchant shipping bound for Britain from southern Spain or the Americas had to cope not only with the familiar North Atlantic weather but also with the German U-boat packs that operated across some three million square miles of the Atlantic. As early as October 1939 a U-boat entered the Royal Navy anchorage at Scapa Flow and sank the battleship ROYAL OAK with the loss of over 800 of her crew. The submarines were soon to be based along the Channel coast of France as that country was overrun, but it was still possible to observe and partially contain them. The situation changed once the whole of France had fallen, enabling the U-boats' HQ to move in June 1940 to Lorient, on the Bay of Biscay with immediate access to the Atlantic. By October the U-boats were carrying out night attacks on the convoys, a thousand ships had been sunk with the loss of 6,000 men by the year's end, and the Germans were confident that it would soon be possible to sink more ships than British yards were capable of replacing. There was already a serious shortage of food, especially of imported wheat for bread, and of many other commodities. The probability of the country being slowly starved into submission as the whole of Europe and North Africa fell into enemy hands did not go unnoticed by the German Navy.

To combat the German threat convoy routes were established across the Atlantic and for the length of the North Sea, through the Straits of Dover and down Channel very early in the war. Convoy assembly ports allowed the exchange of information relating to particular convoys at meetings held ashore immediately prior to departure where sailing orders were clarified. The commodore of the convoy, usually a senior master, added his advice on speed, signalling stragglers, etc., and on keeping station in the appointed positions within the convoy. Ipswich-bound grain and timber ships from the USA and Canada departed from New York or Halifax, Nova Scotia. Vessels laden with raw material for Fisons from Tampa joined convoys from Curacoa (normally for tankers) or New York, while ships coming from Huelva in southern Spain would join the Gibraltar convoys that sailed far out into the Atlantic.

Convoys bound for Britain usually made for the Clyde on the west coast of Scotland, where vessels with orders for Ipswich would join the North Sea convoys round the north of Scotland to Southend, leaving in the approaches to Harwich. More than 3,300 convoys sailed from the HQ at Southend Pier, beginning on 7th September 1939. Only coastal convoys braved the shore guns on the French coast following the Dunkirk Evacuation in late May and early June 1942, when British and Allied troops were taken off the beaches of Northern France by the Navy with the assistance of brave volunteers, many local, in an assortment of small ships that included pleasure craft, fishing boats and sailing barges. From then onwards, ships bound for London were diverted around Scotland, joining the East Coast convoys that were important targets for the German Navy.

The Germans, using fast wooden motor torpedo boats from bases in Holland, Belgium and France, effectively harassed shipping between the Thames Estuary and the Humber, with many actions taking place close to the Suffolk coast. The boats were approximately 100ft in length, able to achieve 33-36 knots and known by the Allies as E-boats (Enemy boats). Defending the Allied shipping were Royal Navy destroyers, corvettes, minesweepers and patrol trawlers. Air escort also had an important part to play in the protection of convoys from the U-boats. The various commands of the Royal Air Force carried the war to the other side of the North Sea, and in due course scores of MTBs and motor gun boats sailed from HMS *BEEHIVE* at Felixstowe.

This then was the background to the activities within the Orwell estuary. Within days of the outbreak of war on 3rd September 1939 Parkeston Quay was taken over by the Admiralty and given the name HMS *BADGER*. It was to be the home port to a number of warships, including some ex-fishing trawlers based there for minesweeping and patrol work. These were soon joined by corvettes, fleet minesweepers and minelayers, a flotilla of destroyers and, for about a year, a small number of submarines plus many auxiliary vessels. The railway-owned passenger vessels that had in peacetime operated from Parkeston Quay were requisitioned as troopships or hospital ships. The result was that the London & North Eastern Railway, the owner of Parkeston Quay, was soon forced through lack of space to operate its cargo services to Bruges, Antwerp, Zeebrugge and Rotterdam from Cliff Quay, Ipswich, during the 'Phoney War', as it was termed in Britain, from December 1939 until 11th May 1940, when the Low Countries were overrun by the German army. With assistance from chartered tonnage, sailings commenced from Ipswich on 11th December 1939 with the arrival of the mv *IMPORT* of Rotterdam. She ran the Rotterdam service until joined by ss *SHERINGHAM* on 12th January, sailing to Antwerp. The accompanying table shows the list of sailings from Ipswich. These continued until hours before Holland was overrun by the German army, the ss *FELIXSTOWE* berthing at Ipswich from Antwerp with the last Continental cargo. One passenger ship, the ss *ST DENIS*, did not have sufficient time to escape from Rotterdam and was scuttled by her crew.

Holland surrendered on 14th May, the realities of war coming considerably closer as various small boats and coasters arrived at Harwich from the Hook. By the 16th, the small Dutch coaster *VEESTER* of Groningen (built in 1931), the Harwich *TRAIN FERRY No.2* and the Dutch salvage tug *ZWARTE ZEE*, at the time of her launching at Kinderdijk in 1933 the largest tug in the world, all arrived in Buttermans Bay via Harwich. *TRAIN FERRY No. 2* was lost off the French coast on 12th June 1940 when attempting to evacuate British personnel, and her two sister ships were purchased for conversion to landing ships in 1940 and renamed HMS *IRIS* and HMS *DAFFODIL*; the latter was sunk by a mine in 1945.

Of the cargo ships running exclusively between Rotterdam and Ipswich for those perilous five months, two were Dutch coasters, the mv *IMPORT*, 199nrt, and the mv *BREM*, 224nrt. The *IMPORT*, which was fresh from the yard, having just been completed at Krimpen a/d Ysel in November 1939, survived the war to trade for N.V. Rotterdam-London Stoomvaart Maats. until 1959, and in 1966 was Greek-owned and registered at Piraeus as *MARIKIA*. The *BREM*, which had been launched at Foxhol in May 1939 as the *FRAM* but was renamed in 1940, was also still at sea in 1966, having been renamed *SEEFALKE* in 1957 for Hamburg owners.

The ss *SHERINGHAM*, launched from Earle's yard at Hull in 1926 for the LNER Harwich cargo services, was operated by the Ministry of War Transport for most of the war years, running between the Clyde and the Bristol Channel. She returned to Harwich after the war, and was broken up in 1958 at Brussels. Somewhat older, the ss *DEWSBURY* had been completed by Earle in 1910 for the Great Central Railway (part of the LNER from 1923) and was transferred to the Harwich-Antwerp service in 1946-47. She was broken up in Holland in 1959.

The ss *FELIXSTOWE*, built by Hawthorn of Leith in 1918 for the Harwich services of the Great Eastern Railway, was hired as a wreck dispersal vessel in 1942. Since there was already a Bangor-class minesweeper bearing the name of *FELIXSTOWE*, the ss *FELIXSTOWE* was renamed *COLCHESTER*; she reverted to her original name when handed back to her owners in 1946. In 1948 she was transferred briefly to British Railways' Weymouth-Channel Islands cargo service before being put on the route between Cairnryan and Larne. She was sold in 1951 to the Limerick S.S. Co. Ltd as the *KYLEMORE*.

In July 1940, as HMS *BADGER* at Parkeston Quay became overloaded, Ipswich became a base for the Auxiliary Patrol, and in September Cliff Quay was designated HMS *BUNTING* with its own senior officer. The depot yacht was originally the auxiliary steel schooner *MERLIN*, 181nrt, built as a yacht at Glasgow in 1897 and renamed HM Yacht *BUNTING* when sent to Ipswich; she was used for officers' accommodation and as a dan layer (marking swept channels with flagged buoys). She was apparently renamed HM Yacht *FREELANCE* in February 1941, at which time the twin-screw motor yacht *FREELANCE*, a vessel built in 1908, was renamed *BUNTING*. To confuse the issue further the *BUNTING*, ex-*FREELANCE*, seems to have been renamed *FREEWILL* at some stage.

As the local fleet of trawlers increased, additional accommodation was required, and on 3rd May 1943 the paddle steamer *EMPEROR OF INDIA* arrived at Cliff Quay to become an accommodation vessel later taking the name HMS *BUNTING*. The *EMPEROR OF INDIA* had been built in 1906 as the *PRINCESS ROYAL* at Thornycroft's yard, Woolston, and after lengthening at their Southampton yard in 1907 she became *EMPEROR OF INDIA* for Cosens & Co. of Weymouth for excursion work on the south coast. She was requisitioned by

One of three sister ships built in 1917 by Armstrong Whitworth on the Tyne for a wartime service from Richborough to Dunkirk, TRAIN FERRY NO.2 was taken over by the Great Eastern Train Ferry Co. Ltd in 1924 for the Harwich to Zeebrugge ferry service. She was lost off the French coast on 12th June 1940 when attempting to evacuate British personnel from France. (A.R.J. Frost)

A public notice attached to the wall of Cranfields' mill in 1939 prohibiting access to the Dock area.

the Admiralty in 1916 for various duties, including minesweeping, and was renamed HMS *MAHRATTA* in 1918, being returned to her owners in 1920. She was taken over again by the Admiralty in December 1939 for minesweeping as *EMPEROR OF INDIA*, and brought home more than 600 soldiers from Dunkirk. Following that event she became an anti-aircraft ship based at Harwich before having her guns removed and becoming an accommodation ship at Ipswich. After the war she was returned to Cosens, being engaged in excursion work until 1956 when she was sold for scrap. On 22nd February 1946 the naval mooring vessel HMS *MOORESS* removed the *EMPEROR OF INDIA*'s semi-permanent moorings from Cliff Quay.

Two Parkeston based trawlers, *LORD MELCHETT* and *RIVER CLYDE*, were the first to arrive at Ipswich for repairs in mid-December 1939. The latter was sunk by a mine off Harwich the following August with the loss of twelve men. During the first three weeks of September 1940 the railway delivered 3,985 tons of coal to Cliff Quay and South West Quay (inside the dock) as the allocation to Ipswich of patrol trawlers, and craft visiting for repairs, rest, watering and coaling greatly increased.

In February 1940 the Ipswich engineering company of Cocksedge & Co. Ltd carried out its first task of hundreds undertaken during the course of the war, repairing the ex-Grimsby trawlers *WILLIAM WESNEY* and *FEZENTA*. The *WILLIAM WESNEY* was sunk by a mine off Orfordness in November 1940. At that time the company began renting land on the SW Quay from the Dock Commission as a workshop. Engineers, or 'dockyard mateys' as they were sometimes called, from Cocksedges and other local firms were to be seen cycling around the docks with a frail basket full of tools on their handlebars and replacement parts tied to their bicycle frames with binder twine. Most of the tasks required the cranage of materials to and from the ships, for which the IDC were paid. The port diver, boat and attendants were frequently hired for rudder and propeller inspections, and sometimes for removing cables and wire that had fouled the propeller. The catalogue of jobs increased with every month until near the end of the war. The work included repairing various machinery aboard, replacement of steel plating, capstans, pumps, gun platforms and guns, funnels, anchors and rafts, plus the loading of kite gear, ammunition, and depth charges when anti-submarine trawlers arrived. By October 1940 the trawl fishing gear had been removed from most trawlers.

The mine has been a part of sea warfare since the seventeenth century. The method used to clear mines from the sea in the early part of the 1939-45 war was similar to trawling for fish, but instead of the trawler towing a net, a saw-edged wire was trailed over the stern to cut the mooring line of a mine that was then exploded on the surface by rifle or gunfire. The 500yd wire was attached to a torpedo-shaped float at the outer end, below which was suspended an 'otter' to veer the sweep wire up to 250 yards to one side of the vessel's course. A 'kite' (made of wood and resembling a box kite), attached to the sweep close to the stern of the trawler, kept the cable under water. A small group of trawlers could then successfully clear a broad channel by sailing the same course, each ship's sweep slightly overlapping the leader's sweep. The safe channel was marked by dan buoys laid by another ship, often a former drifter or requisitioned yacht laden with the flag-topped buoys.

Close to midnight on 21st November 1939 the destroyer HMS *GIPSY*, outward bound from Parkeston Quay with other destroyers was sunk with the loss of some fifty of her crew, including the captain, just off Landguard Fort, within Harwich Harbour, by what turned out to be a magnetic mine dropped from an aircraft. Other vessels were destroyed or damaged by similar mines laid in the shipping channels off the Suffolk coast. Some time elapsed before a means of protecting ships was found, in effect by demagnetising steel vessels by running a cable round the hull and sending a current through it, a process that had to be repeated every six months. Provision was made for degaussing ships in Buttermans Bay, and many vessels, including steel trawlers and Trinity House vessels, were thus protected there. The sailing barge *BLUEBELL*, lying at Pin Mill, which had been sold for a yacht just before the war by farmer Walter Wrinch of Erwarton, was requisitioned by the Admiralty for use as a degaussing vessel in the Bay, and known as HMS *TORCHBEARER* for the duration. Ironically, the term 'degaussing', used in relation to the protection of ships' hulls against magnetic mines, derived its name from the German scientist and mathematician Carl Gauss (1777-1855), who did much work on the theory of magnetism. New ships were built with a permanent cable round the vessel that was continuously charged by the ship's generators.

An early antidote to the magnetic mine, whose detonator was set off by the magnetic field of a ship, was a 'skid', a stout wooden raft aboard which was mounted an electro-magnetic coil to produce a magnetic field around and below it. The 'skid' was towed by a minesweeper. Some of these were brought to Ipswich for repair, but they were not wholly successful as they could only work effectively in quite shallow water.

Another weapon threatening shipping in coastal waters was the acoustic mine, detonated by the sound of a ship's engines within a certain range. These were dealt with by fitting minesweepers with a bell-shaped piece of equipment carried over the bows housing an acoustic hammer known as the 'Kango hammer' that emitted a continuous noise like a pneumatic road drill. The sound coincided with the frequency of a ship's engines, thereby triggering the mine at a safe distance.

The whole assembly was lowered into the sea by a large A-frame suspended over the bow of the minesweeper. A-frames and hammer gear were fitted at Ipswich by Cocksedge & Co. Ltd. Asdic equipment, which provided an echo from an underwater object, was also installed by the company in anti-submarine trawlers; this installation work required the services of a diving crew. The first to be supplied with asdic was probably the ex-Grimsby trawler *FAIRWAY* in April 1941, and at least twenty-six trawlers had been equipped by January 1942.

In an effort to combat the threat of magnetic and acoustic mines to Allied shipping a whole new fleet of non-magnetic wooden minesweepers was constructed, no fewer than thirty-two of them in shipyards at Lowestoft and twenty-four in yards at Wivenhoe and Rowhedge on the River Colne. They were fitted with the LL or double L sweep which consisted of two towed cables through which was passed an electric current that set up a magnetic field astern of the sweeper. The wooden motor minesweepers soon became known as Mickey Mouse Ships from the initial letters of their class; all were given the prefix MMS and a number. Two of these vessels, H.Nl.M.S *BEVELAND* (ex-MMS237) and H.Nl.M.S. *DUIVELAND* (ex-MMS1044), both built at Wivenhoe and named after islands in Zeeland, joined fourteen other Dutch-manned sweepers to form two flotillas operating out of Harwich. Many of the Dutch sailors aboard the flotilla vessels had made their escape from Holland after it had fallen to the Germans. The *BEVELAND* was involved in many sweeping operations along the shipping routes up to Yarmouth and in the Thames Estuary. Several motor minesweepers came up the Orwell to Ipswich for repairs during the course of the war.

By October 1940 at least thirty trawlers and motor boats a month were being supplied with fresh water at Ipswich, and tons of ashes and refuse were carted away. In that month the War Office was charged £370 10s. 11d. for work carried out by Bennett & Snare Ltd of New Street and E.A. Green of St John's Road, Ipswich, for preparations to demolish Cliff Quay and the railway swing bridge over the entrance lock to the Dock should German forces invade. Six decoy submarines, built largely of wood and canvas at Wivenhoe in 1940-41, were moored in the Stour until they were destroyed by the elements.

In January 1941 the work of the port was interrupted briefly by a collision that had nothing to do with the hostilities. The mv *BONNINGTON COURT* of London, 3,012nrt and launched in 1929 at Port Glasgow, had berthed on 17th December 1940, ex-Portland, Oregon, and Vancouver with timber for William Brown, 1,610 tons of wheat for Cranfields and 221 tons of wheat for Marriages of Colchester, the wheat being sent to Colchester in the sailing barges *SALTCOTE BELLE* and *VERONA*. Sailing light on 16th January for the Tyne, *BONNINGTON COURT* collided in the river with F.T. Everards' mv *SPIRALITY*, which was about to enter the Dock from Blyth with coal for Mellonie & Goulder. *SPIRALITY* sank quickly close to the northern end of Cliff Quay. The *BONNINGTON COURT* continued on her journey to the Tyne but was caught by enemy bombers and went down near the Sunk lightvessel on 19th January 1941. The salvage vessel *FOREMOST 18* was summoned from its base at Harwich train ferry pier and by 28th March 534 tons of coal had been recovered and the *SPIRALITY* sufficiently patched to sail to Yarmouth for dry-docking on 13th April. She arrived again with coal for Mellonie & Goulder on 27th August, and continued trading until sold to Belgian shipbreakers in November 1968, exactly thirty-nine years after her launch in November 1939 at Goole.

The *FOREMOST* 18 had played a major but unsuccessful role in salvaging HMS *GIPSY*, the destroyer mentioned earlier. In fact *GIPSY* was gradually broken up until the remains could be dragged clear of the fairway on the

The names of the master and mate of the spritsail barge BLUE MERMAID, *blown up by a magnetic mine off Clacton, on the Merchant Navy memorial.*

Landguard side. She was still visible there until the mid-1960s, when the mudflats and foreshore were reclaimed for the Landguard Container Terminal, which opened in 1967. On 2nd February 1940 the Ministry of Shipping chartered the Dock Commission tug *STRONGHOLD*, built at Goole in 1931, to assist in the work on *GIPSY*. The tug worked from 5.30am to 9.30pm for about two weeks and then went on to general salvage work in the harbour until 18th March. In May the same year *STRONGHOLD* was slipped at St. Clement's Shipyard and refitted for further work with the Ministry within and outside Harwich, in which capacity she served until 27th March 1946. She towed in the ss *GLENFINLAS* of Liverpool after this vessel had been extensively damaged below decks in 1941. The *GLENFINLAS* (4,811nrt) was a large passenger ship owned by Glen Line and built by Hawthorn Leslie of Newcastle in 1917. The vessel had sustained heavy casualties, including several dead, following a serious air attack, near the Sunk lightvessel. In the final accounts to the Ministry an award of £60 was distributed among *STRONGHOLD*'s crew for this service. The Ministry of Shipping later became a part of the Ministry of War Transport, and the contract continued at £160 17s. 0d. plus wages, an agency fee of £54 13s. 10d. per month and Lloyd's annual boiler surveys and insurance at £2 and £3 15s. respectively. *STRONGHOLD* was hired again between May and August 1946 for towing nine LCTs from Woolverstone and Cliff Quay to the harbour, where they were transferred to a sea-going tug.

Worse was to come on the River Orwell on 24th August 1941 when the steamship *SKAGERAK* of London, 753nrt, detonated two parachute mines close to Collimer Point opposite Trimley and sank, breaking into two sections found 200ft apart. Launched in 1921 and originally registered at Copenhagen, she was operated by the MOWT with a mainly Scandinavian crew of twenty-two. Seventeen men were killed, including four British gunners and the Ipswich pilot, James Read, whose body was never found. She was laden with coke ex-Newcastle for Ipswich gasworks, not an unusual cargo if there was a local shortage. Mines were known to have been dropped during the previous night, and the channel was swept and recruits at HMS Ganges searched the riverbank; it is believed that the parachutes were found. Debris from the ship is still visible on the mudflats at low water and the wreck buoy was not removed until the early 1950s because of the time taken to clear the wreckage. Parishioners from Trimley and Levington who were enjoying a sunny and warm Sunday afternoon by the river witnessed the violent explosion and heard the screams of the crew. Coke was gathered from the Trimley shore by local residents for some time to come. The only note relevant to her expected arrival at Ipswich is to be found in the accounts for 25th August under the Special Lock heading: 'Lock not taken, ss SKAGERAK, £1 charged to Lewcock & Pemberton'.

While close to home the magnetic and acoustic mines caused many casualties, German U-boats operating in packs sank many ships sailing in convoy across the Atlantic. As the Battle of the Atlantic was fought between the escorts and the underwater wolfpacks improved U-boats capable of going as far as Freetown in Sierra Leone to intercept traffic much farther south were introduced into service. The increased range of the newer boats was markedly evident on 13th January 1942 when U-123 cruised undetected into New York Bay to find the shoreline, shipping lanes and ships fully illuminated. She had only to wait for an outward-bound convoy to follow and attack at night with devastating results. Fortunately advances in the development of radar by mid-1942 enabled British aircraft fitted with searchlights to find submarines with such success that on 24th May 1943 U-boats were ordered to cease attacking convoys due to increasing losses.

At Ipswich the year 1942 arrived with no sign of peace, although many local companies were faithfully booking advertising space in the next IDC Handbook due in 1943. Cargoes of wheat, timber, pyrites and phosphate continued to arrive at Ipswich. On 15th September 1942, for example, the ss *EMPIRE SPEY* of Glasgow, 2,551nrt, berthed at Cliff Quay from Huelva with 5,055 tons of copper ore, of which 2,064 tons were unloaded to railway trucks and 2,991 tons craned to the Fisons factory hoppers. In addition the vessel unloaded a total of 209 tons of machinery, cork waste, empty mailbags and a Beaufort aeroplane with one wing (damaged), care of Lewcock & Pemberton.

This particular ship, which had visited Ipswich during the earlier part of the war as the *BLAIR SPEY*, may be cited as an example of the extreme conditions endured by merchant ships and their crews during that time. She was launched in 1929 by the Ardrossan Dockyard for a group of Glasgow companies controlled by George Nisbet. She had arrived in the Orwell on 28th December 1939 from New York and discharged her cargo of wheat to barges in Buttermans Bay, sailing for Sunderland on January 7th 1940. She returned on 9th March from Sfax with phosphate of lime for Fison, Packard & Prentice at Cliff Quay, from where she sailed on 22nd March, light for the Tyne.

On 18th October 1940 *BLAIR SPEY* was eastbound across the Atlantic with timber as a part of Convoy SC7, travelling from Sydney, Nova Scotia, to the UK, and comprising thirty-five ships with an inadequate escort. A small pack of U-boats homed in on the convoy and in the space of about three hours twenty ships were sunk. The *BLAIR SPEY* sustained considerable damage from torpedo attacks, and eventually the section forward of the funnel sank with the loss of eighteen men. The stern half remained afloat and was towed all the way to the Clyde, where it received a new fore-part to emerge in March 1942 as the *EMPIRE SPEY* for the Ministry of War Transport. It was in this guise that she berthed at Cliff Quay on 15th September 1942, sailing light for the Tyne on the 23rd. After the war she resumed tramping under her original name.

Following Dunkirk the Auxiliary Patrol of requisitioned fishing vessels and motor boats was quickly formed at ports along the East Coast, most of the crews and skippers staying with their ships. Many had served in the 1914-18 war and were Royal Naval Reservists, and there was a build-up of freshly trained men coming from HMS *EUROPA*, the drafting and training establishment at the Sparrow's Nest in Lowestoft. No fewer than 2,385 names of ex-*EUROPA* men, serving in what had become the Royal Naval Patrol Service and who were lost at sea, are inscribed on the memorial at Lowestoft.

In September 1942 Cocksedge & Co. Ltd provided torpedo tubes for the trawler *JEANNIE McINTOSH*, although whether for use or transportation is not clear. At this period the National Fire Service maintained two fire-floats in the port named *MOSS ROSE* and *JACK SNIPE*.

The Danish-owned ss *GUNVOR MEARSK*, registered at Copenhagen, arrived at Ipswich on 5th October 1942 from Carleton Place on the Ottawa River off the St. Lawrence above Montreal with timber for William Brown & Co., sailing on 13th October for the Tyne. The vessel had been built by W. Gray of West Hartlepool in 1931 as *JOSEPHINE GRAY*. Her name and owners changed in 1934 when she was acquired by A.P. Moller of Copenhagen, but she became London-registered for the war, which she survived to be re-registered afterwards at Aalborg and restored to her Danish owners. Just over two weeks later, the 1920-built ss *JAN* of Bergen berthed at Cliff Quay from Windsor, Nova Scotia, for Brown's. Like *GUNVOR MEARSK*, she had risked the rigours of an Atlantic convoy out of Halifax, as did scores of ships with timber or grain for discharge at Ipswich.

Ipswich bargemen and barges at war

During the 1939-45 conflict, navigation was confined to daylight hours, and closed gates in boom defence systems across the estuaries ensured nothing moved in or out during darkness. There was a boom at Woolverstone on the Orwell, just above the Hard, where one end was made fast to the ex-Ipswich sailing barge *INFLEXIBLE* moored outside the channel. The boom at Harwich stretched across from Landguard, with attendant examination drifters, etc. The main Thames boom of stakes and other obstructions reached six miles from Shoeburyness to the Isle of Sheppey, and another was laid from Canvey Island to the Kent shore. All had movable floating 'gates' formed by buoys connected by chains, and some were equipped with anti-submarine nets. The gates were normally open to traffic from sunrise to sunset. Patrol craft approached barges and other vessels, requiring their details.

When the ss *SKAGERRAK* was mined in the River Orwell in August 1941, a dozen or so barges were anchored at Harwich waiting to get up to Ipswich. Among them were Cranfields' *ORINOCO* and Meux's *PIMLICO*. Once a passage was provisionally cleared, they were towed up all together by a naval tug preceded by a minesweeper.

During 1944-45, having arrived safely in the Thames, there was the immediate threat of V1 flying bombs and V2 rockets. On one occasion a very low V1 passed over *ORINOCO* when she was being towed downriver. Fortunately the gear was on the deck, otherwise the topmast would more than likely have been struck. The V2s, many of which fell in various parts of London, gave no warning; a rush of air was followed by an explosion, that was all. This sound became all too familiar to visiting bargemen.

Generally speaking, the Ipswich barge fleet escaped lightly from the effects

Captain Harold Smy.

of the war. Five of Pauls' barges were sent to Dunkirk during the evacuation of the British Expeditionary Force from France in May/June 1940. The port records show this episode.

Within the following few days all five barges were requisitioned and towed to Dover, ready for the crossing to Dunkirk. Some tugmasters gave the names of barges that were towed and others did not, and it is open to conjecture as to whether the barges were stopped at Sheerness or Gravesend or perhaps reached the docks upriver and were immediately towed to Dover. Both Pauls' big steel barges, *BARBARA JEAN* and *AIDIE*, built at Brightlingsea in the 1920s, had to be left at Dunkirk. The *DORIS* was lost while under tow with two other barges; the *LADY ROSEBERY* also sank when their tug was blown up, and the third of the trio, *PUDGE*, remarkably survived the explosion. All the barge crews escaped, but only two crew members survived from the tug. Tom Polley's younger brother Dennis was the cook aboard *DORIS*, but he was taken off at Dover before the crossing when he was found to be under sixteen. The company's *ENA* and *TOLLESBURY* were left behind but were both brought back separately to Kent, relatively unscathed, by groups of soldiers. *ENA* was taken to Sandwich Flats, where she was found anchored with nobody aboard; *TOLLESBURY* brought up at Ramsgate, where her soldiers were brought ashore in motor boats before the barge was taken up to Gravesend.

After the event, *ENA* was brought back to Ipswich on 10th June from Pegwell Bay and *TOLLESBURY* on 11th June from Gravesend. Both barges, sailed by their usual skippers, went straight on the shipyard for attention. *ENA* sailed again light for London on 22nd July, and *TOLLESBURY* was lightering from Buttermans Bay from 2nd to 7th July, sailing to London on 12th August.

Ipswich man Fred Smy, who started on barges aged fourteen in 1914, carried on working throughout the First World War as a mate, visiting most of the French channel ports, especially Calais, with army materials. In 1922, he became skipper of *NEW TRADER*, owned by the London & Rochester Barge Company Ltd, later becoming master of the same company's *CORONATION* for twenty-three years before moving to the *ROSME*. He was master of her during the Second World War when she struck a mine off the Maplin and sank. Captain Smy managed to save his mate, who was below at the time, and was later awarded the BEM. He carried on until his retirement in 1965 after fifty-one years at sea; he was then master of the same company's fully-powered steel barge *WYVENHOE*, which incidentally was to become the last ex-sailing barge in trade. Fred's brother Harold Smy had previously been skipper of R.&W. Pauls' *BIJOU*, which on 3rd July 1940 was set on fire during an incendiary bomb raid on Mistley and burnt out. Her remains lie on the mudflats to this day. Much of her deck gear that was still servicable was recovered and brought back to Ipswich in the *D'ARCY* on 2nd August 1940.

Harold subsequently became master of Sully's auxiliary motor barge *BEATRICE MAUD*, remaining in her for many years. She had been requisitioned in London on 29th May 1940 for the Dunkirk evacuation. Found off the beaches

Port records showing details of the five Ipswich barges requisitioned for the Dunkirk evacuation.

ARRIVAL	VESSEL	FROM	CARGO	DEPARTURE	TO	SKIPPER
24th May 1940	*AIDIE*	London	Maize	25th May 1940	London light	Harry Potter
24th May	*BARBARA JEAN*	London	Maize	25th May	London light	Charlie Webb
24th May	*ENA*	London	Maize	25th May	London light	Alfred Page
24th May	*TOLLESBURY*	London	Maize	26th May	London light	Lemon Webb
25th May	*DORIS*	London	Maize	26th May	London light	Dick Finbow

at Malo-les-Bains with no crew aboard, the barge was brought back to England by some 300 soldiers, of whom 250 were French. Before the war *BEATRICE MAUD* had been a regular trader to Ipswich, Yarmouth, Battlesbridge and Snape, and she continued a similar pattern after her return from France.

However, the Bristol Channel, the Clyde and Loch Ewe in Scotland were designated reception areas for convoys that had been diverted from the English Channel and the North Sea, and a dozen or so auxiliary-engined barges were sent to the Clyde to assist with lightening the ships, while two went to the Bristol Channel, these being the *SHAMROCK* and *BEATRICE MAUD*. The latter had been much occupied by loading up to 170 tons of brick-rubble from bomb-damaged London to Maldon, Mistley, Colchester and Ipswich during 1942 and 1943. *BEATRICE MAUD* left London under Captain Harold Smy on 18th April 1943, and arrived at Avonmouth on 30th May with a ballast cargo of sand, berthing in Bristol on 1st June. Harold then traded to the northern coastal ports of the West Country and to South Wales including Minehead, Watchet, Llanelly, Port Talbot, Swansea, Cardiff, Newport, Barry, Penarth, Bridgwater, Gloucester, Bideford and Flatholm Island in the Severn. Many of the cargoes were of foodstuffs, but there was also scrap-iron, steel, and tobacco. *BEATRICE MAUD* eventually sailed from Newport with seventy-two tons of coal for Chatham on 9th January 1946, by way of St. Ives, Falmouth, Appledore (to collect her sails that had been put ashore there), Salcombe, Brixham, Weymouth, Cowes Roads and Newhaven, arriving at Chatham on 20th March 1946. Leaving there two days later, she loaded maize in London, arriving at Ipswich on 28th March.

The Colchester-owned barge *CASTANET* struck the wreck of the ss *SKAGERAK* in the Orwell on 6th March 1943. She was wheat laden but some of the cargo was saved. One month later, her sailing gear was recovered by the Ipswich barge *GENERAL JACKSON* from Pin Mill where *CASTANET* lay and was eventually hulked, until being swept across the river to Levington Creek during the gale and flood of 31st January /1st February 1953.

The Months before D-Day

The situation off the East Coast had improved by 1943 due to developments in the British defence systems. Many of the German aircraft that had been laying mines and attacking shipping were diverted to other tasks, and new fleet minesweepers were coming off the ways both at home and abroad, giving some respite to the fleet of requisitioned trawlers. During this period much of the trade was subject to several Government departments, including the Ministry of Supply (sulphuric acid control, fertiliser control, timber control, potato division, non-ferrous metals), the Ministries of Food (including Imported Flour Department), Home Security, War Transport (MOWT) and Health. There was also the London Port Area Grain Committee (LPAGC) monitoring allocations of grain and bags to millers in Suffolk, Essex, Kent and London, with their address on the 5th Floor of Holland House, Bury Street, London EC3.

The coal supply for HMS *BUNTING*'s fleet was maintained by rail until the North Sea became safer, by the middle of the war. From April 1940 to March 1941 there were deliveries every few weeks by the railway, totaling 12,093 tons to the Admiralty's account. Most of it went to a dump on the South-West Quay and had to be transferred as required to Cliff Quay. Throughout the following twelve months to March 1942 trains delivered 13,156 tons of coal, mainly direct to Cliff Quay.

HMS *GANGES* meanwhile received 5,401 tons unloaded to dumps at South-West Quay and Tovells Wharf, where it was loaded to lorries for Shotley. The training of boys had ended by May 1940, the sick bay was in use as a hospital, and the barracks was utilized for the training of conscripted men and boys. Ganges received only 3,757 tons of coal by lorries, loaded from railway trucks, during the similar twelve month period from 1943 to 1944, and about 20 tons was delivered by road to HMS *WOOLVERSTONE*, the name given to the combined operations base at Woolverstone Hall.

The Admiralty's coal consumption had risen at Cliff Quay in the same twelve months from April 1943 to 21,643 tons, an increase of nearly 8,500 tons in two years, reflecting the level of activity by the ships based there. There was some relief though with reduced enemy action, especially by E-boats, in the North Sea by the summer of 1944, no less than 18,980 tons of coal arriving by ship and only 2,663 by rail. The ss *WELSH ROSE*, 252nrt, registered and owned at Liverpool by R. Hughes, built as *BROOKSIDE* at Goole in 1922, brought eighteen cargoes from Humber ports and Blyth. The Hull Gates Shipping Company's ss *MYTONGATE*, 215nrt and launched in 1938 at Willington Quay on the Tyne, discharged twelve cargoes, and the mv *BENGUELA*, built 1936 by the Goole SB Co. Ltd, came with two. Lastly, one cargo arrived in the ss *METHILHILL*, launched by W. Harkess of Middlesbrough as *ARKLESIDE* in 1914.

The ss *EGHOLM*, 754nrt and built in 1924 at Fredrikshavn for D.F.D.S., which arrived from Casablanca in January 1944 with raw materials for fertilizers, was originally registered at Copenhagen but while working for the Allies was registered at Gibraltar. She also carried explosives for the Royal Navy mine depot at Wrabness and these were forwarded by rail, the RN having a private siding serving the depot. Nine tons of 'aircraft' (parts) were unloaded from the Panamanian ss *SVERTE* on 21st February 1944 along with its main cargo of timber from Halifax, Nova Scotia. The ss *CSIKOS*, which arrived from Canada in April 1943, discharged 22 tons of RAF aircraft parts with trucks and wheat. Built as *NORTH PACIFIC* at Joseph L. Thompson's Sunderland yard in 1913, she was sold to the Anglo-Hungarian Shipping Company and renamed in 1934.

Operation Overlord – preparations for D-Day.

The Orwell was one of the assembly areas for landing craft waiting to join the fleet during Operation Overlord, the naval assault phase of which was code-named Neptune. The craft gathered in the Thames Estuary and along the south coast for the intended invasion of France, which began on 6th June 1944, having been postponed one day because of bad weather.

HMS *WOOLVERSTONE*, set up in December 1942 as a combined operations base in Woolverstone Park, was used as a departure point for the new tank landing craft (LCTs) coming directly from numerous yards in ones and twos early in 1944. Some were going straight to the Southampton area, as they were not ready for the initial landing. A contingent of soldiers was stationed at Woolverstone Park constructing dummy LCTs under the trees by daylight and by night at the top of the Hard. These dummy craft had frames of tubular steel covered with suitably painted canvas, and were mounted on small wheels, the flotation being provided by forty-gallon oil drums. They were given ventilators and other fittings, and with gaffs flying the White Ensign were towed down to buoys below Pin Mill. There they remained, and together with other dummy craft on the Deben and Stour gave the impression that any invasion would probably be launched from the East Coast towards Belgium or north-eastern France. Accommodation for personnel at Woolverstone was either in the Hall, more likely for commissioned ranks, or in Nissen huts within the grounds. A broad concrete hard, still surviving and used by Woolverstone yacht marina, was constructed close to the Cat House, where sailing barges had once landed whole cargoes of coal overside for the Hall until the 1920s.

Early in 1944 the nucleus of a batch of seventy-odd tank landing craft (LCTs), not originally intended for Normandy, gathered at Great Yarmouth and Lowestoft to form flotillas. Each completed flotilla consisted of twelve craft, with three flotillas making a squadron. These twin-screw vessels were fitted with petrol main engines because the diesels expected from Paxmans of Colchester were in short supply. The craft were, however, equipped with diesel generators.

During mid-May about seventy-five per cent of those craft then available assembled at Woolverstone to prepare for the anticipated landings on the Continent, all of them commanded by reserve officers, for example professional trawler skippers. The only real exercises consisted of a run up to the bunkering jetty or tanker berth at Cliff Quay and a return to Woolverstone; and sailing to a beach at Felixstowe below the RAF crane pier but just inside the harbour. Here each LCT spent a time on the beach estimated as sufficient to load its proposed cargo, again sailing back to Woolverstone afterwards. The actual loading was done in due course at the same place, and the craft returned loaded to their buoys at Woolverstone. They sailed direct to France early on 5th June 1944. Thereafter the individual landing craft shuttled to and from Normandy when ready, rather than in flotillas, although sailing within the convoy system. Just before Christmas 1944, a few sailed back individually to Woolverstone for repairs and leave, prior to each proceeding elsewhere as required.

On the opposite bank at Orwell Park members of the Seventh Armoured Division, the Desert Rats, trained for the D-Day landings, having arrived back from North Africa early in 1944. During their three to four weeks stay the soldiers spent time water-proofing and oiling their tanks, wrapping canvas around the turrets, and generally preparing for the coming invasion. They left Felixstowe at dusk of D-Day after a delay of two days.

The latter part of the war

Once northern France had been cleared, the Straits of Dover were safe from the E-boats and the big guns at Calais and Boulogne. The Straits were reopened to normal traffic; small vessels, able to hug the Kent coast, had continued to run the gauntlet before the clearance.

On 6th June 1944 the ss *GEOLOGIST* berthed from Alexandria with 2,180 tons of RAF stores care of Movement Control and 45 tons of hessian. This was probably the ship's maiden voyage, having only been completed in March by Lithgows of Port Glasgow for T. & J. Harrison of Liverpool as the latest of their fleet, all of which were named after trades and professions. On 27th July the Greek ss *TAXIARCHIS* of Chios berthed from Casablanca with 6,598 tons of phosphate of lime, discharged to Fison's hoppers and into railway trucks, two tons of 'steel cylinders' discharged into trucks and a ton of bags sent by cart to the Public Warehouse. The *TAXIARCHIS*, launched in September 1913 from Richardson, Ducks' yard at Stockton-on-Tees as the *CALDY* for the Fargrove

Steam Navigation Co. Ltd of Leadenhall Street, London, was one of the many former British ships still sailing at that time. Another interesting British-built ship, the ss *HENRIK IBSEN*, almost forty years old, berthed at the Cliff from Sorel on August 9th with 5,702 tons of wheat for Cranfields, 442 tons for A.A. Gibbons and 122 tons for the LPAGC. She had been completed at Middlesbrough in 1906 for Ibsens of Bergen, although by 1944 she was registered at Stavanger.

The ss *BELGIAN TRADER* of Antwerp arrived on l0th September 1944 from Casablanca laden with 3,937 tons of phosphate of lime. She also had fourteen tons of 'steel cylinders' that were discharged into railway trucks, plus five cases and two handgrips of personal effects.

The Greek ss *NICOLAS*, registered at Cephallonia, arrived on 4th October 1944 from Montreal with forty tons of military stores, 664 tons of wheat for A.A. Gibbons, 607 tons for Marriages, and 4,485 for Cranfields, plus 809 tons of rolled oats and 157 tons of wheat to be loaded to barges and trucks for the London Port Area Grain Committee. The ship sailed light to the Tyne on the 17th.

Trafalgar Day, 21st October 1944, saw the arrival of the Liberty ship ss *MARY PICKERSGILL* at Cliff Quay from Philadelphia and New York via France. She discharged 3,054 tons of Government stores c/o the RAF Embarkation Unit and Movement Control at Dovercourt. As with similar cargoes, in addition to the usual rates for loading cargoes to lorries, trucks or warehouse, charges were raised against Movement Control for chocking bombs in railway trucks.

The *MARY PICKERSGILL* was registered at Baltimore, USA, and was launched there at the Bethlehem-Fairfield Yard in July 1944, three months before her arrival in Ipswich. The Bethlehem Steel Company opened an emergency shipyard in the suburb of Fairfield to accommodate the huge demand for the construction of these vessels, of which they built 385, the first being launched in September 1941. The man behind the mass production of Liberty ships was Henry J. Kaiser, who had the idea of welding prefabricated parts instead of the time-consuming process of riveting individual plates and frames. The construction time for such vessels was under seven weeks from keel laying. More than 2,700 Liberty ships were constructed, and although many were laid up after the war, several were sold to shipping companies, renamed and continued to voyage worldwide. Some later came to Ipswich, in addition to the British wartime standard ships whose names were normally prefixed *EMPIRE*.

The Liberty ship construction programme in the United States was one that produced identical ships. In this country, however, the wartime shipbuilding programme was based on individual shipbuilders producing general types of vessels while avoiding over-standardisation. The classes of vessels that evolved included tramps or cargo vessels, various coaster types, tankers, colliers and tugs. The Admiralty, in addition to being responsible for the building of warships, maintained control of merchant ship construction by issuing licences for ships to be built for private owners, the ships having to conform to specifications. It also directly ordered new ships for operation by merchant shipping companies acting for the Government.

Standardisation of the ships' engines and machinery allowed individual yards to construct vessels with which they were familiar, provided the yard's prototype ships were officially approved. New buildings, under licence in private yards, were under way by early 1940, while the requisition of cargo ships began in January of that year. Details of *EMPIRE* ships coming to Ipswich during 1940-43 are included in the table of deep-sea arrivals at the end of this chapter, the first vessel being the *EMPIRE SNIPE* that berthed on 1st August 1940.

THE PORT AT WAR

351

The ss *EMPIRE GREY* of Shields arrived on 12th November 1944 from Camden, a sub-port of Philadelphia on the Delaware River, with timber for the Ministry of Supply. This was discharged to the quay, to railway trucks, and overside to the river for storage in Gabriel's timber ponds near Stoke Bathing Place. She sailed ten days later with a part-cargo of steel remaining on board for Middlesbrough.

The year 1944 proved to be the definitive turning point of the war, although some military stores continued to roll through Ipswich on the railway from Cliff Quay during 1945. The *EGÉE*, 1,395nrt, a French steamer built in 1940 arrived on 6th January 1945 from Caen, which had been freed early in August 1944. *EGÉE* brought direct from Caen 1,931 tons of equipment and stores that were discharged to trucks and lorries. She sailed light for Harwich on the 15th.

The ss *BELGIAN CAPTAIN* arrived on 20th January 1945 from Bombay with 842 tons of explosives c/o Movement Control, plus 4,675 bags of mail (104 tons), bitumen and acid sludge. A cargo of 100 tons was moved using quayside cranes from No.4 hold to No.5, and 300 tons from No.1 to No.5 hold with cranage and lorries. An unrecorded amount of flour was craned aboard the vessel, ex-lorries. She sailed on the 28th. *BELGIAN CAPTAIN* was launched in 1943 as *EMPIRE CENTAUR*, and she traded under her fourth name into the 1960s. Her running mate *BELGIAN TRADER*, which had arrived in September 1944, was another British standard ship that was completed at Troon in 1942 as *EMPIRE*

Having discarded her wartime shade of overall drab grey, the Liberty Ship SUSAN COLBY *is seen at Cliff Quay about 1957. Built in the East Yard of the New England Shipbuilding Corporation at Portland, Maine, in 1943-44, she was floated out of the basin in which she was constructed in January 1944 rather than being launched down a slipway. At the time the photograph was taken by Mr A.R.J. Frost she had attained a new identity as the* OLGA *of Hamburg.*

LAUNCELOT. Interestingly enough, this vessel was still sailing for Hamburg owners in the mid-1960s as *KETTWIG*.

On the same day that the *BELGIAN CAPTAIN* arrived, the ss *COLCHESTER* berthed from Harwich for coaling. She was better known as the LNER cargo ship *FELIXSTOWE*, the last railway vessel to arrive from Antwerp in May 1940.

Another Liberty ship from the Bethlehem Fairfield Yard in 1943, the *BARBARA FRIETCHIE* of Baltimore, owned by the US Maritime Commission, came into Cliff Quay on 29th January 1945. She discharged timber for the MOS (Timber Control) from Archangel, possibly the first from there since before the war. Most of the timber consisted of boards that had been badly stowed, and it took forty-eight men to turn her round in eleven days.

A Canadian standard ship, the ss *WILLOW PARK* of Montreal, arrived from Quebec on 13th February 1945 with 2,748 tons of wheat for Cranfields, 664 tons for Gibbons and 120 tons to the LPAGC. She was launched in December 1944 at Lauzon on the southern bank of the St. Lawrence, nearly opposite Quebec. Her engine was by Canadian Iron Foundries of Three Rivers, some sixty miles further up the St. Lawrence, and she was one of the 'Park' series of standard ships which, with the 'Forts', were all built in Canada. The ss *FORT COULONGE*, berthed on 6th August 1945 from Casablanca with 5,367 tons of phosphate. She came out of the United Shipyards Ltd works at Montreal in July 1943, and was still at sea in 1966 as the Liberian flagged *SURABAJA STEER* owned by the Steering Line Company of Monrovia. The *WILLOW PARK* returned on April 12th with 3,575 tons of wheat for Cranfields, 442 tons to Gibbons and 243 tons to the LPAGC. Another 'Park' to arrive on 28th April with 4,175 tons of phosphate of lime (discharged to trucks and the factory hoppers) was ss *CATARAQUI PARK*, launched in July 1944 at the Foundation Marine Yard in Pictou, Nova Scotia. She was still working under her fifth name in the mid-1960s.

One of the last big ships from abroad, the ss *RUNSWICK*, owned by Headlam & Son and registered at Whitby, berthed on 10th May 1945 within days of the end of the war in Europe, with deals and 388 sleepers, requiring rental of 109 rods of Cliff Quay by the MOS (Timber Control). The ship arrived from Camden on the Delaware River and sailed light to Sunderland on 2nd June 1945. She had been launched by J.L. Thompson's at their Sunderland yard in 1930.

A handful of *EMPIRE* ships was still coming to Ipswich in 1946 and 1947 after the war had ended. By this time many of the survivors had been disposed of and renamed by various shipping companies, several going to Greece and other flag of convenience countries. One of the last arrivals was the motor tanker *EMPIRE ARROW*, 1,973nrt, from Haifa with motor spirit for the Petroleum Board on 26th February 1947 and again on 11th April from Sheerness. The same ship appeared again exactly four months later as the mv *BRITISH BUGLER* from Haifa, owned by the British Tanker Company Ltd (BP). She was scrapped in 1981 at Kynosauro, Greece.

Another interesting vessel, appearing in January 1946, was the ss *KEILA*, 2,302nrt of Glasgow, from New Brunswick with wheat for Cranfield, Marriage and Gibbons. She came again on 8th March from Casablanca with phoshate of lime. *KEILA* was launched at Sundertand by Joseph L. Thompson & Sons in 1905 as *ZAMORA* for Estonian owners, and registered at Tallinn. Possibly interned for the war, she came under the control of the Ministry of War Transport and was still operated by the Ministry of Transport in 1950 under British managers. Another ship of the same name and Tallinn-registered was built at Budapest in 1960, sailing under the USSR flag.

Bomb damage

Throughout the war, the port and surrounding area remained relatively unscathed from the numerous bombing raids on the town, which caused much death and damage. Many of the dock premises were heavily camouflaged, the buildings being painted with random shapes in various colours in order to deceive the enemy as to their true outline and size, and they remained like this for several years after the war.

Early in the war the dockside buildings and quays had a lucky escape when a cluster of bombs landed but failed to explode. Some weeks later, in October 1940, anti-personnel bombs were dropped on Cliff Quay and Griffin Wharf near to Ransomes & Rapier. The metal casing of the small canister bombs resembled butterfly wings when open, hence the name Butterfly Bomb given to this unpleasant weapon. Their destructive nature when touched resulted in the deaths of six men from the engineering firm and a policeman. During 1941 several high explosive bombs and incendiaries fell on the port. Premises hit included the builder's yard and joinery works of Jepson & Sons situated at Cliff Road and Brown's timber yard at Three Cranes Wharf. It was there that the barge *EXCELSIOR* caught fire; she was damaged beyond repair, and was towed outside the Dock and abandoned on mud flats off Cobbold's brewery. A vessel used as a firefloat in the dock was sunk during one raid, and a fireman died. That same year a large bomb scored a direct hit on Fison's sulphuric acid plant at Cliff Quay, putting it out of action for several months and resulting in acid having to be brought from Flixborough. Cranfields became a casualty of one of the raids made on the port in 1942, a balloon barrage proving to be no deterrent to the Dornier Do.217 that dropped the bomb. Ransomes & Rapier's Waterside Works were hit during one of the bombing missions of 1943 and a gasholder was strafed. On this occasion one of the aircraft taking part in the raid struck the jib of Christopherson's crane at Griffin Wharf and crashed near the lock gates; the pilot was killed.

Staff of Cranfields Brothers formed a fire-fighting team to counter the use of incendiary bombs in air attacks. Some of them are seen here outside the mill with their trailer pump and the cup they have won in a fire-fighting competition.

LNER steamer sailings diverted from Parkeston Quay to Ipswich on outbreak of war.

Date	Ship	Nrt	Por	From		To		Total[1] cargo	Bunker coal (tons)
				Port	Cargo tons	Port	Cargo tons		
11 Dec 1939	mv IMPORT	199	Rotterdam	Rotterdam	357	Rotterdam	31		
19 Dec	mv IMPORT	199	Rotterdam	Rotterdam	327	Rotterdam	13		
27 Dec	mv IMPORT	199	Rotterdam	Rotterdam	345	Rotterdam	15		
1 Jan 1940	mv IMPORT	199	Rotterdam	Rotterdam	141	Rotterdam	2		
8 Jan	mv IMPORT	199	Rotterdam	Rotterdam	311	Rotterdam	73		
12 Jan	ss SHERINGHAM	429	Harwich	Antwerp	77	Antwerp	21		+67
15 Jan	mv LMPORT	199	Rotterdam	Rotterdam	175	Rotterdam	28		
19 Jan	ss SHERINGHAM	429	Harwich	Antwerp	55	Antwerp	26		+75
22 Jan	mv IMPORT	199	Rotterdam	Rotterdam	223	Rotterdam	20		
26 Jan	ss SHERINGHAM	429	Harwich	Zeebrugge	106	Antwerp	31		+69
29 Jan	mv IMPORT	199	Rotterdam	Rotterdam	251	Rotterdam	10		
3 Feb	ss SHERINGHAM	429	Harwich	Zeebrugge		Antwerp		99	+92
4 Feb	mv IMPORT	199	Rotterdam	Rotterdam		Rotterdam		138	
9 Feb	mv BREM	224	Rotterdam	Rotterdam		Rotterdam		178	
11 Feb	mv IMPORT	199	Rotterdam	Rotterdam		Rotterdam		276	
13 Feb	ss SHERINGHAM	429	Harwich	Antwerp		Antwerp		196	+92
15 Feb	mv BREM	224	Rotterdam	Rotterdam		Rotterdam		178	
18 Feb	mv IMPORT	199	Rotterdam	Rotterdam		Rotterdam		280	
21 Feb	ss SHERINGHAM	429	Harwich	Zeebrugge		Antwerp		436	+41
22 Feb	mv BREM	224	Rotterdam	Rotterdam		Rotterdam		208	
26 Feb	mv IMPORT	199	Rotterdam	Rotterdam		Rotterdam		276	
28 Feb	mv BREM	224	Rotterdam	Rotterdam		Rotterdam		250	
28 Feb	ss SHERINGHAM	429	Harwich	Zeebrugge		Antwerp		312	+68
2 Mar	ss FELIXSTOWE	360	Harwich	Zeebrugge		Zeebrugge		434	+39
4 Mar	mv IMPORT	199	Rotterdam	Rotterdam		Rotterdam		315	
4 Mar	ss DEWSBURY	947	Grimsby	Zeebrugge	676[2]	London	Light		+34
5 Mar	ss SHERINGHAM	429	Harwich	Zeebrugge		Zeebrugge		570	+50
6 Mar	mv BREM	224	Rotterdam	Rotterdam		Rotterdam		262	
9 Mar	ss FELIXSTOWE	360	Harwich	Zeebrugge		Antwerp		570	+50
11 Mar	mv IMPORT	199	Rotterdam	Rotterdam		Rotterdam		409	
13 Mar	ss SHERINGHAM	429	Harwich	Antwerp		Zeebrugge		632	+50
15 Mar	mv BREM	224	Rotterdam	Rotterdam		Rotterdam		228	
19 Mar	ss FELIXSTOWE	360	Harwich	Zeebrugge		Antwerp		221	+50
22 Mar	mv IMPORT	199	Rotterdam	Rotterdam		Rotterdam		300	
25 Mar	ss SHERINGHAM	429	Harwich	Antwerp		Antwerp		589	+68
27 Mar	ss FELIXSTOWE	360	Harwich	Antwerp		Antwerp		536	+50
31 Mar	mv BREM	224	Rotterdam	Rotterdam		Rotterdam		257	
1 Apr	ss DEWSBURY	947	Grimsby	Zeebrugge	659	London	Light		+100
3 Apr	mv IMPORT	199	Rotterdam	Rotterdam		Rotterdam		269	
4 Apr	ss SHERINGHAM	429	Harwich	Antwerp		Antwerp		261	+66
6 Apr	ss FELIXSTOWE	360	Harwich	Antwerp		Antwerp		146	+51
9 Apr	mv BREM	224	Rotterdam	Rotterdam		Rotterdam		113t	
11 Apr	ss SHERINGHAM	429	Harwich	Antwerp		Zeebrugge		231	+67
15 Apr	mv IMPORT	199	Rotterdam	Rotterdam		Rotterdam		97	
17 Apr	ss FELIXSTOWE	360	Harwich	Antwerp		Zeebrugge		221	+67
19 Apr	ss SHERINGHAM	429	Harwich	Antwerp		Zeebrugge		136	+66
24 Apr	mv BREM	224	Rotterdam	Rotterdam		Rotterdam		215	
26 Apr	ss FELIXSTOWE	360	Harwich	Antwerp		Zeebrugge		195	+33
27 Apr	mv IMPORT	199	Rotterdam	Rotterdam		Rotterdam		212	
29 Apr	ss SHERINGHAM	429	Harwich	Antwerp		Zeebrugge		282	+66
2 May	mv BREM	224	Rotterdam	Rotterdam		Rotterdam		150	
5 May	ss FELIXSTOWE	360	Harwich	Zeebrugge		Zeebrugge		198t	+51
6 May	mv IMPORT	199	Rotterdam	Rotterdam		Rotterdam		131	
9 May	ss SHERINGHAM	429	Harwich	Zeebrugge	93	Harwich	Light		+58
9 May	mv BREM	224	Rotterdam	Rotterdam	29	Poole	Light		
12 May	ss FELIXSTOWE	360	Harwich	Antwerp	103[3]	Harwich	Light	103	+46

Visits of Royal Navy ships and naval auxiliaries to Ipswich, 1941, 1944 and 1945

Abbreviations used in the tables

ABV   armed boarding vessel
A/P   auxiliary patrol
A/S   anti-submarine
BDV   boom defence vessel
D/L   dan layer
M/S   minesweeper
RCN   Royal Canadian Navy
Tlr.   trawler
TRV   torpedo recovery vessel

Name	Built	Number of Visits		
		1941	1944	1945
ABIDE, RAF drifter, PD 126	1915 Findochty			1
ADONIS, ex-Norwegian tlr. NORDHAV I. Sunk 15.4.1943 by E-boat off Lowestoft.	1915	1		
ALIDA, FD 1912, M/S 1915-19, BDV 1940-45	1915 Dundee	1	1	2
ALISDAIR, Harbour defence patrol craft 1939-45	1937 Amsterdam		1	1
AMSTERDAM, rescue tug (Dutch crew) 1940-44	1937		2	
ANDANES, tlr. A/P 1940, BDV 1941-45	1916	1		
ANN MELVILLE, A 254, M/S 1940-45	1909		1	
ARMANA, tlr. M/S 1940-45	1930	2		
ASTROS, BDV 1939-46	1917	1	2	
BARNEHURST, BDV	1939 Blyth			1
BASSET tlr. Built for Royal Navy, Basset Class A/S	1935	1		1
BASUTO, H 401, tlr. BDV 1940-45	1932 Beverley	1		
BEAUMARIS, Royal Navy Bangor Class MS	1940 Troon			1
BEN TARBERT, HL 21, tlr. Aux/Patrol 1940, BDV 1940, Store carrier 1944	1912 Aberdeen		1	4
BERBERIS ex-LORD HEWART, H 475, purchased 1939	1928 Selby		4	1
BESSIE, tug TID 107			1	1
BOOTLE, Bangor Class M/S	1941 Troon		1	
BRITOMART, Halcyon Class. Sunk 27 Aug 1944 by RAF in Eng. Channel	1938 Devonport DY		1	
BRYHER, Isles Class M/S	1943 Hull			1
BYMS (British Yard Minesweeper) 2014, 2036, 2041, 2047, 2057, 2058, 2194, 2202, 2205, 2206, 2233, 2252, 2257	Built in US, on lent-lease		13	6
CADELLA, GY 221, BDV 1939-46	1913 Selby	1		1
CARINA ex-yacht GOLDEN EAGLE, Ipswich Aux. Patrol	1899		3	2
CARISBROOKE, GY 472, M/S 1939-46	1928 Selby		3	
CASWELL, SA 70, M/S 1940-46	1917 Middlesbrough		2	2
CHAMPION, French tug seized July 1940. Became rescue tug 1940-44.	1892 London		1	
CHARLES HUTSON, RAF Barge. Visit to Ipswich ship yard, 1944	1889 Conyer, Kent		1	

Name	Built	Number of Visits		
		1941	1944	1945
CHEERFUL, RN Algerine Class M/S	1944 H&W Belfast			3
COMMANDER EVANS, H 20, tlr. A/P 1939, D/L 1944-45	1924 Selby	3		
CORALE and COSMIC, RAF lighters			1	
COVENTRY CITY, tlr. A/S 1939-45	1937	1		
DALMATIA, tlr. Purchased as M/S 1939, D/L 1944	1928			1
DESTINN, GY 307, A/P 1940, M/S 1942, water carrier 1943-45	1914 Beverley	5		
DHOON, FD 54, renamed DHOON GLEN 1943 M/S	1915 Selby	1	1	
DONNA NOOK, FD 237, A/P 1939, M/S 1941, sunk in collision with STELLA RIGEL off Harwich 1943.	1915 Selby	1		
DOONIE BRAES, A 881, D/L 1940, M/S 1942-45	1918 Aberdeen	5		
DUNBAR, Royal Navy Bangor Class M/S	1942 Blyth		1	
EARL ESSEX, GY 48, Aux Patrol 1939, M/S 1940-46	1914 Beverley	1		
EDWARD WALMSLEY, FD 412, M/S 1939-46	1919 S. Shields	1	5	
EDWARDIAN, GY 328, M/S 1939-46	1931 Beverley	1	4	2
EDWINA, FD 205, Aux. Patrol M/S. Lost 29/11/41	1915 Dundee	1		
ELFREDA, Catherine Class US M/S	1943			1
EMPIRE MAPLE tug			4	
EMPIRE TAPLEY, 102nrt, Royal Fleet Auxilary, removed oil ex-LCT 5 at Cliff Quay for Harwich				2
ERIDANUS, tlr,, ex-PELICAN, GY 91, fuel carrier 1944	1905 Selby		1	
ETRUSCAN, GY 939, Aux. Patrol 1939, M/S 1940, fuel carrier 1944.	1913 Beverley	1		
EVELYN ROSE, GY tlr., Aux. Patrol 1939, M/S 1941-45		1		
EY 1022			1	
FAIRWAY, GY 488, Aux. Patrol 1940, D/L 1941-46	1918 Selby	5	1	
FAL, HM lighter, collected waste oil ex-BYMSs				1
FELIXSTOWE, Bangor Class Royal Navy M/S		1		
FIREFLY, HM trawler ex-ST JUST 1930, M/S 1939-45			3	1
FLANDRE, GY 598, Aux Patrol, 1940, 1942-45 M/S	1915 Beverley	2		
FLOATING DOCK + KENIA + BESSIE			1	
FORT YORK, built for RCN Royal Navy Bangor Class	1942 Canada			1
FRANC TIREUR, GY 1041, Aux Patrol, M/S 1941. Sunk by E-Boat off Harwich 25/9/43.	1916 Selby	4		
FREIJA, Salvage Vessel of London. Ex-Harwich to Harwich.			1	
FRIENDSHIP, ex-US Navy, Algerine Class	1943 Toronto		1	
GAVA, FD 380, Aux. Patrol 1939, M/S 1942, target towing 1942-46.	1920 Aberdeen	7	1	
GEORGE ADGELL, FD 368, Aux. Patrol 1940, M/S 1941-46	1920 Beverley	2	5	
GEORGE ROBB, A 406, M/S 1939-46	1930 Aberdeen		3	
GIROFLÉE, motor yacht, Aux. Patrol, examination vessel	1935 Greenock	1		
GLEANER, Royal Navy M/S. Ex-survey vessel.	1937 Hartlepool		1	3
GREENFLY, ex-QUANTOCK, H 161, A/S, purchased 1939	1936 Selby			1
GUILLEMOT, Corvette, Kingfisher Class	1939 Dunbarton	1	2	1
HAINAULT, HM tender, ex-Harwich to dock			1	
HALCYON, first of RN Halcyon Class M/S	1933 Clydebank			1
HANNARAY, Isles Class M/S	1944 Beverley		1	1
HARRIS, Royal Navy M/S, Isles Class, ex-GILSAY	1944 Hull		2	
HAYBURN WYKE, FD 99, Aux. Patrol, M/S. Sunk 2/1/45 by torpedo at anchor off Ostend.	1917 Selby	1	2	
HAZARD, Royal Navy Halcyon Class	1937 Hartlepool			2
HERMETRAY, tlr, Royal Navy Isles Class	1944 Selby			2
HILDA COOPER, YH 392, examination service 1939, harbour service 1944-45	1944 Selby	2		
HM TANKER VIC 41 ex-Harwich to Harwich 12/9/44			1	
HORNBEAM, H 116, ex- LORD TRENT, purchased as M/S 1939	1929 Selby			1
HOUND, Royal Navy Algerine Class M/S	1942			1
ILFRACOMBE, Bangor Class Royal Navy M/S	1941	1		
JACINTA, FD 235, Aux. Patrol 1940, M/S 1942, wreck disposal 1944	1915 Selby	5		

APPENDICES

Name	Built	Number of Visits		
		1941	1944	1945
JASON, Halcyon Class M/S	1936 Troon			1
JEANNIE McINTOSH, BCK 209, M/S 1940, Aux. Patrol Drifter 1940-46	1915 Portessie	3	11	
JOHN CATTLING, LO 364, M/S 1939-45	1918 Paisley	1		
KAREN, motor launch			1	
KAREN II, water carrier			4	
KENIA, tug, owner Wm. Watkins, London. Examination vessel 1939, rescue tug 1940-45	1927 Selby		7	1
KINGS GREY, H402, M/S 1939-45	1915 Beverley	6		
KINGSTON OLIVINE, H 209, purchased as A/S tlr 1939	1930 Beverley			1
KITTIWAKE, Kingfisher Class patrol sloop	1936 Woolston		3	2
LADY PHILOMENA, H 167, A/S 1939-45	1936 Beverley			1
LBO 32, 33, 38, 90			4	
LBU 90			1	
LC 4O			1	
LCH 245			1	
LCI (Landing Craft Infantry) 125, 376, 381, 477			4	1
LCIL 216, 509, 512 (Landing craft infantry large)	Built US			4
LCL 131, 181				2
LCM (Landing Craft Mechanised) 1051, 1053, 1054, 1055, 1056, 1057, 1058, 1059, 1130, 1132, 1208, 1239, 1244, 1282, 1287, 1290, 1296, 1297, 1371, 1393			21	
LCP(Landing Craft personnel) 514, 557, both to Woolverstone			2	
LCT (Landing Craft Tank) 1084, 2310			2	
LCT 214 ex-Scarborough with HM stores for RNA station Halesworth				1
LCT 884 to ship yard			1	
LCV (Landing Craft Vehicle) 530, 625			2	
LENNOX, Royal Navy Algerine Class M/S	1943		1	
LEPHRETO, LO 458, M/S 1939, fuel carrier 1944	1917		1	
LESLIE WEST to ship yard. RAF barge	1900 Gravesend		1	
LIBERATOR, ex- HEKLA, GY 118, Aux. Patrol 1940, A/S 1942-45	1929 Selby	6	4	2
LIBRA, GY 687, Aux. Patrol 1939, M/S, fuel carrier 1944-45	1912 Dundee		6	1
LIDDOCH, tlr, Aux. Patrol 1939-41	1919	4		
LLANDUDNO, Royal Navy Bangor Class M/S			1	
LORD ASHFIELD, H 53, M/S 1939-45	1929 Selby			1
LORD BEACONSFIELD, GY 563, Aux. Patrol 1939, M/S 1941-45, wrecked 1945	1915 Selby	1		
LORD MELCHETT, H 1, M/S 1939, D/L 1944-46	1928 Selby		2	1
LOVANIA, GY 700, Aux. Patrol 1940, M/S 1941, towing duty 1945-46	1912 Beverley			1
LST (Landing Ship Tank) 63, 165, 198 (for degaussing), 200, 261, 366, 403 (to Bay for degaussing)			7	
LYDIA LONG, INS 32, M/S 1939, harbour service 1940-45	1918 Lowestoft			1
MALLARD, Kingfisher Class patrol sloop	1936 Banff		3	
MARAIME, motor launch			1	
MARE, LT 362, drifter, M/S 1939-45	1911 Aberdeen	8	4	1
MARION, 715/1896, harbour defence patrol craft	1896 Leith		1	
MARY A HASTIE, Aux. Patrol 1939, M/S 1941-45	1930 Aberdeen	3	4	2
MBL IV to ship yard				1
MFV (Motor Fishing Vessel) 1024, 1079, 1093, 1097, 1537			1	4
MICHAEL GRIFFITH, LO 529, M/S 1939, MDV 1944	1919 Beverley		1	1
MICO, tug			1	
ML (Fairmile B-Class motor launches, 112ft, built 1940-44) 237, 275, 286, 342, 452, 466, 915			5	2
MMS (Motor Minesweeper) 2, 22, 26, 38, 54, 73, 82, 112, 136, 138, 141, 187, 191, 193, 212, 226, 227, 231, 234, 237, 269, 286, 287, 290, 292, 547, 1011, 1014, 1022, 1025, 1031, 1046, 1074, 1081, 1082, 1438, 2149, 2167, 2206, 2233		1	55	14
MMS 1046 to ship yard			1	
MMJ 622				1

Name	Built	Number of Visits		
		1941	1944	1945
MONARCH, 62grt, Royal Fleet Auxilary, probably motor yacht hired as depot ship 1941. Ex-Harwich.			1	
MORAVIA, GY 1018, Aux. Patrol 1940, M/S 1941, mined, sunk 14/3/43	1917	1		
MOUNTJOY, 146nrt, tanker, came with oil for SPEEDWELL	1898 Copenhagen	1		1
MTB (Motor Torpedo Boat) 478, 499, 773, 6739			3	1
NAIRNSIDE, INS 296, drifter 84/1912, M/s 1939, A/P 1940, ferry service 1942-45	1912 Inverness	4		
NESS POINT ((LNER harbour tug at Lowestoft), tender to HMS MARTELLO (Lowestoft) + LCT			1	
NOORDSVARDER, tug, reg. Terschelling, Aux. Patrol 1940, D/L 1944-45	1897 Danzig		1	
NORLAN, BCK 177, drifter, boom tender 1940-45	1914 Buckie	1		
OCEAN EDDY, LH 62, tlr, BDV 1940-45	1929 Aberdeen	1		
OCEAN SCOUT, LT10, drifter, A/P 1939, TRV 1940-45, to Bay for degaussing, 1944	1913	1	1	1
OHM, H 128, M/S 1939-45	1915 Selby		1	
OKINO, GY 1060, tlr, BDV 1940-46, to Bay for degausing 1945	1917 Selby		1	2
ONYX, Royal Navy M/S, Algerine Class	1942 Belfast		1	
ORESTES, Royal Navy M/S, Algerine Class	1942		2	
OVERFLAKKEE (Dutch), ex-MMS 1046 1046				1
OYSTERMOUTH CASTLE, SA 4, M/S 1941-46	1914 Middlesbrough	1		
PATTI, tlr, A/P 1939, M/S 1941-46	1929	2		
PAUL RYKENS, tlr, , reg. Aberdeen, A/S tlr 1939-45	1935 Wesermund	2		
PRINCE VICTOR, GY 569	1910 Selby		1	
PUFFIN, Kingfisher Class patrol sloop	1936 Banff		3	
Q 100, 105, 106, 110, 550		1	4	
RAMPANT, 372 nrt, ex-SS PHAEDRA, renamed EMPIRE SENTINEL, seized 1939	1898 Bremerhaven			1
RATTLESNAKE, Royal Naval Algerine Class M/S	1943			1
RAYMONT, GY 304, A/P 1939, M/S 1940, store carrier 1944-46	1916 Beverley	1		
READY to Bay for degaussing, THV?				1
RED GAUNTLET, LO 33, tlr, M/S 1939, sunk 1943 by E-boat in N. Sea	1930 Stockton	1		
RFA (Royal Fleet Auxiliary), C616, ex-London Admiralty stores				1
RIVER LEVEN, GY 293	1918 Paisley		1	
RML (Fairmile B-Class rescue motor launches, 112 ft) 52O, 532, 544, 546, 547, 553			6	4
RONSO, GY 605, A/P 1939, M/S 1940, fuel carrier 1944-46	1915 Beverley		1	
ROSE-HAUGH, drifter, M/S 1939, degaussing vessel 1940-46	1918 Sandhaven			2
ROSETTE, steam trawler, ex-ROSE, dan-layer 1940, renamed, M/S 1940-45	1911 Aberdeen			1
ROSS, Royal Navy Hunt Class M/S	1919		1	
ROYAL SOVEREIGN, THLV?, for degausing		1		
RYE, Royal Navy Bangor Class M/S	1940 Troon			1
SABINE, BU 1950,tug ex-USA, purchased as rescue tug 1940			1	
SALAMANDER, Royal Navy M/S. Lost 27.8.44 with BRITOMART, both Halcyon Class.	1936 Cowes		1	
SAPPHIRE, BF 322	1910 Montrose	1		
SARAH HIDE, LT 1157, M/S 1939-46	1921 Aberdeen	5	3	
SEAGULL, Halcyon Class M/S	1937 Devonport DY		1	2
SHEARWATER, Kingfisher Class patrol sloop	1939 Cowes		3	3
SHELDRAKE, Kingfisher Class patrol sloop	1937 Woolston		6	1
SHOVA, whaler, D/L 1940, mooring vessel 1942, target towing 1943-46	1912	2		
SIGNA, whaler, D/L 1940-45	1926	1		
SIR GALAHAD, Round Table Class	1941			1
SIR LANCELOT, Round Table Class	1941			1
SORANUS, GY 131, M/S 1940-465	1906 Selby		2	2
SPEEDWELL,. Royal Navy Halcyon Class M/S	1935		1	2
SPINA, whaler, D/L 1940-45	1926	1		
ST MELLONS, rescue tug	1918 Govan		1	
STAR OF THE REALM, GY, ex-NORDSTJERNAN, BDV 1940-46	1917 Selby			1

APPENDICES

Name	Built	Number of Visits		
		1941	1944	1945
STEADFAST, ex-US Navy	1943		1	
STELLA LEONIS, tlr, M/S and D/L	1928	2	1	
STELLA RIGEL, tlr, M/S and D/L	1926		1	
STOUR, naval tlr, Mersey type, ex-*DANIEL FEARALL* (1920)	1917 Selby		6	2
STRATHELLIOT, A 46, Aux. Patrol 1940, store carrier 1942-46	1915 Aberdeen	6		
STRATHMAREE, A 72, Aux-Patrol 1939, store carrier 1942-45	1914 Aberdeen		1	2
SUNBEAM II, LT 304, D/L 1939, TRV 1940-45	1916 Oulton Broad		1	
SURSAY, tlr, Royal Navy Isles Class	1945			1
TANGANYIKA, Royal Navy Algerine Class M/S	1944			1
TATTOO, Catherine Class US M/S	1943			1
TEHANA, LO 132,. M/S 1939, wreck dispersal 1944-46	1929 Selby	1		
THOMAS LEEDS, M 70, M/S 1939-45	1919 Aberdeen	1		
THV (Trinity House Vessel) 71, 85, 90		3		
TID 107 tug				2
TOCOGAY, tlr, Royal Navy Isles Class	1945			1
TUNISIAN, BDV 39, tlr, sunk by mine off Harwich Harbour 1942	1930	1		
TURQUOISE, tlr, A/S	1934	1		1
TYPHOON, tlr, ex-*SYRIAN* until 1940, Aux. Patrol 1939, ABV 1942-45	1918	1		
UGM 122				1
US 509				1
USLC 216, 1512			1	1
VIC 41, HM tanker, ex-Harwich to Harwich 12/9/44			1	
VIC 76 ex-Rowhedge to Bay for degaussing				1
VIDONIA, GY 257, A/P 1940, fuel carrier 1943, sunk in collision 1944	1907 Selby	3		
VIKING BANK, Dutch trawler, M/S 1940-45 (Dutch crew)			3	
VINDELICIA, GY 954, tlr,. Aux.Patrol 1940, fuel carrier 1943, towing duty 1944-45	1913 Beverley	4		
WARSTAR, GY 73, tlr, Aux.Patrol 1940, M/S 1942, fuel carrier 1944-46	1914 Beverley	3		
WATER MAIDENS HML			1	
WDML, water boat ex-Parkeston for distilled water			1	
WELBECK, GY 165, tlr, Aux. Patrol 1940, M/S 1941-46	1917 Selby			2
WHITE MAY HM tanker, once to ship yard 1944			3	1
WIDGEON, Kingfisher Class patrol sloop	1938 Clyde		3	2
WILLA, LT 43, tlr, D/L 1940, harbour service 1942-45	1935 Lowestoft	4	2	
WILLIAM STEPHEN, A 24, Aux.Patrol 1939, M/S 1940, sunk 25/10/43 by E-boat off Cromer.	1917 Aberdeen	1		
WOOLVERSTONE, tender			3	
WYOMING, GY 483, tlr, Aux. Patrol 1939, M/S 1941, sunk 20.5.44 by mine off Harwich.	1915 Selby	2	1	
ZAREBA, ex-*ELLENA*, tlr, M/S 1940, BBV 1944-45	1921		1	

Synopsis of deep-sea arrivals at Ipswich, September 1939 to November 1943

Date	Ship	From	To	Depart to	Cargo	Importer
11 Sep 1939	SZENT GELLERT 2,915 nrt, reg. Budapest	Rosario			Wheat	Cranfield
14 Oct 1939	ss MONKLEIGH 3,104 nrt, reg. London	New Westminster (Canada)			Lumber Lumber	Brown Gabriel
21 Nov 1939	ss GOTTPRID 887 nrt, reg. Mariehamn	Mesane (White Sea)			Timber	MOS
28 Dec 1939	ss BLAIR SPEY Built 1929 Ardrossan 2,521 nrt, reg. Glasgow	New York	BB	Sunderland 7 Jan '40	2647 tons Wheat 1378 tons Wheat 1439 tons Wheat 128 tons Wheat	Cranfield Paul Marriage Rankin
16 Jan 1940	ss KILDALE Built 1924 Sunderland 2,310 nrt, reg. Whitby Bombed & sunk 3 Nov 1940	R Plate	BB	S. Shields 2 Feb	2533 tons Wheat 1185 tons Wheat 129 tons Wheat 1584 tons Wheat 199 tons Wheat	Cranfield Marriage Rankin Paul Pledge (Whitstable)
3 Feb 1940	ss CAPE CORSO Built 1905 Glasgow 2,338 nrt, reg. Glasgow Bombed & sunk 2 May 1942	Santa Fe	BB	Middlesbrough 14 Feb	2090 tons Wheat 138 tons Wheat 749 tons Wheat	Cranfield Paul Marriage
9 Mar 1940	ss BLAIR SPEY Built 1929 Ardrossan 2,521 nrt, reg. Glasgow	Sfax	CQ	Tyne 22 Mar	5899 tons Phos of lime 7.5 tons Camel hair	Fison Lewcock & Pemberton
10 Mar 1940	ss DARCOILER Built 1928 Glasgow 2,544 nrt, reg. Glasgow Torpedoed 28 Sept 1940	Portland (Maine)	BB	Tyne 29 Mar	3688 tons Wheat 828 tonsWheat 1550 tons Wheat	Cranfield Paul Marriage
11 Mar 1940	ss DAYROSE Built 1928 Sunderland 2,605 nrt, reg. Cardiff Torpedoed 14 Jan 1942.	Santa Fe	BB	Hull 31 Mar	2105 tons Wheat 634 tons Wheat 1107 tons Wheat 132 tons Wheat *(note 1)* 2980 tons Maize	Cranfield Paul Marriage Read (Norwich) Paul
28 Mar 1940	ss BARON LOVAT Built 1926 Irvine 2,037 nrt, reg. Ardrossan Torpedoed 6 Jun 1941	Sfax	CQ	Harwich 24 April	5300 tons Phos of lime	Fison
2 Apr 1940	ss KINGSBOROUGH Built 1928 Port Glasgow 2,030 nrt, reg. Glasgow	Huelva	CQ	Cardiff 24 April	4724 tons Copper ore and Pyrites	Fison
26 Apr 1940	ss LANGLEEBROOK Built 1929 Newcastle 2,546 nrt, reg. Newcastle	Philadelphia	BB	Cardiff 8 May	4428 tons Wheat 768 tons Wheat 1771 tons Wheat 133 tons Wheat *(note 2)*	Cranfield Paul Marriage Read (Norwich)
29 Apr 1940	ss PORTUGAL Built 1906 Rostock, reg. Antwerp	Huelva	CQ	Tyne 5 May	4742 tons Pyrites	A/c Customs & Excise
6 May 1940	ss BARON ERSKINE Built 1930 Glasgow 2,216 nrt, reg. Ardrossen Torpedoed 6 Jan 1942	Sfax	CQ	Cardiff 21 May	5300 tons Phos of lime 527 tons Esparto grass 28 tons rags	*(See note 3 for cargo breakdown)*
22 May 1940	ss BARON SALTOUN Built 1927 Irvine 2,041 nrt, reg. Ardrossan Mined 12 June 1940 Cherbourg	Huelva	CQ	Not known 30 May	5406 tons Pyrites	Fison

APPENDICES

Date	Ship	From	To	Depart to	Cargo	Importer
29 May 1940	ss PARTHENON Built 1908 W Hartlepool 2,030 nrt, reg. Chios	San Lorenzo	BB	Hull 5 July	1455 tons Wheat 166 tons Wheat 471 tons Wheat	Cranfield Paul Marriage
30 May 1940	ss EMMA PLEIN Built 1926 Rotterdam 3,155 nrt, reg. Rotterdam	Bahia Blanco	BB	Hull 21 June	975 tons Wheat 6427 tons Barley	Cranfield Paul
5 Jun 1940	ss CZARDA Built 1917 Sunderland 2,352 nrt, reg. Budapest	Sorel	BB	Blyth 20 June	3378 tons Wheat 1426 tons Wheat 825 tons Wheat 128 tons Wheat 387 tons Wheat	Cranfield Paul Marriage Rankin Reckitt & Colman, Nor.
16 Jun 1940	mv AMY LENSON Reg. London	Sfax	CQ	Swansea 28 June	4860 tons Phos of lime 303 tons Esparto grass	Fison T Green, Soho Mills, Bourne End
23 Jul 1940	ss DALEMOOR Built 1922 Newcastle 3,660 nrt, reg. London Mined 15 Jan 1945	Sorel (Qubec)	BB	Harwich 5 Aug	4428 tons Wheat 1575 tons Wheat 996 tons Wheat 110 tons Wheat 471 tons Wheat 128 tons Wheat 110 tons Wheat (note 4) 155 tons Wheat (note5) 155 tons Wheat (note 6)	Cranfield Paul Marriage Pledge (Whitstable) LPAGC Rankin Hooker (Chatham) G. Chitty (Dover) C. Hudson (Ramsgate)
24 Jul 1940	ss EMBASSAGE Built 1935 Sunderland 2,912 nrt, reg. Newcastle Torpedoed 27 Aug 1941	Montreal	BB	Tyne 5 Aug	2657 tons Wheat 5641 tons Wheat	Cranfield Paul
1 Aug 1940	ss EMPIRE SNIPE (see details, EMPIRE shipping table)	Huelva	CQ	Not known	3424 tons Pyrites	Fison
3 Aug 1940	ss BRYNHILD Built 1907 Sunderland 1,348 nrt, reg. London. Mine damage 17 Jul 1942 Gibraltar	Halifax (Canada)	CQ	Not known	3065 loads Timber	Brown
20 Aug 1940	ss DAYROSE Built 1928 Sunderland 2,605 nrt, reg. Cardiff Torpedoed 14 Jan 1942	Rosario	BB	Hull 31 Aug	2021 tons Wheat 110 tons Wheat 534 tons Wheat 3265 tons Maize 305 tons Bran 193 tons Middlings 453 tons Pollards	Cranfield Marriage Paul Paul Paul Paul Paul
22 Aug 1940	ss GRAIGLAS Built 1940 Sunderland 2,548 nrt, reg. Cardiff	Vancouver (Canada)	CQ	Tyne 16 Sept	1235 tons Wheat 6843 loads Timber	Cranfield Brown
8 Oct 1940	ss HAVTOR Built 1930 Porsgrund 867 nrt, reg. Oslo	New Brunswick (Canada)	D	Blyth 18 Oct	2448 loads Timber	Brown
17 Oct 1940	ss SALVUS Built 1928 Newcastle 2,948 nrt, reg. Cardiff Bombed 4 April 1941	R. Plate	BB	Hull 31 Oct	4562 tons Wheat 442 tons Wheat 389 tons Wheat 938 tons Wheat 183 tons Bran 805 tons Pollards 173 tons Middlings 24 tons Wheatgerm	Cranfield Marriage LPAGC Paul Paul Paul Paul Paul
18 Oct 1940	ss BARON KINNAIRD Built 1927 Old Kilpatrick 2,022 nrt, reg. Ardrossan Torpd. 12 Mar 1943 Atlantic	Tampa/Halifax	CQ	Tyne 26 Oct	5000 tons Phos of lime	Fison

Date	Ship	From	To	Depart to	Cargo	Importer
21 Nov 1940	ss EMPIRE KESTREL Built 1919 by Great Lakes Engineering Co. at Ecorse, Michigan for US Shipping Board. 1,617 nrt, reg. London. Acquired by Ministry of Shipping 1940. Torpedoed 1943 off Algiers.	Huelva	CQ	Tyne 7 Nov	3595 tons Pyrites	Fison
7 Dec 1940	ss BARON PENTLAND Built 1927 Irvine 2,044 nrt, reg. Ardrossan Torpedoed 19 Sept 1941	Pictou NS / Sydney NS (Canada)	CQ	Blyth 27 Dec	4214 loads Spruce /Birch	Brown
12 Dec 1940	ss RING Built 1927 Stockholm 622 nrt, reg. Stockholm	Huelva	D	Hull 20 Feb	1659 tons Pyrites	Min. of Supply
17 Dec 1940	ss BONNINGTON COURT Built 1929 Glasgow 3,012 nrt, reg. London Bombed 19 Jan 1941 near Sunk Lightship	Vancouver / Portland (Oregon)	CQ	Tyne 16 Jan	1610 tons Wheat 221 tons Wheat 144 tons Wheat 7065 loads Timber	Cranfields Marriage Paul Brown
10 Jan 1941	mv ALOITH 3,246 nrt, reg. Rotterdam	Vancouver (Canada)	CQ	Hull 17 Feb	8371 loads Timber 500 tons Lead Bars 300 tons Lead Pigs 200 tons Zinc Bars	Brown
28 Jan 1941	ss RUDBY Built 1924 W. Hartlepool 2,989 nrt, reg. W. Hartlepool	Tampa	CQ	Tyne 11 Feb	4973 tons Phos of lime 1131 tons Phos of lime	Fison W. Norfolk Farmers
2 Feb 1941	ss LOKE Built 1915 Stockton 1,431 nrt, reg. Oslo	Halifax	BB	Immingham 14 Mar	1917 tons Wheat 189 tons Wheat 367 tons Wheat	Cranfield Paul Marriage
12 Feb 1941	mv BRABANT 1,287 nrt, reg. Antwerp	R Plate	BB	Immingham Not Known	1003 tons Wheat 1930 tons Maize 313 tons Pollards 431 tons Bran	Cranfield Paul Paul Paul
18 Feb 1941	ss GANYMETES Built 1917 Kinderdijk 1,551 nrt, reg. Amsterdam	Tampa	CQ	Grangemouth 1 Mar	2646 tons Phos of Lime 942 tons Phos of Lime	Fison W. Norfolk Farmers
23 Mar 1941	ss CARA Built 1929 Burntisland 1,078 nrt, reg. Glasgow	Huelva	CQ	Harwich 7 April	2721 tons Pyrites	W. Norfolk Farmers
29 Mar 1941	ss PHOTINIA Built 1938 Sunderland 2,457 nrt, reg. N. Shields Broken up 1974	Halifax	BB	London 6 April	5439 tons Wheat 332 tons Wheat	Cranfield LPAGC
11 Apr 1941	ss BONDE Built Porsgrund 898 nrt, reg. Oslo	Halifax via Methil (part cargo)	D	Harwich 14 April	1576 tons Wheat 282 tons Wheat	Cranfield Paul
18 Apr 1941	ss EMPIRE STRAIT Built 1940 as a collier, W. Hartlepool. 1,574 nrt, reg. Hartlepool. Bomb-damaged off Yarmouth 28 April 1941. Broken up Holland 1960.	Huelva	CQ	Hartlepool 26 Apr	3477 tons Phos of lime	Fison
21 Apr 1941	ss TENAX 2,392 nrt, reg. Glasgow	Halifax (Canada)	BB	Tyne 30 Apr	3200 tons Wheat 1361 tons Wheat 354 tons Wheat 509 tons Wheat	Cranfield Paul Marriage LPAGC

APPENDICES

Date	Ship	From	To	Depart to	Cargo	Importer
1 May 1941	ss SHUNA Built 1915 Sunderland 912 nrt, reg. Glasgow Mined 14 July 1942	Huelva	CQ	Harwich 5 May	1141 tons Pyrites 1217 tons Pyrites	Fison W. Norfolk Farmers
4 May 1941	ss TENNESSEE Built 1921 Copenhagen 1,372 nrt, reg. London Bombed 22 Sept 1942	Portland (Maine)	CQ/D	Tyne 12 May	2471 tons Wheat 470 tons Wheat	Cranfield Paul
9 May 1941	ss ROSSUM Built 1928 Ysel, reg. Amsterdam	Huelva	CQ	Not known	3626 tons Phos of lime	Fison
18 May 1941	ss LOKE Built 1915 Stockton 1,431 nrt, reg. Oslo	Halifax	CQ/D	Not known	3130 tons Wheat 404 tons Wheat	Cranfield Paul
5 Jun 1941	ss RIO BLANCO Built 1922 Blyth 2,510 nrt, reg. London Torpedoed 1 Apr 1942	Boston		Not known	5885 tons Wheat 548 tons Wheat 8 loads Oak Boards	Cranfield Paul Brown
26 Jun 1941	ss NORTH DEVON Built 1924 S. Shields 2,239 nrt reg. Newcastle Bomb damaged 5 Jul 1941	St Johns Newfoundland	BB	Newcastle 4 July	5128 tons Wheat 548 tons Wheat	Cranfield Paul
4 Jul 1941	ss KEILA Built 1905 Sunderland 2,302 nrt, reg. Glasgow	Quebec	BB	Harwich 14 Jul	4252 tons Wheat 1128 tons Wheat	Cranfield Paul
6 Jul 1941	ss SNAR Built 1920 Willington Quay 1,957 nrt reg. Haugesund	Tampa	CQ	Tyne 18 Jul	4693 tons Super phosphate	Fison
24 Jul 1941	ss EUTHALIA Built 1918 Rotterdam 3,023 nrt, reg. Andros Last ship discharged B. Bay	Sorel	BB	Newcastle 2 Aug	3542 tons Wheat 2414 tons Wheat 490 tons Wheat	Cranfield Paul Marriage
28 Jul 1941	ss VANELLUS Built 1921 Sunderland 915 nrt, reg. Liverpool	Huelva	CQ	Harwich 2 Aug	1866 tons Phos of lime 2368 tons Pyrites	W. Norfolk Farmers MOS c/o Lewcock & Pemberton
13 Aug 1941	ss IOANNIS FRANGOS Built 1912 Stockton 2,099 nrt, reg. Chios	Sorel	CQ	Tyne 25 Aug	4059 tons Wheat 653 tons Wheat 221 tons Wheat	Cranfield Paul Marriage
7 Sept 1941	ss LINGE Built 1928 Ysel 1,260 nrt, reg. Rotterdam	Curacoa	D	London 14 Sept	2936 tons Phos of lime	Fison
7 Sept 1941	ss BARON KINNAIRD Built 1927 Old Kilpatrick 2,022 nrt, reg. Ardrossan Torpd. 12 Mar 1943 Atlantic	Tampa	CQ	Tyne 15 Sept	5000 tons Phosphate	Fison
9 Sept 1941	ss LAKE HALLWIL 1,996 nrt, reg. London	Quebec (Canada)	CQ	Tyne 26 Sept	4480 loads Timber	Brown/ MOS
16 Sep 1941	ss SKJOLD Built 1904 Sunderland 797 nrt, reg. London Built for DFDS	St John New Brunswick	D	London 21 Sept	1443 tons Wheat 149 tons Wheat	Cranfield Paul
16 Sep 1941	TENNESSEE Built 1921 Copenhagen 1,371 nrt, reg. London Bombed 22 Sept 1942	Sorel	CQ/D	Harwich 1 Oct	2897 tons Wheat 445 tons Wheat 64 tons Lorries & parts	Cranfield Paul Movement Control

Date	Ship	From	To	Depart to	Cargo	Importer
17 Sept 1941	ss GRADO 1,842 nrt, reg. London	Tampa	CQ	Harwich 30 Sept	3638 tons Phosphate	Fison
11 Oct 1941	ss EMPIRE SCOUT Built 1936 at Lubeck as EILBEK. 1,309 nrt, reg. London. Captured North Atlantic, Nov 1939, while returning to Germany. Acquired by Ministry of Shipping 1940.	Montreal	D	Tyne 17 Oct	2258 tons Wheat 221 tons Wheat	Cranfield Paul
17 Oct 1941	ss LOKE Built 1915 Stockton 1,431 nrt, reg. Oslo	Montreal	CQ	Harwich 25 Oct	3293 tons Wheat 332 tons Wheat	Cranfield Paul
26 Oct 1941	ss ROSSUM Built 1928 Ysel 1,255 nrt, reg. Amsterdam	Curacoa	CQ	Harwich 2 Nov	2960 tons Phos of lime	Fison
16 Dec 1941	ss GLAISDALE Built 1929 Sunderland 2,262 nrt, reg. Whitby	New York	CQ	Hartle-pool 29 Dec	4346 tons Wheat 2916 tons Wheat 117 tons Wheat	Cranfield Paul Marriage
5 Jan 1942	ss JUNO Built 1908 Rotterdam 1,088 nrt, reg. Amsterdam	Curacoa	CQ	Harwich 10 Jan	1910 tons Phosphate	MOS c/o Lewcock & Pemberton
5 Jan 1942	ss OGMORE CASTLE 1,441 nrt, reg. Cardiff	Huelva	CQ	Not known 15 Jan	2060 tons Pyrites 995 tons Pyrites	Fison W. Norfolk Farmers
21 Mar 1942	KATINGO HADJIPATERA Built 1913 Sunderland as SOUTH PACIFIC, 1933 LADY KATHLEEN, 1934 HARRY WALTON, 1935 AVON RIVER, 1937 HARTLAND POINT. 2,307 nrt, reg. Chios	Halifax	CQ	Harwich 29 Mar	5180 tons Wheat 1904 tons Wheat	Cranfield Paul
17 Apr 1942	ss FAR 1,420 nrt, reg. Farsund	Tampa	CQ	Tyne 22 Apr	3205 tons Phosphate	MOS c/o Lewcock & Pemberton
23 April 1942	TIMOK Built 1924 Rotterdam 1,971 nrt, reg. Susak	Baltimore	CQ	Tyne 30 April	3447 tons Wheat 1390 tons Wheat 500 tons Wheat	Cranfield Paul LPAGC
1 May 1942	IOANNIS FRANGOS Built 1912 Stockton 2,099 nrt, reg. Chios	St John New Brunswick		Canada 6 May	4561 tons Wheat 2205 tons Wheat 145 tons Wheat	Cranfield Paul LPGAC
7 May 1942	ss ANNA Built 1919 Greenock 3,193 nrt, reg. Piraeus	St John New Brunswick	CQ	Tyne Not known	6685 tons Wheat	LPAGC
16 May 1942	RADHURST 2,125 nrt, reg. London Torpedoed 21 Feb 1943	Boston	CQ	Sunder-land 22 May	3434 tons Wheat 2010 tons Wheat 442 tons Wheat	Cranfield Paul Gibbons
22 May 1942	ss LINGE Built 1928 Ysel 1,260 nrt, reg. Rotterdam	Curacoa	CQ	Sunder-land 29 May	2900 tons Phosphate	MOS c/o Lewcock & Pemberton
5 Jun 1942	ss EMPIRE CLIFF Built 1940 Goole. Lost 1956 Lisbon to Casablanca.	Canada	CQ	Not known	1044 loads spruce/fir/hemlock/cedar/Columbian pine/redwood	MOS Timber Control
15 Sept 1942	ss EMPIRE SPEY, ex-BLAIR SPEY (see text, Port at War chapter)	Huelva	CQ	Tyne 23 Sept	5055 tons Pyrites +Cork, Beaufort aircraft, empty mailbags, total 209 tons	MOS c/o Lewcock & Pemberton

APPENDICES

Date	Ship	From	To	Depart to	Cargo	Importer
18 Sept 1942	ss *MARGIT* Built 1924 Copenhagen 1,026 nrt, reg. London (reg Copenhagen pre-war)	Parrsboro (Nova Scotia)	CQ	Hull 28 Sept	2594 loads Timber	MOS c/o Lewcock & Pemberton
19 Sep 1942	*EUTHALIA* Built 1918 Rotterdam 3,023 nrt, reg. Andros	Montreal	CQ	Harwich 26 Sept	5607 tons Wheat 4280 tons Wheat 442 tons Wheat 110 tons Wheat	Cranfield Paul Gibbons LPAGC
5 Oct 1942	ss *GUNVOR MAERSK* Built 1931 W Hartlepool 1178 nrt, reg. London	Carleton (Quebec)	CQ	Tyne 13 Oct	2943 loads Timber	Brown
23 Oct 1942	ss *JAN* Built 1920 Lekkerkerk 1,128 nrt, reg. Bergen	Windsor (Nova Scotia) via Halifax	CQ	Tyne 1 Nov	3002 loads Timber	Brown
8 Dec 1942	ss *PETROVSKI* Built 1921 Schiedam 2,285 nrt, reg. Vladivostock	Archangel (Russia)	CQ	Harwich 25 Dec	4665 loads Timber	Brown
1 Mar 1943	*EMPIRE TYNE* Built 1923 Readhead, S. Shields. 2,299 nrt, reg. Newcastle. Requisitioned 1941 by Ministry of War Transport. Broken-up in Hong Kong 1952 as *LINCHCRAG*.	St Johns Newfoundland	CQ	Harwich 9 Mar	4385 tons Wheat 278 tons Wheat 445 tons Wheat	Cranfield LPAGC Gibbons
29 Apr 1943	*CSIKOS* Built 1913 Sunderland 2,468 nrt, reg. Panama	St John s Newfoundland	CQ	Tyne 11 May	4859 tons Wheat 443 tons Wheat 234 tons Wheat 77 tons Lorries 22 tons Aircraft	Cranfield Gibbons LPAHC Movement Control RAF
24 Jun 1943	*NICOLAS* Built 1910 Glasgow 2,910 nrt, reg. Cephalonia	St Johns Newfoundland	CQ	Tyne 1 Jul	5886 tons Wheat 443 tons Wheat 230 tons Wheat	Cranfield Gibbons LPAGC
2 Jul 1943	ss *BRIKA* Built 1929 S. Shields 2,735 nrt, reg. Swansea	Huelva	CQ	Tyne 11 Jul	Copper Ore	MOS Ferts.
16 Jul 1943	ss *MARGIT* Built 1924 Copenhagen 1,026 nrt, reg. London (pre-war reg. Copenhagen)	Halifax (Canada)	CQ	Hull 24 Jul	2551 loads Timber	Brown
29 Jul 1943	ss *EMPIRE GARETH* Built 1942 by Gray, W. Hartlepool. 2,873 nrt, reg. Hartlepool. Broken-up 1968.	Canada	CQ	Tyne 9 Aug	4028 loads Timber	Brown
15 Aug 1943	ss *EMPIRE NIGHTINGALE* Built 1918 Westport USA for US Shipping Board. 3,546 nrt, reg. London. Broken-up Bo'ness Scotland 1953.	Casablanca	CQ	Harwich 26 Aug	Phos of lime	Fison
18 Aug 1943	ss *BEAUREGARD* 3,700 nrt, reg. Philadelphia	Boston	CQ	Leith 7 Sept	3638 tons Wheat 664 tons Wheat 181 tons Wheat 101 tons Lumber 83 tons Dried milk (1,211 barrels) 98 tons Wire rod coils 208 tons Steel bars 97 tons lorry chassis & bodies (46 cases) 981 tons Wool (7368 bales)	Cranfield Gibbons LPAGC Brown Not known Not known Not known Not Known Not known

Date	Ship	From	To	Depart to	Cargo	Importer
31 Aug 1943	ss HJALMER WESSEL Built 1935 Sandefjord 984 nrt, reg. Oslo	Sheet Harbour (Nova Scotia)	CQ	London 7 Sept	2167 loads Timber	Brown
21 Sept 1943	ss BESTIK Built 1920 Bristol 1,568 nrt, reg. Oslo	Halifax	CQ	Harwich 3 Oct	? Steel / timber	Not Known
3 Oct 1943	ss AGIOS GEORGIOS Built 1911 W. Hartlepool 2,721 nrt, reg. Chios	Montreal	CQ	Not known	5175 tons Wheat 664 tons Wheat 221 tons Wheat	Cranfield Gibbons LPAGC
2 Nov 1943	ss NORTH DEVON Built 1924 S. Shields 2,239 nrt, reg. Newcastle Bomb damaged 5 July 1941	Huelva	CQ	Tyne 15 Nov	Copper ore	Not Known
11 Nov 1943	ss EMPIRE BOSWELL Built 1942 by Gray, W. Hartlepool. 1,695 nrt, reg. Hartlepool. Sank 1950.	Casablanca	CQ	Blyth 19 Nov	Phos of lime	MOS
25 Nov 1943	ss NORVANG 2,936 nrt, reg. Bergen	Casablanca	CQ	Harwich 10 Dec	Phos of lime	MOS
28 Nov 1943	THEOMITOR Built 1910 Sunderland 2,750 nrt, reg. Chios	Halifax	CQ	Harwich 10 Dec	5386 tons Wheat 322 tons Wheat 221 tons Wheat 4 tons Tank parts	Cranfield LPAGC Gibbons Not Known

In the fourth column, the abbreviations used are CQ: Cliff Quay; D: Dock; BB: Buttermans Bay.

Note 1. Per mb *BANKSIDE* for Read (Norwich).
Note 2. Per mb *BANKSIDE* for Read (Norwich).
Note 3. Breakdown of *BARON ERSKINE*'s cargo reveals:
        Phosphate of lime   3192 tons (Fison, Packard & Prentice, Ipswich) to factory hoppers
                                     47 tons (Fison, Packard & Prentice) by rail, destination unknown
                             1908 tons (West Norfolk Farmers, Kings Lynn) by rail
                               153 tons (Charles Middleton, Worksop) by rail
                           5300 tons   *Total*
        Rags   13 tons (T. Ford, Snakeley Mills, High Wycombe) by rail
                                 15 tons (J. Dickinson, Crossley Works, Watford) by rail
                                 28 tons   *Total*
        Esparto Grass   200 tons (J. Dickinson, Crossley Works, Watford) by rail
                               102 tons (New Northfleet Paper Mills, Northfleet) by rail
                             101 tons (Horton Kirby Paper Mills, Dartford) by rail
                             124 tons (C. Townsend Hook & Co., Snodland, Kent) by rail
                         527 tons   *Total*

Note 4. Per sb *CASTANET* for Hooker (Chatham).
Note 5. Per sb *H.K.D.* for Chitty (Dover).
Note 6. Per sb *SAVOY* for Hudson (Ramsgate).

Sources

Abstract of the Audited Accounts of Ipswich Corporation from 1 April 1939 to 31 March 1940, published by the East Anglian Daily Times Co. Ltd
An Historical Atlas of Suffolk, edited by David Dymond and Edward Martin, 1988
Ayden, Michael, *Evening Star*, article re George Gladding 12th March 1991
Barfoot, Edna Mary, *Port of Ipswich*, unpublished thesis, 1940s
Blatchly, John, *Eighty Ipswich Portraits: Samuel Read's Early Sketchbook*, Ipswich, 1980
Brown, Haward, Kindred, *Dictionary of Architects of Suffolk Buildings 1800-1914*, 1991
Burtons SROI, HD 2013, HC 449
Cliff Quay Works, Fisons Ltd Fertiliser Division, no date
Cocksedges, SROI, HC 457
Cranes and Ipswich Diesel Works, SROI, HD 2013
Cross, R.L., *Ipswich Markets & Fairs*, Ipswich Corporation 1965
Davis, A.C., *Portland Cement*, Stone Trades Journal 1904
Davis, Ralph, *The Rise of the English Shipping Industry*, David & Charles 1962
Defoe, Daniel, *Tour through the Eastern Counties*, first published 1724
Denton, C.D., letter to *Evening Star*, 13th June 1994
Durant, David, *Life in the Country House*, John Murray, 1996
East Anglian Daily Times, 26th November 1938 and *Evening Star*, 20th October 1988 concerning blockstone
Eighty Years of Enterprise 1869-1949, Ransomes & Rapier
Evening Star, Desert Rats' reunion at Orwell Park, 15th September 2008
Exhibition Catalogue, *River Orwell*, 1959
Fisons's Company History, SROI, HD 1652
Foynes, J.P., *The Battle of the East Coast (1939-1945)*, self-published 1994
Freestone, Jill, & Smith, Richard W., *Ipswich Engines & Ipswich Men*, Over Stoke History Group 1998
Glyde, J.G., *The Moral, Social and Religious Condition of Ipswich in the Middle of the Nineteenth Century*, Ipswich, 1850, reprinted 1971. S.R. Publishers Ltd.
Hudson, Kenneth, *Building Materials*, Longman 1972
Ipswich – Project Orwell, Anglian Water
Ipswich Engineering Society, *History of Engineering in Ipswich*, 1950
Ipswich Engineering Society, *History of Engineering in Ipswich*, 1974
Ipswich Health Reports, 1874-1905
Ipswich Journal, 1814
Ipswich Port Records including Harbour Master's records SROI, EL 1/6/10, Arrivals and Clearance books SROI, EL 1/6/11, and Day Books, Ipswich Transport Museum, ref. 2010/11
Ipswich, its History & Progress 1830-1930, East Anglian Daily Times special supplement.
Kinsey, Gordon, *Martlesham Heath*, Terence Dalton, 1975
Latham, *Timber*, Harrap, 1957
Lloyd's Register, various dates
Malster, R. *A History of Ipswich*, Phillimore, Chichester, 2000
Malster, R. and Jones, R., *A Victorian Vision: The Ipswich Wet Dock Story*, Ipswich Port Authority, Ipswich, 1992
Malster, R. *Ipswich, A Pictorial History*, Phillimore, Chichester, 1991
Malster, R. *Ipswich, Town on the Orwell*, Terence Dalton, Lavenham, 1978
Malster, R. *Some Suffolk Industries, Suffolk Review*, Vol. 5 No.4 Summer 1983, Suffolk Local History Council

Malster, R., *Stowmarket*, Alan Sutton Publishing Ltd.1995
Manorial records for the Manor of Stoke, Ipswich, various dates, SROI
Millgate, Helen, *Mr Brown's War*, Sutton Publishing, 1998
Moffat, A., Air raids in Ipswich, SROI, qs Ips. 940.54
Moffat, Hugh, *Ships and Shipyards of Ipswich 1700-1970*, Malthouse Press, 2002
Musson, A.E. *The Growth of British Industry*, Batsford Academic, 1978
Peter's Ice Cream and the Zagni Family, *Evening Star* 26th February 2001
Ransomes & Rapier's Annual, various 1921-26
Rate Assessment of properties in St Mary Stoke, 1864, SROI, qs Ips 9 (Glyde)
Redstone, Lillian, *Ipswich through the Ages*, East Anglian Magazine, Ipswich, 1948
Russell-Gebbett, Jean, *Henslow of Hitchin*, Terence Dalton, 1977
Smith, Richard W., *Blue Water Sail at Ipswich*, 1997
Smith, Richard W., *The Thames Barge in Suffolk*, Society for Sailing Barge Research, 2006
Souvenir of the Royal Show, 1934
Suffolk Almanac, 1869
Suffolk County Handbook, 1904
Taylor, J.E., *In and About Ancient Ipswich*, Norwich, 1888
Terraine, John, *Business in Great Waters*, Wordworth Edition, 1999
The County Borough of Ipswich, its Growth & Progress, souvenir published by the *East Anglian Daily Times* in 1903, reprinted 1993.
The Eastern Chronology Book of Dates
Vickers Petters, *Daily Herald*, 19th June 1912 and *East Anglian Daily Times* 30th March 1912, SROI, HD 2013
Villiers, Alan, *The Set of the Sails*, Hodder & Stoughton Ltd, 1949
Weightman, Gavin, *The Frozen Water Trade – how ice from New England lakes kept the world cool*, HarperCollins, 2001
Who's Who in Suffolk, 1912.

Index

Illustrations are in **bold** type.
Note: ship's names in this index are naval shore establishments

A
Agent, ship's, 35-8
Aircraft, 238-9
Airy, Sir George Biddell, 273
Aldeburgh, 197
Alexander, Sydney, 35
APCM, 209-10
Argo Line, 31
Armstrong, Samuel, 90
Ashton & Green, 199
Associated British Maltsters, 113, 120
Associated British Ports, 11, 13

B
Bain, Capt. John, 22, 32
Baltic Exchange, 39
Barges, ketch, 223
Barges, Life aboard, 101-4
Barges, owned by Cranfields, 99-100
Barges, refitting, 101-2
Barges, **x**, 1, **7**, 83, 95, 19, 126, 134, 136-8, 140, 141, 152, 157, 160, 194, 195-8, 201-10, 262, 263, 288, 345-7
Baron Line, 158
Bayley, George, 315
Bayley, Jabez, 177,
Beardmore Inflexible, 238-9
Beaumont Quay, Essex, 140
Beaumont, Alfred & Co, 67-8, 195
Bellward, W., 35
Bessey & Palmer, 87
Bevan, Alfred George, 68, 73
Birch, W.M., 72
BOCM, 133, 135-8
Bolton & Laughlin, 193
Bond, Turner & Hurwood, 282
Booth Brothers, 64, 68-9
Bramford, 65, 145-6, 156, 162
Bricks, 193-7
Bridge, Orwell, 32
Bridge, Stoke, 201
Brown, William & Co, 178-80, 184, 192, 199
Bruff, Peter, 269, 315
Budding, Edwin, 273
Bull Motors, 282-3
Bunting, HMS, 339-40
Buoys, navigation, 21
Burton, Son & Sanders, 220, 229-34
Bury St Edmunds, 250
Buttermans Bay, 21,29, 90, 92, 95, 106, 110, 114,

C
Calcium carbide, 172-3
Canadian Cast Container Group, 229
Cargo handling, 249-50
Carlsberg brewery, 127
Catt, Benjamin, 178
Cawoods, 86
Cement manufacture, 204-210
Chaldron measure, 61-2
Christie, F.A., 69-70, **176**, 180, 182
Christopherson, Wilfred, 139, 155
Church, St Peter's, 133
Clark, Kenneth, 220
Clarke, Capt., 31
Claydon, 209-10
Cleopatra's Needle, 50-51
Cliff Quay, 7, 13, 35, 45, 55, 157, 162, 191, 296, 306, **310**, 311, 353
Cliff Quay power station, 35, 162, 265-8, **268**
Coal duties, 63
Coal merchants, 66-87
Coal trade, 1-2, 3, 61-87
Coast Lines, 225-7
Cobbold & Co., 73, 86, 106
Cobbold, John Chevallier, 45, 146
Cockkedge & Co., 86, 280-1, 340-2
Colchester, George Henry, 146
Colchester, V.D., 70, 74, 90, 139, 146, 155, 240
Colchester, William, 146, **147**, 206, 223
Coleman, Ivan, 35
Collier brigs, 61
Consolidated Diesel Co Ltd, 285-6
Containers, 7
Convoy system, 337
Coprolites, 143
Cork lightvessel, 21, 29
Cory, William & Sons Ltd, 35, 78-9, 80
Cowell & Co., 86, 106, 120
Crane Ltd, 283-4
Cranfield Brothers, 89-100, 131, 209, 353
Cranfield, John George, 89, 90

Cranfield, Thomas, 89
Cresswell, Capt. John, 47-60, **48**
Cubitt & Chatterton, 131
Cubitt, William, 201
Curtis, Etheridge, 120

D
Dan Marine, 53, 220
Diesel works, see Consolidated Diesel Co Ltd
Downham Reach, 3, 27, 28
Dunkirk evacuation, 346

E
Eagle Mill, 106, 113
East Anglian Roadstone & Transport, 214-5, 218
Eastern Counties Farmers, see Farmers Co-operative Association
Edible oil and seed trade, 130-1
Edward J. Edwards, 215
Eldred Watkins, **205**, 206-7
Electricity generating, 260-8
Exempt lands, 19

F
Farmers Co-operative Association, Eastern Counties, 128-130
Fawley, 293, 308
Ferry to Stoke, 18
Fertilizers, 143-167
Fish, 243-4
Fison, Edward, 124-5
Fison, James, 145
Fison, Joseph, 89, 93, 124, 145, 153
Fison, Packard & Prentice, 155, 157-162
Flint Wharf Co., 121-2
Fox, C.H. & Son, 18
Fry, Edward, 120
Fulcher, Robert, 175

G
Gabriel, Thomas & Sons, 180
Gabriel, Wade & English, 184, 192
Ganges, HMS, 87, 348
Gasworks, Ipswich, 34, **248**, 249-59
Gibbons, A.A., 93
Gibbons, E. & E.C., 193, 195, **197**, 200, 206
Gipping, river trade, 155-7
Glading, George, 18, 156, **157**
Goldsmith, E.J. & W., 256
Gostling, W., 18
Goulder, Robert, 74-5
Gower, R.E. & C.F., **201**
Grain cargoes, 34, 40, 45-6, 103
Grain terminal, 45
Greenpeace, 60
Greenwich Farm, **306-7**
Griffin Inn, **15**
Griffin Wharf, 42-4, 70, 74, 146, 325, 353
Groom, John, 195
Guano, 144
Guncotton, 164

H
Hain Line, 91, 107, 154
Handford Mill, 132
Hares Creek, 195
Harlands Dock, **19**
Harwich harbour, 106
Harwich, 27-8, 29, 31, 32, 33, 49, 57, 204-6
Hawkes, Capt., 55
Hay cargoes, 221-3
Hog Highland, 193, 195
Holbrook, 195, 196
Hooker, Capt. James, 51
Horlock Dredging Co., 58
Horlock, F.W., 127, 154, 215

I
Ice, 244-7
Ingham, Capt. David, 30, 31
Ipswich Coal Co., 72-3, 84
Ipswich Haven Marina, 12
Ipswich Industrial Co-operative Co., 71-2
Ipswich Malting Co., 116-20, 140, 231
Ipswich Steam Navigation Co., 315
Isaac Lord, 73-4, **85**, 86

J
Jeddah, 31

K
Keeble, Capt. S., 50

Keels, Tyne, 62
Kenney, George, 196
King, A. & Co., 242
King, Walter Burton, 211, 213

L
Landing craft, 348-9
Lash lighters, **174**,
Lawes, J.B., 143
Lawrence, Derek, 35-8
Levington, 28
Lewcock & Pemberton, 35
Liberty ships, 350, **351**
Liebig, Justus von, 143
Lighthouses, Harwich, 21
Lightships, **20**
London & Rochester Barge Co., 135, 173
Londonderry, Marquis of, 62
Lumkin, Bob, 18

M
Madocks, William, 199
Malting & animal feed trade, 105-6, 110, 128
Maltings, 62, 113
Mason family, 132
Mason, Frank, 132
Mason, George, 86, 132-4, 135, 182, 200, 206, 207-10
May family, 219
May, Charles, 273
May, William, 45
Mellonie and Goulder, 35, 70, 74-82
Merchants, salt, 165-6
Meux's brewery, 127-30
Meyer, Montague L., 180
Milling, flour, 89
Molasses, 168-172, 236
Mortimer, Thomas, 106, 127
Motor vehicles, 107-8, 237-8
Moy, Thomas, 83-4
Munton & Fison Ltd, 125

N
Naiad Rowing Club, 14
Neptune Quay, 75, 127, 138

O
Oil trade, 287-313
Ore, river, 140
Orford, 220-3
Orvis, Capt. Jim 'Jemmer', 57
Orwell, port of, 1
Orwell Navigation Service, 9, 21
Orwell Works Works Rowing Club, 14
Ostrich Creek, 211
Owen Parry, 131

P
Packard, Edward, 143-5, 147-8
Papermaking, 132
Parkeston Quay, 338
Pattrick, John, 205-6
Paul, R. & W., 40, 44, 50, 51, 86, 105-16, 135, 195, 318
Pemberton, C., 35
Pendal, J.R. & Sons, 84
Petrel Rowing Club, 13-14
Pigiron, 229, 275
Pilot boats, 28
Pilotage rates, 27-8
Pilots, 27, 30, 32-3
Pin Mill, 203
Pipe, W., 85
Pittock, Capt. Jack, 139
Polley, Capt. Tom, 101-4, **101**
Polley, William, 102
Portland stone, 200-4
Portmadoc, 199
Potato cargoes, 234, **241**
Power stations, 260-8
Pratt, Capt. K., 59
Prentice Brothers, 149, 154
Prentice, Manning, 125, 145-6
Prentice, Thomas, 125-7, 145
Purfleet, 288, 292, 293

R
Rackman, Capt. 48
Railway, 42-6, 64-6, 197, 276-7, 284
Railway, Eastern Union, 42
Railway, Ffestiniog, 199
Railway, Griffin Wharf Branch, 116, 277, 281
Ransome, Frederick, 63

Ransomes & Rapier, 44, 276-80, 284
Ransomes, Sims & Jefferies, 86, 181, 201, 239, 249, 273-6
Read & Page, 211
Reavell Ltd, 281-2
Road materials, 210-18
Rockefeller, John D.,288
Rosher, F., 193, 195

S
Sacker, Sidney, 241
Salt, 165-6
Satim Towage, 58, 59, 60
Sawmills, 176-8, 179-80, 181
Scrap metal, 239-43
Seaham Harbour, 62, 68, 69
Septaria, 104-5
Sewage disposal, 269-72
Shipbuilding, 2-3
Shipping & Coal Co. Ltd, 85
Shotley, 28, 193, 195, **197**
Sizer & Lord, see Isaac Lord
Skinner, H., 240
Slate trade, 131, 199-200
Smith, 'Caps', 18
Smy, Capt. Harold, **346**
Southgate, Walter, 120, 240
St Lawrence Seaway, 96
Standard ships, 160, 161, 186, 350-2
Staton, Rafe, 178
Stoke bathing place, 14, 332
Stoke Sailing Club, 328
Stoke tide mills, 124
Stone dredging, 204-5
Stone, Hector, 140
Stowmarket, 164
Strange, Capt. R., 57
Strood, Kent, 93
Submarines, 330, 331-2, **334**, **335**, **336**
Suffolk Chemical Company, 168-172
Sugar cargoes, 230-3, 234-7
Sugar factory, Ipswich, 65, 234
Sully & Co., 139

T
Threadkell, Capt. Roger, 39-41
Thrutchley, 86
Thurman family, 123
Tiles, 197-8
Timber, 5-6, **6**, 13, 35, 175-193
Timber ponds, 178, 185
Timber raft, 184
Timber trade, 174-92
Tough & Henderson, 103
Tovell, George, 201, 206, 216
Tovells Wharf, 215, **216**, **217**
Tovey, Capt. Ernest 'Delhi', 52
Towage, 42-60, 103
Trinity House, 27, 29, 32
Turner, E.R. & F., 89, 220, 239, 282-3
Twinespinning, 247
Tyrwhitt, Sir Reginald, 331-4

V
Vaux, John, 50

W
Waldringfield, 207-9, **209**
War, First World, 330-6
War, Napoleonic, 177
War, Second World, 159-160, 184, 186, 215-8, 241, 272, 281, 311, 337-53
Washington, Capt. John, 205
Watkins, William, 50
Watts, John, 50
Webber, Samuel, 132
West Bank Terminal, 8-9, **10**, 13, 15, 34, 35, 44, 192
Whaling trade, 2
Woodmancy & Co, 215
Woolpit, 193
Woolverstone, HMS, 348
Wright, Capt. J., 31
Wrinch, Alfred, 180

X
X-lighters, 109, 170

Y
Yachting, 327-9

Z
Zagni, Maria and Napoleone, 247

369

Index of Ships

Names in **bold** are in tables
Illustrations in ***bold italics***

90, steam tug, 55, *56*

A
Aar, *174*
Abercraig, 284
Abide, **355**
Ability, **82**
Abington, **185**
Abraham Rydberg, 57, *59*, **94**
Acclivity, 170
Accretive, **153**
Achatina, *290*
Achilles, 52
Active, 231
Activity, **82**, 236, 293
Actuality, **81**, **82**, **218**
Ada Gane, **70**, 240
Ada, 181
Adam Hill, 244
Adara, 130
Adele J, 234
Adelfotis, **190**
Adherity, 292
Adieu, 130, 279
Admiral Keyes, **255**
Adonis, **355**
Adrian, 332
Advance, **158**
Adventure, **67**
Agatha, 329
Agent Lagoni, **126**
Aghios Georgios, **25**
Agia Marina, 228
Agia Sophia, *161*, 162
Agility, 293
Agioi Anargyroi, **97**
Agios Georgios, **94**, **366**
Agios Viasios, 161, 162
Agnes, **108**
Aidie, **111**, **115**, **346**, 346
Aika, 156
Airdrie, **217**
Aizkarai-Mendi, 157
Alacrity, 81-2, **82**
Alan, **134**, 135, 231
Alaric, 135, **190**, **210**, 212
Alarm, **69**, **70**, **71**, 83, 203, 243
Alaska, **25**
Alassia, **153**
Alastair, 285
Albatros, **158**, **194**, 240
Albatross, **115**, **195**
Albert, **90**, **115**, **288**
Albertina, 147
Alcor, **94**
Alcyone, 68, **69**, **70**, 73
Aldboro', **69**, 87
Alderman, **134**, **210**
Alecto, HMS, ***336***
Alert, **152**
Alexandra, 318
Alf Everard, 79
Alfhem, **242**
Alford, **150**
Alfred, **206**
Algeiba, 214
Algeth, 253
Alice, **108**, **206**, 211
Alice & Ella, **194**
Alice May, **111**, **115**, **208**, **213**,
Alida, **355**
Aline, **134**, **181**, 221
Alioth, 180
Alisdair, **355**
Alisth, **355**
Allegheny, 292
Alma, 316
Aloith, **362**
Alpha, **181**
Alston, 272
Amalthus, 312
Amazon, 49
Amazone, **158**
Amberley, **97**
Ambrizette, *162*
Amelia & Jane, 220
Amerker Brug 1, 53-5, ***184***
Amicitia, 289
Amisade Segundo, ***109***
Amity, 172, 292
Ammonite, **121**, **122**, 147, 151, **152**, 156, 283
Amphion, HMS, **336**
Ampleforth, ***36***
Amslie Park, **189**
Amstelstroom, 78
Amsterdam, **355**
Amy, 220
Amy Lenson, **361**
Andanes, **355**
Andescol, **141**
Andower, **150**
Andromeda, **115**, **152**, **288**
Anglia, 50-1, **115**, **116**, **208**
Ann, **115**, **195**, **288**
Ann Melville, **355**
Anna, **364**
Anna N. Goulandris, **25**
Anna Ramien, 90
Anna Sarah, **67**, **71**, **252**
Anna Wickhorst, 289

Anne De Bretagne, **334**
Annie, **150**, **185**, 246, 254
Annie Crosfield, **150**
Annie Davey, **150**
Antelope, **71**, **72**,
Anteo, 156
Anthony M, 292
Anthony Radcliffe, **108**
Antiquity, **82**
Anvall, **185**
Appian, **190**
Appollo, 53
Apricity, 38
Aptity, 170
Archibald Russell, **56**
Archimedes, **97**
Arcturus, 8, 228
Ardgantock, 238
Ardgarroch, **256**
Ardgen, **242**
Ardwina, *16*, **185**
Aretas, 289
Argo, 9
Argolikos, **94**
Argus, **185**
Ariadne, **181**
Ariel, **69**, **181**
Aristides, **97**
Arkelside, **158**
Armana, **355**
Armathia, **189**
Arneb, 8, 228
Arneborg, 72
Arno, **72**, 107, **149**
Arnold Hirst, 262
Arnotegi-Mendi, 157
Arrow, **134**
Arthur, **72**
Arthur & Eliza, **122**, 270
Arthur Fitger, 118
Arthur James, **121**
Arthurtown, 159
Artieri Giovanni, 120
Ascania, **185**
Ashburton, 242
Ashdene, **217**
Aspasia, **25**
Asperity, 169, 170, 293
Asphodel, 118, **185**
Assiduity, 293
Assurity, 285
Asteria, **218**
Astra, 328
Astrid, **208**, 212
Astros, **355**
Atalanta, 316
Athelbeach, 170, 171, 172
Athelcrest, 171, 172
Athelfoam, 168, 169, 170, 172
Athelmere, 172
Athelstane, 169, 170
Atheltarn, 169, 170, 171,
Athina, **149**
Athlete, **114**, 253
Athole, **70**
Atomicity, **82**
Atonality, 292
Atrato, 129, 281
Audacity, 169, 170
Audrey, **115**, 231
August, **181**, **183**
Augusta, 209
Augusta Mary, **181**, 319
Aureity, 292
Austerity, **218**, 292
Australian, 93
Aveyron, **194**, **195**, 245
Avon, **148**
Avon, 164
Avon River, **364**
Axel, 181, 182
Azariah, 275-6, **279**, **283**, 285, **288**, **288**
Azima, **108**

B
Baines Hawkins, **149**
Balfron, **78**
Balmoral, *324*, 324-5
Baltic Arrow, 228
Baltic Consort, 228
Bangor, **217**
Bangor Bay, *36*, 188
Bankside, **207**
Barbara Brit, 228
Barbara Freitchie, **189**, 352
Barbara Jean, **115**, 279, **346**, 346
Barford, 267
Barnehurst, **355**
Baron Ardrossan, 189
Baron Berwick, **179**, 189
Baron Cochrane, **158**
Baron Dalmeny, **158**
Baron Erskine, 159, **360**
Baron Kelvin, **158**
Baron Kinnaird, 159, **361**, **363**
Baron Loudoun, **111**, 158
Baron Lovat, **360**
Baron Nairn, **158**
Baron Napier, 158

Baron Pentland, **362**
Baron Saltoun, **360**
Baron Yarborough, **189**
Barra Head, **215**, **218**
Basic, 279
Basset, **355**
Baston, **62**
Basuto, **355**
Bayonne, **334**
Beatrice Maud, 346-7
Beaumaris, **355**
Beaumont Belle, **121**, **152**
Beauregard, **94**, **365**
Bede, 135
Bedlormie, 275
Bee, **206**
Beeding, 258
Beeston, **217**
Begonia, **95**
Beinat, **181**
Belford, 227
Belgian Captain, 351
Belgian Trader, 350, 351
Beltor, **4**
Ben Bates, **299**
Ben Harold Smith, **299**
Ben Hebden, 298-9, **299**
Ben Henshaw, 297-9, **298**, **299**
Ben Hittinger, 298-9, **299**
Ben Johnson, 297, **298**, **299**
Ben Olliver, **299**
Ben Read, 298, **298**, **299**
Ben Robinson, 297, **298**, **299**
Ben Sadler, 298, **299**
Ben Tarbert, **355**
Beneficient, 107
Benguela, 348
Benlos, **185**
Berangere, **334**
Berberis, **355**
Berengere, 119
Beric, **99**, 99, 100, 101
Berlin, 106
Bernard Barton, **149**, 150
Bernard Wesch II, 228
Bertha, 241
Beryl, 204
Bessie, **355**, **356**
Bestik, **366**
Betty Anne S, 81
Beveland, HNIMS, 342
Bheestie, 23, 55
Bickley Hall, 259
Bijou, **115**, 115, 212, 346
Birgitta, 136
Birling, 253
Birte O, 82
Bishop Rock, 214
Bitinia, **185**
Black Eyed Susan, 244
Blair Spey, **94**, 344, **360**, **364**
Blanche, 214
Blue Jacket, **200**
Blue Mermaid, 279
Bluebell, 107, 341
Blush Rose, **135**
Bolham, see Sarah Colebrook
Bolstrup, 253
Bombay, **185**
Bona, 151, **152**
Bonde, **94**, **362**
Bonnington Court, **94**, 95, 342, **362**
Bootle, **355**
Borde, 268
Border Firth, 87, **256**
Bore VII, **238**
Bore VIII, **238**
Bore IX, **238**
Bore X, **238**
Bornriff, 112
Borrowdale, 123
Boston Express, 228
Boston Sand, 228
Bothnia, **149**
Botilla Russ, **238**
Bowcombe, 268
BP Alert, **299**
BP Hunter, *303*
Brabant, **94**, **362**
Brackenholm, **71**
Bradfield, 259
Braedale, **78**
Braeside, 285
Bramham, **149**
Brando, 184
Bratsberg, 246
Breezy, 135
Brem, **354**
Brett, 58, 59, 60
Briar Holme, 90
Briarwood, see Gardenia
Bridgeman, 292
Brightlingsea, 23, 322-4, 326
Brika, **365**
Brilliant, 129
Britannia, 89, 123, **210**, 212, 213, 328
Britannic, **152**, **185**, 198, **223**
British Advocate, 304
British Bugler, 352

British Lion, **134**
British Merchant, see Arthur Fitger
British Monarch, **97**
British Oak, 284
British Pluck, **293**
Britomart, HMS, **355**, 358
Briton, **208**
Broadhurst, 258
Broiler, **135**, 135
Bronington, HMS, 15
Broomfleet, 256
Bryher, HMS, **355**
Brynawel, **217**
Brynhild, **361**
Bryntawe, 92
Buckminster, 123
Bullaren, **25**
Bury, **62**
Bushwood, 265, ***266***
Busiris, 136
Bycalla, **152**, 231, **223**

C
Cabby, **81**, 138, **190**, 281
Cadella, **355**
Cairngowan, **149**
Caland, **190**
Calanus, **149**
Calineuse, **200**
Calliope Nicopulo, **133**
Calluna, **185**
Cam, 68
Cambria, 8, 8, 130, **207**, **208**, 284
Cambrian, **200**
Cambronne, **334**
Camellia, 96, **97**, **97**
Camp Debert, see Agia Sophia
Canada, **149**
Candida, 328
Canford Chine, **158**
Canopus, 229, **237**
Cape Corso, **25**, **94**, **360**
Cape Sable, **94**, 189
Caption, **141**
Cara, 159, **362**
Cardinal Wolsey, 316
Cargo Shipper, 173
Carib Prince, **28**
Carina, **208**, **355**
Carisbrooke, **355**
Carisbrooke Castle, see Errol
Carolina, **181**
Caroline, **121**, **122**, 246
Carrasco, **97**
Cassia, **153**
Cast Porcupine, 229
Cast Racoon, 229
Castana, 169, 347
Castle Eden, 184
Castlefield, 90
Caswell, **355**
Cataraqui Park, 352
Cavilla, 106
Cecil Gilders, **141**, 259
Celebrity, **82**
Celerity, **133**
Celtic, 130, **141**, **141**, 203, 279
Celtic Monarch, see James Rolph
Cemsky, 207
Centaur, 151, **152**
Centricity, 259
Centurity, **74**, **82**
Cephalonia, **94**
Cerigo, **133**
Champion, 90, **115**, **181**, **194**, 283, **288**, **355**
Charles & Ann, 271
Charles Hutson, **122**, 233, **355**
Charles L. D., **25**
Charles Treadwell, 160
Charterhouse, **108**
Cheerful, **356**
Chelwood, **266**
Chemical Lausanne, *167*
Chesapeake, **133**
Chingford, **149**
Christiania, 183
Christopher Oldendorf, **242**
Citron, HMS, 332
Citta di Moreale, 38
City Of Agra, **126**
City of Lichfield, **240**
City of Rochester, 322-3
Clan Macfarlane, **119**
Clara, 112
Clareen, 214
Claude, 244
Claus Jurgens, 119-20
Cleopatra, 253
Cliff Quay, *31*, 266-8, ***267***
Clintonia, 93
Cluny Hill, 332
Clyde, **148**, 155
Clyde Firth, **217**
Cock O' The Walk, 73, 150, **152**
Colchester, HMS, see Felixstowe
Colne, **115**
Colombia, 136
Colonia, 99, **99**, **134**
Come On, 147

INDEX OF SHIPS

Commander Evans, **356**
Conan, 159
Condor, 278
Conniscrag, **114**
Consort, **153**
Consul, **121**
Contest, *290*
Continent, **158**
Continuity, **82**
Convoy, **136**, 139, **156**
Co-Operator, **135**
Copsewood, **256**
Corale, **356**
Corbeach, 80, **97**
Corbridge, 80
Cordelia, **312**
Corglen, **266**
Corinthian, 231, 240
Coriolanus, 79, 81
Cormarsh, **266**
Cormead, **266**
Corminster, *80*
Cormist, **266**
Cormoat, **266**, 267
Cormorant, 112
Cormount, **266**, 267
Cormull, 267
Corness, 80
Cornish Coast, **225**
Coronation, **122**, **134**, 346
Corpath, 80
Corsair, **134**
Corsea, **266**
Cortenaer, 240
Cortez, **119**
Cosmic, **356**
Coulouras-Xenos, **25**
County Of Inverness, **119**
Coventry City, **356**
Craigina, **119**
Craiglands, **126**
Craiglwyd, 188
Cremona, **228**
Crofter, **217**
Croham, **217**
Crossbill, 24, **111**, 203
Crouch Belle, **134**
Cruizer, 250
Csikos, **94**, 348, **365**
Cumberland, HMS, 110
Curacoa, **97**
Curly Boy, **181**, **194**
Cutty Sark, 107
Cybeline, **312**
Cydonia, 93, **97**
Cygnet, **122**, 129
Cymric, 203
Czarda, **94**, **111**, **361**

D
D'Arcy, 233, 276, 346
Daffodil, HMS, **338**
Daghestan, **312**
Dagny, **190**
Daisy, **122**
Daisy Maud, **122**
Dalegarth Force, 137
Dalemoor, **94**, **361**
Daleside, **78**
Dalworth, **111**
Dana, **126**, **183**
Daniel Fearall, **359**
Danmark, **149**
Dannebrog, **99**, 99, **100**, **115**, 204, 212
Darcoiler, **94**, **360**
Dartmoor, **148**, 148, 252, **252**
Dauntless, **72**
Davenport, **71**
David, 125
Dawn, **134**
Dayrose, **94**, 112, **360**, **361**
Daystar, **72**, 83, **252**
Deben, **115**, **156**, **122**
Deben II, **155**, 235
Decima, **208**
Dee, 135
Defender, **122**
Delfland, **111**
Delius, 189
Demosthenes, **149**
Dempster, **217**
Desire, 219
Destinn, HMS, **356**
Devon Coast, **225**, **226**
Dewdrop, 147
Dewsbury, **338**, **354**
Dhoon Glen, HMS, **356**
Dhoon, HMS, **356**
Dial, **82**
Dicky, **255**, **256**
Dido, HMS, **331**
Dilston, **263**
Dingwall, **133**
Dinkel, 130
Dinorwic, **126**
Diopside, **242**
Director, 54, **72**
Dispatch, 69
Divara, **189**
Dolphin, **206**
Don Hugo, **149**
Donna Flora, **263**
Donna Nook, **356**
Doonie Braes, HMS, **356**
Dora, 118
Dorando, HMS, **332**
Dorcas, **206**
Doris, 107, **108**, **115**, **210**, 212, 317, 346, **346**
Dorothea, **156**, **194**

Dorothy, **121**, 139, 157, 233
Dorothy Watson, **72**
Dorset Coast, **225**
Dorsetbrook, 258
Douglas, 150
Dover Castle, **122**
Downham, 23, 52
Drechtstroom, 78
Driving Mist, 87
Dryburgh, **263**
Duddon, 68
Duiveland, HNIMS, 342
Dulwich, **94**
Dunbar, **356**
Dungeness, 109
Dunkerque, 151, **152**
Dunn, **62**
Dunnet Head, 215
Dunquerque, **223**
Duquesne, **119**
Durham, **149**
Durhambrook, 258
Durrington, *116*
Dusker, 157
Duva, 108

E
Eagle, **71**
Eaglet, **122**, 123, 220-3, **221**
Eaglet II, **222**
Earl Essex, **356**
East Anglia, **134**, 173
Eastdale, **190**
Eastfield, 91
Eastgate, 90
Eastville, **25**
Eastward, **200**
Eastwood , **122**, 231, 262, **263**
Ebbrix, 87
Ebor, **149**
Echo, 147
Economy, **252**
Eden, 253
Edenside, 78, 202, **252**
Edith, **238**
Edith & Hilda, 118
Edith Mary, 212
Edith May, **136**, **190**, **210**, **213**
Edme, **111**, 233, 276
Edward Walmsley, **356**
Edwardian, **356**
Edwina, **356**
Egee, 351
Egerton, 58
Egholm, **149**, 348
Egton, **94**, 95
Ehrglis, **183**
Eilbek, 110, **364**
El Neptuno, **25**
Elandsgracht, **237**
Eldred Watkins, 209
Elfreda, **356**
Elisa, **108**, **119**
Elisabeth Eff, **246**
Elise Mellonie, *65*, 77, 78, **78**, 155
Eliza, 69, 283
Eliza H, **70**, **72**, **223**
Elizabete, 186
Elizabeth, **181**, **197**, **214**
Elizabeth & Sophia, **121**, **122**, 196
Elizabeth Simpson, 170
Ellen, 243
Ellen & Mary, **206**
Ellen H, 83
Ellena, **359**
Ellie, **183**
Ellin, **25**
Elm Hill, **97**
Eloquence, 72
Elpidophorus, **149**
Elsie Bertha, 209
Emanuele Accame, 118
Embassage, **94**, **361**
Emil Reith, 228
Emily, **108**, **115**, **194**, 243, **288**
Emily Ricket, **121**, **122**
Eminence, **82**
Emma, 204, **210**, 231
Emma Mizzen, **121**, 123
Emma Plein, **94**, **361**
Emma Seager, **122**
Emperor of India, 339-40
Empire Anglesey, 170
Empire Arrow, **352**
Empire Audrey, 170
Empire Boswell, **366**
Empire Cliff, **136**, **364**
Empire Dweller, 170
Empire Frome, 188
Empire Gareth, **365**
Empire Grey, **189**, 351
Empire Harvest, 170
Empire Kestrel, **362**
Empire Mallory, see Bangor Bay
Empire Maple, **356**
Empire Nightingale, **365**
Empire Punch, **241**
Empire Reynard, **241**
Empire Scout, **94**, **364**
Empire Sentinel, **358**
Empire Snipe, 350, **361**
Empire Spey, see Blair Spey, **364**
Empire Strait, **362**
Empire Tapley, **356**
Empire Tedmuir, see Amity
Empire Teguda, 170
Empire Trail, see Loch Maddy
Empire Tyne, **94**, **365**
Empress Of India, **70**
Ena, 101, **108**, *112*, **115**, 115, 212, 346, **346**

Endeavor, **62**, 328
Enfield, 90
Enterprise, 68
Era, 50-1
Eridanus, HMS, **356**
Erik III, **149**
Erling Lindoe, 93
Ermenilda, **150**
Erna Boldt, **149**
Ernest Reyer, **334**
Ernest, 243
Ernesto Ilardi, **119**
Errol, 90
Errwood, 272
Eskwood, **255**
Esme, **133**
Essex, *319*, 319-21
Esso Caernarvon, 293
Esso Dakotah, **292**
Esso Genesee, **292**
Esso Hythe, 293
Esso Inverness, 293
Esso Ipswich, 293
Esso Juniata, **292**
Esso Ottawa, 292
Esso Penzance, 293, *302*
Esso Purfleet, 293
Esso Tioga, **292**
Esterel, **185**
Estrella, see Star
Estrup, **126**
Eswil, 60
Etal, 227
Ethel, **99**, 99, **122**, **135**, **152**, 243
Ethel Ada, 207, 279
Ethel Maud, **121**
Ethelbert, 253
Etoile, 17
Etruscan, **356**
Euphrosyne, 328-9
Eureka, **121**, **122**, **185**
Europa, **151**
Euthalia, **25**, **94**, **363**, 365
Eva Lynch, 154
Evelyn Rose, HMS, **356**
Evelyn, 123, 240
Everards, 158
Evilena, **183**
Excelsior, **99**, 209, 231, 352
Exmoor, **148**, 148
Express, 52
Ey, **356**

F
Fabius, 79
Fair Maid, **67**, 86
Fairway, **356**
Fairy King, **153**
Fairy, **121**, **122**, 123, 140, **140**, 195, *196*, 262
Fal, **356**
Falcon, 50
Falster, **190**
Falstone, 272
Familien Haab, **126**
Fanny, 243, 269
Far, **364**
Farmers Boy, 101
Father Thames, 316
Favorole, 135
Faxfleet, 256, **257**
Fearless, **69**, 69, 73
Federation, **134**
Felice, 120
Felix, **99**, **108**, **223**
Felixstowe, 338-9, 352, **354**, **356**
Fellside, 159
Fenay Lodge, **149**
Fern, **183**, **190**
Ferndene, **82**
Fernwood, **263**
Fezenta, HMT, 340
Fingal, 329
Finland, **183**
Firecrest, 24, **111**, 116
Firefly, **356**
Five Brothers, **134**
Fixity, 237
Flandre, **356**
Fleetwing, **150**
Flid, **183**
Florence, **122**, 179, 275, 327
Flottbek, 157
Flower of Essex, **99**, 99, **185**
Flower Of The Fal, **150**
Fluor, 136
Flying Cloud, 286, *286*
Flying Enterprise, 188
F O Andersen, **183**
Foam, 52, **91**
Fodhla, **78**
Foremost 18, **342**
Formosa, 195
Fort Bedford, 160
Fort Coulange, 160, 352
Fort York, **356**
Fortuna, **182**, **183**
Forward, 332
Fossil, **122**, 147, 151, **152**, 156, **194**
Fox, 275
Foxhound, **134**
Franc Tireur, HMS, **356**
Francis, **69**, 71, 83
Frank Lucey, **121**
Frank M, 293, *298*
Fraternity, **122**
Fred Everard, 79
Frederick William, **111**, **156**
Frederiksborg, 156
Fredheim, **150**

Freelance, 120
Freija, **356**
Freston, 23, 52
Freston Tower, 151, **152**, 220
Frida, **185**, 332
Fridius, **185**
Friends, **62**
Friends of Eliza, 219
Friendship, 73, **223**, *223*, 240, **356**
Frigga, **126**
Fryken, **190**
Fulton, **185**
Function, **141**
Fure Star, 163
Futurity, 237

G
G E Woods, **149**
Gabrielle Wehr, 60
Ganges II, HMS, *335*
Ganymetes, **362**
Gardenia, 96, **97**, **97**, 120
Garlinge, **158**
Garnet, 52
Garoupalia, **97**
Garron Tower, 253
Gava, HMS, **356**
Gazelle, **67**, 67, 141, **141**
Geestdam, 228
Geestdiep, 228
Geestsluis, 228
Geisha, **134**, **208**
Gemine, **149**
General De Boisdeffre, **119**
General De Negrier, **119**
General Jackson, **134**, **185**, 209, 254, 279, 347
General Lee, **153**
Genesta, **152**
Geologist, 349
George, **227**
George & Eliza, **190**
George Adgell, HMS, **356**
George Dittman, **126**
George M. Livanos, **25**
George Robb, HMS, **356**
George Smeed, **208**
Gerald, 284
Gerd, **246**
Germaine, **149**
Germania, **153**
Gertrude, 262
Gilbert, 54
Gillation, **141**, **242**
Gills, **183**
Gilsay, HMS, **356**
Giovani, 289
Gipping, **115**, 151, 155
Gipsy, HMS, 341, 342-3
Giroflée, **356**
Giver, **62**
Glad Tidings, **126**
Gladonia, 259
Gladys, 7, **99**, 99, **100**, 123, **208**
Glaisdale, **94**, **364**
Glanstwyth, 123
Gleaner , **122**, **134**, 173, **356**
Glen Finlas, 57, 343
Glen Rosa, 212, *317*, 317-8
Glenbury, 284
Glencoe, 138
Glenmore, **151**
Gleno, 231, **263**
Glenrosa, **152**
Glenside, **82**
Globe, **108**
Gloriana, 71
Gluckauf, 288
Goddess, 68, **70**
Godspeed, 16
Godwit, **134**, 173
Gold, 259
Goldace, 203
Golden Eagle, **355**
Golden Hinde, 16
Goldrune, **141**
Good Hope, **150**
Good Intent, **122**, **194**
Gosforth, **97**
Gottpride, **360**
Grace, 209
Gracia, 191
Grado, **364**
Grafton, HMS, 15
Graiglas, **94**, **361**
Grand , **242**
Grand Turk, 16
Granta, **266**
Gravelines, **115**, 127, 284
Gravelines I, **111**, **115**
Great Emperor, 52
Greathope, see Queensland
Grecian, 118
Greenfly, HMS, **356**
Greenhithe, **207**
Greta Force, **256**
Greta, **134**
Grieije, **185**
Gros Pierre, **241**
Grunda, **158**
Guardian, **78**
Guelborg, 72
Guillemot , **356**
Guiseppe, **149**
Guiseppe Accame, 108
Gulf Anglia, **150**
Gulf Ipswich, 228
Gundine, **312**
Gundula, **238**, 238
Gunvor Maersk, 345, **365**

Gustav, **181**, **183**
Gustaf Adolf, **181**
Gustav Omer, 52
Gwynhelen, 198, 284
Gyller, 289

H
Hafnia, 130
Hainault, 23, 323, 326, **356**
Halcyon, 279
Halcyon, HMS, **356**
Hallamshire, 150
Hallingdal, **158**
Hammerburg, **185**
Hampshire Coast, **226**
Hand of Providence, 195
Handy, 220
Hannah, 254
Hannaray, HMS, **356**
Hannibal, 112
Hans Borge, **149**
Hanseat, 92
Happy Return, 69, 250
Harald, **149**
Harberton, **111**
Harbinger, 119
Harbor, **185**
Harcourt, **122**
Harfry, **256**
Harleywood, 184
Harlyn, **97**
Harold, 212, **213**
Harris, **356**
Harry Walton, **364**
Hartburn, 92
Hartford, **78**
Hartford Express, 228
Hartland Point, **364**
Harton, 253
Hartside, 253
Harvey, 155
Harwich, 50, 52
Hasewint, 113
Haste Away, 151, **152**
Hausestadt Hamburg, **190**
Havtor, **361**
Haweswater, 272, **272**
Hawkwood, **266**
Haworth, **149**
Hayburn Wyke, HMS, **356**
Hazard, HMS, **356**
Hazelside, **25**
Heather Lea, 76
Heatherpet, 129, 198, **284**, 285-6
Hector, 117, **122**, **140**, 231
Hedley, 69, **166**
Heingar, **94**
Helen & Ernest, 132
Helen Marshall, 87, 213
Helena, 17
Heliopolis Moon, **49**, **53**
Helmsgarth, see Losinj
Helmsman, 292
Heminge, **158**
Hemsley, **62**
Henfield, 258
Henrich Peters, **190**
Henrietta & Leonard Preston, 68, 83
Henrik, **183**
Henrik Ibsen, **94**, 350
Henrika, **150**
Henry, **246**
Her Majesty, 212
Herbert, **134**
Herbertus, **181**
Hercules, 24
Herman Buisman, **190**
Hermetray, **356**
Hermine, **238**
Hero, **62**, **126**
Heron, **111**
Hesper, 73
Heyshott, 268
Hickorol, 310
Hiervery, 289
Highgate, **133**
Highland Queen, **218**
Hilda, **115**, 130, **152**, **223**
Hilda Cooper, HMS, **356**
Hildur, 117-8
Hink, 130
Hippolyte, **181**, **182**
Hjalmer Wessel, **366**
Hjortholm, **149**
Hockley, **121**
Hoegh Silverstar, **160**
Holbeach, 197
Holland, **158**
Holmside, 253, **255**
Holywood, **263**
Homewood, **256**
Hookwood, **263**
Hope, **194**
Hopecrag, **111**
Hopewell, **62**
Hornbeam, **356**
Horsa, **108**
Hound, HMS, **356**
Howard D Troop, **119**
Hudson River, **266**
Hudson Strait, **266**
Humber, **148**
Humber II, 155, **155**
Hunstanworth, **263**
Hunwick, 3, 125
Hycol, 220
Hydra, **246**
Hydraios 111, **242**
Hydrogen, **141**, 141, 254

I
I. Brouncker, **122**
Ida, **108**, **115**, **152**, **252**
Idelia, **72**
Ila, 237, *239*
Ilas, **183**
Ilfracombe, HMS, **356**
Ima, **312**
Imacos, **185**
Imperial, 125, 135
Import, 338, **354**
Indian Chief, 50
Indian Prince, 107
Industry, 135
Inflexible, **213**, 213, 345
Inger Margrethe, 181
Ingrid, 166
Innisbeg, see Broiler
Innisulva, 79
Insistence, **82**
Inta, **312**
Intrepid, **115**, **166**, **210**
Ioannis Frangos, **94**, **363**, **364**
Iona, **149**
Iota, 164, 195
Ipswich, 48-9, 315
Ipswich Pioneer, 227
Ipswich Pioneer II, *34*, 58, 60, 229, *233*,
Ipswich Progress, 227
Ipswich Trader, 217
Irene, 132, **150**, 241
Irene's Emerald, *47*
Irex, **121**
Iris, **181**
Iris, HMS, 338
Irish Oak, **97**
Irish Pine, **97**
Isabel, 77, **152**
Isabella, 148
Isle of Cyprus, **149**
Isle of Hastings, **149**
Isle of Iona, **153**
Isola, 107
Italia, 289
Iverna, **122**, 129
Ivy P, **71**

J
Jacinta, **356**
Jacinth, **151**
Jack Snipe, 345
Jacoba, **185**
Jakkmokk, **185**
James, 164, 219
James & Emma, **166**
James E. Robinson, 238
James Garfield, **71**, **152**
James Tennant, 214
Jan, 345, **365**
Jane, **121**, **122**, 250, 262
Jane Guillon, 90
Jane Knox , **121**, **150**
Janie, **153**
Jantina, **150**
Jantje, 73
Jantje Eppiana, 159
Jarl, **183**
Jaroslav Dabrowski, 228
Jaslo, **228**
Jason, **357**
Jean, **334**
Jean Baptiste, **200**
Jeannie McIntosh, HMS, 345, **357**
Jehovah Jireh, **126**
Jenny, **149**, 231
Jersey Queen, 217
Jesse, 125, **285**
Jewish, **152**
Jim, 218
Joannis Frangos, 23, 96, 113
Jock, **115**, 127
Johannes, **126**
Johannes C. Russ, 180
John, 254
John & Clara, **194**
John & Lillie, 129
John & Margaret, 69, **69**, **200**
John & Thomas, **115**
John Bowes, 253
John Cattling, **357**
John Charrington, 38, **73**, 265
John Clark, **121**
John Evelyn, **134**
John Ewing, **200**
John Lee, **67**
John M, 293, **296**
John Martin, **121**, **122**
John W Arey, 186, **189**
John Williams , **200**
John Wray, **181**
Jolly Bruce, 215
Jolly Frank, 168
Jolly Hugh, 215
Jolly Laura, **78**
Jolly Marie, 198
Jorgan Lapon, **121**, **122**
Joseph, **195**
Joseph Nicholson, **200**
Josephine Magaretha K, **166**
Josh Francis, 130, 259
Joyous, **25**
Jules Gommes, **334**
Julia Wood, **115**, **288**
Julie, **150**
Jumbo, 209
Juniata, 292
Juniper, **206**
Juno, **364**
Justice, 123, **152**, **223**
JW Paulin, **97**

K
Kalamai, 242
Kaliakra, 17
Kalisz, 113
Kalliopi, **25**
Kalmarsund V, *187*, 188
Kardomah, 284
Karen, **357**
Karen II, **357**
Karl Chandris, 161
Kate Fawcett, 150
Kathariotisa, **94**
Katherina, *198*
Katingo Hadjipatera, **94**, **364**
Katvaldis, **94**
Kayeson, **111**
Keila, **94**, 352, **363**
Kemi, **158**
Kenia, 57, **356**, **357**
Kenrix, **263**
Kentbrook, 257
Kildale, **94**, **360**
Kimberley, 99, **99**, **101**, **122**, **134**, **156**
Kimia, 109
King, 135
King Ja Ja, **71**
Kingfisher, 206, 209, 244
Kings Grey, HMS, **357**
Kingsborough, **360**
Kingscote, 253
Kingsley, 253
Kingston Olivine, HMS|, **357**
Kittiwake, HMS, **357**
Kitty, 233
Klondyke, **185**
Knebworth, 156
Knowl Grove, 76
Knowles, **134**
Knud, **149**
Kobe, **111**
Komet, *258*
Konigen Louise, 336
Kozara, *163*
Krasny Profintern, **185**
Kullin, 231
Kurland, **149**
Kyleglen, see Busiris

L
L'Avenir, 110
La Bahia, **97**
La Belle Poule, 17
La Estancia, 95
La Pampa, 95
La Querida, 151, **153**
La Roche Jaquelein, **334**
La Rochefoucauld, **334**
Lady Daphne, **115**, **202**
Lady Elizabeth, 316
Lady Ellen, 117, **121**, **122**
Lady Gwynfred, 284
Lady Iveagh, 90, 123, **126**
Lady Jean, **115**, **202**, **208**
Lady Kathleen, **364**
Lady Louisa Pennant, **200**
Lady Mary, **207**
Lady Maud, **207**, **208**
Lady Middleton, 69
Lady of the Lake, **67**, **70**
Lady of the Wave, **195**, **270**
Lady Philomena, HMS, **357**
Lady Rosebery, 346
Lady Sheena, 82
Lady Sybilla, 82
Lafford, **141**
Lake Dymer, 184
Lake Hallwil, **363**
Lambtonian, 268
Lancashire Coast, 136
Lancaster, **185**, **213**
Lancasterbrook, **218**, 257
Landguard, 29
Langleebrook, **94**, **360**
Larchwood, **256**
Latimer, 119
Launceston, 283
Laura, 73
Laurell, **206**
Laurieston, **263**
Leading Light, 166, 240
Leadsman, 272
Leelite, **78**
Leicesterbrook, 38, **218**
Leif, **246**
Leinster Bay, 228
Len. Piper, **190**
Lena, 28, 135
Lennox, HMS, **357**
Leon Raymundo, 279
Lephreto, HMS, **357**
Leslie West, **357**
Lesrix, **263**
Levant, **153**
Levenwood, **256**
Levnet, 121
Lewis, 129
Liberator, **357**
Libra, **158**, **357**
Lida, 136
Lika, 118
Liddoch, **357**
Lily, **71**
Linchcrag., **365**
Lincolnshire, 257
Lincolnshire, 212
Linge, **363**, **364**
Linton, 256
Lisa- **158**
Lisbeth, **126**
Little England, 51, 52

Little Fred, 132
Little Lady, 243
Little Mystery, 172
Liverpool, 50
Livonia, 131, 231
Lizzie Cory, **126**
Lizzie Lee, **150**
Llandudno, HMS, **357**
Loach, **141**
Lobe, **141**
Locator, **141**
Loch Maddy, 188, *191*
Lodella, **141**
Lodore, 147, **149**
Loke, **94**, **362**, **363**, **364**
Londonbrook, 257
Longfield, 90
Lord Alcester, 68
Lord Ashfield, **357**
Lord Beaconsfield, **115**, **357**
Lord Churchill, **223**, 231
Lord Citrine, 267-8
Lord Eslington, **133**
Lord Haig, 202
Lord Hartington, 235-6
Lord Hewart, **355**
Lord Lansdowne, **70**
Lord Londonderry, 253
Lord Melchett, **357**
Lord Melchett, HMT, 340
Lord Nelson, **213**
Lord Palmerston, **115**
Lord Trent, **356**
Losinj, 188, *192*
Lothair, **223**
Louie Rose, 235
Louise, **134**, 246
Lovania, **357**
Lowlands, **149**
Lucellum, **312**
Lucinda, **200**
Luctor, 130
Lucy Richmond, **70**, 151, **152**
Luddick, **78**
Luffwell, 292
Lulonga, **263**
Lumi, 58
Luminetta, 313
Luminous, 310, 313
Luneberg, **29**
Lungo, **190**
Lunula, **312**, 313
Lusjnealf, **185**
Lux Challenger, 60
Lwow, 136
Lydia, 220
Lydia Long, HMS, **357**
Lymington, **214**, **252**

M
Maarit, 238
Mabel, **108**, **115**, **194**, **288**
Macadam, 216
Macmahon, 119
Madby Ann, **71**
Madcap, **122**, 173
Madge, **181**, **182**
Madrali, 284
Mafeking, **122**
Magdalene, **119**
Maggie, 203
Mahalah, **152**
Maid of Meirion, **200**
Maidstone, HMS, 331
Major, **156**
Malabar, **133**
Malapert, **153**
Malcolm Miller, 16
Mallard, **357**
Malvina, **122**
Manada, 109
Manchester, **62**
Manfred, **185**
Maraime, **357**
March, 244
Mardy , **122**
Mare, **357**
Marechal De Turenne, 119
Marechal De Villars, **334**
Margaret, 87, 125, **194**, **206**
Margarita Weston, **141**
Margeth, **181**
Margit, **238**, **365**
Marguerite Molinos, 119
Marguerite, 212
Maria Catherine, **200**
Maria de Larrinaga, **25**
Maria, **62**, **153**, **206**
Marian, 214
Marian M, **82**
Marianna, **194**
Marianne, **185**
Marie, **150**
Marie Hackfield, 118
Marie May, 130, 138, **190**
Mario Vittporio, **153**
Marion, **357**
Mariquita, 328
Marjorie, **108**, **115**, 116, 127, **128**, 129, 233
Marjorie Mellonie, **76**, **77**, 77, 78, **78**
Market Maid , **67**, 68, 85
Marmaduke, **150**
Marna, 169
Martello, HMS, **358**
Martha, 213
Martha & Ellen, **70**, 83, **150**
Martha Edmonds, **153**
Martha Ellen, **150**
Martien, **190**
Martin, **181**

INDEX OF SHIPS

Martinet, 79
Marwick Head, 215
Mary, 68, **69**, 75, 189
Mary A Hastie, HMS, **357**
Mary Ann, 117, **121**, **122**, **153**, 231
Mary Ashburner, 166
Mary Atkinson, **72**
Mary Eleanor, **150**
Mary Eliezer, 197
Mary Horlock, **149**, 154
Mary Jane, **200**, 270
Mary Johanna, 243
Mary Miller, **150**, 166
Mary Pickersgill, 350
Mary Seymour, 73
Mary Weston, **141**
Marygold, 219
Mascotte, 275
Masonic, **72**
Mathias Picket , **121**, 122
Mathilda, **181**, **238**
Matilda Upton, **71**, 212, **213**, **223**
Maus, **181**
Maximus, *48*, *49*, *53*, 60
May, **99**, 100, **121**, 151, **152**
May, Portland, 202-3
May Cory, **153**
May Flower, **121**, **150**, 219
May Hawthorn, 201
Mayflower, 219
Mayor, **136**
Mayrix, **263**
Maysie, **111**, **134**
Mazeppa, **152**, **223**
Melbourne, 15
Melissa, **213**
Melrose, **263**
Meltemi, 191
Memory, 139, **156**, 279
Menzaleh, **133**
Merisaar, **158**
Merlin, 339
Merneva, **62**
Merrimac, 51-2, **114**, 318
Merry Golden Hind, 323
Meru, 70
Messenger, **200**
Meteor, 328
Mette, **150**
Michael Griffith, **357**
Michael M, **82**
Mico, **357**
Millicent, 147
Millie, **111**, **233**
Millwall, **108**
Millwater, see Elise Mellonie
Mimosa, **185**
Minnie, 275
Minster, 268
Miss Williams, **200**
Mistley, **111**, **115**, **127**, 171, 241
Mobil, **181**
Modesta, 96
Moidart, **263**
Moira M, **82**
Moliere, 118
Mombassa, **149**
Monarch, **358**
Monica M, **82**
Monkleigh, **360**
Moorfoot, 80, **263**
Moravia, **358**
Moss Rose, 345
Motia, 157
Mountain Laurel, **126**
Mountjoy, **358**
Mulberry, 28
Murex, 300, **312**
Muriel, **194**, 262
Mute, , 69, **70**, **72**, **214**, **252**
Myfanwy, **153**
Mystery, **111**, 151, **152**, **213**, 213
Mytilus, **312**, **312**
Mytongate, 348

N

N.E.V.A. , **70**
Nadin, **94**
Nairnside, HMS, **358**
Nancy, 125
Naughton, 130, **141**, 259
Nautilus, **121**, **122**, 147, 151, **152**, 156, **183**, **194**
Navarino, *6*
Naviedale, **158**
Navigator *64*
Neerlandia, 310
Neo, 135
Neptun, **158**
Ness, 92
Ness Point, **358**
Netherton, **153**
Nettle, 332
New Trader, **134**, 346
Newlands, **158**
Newtownards, **255**
Niagara, **134**
Nicholas M, 293
Nicola Dawn, 130, 259
Nicolas, **94**, 350, **365**
Nicos Valmadis, **111**
Nile, **71**, **122**, 129
Ninita, **194**
Niord, 120, **133**
Nitrogen, 254
Njels, **246**
Noblesse, **141**
Noemi, 187
Noordsvarder, **358**
Norcape, 229
Nord, **126**

Nordano, **238**
Nordbalt, 228
Nordhavi, **355**
Nordic Queen, **218**
Nordstjernan, **358**
Norfolk, 318, *318*, 319-21, 326
Norham, **217**
Norlan, **358**
Norman , **185**
Norman Monarch, **133**
Normanhurst, 138
Nornen, **183**
Norsea, 229
Norseman, **71**
Norsky, 229, **232**
North Briton, **149**
North Devon, **94**, 95, **363**, 366
Northdown, 127, **136**
Northgate, **217**
Northumberland, 253-4
Norvang, **366**
Noss Head, 215, **217**
Nova Scotia, **181**
Nova, **238**
Novator, **181**
Novator, 207, 279
Nyborg, **183**

O

Oarsman, 78, **114**
Oban, 135
Oberon, HMS, **17**
Ocean Eddy, HMS, **358**
Ocean Queen, 209, 279
Ocean Scout, HMS, **358**
Ocean, **62**, 119
Octavius, **122**, 231
Odin, **183**, 231
Ogmore Castle, 160, **364**
Ohm, **358**
Oilshipper, 312
Okino, **358**
Olive, 130
Olive Branch, **210**, **213**
Olive May, 242, 286
Onward, **72**, **134**, 206
Onyx, **71**, 86, 275, **358**
Oosterschelde, **158**, *159*
Ootmarsum, **111**
Ophelie, **312**
Ophir, **185**
Opossum, HMS, 15
Orada, **97**
Oranje, 130
Ordinence, **82**
Oread, 317
Orestes, **358**
Orinoco, 99, **100**, 101, 130, **136**, 209, 345
Orion, **122**, **125**, 278, 315
Orlando, **133**
Ortalan, 82
Orwell, 2, 2-3, 48, 86, **108**, **115**, **148**, 155, 177, 315-6, 318
Orwell Tow, 60
Osage, 292
Osceola, 291
Osmussaar **158**
Osprey, **150**
Ossa, 332
Our Boys, **185**
Outwood, 215
Overflakkee, HNIMS, **358**
Oxbird, 24, **78**, **111**, **114**, 115, 241
Oxygen, 139, **190**, 254
Oystermouth Castle, **358**

P

P1, 44, **114**, 254
P4, **22**, **111**, **114**, *118*
Pacific Breeze, 242
Pagarsarri, 154
Panormitis, **111**
Pantelis, 24
Pantias, **111**
Paraguay, **133**
Parma, **238**
Parsifal, **238**, **238**
Parthenon, **94**, **361**
Pass of Ballater, 292
Pass of Balmaha, 292
Pass of Melfort, 311
Patti, **358**
Paul, 243
Paul & Emily, 243
Paul M, **82**
Paul Rykens, **358**
Pauline, 110
Peace, **194**, **195**
Pearl, **71**, **152**, **185**, 213, **213**, **214**, 244, 315
Peerless, **108**
Pegasus, **115**, 212
Pegny, **190**
Pelican, 356
Penchateau, **97**, 228
Pendeen, 95
Penelope, **62**
Penrhyn, **78**
Pepita, 130, 259
Percy Dawson, 272
Percy, **152**
Peter, *41*, 189
Peterbourg, **183**
Petrel, 87, **99**, 209, 279, 284
Petricola, **312**
Petrovski, **365**
Phaeacian, 127, 170, 227, 275
Phaedra, **358**
Phoebus, **149**
Phoenician, 139
Phoenix, **122**

Photinia, **362**
Photinia, **94**
Piaco, 90
Pickle, HMS, 16
Pierre Loti, **334**
Pimlico, 127, **208**, 345
Pin Mill, 323-4, *324*
Pinewood, 38, **266**, 267
Pirola, 82
Plancius, **190**
Plitvice, *163*
Plymouth, **150**
Po, **126**
Pogoria, 17
Polka, 289
Pollux, **97**
Polly, **206**
Polly M, **218**, 241
Poltallock, **119**
Polybius, 155
Pomona, **194**
Pompey, 79
Portlight, **125**, **136**, 233
Portos, **149**
Portugal, **360**
Pride of Ipswich, 157
Pride of the Orwell, **108**, **122**, 283
Pride of the Stour, **122**
Prima, 256
Prima Donna, **195**, 279
Primrose, 23
Primus, 270
Prince Albert, 315
Prince Victor, **358**
Prince, 316
Princess, 233
Princess Royal, 83, 87, **115**, **252**, 288
Probity, 125
Problem, **72**
Prof. Ribaltovsky, **97**
Progress, **181**
Promise, 50
Prompt, **134**
Providence, 69, **72**, **194**, 195, 262
Prowess, **135**, **136**, 138, 169-70
Pudge, **134**, **136**, 138, **185**, **190**, 281, 346
Puffin, **358**
Pylades, **263**
Pyrgos, 191

Q

Quarry, **134**
Quartus, 147
Queen, 38, 67, **67**, **70**
Queen Mary, **108**, **108**
Queen of the Orwell, 317-8
Queen of the South, see Woolwich Belle
Queen of the Thames, 317
Queensland, 85
Quintus, 201

R

R.S. Jackson, **185**
R.W. Wheldon, **114**, 254
Rachel & Julia, **194**
Racia, 54
Radhurst, **94**, **364**
Radix 312
Ragnar, **133**
Rampant, **358**
Ranger, 262
Rathbale, **122**
Rattlesnake, HMS, **358**
Rattray Head, 215
Ratu, **181**
Raven, **134**, **136**
Ravenscraig, 78
Rayford, 87
Raymont, **358**
Ready, **122**, **358**
Reaper, **126**, **153**
Record Reign, **223**, 231, 240, 279
Red Gauntlet, HMS, **358**
Red Tail, 279
Redoubtable, 125, 233
Refloater, 55
Rega, **158**
Regeja, **158**
Regina, **150**
Regum, 203
Rehhorst, *178*, 189
Reindeer, 67, **67**, **71**, 71
Reliance, **111**, 125, 233
Rembrandt, 188
Remercie, **208**, 233
Reminder, **111**, **276**, **277**, 279
Renown, **183**, 206
Repertor, **136**
Repton, 91-2
Resolute, **16**, **153**, 214, 233, 276
Resourceful, 130, 279
Result, **153**
Revenger, **114**
Rheidol Vale, **200**
Rheinland, **183**
Richard, **194**
Richard & Emily, 73
Richard Kelsale, **133**
Richard Lee Barber, 257
Richmond, **194**
Ridgefield, **97**
Riga, 151
Rigley, **62**
Rigoletto, 238
Ring, **362**
Ringmoor, 86, 275
Rio Blanco, **94**, **363**
Rippledyke, 38
Rita, 38
Rivadeluna, **242**

River Clyde, HMT, 340
River Fisher, **218**
River Lady, 323, 326, **327**
River Leven, 396
River Lune, **217**
River Orwell, 38
River Queen, 316
Robert & Thomas, **195**
Robert Adamson, **67**
Robert Owen, 52
Robinia, 123
Robrix, 76
Roch Castle, **223**
Rochester Castle, 231, 240
Rochester City Belle, 322-3
Rocksand, 55
Roderick Dhu, 107
Roffen, **141**
Rogul, **141**
Rohoy, **141**
Roina, **141**
Roma, 275
Ronald
Ronald West, 202, 203, 284
Ronso, **358**
Rosalie, 215
Rose, **70**, **72**, 83, **150**, **227**, **358**
Rose Bud, **152**, **223**
Rose in June, 147
Rose Marie, 136
Rose Middleton, see Niord
Rosebud, 211
Rose-Haugh, **358**
Rosette, **358**
Rosie, 76
Roskilde, **126**
Rosme, 135, 346
Ross, **358**
Rossing, 246
Rossum, **363**, **364**
Rotzburg, **97**
Roxby, 25
Royal Oak, HMS, 337
Royal Sovereign, **358**
Royksund, 112
Rubens, **133**
Rudby, **362**
Rudderman, 254, 292
Rumania, 135
Runic, **141**
Runswick, **189**, 352
Russ, **238**
Rye, HMS, **358**

S

Sabah, 113
Sabine, **358**
Sagacity, **82**, 259
Salamander, **358**
Salmon, 109
Saltcote Belle, **122**, 342
Salvus, **94**, **361**
Samland, **126**
Samuel Bowley, **156**
San Dario, 254
San Eduardo, **312**
San Leonardo, **312**
San Leopoldo, **312**
San Lorenzo, 190
San Macedonio, 311, **312**
San Matteo, 157
San Quirino, 55, 310, **312**
San Roberto, **312**
San Rosendo, 310
San Salvador, **312**
San Tirso, **312**
San Ubaldo, **312**
San Ugon, **312**
San Valerio, **312**
San Zotico, 57
Sandbank, 55
Sandhill, 227
Sandringham, 197
Sanfry, **256**
Santa Margarita, **190**
Sapphire, **358**
Sara, **207**, **208**
Sarah Colebrook, 279
Sarah Davies, **150**
Sarah Hide, **358**
Sarah Lizzie, **252**
Sarah Mcdonald, **200**
Sarah Rowe, **200**
Sarah, **153**, 197
Sarmatia, **158**
Sarnia, 217
Saunter, 170
Sauria, 58
Savill, 197
Saxon, **134**
Scania, **158**
Scarboro', 231
Scarcity, 82, **82**, **218**
Schwan, 241
Scone, 130, **134**, 138
Scoresby, 24, 25, **111**, **111**
Scot, 118
Scotia, **213**
Scottish Glens, **119**
Scottish Heather, 171
Scottish Musician, 171, **312**
Scutola, 289
Sea Spray, **134**
Sea View, **121**
Seaford, **258**, 259
Seagull, 68, **108**, **131**, 151, **358**
Seatoller, **126**
Sebreno, 157
Secret, **200**
Secunda Emilie, 289

Sedgemoor, **67**, 148, **148**, **252**, 252
Seefalke, 85
Senta, **134**
Sepoy, 212
Septimus, 201, **214**
Serapis, **133**
Serb, 112, **115**, **185**
Serenity, **218**
Severn, **155**, 155-6
Severn Side, **141**
Sextus, 79, 81, **122**, 125, 147, 262
Shamrock, **71**, 213
Shamrock IV, 229-30
Shamrock V, 328
Shannon, **148**
Sharon, **126**
Sheafgarth, **263**
Sheaf Spear, **111**
Shearwater, **358**
Shearwater, HMS, 205
Sheikh, **119**
Shelbrit 1, see British Pluck
Sheldergate, **94**
Sheldrake, **358**
Shell Craftsman, **299**
Shell Fitter, **301**
Shell Loader, **296**
Shell Seafarer, **295**
Shellie, **217**
Shell-Mex I, 310-1
Shell-Mex II, 310-1
Shell-Mex IV, 254
Sheringham, 338, **354**
Sherwood, 87
Shield, **134**
Shotton, 86, 275
Shova, **358**
Shuna, **363**
Sicily, 92
Sideris, **97**
Sidon, 289
Siegfried, **238**
Siers Kransen, **246**
Sifka, **153**
Signa, **358**
Signality, **82**
Sigurd, **133**
Sigyn, **133**, 332
Silver Eagle, **200**
Silver Spray, 132
Silver, 130, 259
Simla, 135
Sincerity, **82**
Sindbad, 107
Sir Galahad, HMS, **358**
Sir Lancelot, HMS, **358**
Sir Richard, **134**
Sirius, **181**
Siva, 108, 173
Skaane, **158**
Skagerrak, 23, 257-8, 343-4, 345, 347
Skandiner, **150**
Skarv, 76
Skelwith Force, 137
Skinningrove, **217**
Skjold, **94**, **363**
Skovland, **183**
Slateford, 241
Slesvig, 38
Sliedrecht, 312
Smit Houston, see Solo
S N Madvic, **133**
Snar, **363**
Snowdrop, **252**
Soldat, 136
Solen, **312**
Solo, 60
Solon, 120
Solveig Rickerson, **242**, **243**
Solway Queen, 68
Songvand, **119**
Sonnavind, **97**
Sons of the Thames, 316
Soranus, **358**
Sorlandet, 16
South Pacific, **364**
Southern Belle, **115**, 151
Southport, 159
Southwick, 159, 241
Southwold Belle, 320
Sovereign, 90
Spartan, 118, **153**
Speed, 89
Speedwell, 51, 52, 151, 219, **358**
Speranza, **185**
Speset Fides, 245
Spina, **358**
Spinaway, **194**, **195**
Spinaway C, **7**, **88**, 99, 100, 121, 283
Spinel, **151**
Spirality, 342
Spithead, 279
Spon Acton, **133**
Spray, 52
Spruceland, 188
Squawk, **134**, 157, 173
Sralen, **181**
Srgj, 157, **158**
St Abbs Head, **82**, 215, **218**
St Aidan, 129
St Antonius, 32
St Denis, 338
St Laurent, **200**
St Margaret, **190**
St Mellons, **358**
St Tudwal, 173
Staffordshire, **181**
Staincliffe, 120
Stanley Force, **94**, 112
Stanton, 49

Star, 121, **152**
Star of the Realm, **358**
Star of the Sea, 69, **69**
Startled Fawn, **70**, 73
Stassa, **142**, 143
Steadfast, **359**
Steersman, 254
Stefan, **190**
Stella Leonis, **359**
Stella Rigel, **356**, **359**
Stena Normandica, 31, 229
Stour, 91, **108**, **115**, 148, 151, 155, **155**, **223**, 318, **359**,
Straits of Menai, **108**
Strathelliot, **359**
Strathmaree, **359**
Stratton, 82
Stream Fisher, **217**
Stronghold, 23, 25, 55, 57, **59**, **290**, 343
Strood, , **121**, **122**
Success, 203
Suceava, **97**
Suffolk, 315, 319-21, **322**, 326
Suffolk Coast, **226**
Summer Cloud, **69**
Summity, **218**
Sun XXII, 58, 59
Sunbeam, **122**, **150**, 212
Sunbeam II, **359**
Sundance, 154
Sunflower, 328-9
Sunniside, **255**
Sunnyhill, **78**
Sunrise, **134**
Sunstar, 60
Superga, 311
Supernal, **153**
Surf, **71**
Sursay, HMS, **359**
Susan Colby, **351**
Susan Vittery, **153**
Sussex Belle, **152**, **213**
Svanen, **183**
Svanholm, **149**
Sverker, **158**
Sverte, **189**, 348
Swaantje, **150**
Swallow, **108**, 151, **214**, 231
Sweep, 270, **271**
Sweep II, **270**, 271-2
Swift, 51, **72**, 106, **108**, 140, 151, **214**, 231, 288
Swiftsure, **194**, 211
Swin, 164
Swynfleet, 85, 256, 257
Sylph, **214**
Syrian, **359**
Szent Gellert, **94**, 360

T
T M P, **122**
T.W. Stuart, 68
Tacoma City, 188
Tagus, **133**
Takai Maru, 92
Talon, **97**
Tanganyika, HMS, **359**
Tarquin, 79
Tartary, 170
Tattoo, **359**
Taurus, 109
Taxiarchis, 349
Tay, 275
Tayra, 60
Teesdale, **263**
Teesider, **72**
Tehana, **359**
Telesflora, **149**
Tempesta, see Centurity
Templar, **25**
Tenasserim, 151-2
Tenax, **362**
Tennessee, **94**, **363**
Tern, **108**, 231
Tertius, **122**, **194**, 231, 283
Tessy, **190**
TFC, **185**
Thalatta, **115**, **208**
Thames, 75, **134**, 155
The Baron, 79
The Countess, 79, 257
The Duchess, 79
The Duke, 79, **218**, 257
The Earl, 257
The Emperor, 79
The Exchange, **121**, 195
The Marquis, **82**
The Miller, 130
The Monarch, 79
The Motoketch, 212
The President, **218**
The Sisters, 196, **121**
The Sultan, **263**
The Three Daughters, **134**
The Viceroy, 79
Thekla, **183**
Theomitor, **94**, **366**
Thetis, 38, 98, 112, 118
Thistle, 68, 112, **153**, 328
Thomas, 83, 60, **71**, **156**
Thomas & Annie, **194**
Thomas Adam, **149**
Thomas Leeds, **359**
Thomas Wood, 195
Thora Hafter, 217
Thornhill, **183**
Three Sisters, 271
Thrift, 213, **255**
Thule, **181**
Tiger, **69**
Timok, **94**, **364**
Tintara, **200**

Tirgu Mures, **97**
Tit Bits, **122**
Titan, 118
Tobon, **97**
Tocogay, **359**
Tollesbury, **111**, **115**, 123, **208**, **346**, 346
Tomaso, 289
Topaz, **151**
Topmast 9, 58
Torbay Prince, 323-4
Torchbearer, HMS, 341
Torridge, **62**
Touraine, 119
Trafalgar, 24, 25, **25**
Train Ferry No.2, 338, **339**
Traly, 212
Traviata, **238**
Trebo, 187
Tregantle, **25**
Trelyon, 107
Tremain, 217
Trent River, 18, 24, 79, **154**, **155**, 156-8, 235
Trevarrock, 91
Trevelyan, 91
Treverbyn, 91
Trevilley, 107
Trewyn, 154
Trilby, 130, 141, **141**
Trio, **183**
Tripoli, **97**
Triumph, **69**
Trojan, **208**
Tudor Queen, **218**
Tudor, 93
Tuen, **190**
Tunisian, HMS, **359**
Turquoise, HMS, 213, **359**
Tweed, **224**
Twiggs, **150**
Tymger, **62**
Tyne, **148**, 155
Tynedale, **149**
Typhoon, HMS, **359**
Tyr, **22**

U
Ullswater, **149**
Ulmas, **158**
Una, **213**
Union, 67, **67**, **194**, **195**
Union Fair, **242**
Unionist, **71**
Unique, **122**
Unity, **70**, 131, **152**, **200**, 212
Unknown, 216
Uskole, **97**
Utrecht, 60

V
Vaasa, **238**
Valdivia, 276
Valdora, **122**
Valonia, 203
Valscian, **78**
Vane Tempest, 253, **255**
Vanellus, 159, **363**
Vanguard, **70**
Vanquisher, 310
Varand, **312**
Varmland, **182**
Varuna, **171**, **185**, **190**
Vasa, 150
Vasyaalekseev, **97**
Vaunter, 54
Vechtstroom, 235
Vecta, **69**, 83
Veester, 338
Vega, 241
Velsheda, 328
Vendee, **119**
Venture, **99**, 100, **122**
Venus, **62**
Veravia, 203
Verona, 112, 342
Veronica, **208**
Vertrouwen, 231
Vespasian, 79
Vestanvik, 136
Veturia, **119**
Vianna, 214
Vic 41, **356**, **359**
Vic 76, **359**
Victor, 110
Victoria, **122**, 147, **194**
Victory, **200**
Vicunia, 212
Vidonia, **359**
Vigilant, **190**, 233, 279
Vigour, 29
Viking Bank, **359**
Viking, **190**
Vikingen, 246
Vilja, **242**
Ville du Havre, **334**
Vindelicia, **359**
Ving, **181**
Violet Sybil, 150, **152**
Virgen de Lourdes, 154
Virginia S, **25**
Virgo, **151**
Viscount Castlereagh, **251**, 253, **255**
Visitor, **72**, **252**
Vivid, **134**
Vixen, **206**
Vlaanderen, 310
Vliestroom, 256
Volga 40005, 60
Volmer, **133**
Volunteer, **150**
Vulcan, 275

W
W.R.T., 132
Walter Ulric, 231
Wanderer, 243
Wanja, **185**
War Glen, 184
War Halton, 92
War Leopard, 110
War Syren, 92, 109
Warden Court, **134**
Warden Point, 268
Warrior, **114**
Warstar, HMS, **359**
Warwickbrook, **258**
Washington Irving, 113
Water Lily, 125
Water Maidens, **359**
Waterdale, **167**
Waterloo, 269-70
Waveney, **115**, **148**, **155**, 155, **185**, 283
Waveney II, 235
Waverley, 324-5, **325**
Waziristan, **25**
Welbeck, **359**
Welsh Rose, 348
Wenvoe, **108**
Westall, **134**
Western Belle, 226, **227**
Western Maid, 226, **227**
Westland, 38
Westminster, **25**
Westminsterbrook, 258, **259**
Whale, 240
Whateley Hall, 156-8
Whim, **150**
Whimbrel, **134**
Whinfield, 131
White Heather, 328
White May, **359**
White Swan, **149**
Whitwood, **263**
Whitworth, **263**
Who'd a Thought It, 243
Why Not, **195**, 195, 211, 245
Widgeon, **359**
Wilhemine, **183**
Will Everard, **207**, **208**
Willa, HMS, **359**
William, 86, **115**, 269
William & Lucy, **121**
William Brewster, **189**
William Cleverley, **134**
William Dawson, 263
William Dyer, 214
William Parker, **66**, 67, **67**
William Stephen, **359**
William Wesney, HMT, 340
Willie, **152**, **183**
Willow Park, **94**, 352
Willy, **312**
Wim, **158**, **190**
Winchesterbrook, 258, **259**
Windsor Queen, **218**
Windsorbrook, **40**, 258
Winifred, 86, **134**, 275
Winston Churchill, 16
Wisbech, 279
Witus, **183**
Wolfs Cove, 319
Wolfsburg, **242**
Wolsey, **115**, **210**, **213**
Wolsum, **94**
Wonder, **206**
Woodland, **154**
Woolverstone, HMS, **359**
Woolwich Belle, 318-21, **321**
Woolwich, HMS, 331
Worcesterbrook, 259
Wortha, 59
Worthydown, **238**
Wyoming, **359**
Wyvenhoe, 129, 259, 346, **190**
Wyvisbrook, 92

X
Xylonite, **208**

Y
Yare, 79, **155**, 155-6
Yarmouth Belle, 320
Yarrow, 272
Yewarch, **263**
Yewbank, 215
Yewcroft, **218**
Yewdale, **263**
Yewglen, 159
Yewmount, 85, **263**
Yewtree, **263**
Yewvalley, **263**
Yngaren, **25**
Yokefleet, 256, 257
Yorkbrook, **263**
Yrsa, **126**, **238**

Z
Zaan, 112
Zareba, **359**
Zayda, 289
Zeehonde, 241
Zenobia, **71**, 283
Zephyr, 214
Zeus Ii, **190**
Zorgli, 120
Zuma, **71**, **153**
Zvir, **94**